Lecture Notes in Computer Science 1145
Edited by G. Goos, J. Hartmanis and J. van Leeuwen

Springer
Berlin
Heidelberg
New York
Barcelona
Budapest
Hong Kong
London
Milan
Paris
Santa Clara
Singapore
Tokyo

Radhia Cousot David A. Schmidt (Eds.)

Static Analysis

Third International Symposium, SAS '96
Aachen, Germany, September 24-26, 1996
Proceedings

Springer

Series Editors

Gerhard Goos, Karlsruhe University, Germany

Juris Hartmanis, Cornell University, NY, USA

Jan van Leeuwen, Utrecht University, The Netherlands

Volume Editors

Radhia Cousot
École Polytechnique, Laboratoire d'Informatique
F-91128 Palaiseau Cedex, France
E-mail: radhia.cousot@lix.polytechnique.fr

David A. Schmidt
Kansas State University, Department of Computing and Information Sciences
Manhattan, KS 66506, USA
E-mail: schmidt@cis.ksu.edu

Cataloging-in-Publication data applied for

Die Deutsche Bibliothek - CIP-Einheitsaufnahme

Static analysis : third international symposium ; proceedings / SAS '96, Aachen, Germany, September 24 - 26, 1996. Radhia Cousot ; David A. Schmidt (ed.). - Berlin ; Heidelberg ; New York ; Barcelona ; Budapest ; Hong Kong ; London ; Milan ; Paris ; Santa Clara ; Singapore ; Tokyo : Springer, 1996
(Lecture notes in computer science ; Vol. 1145)
ISBN 3-540-61739-6
NE: Cousot, Radhia [Hrsg.]; SAS <3, 1996, Aachen>; GT

CR Subject Classification (1991): D.1, D.2.8, D.3.2-3,F.3.1-2, F.4.2

ISSN 0302-9743
ISBN 3-540-61739-6 Springer-Verlag Berlin Heidelberg New York

Typesetting: Camera-ready by author
SPIN 10513720 06/3142 - 5 4 3 2 1 0 Printed on acid-free paper

Foreword

Static analysis is increasingly recognised as a fundamental tool for high-performance implementations and verification systems of high-level programming languages. The last two decades have witnessed substantial developments in this area, ranging from theoretical frameworks to the design and implementation of analysers and their application in optimising compilers and program debugging.

The aim of SAS is to promote theory and applications of static analysis as a fundamental tool in high-performance language implementations and program verification. The symposium promotes contacts and information exchange among scientists who share common interests in static analysis for different programming paradigms. Researchers from the fields of concurrent, constraint, functional, imperative, logic and object-oriented programming constitute the audience of SAS.

This volume contains the proceedings of the Third International Static Analysis Symposium (SAS'96), held in Aachen (Germany) during 24–26 September 1996. It succeeds SAS'94, held in Namur (Belgium), SAS'95, held in Glasgow (UK), and the previous international workshops JTASPEFL'91 and WSA'92, which were held in Bordeaux (France), and WSA'93, which took place in Padova (Italy). The proceedings of WSA'93 are published by Springer-Verlag as Lecture Notes in Computer Science, volume 724; those of SAS'94 appear as volume 864 and those of SAS'95 as volume 983.

In response to the call for papers, 79 papers were submitted to SAS'96. All submitted papers were reviewed by at least three experts. The programme committee met on 21st June in Paris and, after lively discussion based on these referee reports, selected 22 high-quality papers (27% acceptation rate). In addition three papers were selected as 'system descriptions' in keeping with a desire to encourage practical experimentation.

At the symposium three invited talks were given by Alex Aiken, Flemming Nielson and Bernhard Steffen. This volume contains the invited presentations, the selected papers and system descriptions.

We thank the programme committee members and the referees for their care in reviewing the submitted papers. They are listed on the following pages.

SAS'96 was hosted together with ALP'96 and PLILP'96 by the Computer Science Department of Aachen University. The conferences were supported by the Association of Logic Programming, Esprit Compulog-Net, RWTH Aachen and SUN Microsystems. We express our gratitude to the local organisers Olaf Chitil, Michael Hanus, Herbert Kuchen, Markus Mohnen, Ulla Oebel, and Frank Zartmann for their contributions to SAS'96.

We also thank Patrick Cousot and Jacques Stern for arranging the Programme Committee meeting at École Normale Supérieure, the computer science laboratory of École Polytechnique (LIX) for the material support, and Beaudouin Le Charlier and Alan Mycroft for passing on their previous experience as SAS chairs.

Paris,
18 July 1996 R. Cousot and D.A. Schmidt

Programme Committee of SAS'96

Radhia Cousot (École Polytechnique, FR), co-chair,
David A. Schmidt (Kansas State University, US), co-chair,

François Bourdoncle (École des Mines de Paris, FR),
Alain Deutsch (INRIA, FR),
Roberto Giacobazzi (Pisa University, IT),
Nicolas Halbwachs (VERIMAG, FR),
Chris Hankin (Imperial College, UK),
Luddy Harrison (Connected Components, US),
Neil D.Jones (DIKU, DK),
Peter Lee (Carnegie Mellon University, US),
Kim Marriott (Monash University, AU),
Jens Palsberg (MIT, US),
Hanne Riis-Nielson (Aarhus University, DK),
Carolyn Talcott (Stanford University, US),
Mads Tofte (DIKU, DK),
Reinhard Wilhelm (Saarbrücken University, DE).

Local Organization Committee

Olaf Chitil, Michael Hanus, Herbert Kuchen, Markus Mohnen, Ulla Oebel and Frank Zartmann.

List of Referees

The Programme Committee wish to express their grateful thanks to the many additional referees:

Ole Agesen, Martin Alt, Torben Amtoft, Peter Holst Andersen, Roberto Bagnara, Dante Baldan, María García de la Banda, Anindya Banerjee, Roberto Barbuti, Denis Bechet, Nick Benton, Bruno Blanchet, Francisco Bueno, Christiansen, Michael Codish, Christopher Colby, Marc-Michel Corsini, Agostino Cortesi, Saumya Debray, Jürgen Dingel, Peter Dybjer, Moreno Falaschi, Karl-Filip Faxén, Christian Fecht, Jean-Claude Fernandez, Gilberto Filè, Alexandre Frey, John Gallagher, Simon Gay, Éric Goubault, Susanne Graf, Philippe Granger, Peter Habermehl, Maria Handjiéva, John Hatcliff, Reinhold Heckmann, Fergus Henderson, Urs Hoelzle, Pierre Jouvelot, Andrew Kelly, Andrew Kennedy, Sergey V. Kotov, Leslie Lamport, Baudouin Le Charlier, Giorgio Levi, Lunjin Lu, Ian Mackie, Florian Martin, Laurent Mauborgne, Torben Mogensen, Bruno Monsuez, George Necula, Joachim Niehren, Kristian Nielsen, Chris Okasaki, Dino Pedreschi, Francesco Ranzato, Antoine Rauzy, Jakob Rehof, Riadh Robbana, Mads Rosendahl, Sabina Rossi, David Sands, Peter Schachte, Helmut Seidl, Manuel Serrano, Peter Sestoft, Olin Shivers, Mihaela Sighireanu, Harald Søndergaard, Morten Heine Sørensen, Christopher Stone, Allen Stoughton, Mikkel Thorup, Peter Van Roy, Franck Védrine, Arnaud Venet, Stephen Weeks, Morten Welinder.

Table of Contents

1 Guests

Constraint-Based Program Analysis 1
Alex Aiken

Semantics-Directed Program Analysis: A Tool-Maker's Perspective 2
Flemming Nielson

Property-Oriented Expansion 22
Bernhard Steffen

2 Contributed Papers

Generalized Dominators for Structured Programs 42
Stephen Alstrup, Peter W. Lauridsen & Mikkel Thorup

Cache Behavior Prediction by Abstract Interpretation 52
Martin Alt, Christian Ferdinand, Florian Martin & Reinhard Wilhelm

Termination Analysis for Offline Partial Evaluation of a Higher Order Functional Language 67
Peter Holst Andersen & Carsten Kehler Holst

Proving Correctness of Constraint Logic Programs with Dynamic Scheduling 83
F.S. de Boer, M. Gabbrielli & C. Palamidessi

Understanding Mobile Agents via a Non-interleaving Semantics for Facile 98
R. Borgia, P. Degano, C. Priami, L. Leth & B. Thomsen

Termination Analysis for Partial Functions 113
Jürgen Brauburger & Jürgen Giesl

A Freeness and Sharing Analysis of Logic Programs Based on a Pre-interpretation 128
Maurice Bruynooghe, Bart Demoen, Dimitri Boulanger, Marc Denecker & Anne Mulkers

Refinement Types for Program Analysis 143
Mario Coppo, Ferruccio Damiani & Paola Giannini

A Comparison of Three Occur-Check Analysers 159
Lobel Crnogorac, Andrew D. Kelly & Harald Søndergaard

Analysis of the Equality Relations for the Program Terms 174
Pavel G. Emelianov

An Even Faster Solver for General Systems of Equations 189
Christian Fecht & Helmut Seidl

Inferring Program Specifications in Polynomial-Time 205
Robert Givan

Automated Modular Termination Proofs for Real Prolog Programs 220
Martin Müller, Thomas Glaß & Karl Stroetmann

Data-Flow-Based Virtual Function Resolution 238
Hemant D. Pande & Barbara G. Ryder

Compiling Laziness Using Projections 255
Ross Paterson

Optimized Algorithms for Incremental Analysis of Logic Programs 270
Germán Puebla & Manuel Hermenegildo

Tractable Constraints in Finite Semilattices 285
Jakob Rehof & Torben Æ. Mogensen

Uniformity for the Decidability of Hybrid Automata 301
Olivier Roux & Vlad Rusu

A Backward Slicing Algorithm for Prolog 317
Stéphane Schoenig & Mireille Ducassé

Combining Slicing and Constraint Solving for Validation of
Measurement Software 332
Gregor Snelting

Subtyping Constrained Types 349
Valery Trifonov & Scott Smith

Abstract Cofibered Domains: Application to the Alias Analysis of
Untyped Programs 366
Arnaud Venet

3 System Descriptions

STAN: A Static Analyzer for CLP($\mathcal{R}$) Based on Abstract Interpretation .. 383
Maria Handjieva

Two Applications of an Incremental Analysis Engine for (Constraint) Logic Programs 385
Andrew D. Kelly, Kim Marriott, Harald Søndergaard & Peter J. Stuckey

PAN – The Prolog Analyzer 387
Martin Müller, Thomas Glaß & Karl Stroetmann

Author Index 389

Constraint-Based Program Analysis

Alex Aiken
Computer Science Division
University of California, Berkeley
Berkeley, CA 94720-1776
aiken@cs.berkeley.edu

Program analysis techniques automatically analyze software, typically either to verify desirable properties (such as type safety) or to gather information for use in program optimization. In the last few years program analyses based on constraint-solving algorithms have become fashionable in the research community. This talk will give a tutorial overview of constraint-based program analysis, including the constraint systems and constraint resolution algorithms used, the theoretical and engineering advantages of constraint approaches, new applications made possible by using constraints, as well as open problems and limitations of current techniques. Examples will be drawn from imperative, object-oriented, functional, and logic programming languages.

Semantics-Directed Program Analysis: A Tool-Maker's Perspective

Flemming Nielson

Computer Science Department, Aarhus University,
Ny Munkegade, DK-8000 Aarhus C, Denmark

WWW: `http://www.daimi.aau.dk/~fn`
E-mail: `fn@daimi.aau.dk`

Abstract. Developing a tool kit for program analysis requires a general metalanguage (or user interface) in which to specify the program analyses, and many past and current approaches are semantics-directed in the sense that they attempt to exploit the structure of the semantics of the program. In this paper we take a tool-maker's perspective at an approach based on two-level semantics, focusing on the flexible way to incorporate and combine a repertoire of program analyses. We conclude by identifying a number of key considerations for the design of semantics-directed frameworks or tool kits for program analysis.

Keywords. Program Analysis, Abstract Interpretation, Denotational Semantics, Two-Level Metalanguages, Tools for Program Analysis.

1 Introduction

The predominant use of program analysis is to enable compilers to generate better code: to supply information about the context in order to generate more specialised code or in order to validate program transformations. While this is by no means the only use of program analysis, it is the only one we shall consider.

The need for tool-making. The lessons from Software Engineering tell us, that to overcome the "software crisis", we need to transform programming from craftmanship into technology. This is facilitated by the construction of general tools (by which we mean computer programs) that embody the knowledge needed to perform a complex task; consequently that task can be performed faster, more reliably, cheaper, more predictably, and by less skilled programmers. Eventually it makes it feasible to construct systems of a complexity that was hardly feasible before.

Let us consider an example from compiler writing. Here regular and context-free grammars are useful for writing the parser module. Indeed there are generally established notations for how to write the context-free grammars; also there is a well developed theory for how to parse various classes of context-free grammars (e.g. LL(1), LR(1), or LALR(1) grammars); and finally there are generally available tools (`yacc`, `ML-yacc`, etc.) that allow to construct the parser module (as a program in C, ML, etc.) directly from the context-free grammar. A similar story applies to regular grammars and their tools (`lex`, `ML-lex`, etc.).

To be useful, a tool should have an easy user interface compared with the complexity of the task being performed. For parsing, the average programmer is probably capable of writing a recursive descent LL(1) parser by hand, but hardly a LALR(1) parser for which tools like `yacc` amply repay the time needed for learning how to use the tool. Next the tool should have a wide area of applicability. This is probably the reason why parser generating tools are generally based on LALR(1) rather than LL(1) since grammars for programming languages are more easily written to conform to the LALR(1) condition than to the LL(1) condition. Also the tool should produce a result of sufficiently high quality that the programmer sees no reason to redo the effort manually. In the case of LALR(1) based parsing, current tools largely live up to this expectation. Finally, the tool should be seen as a constructive way of exploiting existing theories for how to conduct the task at hand.

In the area of compiler writing, where so much research has been conducted, there are disappointingly few tools of general usage, apart from the already mentioned success stories of `lex` and `yacc`. Several tools based on attribute grammars (e.g. [32]) or denotational semantics (e.g. [24]) have been developed for semi-automatic construction of larger parts of compiler front-ends, but none seems to have sustained wide-spread and long-term usage. Also several tools have been developed for semi-automatic construction of compiler back-ends, but hardly any (with the possible exception of `IBURG` [6]) seems to have sustained wide-spread and long-term usage.

Tool-making for program analysis. A similar disappointing outlook applies to tools for program analysis, despite several efforts to construct systems of some generality (e.g. [1, 29, 30, 33]). This is not because of a lack of theoretical developments; indeed there are the methodologies of data flow equations (e.g. [10]), set-based analyses through the generation of constraints (e.g. [7]), abstract interpretation expressed denotationally (e.g. [15]) or operationally (e.g. [3]), annotated type and effect systems (e.g. [28]), and even more general logical systems.

It is important to realise that construction of a tool amounts to defining a user interface: one has to define a *metalanguage* in which to express instances of the problem at hand. The design choices made here are pervasive as illustrated by the following quotes:

– *A good programming language is a conceptual universe for thinking about programming;* Alan Perlis in the Rome Software Development Conference in 1969. (Replace "programming" by "analysis".)

– *A notation is important for what it leaves out;* Joseph E. Stoy in [27].

Thus a metalanguage represents a deliberate design choice concerning which class of languages, and which class of analyses, are at the focus of the development. Therefore different metalanguages may have different capabilities and limitations, and there hardly exists a metalanguage without any limitations whatsoever. Indeed, the price to pay for avoiding all limitations is to have no metalanguage and hence no tool!

We shall therefore accept the need for a metalanguage for program analysis; it should be firmly based on theory and not overly abstract (like using ZF set theory for which it is hardly feasible to implement any tool). To specify an analysis we need

(i) to associate abstract operations with the syntactic constructs, and
(ii) to describe the abstract operations themselves.

Perhaps the most general scenario for *(i)* is the use of many-sorted algebras, where the sorts correspond to the syntactic categories and the operators of the signature to the context-free grammar, although more mundane syntax-directed definitions will do as well. For *(ii)* we still need a metalanguage to describe the interpretation (or many-sorted algebra) of the abstract operations themselves. For inspiration we may look at natural semantics (e.g.[26]), structural operational semantics [25], denotational semantics (e.g. [20]), the syntax-directed frameworks for closure analysis (e.g. [5]), or the semantic frameworks mentioned below.

Overview. First we give an account of two-level metalanguages and their use for compiler construction; Section 2 then ends with a short guide to the literature. Next we present two-level abstract interpretation from a tool-maker's perspective; Section 3 then ends with a short guide to the literature. Finally, we consider how the insights gained provide feed-back to the two-level metalanguages themselves, the general area of domain theoretic program analysis, the wider spectrum of semantics-directed analysis frameworks, and finally the design of tools for analysis.

2 Two-Level Metalanguages

Taking a semantics-directed approach there are several approaches to semantics to choose from: the model-based approaches (including denotational semantics based on domain theory, approaches based on metric spaces, game semantics), the operational approaches (including abstract machines and interpreters, structural operational semantics, natural semantics), and the specification oriented approaches (including Hoare-logics, dynamic and other modal logics, linear logic). There is hardly consensus on what the ideal semantic platform is, and the selection of key contenders change over time. Here we shall consider denotational semantics, that has been used quite effectively to describe (mainly untyped) imperative and functional languages, and that has also been used to describe logic and concurrent languages (through the theory of power-domains).

A tiny denotational metalanguage. A denotational metalanguage is usually taken to be an untyped λ-calculus together with a system of recursive domain equations. By admitting recursive types (for construction of the universal domains) it may alternatively, and profitably, be regarded as a typed λ-calculus. In order to present the overall picture, without spending too much time on the individual technical details, we shall restrict the attention to a subset of the metalanguage usually considered for denotational semantics. In order to prevent any misconceptions, we take the time to state very explicitly, that the development overviewed here is in no way restricted to the tiny denotational metalanguage used in the sequel.

To illustrate our approach we thus decide to consider a simply typed λ-calculus. The types $t \in$ **Type** are given by

$$t ::= B \mid t_1 \times t_2 \mid t_1 \to t_2$$

where $B \in$ **Base** ranges over a set of base types; traditionally these include the booleans *Bool* and the integers *Num*.

The expressions $e \in$ **Exp** are given by

$$e ::= c \mid v \mid \lambda v.e \mid e_1(e_2) \mid \langle e_1, e_2 \rangle \mid \mathit{fst}\ e \mid \mathit{snd}\ e \mid \mathit{if}\ e_0\ e_1\ e_2 \mid \mathit{fix}\ e$$

where $c \in$ **Const** ranges over a set of constants and $v \in$ **Var** ranges over a set of variables; traditionally the constants include the booleans *true* and *false*, the integers, and an addition operator *plus*.

A tiny two-level metalanguage. Let us now move one step further and consider a tiny two-level metalanguage [20]. This is a λ-calculus where types and expressions are characterised as being static (i.e. compile-time) or dynamic (i.e. run-time); when needed we shall use underlining to indicate dynamic entities.

Lambda-calculi with explicit distinctions between static and dynamic have been used for many purposes:

- partial evaluation,
- abstract interpretation, and
- code generation.

Each of these applications pose different demands upon the metalanguage. As a consequence the precise selection of well-formedness conditions to be imposed upon the metalanguage (concerning how to mix static and dynamic entities) is critically dependent upon the application [21]. This explains why the literature contains a family of two-level languages, all related but with different names and features. Here we concentrate on the application to abstract interpretation.

The types $tt \in$ **TType** are now given by

$$tt ::= TB \mid tt_1 \times tt_2 \mid tt_1 \rightarrow tt_2 \mid tt_1 \underline{\times} tt_2 \mid tt_1 \underline{\rightarrow} tt_2$$

where $TB \in$ **TBase** ranges over a set of two-level base types; traditionally these include the static booleans *Bool*, the dynamic booleans $\underline{[Bool]}$, the static integers *Num*, and the dynamic integers $\underline{[Num]}$.

The expressions $te \in$ **TExp** are now given by

$$te ::= tc \mid v \mid \lambda v.te \mid te_1(te_2) \mid \langle te_1, te_2 \rangle \mid fst\ te \mid snd\ te \mid if\ te_0\ te_1\ te_2 \mid fix\ te \mid$$
$$Id \mid te_1 \circ te_2 \mid Curry\ te \mid Apply\langle te_1, te_2 \rangle \mid Tuple\langle te_1, te_2 \rangle \mid Fst \mid Snd \mid$$
$$If\langle te_0, te_1, te_2 \rangle \mid Fix\ te$$

where $tc \in$ **TConst** ranges over a set of two-level constants and $v \in$ **Var** ranges over a set of variables; traditionally the static constants include the static booleans *true* and *false*, the static integers, and an addition operator *plus* operating on static integers. The combinators *Id*, $\circ$, *Curry*, *Apply*, *Tuple*, *Fst*, *Snd*, *If*, and *Fix* relate to the dynamic types and may informally be explained as follows (where we underline the defining formula in order to stress that the combinators operate on dynamic entities):

$$\begin{aligned}
Id &\equiv \underline{\lambda} v.\ v \\
te_1 \circ te_2 &\equiv \underline{\lambda} v.\ te_1 \underline{(} te_2 \underline{(} v \underline{))} \\
Curry\ te &\equiv \underline{\lambda} v_1.\ \underline{\lambda} v_2.\ te \underline{(\langle} v_1, v_2 \underline{\rangle)} \\
Apply\langle te_1, te_2 \rangle &\equiv \underline{\lambda} v.\ te_1 \underline{(} v \underline{)(} te_2 \underline{(} v \underline{))} \\
Tuple\langle te_1, te_2 \rangle &\equiv \underline{\lambda} v.\ \underline{\langle} te_1 \underline{(} v \underline{)}, te_2 \underline{(} v \underline{)\rangle} \\
Fst &\equiv \underline{\lambda} v.\ \underline{fst}\ v \\
Snd &\equiv \underline{\lambda} v.\ \underline{snd}\ v \\
If\langle te_0, te_1, te_2 \rangle &\equiv \underline{\lambda} v.\ \underline{if}\ te_0 \underline{(} v \underline{)}\ te_1 \underline{(} v \underline{)}\ te_2 \underline{(} v \underline{)} \\
Fix\ te &\equiv \underline{\lambda} v.\ \underline{fix}\ te \underline{(} v \underline{)}
\end{aligned}$$

The dynamic constants traditionally include constant functions for producing the dynamic booleans and integers (e.g. $\underline{[\lambda v.true]}$), and an addition operator $\underline{[plus]}$ operating on dynamic integers.

The decision to use combinators rather than underlined λ-notation (as outlined above and in e.g. [16, 20]) is heavily influenced by the application: for partial evaluation and simple forms of abstract interpretation, underlined λ-notation would be quite sufficient, whereas for code generation and more advanced forms of abstract interpretation, the flexibility offered by the combinators proves indispensable. This is partly due to the compositional approach usually taken to two-level metalanguages: we give it a compositional semantics in the best traditions of denotational semantics. Here the use of *categorical combinators* for the dynamic constructs give much more flexibility, as also transpires when interpreting λ-calculi in categories, or when implementing functional languages using combinators. Luckily techniques exist for automatically transforming the ordinary denotational metalanguage to the two-level metalanguage (e.g. [20]).

Parameterised semantics. To illustrate the use of the two-level metalanguage let us consider a small excerpt from a two-level denotational semantics for an imperative language composed of expressions ($exp \in Exp$), commands ($cmd \in Cmd$), variables ($var \in Var$), numerals, booleans etc. To define its semantics in the tradition of denotational semantics we first define some semantic domains:

$$\begin{array}{rcl} loc : Loc & = & Num \\ var : Var & \in & \mathbf{TBase} \\ env : Env & = & Var \to Loc \\ \underline{Val} & = & \underline{[Bool]} \\ \underline{Loc} & = & \underline{[Num]} \\ \underline{State} & = & \underline{Loc \to Val} \end{array}$$

Here we have defined the domain *Loc* to be the domain *Num* of numbers that is already known to be available in **TBase** and we declare that *Var* must be available as well. Next we define the domain *Env* by means of a term from the type part of the metalanguage. Additionally we introduce the metavariables *loc*, *var*, and *env* ranging over the appropriate domains. Finally we define the domain $\underline{Val}$ to equal the domain $\underline{[Bool]}$ known to be available in **TBase**, we define the domain $\underline{Loc}$ to equal the domain $\underline{[Num]}$ of numbers also known to be available, and we define the domain $\underline{State}$ by a term from the type part of the metalanguage. (A more realistic language would have $\underline{Val}$ to be a summand of domains and this is possible in the larger metalanguage considered in the references.) It is important to stress that *Env* is a type in the static part of the metalanguage and $\underline{State}$ is a type in the dynamic part; this corresponds to a compiler handling the environment statically (i.e. at compile-time) while generating code to handle the state dynamically (i.e. at run-time).

Turning to the semantics of expressions we introduce a semantic function $\mathcal{E}$; its functionality is given by means of a term from the type part of the metalanguage:

$$\mathcal{E}[\![exp]\!] \ : \ Env \to \underline{State \to Val \times State}$$

An example semantic clause is given by:

$$\begin{array}{rcl} \mathcal{E}[\![var]\!](env) & = & Tuple\langle get(env(var)),\ Id\rangle \\ \text{where } get & : & Loc \to \underline{State \to Val} \\ get & \in & \mathbf{TConst} \end{array}$$

Here we have used a term from the expression part of the metalanguage to define the semantics of the assignment statement. Additionally we have used an auxiliary function *get*; its functionality is given by means of a term from the type part of the metalanguage; finally it is declared to be a constant that must be available in **TConst**.

Turning to the semantics of commands we introduce a semantic function $\mathcal{C}$:

$$\mathcal{C}[\![cmd]\!] \;:\; Env \rightarrow Loc \rightarrow \underline{State \rightarrow State}$$

A few example clauses are given by:

$$\begin{aligned}
&\mathcal{C}[\![var{:=}exp]\!](env)(loc) \;=\; set(env(var)) \circ \mathcal{E}[\![exp]\!](env) \\
&\qquad \text{where } set \;:\; Loc \rightarrow \underline{Val \times State \rightarrow State} \\
&\qquad\qquad set \;\in\; \mathbf{TConst} \\
&\mathcal{C}[\![\texttt{while}\ exp\ \texttt{do}\ cmd]\!](env)(loc) \;=\; Fix(\lambda c. \\
&\qquad If\langle Fst,\; c \circ \mathcal{C}[\![cmd]\!](env)(loc) \circ Snd,\; Snd\rangle \circ \mathcal{E}[\![exp]\!](env)) \\
&\mathcal{C}[\![\textbf{begin new}\ var;\ cmd\ \textbf{end}]\!](env)(loc) \;= \\
&\qquad \mathcal{C}[\![cmd]\!](env[var \mapsto loc])(next(loc)) \\
&\qquad \text{where } next \;:\; Loc \rightarrow Loc \\
&\qquad\qquad next(loc) \;=\; plus(loc, 1) \\
&\qquad \text{where } \cdots[\cdots \mapsto \cdots] \;:\; (Env \times Var \times Loc) \rightarrow Env \\
&\qquad\qquad \cdots
\end{aligned}$$

Here *next* is defined by a term of the expression part of the metalanguage rather than being declared as a constant that must be available in **TConst**.

For $\cdots[\cdots \mapsto \cdots]$ we then have the possibility of *(i)* either giving a term that defines it, or *(ii)* simply declaring it to be a constant that must be available in **TConst**. In terms of writing the semantic equations, the second choice is surely the easier; in terms of providing an interpretation for the metalanguage, the first choice is surely the easier. In general we believe that the first choice is preferable in that it will pay off in the long term: if a multitude of analyses (or indeed code generations) are to be defined, or if a library of interpretations is to be used for a multitude of programming languages.

It is important to stress that the operations concerning the environment are expressed in the static part of the metalanguage whereas the operations concerning the state are expressed in the dynamic part; as has already been observed above, this corresponds to a compiler handling the environment statically (i.e. at compile-time) while generating code to handle the state dynamically (i.e. at run-time). Furthermore, the meaning of a static operation will be the same regardless of the analysis being specified, whereas the meaning of a dynamic operation will be allowed to vary in accordance with the analysis being specified; similar remarks apply to other uses of the parameterised semantics like specifying code generation or specifying the standard semantics.

The overall approach of parameterised semantics is captured by the following diagram:

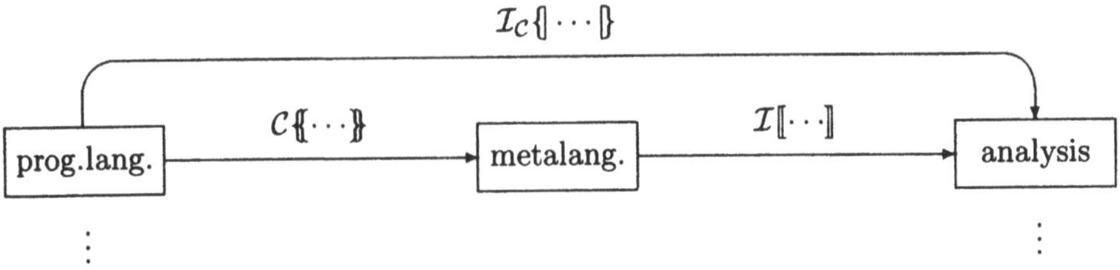

A traditional semantic function, like $\mathcal{I}_C\{\!|cmd|\!\}$ for commands, is "factored" through the metalanguage, as in $\mathcal{I}_C\{\!|cmd|\!\} = \mathcal{I}[\![\mathcal{C}\{\!\{cmd\}\!\}]\!]$. The details of how to obtain $\mathcal{I}[\![\cdots]\!]$ is the subject of the next section.

A tool-makers perspective. Let us end this section by high-lighting the flexibility offered by our sets **TBase** and **TConst** of two-level base types and two-level constants, respectively. We are by no means restricted to letting the two-level base types only contain simple static types like *Bool* and *Num* and simple dynamic types like $\underline{Bool}$ and $\underline{Num}$; it is perfectly feasible to include more complex base types and this is particularly useful for dynamic types. As an example, we might add a type $\underline{Plane}$ for describing points in the plane; since we naturally think of $Plane = Num \times Num$ it might aid the intuition to replace $\underline{Plane}$ by $\underline{Num \times Num}$. In this way the availability of "structured base types" gives a clear separation between:

- those features that will be interpreted compositionally (e.g. $\underline{Num} \;\underline{\times}\; \underline{Num}$), and
- those features that will not (e.g. $\underline{Num \times Num}$).

Similarly, we can admit a dynamic constant $\underline{\lambda(x,y).(-x,y)}$. This flexibility, mentioned already in [15], is often overlooked and we shall return to it in the next section.

In a similar way it may be desirable to have several versions of the dynamic type constructors and their associated operators (e.g. $\underline{\times}'$ and $\underline{\times}''$ together with *Tuple*$'$, *Tuple*$''$, *Fst*$'$ etc.). In this way the analysis tool will allow the user to treat different occurrences of the same type constructor in different ways; in terms of the theoretical developments this hardly poses any new challenges.

Reader's guide. The pragmatics of using two-level metalanguages for compiler writing is explained in [22] (and also Section 6 of [19] and Section 8.2 of [20]); the most up-to-date account of code generation is given in [19]; a recent overview of some of the techniques for automatically transforming the ordinary denotational metalanguage into the two-level metalanguage is given in Chapters 2, 3 and 4 of [20]. A prototype system implementing a number of ideas from [20] is described in [23].

3 Two-Level Abstract Interpretation

We are now ready to give the two-level metalanguage a parameterised denotational semantics suitable for a development of abstract interpretation. For reasons of space we shall take a somewhat cavalier attitude[1] to some of the technical details and instead refer to the references, where the technical details are covered in painstaking detail together with generalisations and extensions of the material presented here. The overall idea is that the static entities are given a fixed semantics whereas the dynamic entities are given a semantics that is parameterised on the specification of an interpretation of the dynamic primitives; this allows to use the same semantic specification with many interpretations (e.g. for specifying different program analyses), and to use the same interpretation for many semantic specifications (e.g. for different programming languages).

Types. The semantics of two-level types $tt \in$ **TType** is defined relative to the type component of an interpretation $\mathcal{I}$ by means of the following equations:

$$\begin{aligned}
\mathcal{I}[\![Num]\!] &= \{\cdots,-1,0,1,\cdots\}_\bot && \text{the flat cpo of integers}\\
\mathcal{I}[\![Bool]\!] &= \{true, false\}_\bot && \text{the flat cpo of booleans}\\
\mathcal{I}[\![tt_1 \times tt_2]\!] &= \mathcal{I}[\![tt_1]\!] \times \mathcal{I}[\![tt_2]\!] && \text{cartesian product}\\
\mathcal{I}[\![tt_1 \rightarrow tt_2]\!] &= \mathcal{I}[\![tt_1]\!] \rightarrow \mathcal{I}[\![tt_2]\!] && \text{monotone or continous functions}\\
\mathcal{I}[\![\underline{B}]\!] &= \mathcal{I}_{\underline{B}}\\
\mathcal{I}[\![tt_1 \,\underline{\times}\, tt_2]\!] &= \mathcal{I}_{\underline{\times}}(\mathcal{I}[\![tt_1]\!], \mathcal{I}[\![tt_2]\!])\\
\mathcal{I}[\![tt_1 \,\underline{\rightarrow}\, tt_2]\!] &= \mathcal{I}_{\underline{\rightarrow}}(\mathcal{I}[\![tt_1]\!], \mathcal{I}[\![tt_2]\!])
\end{aligned}$$

Here the type component of the interpretation $\mathcal{I}$ specifies:

a cpo $\mathcal{I}_{\underline{B}}$ for each dynamic base type $\underline{B} \in$ **TBase**,
a lax functor[2] $\mathcal{I}_{\underline{\times}}$ (over a class of cpo's specified by $\mathcal{I}$), and
a lax functor $\mathcal{I}_{\underline{\rightarrow}}$ (over a class of cpo's specified by $\mathcal{I}$).

As an example, the standard semantics S might have:

$$\begin{aligned}
S_{\underline{[Num]}} &= \{\cdots,-1,0,1,\cdots\}_\bot\\
S_{\underline{[Bool]}} &= \{true, false\}_\bot\\
S_{\underline{\times}}(D_1, D_2) &= D_1 \times D_2\\
S_{\underline{\rightarrow}}(D_1, D_2) &= D_1 \rightarrow D_2
\end{aligned}$$

[1] We assume that the demands on value spaces and functions are chosen in such a way that they interact nicely: one possibility is to use Scott-domains and Scott-continuous functions, and another is to use chain complete partial orders (having least upper bounds of all totally ordered subsets) and monotone functions; in both cases least fixed points exist.

[2] The details of lax functors (called semi-functors in early papers by the author) will not be needed here.

Furthermore, a simple abstract interpretation I might have:

$$\begin{aligned} I_{\underline{[Num]}} &= (\{l \subseteq \{\cdots,-1,0,1,\cdots\} \mid l \text{ is an interval}\}, \subseteq) \\ I_{\underline{[Bool]}} &= (\{\bot, tt, ff, \top\}, \sqsubseteq) \qquad \text{where } \bot \sqsubseteq tt, ff \sqsubseteq \top \\ I_{\underline{\times}}(L_1, L_2) &= L_1 \times L_2 \\ I_{\underline{\rightarrow}}(L_1, L_2) &= L_1 \rightarrow L_2 \end{aligned}$$

Already now we see the flexibility of admitting "structured base types" like $\underline{[Num \times Num]}$; here we might have:

$$\begin{aligned} S_{\underline{[Num \times Num]}} &= S_{\underline{[Num]}} \star S_{\underline{[Num]}} \qquad \text{(smash product)} \\ I_{\underline{[Num \times Num]}} &= (\{l \subseteq \{\cdots,-1,0,1,\cdots\}^2 \mid l \text{ is a convex polygon}\}, \subseteq) \end{aligned}$$

This highlights the difference between a dynamic type like $\underline{[Num] \times [Num]}$, that is to be interpreted compositionally and hence only admits rectangles in the plane (given the choice of $I_{\underline{\times}}$), and a type like $\underline{[Num \times Num]}$ that is not required to be interpreted compositionally, and hence admits much more complex subsets of the plane like the convex polygons of [4]. This flexibility is important for the applicability of a tool for program analysis, but tends to receive less attention in more theoretical studies where one of the research challenges is to increase the descriptive power of compositionally defined dynamic types, so as to reduce the need for "structured base types".

Expressions. The semantics of two-level expressions $te \in$ **TExp** is defined relative to the expression (and type) component of the interpretation $\mathcal{I}$. For the static constructs the equations are:

$$\begin{aligned} \mathcal{I}[\![tc]\!]\rho &= \mathcal{I}_{tc} \\ \mathcal{I}[\![v]\!]\rho &= \rho(v) \\ \mathcal{I}[\![\lambda v.te]\!]\rho &= \lambda d.\ \mathcal{I}[\![te]\!](\rho[v \mapsto d]) \\ \mathcal{I}[\![te_1(te_2)]\!]\rho &= (\mathcal{I}[\![te_1]\!]\rho)(\mathcal{I}[\![te_2]\!]\rho) \\ \mathcal{I}[\![\langle te_1, te_2\rangle]\!]\rho &= (\mathcal{I}[\![te_1]\!]\rho, \mathcal{I}[\![te_2]\!]\rho) \\ \mathcal{I}[\![fst\ te]\!]\rho &= fst(\mathcal{I}[\![te]\!]\rho) \\ \mathcal{I}[\![snd\ te]\!]\rho &= snd(\mathcal{I}[\![te]\!]\rho) \\ \mathcal{I}[\![if\ te_0\ te_1\ te_2]\!]\rho &= \begin{cases} \mathcal{I}[\![te_1]\!]\rho & \text{if } \mathcal{I}[\![te_0]\!]\rho = true \\ \mathcal{I}[\![te_2]\!]\rho & \text{if } \mathcal{I}[\![te_0]\!]\rho = false \\ \bot & \text{if } \mathcal{I}[\![te_0]\!]\rho = \bot \end{cases} \\ \mathcal{I}[\![fix\ te]\!]\rho &= lfp(\mathcal{I}[\![te]\!]\rho) \end{aligned}$$

Here *lfp* is the least fixed point operator (e.g. $lfp(f) = \sqcup_n f^n(\bot)$ for Scott-continous functions). For the dynamic constructs the equations are:

$$\begin{aligned}
\mathcal{I}[\![Id]\!]\rho &= \mathcal{I}_{Id}\\
\mathcal{I}[\![te_1 \circ te_2]\!]\rho &= \mathcal{I}_{\circ}(\mathcal{I}[\![te_1]\!]\rho, \mathcal{I}[\![te_2]\!]\rho)\\
\mathcal{I}[\![Curry\ te]\!]\rho &= \mathcal{I}_{Curry}(\mathcal{I}[\![te]\!]\rho)\\
\mathcal{I}[\![Apply\langle te_1, te_2\rangle]\!]\rho &= \mathcal{I}_{Apply}(\mathcal{I}[\![te_1]\!]\rho, \mathcal{I}[\![te_2]\!]\rho)\\
\mathcal{I}[\![Tuple\langle te_1, te_2\rangle]\!]\rho &= \mathcal{I}_{Tuple}(\mathcal{I}[\![te_1]\!]\rho, \mathcal{I}[\![te_2]\!]\rho)\\
\mathcal{I}[\![Fst]\!]\rho &= \mathcal{I}_{Fst}\\
\mathcal{I}[\![Snd]\!]\rho &= \mathcal{I}_{Snd}\\
\mathcal{I}[\![If\ te_0\ te_1\ te_2]\!]\rho &= \mathcal{I}_{If}(\mathcal{I}[\![te_0]\!]\rho, \mathcal{I}[\![te_1]\!]\rho, \mathcal{I}[\![te_2]\!]\rho)\\
\mathcal{I}[\![Fix\ te]\!]\rho &= \mathcal{I}_{Fix}(\mathcal{I}[\![te]\!]\rho)
\end{aligned}$$

Here the expression component of the interpretation $\mathcal{I}$ specifies the entities

$$\mathcal{I}_{tc}, \mathcal{I}_{Id}, \mathcal{I}_{\circ}, \mathcal{I}_{Curry}, \mathcal{I}_{Apply}, \mathcal{I}_{Tuple}, \mathcal{I}_{Fst}, \mathcal{I}_{Snd}, \mathcal{I}_{If}, \mathcal{I}_{Fix}$$

living in the appropriate spaces; to be formal (see the references) we would need to further index each operator with an identification of the type of that space since for example $\mathcal{I}_{Fst}$ should have versions in $\mathcal{I}[\![tt_1 \underline{\times} tt_2 \underline{\rightarrow} tt_1]\!]$ for all (legal) choices of tt_1 and tt_2.

The standard semantics S might specify e.g.

$$\begin{aligned}
S_{Fst} &= fst\\
S_{\circ}(f_1, f_2) &= \lambda d.\ f_1(f_2(d))\\
S_{If}(f_0, f_1, f_2) &= \lambda d. \begin{cases} f_1(d) & \text{if } f_0(d) = true\\ f_2(d) & \text{if } f_0(d) = false\\ \bot & \text{if } f_0(d) = \bot \end{cases}\\
S_{Fix}(f) &= lfp(f)
\end{aligned}$$

(following the informal explanations of the previous section) and e.g.

$$\begin{aligned}
S_{true} &= true \in S_{\underline{[Bool]}}\\
S_7 &= 7 \in S_{\underline{[Num]}}
\end{aligned}$$

Similarly the analysis I might specify e.g.

$$\begin{aligned}
I_{Fst} &= fst\\
I_{\circ}(h_1, h_2) &= \lambda l.\ h_1(h_2(l))\\
I_{If}(h_0, h_1, h_2) &= h_1 \sqcup h_2 = \lambda l.\ h_1(l) \sqcup h_2(l)\\
I_{Fix}(h) &= lfp(h)
\end{aligned}$$

(following the informal explanations of the previous section) and e.g.

$$\begin{aligned}
I_{true} &= tt \in I_{\underline{[Bool]}}\\
I_7 &= [7, 7] \in I_{\underline{[Num]}}
\end{aligned}$$

Here the conditional ignores the test and simply performs the point-wise union of the results of the "then" and "else" branches; we shall consider more complex choices shortly. Turning to a "structured" constant like $\underline{[\lambda(x, y).(-x, y)]}$ of type $\underline{[Num \times Num] \to [Num \times Num]}$, the standard interpretation might have $S_{[\lambda(x,y).(-x,y)]} = \lambda(d_1, d_2).(-d_1, d_2)$ and the analysis might have $\underline{I_{[\lambda(x,y).(-x,y)]}}$ to be the suitable operation for taking the mirror image of a polygon.

Building-blocks for types. A useful tool for program analysis would contain a large selection of analyses that could be used as building blocks when constructing an analysis. We have already seen a few examples: intervals ($\underline{I_{[Num]}}$), polygons in the plane ($\underline{I_{[Num \times Num]}}$), sets of booleans ($\underline{I_{[Bool]}}$).

On top of this comes the need for *combining* existing analyses to obtain new ones; for this we begin with considering just the property spaces. Suppose that we have a *union* type $tt_1 \underline{+} tt_2$ and that the standard semantics has $S[\![tt_1 \underline{+} tt_2]\!] = S[\![tt_1]\!] \uplus S[\![tt_2]\!]$ where $\uplus$ is a form for disjoint union (that takes care of the least elements). In the parameterised approach this would be recorded by having $S_{\underline{+}}(D_1, D_2) = D_1 \uplus D_2$. An obvious candidate for the analysis would therefore be to use $\uplus$ as well, or rather a slightly modified version that produces complete lattices (e.g. by incorporating a new greatest element). However, the powerset or powerdomain $\mathcal{P}(D_1 \uplus D_2)$ has greater descriptive power than $\mathcal{P}(D_1) \uplus \mathcal{P}(D_2)$ but luckily we have the isomorphism $\mathcal{P}(D_1 \uplus D_2) \cong \mathcal{P}(D_1) \times \mathcal{P}(D_2)$ and this suggest that cartesian product might be a preferable choice. Indeed $L_1 \uplus L_2$ only allows using either a property from L_1 *or* from L_2 (or $\top$ which indicates lack of information), whereas $L_1 \times L_2$ allows using both a property from L_1 *and* from L_2 (with $(\top, \top) = \top$). Therefore a general tool must

- allow to interpret $I_{\underline{+}}$ in several ways (including as $\uplus$ or $\times$).

Next consider the *product* type $tt_1 \underline{\times} tt_2$ where $S[\![tt_1 \underline{\times} tt_2]\!] = S[\![tt_1]\!] \times S[\![tt_2]\!]$, as recorded by $S_{\underline{\times}} = \times$. An obvious candidate for the analysis would therefore be to use $\times$ as well; this leads to analyses in so-called *independent attribute form*. However, $\mathcal{P}(D_1 \times D_2)$ has greater descriptive power than $\mathcal{P}(D_1) \times \mathcal{P}(D_2)$ and this suggests looking for a lax functor $\otimes$ such that $\mathcal{P}(D_1 \times D_2)$ is isomorphic to $\mathcal{P}(D_1) \otimes \mathcal{P}(D_2)$. Luckily a notion of tensor product [12] can be constructed such that it applies to more general complete lattices than those of form $\mathcal{P}(\cdots)$, and such that $\mathcal{P}(D_1 \times D_2) \cong \mathcal{P}(D_1) \otimes \mathcal{P}(D_2)$. Use of the tensor product leads to so-called *relational analyses* of the kind where the precision in each component is described by the component space itself. Therefore a general tool must

- allow to interpret $I_{\underline{\times}}$ in several ways (including as $\times$ or $\otimes$).

Since a relational analysis like "polygons in the plane" does not satisfy the above condition, and is not obtainable using cartesian or tensor products, it would be useful with further possibilities; however, in the absence of this, we need the flexibility of the "structured base types" to allow $\underline{[Num \times Num]}$ such that more "ad-hoc" definitions can be used for the case at hand.

Finally let us consider the *function* type $tt_1 \underline{\rightarrow} tt_2$ where $S_{\underline{\rightarrow}} = \rightarrow$. An obvious candidate therefore is to use $I_{\underline{\rightarrow}} = \rightarrow$ as well and this will give rise to *forward* program analyses; at higher types (e.g. $tt_1 \underline{\rightarrow} (tt_2 \underline{\rightarrow} tt_3)$) they will be inherently independent attribute in nature in that no interplay between the arguments (of type tt_1 and tt_2) can be modelled. In the absence of higher-order entities a *backward* analysis can be obtained by setting $I_{\underline{\rightarrow}} = \leftarrow$, i.e. $I_{\underline{\rightarrow}}(L_1, L_2) = L_1 \leftarrow L_2 = L_2 \rightarrow L_1$; at higher types a general formulation of backwards analyses is still a research issue [8]. However, $\mathcal{P}(D_1 \rightarrow D_2)$ has greater descriptive power than either of $\mathcal{P}(D_1) \rightarrow \mathcal{P}(D_2)$ or $\mathcal{P}(D_2) \rightarrow \mathcal{P}(D_1)$, and this suggest looking for a lax functor $\ominus$ such that $\mathcal{P}(D_1 \rightarrow D_2)$ is isomorphic to $\mathcal{P}(D_1) \ominus \mathcal{P}(D_2)$; additionally, it should apply to more general complete lattices than simply those of form $\mathcal{P}(\cdots)$. This is still an unsolved research problem and therefore we may need the flexibility of the "structured base types" to allow a base type like $\underline{[Num \rightarrow Num \rightarrow Num]}$ in case a more precise ad-hoc analysis can be performed for that particular case. In summary a general tool must

- allow to interpret $I_{\underline{\rightarrow}}$ in several ways (including as $\rightarrow$ or $\leftarrow$).

Building-blocks for expressions. Having constructed the property spaces the next task is to construct the analysis functions themselves. Here we focus on the combinators, because constants like $\underline{[\lambda(x,y).(-x,y)]}$ are intended to be used only when the desired analysis cannot be built compositionally from the primitives provided, just as $\underline{[Num \times Num]}$ is intended to be used only when the desired property spaces cannot be built compositionally from the primitives provided. For each combinator we now suggest one or more "expected forms" [14] that could profitably be offered as building-blocks by the analysis tool.

For *forward analyses* where the dynamic function space is interpreted as ordinary function space, i.e. $I_{\underline{\rightarrow}} = \rightarrow$, it is natural to let an analysis I have:

$$
\begin{aligned}
I_{Id} &= \lambda l.\ l \\
I_{\circ}(h_1, h_2) &= \lambda l.\ h_1(h_2(l)) \\
I_{Curry}(h) &= \lambda l_1.\ \lambda l_2.\ h(l_1, l_2) \\
I_{Apply}(h_1, h_2) &= \lambda l.\ h_1(l)(h_2(l))
\end{aligned}
$$

For *backward analyses* where the dynamic function space is interpreted as "backward function space", i.e. $I_{\underline{\rightarrow}} = \leftarrow$, it is natural to take:

$$
\begin{aligned}
I_{Id} &= \lambda l.\ l \\
I_{\circ}(h_1, h_2) &= \lambda l.\ h_2(h_1(l))
\end{aligned}
$$

This definition is greatly facilitated by the use of combinators for the dynamic level (as opposed to the use of an underlined λ-calculus). Due to the difficulties mentioned previously, the higher-order combinators I_{Curry} and I_{Apply} are best left uninterpreted.

For forward analyses where dynamic product is interpreted by *cartesian product*, i.e. $I_{\underline{\rightarrow}} = \rightarrow$ and $I_{\underline{\times}} = \times$, it is natural to let an analysis I have:

$$I_{Tuple}(h_1, h_2) = \lambda l.\ (h_1(l), h_2(l))$$
$$I_{Fst} = \lambda(l_1, l_2).\ l_1$$
$$I_{Snd} = \lambda(l_1, l_2).\ l_2$$

For forward analyses where dynamic product is interpreted by *tensor product*, i.e. $I_{\underline{\rightarrow}} = \rightarrow$ and $I_{\underline{\times}} = \otimes$, one might have

$$I_{Tuple}(h_1, h_2) = \lambda l.\ cross(h_1(l), h_2(l))$$
$$I_{Fst} = (\lambda(l_1, l_2).\ l_1)^\dagger$$
$$I_{Snd} = (\lambda(l_1, l_2).\ l_2)^\dagger$$

where $cross : L_1 \times L_2 \rightarrow L_1 \otimes L_2$ and $h^\dagger : L_1 \otimes L_2 \rightarrow L$ (whenever $h : L_1 \times L_2 \rightarrow L$) are operations associated with the tensor product. When $L_1 \times L_2$ is $\mathcal{P}(D_1) \times \mathcal{P}(D_2)$ and $L_1 \otimes L_2$ is $\mathcal{P}(D_1 \times D_2)$ this amounts to $cross = \lambda(l_1, l_2).\{(d_1, d_2) \mid d_1 \in l_1, d_2 \in l_2)\}$ and $h^\dagger(Y) = \sqcup\{h(\{d_1\}, \{d_2\}) \mid (d_1, d_2) \in Y\}$. We refer to the references for improvements to the expected form for I_{Tuple} and for expected forms for backward analyses using cartesian product.

For forward analyses a simple-minded approach to interpreting the *conditional* is to ignore the condition and simply merge[3] the results of the two branches:

$$I^1_{If}(h_0, h_1, h_2) = h_1 \sqcup h_2 = \lambda l.\ h_1(l) \sqcup h_2(l)$$

A more precise approach is to use the condition to determine which parts of the argument to be passed to which branch:

$$I^2_{If}(h_0, h_1, h_2) = \lambda l.\ h_1(\mathit{filter}[h_0, tt](l)) \sqcup h_2(\mathit{filter}[h_0, \mathit{ff}](l))$$

Here $\mathit{filter}[h_0, b](l)$ attempts to construct the part of l for which the condition $h_0(l)$ could possibly include the result b. A simple-minded choice therefore is

$$\mathit{filter}[h_0, b](l) = \begin{cases} l & \text{if } h_0(l) \sqsupseteq b \\ \bot & \text{otherwise} \end{cases}$$

and a more precise[4] approach is to take

$$\mathit{filter}[h_0, b](l) = \{a \in A \mid a \sqsubseteq l \wedge h_0(a) \sqsupseteq b\}$$

where A is the set of atoms (a generalisation of singletons).

[3] For maximum precision we use here the least upper bound; coarser analyses would result if it was replaced by a monotone upper bound operator.

[4] A hybrid of this approach is to let the condition be replaced by its actual metalanguage expression; this allows the use of symbolic reasoning in order to achieve even greater precision.

Finally, let us consider the dynamic *fixed point* in the case of forward analyses. For analysis domains of finite height it is possible to use the formula

$$I^1_{Fix}(h) = \sqcup_n\, h^n(\bot)$$

since it is guaranteed to reach the fixed point in a finite number of steps (i.e. $\exists n_0 : \sqcup_n\, h^n(\bot) = h^{n_0}(\bot)$). In the case of analysis domains that are not of finite height there are much better candidate formulae than simply using $h^{n_0}(\top)$ for some natural number n_0. For this let ∇ be a widening operator as defined in [3]: an upper bound operator that additionally satisfies a condition on certain sequences always being finite. Then define

$$I^2_{Fix}(h) = \sqcup_n\, h_\nabla^{\langle n\rangle}$$

where

$$h_\nabla^{\langle 0\rangle} = \bot, \qquad h_\nabla^{\langle n+1\rangle} = \begin{cases} h_\nabla^{\langle n\rangle} & \text{if } h(h_\nabla^{\langle n\rangle}) \sqsubseteq h_\nabla^{\langle n\rangle} \\ h_\nabla^{\langle n\rangle}\ \nabla\ h(h_\nabla^{\langle n\rangle}) & \text{otherwise} \end{cases}$$

One can show that the sequence $(h_\nabla^{\langle n\rangle})_n$ eventually stabilises (i.e. $\exists n_0 : \sqcup_n\, h_\nabla^{\langle n\rangle} = h_\nabla^{\langle n_0\rangle}$) whenever ∇ is a widening operator and hence I^2_{Fix} is obtainable in a finite number of steps. The result obtained in this way can then be further improved using a narrowing operator [3].

Theoretical developments. By now we have covered a good selection of those aspects of two-level abstract interpretation that would be of main interest to the tool-maker, but we have hardly covered any of the rather comprehensive theory needed to ensure that such a tool is well-behaved.

This includes proving that the analyses specified are indeed correct with respect to the semantics; for this a notion of logical relations proves helpful. Correctness relations can frequently be reformulated using representation functions defined inductively on the type structure; for subsets of the metalanguage this allows inducing a best analysis, e.g. the so-called collecting semantics. Closely related to correctness relations are approximation relations between given analyses; these are frequently formulated using Galois connections, and by the type constructors being lax functors, it is possible to build these inductively on the type structure. Correctness and approximation should compose in the sense that approximating an analysis already proved correct should still give rise to a correct analysis; establishing results like these leads to identifying a notion of "level-preserving" types where these results are immediate. Techniques are also needed for changing between analysis methods, e.g. from using the tensor product to using the cartesian product, and here the concept of lax natural transformations is helpful. Finally, the presence of recursive domains in the full metalanguage poses complications of its own.

We refer to the references for coverage of these issues; however, in depth knowledge of this theory is hardly necessary for the user of a tool-kit based on two-level abstract interpretation, in much the same way that in depth knowledge of the theory of context free languages is hardly necessary for the user of `lex` and `yacc`.

Reader's guide. The most up-to-date account[5] of two-level abstract interpretation is given in [18] (with [17] exploring more technical aspects); a reasonably comprehensive account of most of the theory is given in Section 3 of [9].

4 Conclusion

The natural sciences propose theories for describing aspects of the physical world, validate the extent to which the theories describe the physical world, and use the insights gained as feed-back to the development of new theories, overcoming identified shortcomings or attempting to describe additional aspects. Let us conclude in this spirit by extracting some of the insights gained from two-level abstract interpretation and determining what feed-back they might give to the two-level metalanguages themselves, the general area of domain theoretic program analysis, the wider spectrum of semantics-directed analysis frameworks, and finally the design of tools for analysis.

Two-level metalanguages. We have seen that a denotationally based theory of two-level abstract interpretation gives rise to a powerful framework. This framework naturally shares many of the advantages and disadvantages of denotational semantics:

- The adequacy of the two-level metalanguage (for describing the semantics of a programming language) equals the adequacy of denotational semantics itself.

While two-level metalanguages are almost always given a denotational semantics, it is worth stressing that also an operational semantics is feasible (e.g. along the lines of [16]). This opens up for the two-level metalanguage being expanded to a full-fledged functional language; it also opens up for defining two-level notations for completely different programming paradigms [21]:

- The "two-level approach" is *not* inherently restricted to a denotational, domain theoretic, or functional approach.

Domain theoretic program analysis. Taking the domain theoretic approach to program analysis, there are a number of inherent decisions that are worth bringing out:

- abstract interpretation is viewed as abstract computation rather than specification;
- the computational partial order is not fully separated from the approximation partial order (unlike the technically complex [11]), and

[5] Shorter and less technical overviews are given in [15], stressing the metalanguage approach, and [13], overviewing part of the theory, but they no longer convey the full generality of the approach.

– analyses generally model extensional[6] rather than intensional properties.

The first decision is responsible for favouring a framework where the least upper bound (rather than greatest lower bound) is taken when "paths" converge; the second is responsible for mainly modelling safety (or partial correctness) properties; and the third is responsible for the high complexity of implementing some of the analyses specified. It is important to stress that these points apply also to developments based on ordinary denotational metalanguages (e.g. [2])!

Semantics-directed analysis frameworks. Current approaches to defining general frameworks for semantics-directed analysis seem to be mainly based on natural semantics or game semantics; in particular they are largely operational in nature (as would likely be possible for the two-level metalanguage as well).

In assessing these and other approaches it is important to consider the overall applicability of the framework:

– Does it handle a variety of programming *languages*: imperative, functional, object-oriented, logic, concurrent, parallel, and distributed languages, and regardless of whether they are typed or not?
– Does it handle a variety of program *analyses* and does it provide building-blocks for their construction: forwards, backwards, higher-order, independent attribute, and relational analyses?
– Is the *granularity* of the metalanguage adequate: for specification of the analyses, for defining the semantics of the languages, and for conducting the necessary proofs?

Answering the second question involves investigating the extent to which the semantic approach may influence or limit the type of properties that are expressible:

– Does the semantic framework impose limitations upon the kind of properties that can be expressed (e.g. neededness versus strictness, partial versus total properties, and extensional versus intensional properties)?
– Is the choice of properties, and the method of specification, such that efficient realisations are feasible (or do all conceivable realisations have inherently intractable complexity)?

Finally, it is always proper scholarly behaviour to answer the following question:

– To which extent is the new framework better (not just different or "more exciting") than existing approaches, and to what extent have the insights obtained there been incorporated?

[6] An extensional property [31] of a program remains true when the program is replaced by an "equivalent" program (e.g. strictness information), whereas an intensional property may depend on the syntax of the program (e.g. closure information).

Tools for analysis. To determine whether or not a tool is likely to sustain wide-spread and long-term usage it is important to assess its likely performance from the user's point of view. Some considerations were already encountered above:

– Is the user interface easy to understand and of wide applicability: Does it handle a variety of programming *languages* (see above)? Does it handle a variety of program *analyses* and does it provide building-blocks for their construction (see above)?

Then there is the important issue of resource usage (time and space):

– Does the system produce an analysis module faster and more reliably than a manual approach?
– Does the analysis module execute sufficiently fast for the task at hand: Have all relevant algorithmic techniques (e.g. strong components in graphs, binary decision diagrams) been fully exploited? What is the resulting complexity? If modelling extensional properties: would intensional properties be faster to obtain and still be of acceptable quality?

It is much harder to assess the usefulness of the results produced by the system, e.g. how easy it is to exploit them for optimisations in the compiler.

Finally, it is always sound engineering practice to answer the following question:

– To which extent is the new tool better (not just different) than existing systems, and to what extent have the insights obtained there been incorporated?

Awareness of, and responsiveness to, these considerations can only improve the quality of the tool or framework being developed; eventually it just might lead to a tool or framework enjoying wide-spread and long-term usage.

Acknowledgement. This research was funded in part by the DART-project (sponsored by the Danish Natural Science Research Council) and the LOMAPS-project (sponsored by ESPRIT Basic Research). Thanks to Hanne Riis Nielson and Reinhard Wilhelm for providing answers to my questions.

Disclaimer. The references are by no means exhaustive for program analysis; nor is the present treatment of two-level abstract interpretation.

References

1. M. Alt and F. Martin. Generation of Efficient Interprocedural Analyzers with PAG. In *Proc. SAS '95*, SLNCS 983, pages 33–50. Springer-Verlag, 1995.
2. G. L. Burn, C. Hankin, and S. Abramsky. Strictness Analysis for Higher-Order Functions. *Science of Computer Programming*, 7:249–278, 1986.

3. P. Cousot and R. Cousot. Abstract Interpretation: a Unified Lattice Model for Static Analysis of Programs by Construction or Approximation of Fixpoints. In *Proc. 4th POPL*, pages 238–252. ACM Press, 1977.
4. P. Cousot and N. Halbwachs. Automatic Discovery of Linear Restraints Among Variables of a Program. In *Proc. 5th POPL*, pages 84–97. ACM Press, 1978.
5. C. Flanagan and M. Felleisen. The Semantics of Future and Its Use in Program Optimization. In *Proc. POPL '95*, pages 209–220. ACM Press, 1995.
6. C. W. Fraser, D. R. Hanson, and T. A. Proebsting. Engineering a Simple, Efficient Code-Generator Generator. *ACM Letters on Programming Languages and Systems*, 1(3):213–226, 1992.
7. N. Heintze. Set-Based Analysis of ML Programs. In *Proc. LFP'94*, pages 306–317, 1994.
8. J. Hughes. Backward Analysis of Functional Programs. In *Partial Evaluation and Mixed Computation*, pages 187–208. North-Holland, 1988.
9. N. D. Jones and F. Nielson. Abstract Interpretation: a Semantics-Based Tool for Program Analysis. In *Handbook of Logic in Computer Science* volume 4. Oxford University Press, 1995.
10. J. B. Kam and J. D. Ullman. Monotone Data Flow Analysis Frameworks. *Acta Informatica*, 7:305–317, 1977.
11. A. Mycroft and F. Nielson. Strong Abstract Interpretation using Power-Domains. In *Proc. ICALP '83*, SLNCS 154, pages 536–547. Springer-Verlag, 1983.
12. F. Nielson. Tensor Products Generalize the Relational Data Flow Analysis Method. In *Proc. 4th Hungarian Computer Science Conference*, pages 211–225, 1985.
13. F. Nielson. Abstract Interpretation of Denotational Definitions. In *Proc. STACS '86*, SLNCS 210, pages 1–20. Springer-Verlag, 1986.
14. F. Nielson. Expected Forms of Data Flow Analysis. In *Proc. Programs as Data Objects*, SLNCS 217, pages 172–191. Springer-Verlag, 1986.
15. F. Nielson. Towards a Denotational Theory of Abstract Interpretation. In S. Abramsky and C. Hankin, editors, *Abstract Interpretation of Declarative Languages*, pages 219–245. Ellis-Horwood, 1987.
16. F. Nielson. A Formal Type System for Comparing Partial Evaluators. In D. Bjørner, A. P. Ershov, and N. D. Jones, editors, *Partial Evaluation and Mixed Computation*, pages 349–384. North-Holland, 1988.
17. F. Nielson. Strictness Analysis and Denotational Abstract Interpretation. *Information and Computation*, 76:29–92, 1988.
18. F. Nielson. Two-Level Semantics and Abstract Interpretation. *Theoretical Computer Science — Fundamental Studies*, 69:117–242, 1989.
19. F. Nielson and H. R. Nielson. Two-Level Semantics and Code Generation. *Theoretical Computer Science*, 56(1):59–133, 1988.
20. F. Nielson and H. R. Nielson. *Two-Level Functional Languages. Cambridge Tracts in Theoretical Computer Science* volume 34. Cambridge University Press, 1992.
21. F. Nielson and H. R. Nielson. Multi-Level Lambda-Calculi: an Algebraic Description. In *Proc. Dagstuhl Seminar on Partial Evaluation*, SLNCS (to appear). Springer-Verlag, 1996.
22. H. R. Nielson and F. Nielson. Pragmatic Aspects of Two-Level Denotational Meta-Languages. In *Proc. ESOP '86*, SLNCS 213. Springer-Verlag, 1986.
23. H. R. Nielson, F. Nielson, A. Pilegaard, and T. Lange. The PSI System. Technical Report DAIMI IR-114, Department of Computer Science, Aarhus University, Denmark, 1992.

24. L. Paulson. Compiler Generation from Denotational Semantics. In B. Lorho, editor, *Methods and Tools for Compiler Construction*, pages 219–250. Cambridge University Press, 1984.
25. G. D. Plotkin. A Structural Approach to Operational Semantics. Technical Report FN-19, DAIMI, Aarhus University, Denmark, 1981 (reprinted 1991).
26. D. Schmidt. Natural-Semantics-Based Abstract Interpretation. In *Proc. SAS '95*, SLNCS 983, pages 1–18. Springer-Verlag, 1995.
27. J. E. Stoy. *Denotational Semantics: the Scott-Strachey Approach to Programming Language Theory*. MIT Press, 1977.
28. J.-P. Talpin and P. Jouvelot. The Type and Effect Discipline. In *Proc. LICS '92*, pages 162–173, 1992.
29. S. Tjiang and J. Hennessy. Sharlit – a Tool for Building Optimizers. In *Proc. PLDI '92*. ACM Press, 1992.
30. G. V. Venkatesh and C. N. Fischer. Spare: a Development Environment for Program Analysis Algorithms. *IEEE Transactions on Software Engineering*, 1992.
31. A. N. Whitehead and B. Russell. *Principia Mathematica*. Cambridge University Press, 1910 (reprinted 1950).
32. R. Wilhelm. Global Flow Analysis and Optimization in the MUG2 Compiler Generating System. In S. S. Muchnick and N. D. Jones, editors, *Program Flow Analysis: Theory and Applications*, chapter 5. Prentice-Hall, 1981.
33. K. Yi and W. L. Harrison III. Automatic Generation and Management of Interprocedural Program Analyses. In *Proc. POPL '93*, pages 246–259. ACM Press, 1993.

Appendix: The rôle of well-formedness conditions. We already said in Section 2 that a main use of the well-formedness conditions is to formalise the limitations of a given technology for performing the task at hand. A good example is given in [22] (and also Section 6 of [19]) where a version of the metalanguage (called **TMLs**) is used for defining the denotational semantics of a small imperative programming language with procedures. However, the technology for code generation for two-level metalanguages [19] impose additional conditions on the types allowed for dynamic fixed points, and these can be formalised by defining a more restrictive metalanguage (called **TMLsc**). This then suggests systematic transformations upon the denotational semantics in order to transform it from **TMLs** to **TMLsc**. In the case of [22, 19] a main technique is to change the environment: using **TMLs** it is a map from variables to locations (in the store), whereas using **TMLsc** it is a map from variables to pairs of block number and offset. Thus a well-known compiler technology from the implementation of imperative languages is intimately connected to a systematic transformation from one version of the metalanguage to another! This shows promise of being able to understand compiler technology in a much more formal manner than hitherto attempted.

Property-Oriented Expansion

Bernhard Steffen

Universität Passau (Germany)
steffen@fmi.uni-passau.de

Abstract. The paper develops a framework for *property-oriented expansion*, which is much more powerful than the state of the art (motion-based) approaches, supports the combination of transformations, and is open to automatic generation by means of synthesis. The power of our method comes at the price of an exponential worst case complexity, which, however, hardly shows up in practice: usually the algorithm behaves very moderately and provides results, which are essentially of the same size as the argument program. Power and limitations of property-oriented expansion are illustrated by means of algorithms, which are unique in eliminating *all* partial redundancies and *all* partially dead code.

Keywords: data flow analysis, modal logic, partially dead code elimination, optimization, partial redundancy elimination, program expansion, transition systems.

1 Introduction

Classical optimization techniques leave the structure of the argument program invariant. It is the power of code motion within this fixed structure ([MR]), which gives a handle to the elimination of partial redundancies [MR] and partially dead code [KRS1]. However, in contrast to 'full' redundancies [Ki], not all partial redundancies can be eliminated within a given program. Figures 1(left) and 2(left) illustrate the problem: whereas in the first figure it is obvious that there is no optimization potential without modifying the graph structure, the second example shows the disastrous effect of a single (the left most) path, which prohibits the motion of $x := a + b$. The situation is similar for partially dead code elimination.

In this paper we present a framework for *property-oriented expansion* and illustrate its power as well as its current limitations by means of applications to redundancy and dead code elimination. This technique is much more 'aggressive' than the state of the art approaches, the most flexible of which are motion-based, and it supports the combination of transformations, as usually mutually counterproductive effects are separated. Moreover, similar to motion-based approaches [Ste2, Ste3], expansion-based approaches are open to automatic generation by means of synthesis tools.

The point of our application to partial redundancy elimination is the reduction of *partial* redundancy to *total* redundancy by means of *unrolling* and *node splitting*. The effectiveness and correctness of this approach are based on the following two simple observations:

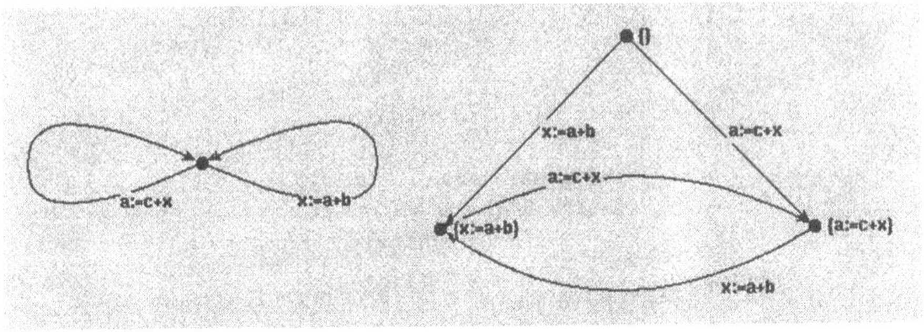

Fig. 1. A minimal example

- There is no difference between redundancy and partial redundancy in the totally expanded computation tree, which results from exhaustive unrolling (expansion) of the underlying program model. This difference is solely due to the join of paths with different histories.
- There are only finitely many different 'redundancy states' for a given program, i.e. situations where different sets of program statements are redundant. Thus there exists a finite bound for the required node splitting and unrolling.

Combined with the fact that total redundancies can easily be eliminated, this finite expansion procedure is already sufficient to eliminate *all* partial redundancies in a program. Our complete algorithm whose power is illustrated in Figures 1(right)[1] and 2(right), also minimizes the *size* of the resulting program. The impact of this minimization is best illustrated in comparison with Figure 2 (middle), which displays the result of the two step basic procedure described above. As the growth of the program size is the limiting fact of our approach, minimization is one of the vital techniques for guaranteeing its practicality.

It is important to note that we are dealing with partial redundancy elimination of *statements* here, and *not* of expressions. Thus we do not need to introduce auxiliaries. However, the standard 'expression elimination' can be fully captured by means of a preprocess inserting such auxiliaries [KRS2].

The application to partially dead code elimination is similar in flavour but requires backward unrolling, which, unfortunately, may introduce additional nondeterminism and blockings (see Figure 7). Thus the execution of such programs requires backtracking until the unique successfully terminating path is found. We conjecture that this problem can be overcome by additional unrolling in combination with a movement of conditions on acyclic parts.

The power of our method comes at the price of a high worst case complexity of its first step, which is proportional to the size of the powerset of the set of assignments considered. However, experience with our implementation indicates

[1] All the presented transformations have been fully automatically computed by means of our implementation.

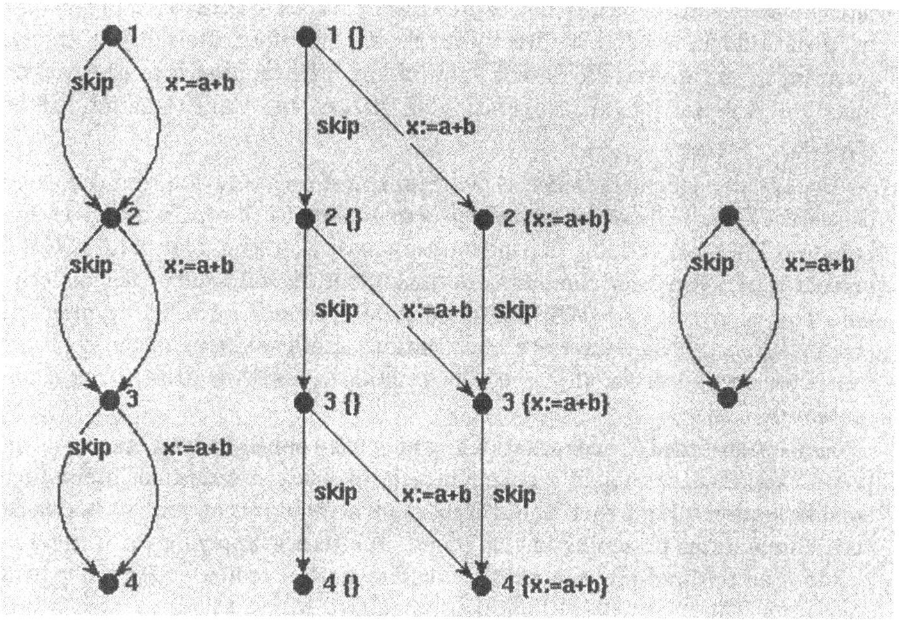

Fig. 2. A 'classical failure' of motion-based approaches

that this exponential factor hardly shows up in practice: usually only a small fraction of the domain of redundancy states is reachable, which guarantees a quite moderate algorithmic behaviour and results which are essentially of the same size as the argument program.

Besides being much more powerful, expansion based optimization has less second order effects[2] than their motion-based counterparts: iterating the application of the redundancy and the dead code elimination procedure yields a program which does neither contain partial redundancies nor partially dead code. Thus in contrast to the motion-based approaches [KRS2], we obtain an optimal solution.

Finally, besides allowing concise specifications of program properties, modal logic can be used as a basis for the automatic generation of data flow analysis algorithms by means of partial evaluation of a *model checker* with respect to the specifying formula [Ste2, Ste3]. Adapting known *synthesis* algorithms [SiCl, MaWo, StMC] a similar generation is also possible for expansion-based algorithms.

Related Work: Foundational backbone of our approach is the construction of the full transition system (later called operational model) corresponding to an abstract interpretation [CC, JoNi] capturing a given program property, like, e.g., redundancy. In contrast to most abstract interpretation-based approaches, our

[2] In [RWZ] the notion of second order effects was introduced to denote the interference between applications of the same kind of optimization. In this paper, we extend the range of this notion to cover interference between different optimizations.

interpretations are typically not expressible as formal abstractions of the underlying data domains, and it directly involves a transformation of the argument program by expansion. We do not know of any other approach to program optimization, where a similar combination of analysis and transformation has been realized.

Usually dependencies between program transformations are resolved at most heuristically: in [ASU] an ad-hoc *phase ordering* among the optimization is chosen based on the most striking dependencies or based on empirical data. [CCo, Cli] present a framework for combining optimizations by combining their underlying data flow analyses, and [WS] a more general approach for ordering interacting optimizations by using interface specifications. However, none of the approaches can cover second order effects of the complexity as they arise in *assignment motion* [KRS2].

Expansion-based transformations, where no code is moved, preserve more properties. Thus they give a better handle to study the mutual interaction of transformations. E.g., even though the partial redundancy and partially dead code eliminations presented in this paper do interact, applying them iteratively provides an optimal program, having neither partial redundancies nor partially dead code. This contrasts with motion-based algorithms, where no 'best' solution is guaranteed to exist [KRS2].

The first two sections establish essentially the same setup as in [Ste2, Ste3]: Section 2 recalls the program representation, and Section 3 the property language. Subsequently, Sections 4 and 5 present our method. While Section 4 concentrates on problem specification, Section 5 presents the corresponding algorithms as well as their essential properties. Finally, Section 6 presents our conclusions and directions for future work.

2 Models for Programs

As in [Ste2, Ste3], we model programs as transition systems, whose states and transitions are labelled with sets of atomic propositions and actions, respectively. Intuitively, atomic propositions describe properties of states, while actions describe (properties of) statements. As usual, the control flow is modelled by the graph structure of the transition system.

Definition 2.1 *A* program model *P is a quintuple* $(\mathcal{S}, \mathcal{A}, \rightarrow, \mathcal{B}, \lambda)$ *where*

1. $\mathcal{S}$ *is a finite set of* nodes *or* program states.
2. $\mathcal{A}$ *is a set of* atoms. *The subsets of* $\mathcal{A}$ *play the role of what is usually called* actions. *We will denote this set of actions by Act.*
3. $\rightarrow \subseteq \mathcal{S} \times Act \times \mathcal{S}$ *is a set of* labelled transitions, *which define the control flow of P.*
4. $\mathcal{B}$ *is a set of* atomic propositions.
5. λ *is a function* $\lambda : \mathcal{S} \rightarrow 2^{\mathcal{B}}$ *that labels states with subsets of* $\mathcal{B}$ *.*

We will write $n \xrightarrow{A} m$ *instead of* $(n, A, m) \in \rightarrow$*, and given* $\alpha \subseteq Act$*, we will call* n *an* α-predecessor *of* m *and* m *an* α-successor *of* n *if* $A \in \alpha$*. The set of all* α*-predecessors and* α*-successors will be abbreviated by* $Pred_\alpha$ *resp.* $Succ_\alpha$[3].

Essentially, a program model is a combination of a standard labelled transition system and a Kripke structure, which allows us to speak about state and statement properties explicitly and separately without using any complicated encodings. Special is only the set structure of the actions allowing us to deal with *abstract interpretations*, which treat concrete statements as sets of properties (cf. [CC]). However, one should abstract from the internal set structure of actions where it is unimportant, like e.g. in Section 3.1 and most of Section 3.2.

Additional Assumption: In the following we assume program models to possess two distinct states **s** (the *start* state) and **e** (the *end* state) satisfying:

1. **s** and **e** do not possess any predecessor and successor, respectively.
2. Every program state is reachable from **s**.
3. **e** is reachable from every program state.

These additional requirements are standard in data flow analysis, and the transformations proposed in this paper are intended to respect this format: even though the basic algorithm of Section 5.1 may introduce multiple end nodes, this format violation is repaired by the subsequent minimization procedure. Admittedly, the situation is much more complicated in Section 5.2, where an appropriate solution to maintain the format is still only conjectured.

Modelling Flow Graphs

Flow graphs are directed graphs whose nodes represent statements (as usual, we will concentrate on assignments and binary branching statements here[4]), and whose edges represent the flow of control. As mentioned above, we can additionally assume that they possess unique start and end nodes.

The simplest way to transform flow graphs into program models is by replacing each *assignment node* by two nodes connected by a transition representing the assignment statement, and each *(binary) branching node* with condition b by a node with two leaving transitions one labelled with b and the other with $\neg\, b$. This transformation increases the number of nodes at most by a factor of 2.

In the following, let $\mathbf{V}$ and $\mathbf{T}$ be sets of program variables and program terms, and $\mathcal{A}_c$ the set containing all assignments of the form $v := t$, where $v \in \mathbf{V}$ and $t \in \mathbf{T}$, as well as all boolean conditions, which may occur as labels of a conditional transition. Furthermore, let $\mathcal{B} =_{df} \{\texttt{start}, \texttt{end}\}$ be a set of atomic propositions, and λ_c the labelling function, which associates the empty set of properties with each node of the model except for $\lambda_c(\mathbf{s}) = \{\texttt{start}\}$ and $\lambda_c(\mathbf{e}) =$

[3] Note that the *Act*-predecessors and *Act*-successors are just the predecessors and successors in the usual sense.

[4] Often, non-deterministic flow graphs are considered, where branching statements are ignored.

{end}. Then the transformed flow graphs form a program model $(\mathcal{S}, \mathcal{A}_c, \rightarrow, \mathcal{B}, \lambda_c)$, where the state labelling just identifies the start and the end state, and the transition labelling the statements and conditions of the original flow graph. We will refer to these models as *concrete* program models.

However, the program models we want to deal with, and which allow an automatic treatment, typically arise as abstractions of concrete program models. A classical abstraction is given by choosing $\mathcal{A}_a = \{\mathtt{mod}(a) \mid a \in \mathcal{A}_c\} \cup \{\mathtt{use}(a) \mid a \in \mathcal{A}_c\} \cup \{\mathtt{occ}(a) \mid a \in \mathcal{A}_c\}$ as the set of transition labels together with the abstraction function $abstr : 2^{\mathcal{A}_c} \rightarrow 2^{\mathcal{A}_a}$. Denoting the left hand side variable of a by $\mathtt{L}(a)$ and its right hand side term by $\mathtt{R}(a)$, this function is defined by:

$$abstr(\{a\}) =_{df} \{\mathtt{mod}(a') \mid \mathtt{L}(a) \text{ is subterm of } \mathtt{R}(a')\}$$
$$\cup \{\mathtt{use}(a') \mid \mathtt{L}(a') \text{ is subterm of } \mathtt{R}(a)\} \cup \{\mathtt{occ}(a)\}$$

and the (additivity) property: $abstr(A) = \bigcup \{ abstr(a) \mid a \in A \}$

Transitions labelled with $\mathtt{mod}(a')$ represent statements that *modify* the value of the right hand side expression of a', and those labelled by $\mathtt{use}(a')$ statements that *use* the left hand side variable of a' in their right hand side expression. Finally, $\mathtt{occ}(a')$ explicitly marks the occurrences of its argument statement. Note that $\mathtt{mod}(a) \wedge \mathtt{occ}(a)$ means that a is a recursive assignment, i.e. $\mathtt{L}(a)$ is subterm of $\mathtt{R}(a)$.

3 The Specification Languages

As in [Ste2, Ste3], we present two specification languages, a *low level* language, which is primary, and a derived *high level* language. Whereas the low level language is the basis for our implementations and used to formally define the semantics of formulas, the high level language is easier to understand and should be used for specification. The essence of the paper can be understood on the basis of the informal presentation of the high level specification language. Thus the reader might skip Section 3.1 containing the formal background.

3.1 Low Level Specifications

Our low-level specification language is essentially a sublanguage of the modal mu-calculus [Koz] characterized by a restricted use of fixpoint constructions. The syntax of our low level specification language is parameterized by denumerable sets *Var*, $\mathcal{B}$ and *Act* of propositional variables, atomic propositions and actions, respectively, where X ranges over *Var*, β over $\mathcal{B}$ and α over subsets of *Act*:
$\Phi ::= tt \mid X \mid \Phi \wedge \Phi \mid \neg\Phi \mid \beta \mid [\alpha]\Phi \mid \overline{[\alpha]}\Phi \mid \nu X.\Phi$

The semantics of formulas is defined with respect to a program model P and an environment e mapping variables to subsets of $\mathcal{S}$ according to the following intuition: every program state satisfies the formula *tt*, while a program state satisfies a variable X if it lies in $e(X)$, and it satisfies $\Phi_1 \wedge \Phi_2$ if it satisfies both Φ_1 and Φ_2. Moreover, a program state satisfies $\neg\Phi$ if it does not satisfy Φ, it satisfies β if it is labelled by a set containing β and it satisfies $[\alpha]\Phi$ if every of its α-successors satisfies Φ. Note that this implies that a program state (node) n satisfies $[\alpha]ff$ exactly when n has no α-successors. Analogously, a program state n satisfies $\overline{[\alpha]}\Phi$ if every α-predecessor satisfies Φ. Thus in analogy, a program state n satisfies $\overline{[\alpha]}ff$ exactly when n has no α-predecessors. The formula $\nu X.\, \Phi$ is a recursive formula and should be thought of as the "largest" solution to the "equation" $X = \Phi$.

As usual, there is a syntactic restriction on expressions of the form $\nu X.\, \Phi$, which ensures the monotonicity of the fixpoint operator: X is required to appear within the range of an even number of negations in Φ. Since P is also finite-state, $\nu X.\, \Phi$ is equivalent to the infinite conjunction $\bigwedge_{i=0}^{\infty} \Phi_i$, where $\Phi_0 = tt$ and $\Phi_{i+1} = \Phi[\Phi_i/X]$ and the substitution $\Phi[\Gamma/X]$ is defined in the standard way.

All this is completely standard, except for the meaning of modalities, which is defined for sets of actions here, rather than just for single actions. This is a convenient generalization, which simplifies the representation of abstract program properties enormously (cf. [BS]).

$$
\begin{aligned}
[\![tt]\!]e &= \mathcal{S} \\
[\![X]\!]e &= e(X) \\
[\![\Phi_1 \wedge \Phi_2]\!]e &= [\![\Phi_1]\!]e \cap [\![\Phi_2]\!]e \\
[\![\neg\Phi]\!]e &= \mathcal{S} \setminus [\![\Phi]\!]e \\
[\![\beta]\!]e &= \{p \in \mathcal{S} \mid \beta \in \lambda(p)\} \\
[\![[\alpha]\Phi]\!]e &= \{p \in \mathcal{S} \mid \forall q \in Succ_{\alpha}(p).\ q \in [\![\Phi]\!]e\} \\
[\![\overline{[\alpha]}\Phi]\!]e &= \{q \in \mathcal{S} \mid \forall p \in Pred_{\alpha}(q).\ p \in [\![\Phi]\!]e\} \\
[\![\nu X.\, \Phi]\!]e &= \bigcup \{S' \subseteq \mathcal{S} \mid S' \subseteq [\![\Phi]\!]e[S'/X]\}
\end{aligned}
$$

Fig. 3. The semantics of formulas.

The formal semantic definition of the logic is given in Figure 3. It maps closed formulas to sets of program states — intuitively, the program states for which the formula is "true". Note that the semantics of $\nu X.\, \Phi$ is based on Tarski's fixpoint theorem [Tar]: its meaning is defined as the greatest fixpoint of a continuous function over the powerset of the set of states. The continuity of this function follows from the syntactic restriction mentioned above, which deals with the problems of negations, and the continuity of the semantic interpretations of the other propositional constructors.

In the following we will write $[\,.\,]$ or $\overline{[\,.\,]}$ instead of $[Act]$ or $\overline{[Act]}$, and $p \models_e \Phi$ if p satisfies Φ with respect to e, i.e. if $p \in [\![\Phi]\!]e$, and we will omit reference to

e whenever Φ is closed. Moreover, as usual, we can define the following duals to the operators of our language and the implication operator $\Rightarrow$ by:

$$\begin{aligned}\Phi_1 \vee \Phi_2 &= \neg(\neg\Phi_1 \wedge \neg\Phi_2)\\ \langle\, \alpha \,\rangle\, \Phi &= \neg[\, \alpha \,]\, (\neg\Phi)\\ \overline{\langle\, \alpha \,\rangle}\, \Phi &= \neg\overline{[\, \alpha \,]}\, (\neg\Phi)\\ \mu X.\, \Phi &= \neg\, \nu X.\, \neg(\Phi[\neg X/X])\\ \Phi \Rightarrow \Psi &= \neg\Phi \vee \Psi\end{aligned}$$

Our low level specification language consists of all *closed* and *guarded* formulas, where no variable occurs free inside the scope of a fixpoint expression.[5] Closed means that all variables are bound by a fixpoint operator, and guarded that they all occur inside the range of a modality.

3.2 High Level Specifications

The recursive proposition constructors add a tremendous amount of expressive power to the logic (cf. [EL, Ste1]). For example, they allow the description of invariance (or *safety*) and eventuality (or *liveness*) properties. However, general fixpoint formulas are often unintuitive and difficult to understand. Our specifications are therefore based on the intuitively easy to understand derived "Henceforth" and "Possibly" operators of the temporal logic CTL (see [CES]):

$$\mathbf{AG}\, \Phi = \nu X.\, (\Phi \wedge [\,.\,]\, X) \text{ and } \mathbf{EF}\, \Psi = \mu X.\, (\Phi \vee \langle\,.\,\rangle\, X)$$

and their past-time counterparts:

$$\overline{\mathbf{AG}}\, \Phi = \nu X.\, (\Phi \wedge \overline{[\,.\,]}\, X) \text{ and } \overline{\mathbf{EF}}\, \Psi = \mu X.\, (\Phi \vee \overline{\langle\,.\,\rangle}\, X)$$

Intuitively, a given program state s satisfies $\mathbf{AG}\ \Phi$ if Φ holds in every state reachable from s, and it satisfies $\mathbf{EF}\,\Phi$, the dual "Possibility" property, if a state satisfying Φ may be reached. The other two operators simply concern the same properties for the inverted flow of control in the program model.

In order to obtain the required expressive power, these basic versions must be parameterized in their 'next step' potential.

$$\begin{aligned}&\mathbf{AG}_A\, \Phi = \nu X.\, (\Phi \wedge [\, A \,]\, X) \text{ and } \mathbf{EF}_A\, \Psi = \mu X.\, (\Phi \vee \langle\, A \,\rangle\, X)\\ &\overline{\mathbf{AG}}_A\, \Phi = \nu X.\, (\Phi \wedge \overline{[\, A \,]}\, X) \text{ and } \overline{\mathbf{EF}}_A\, \Psi = \mu X.\, (\Phi \vee \overline{\langle\, A \,\rangle}\, X)\end{aligned}$$

The difference between $\mathbf{AG}\ \Phi$ and $\mathbf{AG}_A\ \Phi$ simply concerns the notion of reachability. Whereas every step is allowed in the former formula, reachability for $\mathbf{AG}_A\ \Phi$ means reachability via steps in A. As will be seen in the next section, this parameterization is rather powerful.

As in [Ste2], our high level specification language arises from the low level specification language by replacing the general fixpoint operator with the four operators established above. This language is quite expressive and allows concise specifications for a wide class of program properties.

---

[5] The point of this condition is to avoid the possibility of *alternated nesting* [EL]. Of course, there are weaker conditions to guarantee this, but they are unnecessarily complicated for our purpose.

4 Specifying Global Properties

The global properties of interest only concern the set of terminating program executions, i.e., paths through the program model reaching the end node. E.g., we consider an assignment as guaranteed to be executed, if it appears on each path to **e**. Thus a preceding loop without this assignment does not harm, as we are not interested in program execution staying within this loop. This implicit fairness constraint is best expressed using the following indirect specification style, which is characterized by double negation:

> **Indirect Specification Style:** Instead of "on each path to y there will be an x", we equivalently specify "y cannot be reached on paths where x is not visible".

In the following considerations the sets $\mathcal{A}_c^P$ of all statements (statement patterns) and $\mathbf{V}^P$ of all variables appearing in the considered argument program are of importance, as their finiteness is the key to termination and decidability. Moreover we adopt the following

Convention: $[\alpha]tt$ and $\overline{[\alpha]}tt$ are abbreviated by α and $\overline{\alpha}$, respectively.

4.1 Redundancy-Related Properties

Intuitively, *a statement is redundant at a program point, if it is guaranteed that its 'value' has been computed in every possible computation reaching this point.* More formally, this notion can be approximated by saying that

> *A statement is redundant at a program point, if it has been executed in every possible computation reaching this point, and after the last execution, the value of the right hand side expression has not been changed until the point is reached.*

Concentrating on non-recursive statements,[6] can be reformulated according to the indirect specification style as follows:

> *A statement is redundant, if going in the reverse direction of the control flow, it is not possible to reach the start state or a point of* modification *without meeting another occurrence of the statement first.*

The latter two verbal formulations are already quite 'heavy', and leave still room for misunderstandings. In contrast, using modal logic, the following one line specification makes the last formulation totally precise:

$$\overline{\mathbf{AG}}_{\neg\mathtt{occ}(a)}\ \neg(\overline{\mathtt{mod}}(a) \vee \mathtt{start}) \qquad \text{REDUNDANT}(a)$$

In contrast, *partial* redundancy, i.e., the existence of a path on which the statement is redundant, can be given in a direct style:

---

6 Recursive assignments are never redundant. Thus we can assume that all the considered assignments are non-recursive.

$\overline{\mathbf{EF}}_{\neg \mathtt{mod}(a)}\ \overline{\mathtt{occ}}(a)$ PARTIALLY REDUNDANT(a)

Requiredness, the negation of redundance, can systematically be put into *positive normal form*, which in our case results in the following comparatively easy to comprehend specification:

$\overline{\mathbf{EF}}_{\neg \mathtt{occ}(a)}\ \overline{\mathtt{mod}}(a) \vee \mathtt{start}$ REQUIRED(a)

and *total* requiredness, as the negation of partial redundance:

$\overline{\mathbf{AG}}_{\neg \mathtt{mod}(a)}\ \neg\overline{\mathtt{occ}}(a)$ TOTALLY REQUIRED(a)

Goal of partial redundancy elimination is to obtain a program where all statements are totally required (not partially redundant). This property of the resulting program, which we will call *universal requiredness*, can be formally expressed as follows:

UNIVERSAL REQUIREDNESS:

$\forall a \in \mathcal{A}_c^P.\ \mathbf{AG}\,(\mathtt{occ}(a) \Rightarrow \text{TOTALLY REQUIRED}(a))$

As $\mathcal{A}_c^P$ is finite, this property can easily be verified via model checking [Ste2]. However, up to now no technique has been available to guarantee this property, i.e., to eliminate all partial redundancies.

4.2 Liveness-Related Properties

Intuitively, *a statement is dead at a program point, if the value it assigns to its left hand side variable is superfluous for every program execution touching this point.* Similar to the previous section, this can be made precise as follows:

$\mathbf{AG}_{\neg \mathtt{mod}(a)}\ \neg(\mathtt{use}(a) \vee \mathtt{end})$ DEAD(a)

As before, the complementary notion, *partial* death, i.e., the existence of a path on which the statement is dead, can be specified in a direct style:

$\mathbf{EF}_{\neg \mathtt{use}(a)}\ \mathtt{mod}(a)$ PARTIALLY DEAD(a)

Following the line of Section 4.1, we arrive at the comparatively easy to comprehend specification for *liveness*, as the negation of death:

$\mathbf{EF}_{\neg \mathtt{mod}(a)}\ (\mathtt{use}(a) \vee \mathtt{end})$ LIVE(a)

and *total* liveness, as the negation of partial death:

$\mathbf{AG}_{\neg \mathtt{use}(a)}\ \neg\mathtt{mod}(a)$ TOTALLY LIVE(a)

Goal of partially dead code elimination is to obtain a program where all statements are totally live (not partially dead). This property of the resulting program, which we will call *universal liveness*, can be formally expressed as follows:

UNIVERSAL LIVENESS:

$\forall a \in \mathcal{A}_c^P.\ \mathbf{AG}\,(\mathtt{occ}(a) \Rightarrow \text{TOTALLY LIVE}(a))$

As before for redundancy elimination, this property can be automatically checked by means of model checking, however, up to now no technique has been available to eliminate all partially dead code.

5 Property-Oriented Expansion

In this section we show how to fully eliminate partial redundancies and partially dead code by property-driven unrolling (expansion) and elimination. We will start our considerations along the discussion of partial redundancy, which can be regarded as a particularly natural application of our technique. Subsequently, we will discuss how this technique can be extended to dead code elimination. In contrast to partial redundancy elimination, where the expansion follows the usual flow of control and is therefore 'harmless', being based on a backward analysis, this application requires a backward unrolling, which may destroy determinism and introduce deadlock. Thus further techniques are required to re-establish the original degree of determinism. Finally, we discuss the interference between these two optimizations, before we address the automatic generation of expansion-based algorithms.

5.1 Partial Redundancy Elimination

Redundancy elimination is well-understood since Kildall [Ki], and there has been a lot of work on partial redundancy elimination elaborating on Morel/Renvoise's seminal paper [MR]. However, in contrast to 'full' redundancies, no algorithm has been proposed yet to eliminate *all* partial redundancies. Figure 2 illustrates this situation: all known techniques are stuck with the program model on the left, whereas our method will produce the desired solution displayed on the right. In fact, all the examples discussed in this paper are of this kind.

The point of our algorithm is to reduce partial redundancy to total redundancy, i.e., to transform each argument program in such a way that redundancy and partial redundancy coincide, which can be logically expressed as

$$\forall a \in \mathcal{A}_c^P.\ \mathbf{AG}(\text{PARTIALLY REDUNDANT}(a) \ \Rightarrow \text{REDUNDANT}(a))$$

which is equivalent to

$$\forall a \in \mathcal{A}_c^P.\ \mathbf{AG}(\text{REQUIRED}(a) \ \Rightarrow \text{TOTALLY REQUIRED}(a))$$

Two simple observations deliver the key to this transformation:

- There is no difference between redundancy and partial redundancy in the totally expanded computation tree, which results from exhaustive unrolling (expansion) of the underlying program model. This difference is solely due to the join of paths with different histories.
- There are only finitely many different 'redundancy states' for a given program, i.e. situations where different sets of program statements are redundant.

Thus 'partiality' can effectively be removed, making the following redundancy elimination algorithm effective as well:

Basic Algorithm: Complete Elimination of Partial Redundancies

1. Expand the program model in such a way that each node is labelled with its precise 'redundancy state'. This can be achieved by splitting nodes in the program model, whenever a new redundancy state is reached.
2. Eliminate all total redundancies in the expanded graph.

In order to put the algorithm on a formal footing, we define as suggested above:

- the domain $\mathbf{R}$ of all redundancy states, which is given by the powerset $2^{\mathcal{A}_c^P}$ of the set of all statements (statement patterns) appearing in the program.
- an abstract semantic function (property transformer) $f_r : \mathcal{L} \to (\mathbf{R} \to \mathbf{R})$, defined by:
  - For all conditions a and all $R \in \mathbf{R}$: $f_r(a)(R) = R \cup \{a\}$
  - For all assignments $x := t$ and all $R \in \mathbf{R}$:

$$f_r(a)(R) = (R \cup \{x := t\}) \setminus \{\, a \,|\, x \text{ appears in } \mathtt{R}(a) \,\}$$

The intuition behind this definition is as follows: the domain $\mathbf{R}$ is intended to express the set of assignments being redundant at the current state of the program execution, while f_r is intended to model the effect of a statement execution on the redundancy information. The first clause in the definition of f_r models the fact that the occurrence of a condition (transition) makes the subsequent test of the same condition redundant, while it maintains all the current redundancy information. The second clause additionally keeps track of the destructive character of assignments: an assignment to a variable x 'revives' all statements whose right hand side expression depends on x.

f_r defines an abstract semantics for program models, which can be exploited to define a corresponding *operational model*, whose nodes consist of pairs, where the first components are nodes of the program model and the second components are redundancy states, i.e., elements of $\mathbf{R}$. These models are precisely the expanded program models mentioned in the first step of the basic algorithm. They can be constructed on-the-fly by successively executing the following four steps:

1. Set $(\mathbf{s}, \emptyset)$ to be a reachable node of the operational model.
2. Take a not yet processed reachable node (n, R) of the operational model and mark it as already processed.
3. For each transition t of the program model from n to some state n' labelled with some statement a consider $(n', f_r(a)(R))$, and add it to the set of reachable nodes whenever it is new. Moreover add an a-labelled transition from (n, R) to $(n', f_r(a)(R))$ to the operational model.
4. Continue with the second step until all reachable nodes are processed.

As $2^{\mathcal{A}_c^P}$ is finite for each program, this procedure will always terminate and therefore constitute the first step of the basic variant of our algorithm. The second step now simply consists of a program traversal, where a statement label of a transition from (n, R) to $(n', f_r(a)(R))$ is replaced by `skip`, whenever it lies in R. According to this construction it is rather straightforward to show the following theorem, which manifests the extreme power of this optimization:

Theorem 5.1 (Redundancy) *The basic algorithm terminates with a program which does not contain any partial redundancy, i.e., which satisfies the universal requiredness property:*

$$\forall a \in \mathcal{A}_c^P.\ \mathbf{AG}\,(\mathsf{occ}(a) \Rightarrow \mathit{TOTALLY\ REQUIRED}(a))$$

Applying standard techniques from automata and concurrency theory, this basic algorithm can be extended to also minimize the program size in two steps:

1. *Elimination of the* `skip` *edges*: this can be done by techniques known as ε-elimination in the above mentioned theories.
2. *Minimization up to bisimulation*: This minimization produces a state (node) minimal program model which exactly maintains the degree of non-determinism of its argument program. In the case of a deterministic input, the corresponding minimal deterministic program model is generated.

Adding these two steps, which are of low polynomial complexity, to the basic algorithm, we obtain:

Corollary 5.2 (Minimality) *Given a deterministic program, the complete four step algorithm for redundancy elimination terminates with a minimal deterministic program model, which does not contain any partial redundancy.*

The power of the four step algorithm comes at the price of a high worst case complexity of its first step, which is proportional to the size of the powerset of the set of assignments considered. However, it is our experience that this exponential factor hardly shows up in practice: Usually only a small fraction of the domain of redundancy states is reachable, which guarantees a quite moderate algorithmic behaviour and results which are essentially of the same size as the argument program. Figure 4 (left) shows a refined version of the motivating example of Figure 2 containing conditions and assignments at the edges previously associated with `skip`. Our complete algorithm produces the result displayed in Figure 4 (right), after having constructed the intermediate program model of Figure 5 by means of the basic algorithm.

5.2 Partially Dead Code Elimination

The basic idea behind our dead code elimination algorithm is as in the previous section, and its formal ingredients are given by:

- the domain $\mathbf{D}$ of all dead assignment states, which is given by the powerset $2^{\mathbf{V}^P}$ of the set of all variables appearing in the program.
- An abstract semantic function $f_d : \mathcal{L} \rightarrow (\mathbf{D} \rightarrow \mathbf{D})$, defined by:

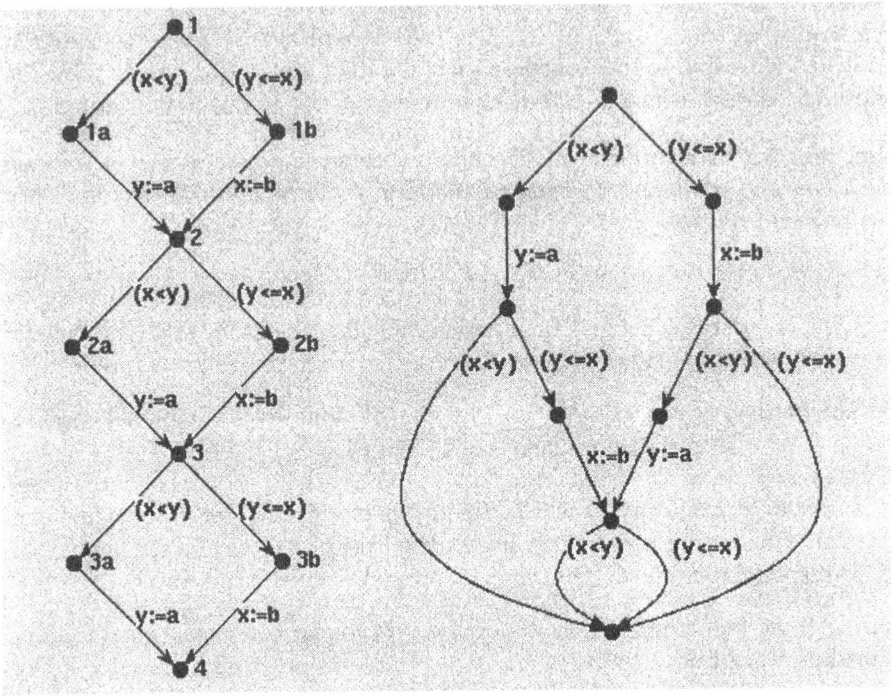

Fig. 4. A refined version of the 'classical failure'

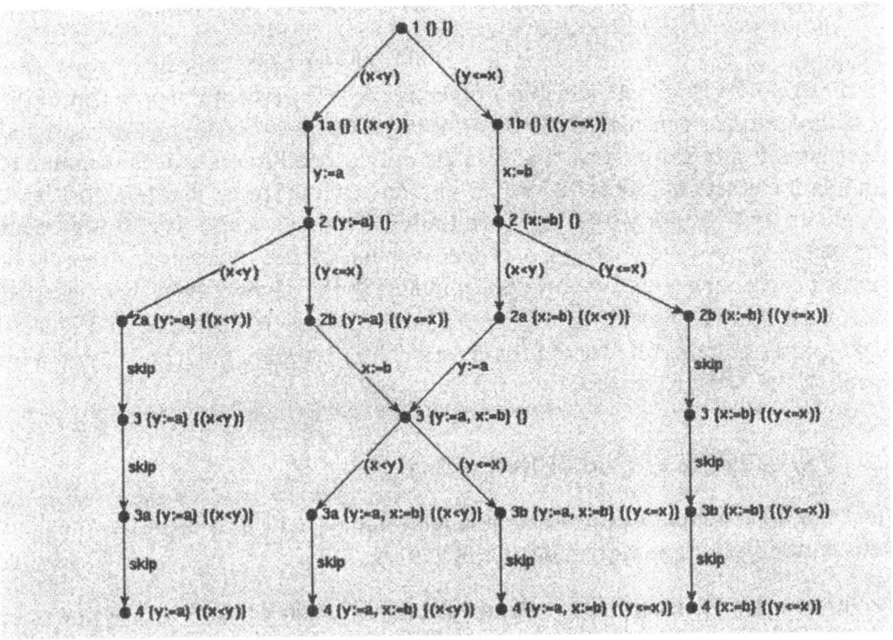

Fig. 5. The intermediate program model for Figure 4

- For all conditions a and all $D \in \mathbf{D}$:

  $f_d(a)(D) = D \setminus \{y \mid y \text{ appears in } \mathtt{R}(a)\}$
- For all assignments $x := t$ and all $D \in \mathbf{D}$:

  $f_d(a)(D) = (D \cup \{x\}) \setminus \{y \mid y \text{ appears in } \mathtt{R}(a)\}$

The intuition behind the definition is based on the idea of an execution in reverse direction, i.e., opposite to the usual flow of control, which captures the fact that dead code elimination requires a backward analysis. The domain **D** is intended to express the set of variables, which are dead, i.e., whose values are not required in any continuation of a program execution, while f_d is intended to model the 'backward' effect of a statement execution on this information. The first clause in the definition of f_d expresses the fact that the occurrence of a condition (transition) reviewes all variables occurring in it. The second clause additionally keeps track of the destructive character of assignments: the variable x is dead directly before any non-recursive assignment to x.

Using these entities, the dead code elimination algorithm evolves essentially in the same fashion as the redundancy elimination algorithm above. However, besides just working in the direction opposite to the control flow, the separation of analysis and elimination, which works for redundacy elimination, causes second order effects: a statement may have caused 'live' during the analysis, even though it is itself dead. Thus after its elimination, the results of the analysis are no longer true and must be recomputed. For so-called *faint code*, i.e., code (in a loop) whose liveness is caused by its own existence [GMW, HDT], this problem cannot even be resolved by iteration. However, the problem can be resolved by merging the analysis and elimination phase, which in fact prohibits any second order effect:

Merged Algorithm: Complete Elimination of Partially Dead Code

1. Set $(\mathbf{e}, \emptyset)$ to be a reachable node of the operational model.
2. Take a not yet processed reachable node (n, D) of the operational model and mark it as already processed.
3. For each transition t of the program model from some state n' to n labelled with some statement a,
   - set $\mathbf{a} := \mathtt{skip}$ if a is dead according to D, and $\mathbf{a} := a$ otherwise,
   - consider $(n', f_d(\mathbf{a})(D))$, and add it to the set of reachable nodes whenever it is new. Moreover add an **a**-labelled transition from $(n', f_d(\mathbf{a})(D))$ to (n, D) to the operational model.
4. Continue with the second step until all reachable nodes are processed.

One easily observes that the merged algorithm has no second order effects, i.e., one application provides the full effect, and every subsequent application leaves the program completely invariant. Moreover, it is obvious that the algorithm will change every program possessing partially dead code. Thus together we obtain:

Theorem 5.3 (Death) *The merged algorithm terminates with a program having no partially dead code, i.e., which satisfies the universal liveness property:*

$\forall a \in \mathcal{A}_c^P.\ \mathbf{AG}\,(\mathsf{occ}(a) \Rightarrow \mathit{TOTALLY\ LIVE}(a))$

Unfortunately, this is the end of the good news, which are supported by the example in Figure 6. Here the left most program model is transformed into the intermediate model by means of the basic algorithm, and successively 'collapsed' by the minimization procedure described in the previous section to the (desired) program model on the right. The general problem shows already up in the in-

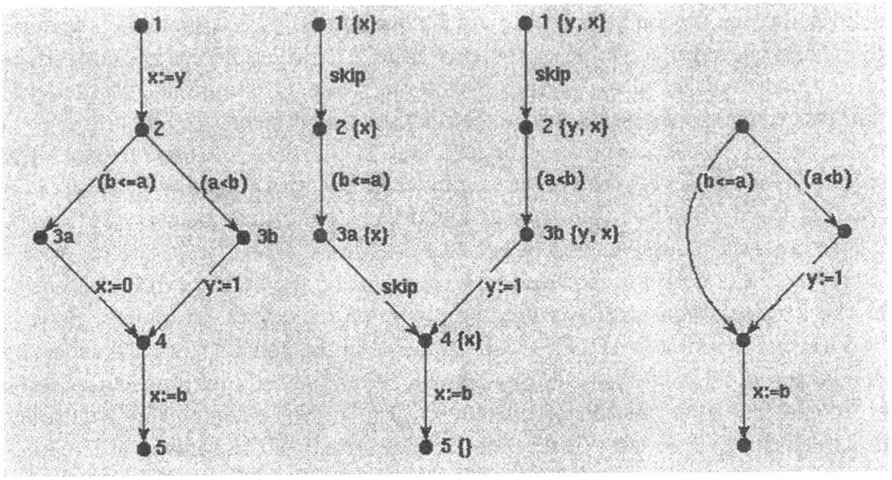

Fig. 6. The good case

termediate program model: it has two start nodes, which can be chosen non-deterministically. Thus even though we started with a deterministic program, the result is non-deterministic. Moreover, as the number of successful paths is not changed by the transformation, depending on the initial values, one of these paths is going to deadlock. Luckily, minimization of the concrete program model up to language equivalence eliminates this non-determinism.[7]

Unfortunately, Figure 7, which simply arises from replacing the third statement of the right path by $y := x$ in Figure 6, shows that minimization is insufficient to repair the defect in general. Nevertheless, we consider this transformation as very interesting, in particular as there are strong indications that this defect can be healed by further expansion together with some motion of conditions in acyclic parts of the program model.

Independently of the problems with the increased non-determinism, we have the following interesting property.

Theorem 5.4 (Combined Optimization) *Iterating the redundancy elimination procedure*[8] *and the dead code elimination procedure until stability, yields a*

[7] Note that the notion of non-determinism for programming languages does not coincide with the corresponding automata theoretical notion.

[8] Modified to deal with several start nodes.

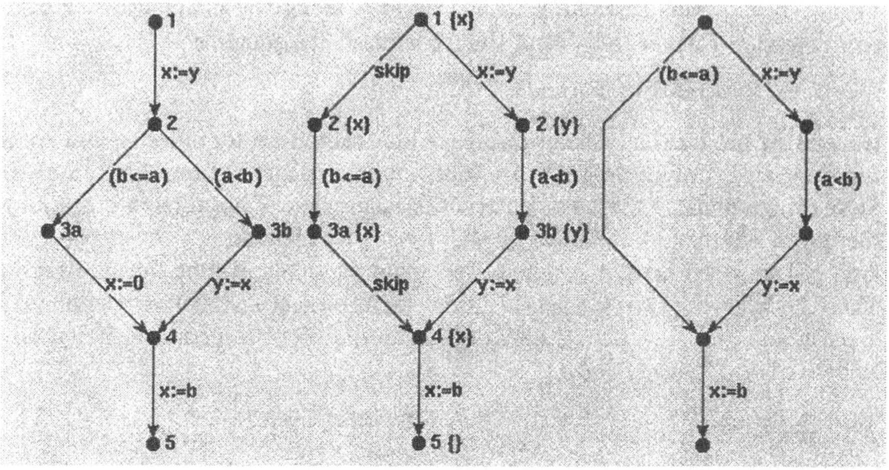

Fig. 7. The bad case

program which does neither contain partial redundancies nor partially dead code.

Sketch of the Proof: As both component procedures only stabilize if their goal is satisfied, i.e., no partial redundancy resp. no partially dead code is left, one must only prove termination, which is a consequence of the fact that there is a uniform bound for the size of the constructed models.

5.3 Automatic Generation of Optimizations by Expansion

Besides being a valuable aid to concisely specifying program properties, modal logic can be used as a basis for the automatic generation of data flow analysis algorithms by means of partial evaluation of a *model checker* with respect to the specifying formula [Ste2, Ste3]. This idea led to an implementation of an algorithm that takes a modal logical specification as an input and produces a corresponding data flow analysis algorithm [KKKS]. E.g., getting $\overline{\mathbf{EF}}_{\neg mod(a)}\ \overline{\mathtt{occ}}(a)$ as an input, this algorithm delivers a partial redundancy checker marking each partially redundant assignment of its input program.

Thus the question arises to what extent is optimization by expansion open to such a kind of generation, i.e., does there exist an algorithm that, given a modal logical formula, produces an elimination by expansion algorithm. Key to such an algorithm are the logical characterization of the structure of concrete program models together with the existence of a model construction algorithm for a certain modal logics. Given a modal formula of a specific format, these algorithms synthesize a (program) model satisfying this formula. Thus in contrast to data flow analysis generation, which was based on model checking, expansion-based algorithms can be generated on top of an appropriate *model synthesis* algorithm.

The rest of this section sketches this idea along the elimination of partial redundancies. First ingredient of the 'generator' is a compiler

charf: *Programs* $\rightarrow$ *Formulas*

translating program models into so-called characteristic formulas, which specify the programs' branching structure, but not their degree of unrolling [Ste1, SI]. Second ingredient is a model construction algorithm. Even though current synthesis procedures [SiCl, MaWo, StMC] for modal logic do not cover exactly the kind of logic used here, it is possible to adapt these algorithms to this situation. Thus the following two step specification can be seen as an 'effective template' for expansion-based algorithms, which on instantiation of a modal property works as desired.

Automatic Generation:

Synthesize a program model for charf(P) $\wedge$ *'Modal Property'*

E.g., instantiating *'Modal Property'* with

$$\forall a \in \mathcal{A}_c^P.\ \mathbf{AG}(\text{PARTIALLY REDUNDANT}(a) \Rightarrow \text{REDUNDANT}(a))$$

yields a program that transforms each input program model into an expanded version, where each partial redundancy is in fact total. Thus it realizes the first step of our basic algorithm, which is the key to the idea of expansion-based optimization.

The situation is more complicated, if we also want to cover transformations like partially dead code elimination. This requires the treatment of backward modalities, and it introduces the possibility of *failure*. Whereas the existence of a program model for the above mentioned specification for redundancy elimination is always guaranteed to exist,

$$\text{charf}(P) \wedge \forall a \in \mathcal{A}_c^P.\ \mathbf{AG}(\text{LIVE}(a) \Rightarrow \text{TOTALLY LIVE}(a))$$

does not necessarily have a model, indicating that the characteristic formula and the requirement of 'partiality' elimination are inconsistent. This observation reflects the fact that 'partiality' elimination may change the degree of determinism in a way, which cannot be repaired without violating charf(P). As mentioned above, we conjecture that condition movement, which in fact violates charf(P), but in a controlled way, is the transformation of choice here.

6 Conclusions and Perspectives

A framework for *property-oriented expansion* has been developed, which is much more powerful than the state of the art (motion-based) approaches, supports the combination of transformations, and is open to automatic generation by means of synthesis. Central limitation to this approach is its exponential worst case complexity, which, however, hardly shows up in practice: usually the algorithm behaves moderately and provides results, which are essentially of the same size as the argument program. This 'good' behaviour can be supported by pre-analyses, e.g., limiting the considered redundancy states to the set of statements known to be partially redundant in the argument program.

Nevertheless, the worst case complexity can strike back as is best illustrated by looking at a program model consisting of one state with loops for n mutually independent and non-recursive statements. In this program all the 2^n redundancy states are in fact reachable. Even though patterns like this do not seem typical for sequential programs, they often appear in concurrent programs as the result of the underlying *interleaving semantics*. We are therefore considering *partial order*-based program representations together with the suppression of equivalent computation paths in order to limit the complexity for these kind of program patterns [God].

Finally, we are currently considering other applications of property oriented expansion for imperative programs, like constant propagation and folding, and other application areas, like e.g., functional languages.

Acknowledgement

I am very grateful to Jürgen Kreileder, Thomas Braun, Christian Wiesner for implementing the presented algorithm. Their experiments led to valuable feedback and to the pictures displayed in the paper. Moreover, I would like to thank Gerald Lüttgen, Jens Knoop, Oliver Rüthing, Tiziana Margaria, Michael von der Beeck for fruitful discussion and proof reading.

References

[ASU] A.V. Aho, R. Sethi,J.D. Ullman. *Compilers: Principles, Techniques and Tools*, Addison-Wesley, 1985.

[BS] J. Bradfield, C.Stirling. *Local Model Checking for Infinite State Spaces.* LFCS Report Series ECS-LFCS-90-115, June 1990

[CC] P. Cousot, R. Cousot. *Abstract interpretation: A unified Lattice Model for static Analysis of Programs by Construction or Approximation of Fixpoints.* In Proceedings 4th POPL, Los Angeles, California, January, 1977

[CCo] C. Click, K.D. Cooper. *Combining Anlyses, Combining Optimizations*, ACM TOPLAS N.2, Vol.17, pp.181 - 196, 1995

[CES] E. Clarke, E.A. Emerson, A.P. Sistla. *Automatic Verification of Finite State Concurrent Systems using Temporal Logic Specifications: A Practical Approach.* In Proceedings 10th POPL'83, 1983

[Cli] C. Click. *Combining Analyses, Combining Optimizations*, Ph.D. Thesis, Rice University, Houston, TX, 1995, 149 pages.

[EL] E. Emerson, J. Lei, *Efficient model checking in fragments of the propositional mu-calculus.* In Proceedings LICS'86, 267-278, 1986

[GMW] R. Giegerich, U. Möncke, R. Wilhelm. *Invariance of Approximative Semantics with Respect to Program Transformations*, Informatik-Fachberichte 50, pp. 1-10, Proc. of the third Conference of the European Co-operation in Informatics, Springer, 1981.

[God] P. Godefroit. *Partial-Order Methods for the Verification of Concurrent Systems.* LNCS Monography, LNCS 1032, 1996.

[HDT] S. Horwitz, A. Demers, T. Teitelbaum. *An Efficient General Iterative Algorithm for Data Flow Analysis*, Acta Informatica, vol. 24, pp. 679 - 694, 1987.

[Ki] G. A. Kildall. *A unified approach to global program optimization.* In *Conf. Rec. 1st ACM Symposium on Principles of Programming Languages (POPL'73)*, pages 194 – 206. ACM, New York, 1973.

[KKKS] M. Klein, J. Knoop, D. Koschützki, B. Steffen. *DFA & OPT*-METAFrame : *A Toolkit for Program Analysis and Optimization* (Tool description) - Proc. TACAS'96, Int. Workshop on Tools and Algorithms for the Construction and Analysis of Systems, Passau, LNCS 1055 Springer, pp. 418-421

[Koz] D. Kozen. *Results on the Propositional mu-Calculus.* TCS 27, 333-354, 1983

[KRS1] J. Knoop, O. Rüthing, B. Steffen. *Partial Dead Code Elimination*, SIGPLAN PLDI Conference'94, *ACM SIGPLAN Notices 29*, Orlando, June 1994

[KRS2] J. Knoop, O. Rüthing, B. Steffen. *The Power of Assignment Motion*, Proc. of the ACM SIGPLAN'95 Conference on Programming Language Design and Implemantion (PLDI'95), La Jolla, California, June 1995, *SIGPLAN Notices 30*, 6 (1995), 233 - 245

[MaWo] Z. Manna, P. Wolper. "*Synthesis of Communicating Processes from Temporal Logic Specifications*," ACM TOPLAS Vol.6, N.1, Jan. 1984, pp.68-93.

[MR] E. Morel, C. Renvoise. *Global Optimization by Suppression of Partial Redundancies.* Communications of the ACM 22, 96-103, 1979

[JoNi] N.D. Jones, F. Nielson. *Abstract Interpretation: A Semantics-Based Tool for Program Analysis.* In *Handbook of Logics in Computer Science*, Vol. 4, pp. 527 - 637, Oxford University Press, 1995.

[RWZ] B.K. Rosen, M.N. Wegman, F.K. Zadeck. *"Global Value Numbers and Redundant Computations"*. 15th POPL, San Diego, California, 12 - 27, 1988

[SI] B. Steffen, A.Ingolfsdottir. *Characteristic Formulae for Finite State Processes*, International Journal on Information and Computation, Vol. 110, No. 1, 1994

[SiCl] A.P. Sistla, E.M. Clarke. "*The Complexity of the Propositional Linear Temporal Logics*," Journal of the ACM, Vol.32, N.3, July 1985, pp.733-749.

[Ste1] B. Steffen. *Characteristic Formulae.* Proceedings of the International Colloquium on Automata, Languages and Programming, ICALP'89, LNCS 372, 1989

[Ste2] B. Steffen. *Data Flow Analysis as Model Checking.* Proceedings of the International Concerence on Theoretical Aspects of Computer Software, TACS'91, LNCS 526, 1991

[Ste3] B. Steffen. *Generating Data Flow Analysis Algorithms from Modal Specifications*, International Journal on Science of Computer Programming, N. 21, 1993, pp. 115-139.

[StMC] B. Steffen, T. Margaria, A. Claßen. *Heterogeneous Analysis and Verification for Distributed Systems*, In "SOFTWARE: Concepts and Tools", vol. 17, N.1, pp. 13-25, Springer Verlag, 1996.

[Tar] A. Tarski. *A Lattice-Theoretical Fixpoint Theorem and its Applications.* Pacific Journal of Mathematics, v. 5, 1955.

[WS] D. Whitfield, M.L. Soffa. *An Approach to Ordering Optimizing Transformations*, Proc. 2nd ACM SIGPLAN Symposium on Principles & Practice of Parallel Programming (PPOPP), Seattle, Washington, SIGPLAN Notes *25*,3, pp.137 - 147, March 1990.

Generalized Dominators for Structured Programs

Stephen Alstrup[1] and Peter W. Lauridsen[1] and Mikkel Thorup[1]

Department of Computer Science, University of Copenhagen, Universitetsparken 1, DK-2100 Copenhagen, Denmark (e-mail : stephen,waern,mthorup@diku.dk, www : http://www.diku.dk/~stephen,~mthorup)

Abstract. Recently it has been discovered that control flow graphs of structured programs have bounded treewidth. In this paper we show that this knowledge can be used to design fast algorithms for control flow analysis. We give a linear time algorithm for the problem of finding the immediate multiple-vertex dominator set for all nodes in a control flow graph. The problem was originally proposed by Gupta (Generalized dominators and post-dominators, ACM Symp. on Principles of Programming Languages, 1992). Without the restriction of bounded treewidth the fastest algorithm runs in $O(|V| * |E|)$ on a graph with $|V|$ nodes and $|E|$ edges and is due to Alstrup, Clausen and Jørgensen (An $O(|V| * |E|)$ Algorithm for Finding Immediate Multiple-Vertex Dominators, accepted to Information Processing Letters).

1 Introduction

Constructing dominator trees for control flow graphs $G(V, E, s)$ has been investigated in many papers (see e.g. [8, 9, 11, 13, 14]) in connection with global flow analysis and program optimization. Recently Gupta [6, 7] extended the problem to finding generalized dominator trees which can be use for e.g. propagating loop invariant statements out of loops in cases, where no single node dominates the loop exit, but where a union of nodes together dominates the exit. The generalized dominator tree is constructed by adding to each node in the dominator tree, information about the immediate multiple-vertex dominator, *imdom*, for the node. In [6] an $O(n * 2^n * |V| + |V|^n)$ algorithm is given for computing the *imdom*-set for all nodes, where n is the largest cardinality of any *imdom*-set. Later Sreedhar and Gao have given an $O(|E|^2)$ algorithm [4] using a new representation for flow graphs [5]. The fastest algorithm so far runs in $O(|V| * |E|)$ time and is due to Alstrup, Clausen and Jørgensen [2]. In this paper we give a linear time algorithm for the same problem for structured programs which recently have been shown to have control flow graphs with bounded treewidth (see fact 1 below which is a result due to Thorup [15]). We use a general framework in this paper which is summarized in theorem 15 showing the strongness of using bounded treewidth. The theorem can thus be used as a basic tool for the design of control flow analysis algorithms.

2 Definitions

Let $G(V, E, s)$ be a control flow graph [1] with start node s. The nodes and the edges for G are denoted as $V(G)$ and $E(G)$ respectively. If Y is a subset of nodes of $V(G)$ then $G[Y]$ is the graph induced by the nodes in Y, hence $E(G[Y]) = \{(v, w) | v, w \in Y \wedge (v, w) \in E(G)\}$. If $(v, w) \in E(G)$ we say that v is a predecessor of w. Node v dominates node w if and only if all paths from s to w pass through v. The dominance relation is reflexive and transitive, and can be represented by a tree, called the dominator tree. The generalized dominator tree is constructed by adding an additional parent to each of the nodes in the dominator tree. The additional node for the node v is holding the immediate multiple-vertex dominator for the node v, $imdom(v)$, which is the minimum set of predecessors of v which together dominates v. More precisely $imdom(v)$ is defined by the following three conditions:

1. $imdom(v) \subseteq predecessors(v) = \{w | (w, v) \in E(G)\}$.
2. Any path from s to v contains a node $w \in imdom(v)$.
3. For each node $w \in imdom(v)$ a path from s to v exists which contains w and does not contain any other node in $imdom(v)$.

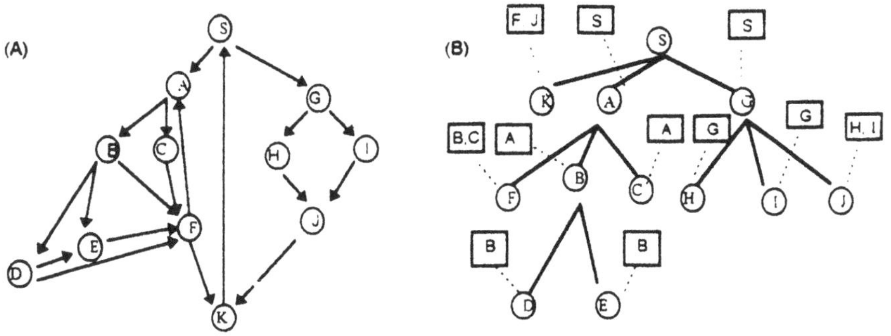

Fig. 1. (A) A sample graph. (B) The expanded dominator tree for the graph. The rectangles are holding the imdom-sets for the nodes.

3 Structured programs have small treewidth

The usefulness of the linear algorithm given in this paper can be seen from the following fact due to Thorup [15]:

Fact 1 *Control flow graphs for structured programs have* (≤ 6) *treewidth, e.g.*

- *Goto-free Algol [12] and Pascal [16] programs have* (≤ 3) *treewidth control flow graphs.*
- *All Modula-2 [17] programs have* (≤ 5) *treewidth control flow graphs.*
- *Goto-free C [10] programs have* (≤ 6) *treewidth control flow graphs.*

Without short circuit evaluation, each of the above treewidths drops by one.

In the following we give the definition of treewidth and describe previous work with bounded treewidth, which will be used to decompose the control flow graph for the algorithm presented in the next section.

Definition 1. A *tree decomposition* of a graph $G = (V, E)$ is a pair (X, T) where $T = (V(T), E(T))$ is a tree and X is a family $\{X_i | i \in V(T)\}$ of subsets of $V(G)$ such that

1. $\bigcup_{i \in V(T)} X_i = V(G)$.
2. for all edges $(v, w) \in E(G)$, there exists an $i \in V(T)$ with $v \in X_i$ and $w \in X_i$.
3. for all $i, j, k \in V(T)$: if j is on the path from i to k in T, then $X_i \cap X_k \subseteq X_j$.

The *width* of a tree decomposition is $\max_{i \in V(T)} |X_i| - 1$. The *treewidth* of a graph G is the minimum width over all possible tree decompositions of G.

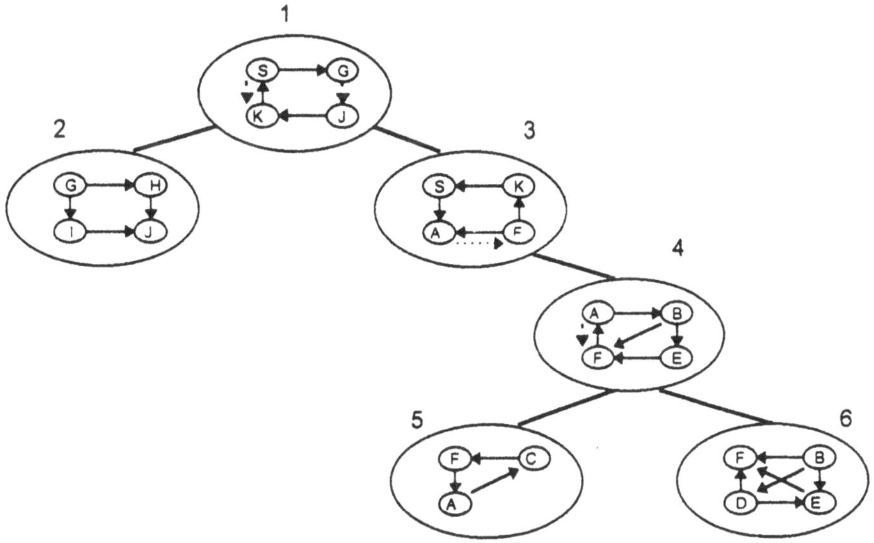

Fig. 2. A tree decompostion of the graph in fig. 1. The tree nodes are numbered 1..6. The dotted edges are $TC^{\uparrow}(i)$-edges, which will be defined in the following.

From fact 1 and definition 1 we have that a control flow graph can be decomposed for examination of small fractions of the graph, and the following fact due to Bodlaender [3] solves the problem of constructing the tree decomposition.

Fact 2 *1. For all constants $t \in \mathcal{N}$, there exist a linear time algorithm which tests whether a given graph G with n nodes has treewidth $(\leq t)$ and if so, outputs a tree decomposition (X, T) of G with width $(\leq t)$, where $|V(T)| = n - t$.*

2. We can in linear time convert (X, T) into another tree decomposition (X_b, T_b) of G with width t, where T_b is a binary tree and $|V(T_b)| \leq 2(n - t)$.

The second part follows by the usual binarization of an arbitrary tree.

In the following section we will use a binary tree decomposition, using any node from the tree which includes the start node as root (the rooted tree can be binarized by adding at most one more node to the tree). For a tree node i we use the names $Parent(i)$, $Sibling(i)$, $Left(i)$ and $Right(i)$ for the parent, sibling and children respectively of i. Furthermore we follow the convention that $X_j = \emptyset$ if $j \notin V(T)$.

4 Algorithm

In [2] the problem of finding immediate multiple-vertex dominator (*imdom*) is reduced to a reachability problem for each node in the graph. More specifically $imdom(v)$ is found by first marking all predecessors of v. Next a search method (e.g. depth first) is used to find all nodes which are reachable from s without passing marked nodes. The marked nodes found by this search equals $imdom(v)$. We will refer to this algorithm as the ACJ-algorithm. In this section we assume that a rooted binary tree decomposition of the graph, in which the start node belongs to the root, is given. We can therefore restrict the search in the ACJ-algorithm to a subgraph induced by a tree node to which is added edges containing the necessary reachability information from the rest of the graph. This additional information can be computed simultaneously for all tree nodes by a constant number of graph traversals. To be more specific we traverse the graph by examining the tree nodes first in a bottom-up fashion and then in a top-down fashion in order to find some restricted transitive closures for each tree node. Furthermore we traverse the graph in order to determine reachability from the start node under different constraints and finally we collect the *imdom*-sets. In the rest of this section we denote the tree decomposition of $G(V, E, s)$ as (X, T). We use the term "nodes reachable from v without *passing* nodes from Y", to restrict reachability to paths, on which only v and the node reached can belong to Y.

Definition 2. For a tree node i we define $X_i^{\uparrow}$ as the nodes in descendants of i, hence $X_i^{\uparrow} = \{u | u \in X_j \wedge j \text{ is a descendant of } i\}$. Similarly we define $X_i^{\downarrow}$ as the nodes in X_i and the nodes from tree nodes which are not a descendant of i, hence $X_i^{\downarrow} = \{u | u \in X_j \wedge (j = i \vee j \text{ is not a descendant of } i)\}$ (note that if i is the root node then $X_i^{\downarrow} = X_i$ and if i is a leaf then $X_i^{\uparrow} = X_i$).

4.1 Bottom-Up Closures

Definition 3. For a tree node i and a node $v \in X_i$ we define $TC^{\uparrow}(i, v)$ as the nodes in X_i reachable from v in the subgraph $G[X_i^{\uparrow}]$ without passing nodes from X_i. Furthermore we define $TC^{\uparrow}(i) = \{(v, w) | v, w \in X_i \wedge w \in TC^{\uparrow}(i, v)\}$.

Note that this definition and the following definitions introduce self-loops. These edges are only added to simplify the definitions and will be ignored in the following.

Lemma 4. *$TC^{\dagger}(i,v)$ are the nodes in X_i reachable from v without passing nodes in X_i in the graph $G[X_{Left(i)} \bigcup X_{Right(i)} \bigcup X_i]$ to which are added the edges in $TC^{\dagger}(Left(i)) \bigcup TC^{\dagger}(Right(i))$.*

Proof. If i is a leaf the lemma is trivially true. Assume therefore i is not a leaf. We will first show that all nodes belonging to $TC^{\dagger}(i,v)$ are reachable from v. Assume $w \in TC^{\dagger}(i,v)$. If $(v,w) \in E(G[X_i])$ then w is obviously reachable, so let $P = v, y_1, ..., y_k, w$ be a path implying $w \in TC^{\dagger}(i,v)$. By definition 3 no y_j is in X_i and therefore by definition 1.3 y_1 and y_k are in $X_{Left(i)}$ or $X_{Right(i)}$. Assume without loss of generality that y_1, y_k are in $X_{Left(i)}$. By induction we can find all nodes in $X_{Left(i)}$ reachable from y_1 in $G[X^{\dagger}_{Left(i)}]$ and as a special case we can find y_k. The path P is therefore represented in the graph.
We now show that all nodes reachable from v are in $TC^{\dagger}(i,v)$. The only way for this not to be the case would be if one of the additional edges concealed a node from X_i. This is however impossible by definition 1.3. □

By lemma 4 we can find $TC(i)$ for each tree node i by performing simple searches in all tree nodes in a bottom-up fashion. This information can now be used for finding a Restricted Transitive Closure (RTC) for each tree node bottom-up. We define RTC as follows:

Definition 5. For a tree node i and nodes $v, w \in X_i$ we define $RTC^{\dagger}(i,v,w)$ as the nodes in X_i reachable from w in the subgraph $G[X_i^{\dagger}]$ without passing v or any predecessors of v. Furthermore we define $RTC^{\dagger}(i,v) = \{(w,u) | w, u \in X_i \wedge u \in RTC^{\dagger}(i,v,w)\}$.

Lemma 6. *$RTC^{\dagger}(i,v,w)$ are the nodes in X_i reachable from w without passing v or any predecessors of v in the graph $G[X_{Left(i)} \bigcup X_{Right(i)}) \bigcup X_i]$ to which are added the edges:*
$TC^{\dagger}(Left(i))$, if $v \notin X_{Left(i)}$ and $RTC^{\dagger}(Left(i),v)$ otherwise
$TC^{\dagger}(Right(i))$, if $v \notin X_{Right(i)}$ and $RTC^{\dagger}(Right(i),v)$ otherwise

Proof. If i is a leaf the lemma is trivially true. Assume therefore that i is not a leaf. We will first prove that the nodes found belong to $RTC^{\dagger}(i,v,w)$. To prove this we only need to prove that none of the additional edges can conceal a predecessor of v. If $v \notin X_{Left(i)} \wedge v \notin X_{Right(i)}$ then all predecessors of v in $X_i^{\dagger}$ will belong to X_i and none of the additional edges can conceal a predecessor of v by definition 1.3. If $v \in X_{Left(i)}$ by induction we have that the edges in $RTC^{\dagger}(Left(i),v)$ do not conceal predecessors of v. The case where $v \in X_{Right(i)}$ is analogous. In order to prove that all nodes are found assume that $u \in RTC^{\dagger}(i,v,w)$. If $v \notin X_{Left(i)} \wedge v \notin X_{Right(i)}$ then all paths from w to u in $G[X_i^{\dagger}]$ are represented in the graph by lemma 1. If $v \in X_{Left(i)}$ then by induction all paths from w in $G[X^{\dagger}_{Left(i)}]$ which avoids predecessors of v are represented. Since the only possible remaining paths have to be in $G[X_i]$ all paths which meets the requirements are represented in the graph. The case where $v \in X_{Right(i)}$ is again analogous. □

According to lemma 6 the set $RTC^{\uparrow}(i,v,w)$ can be found by performing the ACJ-algorithm with w as the start node on the graph described in the lemma.

4.2 Top Down Closures

Definition 7. For a tree node i and a node $v \in X_i$ we define $TC^{\downarrow}(i,v)$ as the nodes in X_i reachable from v in the subgraph $G[X_i^{\downarrow}]$ without passing nodes in X_i. Furthermore we define $TC^{\downarrow}(i) = \{(v,w)|v,w \in X_i \wedge w \in TC^{\downarrow}(i,v)\}$.

Lemma 8. *$TC^{\downarrow}(i,v)$ are the nodes in X_i reachable from v in the graph $G[X_{Parent(i)} \bigcup X_{Sibling(i)} \bigcup X_i]$ to which are added the edges $TC^{\downarrow}(Parent(i)) \bigcup TC^{\uparrow}(Sibling(i))$ without passing nodes in X_i.*

Proof. The lemma is analogous to lemma 4 except that in lemma 4 $X_{Left(i)} \bigcap X_{Right(i)} \subseteq X_i$ whereas $(X_{Parent(i)} \bigcap X_{Sibling(i)}) \backslash X_i$ is not necessarily empty. It is however easily verified that these nodes does not affect the correctness. □

Analogously to the bottom-up closure we define a restricted transitive closure top-down:

Definition 9. For a tree node i and nodes $v,w \in X_i$ we define $RTC^{\downarrow}(i,v,w)$ as the nodes in X_i reachable from w in the subgraph $G[X_i^{\downarrow}]$ without passing v or any predecessors of v. Furthermore we define $RTC^{\downarrow}(i,v) = \{(w,u)|w,u \in X_i \wedge u \in RTC^{\downarrow}(i,v,w)\}$.

Lemma 10. *$RTC^{\downarrow}(i,v,w)$ are the nodes in X_i reachable from w without passing v or any predecessors of v in the graph $G[X_{Parent(i)} \bigcup X_{Sibling(i)} \bigcup X_i]$ to which are added the edges:*
$TC^{\downarrow}(Parent(i)) \bigcup TC^{\uparrow}(Sibling(i))$, if $v \notin X_{Parent(i)}$.
$RTC^{\downarrow}(Parent(i),v) \bigcup TC^{\uparrow}Sibling(i)$, if $v \notin X_{Sibling(i)} \wedge v \in X_{Parent(i)}$.
$RTC^{\downarrow}(Parent(i),v) \bigcup RTC^{\uparrow}(Sibling(i),v)$, if $v \in X_{Sibling(i)}$.

Proof. Apart from the difference mentioned in the proof for lemma 8, lemma 10 differs only from lemma 6 in that the case $v \in X_{Sibling(i)} \wedge v \notin X_{Parent(i)}$ cannot occur. The proof for lemma 10 is otherwise analogous to the proof of lemma 6 and is therefore omitted. □

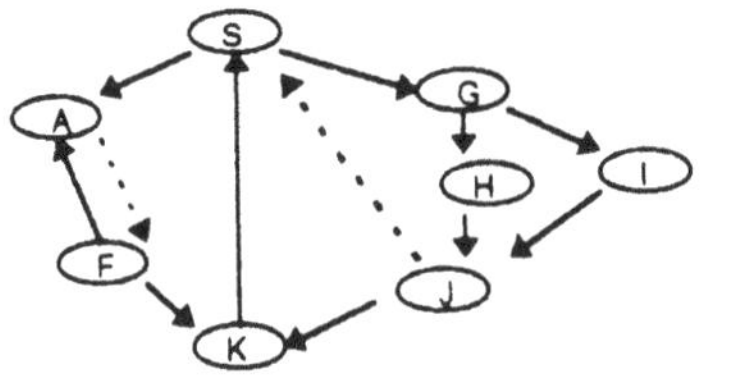

Fig. 3. Search graph for finding $RTC^{\downarrow}(2,G)$ for treenode 2: $(J,S) \in RTC^{\downarrow}(1,G)$ and $(A,F) \in TC^{\uparrow}(3)$.

4.3 Reachability

With both the top-down and bottom-up closure edges in hand, all information about paths between nodes in a tree node, which does not pass through nodes from the tree node is obtainable. We therefore only need to know which nodes are reachable from s in each tree node.

Definition 11. For a tree node i we define $STC(i)$ as the nodes in X_i reachable from s in the subgraph $G[X_i^{\downarrow}]$ by a path, on which the last node is the only node from X_i.

Lemma 12. *$STC(i) = \{s\}$, if i is the root node. Otherwise let H be the graph $G[X_{Parent(i)} \bigcup X_{Sibling(i)}]$ to which are added the edges $TC^{\downarrow}(Parent(i)) \bigcup TC^{\uparrow}(Sibling(i))$. Then $STC(i)$ are the nodes in X_i reachable from nodes in $STC(Parent(i))$ by a path P in H, such that the last node on P is the only node in X_i.*

Proof. The proof is similar to the proof of lemma 8 and is therefore omitted. □

Definition 13. For a tree node i and a node $v \in X_i$ we define $RSTC(i, v)$ as the nodes in X_i reachable from s in the graph G by a path on which only the last node allowed to be v or any predecessor of v.

Lemma 14. *If $v \notin X_{Parent(i)}$ then $RSTC(i, v)$ are the nodes reachable from a node in $STC(i)$ by a path, on which only the last node is allowed to be v or any predecessor of v, in the graph $G[X_i]$ to which are added the edges $RTC^{\uparrow}(i, v) \bigcup RTC^{\downarrow}(i, v)$. Otherwise if $v \in X_{Parent(i)}$ then $RSTC(i, v)$ are the nodes reachable from a node in $RSTC(Parent(i), v) \bigcap X_i$ by a path, on which only the last node is allowed to be v or any predecessor of v, in the graph $G[X_i]$ to which are added the edges $RTC^{\uparrow}(i, v)$.*

Proof. If $v \notin X_{Parent(i)}$ then all predecessors of v in $G[X_i^{\uparrow}]$ are in X_i and therefore a path exists from s to all nodes in $STC(i)$ which avoids v and predecessors of v. This observation together with definitions 5, 9 and 11 establishes the first case. The second case follows directly from the same definitions and the definition of $RSTC$ by induction. □

4.4 Closure of a tree node

In this subsection we will summarize the information defined in the previous subsections. The theorem below shows that it is possible in linear time to preprocess a graph with bounded treewidth, so as to "close" each tree node. In other words we can ensure that certain paths, restricted in different ways, between or to nodes of a tree node, are represented in the tree node. The theorem can thus be used for the development of efficient algorithms in graphs with bounded treewidth.

Theorem 15. *Given a graph $G(V, E, s)$ with treewidth t and a binary tree decomposition of G we can preprocess G in linear time, so that for each preprocessed tree node i:*

1. *For each node $v \in X_i$ the set of nodes in X_i reachable from v without passing other nodes in X_i is known. The preprocessing has complexity $O(|V|t^3)$*
2. *For each node pair $v, w \in X_i$ the set of nodes in X_i reachable from w without passing v or any predecessors of v is known. The preprocessing has complexity $O(|V|t^4)$.*
3. *All nodes in X_i reachable from the start node s by a path on which the last node is the only node from X_i are known. The preprocessing has complexity $O(|V|t^3)$*
4. *For each node $v \in X_i$ all nodes in X_i reachable from the start node s by a path, on which only the last node is allowed to be v or any predecessor of v, are known. The preprocessing has complexity $O(|V|t^4)$.*

Proof. To obtain the information in 2 and 3, the information in 1 has to be available. Similarly the information in 4 requires the information in 1,2 and 3.

1. By lemma 4 we can find all paths between nodes of X_i which passes through proper descendants of i, by performing, for each node in X_i, a simple search in a graph induced by 3 tree nodes containing at most $3t$ nodes. The complete search for each tree node can thus be done in $O(t^3)$-time and since there are $O(|V|)$ tree nodes the complexity is established. By lemma 8 we can find all paths which passes "above" a tree node analogously.
2. By lemma 6 we can find all paths avoiding v and predecessors of v in the subgraph spanned by the tree nodes in the subtree rooted at i, by performing the ACJ-algorithm with w as start node. Thus the ACJ-algorithm with complexity $O(t^3)$ has to be run for each node in X_i. Since there are at most t nodes in X_i and $O(|V|)$ tree nodes the complexity is established. Again we can find all paths in the graph "above" i analogously.
3. By performing a similar search as in 1 in each tree node in a top-down fashion, we can find the nodes required.
4. By performing the ACJ-algorithm analogously to 2 in each tree node in a top-down fashion, we can find the nodes required.

□

4.5 Finding Imdom-sets

We will now present the main theorem for finding the *imdom*-sets.

Theorem 16. *$Imdom(v) = \{w | (w, v) \in E(G) \wedge w \in \bigcup_{i \in V(T)} RSTC(i, v)\}$, where $RSTC(i, v) = \emptyset$, if $v \notin X_i$.*

Proof. Let I denote the right hand side of the expression. We will prove the theorem by showing that I satisfies the three conditions in the definition of *imdom*.

1. Obvious.
2. Assume that a path from s to v exists which does not include any node in I. Let w denote the predecessor of v first reached on the path. Since the path from s to w does not include any predecessors of v, w must belong to $RSTC(j, v)$ for a tree node j to which both v and w belong, contradicting that $w \notin \bigcup_{i \in V(T)} RSTC(i, v)$.
3. Follows directly from the definition of $RSTC$. □

Theorem 17. *Given a control flow graph $G(V, E, s)$ with treewidth t and a binary tree decomposition (X, T) of G, we can find imdom(v) for each node $v \in V$ in linear time.*

Proof. By theorem 15 we can compute $RSTC(i, v)$ for each pair $i \in V(T)$, $v \in V$ in $O(|V|t^4)$-time. By theorem 16 we can find the *imdom*-sets for each node v by traversing the tree and for each tree node i collect the nodes which are predecessors of v and belong to $RSTC(i, v)$ (the collection of nodes belonging to *imdom*-sets for all nodes can of course be done simultaneously). □

References

1. A.V. Aho, R. Sethi, and J.D. Ullman. *Compilers: Principles, Techniques and Tools.* Addison-Wesley, 1986.
2. S. Alstrup, J. Clausen, and K. Jørgensen. An $O(|V| * |E|)$ algorithm for finding immediate multiple-vertex dominators. Technical Report DIKU-TR-96/4, Deparment of Computer Science, University of Copenhagen, 1996. Revised version with minor change accepted to Information Processing Letters.
3. H. Bodlaender. A linear time algorithm for finding tree-decompositions of small treewidth. In *Proc. 25th ACM. Symp. on theory of Comp.(STOC'93)*, pages 226–234, 1993.
4. G.R. Gao, Y.-F Lee, and V.C. Sreedhar. DJ-graphs and their application to flowgraph analyses. Technical Report 70, McGill University, School of Computer Science, ACAPS, May 1994.
5. G.R. Gao and V.C. Sreedhar. A linear time algorithm for placing ϕ-nodes. In *ACM Symp. on the Principles of Programming Languages (POPL'95)*, volume 22, pages 62–73, January 1995.
6. R. Gupta. Generalized dominators and post-dominators. In *ACM Symp. on Principles of Programming Languages (POPL'92)*, volume 19, pages 246–257, 1992.
7. R. Gupta. Generalized dominators. *Information processing letters*, 53:193–200, 1995.
8. D. Harel. A linear time algorithm for finding dominator in flow graphs and related problems. In *Proc. 17th Ann. ACM Symp. on theory of Comp. (STOC'85)*, pages 185–194, 1985.
9. M.S. Hecht and J.D. Ullman. A simple algorithm for global data flow analysis of programs. *SIAM J. Comput.*, 4:519–532, 1975.
10. B.R. Kernighan and D.M. Ritchie. *The C programming language*. Prentice–Hall, New-Jersey, 1978.
11. T. Lengauer and R.E. Tarjan. A fast algorithm for finding dominators in a flowgraph. *ACM Trans. Programming Languages Systems*, 1:121–141, 1979.

12. P. Naur. Revised report on the algorithmic language algol 60. *Comm. ACM*, 1(6):1–17, 1963.
13. P.W. Purdom and E.F. Moore. Immediate predominators in a directed graph. *Comm. ACM*, 15(8):777–778, 1972.
14. R.E. Tarjan. Finding dominators in directed graphs. *SIAM J. Comput.*, 3(1):62–89, 1974.
15. M. Thorup. Structured programs have small tree-width and good register allocation. Technical Report DIKU-TR-95/18 (revised version), Deparment of Computer Science, University of Copenhage, 1995.
16. N. Wirth. The programming language pascal. *Acta informatica*, 1:35–63, 1971.
17. N. Wirth. *Programming in modula-2(3rd corr.ed)*. Springer–verlag, Berlin, New York, 1985.

Cache Behavior Prediction by Abstract Interpretation

Martin Alt, Christian Ferdinand, Florian Martin, and Reinhard Wilhelm

Universität des Saarlandes / Fachbereich Informatik
Postfach 15 11 50 / D-66041 Saarbrücken / Germany
Phone: +49 681 302 5573 Fax: +49 681 302 3065
{alt,ferdi,florian,wilhelm}@cs.uni-sb.de
http://www.cs.uni-sb.de/users/{alt,ferdi,martin,wilhelm}

Abstract. Abstract Interpretation is a technique for the static analysis of dynamic properties of programs. It is semantics based, that is, it computes approximative properties of the semantics of programs. On this basis, it allows for correctness proofs of analyzes. It thus replaces commonly used ad hoc techniques by systematic, provable ones, and it allows the automatic generation of analyzers from specifications as in the Program Analyzer Generator, PAG.

In this paper, abstract interpretation is applied to the problem of predicting the cache behavior of programs. Abstract semantics of machine programs for different types of caches are defined which determine the contents of caches. The calculated information allows to sharpen worst case execution times of programs by replacing the worst case assumption 'cache miss' by 'cache hit' at some places in the programs. It is possible to analyse instruction, data, and combined instruction/data caches for common (re)placement and write strategies. The analysis is designed generic with the cache logic as parameter.

Keywords: abstract interpretation, program analysis, cache memories, real time applications, worst case execution time prediction.

1 Cache Memories and Real-Time Applications

Caches are used to improve the access times of fast microprocessors to relatively slow main memories. They can reduce the number of cycles a processor is waiting for data by providing faster access to recently referenced regions of memory[1].

Programs with hard real time constraints have to be subjected to a schedulability analysis by the compiler [17, 6]; it has to be determined whether all timing constraints can be satisfied. WCETs (Worst Case Execution Times) for processes have to be used for this. For hardware with caches, the appropriate worst case assumption is that all accesses miss the cache. This is an overly pessimistic assumption which leads to a waste of hardware resources.

[1] Hennessy and Patterson [8] describe typical values for caches in 1990 workstations and minicomputers: Hit time 1–4 clock cycles (normally 1); Miss penalty 8–32 clock cycles.

Correct information about the contents of the cache at program points could help to sharpen the worst case execution times. Such information can be computed by an abstract interpretation statically collecting information about cache contents. The way this information is computed, an abstraction of the concrete semantics of the programs, depends on the type of cache regarded and the cache replacement strategy. Several abstract semantics are described, for different types of caches.

2 Program Analysis by Abstract Interpretation

Program analysis is a widely used technique to determine runtime properties of a given program without actually executing it. There is a common theory for all program analyses called abstract interpretation [5]. With this theory, termination and correctness of a program analysis can be easily proven. According to this theory a program analysis is determined by an *abstract semantics.*

The program analyzer generator PAG [1] offers the possibility to generate a program analyzer from a description of the abstract domain and of the abstract semantic functions. These descriptions are given in two high level languages, which support the description even of complex domains and semantic functions. The domain can be constructed from some simple sets like integers by operators like building power sets or by constructing of functions. The semantic functions are described in a functional language which combines high expressiveness with efficient implementation. Additionally one has to write a join function combining two incoming values of the domain into a single one. This function is applied whenever a point in the program has two (or more) possible execution predecessors.

For the analysis of programs with (recursive) procedures PAG supports the *functional approach* and the *call string approach* [15].

3 Related Work

The computation of WCETs for real-time programs is an ongoing research activity. Park and Shaw [12] describe a method to derive WCETs from the structure of programs. In [13] Puschner and Koza propose methods to guide the computation of WCETs by user annotations. Both approaches do not take cache behavior into account.

An overview of 'Cache Issues in Real-Time Systems' is given in [3]. We restrict our examination here to the intrinsic cache behavior. In [10] Arnold, Mueller, Whalley, and Harmon describe a data flow analysis for the prediction of instruction cache behavior of programs for direct mapped caches.

A method for the data cache analysis by graph coloring is described in [11, 14]. Similar to the Chow-Hennessy register allocator, variables are allocated to cache lines. The objective of the analysis is to show that throughout the live range of a cache line, no other memory access interferes with this particular cache line.

In [9] a general framework is described for the computation of WCETs of programs in the presence of pipelines and cache memories. Two kinds of pipeline and cache state information are associated with every program construct for which timing equations can be formulated. One describes the pipeline and cache state when the program construct is finished. The other one can be combined with the state information from the previous construct to refine the WCET computation for that program construct. An approximation to the solution for the set of timing equations has been proposed.

4 Cache Memories

A cache can usually be characterized by three major parameters:

- *capacity* is the number of bytes it may contain.
- *line size* (also called block size) is the number of contiguous bytes that are transferred from memory on a cache miss. The cache can hold at most *capacity*/*line size* blocks.
- *associativity* is the number of cache locations where a particular block may reside. *capacity*/(*line size* $*$ *associativity*) is the number of *sets*[2] of a cache.

If a block can reside in any cache location, then the cache is called *fully associative*. If a block can reside in exactly one location, then it is called *direct mapped*. If a block can reside in exactly A locations, then the cache is called *A-way set associative* [16]. The fully associative and the direct mapped cache are special cases of the A-way set associative cache where $A = n$ and $A = 1$ rsp.

5 Concrete Semantics

In the following, we consider a cache as a set of cache lines $L = \{l_0, \ldots, l_{n-1}\}$, where $n =$ (*capacity*/*line size*). The store $S = \{s_0, \ldots, s_{m-1}\}$ is divided into blocks of size *line size*, so that one memory block can be transferred into one cache line. The locations where a memory block may reside in the cache depend on the level of associativity of the cache memory. This is formalized by a relation between cache lines and memory blocks.

Definition 1 mapping relation. A mapping relation $\mathcal{M} \subseteq L \times S$ is a subset of the cartesian product of caches and stores. It defines the cache lines that may hold a particular memory block. The meaning of an element $(l, s) \in \mathcal{M}$ of a mapping relation is: the memory block s may be stored in cache line l.

Example 1 special mappings. The following mappings describe common cache organizations:

- *fully associative mapping*: $\mathcal{M}_{assoc} = L \times S$. A memory block may be held by any cache line
- *direct mapping*: $\mathcal{M}_{direct} = \{(l_i, s_x) \mid i = (x\%n), x \in \{0, \ldots, m-1\}\}$. % denotes the modulo division. A memory block may reside in exactly one cache line[3]
- *A-way set associative mapping*:
  $\mathcal{M}_{A-way} = \bigcup_{a=0}^{A-1} \{(l_i, s_x) \mid i = (x\%(n/A)) * A + a, x \in \{1, \ldots, m\}\}$.
  A memory block may reside in exactly A cache lines

[2] A *set* can be considered as a fully associative subcache.

[3] The 'address' within the cache (and thereby the cache line) is usually determined by the lowest N bits of the address of a memory block, where *capacity* $= 2^N$.

For the absence of any memory block in a cache line, we introduce a new element I; $S' = S \cup \{I\}$.

Definition 2 concrete cache state. A *(concrete) cache state* is a mapping $c : L \to S'$. C_c denotes the set of all concrete cache states.

In the case of an A-way set associative or fully associative cache, a cache line has to be selected for replacement when the cache is full and the processor requests further data. This is done according to a replacement strategy. Common strategies are *LRU* (Least Recently Used), *FIFO* (First In First Out), and *random*.

The replacement strategy is integrated into the *update* function that models the effects of referencing the cache.

Definition 3 cache update. A cache update function $\mathcal{U}_{\mathcal{M}} : C_c \times S \to C_c$ is a function from a concrete cache state and a memory block to a concrete cache state.

Accesses to caches can be modeled in the following ways:

- *direct mapped cache*: $\mathcal{U}_{\mathcal{M}_{direct}}(c, s_x) = c[l_i \mapsto s_x]$ where $i = (x\%n)$; where $c(l) = s$ means cache line l holds memory block s; and $c(l) = I$ means cache line l holds no valid memory block.
- *fully associative cache with LRU replacement strategy*:

$$\mathcal{U}_{\mathcal{M}_{assoc}}(c, s) = \begin{cases} [\, l_0 \mapsto s, \\ \quad l_i \mapsto c(l_{i-1}) \mid i = 1 \ldots h, \\ \quad l_i \mapsto c(l_i) \mid i = h+1 \ldots n-1 \;]; \text{ if } \exists l_h : c(l_h) = s \\ [\, l_0 \mapsto s, \\ \quad l_i \mapsto c(l_{i-1}) \text{ for } i = 1 \ldots n-1 \,]; \text{ otherwise} \end{cases}$$

  The order of the cache lines $l_1, l_2, \ldots$ is used to express the relative age of a memory block. The least recently referenced memory block is put in the first position. If the memory block has not been in the cache already, the 'oldest' memory block is removed from the cache.
- *A-way set associative cache with LRU replacement strategy*:

$$\mathcal{U}_{\mathcal{M}_{A-way}}(c, s) = c'$$

$$c' = \begin{cases} c[\, l_j \mapsto s, \\ \quad l_i \mapsto c(l_{i-1}) \mid i = j+1 \ldots h, \\ \quad l_i \mapsto c(l_i) \mid i = h+1 \ldots (j+A-1) \quad]; \\ \quad \text{where } \{(l_j, s), \ldots, (l_{j+A-1}, s)\} \\ \qquad \subset \mathcal{M}_{A-way} & \text{if } \exists l_h : c(l_h) = s \\ c[\, l_j \mapsto s, \\ \quad l_i \mapsto c(l_{i-1}) \mid i = j+1 \ldots (j+A-1) \,]; \\ \quad \text{where } \{(l_j, s), \ldots, (l_{j+A-1}, s)\} \\ \qquad \subset \mathcal{M}_{A-way} & \text{otherwise} \end{cases}$$

  An A-way set associative cache is partitioned into n/A *fully associative sets*. The *fully associative set* $\{l_j, \ldots, l_{j+A-1}\}$ is treated as the fully associative cache above. For all cache lines that are not in in the *set*, the cache state remains unchanged.

We represent programs by control flow graphs consisting of nodes and typed edges. The nodes represent *basic blocks*[4]. For each basic block it is known which memory blocks it references[5], i.e. there exists a mapping from control flow nodes to a list of memory blocks: $\mathcal{L} : V \rightarrow S^*$. The execution of a basic block successively loads all memory its blocks into the cache.

We can describe the working of a cache by the aid of the update functions $\mathcal{U}_\mathcal{M}$. It is applied for all memory references of a control flow node by walking in the control flow graph according to the execution of a program. The effect of a control flow node n, on a cache state c is[6]: $[\![n]\!]_\mathcal{M} c = \mathcal{U}_\mathcal{M}\ (\ldots(\mathcal{U}_\mathcal{M}\ (c, s_1))\ldots)s_x$ where $\mathcal{L}\ (n) = [s_1, \ldots, s_x]$.

The cache state at a computation point t_m is the composition of functions related to the elements of the trace $(t_1, \ldots, t_m)$ applied to the initial cache state $\perp_\mathcal{M}$ that maps all cache lines to I: $[\![(t_1, \ldots, t_m)]\!]'_\mathcal{M} \perp_\mathcal{M}$ where $[\![(t_1, \ldots, t_m)]\!]'_\mathcal{M} = ([\![(t_1, \ldots, t_{m-1})]\!]'_\mathcal{M} \circ [\![t_m]\!]_\mathcal{M})$ and $[\![\emptyset]\!]'_\mathcal{M} = \mathbf{id}$.

6 Abstract Semantics

In order to generate a program analyzer, the program analyzer generator PAG requires the specification of an abstract domain, abstract semantic functions, and a join function. The domain for our abstract interpretation is given by the *abstract cache states*:

Definition 4 abstract cache state. An *abstract cache state* $\hat{c} : L \rightarrow 2^{S'}$ is a mapping from the cache lines into the powerset of the memory blocks. $\hat{C}$ denotes the set of all abstract cache states.

The abstract semantic function describes the effects of a control flow node on an element of the abstract domain. The **abstract cache update** function $\hat{\mathcal{U}}_\mathcal{M}$ for abstract cache states is a canonical extension of the cache update function $\mathcal{U}_\mathcal{M}$ on concrete cache states:

- *direct mapped cache:* $\hat{\mathcal{U}}_{\mathcal{M}_{direct}}(\hat{c}, s_x) = \hat{c}[l_i \mapsto \{s_x\}]$ where $i = (x\%n)$
- *fully associative cache with LRU replacement strategy:* $\hat{\mathcal{U}}_{\mathcal{M}_{assoc}}(\hat{c}, s) = \hat{c}'$

$$\hat{c}' = \begin{cases} [\, l_0 \mapsto \{s\}, & \\ \ \ l_i \mapsto \hat{c}(l_{i-1}) - \{s\} \mid i = 1 \ldots h, & \\ \ \ l_i \mapsto \hat{c}(l_i) - \{s\} \mid i = h+1 \ldots n-1]; & \text{if } \exists l_h : \hat{c}(l_h) = \{s\} \\ [\, l_0 \mapsto \{s\}, l_i \mapsto \hat{c}(l_{i-1}) - \{s\} \text{ for } i = 1 \ldots n-1]; & \text{otherwise} \end{cases}$$

- *A-way set associative cache with LRU replacement strategy:*

$$\hat{\mathcal{U}}_{\mathcal{M}_{A-way}}(\hat{c}, s) = \hat{c}'$$

[4] A basic block is a sequence (of fragments) of instructions in which control flow enters at the beginning and leaves at the end without halt or possibility of branching except at the end. For our cache analysis, it is most convenient to have one memory reference per control flow node. Therefore, our nodes may represent the different fragments of machine instructions that access memory.

[5] This is very restricted. See Section 9.1 for weaker restrictions.

[6] In the literature on abstract interpretation (e.g. [18]), our concrete semantics is usually referred to as auxiliary semantics, which is sometimes constructed for the purpose of defining an appropriate abstract semantics.

$$\hat{c}' = \begin{cases} \hat{c}[\, l_j \mapsto \{s\}, \\ \quad l_i \mapsto \hat{c}(l_{i-1}) - \{s\} \mid i = j+1 \ldots h, \\ \quad l_i \mapsto \hat{c}(l_i) - \{s\} \mid i = h+1 \ldots (j+A-1) \quad]; \\ \quad \text{where } \{(l_j, s), \ldots, (l_{j+A-1}, s)\} \\ \qquad \subset \mathcal{M}_{A-way} & \text{if } \exists l_h : \hat{c}(l_h) = \{s\} \\ \hat{c}[\, l_j \mapsto \{s\}, \\ \quad l_i \mapsto \hat{c}(l_{i-1}) - \{s\} \mid i = j+1 \ldots (j+A-1)\,]; \\ \quad \text{where } \{(l_j, s), \ldots, (l_{j+A-1}, s)\} \\ \qquad \subset \mathcal{M}_{A-way} & \text{otherwise} \end{cases}$$

On control flow nodes with at least two[7] predecessors, *join*-functions are used to combine the abstract cache states.

Definition 5 join function. A *join function* $\hat{\mathcal{J}}_{\mathcal{M}} : \hat{C} \times \hat{C} \mapsto \hat{C}$ is a binary function on abstract cache states.

6.1 Join Functions for Direct Mapped Caches

For the direct mapped cache, Mueller at al. [10, 2] use the following join functions: $\hat{\mathcal{J}}_{\mathcal{M}_{direct}}(\hat{c}_1, \hat{c}_2) = \hat{c}$ where $\hat{c}(l) = \hat{c}_1(l) \cup \hat{c}_2(l)$.

$\hat{c}$ computes for each cache line l a set of possible contents. If a cache line l on two different paths with cache states $\hat{c}_1$ and $\hat{c}_2$ holds different memory blocks $\hat{c}_1(l) = \{s_x\}$, $\hat{c}_2(l) = \{s_y\}$, and $x \neq y$, the set $\hat{c}(l) = \{s_x, s_y\}$ means that the cache line l holds either memory block s_x or s_y.

The goal is to determine for every control flow node n whether the references to the memory $\mathcal{L}\ (n)$ will result in cache hits or cache misses.
This can be computed from the abstract semantics by:

- if a memory block s is not in $\hat{c}(l)$ for an arbitrary l then it is definitely not in any cache line.
  This memory reference will *always miss* the cache.
- if $\hat{c}(l) = \{s\}$ for a cache line l then s is definitely in cache line l.
  This memory reference will *always hit* the cache.
- if $\hat{c}(l) = \{I, s\}$ for a cache line l then s is definitely in cache line l for the second and all following executions of n.

In [2] references to instruction caches are further categorized taking the loop nesting level of the instruction into account. An instruction within a loop is called *first miss* if the first reference to the instruction is a cache miss and all remaining references during the execution of the loop are cache hits. Likewise, a *first hit* indicates that the first reference to the instruction will be a hit and all remaining references during the execution of the loop will be misses (see Table 1). This categorization of instructions is used in a timing tool to compute the WCET of a program.

For fully associative caches and set associative caches, two different join functions have to be used. For the identification of 'always hits', the join function corresponds to set intersection, and for the identification of 'always miss', the join function corresponds to set union.

---

[7] Our join functions are associative. On nodes with more than two predecessors, the join function is used iteratively.

Other program lines in the loop that map to the same cache line	The instruction is always executed in the loop and is in cache initially	In the worst case treat the instruction as:
no	no	first miss
no	yes	always hit
yes	no	always miss
yes	yes	first hit

Table 1. Categorizations of Instructions for the WCET analysis according to [2].

During the analysis for direct mapped caches there never occur empty sets. The interpretation of sets of one element is equivalent under union and intersection: $\#(A \cup B) = 1$ and $A \neq \emptyset$ and $B \neq \emptyset \Rightarrow (A \cup B) = (A \cap B)$.

6.2 Join Functions for Fully Associative Caches with LRU Replacement

For the fully associative cache with LRU replacement strategy we can use the following join function to determine if a memory block s is in the cache at a control flow node n: $\hat{\mathcal{J}}^{\cap}_{\mathcal{M}_{assoc}}(\hat{c}_1, \hat{c}_2) = \hat{c}$ where

$$\hat{c}(l_x) = \{s_i \mid \exists l_a, l_b \text{ with } s_i \in \hat{c}_1(l_a), s_i \in \hat{c}_2(l_b) \text{ and } x = max(a, b)\}.$$

The position of the memory blocks in the abstract cache state, i.e. the number of the cache line, represents the relative age of a memory block. If a memory block s has two different relative ages in two abstract cache states, i.e. is in different positions $s \in \hat{c}_1(l_x)$ and $s \in \hat{c}_2(l_y)$ then the join function takes the oldest relative age, i.e. the highest position.

Example 2 $\hat{\mathcal{J}}^{\cap}_{\mathcal{M}_{assoc}}$.

	l_0	l_1	l_2	l_3
$\hat{c}_1$	$\{s_a\}$	$\{s_b\}$	$\{s_c\}$	$\{s_d\}$
$\hat{c}_2$	$\{s_c\}$	$\{s_e\}$	$\{s_a\}$	$\{s_d\}$
$\hat{\mathcal{J}}^{\cap}_{\mathcal{M}_{assoc}}(\hat{c}_1, \hat{c}_2)$	$\{\}$	$\{\}$	$\{s_c, s_a\}$	$\{s_d\}$

An abstract cache state $\hat{c}$ at a control flow node n can be interpreted in the following way:

- If $s \in \hat{c}(l)$ for a cache line l then s is definitely in the cache. A reference to s will ***always hit*** the cache.
- If $s \in \hat{c}(l_x)$ then s will remain in the cache for at least $(\frac{capacity}{line\ size} - x)$ cache updates that put a 'new' element into the cache.

To determine if a memory block s is never in the cache at a control flow node n we use the join functions: $\hat{\mathcal{J}}^{\cup}_{\mathcal{M}_{assoc}}(\hat{c}_1, \hat{c}_2) = \hat{c}$ where $\hat{c}(l) = \hat{c}_1(l) \cup \hat{c}_2(l)$
Here we have the same join function as for the direct mapped cache.

An abstract cache state $\hat{c}$ at a control flow node n can be interpreted in the following way:

- if a memory block s is not in $\hat{c}(l)$ for an arbitrary l then it is definitely not in any cache line. This memory reference will ***always miss*** the cache.
- If $s \in \hat{c}(l_x)$ with x minimal then s will remain in the cache for at most $(\frac{capacity}{line\ size} - x)$ cache updates that put a 'new' element into the cache.

6.3 Join Functions for A-way Set Associative Caches with LRU Replacement

For the A-way set associative cache with LRU replacement strategy we can use the following join function to determine if a memory block s is in the cache at a control flow node n: $\hat{\mathcal{J}}^{\cap}_{\mathcal{M}_{A-way}}(\hat{c}_1, \hat{c}_2) = \hat{c}$ where

$$\hat{c}(l_x) = \{s_i \mid \exists l_a, l_b \text{ with } s_i \in \hat{c}_1(l_a), s_i \in \hat{c}_2(l_b) \text{ and } x = max(a,b)$$
$$\text{and } (l_a, s_i), (l_b, s_i), (l_x, s_i) \in \mathcal{M}_{A-way}\}.$$

An A-way set associative cache is partitioned into n/A fully associative sets. $\hat{\mathcal{J}}^{\cap}_{\mathcal{M}_{A-way}}(\hat{c}_1, \hat{c}_2)$ corresponds to the application of $\hat{\mathcal{J}}^{\cap}_{\mathcal{M}_{assoc}}$ to the fully associative sets of $\hat{c}_1$ and $\hat{c}_2$.

Example 3 $\hat{\mathcal{J}}^{\cap}_{\mathcal{M}_{A-way}}$. Let $\{l_0, l_1\}$ and $\{l_2, l_3\}$ be the fully associative sets of a two-way set associative cache with 4 lines.

	l_0	l_1	l_2	l_3
$\hat{c}_1$	$\{s_a\}$	$\{s_b\}$	$\{\}$	$\{s_e, s_d\}$
$\hat{c}_2$	$\{s_c\}$	$\{s_a\}$	$\{s_d\}$	$\{s_f\}$
$\hat{\mathcal{J}}^{\cap}_{\mathcal{M}_{assoc}}(\hat{c}_1, \hat{c}_2)$	$\{\}$	$\{s_a\}$	$\{\}$	$\{s_d\}$

An abstract cache state $\hat{c}$ at a control flow node n can be interpreted in the following way:

- If $s \in \hat{c}(l)$ for a cache line l then s is definitely in the cache. A reference to s will *always hit* the cache.
- If $s \in \hat{c}(l_x)$ and $\{l_j, \ldots, l_c, \ldots, l_{j+A-1}\}$ is the fully associative set of the cache with $j \leq x \leq j + A + 1$, then s will remain in the cache for at least $(j + A - 1) - x$ cache updates that put a 'new' element into the cache.

To determine if a memory block s is never in the cache at a control flow node n we use the same join functions and the same interpretation as in the fully associative case: $\hat{\mathcal{J}}^{\cup}_{\mathcal{M}_{A-way}} = \hat{\mathcal{J}}^{\cup}_{\mathcal{M}_{assoc}}$.

7 Analysis of Loops

Loops are of special interest, since many programs spend most of their runtime within loops. In a control flow graph, a loop is represented as a cycle. The *start node* of a loop has two incoming edges. One represents the entry into the loop, the other represents the control flow from the end of the loop to the beginning of the loop. The later is called *loop edge*[8].

A loop usually iterates more than once. Since the execution of the loop body usually changes the cache contents, it is useful to distinguish the first iteration from all others. This could be achieved by virtually unrolling each loop once.

Example 4. Let us consider a sufficiently large fully associative data cache with LRU replacement strategy and the following program fragment:

```
/* Variable x not in the data cache */
for i:=1 to .. do  ... y:=x  ... end
```

[8] We consider here loops that correspond to the loop constructs of 'higher programming languages'. Program analysis is not restricted to this, but will produce more precise results for programs with well behaved control flow.

In the first execution of the loop, the reference to **x** will be a cache miss, because **x** is not in the cache. In all further iterations the reference to **x** will be a cache hit, if the cache is sufficiently large to hold all variables referenced within the loop.

For the abstract interpretation, the join function $\hat{\mathcal{J}}^{\cap}_{\mathcal{M}_{assoc}}$ combines the abstract cache states at the start node of the loop. Since the join function is 'similar' to set intersection, the combined abstract cache state will never include the variable **x**, because **x** is not in the abstract cache state before the loop is entered. For a WCET computation for a program this is a safe approximation, but nevertheless not very good.

Loop unrolling would overcome this problem. After the first unrolled iteration, **x** would be in the abstract cache state and would be classified as always hit.

For nested loops, loop unrolling can be an expensive transformation which is exponential in the nesting depth. This problem is similar to the problem of analyzing procedures in program analysis, for which solutions exist (see Section 2).

For our analysis of cache behavior we transform loops into procedures to be able to use the existing methods and tools[9] (see Figure 1).

```
...
while P do
      BODY        ==>        ...
end;                         loop_L();  (1)
```

```
proc loop_L();
if P then
  BODY
  loop_L();        (2)
end
```

Fig. 1. Loop transformation.

7.1 Callstring Approach

There are only a finite number of cache lines and for each program a finite number of memory blocks. This means, the domain of abstract cache states $\hat{c} : L \to 2^{S'}$ is finite. Additionally, the abstract cache update functions $\hat{\mathcal{U}}$ and the join functions $\hat{\mathcal{J}}$ are monotonic. This guarantees that abstract interpretations with both the callstring approach and the functional approach will terminate.

In the callstring approach, the high complexity of the functional approach can be circumvented. If we restrict the callstring length to 1 (*callstring*(1)), then for each transformed loop only two different incoming abstract cache states are considered: One for the call to the loop–procedure at the original place of the loop in the program (1) (see Figure 1); and one for the recursive call of the loop-procedure (2). The first call corresponds to the first iteration of the loop. The second call corresponds to all other iterations of the loop.

This means, we can interpret the abstract cache states $\hat{c}_f$ for the first iteration and $\hat{c}_o$ for all other iterations at a control flow node n within the loop–procedure according to Table 2. Note: For A-way set associative caches and fully associative caches the determination of 'always hit' and 'always miss' requires analysis with both $\hat{\mathcal{J}}^{\cap}_{\mathcal{M}}$ and $\hat{\mathcal{J}}^{\cup}_{\mathcal{M}}$. We call the analysis with $\hat{\mathcal{J}}^{\cap}_{\mathcal{M}}$ **must analysis** because it computes all blocks that must be in the cache. And we call the analysis with $\hat{\mathcal{J}}^{\cup}_{\mathcal{M}}$ **may analysis** because it computes all blocks that may be in the cache.

[9] Ludwell Harrison III [7] also proposed this transformation for the analysis of loops.

Interpretation of the abstract cache state $\hat{c}_f$ for a reference to a memory block s:	Interpretation of the abstract cache state $\hat{c}_o$ for a reference to a memory block s:	Combination of $\hat{c}_f(s)$ and $\hat{c}_o(s)$:
always hit	always hit	always hit
always miss	always hit	first miss
always miss	always miss	always miss
always hit	always miss	first hit
always hit	–	first hit
always miss	–	always miss
–	always hit	first miss
–	always miss	always miss
–	–	always miss

Table 2. Interpretation of abstract cache states for callstring(1). The second part describes the categorization for a WCET analysis according to Table 1 if no classification into 'always hit' and 'always miss' is possible.

7.2 Functional Approach

During the analysis of a program, PAG tabulates for each procedure (and each loop that has been transformed into a procedure) all abstract cache states within the procedure for all different incoming abstract cache states.

This computes the same values as if the loops had been unrolled. In the worst case, the exponential growth in program code of the loop unrolling corresponds to exponentially many different incoming abstract cache states that are tabulated during the analysis. But often, there are much less different incoming abstract cache states than unrolled loop bodies for a deeply nested loop nest.

The functional approach gives the most detailed results for the abstract interpretation but may be very expensive.

8 Example

We consider must and may analysis for a fully associative data cache of 4 lines for the following program fragment of a loop, where $..x..$ stands for a construct that references variable x:

`while` $..e..$ `do` $..b..; ..c..; ..a..; ..d..; ..c..$ `end`

The control flow graph and the result of the analysis with callstring(1) are shown in Figure 2. We assume that each variable fits exactly into one cache line. The nodes of the control flow graph are numbered 1 to 6, and each node is marked with the variable it accesses (a, b, c, d, e). For the analysis, we assume the loop has been implicitly transformed into a procedure according to Figure 1.

Each node is marked with the abstract cache states (in the same format as in Example 2) computed by the PAG–generated analyzer immediately before the abstract cache states are updated with the memory references. The loop entry edge is marked with the incoming abstract cache states. The loop exit edge is marked with the outgoing abstract cache states.

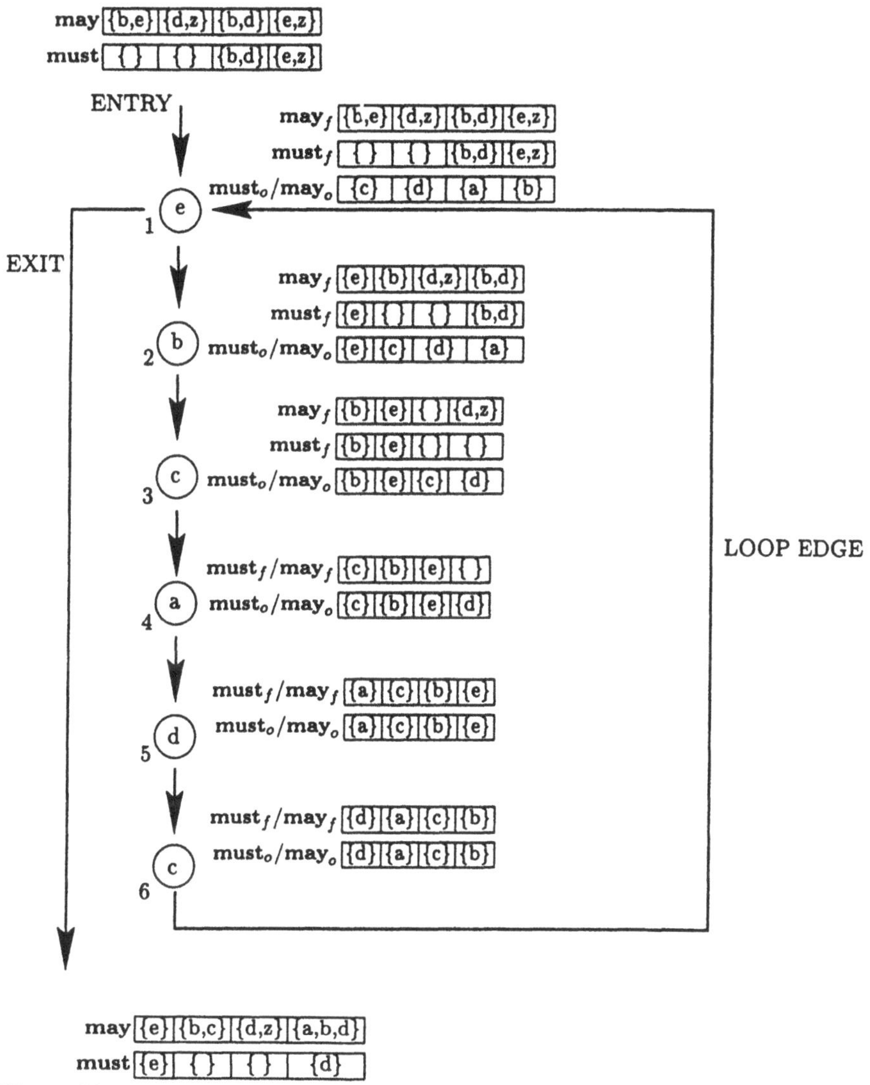

Fig. 2. Must and may analysis for a fully associative data cache with callstring(1). **must** and **may** are the abstract cache states for the must and the may analysis. $\mathbf{must}_f$ and $\mathbf{may}_f$ are the abstract cache states for the first loop iteration. $\mathbf{must}_o$ and $\mathbf{may}_o$ are the abstract cache states for all other iterations. The abstract cache states can be interpreted for each variable reference according to Table 2:

(Node,Variable)	Interpretation
(1,*e*), (2,*b*)	first hit
(3,*c*)	first miss
(4,*a*), (5,*d*)	always miss
(6,*c*)	always hit

9 Data Caches and Combined Data/Instruction Caches

9.1 Scalar Variables

In the current design, the work is limited to the prediction of memory references to addresses that can be determined at analysis time. This allows for example for the prediction of instruction cache behavior.

Our analysis can also be used to predict the behavior of data caches or combined instruction/data caches for programs that use only scalar variables.

For this kind of programs, it is possible to compute for each data reference to a procedure parameter or a local variable the address within the procedure stack frame by a static stack level simulation [18]. For each call to a procedure, the address of the procedure stack frame depends only on a statically computable offset to the procedure stack frame of the caller.

For our abstract interpretation, we extend the function that maps control flow nodes to the list of referenced memory blocks by an argument that is the set of possible absolute stack frame addresses[10]: $\mathcal{L}' : V \times 2^{\mathbb{N}_0} \to S^*$.

Additionally, we assume a function $\mathcal{H}$ that maps call nodes to their relative stack frame offset or stack height: $\mathcal{H} : V \to \mathbb{N}_0$.

All abstract semantic functions and join functions have to be defined on pairs of abstract cache states and sets of actual stack frame addresses:
$\hat{\mathcal{U}}'_{\mathcal{M}} : \hat{C} \times 2^{\mathbb{N}_0} \times S \to \hat{C} \times 2^{\mathbb{N}_0}$ and $\hat{\mathcal{J}}'_{\mathcal{M}} : (\hat{C} \times 2^{\mathbb{N}_0}) \times (\hat{C} \times 2^{\mathbb{N}_0}) \to (\hat{C} \times 2^{\mathbb{N}_0})$
Only the abstract semantic function for procedure calls[11] have to change the actual stack frame address.

$$\hat{\mathcal{U}}'_{\mathcal{M}}(\hat{c}, s, \{h_1, \ldots, h_x\}) = \begin{cases} \Big(\hat{\mathcal{U}}_{\mathcal{M}}(\hat{c}, s), \{h_1 + \mathcal{H}(n), \ldots, h_x + \mathcal{H}(n)\}\Big) \\ \qquad\qquad\qquad\qquad\qquad\qquad \text{for a call node } n \\ \Big(\hat{\mathcal{U}}_{\mathcal{M}}(\hat{c}, s), \{h_1, \ldots, h_x\}\Big) \qquad \text{otherwise} \end{cases}$$

$$\hat{\mathcal{J}}'_{\mathcal{M}}((\hat{c}_1, H_1), (\hat{c}_2, H_2)) = \Big(\hat{\mathcal{J}}_{\mathcal{M}}(\hat{c}_1, \hat{c}_2), H_1 \cup H_2\Big)$$

For programs without recursive procedures, there are only finitely many stack frame addresses. This guarantees termination of the abstract interpretation. With the functional approach and the callstring approach where the procedure nesting depth of the program does not exceed the callstring length, the sets of stack frame addresses for the $\hat{\mathcal{U}}'$ and $\hat{\mathcal{J}}'$ functions contain always exactly one element. This means there is no loss of information.

For programs with recursive procedures, the number of stack frame addresses may grow infinitely during the analysis so that the analysis does not terminate. Cousot and Cousot [4] proposed a technique called *'widening'* that speeds up the analysis.

We use a 'widening' function ∇ to restrict the number of stack frame addresses. When during the analysis the number of elements in a set of stack frame

[10] This works for C-type languages where all procedures are 'global'. PASCAL-like languages with local procedures referencing local variables of other procedures can't be modeled in this way.

[11] This holds only for procedures of the original program. The newly introduced loop-procedures do not change the procedure stack frame address.

addresses exceeds a given limit R, ∇ replaces this set by $\mathbb{N}_0$[12]. This can only occur when the join function is applied.

$$\nabla(\{h_1,\ldots,h_x\}) = \begin{cases} \{h_1,\ldots,h_x\} \text{ if } x \leq R \\ \mathbb{N}_0 \qquad \text{otherwise} \end{cases}$$

An occurrence of $\mathbb{N}_0$ means a total loss of information on the stack frame address. Accordingly, the update and join functions can not compute any relevant information, but map all abstract cache states to the most undefined cache state $\top_{\mathcal{M}}$: $\hat{\mathcal{U}}'_{\mathcal{M}}(\hat{c}, s, \mathbb{N}_0) = \hat{\mathcal{J}}'_{\mathcal{M}}((\hat{c}_1, \mathbb{N}_0), (\hat{c}_2, H)) = \hat{\mathcal{J}}'_{\mathcal{M}}((\hat{c}_1, H), (\hat{c}_2, \mathbb{N}_0)) = (\top_{\mathcal{M}}, \mathbb{N}_0)$.

$$\top_{\mathcal{M}_{direct}} = \top^{\cup}_{\mathcal{M}_{assoc}} = \top^{\cup}_{\mathcal{M}_{A-way}} = [l_i \mapsto S \mid i = 1\ldots n]$$

$$\top^{\cap}_{\mathcal{M}_{assoc}} = \top^{\cap}_{\mathcal{M}_{A-way}} = [l_i \mapsto \{\} \mid i = 1\ldots n]$$

9.2 Writes

So far, we have ignored writing to a cache and only considered reading from a cache. There are two common cache organizations with respect to writing to the cache [8]:

- *Write through:* On a cache write the data is written to both the memory block and the corresponding cache line.
- *Write back:* The data is written only to the cache line. The modified cache line is written to main memory only when it is replaced. This is usually implemented with a bit (called *dirty bit*) for each cache line that indicates if the cache line has been modified.

The execution time of a store instruction often depends on whether the memory block that is written is in the cache (*write hit*) or not (*write miss*). For the prediction of hits and misses we can use our analysis. There are two common cache organizations with respect to write misses:

- *Write allocate:* The block is loaded into the cache. This is generally used for write back caches.
- *No write allocate:* The block is not loaded into the cache. The write changes only the main memory. This is often used for write through caches.

Writes to write through/write allocate caches can be treated as reads. For no write allocate caches, the update functions have to be adapted. For A-way set associative caches ($A > 1$) and fully associative caches, a write access to a block s is treated as a read access, if s is already in the concrete or abstract cache state. Otherwise, and for direct mapped caches[13], the write access is ignored, i.e. the update functions is the identity function for this case.

Write back caches write a modified line to memory when the line is replaced. The timing of a load or store instruction may depend on whether a modified or an unmodified line is replaced[14]. To keep track of modified cache lines, we extend

[12] PAG includes a *'negative'* set representation, so that this operation is efficiently implemented.

[13] This is to preserve the interpretation of sets of one element as always hits.

[14] Many cache designs use write buffers that hold a limited number of blocks. Write buffers may delay a cache access, when they are full or data is referenced that is still in the buffer. To analyze the behavior of the write buffers possible 'write backs' have to be determined.

the cache states by a 'dirty' bit, where d means modified, p means unmodified[15]: $c : L \to \{d,p\} \times S'$ and $\hat{c} : L \to 2^{\{d,p\} \times S'}$.
The update functions distinguish reads and writes. The dirty bit is set to d only on writes:

$$\begin{aligned} \mathcal{U}_{\mathcal{M}} &: C_c \times (\{r,w\} \times S) \to C_c \\ \hat{\mathcal{U}}_{\mathcal{M}} &: \hat{C} \times (\{r,w\} \times S) \to \hat{C} \\ \hat{\mathcal{U}}'_{\mathcal{M}} &: \hat{C} \times 2^{\mathbb{N}_0} \times (\{r,w\} \times S) \to \hat{C} \times 2^{\mathbb{N}_0} \end{aligned}$$

Let n be a control flow node, s_a be one read or write memory reference at n, $\hat{c}_1^{\cup}$ the abstract cache state for the *may* analysis immediately before s_a is referenced, and $\hat{c}_2^{\cup} = \hat{\mathcal{U}}_{\mathcal{M}}(\hat{c}_1^{\cup}, m, s_a), m \in \{r,w\}$ the abstract cache state immediately after s_a was referenced, $\hat{c}_1^{\cap}$ the abstract cache state for the *must* analysis immediately before s_a is referenced, and $\hat{c}_2^{\cap} = \hat{\mathcal{U}}_{\mathcal{M}}(\hat{c}_1^{\cap}, m, s_a), m \in \{r,w\}$ the abstract cache state immediately after s_a was referenced. Let l_x the cache line where s_a has been stored in $\hat{c}_2^{\cup}$. Then $\hat{c}_1^{\cup}(l_x)$ contains all possible memory blocks that may have been replaced by s_a.

- If $\{s \mid (d,s) \in \hat{c}_1^{\cup}(l_x)\} = \emptyset$, then no dirty memory block has been replaced. This reference has definitively caused **no write back**.
- If there is a dirty line $s \in \{s \mid (d,s) \in \hat{c}_1^{\cup}(l_x)\}$ and s is an always hit in $\hat{c}_1^{\cap}$ and s is a always miss in $\hat{c}_2^{\cup}$, then a dirty memory block has been replaced. This reference has definitively caused a **write back**.
- If $\{s \mid (d,s) \in \hat{c}_1^{\cup}(l_x)\} \neq \emptyset$ then for a WCET analysis we have to consider a possible write back.

The identified (possible) write backs can be used in another abstract interpretation similar to the cache analysis for the prediction of the write buffer behavior.

10 State of the Implementation and Future Work

The presented techniques have been validated with an ANSI-C frontend that has been interfaced to PAG. We are currently developing a PAG interface for executables based on the Wisconsin architectural research tool set (WARTS).

11 Conclusion

We have described several semantics of programs executed on machines with several types of one level caches. Abstract interpretations based on these semantics statically analyze the intrinsic cache behavior of programs. The information computed allows interpretations such as 'always hit', 'always miss', 'first hit', 'first miss', and 'write back'. It can be used to improve execution time calculations for programs. The analyses are specified as needed by the program analyzer generator PAG.

Acknowledgements

We like to thank Susan Horwitz for making available the ANSI-C frontend, and Mark D. Hill, James R. Larus, Alvin R. Lebeck, Madhusudhan Talluri, and David A. Wood for making available the Wisconsin architectural research tool set (WARTS).

[15] For the abstract interpretation: $d > p$ and $\top_{\{d,p\}} = d$.

References

1. Martin Alt and Florian Martin. Generation of efficient interprocedural analyzers with PAG. In *SAS'95, Static Analysis Symposium*, pages 33–50. Springer-Verlag LNCS 983, September 1995.
2. Robert Arnold, Frank Mueller, David B. Whalley, and Marion Harmon. Bounding worst-case instruction cache performance. In *IEEE Symposium on Real-Time Systems*, pages 172–181, Dec 1994.
3. Swagato Basumallick and Kelvin Nilsen. Cache issues in real-time systems. In *Proceedings of the 1994 ACM SIGPLAN Workshop on Language, Compiler and Tool Support for Real-Time Systems*, June 1994.
4. P. Cousot and R. Cousot. Static determination of dynamic properties of programs. In *Proceedings of the second International Symposium on Programming*, pages 106–130, Dunod, Paris, France, 1976.
5. P. Cousot and R. Cousot. Abstract interpretation: a unified lattice model for static analysis of programs by construction or approximation of fixpoints. In *Conference Record of the 4th ACM Symposium on Principles of Programming Languages*, pages 238–252, Los Angeles, CA, January 1977.
6. Wolfgang A. Halang and Krzysztof M. Sacha. *Real-Time Systems.* World Scientific, 1992.
7. Ludwell Harrison. *Personal communication on Abstract Interpretation, Dagstuhl Seminar*, 1995.
8. J.L Hennessy and D.A. Patterson. *Computer Architecture: A Quantitative Approach.* Morgan Kaufmann, 1990.
9. Sung-Soo Lim, Young Hyun Bae, Gye Tae Jang, Byung-Do Rhee, Sang Lyul Min, Chang Yun Park, Heonshik Shin, Kunsoo Park, Soo-Mook Moon, and Chong Sang Kim. An accurate worst case timing analysis for risc processors. *IEEE Transactions on Software Engineering*, 21(7):593–604, July 1995.
10. Frank Mueller, David B. Whalley, and Marion Harmon. Predicting instruction cache behavior. In *Proceedings of the 1994 ACM SIGPLAN Workshop on Language, Compiler and Tool Support for Real-Time Systems*, June 1994.
11. Kelvin D. Nilsen and Bernt Rygg. Worst-case execution time analysis on modern processors. In *Proceedings of the 1995 ACM SIGPLAN Workshop on Language, Compiler and Tool Support for Real-Time Systems*, June 1995.
12. Chang Yun Park and Alan C. Shaw. Experiments with a program timing tool based on source-level timing schema. *IEEE Computer*, 25(5):48–57, May 1991.
13. P. Puschner and Ch. Koza. Calculating the maximum execution time of real-time programs. *Real-Time Systems*, 1:159–176, 1989.
14. J. Rawat. Static analysis of cache performance for real-time programming. Masters thesis, Iowa State University, May 1993.
15. Micha Sharir and Amir Pnueli. Two approaches to interprocedural data flow analysis. In Steven S. Muchnick and Neil D. Jones, editors, *Program Flow Analysis: Theory and Applications*, chapter 7, pages 189–233. Prentice-Hall, 1981.
16. A.J. Smith. Cache memories. *ACM Computing surveys*, 14(3):473–530, Sep 1983.
17. Alexander D. Stoyenko, V. Carl Hamacher, and Richard C. Holt. Analyzing hard-real-time programs for guaranteed schedulability. *IEEE Transactions on Software Engineering*, 17(8), August 1991.
18. Reinhard Wilhelm and Dieter Maurer. *Compiler Design.* International Computer Science Series. Addison–Wesley, 1995.

Termination Analysis for Offline Partial Evaluation of a Higher Order Functional Language

Peter Holst Andersen
Department of Computer Science,
University of Copenhagen,
txix@diku.dk

Carsten Kehler Holst
Prolog Development Center
kehler@pdc.dk

Abstract. One of the remaining problems on the path towards fully automatic partial evaluation is ensuring termination of the specialization phase. In [10] we gave a termination analysis which could be applied to partial evaluation of first-order strict languages, using a new result about inductive arguments (loosely: if whenever something grows, something gets smaller then the program will only enter finitely many different states). In this paper we extend this work to cover higher-order functional languages. We take an operational approach to the problem and consider the closure representation of higher-order functions to perform a combined data- and control-dependency analysis. The result of this analysis is then used, as in the first-order case, to decide which arguments need to be dynamic to guarantee termination of partial evaluation of the analysed program. The new methods have been tested on a variety of programs, and will be incorporated in a future release of the Similix partial evaluator for Scheme.

Keywords: partial evaluation, termination, abstract interpretation, size analysis.

1 Introduction

For partial evaluation to be successful as an automatic tool for non-specialist users, the user must be able to use it as a "black box" similar to the way optimizing compilers are used today. So termination must be ensured.

Almost all of today's offline partial evaluators have unsafe termination properties (i.e., they are not guaranteed to terminate). The reason for this is an apparently unavoidable conflict between two desirable properties: A partial evaluator should *terminate* on every program p and static data s, and it should be *computationally complete*, meaning that it should compute *all* of p's actions that depend only on s.

Many successful partial evaluators have prioritized computational completeness over termination (e.g., Similix [1, 5], Schism [6], and C-Mix [2, 3]). In this paper we show that termination can be achieved even for higher-order languages with an acceptable loss of computational completeness.

The sources of nontermination are *infinite specialization* (an attempt to create an infinitely large specialized program) and *completely static loops* (loops in p that depend only on the static input s). We develop an analysis for a higher order untyped strict functional language (e.g., Scheme) that is used to change some of the binding times in the program from static to dynamic, in such a way that partial evaluation of the program only enters finitely many different configurations. This, together with memoization, guarantees termination of partial evaluation.

The analysis is based on the same foundation as Holst's analysis for a first-order language [10], which works as follows: First an approximation of the program's control- and data-flow during partial evaluation is computed. The approximation gives information about which variables depend on which, and whether they grow or get smaller along the possible evaluation paths. The gathered information is then used to generalize[1] variables for which upper bounds cannot be guaranteed. To adopt the approach from [10] to a higher-order language (or any other language for that matter), "all" we have to do is to devise an analysis that collects an approximation of the program's control- and data-flow, and then apply the main result from [10]. The problem is to collect an interesting approximation.

Termination of computationally complete partial evaluation in general is undecidable (an easy consequence of Rice's Theorem [13]). Therefore the analysis will make a *safe approximation*, that is guaranteed to detect all infinite loops, but may classify some loops as infinite even though they will always terminate. This corresponds to the safety condition found in other abstract interpretations, e.g., strictness analysis. However, in strictness analysis even a little information can be useful, whereas our analysis is uninteresting unless it solves the problem for a large class of programs. Therefore, the development of the analysis has mainly been driven by experimentation with small programs containing non-trivial recursion and usages of higher-order functions. This approach was motivated by the belief that, if the analysis can handle these small, but complex programs satisfactory, then it can handle real programs as well. Experiments show that the analysis is strong enough to detect that partial evaluation of non-trivial interpreters using higher-order features will terminate, and at the same time all interpretive overhead will be specialized away.

A related problem, which we will not address in this paper, is *abnormal termination* of partial evaluation (errors occurring while executing static code). The problem has been fixed in Similix [1], which generates code to produce the error at run time when encountering an erroneous static expression.

Outline of the Paper. The paper presents an overview of the analysis. Non-essential technical details have been left out to give room for a report of several practical experiments. We give an account of how the analysis was developed

[1] To generalize a variable means "to change its binding time from static to dynamic."

through trial and error in the hope that others may benefit from our experience. A more detailed description can be found in the technical report [4].

Section 2 defines the subject language used in this paper. Section 3 describes how quasi-termination forms the foundation of the termination analysis. Section 4 gives an overview of the termination analysis, and lists the component analyses on which it is based. Section 5 describes the development history of the analysis. Section 6 reports the results of applying the analysis to a number of different programs. Section 7 gives the central technical details. Section 8 concludes and describes related and future work.

Contributions of this Paper. The work presented here is an extension of [10], its main contributions are handling of the higher order case, and we hope, a more intuitive presentation of the ideas. The work also includes an evaluation of the analysis based on empirical results. Finally, we expect that the analysis can serve as a template for other similar analyses.

Prerequisites. This paper requires knowledge of partial evaluation corresponding to for example [11, Part II].

2 Language

We are essentially dealing with the untyped lambda-calculus augmented with named functions. Initially the program is lambda-lifted and the arguments are tupled, so each function has two arguments; a tuple with the free variables and one with the lambda bound. Thus, the lambda expression $\lambda x.y\ x$ becomes $\text{Clo}(l, \langle y \rangle)$ where l is a freshly generated label (function) with the definition $l(y)(x) = y\ x$. Likewise, a function call $f(e_1, \ldots, e_n)$ becomes $\text{Clo}(f, \langle\rangle)(e_1, \ldots, e_n)$.

When we use binding-time information we annotate the program by underlining the dynamic expressions. The termination analysis relies on the fact that the program is *well-annotated* [11].

3 Quasi-Termination

In this section we define quasi-termination, state a central theorem giving a sufficient condition for a program to be quasi-terminating, give some intuition behind the principles on which the termination analysis is based, and introduce key terminology used in this paper. The material presented in this section can also be found in Holst [10], which contains a proof of Theorem 3.1.

Configurations. A *configuration* is composed of a *program point* identifying a position in a program, and the values of the variables at that point.

We can think of evaluation of a flowchart program as going through a sequence of configurations, where each configuration c_i is composed by a label and a mapping of variables to values.

$$c_1 \rightarrow c_2 \rightarrow \cdots \rightarrow c_n$$

It should be clear that each configuration uniquely determines the rest of the sequence. A program is terminating if the sequence of configurations is finite for all inputs. A program is *quasi-terminating* if it for any input only enters finitely many different configurations.

In pure functional programs a program point could be identified by an expression in the program, and a configuration would then be an (expression, environment) pair. Instead of considering a sequence of configurations it would be more natural to consider evaluation trees (finite or infinite) with (expression, environment) pairs as nodes, and with a subtree for each subevaluation. Each node uniquely determines the subtree of which it is the root. If the tree is finite for all input, then the program is terminating. This does not necessarily mean that the result is well defined, e.g., it might terminate with an error (typically something along the lines of "`can't take car of nil`"). If the tree only contains finitely many different nodes for any input, then the program is quasi-terminating. Clearly this does not imply that the tree is finite.

Applying König's lemma "In a finitely branching infinite tree some paths will be infinite" makes it possible to consider paths in a tree instead of the whole tree. If all paths are finite the tree will be finite, and if all paths contain only finitely many different nodes, the tree as a whole will contain only finitely many different nodes.

In the following example f is an obviously non-terminating, but quasi-terminating program, whereas g is neither a terminating nor a quasi-terminating program.

$$f(x) = f(x)$$
$$g(x) = g(x+1)$$

Transitions. If for some input a program goes through configurations c_1, c_2, and c_3 in that order, we say that there is a *transition* from configuration c_1 to c_2, one from c_2 to c_3, and one from c_1 to c_3. We call the "smallest" transitions *1-step* or *simple* transitions and the others *composite* transitions. Since the proof for Theorem 3.1 argues that if the program goes through only finitely many 1-step transitions then it is terminating, it is important that the 1-step transitions are primitive, meaning they only take finite time.

In our lambda-lifted language we will use function calls as 1-step transitions. They are primitive, since a function cannot loop without calling itself. In our language a transition is a mapping between environments, or argument tuples. The set of all 1-step transitions defined by a program is the collection of all the function calls that can occur during any run. It is important to notice that the set of all transitions in a program is not the set of 1-step transitions but the transitive closure of these.

An *endotransition* is a transition from a program point back to itself. This need not be a 1-step transition.

Example 1. Consider the following programs operating on natural numbers:

$$f(x,y) = \textit{if } y = 1 \textit{ then } y \textit{ else } f(x+1, y-1)$$
$$g(x,y) = \textit{if } y = 1 \textit{ then } g(2,x) \textit{ else } g(x+1, y-1)$$

When f is called with $(2,5)$ the evaluation goes through the following sequence of configurations, where each arrow denotes a 1-step transition equivalent to a call in the program:

$$f(2,5) \to f(3,4) \to f(4,3) \to f(5,2) \to f(6,1)$$

If we, for example, compose the first two 1-step transitions we get a composite transition from $f(2,5)$ to $f(4,3)$.

Inductive Arguments. We focus our interest on inductive arguments (i.e., arguments or argument positions, that depend on themselves). Consider the endotransition, which comes from a direct call from h to itself somewhere in its body:

$$h(a,b) = \ldots\ h(A,B)\ \ldots$$

If $A < a$ we say that a (in the sense "the first argument position") is *in situ decreasing.* $A < a$ should be read as "for all possible values of a this transition gives rise to a value of A that is strictly less than that of a." If the same holds for B (i.e., if $B < a$) then b is said to be *decreasing.* If we only can guarantee $A \leq a$ we say the argument is *in situ weakly decreasing*, or *in situ equal.* Similarly, if $B \leq a$ then b is said to be *weakly decreasing* or *equal.* If we cannot guarantee that the argument is at most equal we consider it an *increasing* argument (this is safe if imprecise). If an increasing argument depends on itself it is *in situ increasing.*

In the example above the call $f(x+1, y-1)$ has an in situ increasing first argument and an in situ decreasing second argument. Since all the transitions in f has this form Theorem 3.1 tells us that f is quasi-terminating.

Theorem 3.1 requires the in situ decreasing parameters controlling the loops to be *bounded*[2] for the program to be quasi-terminating. The reason behind this requirement is illustrated by the function g in the example above. We have an endotransition from g to itself, where y is in situ decreasing and x is in situ increasing, but the program is not quasi-terminating. Consider for example the following infinite evaluation path:

$$\underline{g(2,2)} \to g(3,1) \to \underline{g(2,3)} \to g(3,2) \to g(4,1) \to \underline{g(2,4)} \to \ldots$$

The problem is that y is reset every once in a while (at the underlined configurations) to a value on which there is no bound.

The rest of this paper attempts to bring us in position to use the main result of Holst [10] stated below. The problem is to collect an interesting approximation of the set of transitions.

Theorem 3.1 *Consider all transitions defined by a given program (composite as well as simple). Assume the domains are finitely downwards closed*[3] *with respect to some size ordering. Then the program is quasi-terminating if every endotransition with an in situ increasing argument, also has a bounded in situ decreasing argument.*

[2] An argument is said to be *bounded*, if it has an upper bound for every run.

[3] A domain is finitely downwards closed if for any value the set of values smaller than it is finite. This is strictly stronger than the descending chain condition [8].

The Connection to Partial Evaluation. Let $trans_p$ be the set of all transitions during partial evaluation of a well-annotated program p. The dynamic variables do not occur in $trans_p$, as they do not take on any values during partial evaluation. If every endotransition in $trans_p$ with an in situ increasing argument, also has a bounded in situ decreasing argument, then the program will only enter finitely many different configurations during partial evaluation.

Termination of partial evaluation of the program can now be ensured by memoizing the configurations. Note that completely static configurations must be memoized as well, otherwise a static loop could cause non-termination. This differs from what is normally done in partial evaluation, where only configurations that lead to specialized program points are memoized.

The objective of the termination analysis is to change some of the binding times to dynamic, such that the "offending" or "dangerous" arguments do not appear in $trans_p$.

4 Overview of the Termination Analysis

In this section we give an overview of the termination analysis including brief descriptions of the analyses on which it is based. The diagram below illustrates the dependencies between the various analyses.

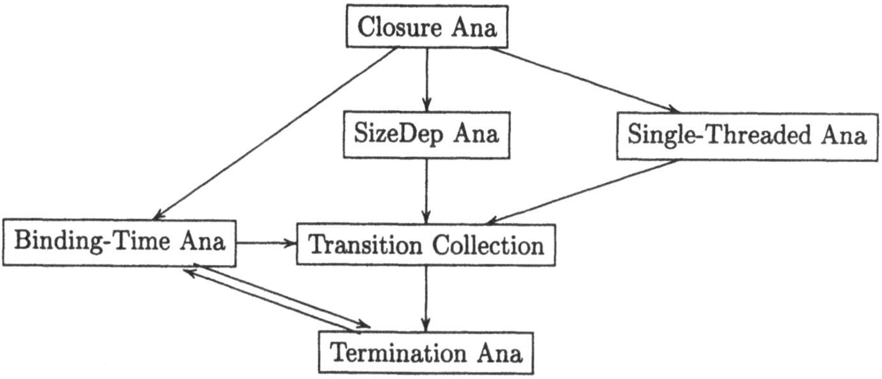

Closure Analysis. The net result of the closure analysis [14, 5], is a safe approximation of which closures a given expression can evaluate to. In addition to tracing the flow of closures, we also trace the flow of first-order values (i.e., the analysis detects if a given expression can evaluate to a first-order value).

Binding-Time Analysis. The binding-time analysis produces a well-annotated version of the program.

Single-Threaded Analysis. This analysis identify *single-threaded* closures (i.e., closures that are applied at most once). The information gathered can be used to get higher precision when tracing flow in the program.

The analysis of Turner, Wadler, and Mossin [15] can be used to detect single-threaded closures.

Size and Dependency Analysis. The size analysis is a data-dependency analysis; which part of the arguments is the value build from, and how. The dependency analysis is a standard control-dependency analysis, which collects information about which part of the arguments the value depends on.

Transition Collection. Once the size information and dependency information have been obtained, an approximate 1-step transition is collected for each reachable call in the program[4]. Then the entire approximate set of transitions is generated by taking the transitive closures of all compositions of these.

Termination Analysis. We notice that an argument that does not depend on an in situ increasing argument must be bounded. So given a well-annotated program and an approximation of the set of transitions, we ensure termination of partial evaluation by repeating the following three steps until the annotations stabilize:

1. Generalize in situ increasing arguments occurring in endotransitions without a static bounded in situ decreasing argument.
2. Update the annotations to ensure that the program is well-annotated.
3. Redo the transitions collection and termination analysis.

This ensures that partial evaluation of the program will only enter finitely many different configurations.

5 Development History

In this section we give an account of how we developed the analysis focusing on the size and dependency analysis and the transition collection, since they are solving the core problems. First, we give a description of the first-order analysis, which served as a basis for the development. Second, we describe how a simple extension tames the control-flow problem in higher-order programs. Third, we describe a plausible but, as it turned out, unsuccessful attempt to deal with higher-order data flow using bounded trees. Fourth, we show how grammars solve most of the problems. Finally, we show how the remaining problems can be solved by taking binding times and single-threaded closures into account.

The First-Order Analysis. The result of the size and dependency analysis in the first order case is, for each function, a (*size*, *dep*) pair describing how the return value relates to the parameters. Informally, the *dep* value is a set of argument positions identifying which of the parameters the return value depends on (including control dependency). Again informally, the *size* is a set of "basic" size values, which come in three guises: $D(i)$, $E(i)$, and I, where i is an argument position; the ith parameter. $D(i)$ means that the return value is guaranteed to be less that the ith parameter, $E(i)$ means "less than or equal", and I means that we cannot ensure anything. The meaning of a set of basic size values is the

[4] Assuming, as usual, that every conditional branch can go either way.

disjunction of the size values. The size value only describes data dependency and not control dependency. Consider the following functions:

$$\begin{aligned} f(x,y) &= g(x,x,y) \\ g(x,y,z) &= \text{if } z \text{ then } car\ x \text{ else } car\ y \end{aligned}$$

The return value of g becomes $\langle(\{D(1),D(2)\},\{1,2,3\})\rangle$, meaning it is either smaller than x or smaller than y and it depends on x, y, and z. Why the either-or case is interesting should be clear when considering f whose return value becomes $\langle(D(1),\{1,2\})\rangle$.

Once the size and dependency information has been collected, an approximate 1-step transition is collected for each reachable call in the program. The size and dependency information is needed in case of calls that pass the return value of some function as a parameter to another (e.g., $f(g(x,y),z)$). A transition consists of two function names (the caller and the callee) and a tuple of (*size*, *dep*) pairs, which describes how the callee's parameters relate to the caller's parameters. For example, the call $f(x,y) = g(x,x,y)$ would give rise to the following transition: $(\langle f,g\rangle,\langle E(1),E(1),E(2)\rangle)$ (the dependency information has been omitted for readability).

If the program contains calls between two functions with different size-dep characteristics, a 1-step transition is collected for each call. This is crucial for the precision of the analysis. Consider the following two transitions: $\langle D(1),E(2)\rangle$, and $\langle E(1),D(2)\rangle$. If we only collected one transition for each function pair it would have to be $\langle E(1),E(2)\rangle$, and we would not detect that the arguments are decreasing.

Once we have collected the 1-step transitions, we take the transitive closure of all compositions of these to get an approximation of the program's control and data flow.

Example 2. The functions

$$\begin{aligned} f(x) &= g(x, cons\ x\ x) \\ g(x,y) &= h(hd\ y, hd\ x, x) \end{aligned}$$

give rise to the following 1-step transitions:

$$t_1 = (\langle f,g\rangle,\langle E(1),I\rangle), \quad t_2 = (\langle g,h\rangle,\langle D(2),D(1),E(1)\rangle)$$

When t_1 and t_2 are composed we get the following transition:

$$\begin{aligned} t_2 \circ t_1 &= (\langle f,h\rangle,\langle D(2),D(1),E(1)\rangle \circ \langle E(1),I\rangle) \\ &= (\langle f,h\rangle,\langle D(2)\circ\langle E(1),I\rangle, D(1)\circ\langle E(1),I\rangle, E(1)\circ\langle E(1),I\rangle\rangle) \\ &= (\langle f,h\rangle,\langle I,D(1),E(1)\rangle) \end{aligned}$$

The transition describes a transfer of control from f to h, and shows how h's parameters relate to f's parameters. We can verify that we have composed the transitions correctly by unfolding the call to g: $f(x) = h(hd\ (cons\ x\ x), hd\ x, x)$. Note that we are unable to detect that the first argument to h is actually equal to x. However, it turns out that the techniques developed in this paper for handling higher-order values also apply to data structures, so the example does not prove to be a problem.

Transitions represent functions from argument tuples to argument tuples, and size descriptions represent functions from argument tuples to values, thus the composition of $\langle D(2), D(1), E(1)\rangle$ with $\langle E(1), I\rangle$ is found by composing each element of the former tuple with the latter. For example, the composition $D(2) \circ \langle E(1), I\rangle$ denotes a value that is increased first and then decreased. Since the size description does not tell how much the value is increased respectively decreased the result of the composition has to be I. The other compositions are computed using similar reasoning.

The Higher-Order Case. A major difference between first-order and higher-order programs is the complexities involved in determining the control flow. In the first-order case control flow is deterministic except for conditionals where both branches must be considered. In the higher-order case the flow at every application is undetermined, since the function can be any of a number of different abstractions in the program.

Another problem is that the data flow is obscured when calls and returns cause data to flow in and out of closures. As we saw above this also occurs when dealing with data structures (i.e., *hd* (*cons* x x)): When a (potentially complex) structure is taken apart it is difficult to tell where the different parts originate from.

The Simple Higher-Order Analysis. We started out trying to solve the control-flow problem, without addressing the data-flow problem (data flowing in and out of closures). We had the hope that most flow would be determined by first-order values (e.g., the decomposition of an expression in an interpreter) so that it would not matter that the analysis was conservative in the handling of higher-order values.

The simple higher-order analysis uses the same domains as the first-order analysis, so we just need to extend the analysis to handle the two new language constructs: abstraction and application. The size description of an abstraction is simply I (which makes sense, since an abstraction builds something) and the dependency description consists of a list of the free variables. The size-dep description of an application is found by taking the least upper bound of all possible calls (the closure analysis is used to determined which abstractions can flow to the application). The free variables in the calls are described by I, since the size-dep domains are inadequate for obtaining more detailed information.

Similarly, at each application we collect a 1-step transition for each of the abstractions that can flow to the application, and again the free variables are described by I. Since partial evaluation evaluates under dynamic abstractions we also collect a 1-step transition at each abstraction. Notice that the simple higher-order analysis does not use the binding-time information, so it must take into account that a given abstraction might become dynamic.

Experiments with the analysis showed that it is able to detect control flow with acceptable precision, whereas more precision is needed in the handling of data flow. The following example illustrates the kind of data flow the analysis is unable to detect:

$$\begin{aligned} f(x,y) &= g(\lambda z.hd\ x, y) \\ g(c,y) &= c\ y \end{aligned}$$

The return value of f becomes I, when in fact it is smaller than x. The reason is that at the application of the closure we know absolutely nothing about the free variable x (a variable in another environment), so we have to make the conservative assumption that the result is increasing.

Improving the Representation of Higher-Order Values. A closure is represented as a label and a tuple with the value of the free variables; in general a tree. An obvious abstraction of this gives rise to an infinite tree augmented with a size-dep value at each node describes the return value of functions more accurately than the simple size-dep values.

We present two different finite representations of the infinite trees, namely (1) cutting off the trees at depth k and (2) approximation using grammars [12]. The depth bound was tried first, in the hope that it would be sufficiently precise and simpler to implement than grammars, however, neither turned out to be the case.

The k-Bounded Analysis. The infinite tree is made finite by cutting it off at depth k, and attributing each remaining node with an extra size-dep value, which approximates the subtree (of the infinite tree) of which it is root.

Experiments showed that that there *is* a need to handle recursively built structures (and the values they contain). Furthermore, the k-bounded analysis turned out to be more complicated to implement than the grammar-based analysis.

The Grammar-Based Analysis. The infinite tree is approximated by a grammar that contains one rule for each label in the tree. Thus, a label that appears in two different contexts in the tree will be approximated by one rule in the grammar. We have chosen this representation for simplicity. The domains in more detail:

$$\begin{aligned} \text{SizeDep}^- &= \mathcal{P}(\text{Label} \times \text{Size} \times \text{Dep}) \\ \text{Gram} &= \text{Label} \mapsto (\text{SizeDep}^-)^* \\ \text{SizeDep} &= \text{SizeDep}^- \times \text{Gram} \end{aligned}$$

A SizeDep value consists of a grammar and a set of triples $\langle label, size, dep \rangle$ — one for each label the described function can return ($\mathcal{P}$ is the Hoare power domain). We use a power domain to be able to get a more precise description of functions that can return more than one kind of value (e.g., two differently labeled lambdas). Note that a label also can denote a first-order value. For example, the abstract value (the size-dep information has been omitted for readability)

$$\{l_1\},\ [l_1 \mapsto \langle \{FO\}, \{l_1, l_2\} \rangle,\ l_2 \mapsto \langle\rangle]$$

denotes a l_1-closure, where the first free variable of the closure is a first-order value, and the second is either an l_1- or an l_2-closure. l_2 has no free variables.

Recall that dependency (both data and control-dependency) in the first-order analysis was represented using argument positions. To use the extra precision the grammars give us, we need a more refined way to express dependency. Therefore, we extend the size domain with the forms $D(i\ l\ j)$ and $E(i\ l\ j)$, where i refers to the ith parameter, l is a label identifying an abstraction, and j refers to the jth free variable in the abstraction. For example, $D(1\ l_1\ 2)$ denotes a function whose return value is always less than the second free variable of an l_1-closure found in the function's first argument. Notice the close correspondence between the meaning of size values and the meaning of grammars. This correspondence makes it easy to compose SizeDep values.

Using Binding-Time Information. Below is the extract of a lambda interpreter:

$$\begin{aligned} int(e,\rho) = &\text{ if } car\ e = \text{'}Var \text{ then } \rho(cdr\ e)\\ &\text{ else if } car\ e = \text{'}Lam \text{ then } \lambda x.int(caddr\ e,\ update(cadr\ e,\ x,\ \rho))\\ &\text{ else } int(cadr\ e,\ \rho)\ int(caddr\ e,\ \rho) \end{aligned}$$

Specialization of *int* with respect to some expression e will terminate, because something gets smaller in every transition during partial evaluation. However, the analysis, as it has been developed so far, is unable to detect this. The reason is that *int* is *not* quasi-terminating under normal evaluation (consider the call sequence spawned by interpretation of the term $(\lambda x.x\ x)\ (\lambda x.x\ x)$).

The problem can be fixed by taking the binding-times into account when collecting transitions: Since the application in the last else-branchi n *int* is dynamic, it does not give rise to any transitions during partial evaluation, so they can safely be ignored. Using this extra information the analysis is able to detect that partial evaluation of the interpreter indeed terminates.

Note that taking the binding times into account introduces a cyclic dependency between the binding-time analysis, the transition collection, and the termination analysis (See the overview diagram in Sect. 4).

Using Single-Threaded Information. In order to get a more precise description of the free variables in an abstraction, it is sometimes beneficial to pretend that the calls inside a given abstraction is performed directly instead of via an application later during evaluation. At the abstraction one can collect a more accurate description of the free variables, whereas little is known about the lambda-bound variables. At the application the situation is the reverse. Since we are not interested in the size-dep relationship of the dynamic variables the result of the analysis can be improved by collecting transitions inside abstractions whose lambda-bound variables are dynamic. However, it is only safe to do so if the abstraction can at most be applied once (i.e., if it is single threaded), otherwise an infinite loop will be overlooked in case the closure is copied an unbounded number of times (consider the example above).

6 Experiments

In this section we shall report the result of applying the various versions of the analysis to a number of different programs, that contain non-trivial recursion and usages of higher-order features. The analysis is implemented in Gofer and is fully automatic except for the binding-time and single-threaded analyses.

The PE column indicates whether or not partial evaluation of the program is guaranteed to terminate (using the obvious binding-time division of the initial parameters); T indicates termination and N indicates possible non-termination.

The S, G, and G+ columns contain the results of running three different versions of the analysis, namely the simple higher-order analysis (S), which uses the simple size-dep domains, the grammar based analysis (G), and finally the grammar-based analysis that also takes binding-time and single-threaded information into account (G+).

A $\surd$ indicates that the analysis detects that specialization of the program always will terminate (when that is the case), or that the analysis safely detects that it may loop (in case of the ho.letrec program). A $\div$ indicates that the analysis performs one or more unnecessary generalizations — not that the analysis produces a wrong result.

Program	PE	S	G	G+	Description
flatten	T	$\div$	$\div$	$\surd$	Flatten a list of lists, written in cps
kmp	T	$\surd$	$\surd$	$\surd$	naive pattern matcher[5]
closure	T	$\div$	$\surd$	$\surd$	extraction of static data from a closure
fo	T	$\surd$	$\surd$	$\surd$	int. for a first-order language with let
fo.func	T	$\surd$	$\surd$	$\surd$	"fo" extended with named functions
goto	T	$\surd$	$\surd$	$\surd$	int. for a goto-language
goto.while	T	$\div$	$\div$	$\div$	int. for a goto-language with while
ho	T	$\div$	$\div$	$\surd$	lambda interpreter
ho.cbn	T	$\div$	$\div$	$\surd$	call-by-name lambda interpreter
ho.cps	T	$\div$	$\div$	$\surd$	lambda interpreter written in cps
ho.let	T	$\div$	$\div$	$\surd$	"ho" extended with let
ho.func	T	$\div$	$\div$	$\surd$	"ho.let" extended with named functions
ho.letrec	N	$\surd$	$\surd$	$\surd$	"ho" extended with letrec

The simple higher-order analysis is able to detect that partial evaluation of fo terminates, which is encouraging since fo uses higher-order functions to represent the environment.

By inspection of the flatten example and most of the ho examples, it is obvious that use of binding-time and single-threaded information is crucial for getting accurate results. The analysis safely detects that ho.letrec may loop (e.g., if it is specialized with respect to the expression (*letrec x x*)).

[5] The result of specializing the naive pattern matcher is a Knuth-Morris-Pratt matcher (originally achieved by Consel and Danvy [7]).

The analysis is unable to detect that partial evaluation of goto.while terminates. The reason is that the interpretation of the while-construct is implemented by adding the body of the loop to the while statement and interpreting the result. In order to handle this example we would need a richer size measure.

In conclusion: The analysis is strong enough to detect that partial evaluation of non-trivial interpreters using higher-order features will terminate.

7 Central Technical Details

In this section we present selected technical details of the size analysis and the transition collection. A complete description of the analyses can be found in the technical report [4].

The Grammar-Based Size-Analysis. The central part of the size analysis is given below. A variable $x_{i,j}$ is described by the *identity* size-dep value for the values $x_{i,j}$ may evaluate to (i.e., *id* constructs a grammar that describes the structures of $x_{i,j}$'s possible values and inserts the relevant equal E(•) values at every node).

$$\mathcal{S} : \text{AnnExp} \to \text{Fenv} \to \text{SizeDep}$$
$$\phi : \text{Fenv} = \text{Fnames} \to \text{SizeDep}$$

$$\begin{aligned}
\mathcal{S}[\![x_{i,j}]\!]\phi &= id(x_{i,j})\\
\mathcal{S}[\![Clo(f_i, \langle e_1, \ldots, e_n\rangle)]\!]\phi &= \langle f_i, \mathrm{I}, [f_i \mapsto \langle \mathcal{S}[\![e_1]\!]\phi \downarrow_{\text{SizeDep}^-}, \ldots\rangle] \\
&\qquad \sqcup \textstyle\bigsqcup_j \mathcal{S}[\![e_j]\!]\phi \downarrow_{\text{Gram}}\rangle\\
\mathcal{S}[\![e\ (e_1, \ldots, e_n)]\!]\phi &= \textstyle\bigsqcup\{\, \phi(l) \circ^{\sharp} \langle x_{l1}, \ldots, x_{lm}, \mathcal{S}[\![e_1]\!]\phi, \ldots \mathcal{S}[\![e_n]\!]\phi\rangle \mid \\
&\qquad \langle l, _, _\rangle \in \alpha,\ l \neq FO,\ arity(l) = n\}\\
&\quad \text{where } (\alpha, G) = \mathcal{S}[\![e]\!]\phi\\
&\qquad \langle \alpha_{l1}, \ldots, \alpha_{lm}\rangle = G(l)\\
&\qquad x_{li} = normalize(\alpha_{li}, G)
\end{aligned}$$

Recall that the program has been lambda lifted prior to running the size analysis and that an abstraction appears in the program as the creation of a closure $Clo(f_i, \langle e_1, \ldots, e_n\rangle)$. A f_i-closure is described by a SizeDep value whose grammar maps f_i to a tuple of SizeDep$^-$ values describing the free variables. Since the free variables may contain closures as well, their grammars are collected.

For an application $e\ (e_1, \ldots, e_n)$ we compose each closure of the right arity e can evaluate to with a tuple describing the arguments and take the least upper bound of the results. The description of the free variables are found by first looking up the relevant entry in the grammar: α_{li} (a SizeDep$^-$ value) and then selecting the entries from the grammar that are sufficient for describing α_{li} (the normalization step).

Abstract Transition Semantics. The abstraction transition semantics, which collects abstract 1-step transitions and compositions of these, is given below.

$$\text{AbsTrans} = \text{Fnames} \times \text{Fnames} \mapsto \mathcal{P}(\text{SizeDep}^*)$$
$$\mathcal{CS}_* : \text{AnnExp} \to \text{Fenv} \to \text{AbsTrans}$$

$$\begin{array}{ll}
\mathcal{CS}_{f_i}[\![\mathit{Clo}(f_j, \langle e_1, \ldots, e_n\rangle)]\!]\phi = \bigsqcup_k \mathcal{CS}_{f_i}[\![e_k]\!]\phi \\
\mathcal{CS}_{f_i}[\![\underline{\mathit{Clo}}(f_j, \langle e_1, \ldots, e_n\rangle)]\!]\phi = \bigsqcup_k \mathcal{CS}_{f_i}[\![e_k]\!]\phi \sqcup \\
\qquad [\langle f_i, f_j\rangle \mapsto \langle \mathcal{S}[\![e_1]\!]\phi, \ldots, \mathcal{S}[\![e_n]\!]\phi, \bot, \ldots, \bot\rangle] \\
\mathcal{CS}_{f_i}[\![e\ (e_1, \ldots, e_n)]\!]\phi & = \mathcal{CS}_{f_i}[\![e]\!]\phi \sqcup \bigsqcup_j \mathcal{CS}_{f_i}[\![e_j]\!]\phi \sqcup \\
& \quad [\langle f_i, f_j\rangle \mapsto \langle \tau_1, \ldots, \tau_m, \mathcal{S}[\![e_1]\!]\phi, \ldots, \mathcal{S}[\![e_n]\!]\phi\rangle \mid \\
& \quad \mathit{Clo}(f_j, \langle \tau_1, \ldots, \tau_m\rangle) \in \mathcal{S}[\![e]\!]\phi \downarrow_{\text{SizeDep}^-}, \\
& \quad \text{arity}(f_j) = n] \\
\mathcal{CS}_{f_i}[\![e\ \underline{@}\ (e_1, \ldots, e_n)]\!]\phi & = \mathcal{CS}_{f_i}[\![e]\!]\phi \sqcup \bigsqcup_j \mathcal{CS}_{f_i}[\![e_j]\!]\phi
\end{array}$$

$$\begin{array}{ll}
\phi_p & = \mathit{fix}\ \lambda\phi.[f_i \mapsto \mathcal{S}[\![e_i]\!]\phi \mid f_i(\ldots)(\ldots) = e_i \in p] \\
\mathit{1\text{-}atrans}_p & = \bigsqcup_i \mathcal{CS}_{f_i}[\![e]\!]\phi_p, \text{ where } f_i(\ldots)(\ldots) = e \in p, \text{ and } f_i \text{ is reachable} \\
\mathit{atrans}_p & = \mathit{fix}\ \lambda T.(\ [\langle f_i, f_k\rangle \mapsto t_2 \circ^\sharp t_1 \mid [\langle f_i, f_j\rangle \mapsto t_1], [\langle f_j, f_k\rangle \mapsto t_2] \in T] \\
& \qquad \sqcup\ \mathit{1\text{-}atrans}_p)
\end{array}$$

The non-trivial entries in the abstract semantics are those for application and the creation of closures. Notice how static closure creation match static application, and residual closure creation match residual application: A static closure creation gives rise to transitions at application time and not at creation time, whereas residual closure creation contribute at creation time but not when applied.

During partial evaluation of a residual creation of a closure $\underline{\mathit{Clo}}(f_j, \ldots)$, a transition to f_j occurs, because the specializer evaluates the body of f_j (yielding a reduced expression). To model this behavior we collect an abstract transition from the calling function to f_j in which the lambda-bound variables are described by $\bot$ (because they are dynamic).

Static application generates a transition for each closure of the right arity. The description of the free variables are taken from the grammar describing the closure and the description of the lambda-bound variables from the actual arguments.

Termination Analysis. We use the result of the abstract transition semantics to determine which variables may be in situ increasing and which are guaranteed to be in situ decreasing: Given an endotransition $t \in \mathit{atrans}_p(f_i, f_i)$ we classify the variable $x_{i,j}$ as in situ increasing if $\exists \langle \_, s, d\rangle \in \pi_j(t)$, where $s = \mathrm{I}$ and $j \in d$, and as in situ decreasing if $\forall \langle \_, s, \_\rangle \in \pi_j(t) : s = \bot$, $s = \mathrm{D}(j)$, $s = \mathrm{D}(j\ f\ k)$, or $s = \mathrm{E}(j\ f\ k)$ for some $f \in \text{Fnames}, k \in \{1, \ldots, \mathit{fv}(f)\}$.

It is obvious that $x_{i,j}$ is in situ decreasing if it is described by $\mathrm{D}(j)$. It is less obvious that the abstract value $\mathrm{E}(j\ f\ k)$ also guarantees this. Recall that $\mathrm{E}(j\ f\ k)$ means that value is weakly decreasing of the kth free variable in an l-closure taken from $x_{i,j}$. Since closures are treated as data structures, $\mathrm{E}(j\ f\ k)$ describes a substructure of $x_{i,j}$, which implies that $x_{i,j}$ is in situ decreasing.

8 Related Work, Conclusion, and Future Work

Related Work. Jones, Gomard and Sestoft [11] present a termination analysis for a flowchart language, and Jones and Glenstrup [9] give efficient algorithms for implementing a termination analysis for a tail-recursive first-order language. Both analyses use techniques similar to ours to reason about increasing and decreasing variables. However, where we classify variables that may be unbounded as dynamic until no changes occur, they start by a division of dubious and dynamic variables, and classify dubious variables as static when they can be guaranteed to be bounded, and in the end classify the remaining dubious variables as dynamic. Loosely, one can say that they approach the fixpoint from the bottom, where we approach it from the top. It is unclear whether we end up with the same fixpoint.

Conclusion. We have extended the first-order analysis of Holst [10] to the higher order case, thereby taking an step towards fully automatic partial evaluation of higher-order functional languages. Our analysis is strong enough to handle values flowing in and out of closures, however the analysis sometimes fail to recognize in situ decreasing parameters due to the inevitable aliasing, which is necessary to obtain a finite description.

The analysis has been developed hand in hand with our experimental implementation of the analysis[6]. This has made it possible for us to focus on practical usefulness, in the sense that the analysis should be strong enough to handle a large class of interesting programs. The focus has not been on speed, elegance, or an extensive correctness proof. In our opinion this has been an essential choice. We had to go through four major revisions of the analysis before our implementation was capable of handling a sufficiently large class of interesting programs to be of interest in a real partial evaluator. Our experiments with the implementation of the analysis on interpreters written in different styles indicates, that the analysis is precise enough. The current implementation is too slow to be of use on programs of realistic size, but in our opinion we are not up against any inherent complexity problem; just a slow implementation.

Future Work. The techniques presented in this paper rely heavily on the use of finitely downwards closed domains in the subject program, and it is not clear how they can be extended to domains, that do not have a natural well-founded size ordering.

The extension to structured datatypes is straightforward, e.g., for pairs simply add a label for each cons in the program and collect the size information using the same techniques as for closures.

Before the analysis can be integrated into Similix efficient algorithms must be developed. We expect that the algorithms of Jones and Glenstrup can be extended to serve this purpose.

---

[6] Thanks to Mark P. Jones for providing Gofer, without which it would have been impossible to conduct quite as many experiments as we did.

Acknowledgements. Our thanks to Neil D. Jones and Arne Glenstrup for much needed sparring and helpful comments.

References

1. The Similix system, version 5.1. 1995.
2. Lars Ole Andersen. Binding-time analysis and the taming of C pointers. In David Schmidt, editor, *Proc. of ACM Symposium on Partial Evaluation and Semantics-Based Program Manipulation, PEPM'93*, pages 47–58, 1993.
3. Lars Ole Andersen. *Program Analysis and Specialization for the C Programming Language.* PhD thesis, DIKU, University of Copenhagen, May 1994. (DIKU report 94/19).
4. Peter Holst Andersen and Carsten Kehler Holst. *Termination Analysis for Offline Partial Evaluation of a Higher Order Functional Language.* Technical Report, DIKU, University of Copenhagen, Denmark, 1996. To appear.
5. Anders Bondorf and Jesper Jørgensen. *Efficient analyses for realistic off-line partial evaluation: extended version.* Technical Report 93/4, DIKU, University of Copenhagen, Denmark, 1993.
6. Charles Consel. A tour of Schism: a partial evaluation system for higher-order applicative languages. In David Schmidt, editor, *ACM SIGPLAN Symposium on Partial Evaluation and Semantics Based Program Manipulation*, pages 145–154, June 1993.
7. Charles Consel and Olivier Danvy. Partial evaluation of pattern matching in strings. *Information Processing Letters*, 30:79–86, January 1989.
8. B. A. Davey and H. A. Priestley. *Introduction to Lattices and Order. Cambridge Mathematical Textbooks*, Cambridge University Press, 1990.
9. Arne J. Glenstrup and Neil D. Jones. BTA algorithms to ensure termination of off-line partial evaluation. In *Andrei Ershov Second International Conference "Perspectives of System Informatics"*, Lecture Notes in Computer Science, 1996. Upcoming.
10. Carsten Kehler Holst. Finiteness analysis. In John Hughes, editor, *Functional Programming Languages and Computer Architectures*, pages 473–495, ACM, Springer-Verlag, Cambridge, Massachusetts, USA, August 1991.
11. Neil D. Jones, Carsten Gomard, and Peter Sestoft. *Partial Evaluation and Automatic Program Generation. C.A.R. Hoare, Series Editor*, Prentice Hall International, International Series in Computer Science, June 1993. ISBN number 0-13-020249-5 (pbk).
12. Neil D. Jones and Steven S. Muchnick. Flow analysis and optimization of Lisp-like structures. In Steven S. Muchnick and Neil D. Jones, editors, *Program Flow Analysis: Theory and Applications*, chapter 4, pages 102–131, Prentice-Hall, 1981.
13. H.G. Rice. Classes of recursively enumerable sets and their decision problems. *Transaction of the AMS*, 89:25–59, 1953.
14. Peter Sestoft. *Replacing Function Parameters by Global Variables.* Master's thesis, DIKU, University of Copenhagen, Denmark, October 1988. 107 pages.
15. David N. Turner, Philip Wadler, and Christian Mossin. Once upon a type. In *7'th International Conference on Functional Programming and Computer Architecture*, pages 1–11, ACM Press, La Jolla, California, June 1995.

Proving Correctness of Constraint Logic Programs with Dynamic Scheduling

F.S. de Boer* M. Gabbrielli‡ C. Palamidessi§

Abstract. A general framework based on Hoare logic is introduced for specifying and reasoning about Constraint Logic Programs with dynamic scheduling. The framework consists of a mixed formalism of programs in a ccp-like language, on the one hand, and correctness properties of the Hoare logic, on the other hand. In this formalism delay conditions are viewed as a specific class of correctness properties. In the construction of the proof-system we follow the lines of a previous proof-system we developed for concurrent constraint programming, which was sound, but not complete (for ccp). Due to the different kind of choice used in CLP, on the contrary, the system considered here is both sound and complete.

1 Introduction

Most of the existing (constraint) logic programming systems use a flexible selection rule which allows to dynamically delay (or suspend) the selection of atoms until the arguments are sufficiently instantiated. This dynamic scheduling is obtained by adding so-called *delay declarations* to program clauses. Delay declarations, introduced by Naish in [16], allow to run the calls more efficiently, to prevent run-time errors and to enforce termination. In Constraint Logic Programming (CLP for short) they are used also to postpone the evaluation of constraints which are "too hard" for the solver. For example, in CLP($\Re$) non-linear arithmetic constraints are delayed until they become linear. More generally, they provide the programmer with a better control over computations and, similarly to guards in concurrent logic languages, allow one to express some degree of synchronization among the different processes (i.e. atoms) in a program. The practical relevance of delay declarations is demonstrated by the fact these declarations (or similar ones) are implemented in languages as Sicstus Prolog [5], ECLiPSe [20], Gödel [7] and in many CLP systems [10].

From the semantic viewpoint, the fact that an atom can be delayed until certain conditions are satisfied introduces some complications similar to those arising in concurrent languages. The operational semantics of logic programs with dynamic scheduling has been discussed by Naish [17] while their denotational semantics has been investigated by Marriott et al. [15, 14]. Recently also the issue of correctness has received some attention. Apt and Luitjes [2] have investigated deadlock freedom, occur check freedom, termination and absence of builtins' errors in presence of delay declarations. Termination has also been studied by Marchiori and Teusink [13] and

* Universiteit Utrecht, Department of Computer Science, Padualaan 14, De Uithof, 3584 CH Utrecht, The Netherlands. frankb@cs.ruu.nl

‡ Università di Pisa, Dipartimento di Informatica, Corso Italia 40, 56125 Pisa, Italy. gabbri@di.unipi.it

§ Università di Genova, DISI, Via Dodecaneso, 35, 16146 Genova, Italy. catuscia@disi.unige.it

by Lüttringhaus [12]. In particular, the latter paper describes an algorithm which, given a program, generates automatically delay declarations which ensure termination. However, as far as we know, the issue of partial correctness, namely the fact that the computed constraints correspond with the intended meaning of the program, has not been considered yet.

In particular, while the declarative meaning of (constraints) logic programs is well understood in terms of first-order logic theories, the logical meaning of delay declarations has not been addressed yet. In fact, if we have a program `P` defining a predicate `p(X)`, then (the constraints computed by the query) `p(X)` will satisfy certain properties which can be derived logically from the theory of `P`. Thus, considering for instance logic programs, one can reason about program correctness by simply using the least Herbrand model [1]. If we now add the delay declaration `DELAY p(X) UNTIL Condition(X)` then what can we say about the properties satisfied by `p(x)` in the new program? In this paper we show that, if `p(x)` in `P` satisfies a property ϕ, then under the delay declaration it will satisfy the property `Condition(x)` $\rightarrow \phi$. In other words, the logical meaning of delay declarations can be understood as logical implication.

More generally, in this paper we introduce a general framework based on Hoare logic for specifying and reasoning about the partial correctness of constraint logic programs with delay declarations. The framework consists of a mixed formalism of programs on the one hand, and correctness properties of the Hoare logic, on the other hand. In order to prove the soundness and completeness of the system it is convenient to deal with a more "algebraically structured" language. To this end we translate CLP into a sort of concurrent constraint programming language (ccp for short), which we call δ-ccp, and which is basically an extension of ccp with local choice (also called angelic ccp) [11]. The extension consists in allowing the presence of delay conditions in the "ask" construct. Such an extension enhances the expressive power, but preserves the nice properties of local ccp, in particular the denotational semantics can still be defined in a simple way by using closure operators, following [11]. We use the denotational semantics as a guideline for the development of a compositional proof-system, where "compositional" means that the correctness (or specification) of a composite program can be derived directly from the correctness (or specifications) of its immediate constituents. This abstraction from the internal structure of the components of a program is crucial in mastering the complexity of large programs and supports the methodology of top-down design.

The proof-system is parametric wrt a theory of properties based on the elements of the constraint system, a class of user-defined properties (including the delay conditions), and the connectives of the propositional calculus. Differently from the system developed in [3], here we can use classical logic to reason about properties. This is mainly due to the fact that we deal with the local variables of CLP just by variable-renaming, hence we don't need to impose a cylindrification operator on properties. Thus, a specific theory is constituted by a set of proper axioms, which represent the entailment relations among the constraints and the user-defined properties, plus the laws of predicate calculus. We prove that our proof-system is sound and complete by using the denotational semantics. Thanks to its simplicity, this proof turns out to be (relatively) easy. It is worth noticing that, on the contrary, the proof-system defined in [3] for ccp is sound but incomplete. This is because ccp has global choice, whereas the kind of nonderminism of CLP can be modeled by local choice, even if we add the delay declarations.

2 Preliminaries

Both CLP and ccp frameworks are defined parametrically wrt to some notion of constraint system. In the standard CLP setting constraints are essentially first order formulas built up by using predicate symbols which have a predefined interpretation (e.g. equations on the term algebra or inequalities over the reals). A more abstract view is followed in [18] by formalizing the notion of constraint system along the guidelines of Scott's treatment of information systems and by using notions from cylindric algebras [8] to formalize the hiding operator and the renaming of variables. In the following we introduce only the basic definition of cylindric constraint system. We refer to [19] for more details concerning its construction and properties. We assume given a (denumerable) set of variables *Var* with typical elements $x, y, z, \ldots$.

Definition 1. Let $\langle C, \leq, \sqcup, true, false\rangle$ be a complete algebraic lattice. Assume that for each $x \in Var$ a function $\exists_x : C \to C$ is defined such that for any $c, d \in C$:

(i) $c \vdash \exists_x(c)$, (ii) if $c \vdash d$ then $\exists_x(c) \vdash \exists_x(d)$,
(iii) $\exists_x(c \sqcup \exists_x(d)) = \exists_x(c) \sqcup \exists_x(d)$, (iv) $\exists_x(\exists_y(c)) = \exists_y(\exists_x(c))$.

Moreover assume that for x, y ranging in *Var*, C contains the constraints d_{xy} (so-called diagonal elements) which satisfy the following axioms:

(v) $true \vdash d_{xx}$, (vi) if $z \neq x, y$ then $d_{xy} = \exists_z(d_{xz} \sqcup d_{zy})$,
(vii) if $x \neq y$ then $d_{xy} \sqcup \exists_x(c \sqcup d_{xy}) \vdash c$.

Then $\mathbf{C} = \langle C, \leq, \sqcup, true, false, Var, \exists_x, d_{xy}\rangle$ is a *cylindric constraint system*.

Following the standard terminology and notation, instead of $\leq$ we will refer to its inverse relation, denoted by $\vdash$ and called *entailment* (so, $\forall c, d \in C.\ c \vdash d \Leftrightarrow d \leq c$). When considering first order formulas as constraints (e.g. in the examples) we will use $\wedge$ instead of the $\sqcup$, since in this case the least upper bound $\sqcup$ corresponds to logical conjunction. In the sequel we will identify a system $\mathbf{C}$ with its underlying set of constraints C and we will denote $\exists_x(c)$ by $\exists_x c$. We define the set $fv(c)$ of the free variables which appear in the constraint c as $fv(c) = \{x \mid \exists_x c \neq x\}$. Then, given a constraint c which contains finitely many free variables, we denote by $\exists_{-x}c$ the existential closure of c with the exception of the variable x which remains unquantified, i.e. $\exists_{-x}c$ is a shorthand for $\exists_{x_1} \ldots \exists_{x_n} c$ where $\{x_1, \ldots, x_n\} = fv(c) \setminus \{x\}$. Moreover we denote by $c[x/y]$ the constraint $\exists_y(c \sqcup d_{xy})$ which represents abstractly the constraint obtained from c by renaming the variable x for y. Previous notations are extended to tuples of distinct variables in the obvious way.

As previously mentioned, many CLP languages use delay declarations to dynamically delay (or suspend) the selection of atoms until the arguments are sufficiently instantiated. In the following we briefly introduce the terminology and the basic notions for these languages. For CLP we refer to the original paper [9] by Jaffar and Lassez and to the survey [10] by Jaffar and Maher. We let $vars(e)$ to denote the set of variables which appear in the syntactic expression e and we denote by $\overline{x}$ a tuple of distinct variables. An atom of the form $p(\overline{x})$ is called pure and a conjunction of pure atoms which do not share variables with each other will be often denoted by Q. CLP queries and clauses have the form c, Q and $p(\overline{x}) \leftarrow c, Q$ respectively, where

c is a constraint different from *false* and $vars(Q) \cap \overline{x} = \emptyset$[1]. A program, as usual, is a set a clauses. Given a program P and a pure atom A, we denote by $defn_P(A)$ the set of variant of clauses in P which have A as head[2]. A derivation step for a query c, Q in a program P consists in replacing an atom A in Q with the body of a clause $cl \in defn_P(A)$ provided that the constraint in cl is consistent with c and no variable clash occurs. We denote by $\leadsto_P$ the relation on queries corresponding to derivation steps in the program P. We denote by $\leadsto_P^*$ the reflexive and transitive closure of $\leadsto_P$, i.e. the relation corresponding to derivations. We do not make any assumption on the selection rule which is used to select the atom to be rewritten, since this allows us to model also parallel executions.

Naish [16] first introduced delay declarations in logic languages by using `wait` constructs in MU-Prolog. Here we follow loosely the syntax used in the language Gödel and consider declarations of the form `DELAY p(X̄) UNTIL Condition(X̄)` where `Condition(X̄)` is a formula in some assertion language. The meaning of such a declaration is that the atom `p(Ȳ)` can be selected in a resolvent c, Q only if the constraint c which has been produced so far in the derivation satisfies the condition `Condition(Ȳ)`. For example, considering such a numerical constraint system as the one used in CLP($\Re$), the declaration `DELAY p(X) UNTIL X > 0` means that `p(X)` can be selected in a resolvent c, Q only if c forces `X` to assume values greater than 0.

In our setting delay conditions can be formalized as follows. We assume given a set of conditions Δ, with typical elements $\delta(\overline{x})$, $\delta_1(\overline{x})\ldots$, whose syntax we do not further specify since this is not relevant to our results. Then we assume that an interpretation for conditions is given in the form of a function $I : \Delta \to \wp(\mathcal{C})$ which, for each condition, returns the set of constraints which satisfy it. In other words, we say that c satisfies $\delta(\overline{x})$ iff $c \in I(\delta(\overline{x}))$. The existing programming systems assume that if an atom is not delayed then adding more information will never cause it to delay, i.e. if c satisfies $\delta(\overline{x})$ and $d \vdash c$ then d satisfies $\delta(\overline{x})$. Thus, we also make the same assumption and require that, for each $\delta(\overline{x}) \in \Delta$, $I(\delta(\overline{x}))$ isan upward closed set, i.e. $I(\delta(\overline{x})) = \uparrow I(\delta(\overline{x}))$ where $\uparrow$ is the obvious extension to set of constraints of the operator defined on $\mathcal{C}$ by $\uparrow c = \{d \mid c \leq d\}$. Furthermore, delay conditions are usually assumed to be consistent wrt renaming, i.e. if $c \in I(\delta(\overline{x}))$, then $c[\overline{y}/\overline{x}] \in I(\delta(\overline{y}))$. We make this assumption too. We assume that for each predicate symbol exactly one delay declaration is given (multiple declarations can be obtained by using logical connectives in the syntax of conditions). When the condition holds vacuously (i.e. when $I(\delta(\overline{x})) = \mathcal{C}$) we simply omit the declaration. Now, given a declaration `DELAY p (X̄) UNTIL δ(X̄)` for the predicate symbol p, an atom `p(Ȳ)` can be selected in the resolvent c, Q only if $c \in I(\delta(\overline{Y}))$. In the following we will implicitly consider only CLP derivations in which the selection of atoms in resolvents respects the above rule.

The result of a finite (maximal) derivation for a query, usually called answer constraint, consists of the constraint obtained from the one accumulated in the derivation by disregarding the information on the local variables, i.e. by existentially quantifying the variables which do not appear in the query. Thus we will consider the following

---

[1] We use this syntax since it simplifies the parameter passing mechanism. Note that this is not a restriction, since the presence of generic terms as arguments to predicate symbols can be expressed via the constraints.

[2] A variant of a clause cl is obtained by replacing the tuple $\overline{x}$ of all the variables appearing in cl for another tuple $\overline{y}$ of (distinct) variables.

notion of observables. Given a program P and a query c, Q we define

$$\mathcal{O}_{clp}(P,Q,c) = \{\exists_{-vars(c,Q)}d \mid \text{ there exists a derivation } c,Q \rightsquigarrow_P^* d,Q' \not\rightsquigarrow\}.$$

Note that we consider here also results of deadlocked computations, i.e. of those computation which end up in a resolvent d, Q' where Q' is non-empty and cannot be further reduced because the delay conditions are not satisfied.

3 CLP with dynamic scheduling as a ccp-like language

In this section we show how constraint logic programs with dynamic scheduling can be translated into a ccp-like language in a quite natural way.

The basic idea underlying ccp languages is that computation progresses via monotonic accumulation of information in a global store. Information is produced by the concurrent and asynchronous activity of several agents which can add (tell) a constraint to the store. Dually, agents can also check (ask) whether a constraint is entailed by the store, thus allowing synchronization among different agents. Differently from the standard ccp setting, here we assume that delay conditions are arguments to ask actions. As we show later, this allows us to formulate in a natural way the delay mechanism by using the ask evaluation. Tell actions instead also in our case have standard constraints as arguments, since we use tell's evaluation to simulate the accumulation of constraints in CLP derivations. A notion of locality is obtained in ccp by introducing the agent $\exists x A$ which behaves like A, with x considered *local* to A. We do not use such an explicit operator: analogously to the standard CLP setting, locality is introduced implicitly by assuming that if a process is defined by $p(\overline{x}) \leftarrow A$ and a variable y in A does not appear in $\overline{x}$, then y has to be considered local to A. This will simplify the parameter passing mechanism and therefore our proof-system for partial correctness.

The $\parallel$ operator, both in ccp and in our case, allows one to express parallel composition of two agents and it is usually described in terms of interleaving. Finally (local) non-determinism arises by introducing an (associative and commutative) *choice operator* $+$: the agent $A + B$ nondeterministically selects either A or B and then behaves as the selected agent. Usually ccp languages adopt *global non-determinism* which is more expressive than the local one. In fact in the global case the external environment can affect the choice, since only those branches whose guards are enabled can be selected. On the other hand, as shown in [11], local ccp has a very simple denotational model based on closure operators. Since CLP with dynamic scheduling has only local non-determinism, we use here this restricted form of non-determinism. In this way we have a simple semantic basis for our calculus. Thus we end up with the following syntax for δ-ccp.

Definition 2. Let $\mathcal{C}$ be a constraint system and let Δ be a set of delay conditions. The syntax of *declarations* and *agents* is given by the following grammar:

$$\begin{array}{lll} \text{Declarations} & D ::= \epsilon \mid p(\overline{x}) : -A \mid D, D \\ \text{Agents} & A ::= \mathit{stop} \mid \mathit{tell}(c) \mid \mathit{ask}(\delta(\overline{x})) \rightarrow A \mid A + A \mid A \parallel A \mid p(\overline{x}) \\ \text{Processes} & P ::= D.A \end{array}$$

where c is a finite element in $\mathcal{C}$ and $\delta(\overline{x}) \in \Delta$. A δ-ccp *process* $D.A$ is supposed to be *closed*, i.e. we assume that each predicate symbol occurring in D or in A is defined in

D. Furthermore, we assume that D contains at most one declaration for each predicate symbol.

The operational model of δ-ccp can be described by a transition system $T = (Conf, \longrightarrow)$ as follows. The configurations (in) *Conf* are pairs consisting of a process, and a constraint in C representing the common *store*. The transition relation $\longrightarrow \subseteq Conf \times Conf$ is described by the (least relation satisfying the) rules **R1-R5** of Table 1 where we assume given a set D of declarations and an interpretation $I : \Delta \rightarrow \wp(C)$ for delay conditions. The transition relation is essentially the same defined for local choice ccp [11]: According to rule **R4**, the *choice* operator gives rise to local (or internal) non-determinism, since the agent $A + B$ nondeterministically selects one of the two components and the environment cannot control the choice.

As in ccp, the action $ask(\delta(\overline{x}))$ represents a guard, i.e. a test on the current store c, whose execution does not modify c. However, we say that $ask(\delta(\overline{x}))$ is *enabled* in c iff $c \in I(\delta(\overline{x}))$, i.e. if c satisfies the delay condition $\delta(\overline{x})$. Thus, as shown in rule **R2**, if $ask(\delta(\overline{x}))$ is enabled in the current store then the agent $ask(\delta(\overline{x})) \rightarrow A$ can proceed in the computation and behaves as A. Otherwise the agent suspends, waiting for other (parallel) agents to add information to the store. Clearly this mechanism allows us to simulate the delay evaluation previously described for CLP. Another difference with standard ccp is that in rule **R5**, analogously to the case of CLP, we assume that all the variables which appear in the pure atoms contained in $p(\overline{x}) : -A$ are distinct and we denote by $defn_D(p(\overline{x}))$ the set of variants of declarations in D which have $p(\overline{x})$ as head. We assume also the presence of a renaming mechanism that takes care of using fresh variables each time a clause is considered (in **R5**)[3].

Using the transition system in Table 1 we can now define the standard notion of observables as the results of finite computations. As in the case of CLP observables, we do not consider the values of local variables in the results. We denote by $\longrightarrow^*$ the reflexive and transitive closure of the relation $\longrightarrow$.

Definition 3. Let $D.A$ be a δ-ccp process and C be a constraint system. The observables of $D.A$, wrt an initial store $c \in C$, are

$$\mathcal{O}_{ccp}(D.A, c) = \{\exists_{-vars(A,c)} d \mid \text{ there exists } \langle D.A, c\rangle \longrightarrow^* \langle D.B, d\rangle \not\longrightarrow\}.$$

A CLP program can be seen as a δ-ccp program essentially by identifying atoms with agents, constraints with tell agents, conjunction with parallel composition, and disjunction (of clauses) with nondeterministic choice. Clearly there remain some differences, mainly due to the different underlying computational model. In fact, in CLP a consistency test is done at each derivation step in order to prevent (finitely) failing computation, while this is not the case for δ-ccp and for the so-called "eventual tell" ccp languages. However these differences are not relevant to the issue of partial correctness.

As for delay declarations it is quite natural to simulate them by using the *ask* mechanism previously mentioned. So we can formally define the translation τ from CLP with dynamic scheduling to δ-ccp as follows. Given a CLP query $c, A_1, \ldots, A_n$

[3] For the sake of simplicity we do not describe this renaming mechanism in the transition system. The interested reader can find in [19] and [4] various formal approaches to this problem.

R1 $\langle D.tell(c), d\rangle \longrightarrow \langle D.Stop, c \sqcup d\rangle$
R2 $\langle D.ask(\delta(\bar{x})) \rightarrow A, c\rangle \longrightarrow \langle D.A, c\rangle \quad c \in I(\delta(\bar{x}))$
R3 $\dfrac{\langle D.A, c\rangle \longrightarrow \langle D.A', c'\rangle}{\begin{array}{l}\langle D.A \parallel B, c\rangle \longrightarrow \langle D.A' \parallel B, c'\rangle \\ \langle D.B \parallel A, c\rangle \longrightarrow \langle D.B \parallel A', c'\rangle\end{array}}$
R4 $\begin{array}{l}\langle D.A + B, c\rangle \longrightarrow \langle D.A, c\rangle \\ \langle D.A + B, c\rangle \longrightarrow \langle D.B, c\rangle\end{array}$
R5 $\langle D.p(\bar{x}), c\rangle \longrightarrow \langle D.A, c\rangle \qquad p(\bar{x}) : -A \in defn_D(p(\bar{x}))$

Table 1. The transition system for δ-ccp.

we obtain an δ-ccp agent defined by

$$\tau(c, A_1, \ldots, A_n) = tell(c) \parallel A_1 \parallel \ldots \parallel A_n$$

(here and in the following we omit parenthesis since the operators $\parallel$ and $+$ are associative). As for programs, if the CLP program P consists of the clauses $\mathtt{p}(\bar{\mathtt{x}}) \leftarrow \mathtt{c_i}, \mathtt{Q_i}$, with $i \in [1, n]$, defining a single predicate p and of the delay declaration DELAY $\mathtt{p}(\bar{\mathtt{x}})$ UNTIL $\delta(\bar{\mathtt{x}})$, then $\tau(P)$ is the δ-ccp declaration

$$p(\bar{x}) : -ask(\delta(\bar{x})) \rightarrow (\tau(c_1, Q_1) + \ldots + \tau(c_n, Q_n)).$$

This can be extended to programs defining several predicates in the obvious way. The equivalence of the original CLP program with the translated one is expressed by the following.

Proposition 4. *Let P be a CLP program with delay declarations and c, Q be a query where $c \in C$ ($c \neq false$) is the input constraint. Then*

$$\mathcal{O}_{clp}(P, Q, c) = \mathcal{O}_{ccp}(\tau(P).\tau(Q), c) \setminus \{false\}.$$

Given the previous proposition, any partial correctness result which holds for δ-ccp can be immediately applied to CLP programs with delay declarations. Therefore in the following we will focus on δ-ccp programs.

Example 1. As an example of translation of a CLP program into δ-ccp we consider now a not-so-trivial program which we will use again later to illustrate an application of our verification method. This program takes two lists `Li` and `Lp` representing the nodes obtained from the in-order and pre-order traversal of a binary tree `T`, respectively, and returns `T`. A tree with root `a`, left subtree `Tl`, and right subtree `Tr`, will be represented by the term `(a,Tl,Tr)`; the empty tree will be represented by `()`.

The idea is the following: If the lists are empty, then `T` will be the empty tree. Otherwise, we pick the first element `X` of `Lp`, which will become the root of `T`, and we split `Li` in two parts: the sublist `Lil` of the elements to the left of `X`, and the sublist

Lir of the elements to the right of X. By comparing recursively Lil and the tail of Lp we will obtain the left subtree Tl of T and a residual list Lpr of the rightmost elements of Lp which have not been used for the construction of Tl. By comparing recursively Lir and Lpr we will obtain the right subtree Tr of T. Generally this second recursive call will also produce a residual list L of the rightmost elements of Lpr which have not been used for the construction of Tr.

```
tree(Li,Lp,T) ← L=[], tree&residual(Li,Lp,T,L).

tree&residual(Li,Lp,T,L) ← Li=[], T=(), L=Lp.
tree&residual(Li,Lp,T,L) ← Li = [Y|Lit], Lp = [X|Lpt], T = (X,Tl,Tr),
                            split(X,Li,Lil,Lir),
                            tree&residual(Lil,Lpt,Tl,Lpr),
                            tree&residual(Lir,Lpr,Tr,L).

split(X,L,Ll,Lr) ← L =[X|Lr], Ll=[].
split(X,L,Ll,Lr) ← L=[Y|Lt], X ≠ Y, Ll=[Y|Llt], split(X,Lt,Llt,Lr).
```

A sequence of constraints, in a clause or in a goal, is to be interpreted as their logical conjunction (join). For instance Li=[], T=(), L=Lp corresponds to Li=[] ∧ T=() ∧ L=Lp. The delay declarations for this program are:

```
DELAY tree&residual(Li,Lp,_,_) UNTIL nonvar(Li) ∧ nonvar(Lp).
DELAY split(X,L,_,_) UNTIL ground(X) ∧ ∃ Y: ∃ Lt: L=[Y|Lt] ∧ ground(Y).
```

The translation of this program into δ-ccp gives the following:

$tree(Li, Lp, T)$:- $tell(L = [\,]) \parallel tree\&residual(Li, Lp, T, L)$

$tree\&residual(Li, Lp, T, L)$:- $ask(nonvar(Li) \wedge nonvar(Lp)) \rightarrow$
$tell(Li = [\,] \wedge T = () \wedge L = Lp)$
$+$
$(\, tell(Li = [Y|Lit] \wedge Lp = [X|Lpt] \wedge T = (X, Tl, Tr)) \parallel split(X, Li, Lil, Lir) \parallel$
$tree\&residual(Lil, Lpt, Tl, Lpr) \parallel tree\&residual(Lir, Lpr, Tr, L)\,)$

$split(X, L, Ll, Lr)$:- $ask(ground(X) \wedge \exists Y : \exists Lt : L = [Y|Lt] \wedge ground(Y)) \rightarrow$
$tell(L = [X|Lr] \wedge Ll = [\,])$
$+$
$(\, tell(L = [Y|Lt] \wedge X \neq Y \wedge Ll = [Y|Llt]) \parallel split(X, Lt, Llt, Lr)\,)$

4 Partial correctness

In this section we formalize the concept of partial correctness for δ-ccp programs. To this aim we first define the correctness properties to be used in the specification logic. Then we define validity of assertions in terms of a strongest postcondition semantics.

Intuitively, a property expresses some common feature of the results of (finite) computations. Since in our case results are constraints it is natural to consider a property as a set of basic constraints, namely the set of all those constraints which satisfy the property itself. In order to define a specification logic we need some syntactic representation of properties. As far as tell operations are concerned, we can simply consider a language consisting of (a syntactic representation of) constraints themselves, together with the usual connectives of the predicate calculus. However, in the specification logic we need to represent also delay conditions, plus other user-defined predicates which have an intentional meaning, defined by the user, to specify properties of the computation. For example, given a numerical constraint system such as $\Re$, one could need the property $fact(x, y)$ which is satisfied by all the constraints forcing x to be the factorial of y. These properties usually correspond to an infinite set of constraints, hence they cannot be represented in the language above as we would need an infinite disjunction. Therefore we consider as basic properties also *user defined predicates*. These are predicates introduced by the user, together with an interpretation which identify them with a specific set of basic constraints. We denote by U the set of user defined properties, with typical elements $u(\overline{x}), u_1(\overline{x})\ldots$ and we assume that $\Delta \subseteq U$. Thus the language of properties is defined as follows.

Definition 5. Given a constraint system C and a set of user defined predicates U, the language of properties is defined by the following grammar, where $c \in C$ and $u(\overline{x}) \in U$:

$$\phi ::= c \mid u(\overline{x}) \mid \phi \wedge \psi \mid \neg\phi.$$

Logical disjunction ($\vee$) and implication ($\rightarrow$) are defined in the usual way: $\phi \vee \psi =_{\mathrm{df}} \neg(\neg\phi \wedge \neg\psi)$ and $\phi \rightarrow \psi =_{\mathrm{df}} \neg\phi \vee \psi$. A constraint c viewed as a property will be interpreted as the set of constraints d that entail c, i.e. as the upward closure $\uparrow c$ of c in C (wrt the $\leq$ ordering). Thus a constraint d satisfies the basic property c iff $d \in \uparrow c$. For user defined predicates, we assume given an interpretation $I : U \rightarrow \wp(C)$ which defines their meaning. Thus a user defined property $u(\overline{x})$ is satisfied by a constraint c iff $c \in I(u(\overline{x}))$. We assume that I is consistent wrt variable renaming, i.e. $c \in I(u(\overline{x}))$ iff $c[\overline{y}/\overline{x}] \in I(u(\overline{y}))$. Moreover, as previously mentioned, for $\delta(\overline{x}) \in \Delta$ we assume that $I(\delta(\overline{x})) = \uparrow I(\delta(\overline{x}))$. The logical operations of conjunction and negation are interpreted in the classical way by their corresponding set theoretic operations of intersection and complement: Thus a constraint c satisfies a property $\phi \wedge \psi$ iff it satisfies both ϕ and ψ, and a constraint c satisfies a property $\neg\phi$ iff c does not satisfy ϕ. Formally, the semantics of properties is defined as follows:

Definition 6. The semantics of properties is given by a function $[\![\cdot]\!]$ which maps properties into non-empty sets of constraints and it is defined as follows:

$$\begin{array}{llll} [\![c]\!] & = \uparrow c & \qquad [\![u(\overline{x})]\!] & = I(u(\overline{x})) \\ [\![\neg\phi]\!] & = (C \setminus [\![\phi]\!]) \cup \{false\} & \qquad [\![\phi \wedge \psi]\!] & = [\![\phi]\!] \cap [\![\psi]\!]. \end{array}$$

The semantics of a property is parametric wrt C and I. We omitted them from the notation just for the sake of simplicity. Note also that the semantic domain is a boolean algebra of non-empty sets of constraints, where $\{false\}$ represents the least element (this justifies the above definition of $[\![\neg\phi]\!]$ as $(C \setminus [\![\phi]\!]) \cup \{false\}$ instead than simply $C \setminus [\![\phi]\!]$). The reason why we consider non-empty sets only is merely technical: it allows for a more direct correspondence with the semantics of δ-ccp.

Definition 7. A property ϕ is called valid, notation $\models_{C,I} \phi$, iff every constraint satisfies the property, i.e. $[\![\phi]\!] = C$, where C is the given constraint system and I is the given interpretation for user defined properties.

Since we are in a boolean algebra, the validity of a property can be proved simply by the inference system of the predicate logic, on the set of proper axioms specifying the relations among the basic elements of the algebra. These are the sets corresponding to user-defined predicates and constraints, hence we assume an axiom of the form $c \rightarrow d$ for each pair of constraints c, d such that $d \leq c$, and an axiom of the form $c \rightarrow u(\tilde{x})$ for each constraint c, user-defined predicate $u(\tilde{x})$, such that $c \in I(u(\tilde{x}))$.

If we indicate by $Ax(C, I)$ the collection of all these axioms, then we have

Proposition 8. $\models_{C,I} \phi$ *iff* $Ax(C, I) \vdash \phi$, *where* $\vdash$ *is the derivability relation in the predicate calculus.*

We conclude this section by discussing the relation between the logic of the properties and the logic implicit in the underlying constraint system. It should be clear that the former is a richer logic. The only connective which is present also in the constraint system is $\wedge$, in fact $c \sqcup d$ and $c \wedge d$ are equivalent. But for the other connectives this is not true in general. The $\vee$ does not correspond to the greatest lower bound $\sqcap$ in C. In fact $(c \vee d) \rightarrow (c \sqcap d)$ is valid, but the reverse is not, since every constraint which satisfy $(c \vee d)$ should entail c or d, while this is not the case for $(c \sqcap d)$. Analogously, if we have a form of negation in C, this is in general a weaker form of negation than $\neg$. For instance, if we have the constraints $x = 0$ and $x \neq 0$, this only means that $x = 0 \sqcup x \neq 0$ is *false*, but doesn't generally mean that $x = 0 \sqcap x \neq 0$ is *true* (it could be, for instance, a constraint saying that x is ground). Thus $x \neq 0 \rightarrow \neg x = 0$ is valid, but the reverse is not, and $x = 0 \vee \neg x = 0$ is valid, but $x = 0 \vee x \neq 0$ is not. In particular, the latter is satisfied by a constraint c only if c entails $x = 0$ or c entails $x \neq 0$. We introduce now our language for specifying correctness assertions.

Definition 9. A *partial correctness assertion* is a construct of the form $D.A \; sat \; \phi$ where $D.A$ is a δ-ccp process and ϕ is a property. The semantic of an assertion $D.A \; sat \; \phi$ is given as follows: $\models D.A \; sat \; \phi$ iff $SP(D.A) \subseteq [\![\phi]\!]$, where $SP(D.A) =_{def} \{d \mid$ there exists $c \in C$ s.t. $d \in \mathcal{O}_{ccp}(D, A, c) \}$.

Intuitively $\models D.A \; sat \; \phi$, i.e. $D.A \; sat \; \phi$ is valid, iff every terminating computation of $D.A$ (for any input) results in a constraint which satisfies the property ϕ. The set $SP(D.A)$ actually describes the *strongest postcondition* of the process $D.A$ with respect to the precondition *true*, since every constraint satisfies the property *true*.

5 A proof-system for δ-ccp

In this section we develop a proof-system for δ-ccp following the lines of the one defined in [3] for ccp. To this aim, it is convenient to give first a compositional characterization of the semantics $SP(D.A)$. It comes out that we can use nearly the same denotational construction as the one introduced by Jagadeesan et al. in [11] for local ccp. This is worth noticing, since δ-ccp has more expressive power than local ccp, for it allows tests (ask guards) on (upward closed) properties. For example, we could test that the store contains the maximal information on x (a generalization of the notion of groundness) by using a guard $ask(g(x))$ where the interpretation of $g(x)$ is defined as $g(x) = \{c \mid$ for every d. $\exists_{-x} d \vdash \exists_{-x} c$ implies $\exists_{-x} c \vdash \exists_{-x} d\}$.

However, even though δ-ccp can be seen as a "lifted ccp", i.e. a ccp language defined on a lifted constraint system $\wp(C)$, yet the results of computations can be considered as constraints in C. Thus we can define the following denotational semantics.

Definition 10. Let $\wp_f(C)$ denote the collection of the subsets of C containing *false*, and let *Env* denote the set of environments, namely functions e which associate to each procedure name p and to each tuple $\bar{x}$ an element of $\wp_f(C)$, with the property that $e(p)(\bar{y}) = e(p)(\bar{x})[\bar{x}/\bar{y}]$. The denotational semantics of δ-ccp is expressed by the function $[\![\cdot]\!] : Declarations \times Agents \to Env \to \wp_f(C)$ defined by the equations in Table 2, where μ denotes the least fixpoint wrt subset inclusion and $\mathbb{E}$ is the cylindrification operator on sets of constraints, namely $\mathbb{E}_x(C) = \{c \mid \exists_x c = \exists_x d \text{ for some } d \in C\}$.

D0 $[\![D.stop]\!](e) = C$

D1 $[\![D.tell(c)]\!](e) = \uparrow c$

D2 $[\![D.ask(\delta(\bar{x})) \to A]\!](e) = (C \setminus I(\delta(\bar{x}))) \cup (I(\delta(\bar{x})) \cap [\![D.A]\!](e))$

D3 $[\![D.A \parallel B]\!](e) = [\![D.A]\!](e) \cap [\![D.B]\!](e)$

D4 $[\![D.A + B]\!](e) = [\![D.A]\!](e) \cup [\![D.B]\!](e)$

D5 $[\![D.p(\bar{x})]\!](e) = e(p)(\bar{x}) \qquad p \notin D$

D6 $[\![D.p(\bar{x})]\!](e) = \mu\Psi$
where $\Psi(f) = \mathbb{E}_{-\bar{x}}[\![D \setminus \{p\}.A]\!](e[p/f](\bar{x}))$, $p(\bar{x}) : -A \in defn_D(p(\bar{x}))$

Table 2. Strongest postcondition semantics of δ-ccp

In equations **D5** and **D6** $p \notin D$ means that D does not contain any declaration for p, while $D \setminus \{p\}$ denotes the program obtained from D by removing the declaration for p. Note that the environment is used only in the fixpoint construction, but it is not relevant in the semantics of a process, since a process is closed (wrt procedure names) by definition. Namely we have that, for any process $D.A$ and for every pair of environments e and e', $[\![D.A]\!](e) = [\![D.A]\!](e')$ holds. Therefore we can denote the semantics of a process $D.A$ simply by $[\![D.A]\!]$. Using the lifting described above we now obtain the following result.

Proposition 11. *For any process $D.A$ we have $SP(D.A) = [\![D.A]\!]$.*

As discussed in [3], the denotational semantics allows us to obtain the proof-system by simply "mirroring" the equations. In fact the operators of the language are modeled in these equations by standard set theoretic notions which in the specification logic get replaced by the corresponding logical notions. Table 3 contains the rules of the calculus for assertions of the form $D.A\ sat\ \phi$. Rules **C0-C6** are given in the usual natural deduction style and are self explaining since they are obtained essentially by a logical reading of equations **D0-D6**, i.e. by turning $\cup$ into $\vee$ and $\cap$ into $\wedge$. It is also worth noticing that they provide a logical meaning for the operators of the language: action prefixing ($\to$) corresponds to implication (still denoted by $\to$), parallel composition to conjunction and choice to disjunction. Reasoning about recursion is formalized in terms of the meta-rule **C6** (Scott-induction) which allows to conclude that the agent

$p(\overline{x})$ satisfies a property ϕ whenever the body of $p(\overline{x})$ satisfies the same property assuming the conclusion of the rule. Also here we assume to choose an instance of the definition of p such that all local variables are fresh wrt $\overline{x}$ and ϕ. Finally, we have the consequence rule **C7** for weakening a property. This rule allows to include in the reasoning process information about the underlying constraint system and the user-defined predicates.

C0 $D.stop\ sat\ true$

C1 $D.tell(c)\ sat\ c$

C2 $\dfrac{D.A\ sat\ \phi}{D.ask(\delta(\overline{x})) \to A\ sat\ \delta(\overline{x}) \to \phi}$

C3 $\dfrac{D.A\ sat\ \phi \quad D.B\ sat\ \psi}{D.A \parallel B\ sat\ \phi \wedge \psi}$

C4 $\dfrac{D.A\ sat\ \phi \quad D.B\ sat\ \psi}{D.A + B\ sat\ \phi \vee \psi}$

C5 $\dfrac{D.p(\overline{x})\ sat\ \phi}{D.p(\overline{y})\ sat\ \phi[\overline{x}/\overline{y}]}$

C6 $\dfrac{D \setminus \{p\}.p(\overline{x})\ sat\ \phi \vdash D \setminus \{p\}.A\ sat\ \phi}{D.p(\overline{x})\ sat\ \phi}\ p(x) : -A \in defn_D(p(\overline{x}))$

C7 $\dfrac{D.A\ sat\ \phi \quad Ax(C,I) \vdash \phi \to \psi}{D.A\ sat\ \psi}$

Table 3. A calculus for δ-ccp

We illustrate now the formal justification of the above calculus, namely its soundness and completeness.

Theorem 12 Soundness. *If $D.A\ sat\ \phi$ can be derived by the inference system in Table 3, then $\models D.A\ sat\ \phi$ holds.*

Completeness of the system is proved in the sense of Cook ([6]): We assume the expressibility of the strongest postcondition of a process $D.A$, i.e. that there exists a property ϕ such that $SP(D.A) = [\![\phi]\!]$, and that we are able to prove all the valid relations of the formulas involving ϕ. In the case of CLP, in general ϕ can be expressed with a predicate defined recursively via clauses.

Theorem 13 Completeness. *If $\models D.A\ sat\ \phi$, then $D.A\ sat\ \phi$ can be derived by the inference system in Table 3.*

The above results can be applied in a direct way to CLP programs with delay declarations by using Proposition 4. Thus we have the following result where, for the if part, we make the same assumptions made above for the completeness theorem.

Corollary 14. *Let P be a CLP program with delay declarations, c, Q be a query and ϕ a property. Then $\tau(P).\tau(Q)$ sat ϕ can be derived by the inference system in Table 3 iff* $\bigcup_{c\in\mathcal{C}} \mathcal{O}(P,Q,c) \cup \{false\} \subseteq [\![\phi]\!]$.

So we can prove that $\tau(P).\tau(Q)$ satisfies the property ϕ iff any finite non-failing computation for the query c, Q, for any constraint c, in the CLP program P, produces an answer constraint which satisfies ϕ.

Example 2. We give now an example of the use of our proof system to prove properties of programs. Consider again the program in Example 1. We want to prove the following property:

$$tree(Li, Lp, T) \;\; sat \;\; (ground(Li) \wedge ground(Lp)) \rightarrow (samenodes(Li, T) \wedge samenodes(Lp, T))$$

where $somenodes(L,T)$ holds iff L and T have the same elements. Let's denote by ϕ the property $(ground(Li) \wedge ground(Lp)) \rightarrow (samenodes(Li,T) \wedge samenodes(Lp,T))$. By the rule for the procedure call (**C6**) it is sufficient to prove that

$$tell(L = [\,]) \parallel tree\&residual(Li, Lp, T, L) \;\; sat \;\; \phi.$$

By the rule for the weakening (**C7**) it is sufficient to consider

$$tell(L = [\,]) \parallel tree\&residual(Li, Lp, T, L) \;\; sat \;\; L = [\,] \wedge \psi,$$

where ψ is the property $(ground(Li) \wedge ground(Lp)) \rightarrow (samenodes(Li,T) \wedge samenodes(Lp \setminus L, T))$, with $Lp \setminus L$ denoting the nodes of Lp minus the nodes of Li. By the parallel rule (**C3**) and the tell rule (**C1**) we reduce the proof to

$$tree\&residual(Li, Lp, T, L) \;\; sat \;\; \psi.$$

We can now apply the rule for the procedure call, thus reducing the proof to

$$ask(nonvar(Li) \wedge nonvar(Lp)) \rightarrow A_1 + A_2 \;\; sat \;\; \psi$$

where A_1 is the process $tell(Li = [\,] \wedge T = () \wedge \; L = Lp)$ and A_2 is the process

$$tell(Li = [Y|Lit] \wedge Lp = [X|Lpt] \wedge T = (X, Tl, Tr)) \parallel split(X, Li, Lil, Lir) \parallel$$
$$tree\&residual(Lil, Lpt, Tl, Lpr) \parallel tree\&residual(Lir, Lpr, Tr, L).$$

Remember that to make this last proof we can use the assumption

$$tree\&residual(Li, Lp, T, L) \; sat \; \psi, \tag{1}$$

as it is allowed by the Rule **C6**. Observe now that $\psi \equiv (nonvar(Li) \wedge nonvar(Lp)) \rightarrow \psi$, thus using the ask rule (**C2**) we reduce the proof to

$$A_1 + A_2 \;\; sat \;\; \psi$$

Consider that $\psi \equiv (\psi \wedge Li = [\,]) \vee (\psi \wedge Li \neq [\,])$, and that $\psi \wedge Li = [\,] \equiv Li = [\,] \wedge T = () \wedge Lp \subseteq L$ (where $Lp \subseteq L$ means that the elements of Lp are contained in the elements of L). From Rule **C1** we have

$$A_1 \equiv tell(Li = [\,] \wedge T = () \wedge \; L = Lp) \;\; sat \;\; Li = [\,] \wedge T = () \wedge Lp \subseteq L,$$

hence for the parallel rule it is sufficient to prove that $A_2 \;\; sat \;\; \psi \wedge Li \neq [\,]$.

Observe that $\psi \wedge Li \neq [\,]$ is implied by the condition $\eta \equiv$

$$(Li = [Y|Lit] \wedge Lp = [X|Lpt] \wedge T = (X, Tl, Tr)) \wedge$$
$$((ground(X) \wedge ground(Li)) \rightarrow Li = Lil * X * Lir \wedge$$
$$((ground(Lil) \wedge ground(Lpt)) \rightarrow (samenodes(Lil, Tl) \wedge samenodes(Lpt \setminus Lpr, Tl))) \wedge$$
$$((ground(Lir) \wedge ground(Lpr)) \rightarrow (samenodes(Lir, Tr) \wedge samenodes(Lpr \setminus L, Tr)))$$

(here $Lil * X * Lir$ represents the concatenation of Lil, X, and Lir), hence by the weakening rule it is sufficient to prove that A_2 *sat* η. This can be done by using the parallel rule, and then proving:

- $tell(Li = [Y|Lit] \wedge Lp = [X|Lpt] \wedge T = (X, Tl, Tr))$ *sat* $(Li = [Y|Lit] \wedge Lp = [X|Lpt] \wedge T = (X, Tl, Tr))$. By the tell rule.
- $tree\&residual(Lil, Lpt, Tl, Lpr)$ *sat* $(ground(Lil) \wedge ground(Lpt)) \rightarrow (samenodes(Lil, Tl) \wedge samenodes(Lpt \setminus Lpr, Tl))$. By the assumption (1), and the renaming rule (C5).
- $tree\&residual(Lir, Lpr, Tr, L)$ *sat* $(ground(Lir) \wedge ground(Lpr)) \rightarrow (samenodes(Lir, Tr) \wedge samenodes(Lpr \setminus L, Tr))$. Like before.
- $split(X, Li, Lil, Lir)$ *sat* $(ground(X) \wedge \exists Y : \exists Lt : L = [Y|Lt] \wedge ground(Y)) \rightarrow Li = Lil * X * Lir$. We leave this for exercise to the reader.

6 Conclusion and future work

We presented a correct and complete compositional proof-system for proving partial correctness of CLP programs with delay declarations. Several extensions and different applications are possible.

Firstly, since we have presented a calculus for the strongest postcondition wrt the precondition *true*, a natural extension would be to consider arbitrary preconditions, i.e. to give a calculus for triples of the form $\{\psi\}\ D.A\ \{\phi\}$ in the classical Hoare-logic style. As shown in [3], if preconditions are described by upward closed properties (i.e. they are expressed by formulas involving constraints, conjunctions and disjunctions only) then triples are not more expressive than the assertions considered in previous sections, since proving the triple $\{\psi\}\ D.A\ \{\phi\}$ is equivalent to prove $D.A$ *sat* $\psi \rightarrow \phi$. On the other hand, in general our system does not allow us to prove triples in which the precondition contains negation. Introducing preconditions containing negation is not straightforward, since the stronger postcondition semantics in this case is not any more compositional.

Secondly, since properties could be expressed in a CLP language itself, our calculus could be used to prove equivalence of programs and "internal" properties of programs. For example, given the usual REVERSE program defining the predicate `reverse(s,t)` which reverses a list, one could easily prove the symmetricity of the predicate, i.e. that REVERSE.`reverse(s,t)` *sat* REVERSE.`reverse(t,s)`.

Thirdly, we can use our calculus for the transformational design of programs. The main idea underlying the transformational approach to the design of programs is the stepwise refinement of specifications into programs. To express the stepwise construction of a program usually the formalism of *mixed terms* is introduced, i.e. terms that are constructed out of programs and specifications. In the case of δ-ccp programs we can easily have a unified formalism both for programs and properties.

In such a formalism an assertion of the from P *sat* ϕ corresponds to the implication $P \rightarrow \phi$ and thus models the *refinement (or implementation)*: A (mixed) term Φ *refines* a mixed term Ψ iff $\Phi \rightarrow \Psi$ holds. So, a derivation of a process P from a specification ϕ in this approach corresponds with proving (using our calculus) the sequence $P \equiv \Phi_n \rightarrow \ldots \rightarrow \Phi_1 \equiv \phi$ of implications between mixed terms $\Phi_1, \ldots \Phi_n$ where Φ_1 is the given specification ϕ and Φ_n denotes the derived program.
Acknowledgments: This work was partially supported by the HCM Project "EXPRESS".

References

1. K. R. Apt. Declarative Programming in Prolog. In D. Miller, editor, *Proceedings of the Int'l Symposium on Logic Programming*, The MIT Press, pages 11–35x, 1993.
2. K. R. Apt and I. Luitjes. Verification of logic programs with delay declarations. In A. Borzyszkowski and S. Sokolowski, editors, *Proc. of AMAST*, LNCS, pages 1–19, Berlin, 1995. Springer-Verlag.
3. F.S. de Boer, M. Gabbrielli, E. Marchiori, and C. Palamidessi. Proving Concurrent Constraint Programs Correct. In *Proc. of Twentyfirst POPL*, ACM Press, 1994.
4. F.S. de Boer and C. Palamidessi. A Fully Abstract Model for Concurrent Constraint Programming. In S. Abramsky and T.S.E. Maibaum, editors, *Proc. of TAPSOFT/CAAP, LNCS 493*, pages 296–319. Springer-Verlag, 1991.
5. M. Carlsson. *SICStus Prolog User's Manual.* Po Box 1263, S-16313 Spanga, Sweden, February 1988.
6. S.A. Cook. Soundness and completeness of an axiom system for program verification. *SIAM J. Computation*, 7(1):70–90, 1978.
7. P. M. Hill and J. W. Lloyd. *The Gödel programming language.* The MIT Press, 1994.
8. L. Henkin, J.D. Monk, and A. Tarski. *Cylindric Algebras (Part I).* North-Holland, 1971.
9. J. Jaffar and J.-L. Lassez. Constraint Logic Programming. In *Proc. of POPL*, pages 111–119. ACM Press, 1987.
10. Joxan Jaffar and Michael J. Maher. Constraint logic programming: A survey. *Journal of Logic Programming*, 19/20:503–581, 1994.
11. R. Jagadeesan, V.A. Saraswat, and V. Shanbhogue. Angelic non-determinism in concurrent constraint programming. Technical report, Xerox Park, 1991.
12. S. Lüttringhaus-Kappel. Control generation for logic programs. In D.S. Warren, editor, *Proc. Tenth Int'l Conf. on Logic Programming*, pages 478–495. MIT Press, 1993.
13. E. Marchiori and F. Teusink. Proving termination of logic programs with delay declarations. In J. Lloyd, editor, *Proc. of ILPS.* MIT Press, 1995.
14. K. Marriott, M. Falaschi, M. Gabbrielli and C. Palamidessi. A simple semantics for logic programming languages with delay. In R. Kotagiri, editor, Proc. Eighteenth Australian Computer Science Conf., *Australian Computer Science Comm.* **17** (1): 356–363, 1995.
15. K. Marriott, M. Garcia de la Banda and M. Hermenegildo. Analyzing Logic Programs with Dynamic Scheduling. *Proc. of POPL*, pages 240–253. ACM Press, 1994.
16. L. Naish. An introduction to MU-Prolog. Technical Report 82/2, The University of Melbourne, 1982.
17. L. Naish. *Negation and Control in Prolog*, LNCS 238, Springer-Verlag, 1985.
18. V.A. Saraswat and M. Rinard. Concurrent constraint programming. In *Proc. of POPL*, pages 232–245, 1990.
19. V.A. Saraswat, M. Rinard, and P. Panangaden. Semantics foundations of Concurrent Constraint Programming. In *Proc. of POPL*, 1991.
20. Mark Wallace and André Veron. Two problems – two solutions: One system – ECLiPSe. In *Proc. IEEE Colloquium on Advanced Software Technologies for Scheduling*, London, 1993.

Understanding Mobile Agents via a Non-Interleaving Semantics for Facile *

R. Borgia[1], P. Degano[1], C. Priami[1], L. Leth[2] and B. Thomsen[2]

[1] Dipartimento di Informatica, Università di Pisa
Corso Italia 40, I-56100 Pisa, Italy
{degano,priami}@di.unipi.it
[2] European Computer-Industry Research Centre
Arabellastr. 17, D-81925 Munich, Germany
{lone,bt}@ecrc.de

Abstract. Mobile agents, i.e. pieces of programs that can be sent around networks of computers, are starting to appear on the Internet. Such programs may be seen as an enrichment of traditional distributed computing. Since mobile agents may carry communication links with them as they move across the network, they create very dynamic interconnection structures that can be extremely complex to analyse. In this paper we analyse a fragment of a system based on the mobile agent principle written in the Facile programming language. We propose a Structural Operational Semantics (SOS) for Facile, giving a proved transition system that records encodings of the derivation trees of transitions in their labels. This information allows us to easily recover non-interleaving semantics for Facile by looking only at the labels of transitions. We use the new Facile semantics to debug an agent based system. This example is a scaled down version of a system demonstrated at the European IT Conference Exhibition in Brussels, 1995.

1 Introduction

With the emergence of mobile agent based systems a new class of applications has started to roam the information highway. Mobile agent based systems bring the promise of new, more advanced and more flexible services and systems. Mobile agents are self-contained pieces of software that can move between computers on a network. Agents can serve as local representatives for remote services, provide interactive access to data they accompany, and carry out tasks for a mobile user temporarily disconnected from the network. Agents also provide a means for the set of software available to a user to change dynamically according to the user's needs and interests [16].

Mobile agents brings with them the fear of viruses, Trojan horses and other nasties. To avoid viruses, Trojan horses and the like the main approach to agent

* Work partially supported by ESPRIT Basic Research Action 8130 - LOMAPS

based systems is based on development of safe languages, i.e. languages that do not allow peek and poke, unsafe pointer manipulations and unrestricted access to file operations. This is often achieved through interpreted languages. Java[11], Safe-TCL[8], Telescript[20] are examples of this approach.

Even when the fear of viruses has been eliminated, mobile agent systems may be a magnitude more complex to develop than traditional client/server applications since it is very easy to create agents that will counter act each other or inadvertently "steal" resources from other agents. Since an agent can move from place to place, it can be very hard to trace the execution of such systems and special care must be taken when constructing such systems.

However, apart from being safe languages in the above sense, the mentioned languages are rather traditional, based on the object oriented paradigm and/or traditional imperative scripting language techniques, thus these languages offer very little support for the analysis of systems.

Facile [9, 10, 17, 19] is a viable alternative to the above mentioned languages. Facile is a multi-paradigm programming language combining functional and concurrent programming. The language is conceived for programming of reactive systems and distributed systems, in particular the construction of systems based on the emerging mobile agent principle since processes and channels are naturally treated as first class objects. Facile provides safe execution of mobile agents because they only have access to resources they have been given explicitly. Facile offers integration of different computational paradigms in a clean and well understood programming model that allows formal reasoning about program behaviour and properties.

Although Facile is still in an experimental phase, it is mature enough that it has been used successfully to implement some larger distributed applications. One example is the Calumet teleconferencing system [14, 15], which supports cooperative work through real-time presentations of visual and audio information across wide area networks, and Einrichten [1], an application that melds distribution, sophisticated graphics, and live video to permit collaborative interior design work for widely-separated participants. The latter application was demonstrated at the 1995 G7 technology summit in Brussels. Another example, the Mobile Service Agent (MSA) demonstration [18], given at the EITC'95 Exhibition in Brussels, is the subject for analysis in this paper.

Facile may be viewed as an extension of λ-calculus with primitives for concurrency, communication and distribution. The language has a binding operator (λ-abstraction) to define (possibly higher-order) functions. Functions, processes and channels may be either the result of the evaluation or the arguments of expressions.

Facile handles concurrency through dynamic definition of processes, channels and virtual processing units (called nodes). Processes exchange messages with send and receive primitives along channels that are explicitly managed. Communication is synchronous.

The functional and the concurrent parts of Facile are strongly integrated: processes evaluate expressions to values while expressions may activate processes or return channels and node identifiers.

The semantics of Facile has been studied quite extensively [9, 10, 17, 12, 2], focusing on defining the (abstract) execution of programs in terms of transition systems, reduction systems or abstract machines or are concerned with the development of program equivalences. So far the approach to semantics for Facile has been based on the interleaving approach to modeling concurrency.

In this paper we present a non interleaving semantics for Facile. The presentation of this non-interleaving semantics for Facile is based on the parametric approach introduced in [6, 7]. We adopt a very concrete (SOS) transition system whose transitions are labelled by encodings of their proofs. We then instantiate it to non-interleaving semantics through relabelling functions, which maintain only the relevant information in the labels. This approach allows us to use the standard definitions and tools developed for the interleaving case. In this paper we restrict our attention to the non distributed part of the Facile language because this suffices for the discussion of the present case-study. The full version of Facile is dealt with in the full paper [4] and in [13].

Furthermore, we use the non interleaving semantics for Facile to debug the behaviour of a mobile agent based system written in Facile. The system we analyse is a scaled down version of a problem with causal dependencies of higher order processes and mobile channels. It originally arose in the code for the Mobile Service Agent demonstration. Using "traditional" debugging techniques it took two weeks to track the problem down.

We would like to point out that in this paper we will address the question of analysis of "real code". The advantage of our approach is that there will be no gap between model and implementation of a system. This is in sharp contrast to traditional analysis of systems. Here the analysis takes place in a formal model of the system, but the system itself is implemented in a traditional programming language without formal foundation, thus there is inevitably a gap between the formal model and the running code. Our approach is independent of the type of system being analysed; it applies to mobile agents, client/server or other concurrent programs.

The rest of this paper is organised as follows: Section 2 introduces the syntax of core Facile and in section 3 a Proved Transition System semantics is defined. Section 4 defines the notion of causality which may be derived from the Proved Transition System semantics. In section 5 we apply the mathematical framework to a case study derived from a larger mobile agent based application implemented in Facile. Finally, in section 6 we give some concluding remarks.

2 Facile

In this paper, we only consider the concurrent functional core of Facile. This core contains the set of constructs which is sufficient to define any Facile program running on a single virtual node. We refer to [17, 12] for details about physical distribution in Facile. The syntax consists of two parts: expressions (functions) E and behaviour expressions (processes) BE. Expressions are statically typed, and t ranges over types. We assume that all expressions are correctly typed. The type system is reported in [9]. Note that processes have no type. The syntax is given below.

$$v ::= x \mid c \mid \lambda x.e \mid \texttt{code}(be)$$

$$e ::= v \mid e_1 e_2 \mid \texttt{spawn}(be) \mid \texttt{channel}(t) \mid e!e \mid e?$$

$$be ::= \texttt{terminate} \mid \texttt{activate}(be) \mid be \| be \mid be + be$$

Val (ranged over by v) denotes the set of syntactic values. Values are a subclass of expressions without free variables. Values can be passed as parameters to functions or be communicated between processes, possibly residing on different nodes in a system.

We assume a countable set of variables denoted by $x, x_i, \ldots$. Constants are ranged over by c, and these include integers, booleans, channel-valued constants, node identifiers and a distinguished, dummy value `triv`. Predefined operators such as `if-then-else` are denoted by c as well. We assume that all operations are in curried form to avoid the introduction of tuples and product types. Functions are defined and manipulated in λ-calculus style with abstractions and applications. λ is a variable binder with the usual notion of free and bound variables. The set of free variables of an expression is denoted by fn. fn is structurally extended to behaviour expressions and distributed behaviour expressions. Substituting an expression for a variable with the usual avoidance of accidental binding is denoted by $e[e'/x]$. For a formal definition of these concepts see [9]. Normally we only need to substitute values for variables. The `code` construct transforms a process into a value that can be used in the functional style. More precisely, $\texttt{code}(be)$ is a process closure whose behaviour is described by be. A new channel on which we can transmit values of type t is generated by $\texttt{channel}(t)$. The send operation $e_1!e_2$ sends the value resulting from the evaluation of e_2 along the channel resulting from the evaluation of e_1. The operation returns the value `triv` when the receiver gets the value. The receive operation $e?$ returns the value read on the channel resulting from the evaluation of e. The evaluation of $\texttt{spawn}(be)$ returns the value `triv`. The spawning operation has the effect of concurrently executing the process specified by be on the current virtual node.

Unlike evaluation of expressions, the execution of behaviour expressions does not produce values. The simplest process is `terminate` which does nothing. The process $\texttt{activate}(e)$ activates the evaluation of the expression e. The operator $\|$ describes the parallel composition of processes allocated on the same virtual node. The operator $+$ denotes nondeterministic choice.

The core of Facile has no operator for sequentialisation of expressions or processes. The term $e_1.e_2$ is implemented in the core language as:

$$e_1.e_2 \equiv (\lambda x.e_2)e_1 \qquad \mathit{if}\ x \notin fn(e_2)$$

where $fn(e)$ denotes the free variables of e. The term $e.be$ is translated as

$$e.be \equiv \mathtt{activate}((\lambda x.\mathtt{code}(be))e) \qquad \mathit{if}\ x \notin fn(be)$$

In the following we will use sequentialisation to simplify the representation of Facile systems. When the direction of communication is immaterial we may simply write $a.be$ and a instead of $a.\mathtt{terminate}$.

The behaviour of Facile programs is defined in SOS style by the operational semantics in [17]. This semantics has transitions on the form: $K, N, e \xrightarrow{\ell}_e K', N', e'$ and $K, N, be \xrightarrow{\ell}_{be} K', N', be'$ where K and N are sets used to keep track of generated channels and nodes. We shall not report the "standard" SOS here, but refer the reader to [17]. In the following section we introduce an alternative operational semantics based on Proved Transition Systems semantics.

3 Proved Transition System

In this section we define the proved operational semantics of core Facile following [13]. The interested reader can find the semantics of the full language in [4]. To simplify the definition of causal semantics of core Facile, we assume that $||$ is right associative. We start with the definition of actions.

Definition 1. Let $\{k \in \mathcal{S}_t\}$ be the set of channels of type t, and let $\mathcal{S}$ be the set of all channels. The set Act of actions is:

$$\{k(v), \overline{k(v)}\} \cup \{\tau\} \cup \{(\tau, k) \ : k \in \mathcal{S}\} \cup \{\Phi(be) \ : be \in BE\}$$

The first set will sometimes be referred to as $Comm$. Elements of Act are denoted as $\mu, \mu_i, \mu', \ldots$.

The label (τ, k) is caused by $\mathtt{channel}(t)$ and contains the name of the new channel. The label $\Phi(be)$ represents the creation of a new process to be activated by $\mathtt{spawn}(be)$

Following the developments in [6, 7], we extend actions with the parallel structure of the process which executes them.

Definition 2. Let $\mu \in Act$, and $\vartheta \in \{||_0, ||_1\}^*$. The set Θ of *proof terms* is:

$$\{\vartheta\mu\} \cup \{\vartheta\langle\vartheta_0\lambda, \vartheta_1\bar{\lambda}\rangle \ : \lambda \in Comm\}$$

Elements of Θ are denoted as $\theta, \theta_i, \theta', \ldots$.

Function $\ell : \Theta \rightarrow Act$ defined below is used to recover the action starting from a proof term.

$$\ell(\mu) = \mu \; ; \quad \ell(\langle \vartheta_0 \lambda, \vartheta_1 \bar{\lambda} \rangle) = \tau \; ; \quad \ell(\vartheta \theta) = \ell(\theta)$$

We extend the involution $^{-}$ to ℓ by stipulating $\overline{\ell(\theta)} = \overline{k(v)}$ *iff* $\ell(\theta) = k(v)$

The proof term $\vartheta\mu$ is the label of a generic action μ executed by a process whose position is encoded by ϑ ($||_0$ and $||_1$ denotes the left and right part of a parallel composition, respectively). The synchronisation of two processes is labelled $\vartheta\langle \vartheta_0 \lambda, \vartheta_1 \bar{\lambda} \rangle$. We need an auxiliary function $\mathcal{C}$ that returns the channel valued constants in a Facile program. When creating a new channel name, the function is used to check whether this name is already in use. The function $\mathcal{C}$ works recursively through expressions and behaviour expressions.

Definition 3. The function $\mathcal{C}$, from expressions and behaviour expressions to the set of all channels, is defined by structural induction as follows:

$$\mathcal{C}(x) = \emptyset \qquad \mathcal{C}(c) = \begin{cases} \{c\} & \text{if } c \in \mathcal{S} \\ \emptyset & \text{otherwise} \end{cases}$$

$$\mathcal{C}(\lambda x.e) = \mathcal{C}(e) \qquad \mathcal{C}(e_1 e_2) = \mathcal{C}(e_1) \cup \mathcal{C}(e_2)$$

$$\mathcal{C}(\texttt{channel}(t)) = \emptyset \qquad \mathcal{C}(e_1!e_2) = \mathcal{C}(e_1) \cup \mathcal{C}(e_2)$$

$$\mathcal{C}(e?) = \mathcal{C}(e) \qquad \mathcal{C}(\texttt{code}(be)) = \mathcal{C}(be)$$

$$\mathcal{C}(\texttt{spawn}(be)) = \mathcal{C}(be) \qquad \mathcal{C}(be_1 \, || \, be_2) = \mathcal{C}(be_1) \cup \mathcal{C}(be_2)$$

$$\mathcal{C}(be_1 \, + \, be_2) = \mathcal{C}(be_1) \cup \mathcal{C}(be_2) \qquad \mathcal{C}(\texttt{activate}(e)) = \mathcal{C}(e)$$

$$\mathcal{C}(\texttt{terminate}) = \emptyset$$

We now define the proved transition system of Facile.

Definition 4.
The proved transition system of Facile is the triple $PTS = \langle T, \Theta, \longrightarrow_{be} \rangle$ where T is the set of closed Facile programs, Θ is the set of proof terms, and $\longrightarrow_{be}$ is the transition relation defined in Tables 1 and 2.

Here we examine the rules of expressions (Tab. 1). The creation of a new channel returns the name of that channel. We must ensure that the new name is not already in use elsewhere in the program to avoid name confusion. Since the channel generated by `channel`(t) is recorded in the labels of transitions (see rule 4.), we perform the name clash check at each derivation step by checking the condition $\ell(\theta) = (\tau, k) \;\Rightarrow\; k \notin \mathcal{C}(-)$. The same condition is applied in the rules for parallel composition of processes. Note that in rule 3.*a* the above condition is not needed because channel names have already been checked inductively during the derivation of the premise.

The $\Phi(be)$ label in rule 5 represents the creation of a new process be by `spawn`(be).

Consider the rules of behaviour expressions. The tag $||_0$ in rule 7.a and $||_1$ in rule 7.b means that the left, respectively the right, component of a parallel

$$1.a : \frac{e_1 \xrightarrow{\theta}_e e_1'}{e_1 e_2 \xrightarrow{\theta}_e e_1' e_2}, \begin{cases} \ell(\theta) = (\tau, k) \Rightarrow \\ k \notin C(e_2) \end{cases} \qquad 1.b : \frac{e_2 \xrightarrow{\theta}_e e_2'}{v e_2 \xrightarrow{\theta}_e v e_2'}, \begin{cases} \ell(\theta) = (\tau, k) \Rightarrow \\ k \notin C(v) \end{cases}$$

$$2.a : \frac{e_1 \xrightarrow{\theta}_e e_1'}{e_1 ! e_2 \xrightarrow{\theta}_e e_1' ! e_2}, \begin{cases} \ell(\theta) = (\tau, k) \Rightarrow \\ k \notin C(e_2) \end{cases} \qquad 1.c : (\lambda x.e)v \xrightarrow{\tau}_e e[v/x]$$

$$2.b : \frac{e_2 \xrightarrow{\theta}_e e_2'}{k!e_2 \xrightarrow{\theta}_e k!e_2'}, \begin{cases} \ell(\theta) = (\tau, h) \Rightarrow \\ h \neq k \end{cases} \qquad 2.c : k!v \xrightarrow{\overline{k(v)}}_e \mathtt{triv}, \begin{cases} k \in S_t \\ \emptyset \vdash v : t \end{cases}$$

$$3.a : \frac{e \xrightarrow{\theta}_e e'}{e? \xrightarrow{\theta}_e e'?} \qquad 3.b : \ k? \xrightarrow{k(v)}_e v, \begin{cases} k \in S_t \\ \emptyset \vdash v : t \end{cases}$$

$$4. : \mathtt{channel}(t) \xrightarrow{(\tau,k)}_e k, \ k \in S_t \qquad 5. : \mathtt{spawn}(be) \xrightarrow{\Phi(be)}_e \mathtt{triv}$$

Table 1. Proved function expressions of Facile.

composition moves. When two processes be_1 and be_2 communicate (rule 8), the label on the transition is the pair of the actions performed by the two partners θ_1 and θ_2, decorated with their positions $||_0$ and $||_1$, respectively.

The nondeterministic choice + does not change the labels (rules 9.a-b) because the non interleaving relations, in which we are interested, are interpretations of the parallel structure of processes only. There is no need for checking channel names in rules 9.a-b, because the choice operator discards either summand be_2 or be_1. Assume that be_1 generates a channel k which already exists in be_2. Since the rule discards be_2, there is no name clash and the name can be re-used. The symmetric case is similar.

Note that creation of processes alters the structure of programs. The creation of a new process be by **spawn**(be) causes be to be put in parallel with the processes that already run on the current node:

$$\mathtt{spawn}(be).\alpha || (be_1 || be_2) \xrightarrow{\tau} ((\alpha || be) || (be_1 || be_2))$$

To get a feeling for the intuition behind proof terms consider the computation in Fig. 1: The label $||_0 \tau$ of the first transition says that the process at position $||_0$ performs an internal action τ. Since $||$ is right-associative, the transition comes from the **spawn**(be_1) prefix.

The last transition is a communication. Its label shows that v is transmitted along channel k. The sender and the receiver are located at $||_1||_0$ and $||_1||_1$, respectively. Assume that the residual γ of the receiver is influenced by the value v. Then γ becomes γ'.

We end this section with a proposition that relates the original [17] and the proved semantics of Facile. The proof is by induction on the rules that define

$$6.a: \frac{e \xrightarrow{\theta}_{e} e'}{\texttt{activate}\, e \xrightarrow{\theta}_{be} \texttt{activate}\, e'} \quad 6.b: \frac{e \xrightarrow{\vartheta\Phi(be)}_{e} e'}{\texttt{activate}\, e \xrightarrow{\vartheta\tau}_{be} \texttt{activate}\, e' || be}$$

$$6.c: \texttt{activatecode}(be) \xrightarrow{\tau}_{be} be \quad 7.a: \frac{be_1 \xrightarrow{\theta}_{be} be_1'}{be_1 \,||\, be_2 \xrightarrow{||_0\theta}_{be} be_1' \,||\, be_2}, \begin{cases} \ell(\theta) = (\tau, k) \Rightarrow \\ k \notin C(be_2) \end{cases}$$

$$7.b: \frac{be_2 \xrightarrow{\theta}_{be} be_2'}{be_1 \,||\, be_2 \xrightarrow{||_1\theta}_{be} be_1 \,||\, be_2'}, \begin{cases} \ell(\theta) = (\tau, k) \Rightarrow \\ k \notin C(be_1) \end{cases}$$

$$8.: \frac{be_1 \xrightarrow{\theta_1}_{be} be_1' \quad be_2 \xrightarrow{\theta_2}_{be} be_2'}{be_1 \,||\, be_2 \xrightarrow{\langle ||_0\theta_1, ||_1\theta_2 \rangle}_{be} be_1' \,||\, be_2'}, \ \ell(\theta_1) = \overline{\ell(\theta_2)}$$

$$9.a: \frac{be_1 \xrightarrow{\theta}_{be} be_1'}{be_1 + be_2 \xrightarrow{\theta}_{be} be_1'} \quad 9.b: \frac{be_2 \xrightarrow{\theta}_{be} be_2'}{be_1 + be_2 \xrightarrow{\theta}_{be} be_2'}$$

Table 2. Proved behaviour expressions of Facile.

$$\texttt{spawn}(be_1).\alpha || k\,!\,v.\beta || k\,?.\gamma$$
$$\Big\downarrow\, ||_0\tau$$
$$(\alpha || be_1) || k\,!\,v.\beta || k\,?.\gamma$$
$$\Big\downarrow\, ||_1 \langle ||_0 \overline{k(v)}, ||_1 k(v) \rangle$$
$$(\alpha || be_1) || \beta || \gamma'$$

Fig. 1. A computation of a Facile program.

the transition relations and the proof can be found in [13].

Proposition 5. *Let* $\xrightarrow{\mu}$ *and* $\xrightarrow{\theta}_{be}$ *be the standard and the transition relations in Def. 4, respectively. Then,*

$$K, N, be \xrightarrow{\mu} K', N', be' \Leftrightarrow \exists\theta \,.\, be \xrightarrow{\theta}_{be} be' \wedge \ell(\theta) = \mu$$

4 Causality

We define process causality by interpreting the parallel structure of processes. Therefore, we consider the prefix of proof terms made up of $||_i$. For the sake of readability, we distinguish between communications and other operations. Following this scheme we define two dependency relations and then we compose them to obtain process causality.

Definition 6. Let $P_0 \xrightarrow{\theta_0}_p P_1 \xrightarrow{\theta_1}_p \ldots \xrightarrow{\theta_n}_p P_{n+1}$ be a proved computation and let $\theta_n = \vartheta'\mu'$. Then, θ_n has a direct dependency on θ_h ($\theta_h \sqsubseteq_1^1 \theta_n$) iff $\theta_h = \vartheta\mu$ and ϑ is a prefix of ϑ'. The dependencies of θ_n are obtained by the reflexive and transitive closure of $\sqsubseteq_1^1$, i.e., $\sqsubseteq_1 = (\sqsubseteq_1^1)^*$.

The following definition deals with communications.

Definition 7. Let $P_0 \xrightarrow{\theta_0}_p P_1 \xrightarrow{\theta_1}_p \ldots \xrightarrow{\theta_n}_p P_{n+1}$ be a proved computation, and hereafter let i, as well as j, be either 0 or 1. Then, θ_n has a direct dependency on θ_h ($\theta_h \sqsubseteq_2^1 \theta_n$) iff either

- $\theta_h = \vartheta\langle\vartheta_0\lambda_0, \vartheta_1\lambda_1\rangle$, $\theta_n = \vartheta_2\mu$ and $\vartheta\vartheta_i\lambda_i \sqsubseteq_1 \theta_n$; or
- $\theta_h = \vartheta_2\mu$, $\theta_n = \vartheta\langle\vartheta_0\lambda_0, \vartheta_1\lambda_1\rangle$, $\theta_h \sqsubseteq_1 \vartheta\vartheta_i\lambda_i$ and λ_i is a send; or
- $\theta_h = \vartheta\langle\vartheta_0\lambda_0, \vartheta_1\lambda_1\rangle$, $\theta_n = \vartheta'\langle\vartheta'_0\lambda'_0, \vartheta'_1\lambda'_1\rangle$, $\vartheta\vartheta_i\lambda_i \sqsubseteq_1 \vartheta'\vartheta'_j\lambda'_j$, and λ'_j is a send.

The dependencies of θ_n are obtained by the reflexive and transitive closure of $\sqsubseteq_2^1$, i.e., $\sqsubseteq_2 = (\sqsubseteq_2^1)^*$.

Process causality is obtained as the reflexive and transitive closure of the two relations above, i.e.

$$\sqsubseteq_p = (\sqsubseteq_1 \cup \sqsubseteq_2)^*.$$

From the proved transition system semantics we may derive many different kinds of information such as locality, precedence, enabling, independence and causality. In this paper we only study causality since it suffices for analysis of the system we want to debug (see section 5). For definitions and examples of the other mentioned relations we refer to [4, 13].

5 Analysis of a Mobile File Browser Agent

The following is a scaled down version of a problem with causal dependencies of higher order processes and mobile channels. It originally arose in the code for the Mobile Service Agent demonstration given at the EITC'95 Exhibition. Using "traditional" debugging techniques it took two weeks to track down the problem.

The problem is the following. We have an agent server that can be called to deliver a client (FB) to the user and leave behind a server (FTP). There is a mistake in the FTP server in the sense that it should have been recursive to handle several calls from the FB client. However, there is also a mistake in the overall system, namely that all client/server pairs share the same channel. Thus even though there is a mistake in the FTP server, the system may continue to operate as long as we request more FB clients. Indeed each time we request an FB client we generate a new FTP server which is waiting on the same channel, thus an old FB client may "steal" the new FTP server from a new FB client.

Below we give the Facile code, both for running code (typewritten) in the Facile Antigua Release [19], and a version written in core Facile (italic). We omit parts not relevant to our discussion. The system activates the two processes FBS and AC. Process AC is busy waiting for an agent request. When the request arrives, AC creates a channel (**reqch**) and sends it to process FBS along their common channel **getch**. Now process AC is waiting for an agent from FBS. Once the process FBS has received the channel name on which AC is waiting for the agent, FBS sends process FB to AC together with the needed channels. Then it activates an FTP server on its node and restarts. Process AC activates the client FB on its node and resumes. Now the interaction is between FTP and FB as follows. The client waits for a request on channel **getinfo**, then creates the channel on which it wants to receive the service (**repch**) and sends it to FTP. Then it waits for the service. The FTP server receives the channel on which it sends the answer to FB, then prints a message to say that the connection is established and sends the answer. At this point the FTP server terminates. The FB client receives the answer, prints a message to say that the interaction is finished and reactivates itself. Since channel **reqch** is global and the client FB is a recursive process while FTP is not, the problem described at the beginning of this section may arise. Note that even if the FTP server is made recursive, there would still not be the wanted correspondence between pairs of FTP servers and file browsers FB.

```
(* Declarations *)
proc FB (getinfo,reqch) =
  let val _ = receive getinfo (* just to keep it waiting until asked *)
      val repch = channel ()
      val _ = send(reqch,repch)
      val _ = receive repch
      val _ = print "Got handshake from server\n"
  in activate FB (getinfo,reqch)
  end
```

$$FB(getinfo,reqch)=getinfo?.(\lambda repch.reqch!repch.repch?.FB(getinfo,reqch))channel$$

```
proc FTP reqch =
  let val repch = receive reqch
      val _ = print "Request from client\n"
  in send(repch,());terminate
  end
```

$$FTPreqch=(\lambda repch.repch!.terminate)reqch?$$

```
proc FBS (getch,reqch,getinfo) =
  let val fbch = receive getch
```

```
      val _ = send(fbch,FB(getinfo,reqch))
      val _ = spawn (FTP reqch)
  in activate FBS (getch,reqch,getinfo)
  end
```

$FBS(getch,reqch,getinfo) {=} (\lambda fbch.fbch!FB(getinfo,reqch).$

$spawn(FTPreqch).FBS(getch,reqch,getinfo))getch?$

```
proc AC (getag,getch) =
  let val _ = receive getag (* just to keep it waiting until asked *)
      val reqch = channel ()
      val _ = send(getch,reqch)
      val FBCagent = receive reqch
  in spawn FBCagent;
     activate AC (getag,getch)
  end
```

$AC(getag,getch) {=} getag?.(\lambda reqch.getch!reqch.(\lambda FBCagent.spawn(FBCagent).$

$AC(getag,getch))reqch?)channel$

```
(* Body *)
val getag = channel (): unit channel
val getinfo = channel (): unit channel

let
  val reqch = channel ()
  val getch = channel ()
in spawn (FBS (getch,reqch,getinfo));
   spawn (AC (getag,getch))
end
```

$(\lambda reqch.\lambda getch.spawn(FBC(getch,reqch,getinfo)).spawn(AC(getag,getch)))channel)channel$

We now show how the error in the first version of the system can easily be singled out by using a causal relation between transitions. The idea is that the operations *val _ = print "Request from client n"* executed by any FTP server must be independent of one another. In fact, FTP serves and terminates. When the FB client interacts with two servers, thus leaving another client without its server, there is a chain of two actions and the first causes the second.

As an example consider the computation in Fig. 2 extracted from the transition system of the incorrect code. Assume that two FTP servers and two FB clients have been activated, and that client FB_1 steals the server of FB_2.

spawn(FBS).spawn(AC)

$\downarrow \tau$

(spawn(AC)$\|FBS$)

$\downarrow \|_0 \tau$

((terminate$\|AC$)$\|FBS$)

$\vdots$

((terminate$\|((AC\|FB_2)\|FB_1))\|((FBS\|FTP_2)\|FTP_1)) = s_0$

$\downarrow \ (\|_0\|_1 \|_1 \overline{reqch(repch)}, \|_1 \|_1 reqch(repch))$

$\theta_1 \downarrow \ \|_1 \|_1 request\ client\ 1$

$\theta_2 \downarrow \ (\|_0\|_1 \|_1 repch, \|_1 \|_1 \overline{repch})$

((terminate$\|((AC\|FB_2)\|FB_1))\|((FBS\|FTP_2)\|$terminate)) = s_1$

$\theta_3 \downarrow \ (\|_0\|_1 \|_1 \overline{reqch(repch)}, \|_1 \|_0 \|_1 reqch(repch))$

$\theta_4 \downarrow \ \|_1 \|_0 \|_1 request\ client\ 2$

$\vdots$

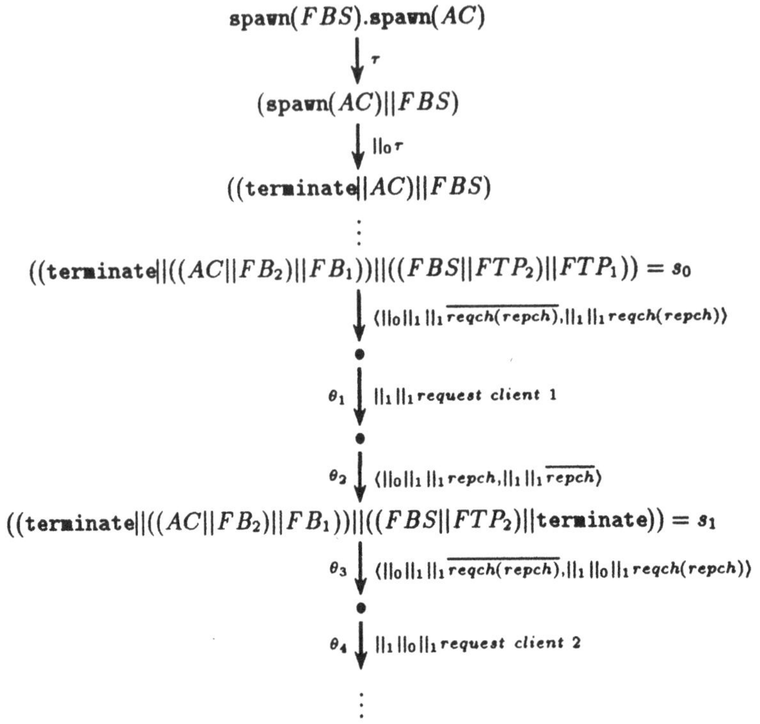

Fig. 2. A computation of the client-server system for mobile agents.

Process causality establishes that

$$\theta_1 = \|_1\|_1\ request\ client\ 1 \sqsubseteq_p \|_1\|_0\|_1\ request\ client\ 2$$

due to the inheritance of causal dependencies through communications. Indeed, $\theta_3 \sqsubseteq_p \theta_4$ because the reader of θ_3 has the same proof part of θ_4; in turn, the writer of θ_3 depends on (the reader of) θ_2, hence $\theta_2 \sqsubseteq_p \theta_3$. Since θ_1 causes (the writer of) θ_2, we have $\theta_1 \sqsubseteq_p \theta_2$. By transitivity, $\theta_1 \sqsubseteq_p \theta_4$. This causal dependency makes evident the misuse of channels.

A first attempt to repair the error was to make FTP recursive through the code

```
proc FTP reqch =
  let val repch = receive reqch
      val _ = print "Request from client\n"
  in send(repch,());activate FTP reqch
  end
```

$FTPreqch=(\lambda repch.repch!.activateFTPreqch)reqch?$

However, the same computation in Fig. 2 can still occur, apart from state s_1 that now becomes equal to s_0. This shows that FTP servers are not private to FB clients. A way out is to make sure that each pair of FTP server and FB shares a private channel. It is implemented by replacing FTP by the above recursive version, and replacing FBS and the body by

```
proc FBS (getch,getinfo) =
  let val fbch = receive getch
      val reqch = channel ()
      val _ = send(fbch,FB(getinfo,reqch))
      val _ = spawn (FTP reqch)
  in activate FBS (getch,getinfo)
  end
```

$FBS(getch,getinfo)=(\lambda fbch.(\lambda reqch.fbch!FB(getinfo,reqch).spawn(FTPreqch).$

$FBS(getch,reqch,getinfo))channel)getch?$

and by, respectively

```
val getag = channel (): unit channel
val getinfo = channel (): unit channel

let
  val getch = channel ()
in spawn (FBS (getch,getinfo));
   spawn (AC (getag,getch))
end
```

$(\lambda getch.spawn(FBC(getch,getinfo)).spawn(AC(getag,getch)))channel$

Now, it is straightforward to prove that a client FB_i communicates with a server FTP_i along a private channel, generated by the same i^{th} activation of FBS that creates FB_i and FTP_i. As any FTP has only one channel, it can serve only its client, and vice versa. Hence the problem has been solved and the bug has been fixed.

6 Conclusion

In this paper we have presented a new operational semantics for the Facile programming language based on the notion of proved transition systems. From this semantics it is possible to derive many different types of information. We have used the semantics to derive information about causal dependencies in Facile programs. The framework is applied to a case study derived from a successful demonstration of agent programming in Facile.

Other types of information that may be derived from the proved semantics, but these were not needed for the analysis presented in this paper. Some of these are studied in the full paper [4].

The proved semantics for Facile is an interesting example of what can be achieved with a programming language based on strong formal foundations since it allows the formal reasoning about properties to be related directly to the running program and thus eliminates the model/running program gap that normally exists in systems with formal specifications, but implementations in traditional programming languages.

Furthermore, since the proved semantics for Facile is based on "normal" transition system definitions (although the labels carry a lot more information) it is possible to (re)-use existing verifier tools like *CWB* [5] and *YAPV* [3]. In particular, the latter has been used to derive the proved computations used here, and to handle machanically the long wired labels.

References

1. K. Ahlers, D. E. Breen, C. Crampton, E. Rose, M. Tucheryan, R. Whitaker, and D. Greer. An augmented vision system for industrial applications. In *SPIE Photonics for Industrial Applications Conference Proceedings*, October 1994.
2. R. Amadio, L. Leth, and B. Thomsen. From a concurrent λ-calculus to the π-calculus. In *Proceedings of FCT'95*, 1995. Full version in technical report ECRC-95-18.
3. A. Bianchi, S. Coluccini, P. Degano, and C. Priami. An efficient verifier of truly concurrent properties. In V. Malyshkin, editor, *Proceedings of PaCT'95, LNCS 964*, pages 36–50. Springer-Verlag, 1995.
4. Roberta Borgia, Pierpaolo Degano, Corrado Priami, Lone Leth, and Bent Thomsen. Understanding mobile agents via a non-interleaving semantics for Facile. Technical Report ECRC-96-4, European Computer-Industry Research Centre, 1996.
5. R. Cleaveland, J. Parrow, and B. Steffen. The concurrency workbench: A semantics-based tool for the verification of concurrent systems. *ACM Transaction on Programming Languages and Systems*, pages 36–72, 1993.
6. P. Degano and C. Priami. Proved trees. In *Proceedings of ICALP'92, LNCS 623*, pages 629–640. Springer-Verlag, 1992.
7. P. Degano and C. Priami. Causality for mobile processes. In *Proceedings of ICALP'95, LNCS 944*, pages 660–671. Springer-Verlag, 1995.
8. Felix Gallo. Agent-Tcl: A white paper. Posted to the `safe-tcl@cs.utk.edu` mailing list, December 1994. Draft document.
9. A. Giacalone, P. Mishra, and S. Prasad. Facile: A symmetric integration of concurrent and functional programming. *International Journal of Parallel Programming*, 18:121–160, 1989.

10. A. Giacalone, P. Mishra, and S. Prasad. Operational and algebraic semantics for Facile: A symmetric integration of concurrent and functional programming. In *Proceedings ICALP'90, LNCS 443*, pages 765–780. Springer-Verlag, 1990.
11. James Gosling and Henry McGilton. The Java language environment. White paper, May 1995. Sun Microsystems, 2550 Garcia Avenue, Mountain View, CA 94043, USA. Available at `http://java.sun.com/`.
12. L. Leth and B. Thomsen. Some Facile Chemistry. *Formal Aspects of Computing, Volume 7, Number 3*, pages 314–328, 1995.
13. C. Priami. *Enhanced Operational Semantics for Concurrency*. PhD thesis, Dipartimento di Informatica, Università di Pisa, March 1996. Available as Tech. Rep. TD-08/96.
14. J.-P. Talpin. The Calumet Experiment in Facile - A Model for Group Communication and Interaction Control in Cooperative Applications. Technical Report ECRC-94-26, European Computer-Industry Research Centre, 1994.
15. J.-P. Talpin, P. Marchal, and K.: Ahlers. Calumet - A Reference Manual. Technical Report ECRC-94-30, European Computer-Industry Research Centre, 1994.
16. B. Thomsen, F. Knabe, L. Leth, and P.-Y. Chevalier. Mobile agents set to work. *Communications International*, July 1995.
17. B. Thomsen, L. Leth, and A. Giacalone. Some Issues in the Semantics of Facile Distributed Programming. In *Proceedings of the 1992 REX Workshop on "Semantics: Foundations and Applications"*, LNCS 666. Springer-Verlag, 1992.
18. B. Thomsen, L. Leth., F. Knabe, and P.-Y. Chevalier. Mobile agents. Technical Report ECRC-95-21, European Computer-Industry Research Centre, 1995.
19. B. Thomsen, L. Leth, S. Prasad, T.-M. Kuo, A. Kramer, F. Knabe, and A. Giacalone. Facile Antigua Release Programming Guide. Technical Report ECRC-93-20, European Computer-Industry Research Centre, 1993.
20. James E. White. Telescript technology: The foundation for the electronic marketplace. General Magic white paper, 2465 Latham Street, Mountain View, CA 94040, 1994.

Termination Analysis for Partial Functions*

Jürgen Brauburger and Jürgen Giesl

FB Informatik, TH Darmstadt, Alexanderstr. 10, 64283 Darmstadt, Germany
E-mail: {brauburger|giesl}@inferenzsysteme.informatik.th-darmstadt.de

Abstract. This paper deals with automated termination analysis for *partial functional programs*, i.e. for functional programs which do not terminate for each input. We present a method to determine their *domains* (resp. non-trivial subsets of their domains) *automatically*. More precisely, for each functional program a *termination predicate* algorithm is synthesized, which only returns true for inputs where the program is terminating. To ease subsequent reasoning about the generated termination predicates we also present a procedure for their simplification.

1 Introduction

Termination of algorithms is a central problem in software development and formal methods for termination analysis are essential for program verification. While most work on the automation of termination proofs has been done in the areas of *term rewriting systems* (for surveys see e.g. [Der87, Ste95]) and of *logic programs* (e.g. [UV88, Plü90, SD94]), in this paper we focus on *functional programs*.

Up to now all methods for automated termination analysis of functional programs (e.g. [BM79, Wal88, Hol91, Wal94b, NN95, Gie95b, Gie95c]) aim to prove that a program terminates for *each* input. However, if the termination proof fails then these methods provide no means to find a (sub-)domain where termination is provable. Therefore these methods cannot be used to analyze the termination behaviour of *partial* functional programs, i.e. of programs which do not terminate for all inputs [BM88].

In this paper we automate Manna's approach for termination analysis of "partial programs" [Man74]: For every algorithm defining a function f there has to be a *termination predicate*[1] θ_f which specifies the "admissible input" of f (i.e. evaluation of f must terminate for each input admitted by the termination predicate). But while in [Man74] termination predicates have to be provided by the user, in this paper we present a technique to synthesize them *automatically*.

In Section 2 we introduce our functional programming language and sketch the basic approach for proving termination of algorithms. Then in Section 3 we show the requirements termination predicates have to satisfy and based on these requirements we present a procedure for the automated synthesis of termination

* This work was supported by the Deutsche Forschungsgemeinschaft under grant no. Wa 652/7-1 as part of the focus program "Deduktion".

[1] Instead of "termination predicates" Manna uses the notion of "input predicates".

predicates[2] in Section 4. The generated termination predicates can be used both for further automated and interactive program analysis. To ease the handling of these termination predicates we have developed a procedure for their simplification which is introduced in Section 5. Finally, we give a summary of our method and illustrate its power with a collection of examples (Section 6).

2 Termination of Algorithms

In this paper we regard an eager first-order functional language with (free) algebraic data types. To simplify the presentation we restrict ourselves to non-parameterized types and to functions without mutual recursion (see the conclusion for a discussion of possible extensions of our method).

As an example consider the algebraic data type nat for natural numbers. Its objects are built with the *constructors* 0 and succ and we use a *selector* pred as an inverse function to succ (with $\mathsf{pred}(\mathsf{succ}(x)) = x$ and $\mathsf{pred}(0) = 0$, i.e. pred is a total function). To ease readability we often write "1" instead of "succ(0)" etc. For each data type s there must be a pre-defined equality function "=" : $s \times s \to \mathsf{bool}$. Then the following algorithm defines the subtraction function:

$$\begin{array}{l} \textit{function}\ \mathsf{minus}(x, y : \mathsf{nat}) : \mathsf{nat} \Leftarrow \\ \quad \textit{if}\ \ x = y\ \ \textit{then}\ 0 \\ \qquad\qquad\quad \textit{else}\ \ \mathsf{succ}(\mathsf{minus}(\mathsf{pred}(x), y)). \end{array}$$

In our language, the body q of an algorithm "*function* $\mathsf{f}(x_1 : s_1, \ldots, x_n : s_n) : s \Leftarrow q$" is a term built from the variables $x_1, \ldots, x_n$, constructors, selectors, equality function symbols, function symbols defined by algorithms, and conditionals (where we write "*if* t_1 *then* t_2 *else* t_3" instead of "*if*(t_1, t_2, t_3)"). These conditionals are the only functions with non-eager semantics, i.e. when evaluating "*if* t_1 *then* t_2 *else* t_3", the (boolean) term t_1 is evaluated first and depending on the result of its evaluation either t_2 or t_3 is evaluated afterwards.

To prove *termination* of an algorithm one has to show that in each recursive call a given *measure* is decreased. For that purpose a *measure function* $|.|$ is used which maps a tuple of data objects $t_1, \ldots, t_n$ to a natural number $|t_1, \ldots, t_n|$. In the following we often abbreviate tuples $t_1, \ldots t_n$ by t^*.

For example, one might attempt to prove termination of minus with the *size* measure $|.|_\#$, where the size of an object of type nat is the number it represents (i.e. the number of succ's it contains). So we have $|0|_\# = 0$, $|\mathsf{succ}(0)|_\# = 1$ etc. As minus is a binary function, for its termination proof we need a measure function on pairs of data objects. Therefore we extend the size measure function to pairs by measuring a pair by the size of the first object, i.e. $|t_1, t_2|_\# = |t_1|_\#$. Hence, to prove termination of minus we now have to verify the following inequality for

[2] Strictly speaking, we synthesize *algorithms* which compute termination predicates. For the sake of brevity sometimes we also refer to these algorithms as "termination predicates".

all instantiations of x and y where $x \neq y$ holds[3]:

$$|\mathsf{pred}(x), y|_\# < |x, y|_\#. \tag{1}$$

But the algorithm for minus does not terminate for all inputs, i.e. minus is a *partial* function (in fact, $\mathsf{minus}(x, y)$ only terminates if the number x is not smaller than the number y). For instance, the call $\mathsf{minus}(0, 2)$ leads to the recursive call $\mathsf{minus}(\mathsf{pred}(0), 2)$. As $\mathsf{pred}(0)$ is evaluated to 0, this results in calling $\mathsf{minus}(0, 2)$ again. Hence, evaluation of $\mathsf{minus}(0, 2)$ is not terminating. Consequently, our termination proof for minus must fail. For example, (1) is not satisfied if x is 0 and y is 2.

Instead of proving that an algorithm terminates for *all* inputs (*absolute* termination), in the following we are interested in finding subsets of inputs where the algorithms are terminating. Hence, for each algorithm defining a function f we want to generate a *termination predicate* algorithm θ_f where evaluation of θ_f always terminates and if θ_f returns true for some input t^* then evaluation of $\mathsf{f}(t^*)$ terminates, too.

Definition 1. Let $\mathsf{f} : \mathsf{s}_1 \times \ldots \times \mathsf{s}_n \to \mathsf{s}$ be defined by a (possibly non-terminating) algorithm. A *total* function $\theta_\mathsf{f} : \mathsf{s}_1 \times \ldots \times \mathsf{s}_n \to \mathsf{bool}$ is a **termination predicate** for f iff for all tuples t^* of data objects, $\theta_\mathsf{f}(t^*) = \mathsf{true}$ implies that the evaluation of $\mathsf{f}(t^*)$ is terminating.

Of course the problem of determining the *exact* domains of functions is undecidable. As we want to generate termination predicates automatically we therefore only demand that a termination predicate θ_f represents a *sufficient* criterion for the termination of f's algorithm. So in general, a function f may have an infinite number of termination predicates and false is a termination predicate for each function. But of course our aim is to synthesize weaker termination predicates, i.e. termination predicates which return true as often as possible.

3 Requirements for Termination Predicates

In this section we introduce two requirements that are sufficient for termination predicates, i.e. if a (terminating) algorithm satisfies these requirements then it defines a termination predicate for the function under consideration. A procedure for the automated synthesis of such algorithms will be presented in Section 4.

First, we consider simple partial functions like minus (Section 3.1) and subsequently we will also examine algorithms which call other partial functions (Section 3.2).

3.1 Termination Predicates for Simple Partial Functions

We resume our example and generate a termination predicate θ_minus such that evaluation of $\mathsf{minus}(x, y)$ terminates if $\theta_\mathsf{minus}(x, y)$ is true. Recall that for proving absolute termination one has to show that a certain measure is decreased in

[3] We often use "$t \neq r$" as an abbreviation for $\neg(t = r)$, where the boolean function $\neg$ is defined by an (obvious) algorithm.

each recursive call. But as we illustrated, the algorithm for minus is not always terminating and therefore inequality (1) does not hold for all instantiations of x and y which lead to a recursive call. Hence, the central idea for the construction of a termination predicate θ_{minus} is to let θ_{minus} return true only for those inputs x and y where the measure of x and y is greater than the measure of the corresponding recursive call and to return false for all other inputs. So if evaluation of $\mathsf{minus}(x, y)$ leads to a recursive call (i.e. if $x \neq y$ holds), then $\theta_{\mathsf{minus}}(x, y)$ may only return true if the measure $|\mathsf{pred}(x), y|_{\#}$ is smaller than $|x, y|_{\#}$. This yields the following requirement for a termination predicate θ_{minus}:

$$\theta_{\mathsf{minus}}(x, y) \wedge x \neq y \rightarrow |\mathsf{pred}(x), y|_{\#} < |x, y|_{\#}. \tag{2}$$

For example, the function defined by the following algorithm satisfies (2):

$$\begin{array}{l} \textit{function}\ \theta_{\mathsf{minus}}(x, y : \mathsf{nat}) : \mathsf{bool} \Leftarrow \\ \quad \textit{if}\ \ x = y\ \ \textit{then}\ \mathsf{true} \\ \qquad\qquad\qquad\ \ \textit{else}\ \ |\mathsf{pred}(x), y|_{\#} < |x, y|_{\#}. \end{array}$$

This algorithm for θ_{minus} uses the same case analysis as minus. Since minus terminates in its non-recursive case (i.e. if $x = y$), the corresponding result of θ_{minus} is true. For the recursive case (if $x \neq y$), θ_{minus} returns true iff $|\mathsf{pred}(x), y)|_{\#} < |x, y|_{\#}$ is true. We assume that each measure function $|.|$ is defined by a (terminating) algorithm. Hence, in the result of the second case θ_{minus} calls the algorithm for the computation of the size measure $|.|_{\#}$ and it also calls a (terminating) algorithm to compute the less-than relation "<" on natural numbers.

So in general, given an algorithm for f we demand the following requirement for termination predicates θ_{f} (where $|.|$ is an arbitrary measure function):

$$\begin{array}{l} \text{If evaluation of } \mathsf{f}(t^*) \text{ leads to a recursive call } \mathsf{f}(r^*), \\ \text{then } \theta_{\mathsf{f}}(t^*) \text{ may only return true if } |r^*| < |t^*| \text{ holds.} \end{array} \tag{Req1}$$

However, (Req1) is not a *sufficient* requirement for termination predicates. For instance, the function θ_{minus} defined above is not a termination predicate for minus although it satisfies requirement (Req1). The reason is that $\theta_{\mathsf{minus}}(1, 2)$ returns true (as $|\mathsf{pred}(1), 2|_{\#} < |1, 2|_{\#}$ holds). But evaluation of $\mathsf{minus}(1, 2)$ is not terminating because its evaluation leads to the (non-terminating) recursive call $\mathsf{minus}(0, 2)$.

This non-termination is not recognized by θ_{minus} because $\theta_{\mathsf{minus}}(1, 2)$ only checks if the arguments $(0, 2)$ of the *next* recursive call of minus are smaller than the input $(1, 2)$. But it is not guaranteed that *subsequent* recursive calls are also measure decreasing. For example, the next recursive call with the arguments $(0, 2)$ will lead to a subsequent recursive call of minus with the same arguments, i.e. in the subsequent recursive call the measure of the arguments remains the same. For that reason $\theta_{\mathsf{minus}}(1, 2)$ evaluates to true, but application of θ_{minus} to the arguments $(0, 2)$ of the following recursive call yields false.

Therefore in addition to (Req1) we must demand that a termination predicate θ_{f} remains valid for each recursive call in f's algorithm. This ensures that subsequent recursive calls are also measure decreasing:

$$\text{If evaluation of } \mathsf{f}(t^*) \text{ leads to a recursive call } \mathsf{f}(r^*), \text{ then } \theta_{\mathsf{f}}(t^*) \text{ may only return true if } \theta_{\mathsf{f}}(r^*) \text{ is also true.} \tag{3}$$

In our example, to satisfy the requirements (Req1) and (3) we modify the result of θ_{minus}'s second case by demanding that θ_{minus} also holds for the following recursive call of minus:

$$\begin{array}{l} \textit{function } \theta_{\mathsf{minus}}(x, y : \mathsf{nat}) : \mathsf{bool} \Leftarrow \\ \quad \textit{if } \; x = y \; \textit{ then } \mathsf{true} \\ \qquad\qquad\quad \textit{else } \; |\mathsf{pred}(x), y|_{\#} < |x, y|_{\#} \; \wedge \; \theta_{\mathsf{minus}}(\mathsf{pred}(x), y). \end{array}$$

In this algorithm we use the boolean function symbol $\wedge$ to ease readability, where $\varphi_1 \wedge \varphi_2$ abbreviates "*if* φ_1 *then* φ_2 *else* false". Hence, the semantics of the function $\wedge$ are *not* eager. So terms in a conjunction are evaluated from left to right, i.e. given a conjunction $\varphi_1 \wedge \varphi_2$ of boolean terms (which we also refer to as "formulas"), φ_1 is evaluated first. If the value of φ_1 is false, then false is returned, otherwise φ_2 is evaluated and its value is returned. Note that we need a *lazy* conjunction function $\wedge$ to ensure termination of θ_{minus}. It guarantees that evaluation of $\theta_{\mathsf{minus}}(x, y)$ can only lead to a recursive call $\theta_{\mathsf{minus}}(\mathsf{pred}(x), y)$ if the measure of the recursive arguments $|\mathsf{pred}(x), y|_{\#}$ is smaller than the measure of the inputs $|x, y|_{\#}$.

The above algorithm really defines a termination predicate for minus, i.e. θ_{minus} is a total function and the truth of θ_{minus} is sufficient for the termination of minus. This algorithm for θ_{minus} was constructed in order to obtain an algorithm satisfying the requirements (Req1) and (3). In Section 4 we will show that this construction can easily be automated. A closer look at θ_{minus} reveals that we have synthesized an algorithm which computes the usual greater-equal relation "$\geq$" on natural numbers. As $\mathsf{minus}(x, y)$ is *only* terminating if x is greater than or equal to y, in this example we have even generated the weakest possible termination predicate, i.e. θ_{minus} returns true not only for a subset but for *all* elements of the domain of minus.

3.2 Algorithms Calling Other Partial Functions

In general (Req1) and (3) are not sufficient criteria for termination predicates. These requirements can only be used for algorithms like minus which (apart from recursive calls) only call other *total* functions (like $=$, succ, and pred).

In this section we will examine algorithms which call other *partial* functions. As an example consider the algorithm for $\mathsf{list\_minus}(l, y)$ which subtracts the number y from all elements of a list l. Objects of the data type list are built with the constructors empty and add, where $\mathsf{add}(x, k)$ represents the insertion of the number x into the list k. We also use the selectors head and tail, where head returns the first element of a list and tail returns a list without its first element (i.e. $\mathsf{head}(\mathsf{add}(x, k)) = x$, $\mathsf{head}(\mathsf{empty}) = 0$, $\mathsf{tail}(\mathsf{add}(x, k)) = k$, $\mathsf{tail}(\mathsf{empty}) = \mathsf{empty}$).

$$\begin{array}{l}
\textit{function}\ \mathsf{list_minus}(l : \mathsf{list}, y : \mathsf{nat}) : \mathsf{list} \Leftarrow \\
\quad \textit{if}\ \ l = \mathsf{empty}\ \ \textit{then}\ \mathsf{empty} \\
\qquad\qquad\qquad\qquad \textit{else}\ \ \mathsf{add}(\mathsf{minus}(\mathsf{head}(l), y), \mathsf{list_minus}(\mathsf{tail}(l), y)).
\end{array}$$

We construct the following algorithm for $\theta_{\mathsf{list\_minus}}$ by measuring pairs $|l, y|_\#$ by the *size* of the first object $|l|_\#$ again, where the size of a list is its length.

$$\begin{array}{l}
\textit{function}\ \theta_{\mathsf{list_minus}}(l : \mathsf{list}, y : \mathsf{nat}) : \mathsf{bool} \Leftarrow \\
\quad \textit{if}\ \ l = \mathsf{empty}\ \ \textit{then}\ \mathsf{true} \\
\qquad\qquad\qquad\qquad \textit{else}\ \ |\mathsf{tail}(l), y|_\# < |l, y|_\# \wedge \theta_{\mathsf{list_minus}}(\mathsf{tail}(l), y).
\end{array}$$

But although this algorithm defines a function which satisfies (Req1) and (3), it is not a termination predicate for list_minus. The reason is that $\theta_{\mathsf{list\_minus}}(\mathsf{add}(0, \mathsf{empty}), 2)$ evaluates to true because the size of the empty list is smaller than the size of $\mathsf{add}(0, \mathsf{empty})$. But evaluation of $\mathsf{list\_minus}(\mathsf{add}(0, \mathsf{empty}), 2)$ is not terminating as it leads to the (non-terminating) evaluation of $\mathsf{minus}(0, 2)$.

The problem is that $\theta_{\mathsf{list\_minus}}$ only checks if *recursive* calls of list_minus are measure decreasing but it does not guarantee the termination of *other* algorithms called. Therefore we have to demand that $\theta_{\mathsf{list\_minus}}$ ensures termination of the subsequent call of minus, i.e. in the second case $\theta_{\mathsf{list\_minus}}(l, y)$ must imply $\theta_{\mathsf{minus}}(\mathsf{head}(l), y)$.

So we replace (3) by a requirement that guarantees the truth of $\theta_{\mathsf{g}}(r^*)$ for *all* function calls $\mathsf{g}(r^*)$ in f's algorithm (i.e. also for functions g different from f):

If evaluation of $\mathsf{f}(t^*)$ leads to a function call $\mathsf{g}(r^*)$, then $\theta_{\mathsf{f}}(t^*)$ may only return true if $\theta_{\mathsf{g}}(r^*)$ is also true. (Req2)

Note that (Req2) must also be demanded for non-recursive cases. The function $\theta_{\mathsf{list\_minus}}$ defined by the following algorithm satisfies (Req1) and the extended requirement (Req2):

$$\begin{array}{l}
\textit{function}\ \theta_{\mathsf{list_minus}}(l : \mathsf{list}, y : \mathsf{nat}) : \mathsf{bool} \Leftarrow \\
\quad \textit{if}\ \ l = \mathsf{empty}\ \ \textit{then}\ \mathsf{true} \\
\qquad\qquad\qquad\qquad \textit{else}\ \ \theta_{\mathsf{minus}}(\mathsf{head}(l), y) \wedge |\mathsf{tail}(l), y|_\# < |l, y|_\# \wedge \theta_{\mathsf{list_minus}}(\mathsf{tail}(l), y).
\end{array}$$

The above algorithm in fact defines a termination predicate for list_minus. Analyzing the algorithm one notices that $\theta_{\mathsf{list\_minus}}(l, y)$ returns true iff all elements of l are greater than or equal to y. As evaluation of $\mathsf{list\_minus}(l, y)$ only terminates for such inputs, we have synthesized the weakest possible termination predicate again.

Note that algorithms may also call partial functions in their *conditions*. For example consider the algorithm for half which calls minus in its conditions:

$$\begin{array}{l}
\textit{function}\ \mathsf{half}(x : \mathsf{nat}) : \mathsf{nat} \Leftarrow \\
\quad \textit{if}\ \ \mathsf{minus}(x, 2) = 0\ \ \textit{then}\ 1 \\
\qquad\qquad\qquad\qquad \textit{else}\ \ \mathsf{succ}(\mathsf{half}(\mathsf{minus}(x, 2))).
\end{array}$$

This algorithm does not terminate for the inputs 0 or 1, since in the conditions the term minus$(x, 2)$ must be evaluated. Therefore due to (Req2), θ_{half} must ensure that all calls of the partial function minus in the conditions are terminating, i.e. $\theta_{\mathsf{half}}(x)$ must imply $\theta_{\mathsf{minus}}(x, 2)$. The following algorithm for θ_{half} satisfies both requirements (Req1) and (Req2):

function $\theta_{\mathsf{half}}(x : \mathsf{nat}) : \mathsf{bool} \Leftarrow$
  $\theta_{\mathsf{minus}}(x, 2) \;\wedge\; (\mathit{if}\;\; \mathsf{minus}(x, 2) = 0$
    then true
    else $\theta_{\mathsf{minus}}(x, 2) \wedge |\mathsf{minus}(x, 2)|_{\#} < |x|_{\#} \wedge \theta_{\mathsf{half}}(\mathsf{minus}(x, 2)))$.

The above algorithm first checks if the call of the algorithm minus in the conditions of half is terminating. If the corresponding termination predicate $\theta_{\mathsf{minus}}(x, 2)$ is false, then θ_{half} also returns false. Otherwise, evaluation of θ_{half} continues as usual.

This algorithm really defines a termination predicate for half. Analysis of θ_{half} reveals that we have synthesized the "even"-algorithm (for numbers greater than 0) which again is the weakest possible termination predicate for half.

The following lemma states that the two requirements we have derived are in fact sufficient for termination predicates.

Lemma 2. *If a total function* θ_{f} *satisfies the requirements (Req1) and (Req2) then* θ_{f} *is a termination predicate for* f.

Proof. Suppose that there exist data objects t^* such that $\theta_{\mathsf{f}}(t^*)$ returns true but evaluation of $\mathsf{f}(t^*)$ does not terminate. Then let t^* be the smallest such data objects, i.e. for all objects r^* with a measure $|r^*|$ smaller than $|t^*|$ the truth of $\theta_{\mathsf{f}}(r^*)$ implies termination of $\mathsf{f}(r^*)$.

As we have excluded mutual recursion we may assume that for all other functions g (which are called by f) the predicate θ_{g} really is a termination predicate. Hence, requirement (Req2) ensures that evaluation of $f(t^*)$ can only lead to terminating calls of *other* functions g. Therefore the non-termination of $f(t^*)$ cannot be caused by another function g.

So evaluation of $\mathsf{f}(t^*)$ must lead to recursive calls $\mathsf{f}(r^*)$. But because of requirement (Req1), r^* has a smaller measure than t^*. Hence, due to the minimality of t^*, $\mathsf{f}(r^*)$ must be terminating (as (Req2) ensures that $\theta_{\mathsf{f}}(r^*)$ also returns true). So the recursive calls of f cannot cause non-termination either. Therefore evaluation of $\mathsf{f}(t^*)$ must also be terminating. □

4 Automated Generation of Termination Predicates

In this section we show how algorithms defining termination predicates can be synthesized automatically. Given a functional program f, we present a technique to generate a (terminating) algorithm for θ_{f} satisfying the requirements (Req1) and (Req2). Then due to Lemma 2 this algorithm defines a termination predicate for f.

Requirement (Req2) demands that θ_f may only return true if evaluation of all terms in the conditions and results of f is terminating. Therefore we extend the idea of termination predicates from *algorithms* to arbitrary *terms*.

Hence, for each term t we construct a boolean term $\Theta(t)$ (a *termination formula* for t) such that evaluation of $\Theta(t)$ is terminating and $\Theta(t)$ = true implies that evaluation of t is also terminating[4]. For example, a termination formula for $\mathsf{half}(\mathsf{minus}(x,2))$ is $\theta_{\mathsf{minus}}(x,2) \wedge \theta_{\mathsf{half}}(\mathsf{minus}(x,2))$, because due to the eager nature of our functional language in this term minus is evaluated before evaluating half. So termination formulas have to guarantee that a subterm $\mathsf{g}(r^*)$ is only evaluated if $\theta_{\mathsf{g}}(r^*)$ holds. In general, *termination formulas* are constructed by the following rules:

$$\begin{aligned}
&\Theta(x) &&:\equiv \text{true}, && \text{for variables } x, \quad \text{(i)}\\
&\Theta(\mathsf{g}(r_1,\ldots,r_n)) &&:\equiv \Theta(r_1)\wedge\ldots\wedge\Theta(r_n)\wedge\theta_{\mathsf{g}}(r_1,\ldots,r_n), && \text{for functions } \mathsf{g}, \quad \text{(ii)}\\
&\Theta(\mathit{if}\ r_1\ \mathit{then}\ r_2\ \mathit{else}\ r_3) &&:\equiv \Theta(r_1)\wedge \mathit{if}\ r_1\ \mathit{then}\ \Theta(r_2)\ \mathit{else}\ \Theta(r_3). && \quad \text{(iii)}
\end{aligned}$$

Note that in rule (ii), if g is a constructor, a selector, or an equality function, then we have $\theta_{\mathsf{g}}(x^*)$ = true, because those functions are total.

To satisfy requirement (Req2) θ_f must ensure that evaluation of all terms in the body of an algorithm f terminates. So if f is defined by the algorithm "*function* $\mathsf{f}(x_1 : s_1,\ldots,x_n : s_n) : s \Leftarrow q$", then θ_f has to check whether the termination formula $\Theta(q)$ of f's body is true.

But the body of f can also contain recursive calls $\mathsf{f}(r^*)$. To satisfy requirement (Req1) we must additionally ensure that the measure $|r^*|$ of recursive calls is smaller than the measure of the inputs $|x^*|$. Therefore for recursive calls $\mathsf{f}(r^*)$ we have to change the definition of *termination formulas* as follows:

$$\Theta(\mathsf{f}(r_1,\ldots,r_n)) :\equiv \Theta(r_1)\wedge\ldots\wedge\Theta(r_n)\wedge|r_1,\ldots,r_n| < |x_1,\ldots,x_n| \wedge \theta_{\mathsf{f}}(r_1,\ldots,r_n) \quad \text{(iv)}$$

In this way we obtain the following procedure for the generation of termination predicates.

Theorem 3. *Given an algorithm "function* $\mathsf{f}(x_1 : s_1,\ldots,x_n : s_n) : s \Leftarrow q$*", we define the algorithm "function* $\theta_f(x_1 : s_1,\ldots,x_n : s_n) : \mathsf{bool} \Leftarrow \Theta(q)$*", where the termination formula* $\Theta(q)$ *is constructed by the rules (i) - (iv). Then this algorithm defines a termination predicate* θ_f *for* f *(i.e. this algorithm is terminating and if* $\theta_f(t^*)$ *returns* true*, then evaluation of* $\mathsf{f}(t^*)$ *is also terminating).*

Proof. By the definition of termination formulas, algorithms generated according to Theorem 3 are *terminating*, because evaluation of $\theta_f(t^*)$ can only lead to a *recursive* call $\theta_f(r^*)$ if the measure $|r^*|$ is smaller than $|t^*|$ and because calls of *other* functions $\mathsf{g}(s^*)$ can only be evaluated if $\theta_{\mathsf{g}}(s^*)$ holds.

Moreover, by construction the generated algorithm defines a function θ_f which satisfies the requirements (Req1) and (Req2) we presented in Section 3. Due to

[4] More precisely, this implication holds for each substitution σ of t's variables by data objects: For all such σ, evaluation of $\sigma(\Theta(t))$ is terminating and $\sigma(\Theta(t))$ = true implies that the evaluation of $\sigma(t)$ is also terminating.

Lemma 2 this implies that θ_f must be a termination predicate for f, i.e. it is total and it is sufficient for termination of f. □

The construction of algorithms for termination predicates according to Theorem 3 can be directly automated. So by this theorem we have developed a procedure for the automated generation of termination predicates. For instance, the termination predicate algorithms for minus, list_minus, and half in the last section were built according to Theorem 3 (where for the sake of brevity we omitted termination predicates for *total* functions because such predicates always return true). As demonstrated, the generated termination predicates often are as weak as possible, i.e. they often describe the *whole* domain of the partial function under consideration (instead of just a sub-domain).

5 Simplification of Termination Predicates

In the last section we presented a method for the automated generation of algorithms which define termination predicates. But sometimes the synthesized algorithms are unnecessarily complex. To ease subsequent reasoning about termination predicates in the following sections we introduce a procedure to *simplify* the generated termination predicate algorithms which consists of four steps.

5.1 Application of Induction Lemmata

First, the well-known induction lemma method by *R. S. Boyer* and *J S. Moore* [BM79] is used to eliminate (some of) the inequalities $|r^*| < |x^*|$ (which ensure that recursive calls are measure decreasing) from the termination predicate algorithms. Elimination of these inequalities simplifies the algorithms considerably and often enables the execution of subsequent simplification steps.

An *induction lemma* points out that under a certain hypothesis δ some operation drives some measure down, i.e. induction lemmata have the form

$$\delta \longrightarrow |r^*| < |x^*|.$$

In the system of Boyer and Moore induction lemmata have to be provided by the *user*. However, *C. Walther* presented a method to generate a certain class of induction lemmata for the *size* measure function $|.|_\#$ *automatically* [Wal94b] and we recently generalized his approach towards measure functions based on arbitrary *polynomial norms* [Gie95b]. For instance, the induction lemma needed in the following example can be synthesized by Walther's and our method.

While Boyer and Moore use induction lemmata for absolute termination proofs, we will now illustrate their use for the simplification of termination predicate algorithms. As an example consider the following algorithm:

function quotient(x, y : nat) : nat $\Leftarrow$
  if $x < y$ *then* 0
        else succ(quotient(minus(x, y), y)).

Using the procedure of Theorem 3 the following termination predicate algorithm is generated. In this algorithm we again neglect the call of the termination predicate $\theta_<$ as "$<$" is defined by an (absolutely) terminating algorithm and therefore $\theta_<$ always returns true.

function $\theta_{\mathsf{quotient}}(x, y : \mathsf{nat}) : \mathsf{bool} \Leftarrow$
  if $x < y$ *then* true
    else $\theta_{\mathsf{minus}}(x, y) \wedge |\mathsf{minus}(x, y), y|_{\#} < |x, y|_{\#} \wedge \theta_{\mathsf{quotient}}(\mathsf{minus}(x, y), y)$.

We know that in the result of $\theta_{\mathsf{quotient}}$ the term $\mathsf{minus}(x, y)$ will only be evaluated if this evaluation is terminating, i.e. if $\theta_{\mathsf{minus}}(x, y)$ holds. So in order to eliminate the inequality occurring in the result of $\theta_{\mathsf{quotient}}$'s second case, we look for an induction lemma which states that provided minus is terminating the measure of $|\mathsf{minus}(x, y), y|_{\#}$ is smaller than $|x, y|_{\#}$ under some hypothesis δ. Hence, we search for an induction lemma of the form

$$\theta_{\mathsf{minus}}(x, y) \wedge \delta \rightarrow |\mathsf{minus}(x, y), y|_{\#} < |x, y|_{\#}.$$

For instance, we can use the following induction lemma which states that (provided $\mathsf{minus}(x, y)$ terminates) the result of $\mathsf{minus}(x, y)$ is smaller than its first argument x, if both x and y are not 0:

$$\theta_{\mathsf{minus}}(x, y) \wedge x \neq 0 \wedge y \neq 0 \rightarrow |\mathsf{minus}(x, y), y|_{\#} < |x, y|_{\#}.$$

As in the result of $\theta_{\mathsf{quotient}}$ the truth of $\theta_{\mathsf{minus}}(x, y)$ is guaranteed before evaluating the inequality $|\mathsf{minus}(x, y), y|_{\#} < |x, y|_{\#}$ we can now replace this inequality by $x \neq 0 \wedge y \neq 0$ which yields the following simplified algorithm:

function $\theta_{\mathsf{quotient}}(x, y : \mathsf{nat}) : \mathsf{bool} \Leftarrow$
  if $x < y$ *then* true
    else $\theta_{\mathsf{minus}}(x, y) \wedge x \neq 0 \wedge y \neq 0 \wedge \theta_{\mathsf{quotient}}(\mathsf{minus}(x, y), y)$.

So in general, if the body of an algorithm contains an inequality $|r^*| < |x^*|$ which will only be evaluated under the condition ψ, then our simplification procedure looks for an induction lemma of the form

$$\psi \wedge \delta \rightarrow |r^*| < |x^*|.$$

If such an induction lemma is known (or can be synthesized) then the inequality $|r^*| < |x^*|$ is replaced by δ.

5.2 Subsumption Elimination

In the next simplification step *redundant terms* are *eliminated* from the termination predicate algorithms. Recall that θ_{minus} computes the greater-equal relation "$\geq$" on natural numbers. Hence the condition of $\theta_{\mathsf{quotient}}$'s second case implies the truth of $\theta_{\mathsf{minus}}(x, y)$, i.e. we can verify

$$x \not< y \rightarrow \theta_{\mathsf{minus}}(x, y). \qquad (4)$$

For that reason the *subsumed term* $\theta_{\mathsf{minus}}(x, y)$ may be eliminated from the second case of $\theta_{\mathsf{quotient}}$ which yields

$$\begin{aligned} &\textit{if } x < y \textit{ then } \mathsf{true} \\ &\qquad\qquad \textit{else } x \neq 0 \wedge y \neq 0 \wedge \theta_{\mathsf{quotient}}(\mathsf{minus}(x,y),y). \end{aligned}$$

Note that evaluation of the terms $x \neq 0$ and $y \neq 0$ is always terminating (i.e. their termination formulas $\Theta(x \neq 0)$ and $\Theta(y \neq 0)$ are both true). Hence, the order of the terms $x \neq 0$ and $y \neq 0$ can be changed without affecting the semantics of $\theta_{\mathsf{quotient}}$. Then in the result of $\theta_{\mathsf{quotient}}$'s second case the term $x \neq 0$ will only be evaluated under the condition $x \not< y \wedge y \neq 0$. But this condition again implies the truth of $x \neq 0$, i.e. we can easily verify

$$x \not< y \wedge y \neq 0 \rightarrow x \neq 0. \tag{5}$$

Hence, the *subsumed term* $x \neq 0$ can also be eliminated which results in the following algorithm for $\theta_{\mathsf{quotient}}$:

$$\begin{aligned} &\textit{function } \theta_{\mathsf{quotient}}(x, y : \mathsf{nat}) : \mathsf{bool} \Leftarrow \\ &\quad \textit{if } x < y \textit{ then } \mathsf{true} \\ &\qquad\qquad \textit{else } y \neq 0 \wedge \theta_{\mathsf{quotient}}(\mathsf{minus}(x,y),y). \end{aligned}$$

According to [Wal94b] we call formulas like (4) and (5) *subsumption formulas*. So in general, if a term ψ_2 will only be evaluated under the condition ψ_1 and if the subsumption formula $\psi_1 \rightarrow \psi_2$ can be verified, then our simplification procedure replaces the term ψ_2 by true. (Subsequently of course, in a conjunction the term true may be eliminated.)

For the automated verification of subsumption formulas an *induction theorem proving system* is used (e.g. one of those described in [BM79, Bi$^+$86, Bu$^+$90, Wal94a]). For instance, the subsumption formula (4) can be verified by an easy induction proof and subsumption formula (5) can already be proved by case analysis and propositional reasoning only.

5.3 Recursion Elimination

To apply the following simplification step recall that $\varphi_1 \wedge \varphi_2$ is an abbreviation for "*if* φ_1 *then* φ_2 *else* false". Hence, the algorithm for $\theta_{\mathsf{quotient}}$ in fact reads as follows:

$$\begin{aligned} &\textit{function } \theta_{\mathsf{quotient}}(x, y : \mathsf{nat}) : \mathsf{bool} \Leftarrow \\ &\quad \textit{if } x < y \textit{ then } \mathsf{true} \\ &\qquad\qquad \textit{else } (\textit{if } y \neq 0 \textit{ then } \theta_{\mathsf{quotient}}(\mathsf{minus}(x,y),y) \\ &\qquad\qquad\qquad\qquad\qquad \textit{else } \mathsf{false}). \end{aligned}$$

So this algorithm has three *cases*, where the first case has the *result* true which is only evaluated under the *condition* $x < y$, the second case has the result $\theta_{\mathsf{quotient}}(\mathsf{minus}(x,y),y)$ and the corresponding condition $x \not< y \wedge y \neq 0$, and the third case has the result false and the condition $x \not< y \wedge y = 0$.

Now we *eliminate* the *recursive call* of $\theta_{\mathsf{quotient}}$ according to the *recursion elimination* technique of Walther [Wal94b]. If we can verify that evaluation of a recursive call $\theta_f(r^*)$ always yields the same result (i.e. it always yields true or it always yields false) then we can replace the recursive call $\theta_f(r^*)$ by this result. In this way it is possible to replace the recursive call of $\theta_{\mathsf{quotient}}$ by the value true. The reason is that each recursive call $\theta_{\mathsf{quotient}}(\mathsf{minus}(x,y),y)$ evaluates to true.

More precisely, the parameters $(\text{minus}(x,y), y)$ of the recursive call either satisfy the condition of θ_{quotient}'s first case (i.e. $\text{minus}(x,y) < y$) or they satisfy the condition of θ_{quotient}'s second case (i.e. $\text{minus}(x,y) \not< y \wedge y \neq 0$). This property is expressed by the following formula:

$$x \not< y \wedge y \neq 0 \;\rightarrow\; \text{minus}(x,y) < y \vee (\text{minus}(x,y) \not< y \wedge y \neq 0). \qquad (6)$$

As the arguments of recursive calls always satisfy the condition of the first (non-recursive) or the second (recursive) case, due to the termination of θ_{quotient} after a finite number of recursive calls θ_{quotient} will be called with arguments that satisfy the condition of the first non-recursive case. Hence, the result of the evaluation is true. Therefore the recursive call of θ_{quotient} can in fact be replaced by true which yields the following non-recursive version of θ_{quotient}:

function $\theta_{\text{quotient}}(x, y : \text{nat}) : \text{bool} \Leftarrow$
  if $x < y$ *then* true
    else (*if* $y \neq 0$ *then* true
      else false)

resp.

function $\theta_{\text{quotient}}(x, y : \text{nat}) : \text{bool} \Leftarrow$
  if $x < y$ *then* true
    else $y \neq 0$.

In general, let R be a set of recursive θ_{f}-cases with *results* of the form $\theta_{\text{f}}(r^*)$ and let b be a boolean value (either true or false). Our simplification procedure replaces the recursive calls in the R-cases by the boolean value b, if for each case in R evaluation of the result $\theta_{\text{f}}(r^*)$ either leads to a non-recursive case with the result b or to a recursive case from R.

Let Ψ be the set of all *conditions* from non-recursive cases with the result b and of all conditions from R-cases. Then one has to show that the arguments r^* satisfy one of the conditions $\varphi \in \Psi$, i.e. $\varphi[x^*/r^*]$ must be valid (where $[x^*/r^*]$ denotes the substitution of the formal parameters x^* by the terms r^*). Hence, for each case in R with the *condition* ψ the following *recursion elimination formula* has to be verified:

$$\psi \rightarrow \bigvee_{\varphi \in \Psi} \varphi[x^*/r^*].$$

Again, for the automated verification of such formulas an (induction) theorem prover is used. For instance, formula (6) can already be verified by propositional reasoning only.

5.4 Case Elimination

In the last simplification step one tries to replace conditionals by their results. More precisely, regard a conditional of the form "*if* φ_1 *then* true *else* φ_2" which will only be evaluated under a condition ψ. Now the simplification procedure tries to replace this conditional by the result φ_2. For that purpose the procedure has to check whether φ_2 also holds in the *then*-case of the conditional, i.e. it tries to verify the *case elimination formula*

$$\psi \wedge \varphi_1 \;\rightarrow\; \varphi_2.$$

If this implication can be proved (and if the condition $\neg\varphi_1$ is not necessary to ensure termination of φ_2's evaluation, i.e. if $\psi \rightarrow \Theta(\varphi_2)$), then the conditional is replaced by φ_2. Of course, conditionals of the form "*if* φ_1 *then* φ_2 *else* true" can be simplified in a similar way.

In our example, the case elimination formula $x < y \rightarrow y \neq 0$ can be verified. Moreover, as evaluation of $y \neq 0$ is always terminating (i.e. $\Theta(y \neq 0)$ is true), the condition $x \not< y$ is not necessary to ensure termination of that evaluation. Therefore the conditional in the body of $\theta_{\mathsf{quotient}}$'s algorithm is now replaced by $y \neq 0$. In this way we obtain the final version of $\theta_{\mathsf{quotient}}$:

$$\textit{function}\ \theta_{\mathsf{quotient}}(x, y : \mathsf{nat}) : \mathsf{bool} \Leftarrow \quad y \neq 0.$$

Using the above techniques this simple algorithm for $\theta_{\mathsf{quotient}}$ has been constructed which states that evaluation of $\mathsf{quotient}(x, y)$ terminates if y is not 0. This example demonstrates that our simplification procedure eases further automated reasoning about termination predicates significantly and it also enhances the readability of the termination predicate algorithms.

Summing up, the procedure for simplification of termination predicate algorithms works as follows: First, induction lemmata are used to *replace inequalities* by simpler formulas. Then the procedure eliminates *subsumed terms* and *recursive calls*. Finally, *cases* are *eliminated* by replacing conditionals by their results if possible.

This simplification procedure for termination predicates works *automatically*. It is based on a method for the synthesis of induction lemmata [Wal94b, Gie95b] and it uses an induction theorem prover to verify the subsumption, recursion elimination, and case elimination formulas (which often is a simple task).

6 Conclusion

We have presented a method to determine the domains (resp. non-trivial subdomains) of partial functions automatically. For that purpose we have *automated* the approach for termination analysis suggested by Manna [Man74]. Our analysis uses *termination predicates* which represent conditions that are sufficient for the termination of the algorithm under consideration. Based on sufficient requirements for termination predicates we have developed a procedure for the automated synthesis of termination predicate algorithms. Subsequently we introduced a procedure for the simplification of these generated termination predicate algorithms which also works automatically.

The presented approach can be used for polymorphic types, too, and an extension to mutual recursion is possible in the same way as suggested in [Gie96] for absolute termination proofs. Termination analysis can also be extended to higher-order functions by inspecting the decrease of their first-order arguments, cf. [NN95]. To determine non-trivial subdomains of higher-order functions which are not always terminating, in general one does not only need a termination predicate for each function f but one also has to generate termination predicates for the (higher-order) *results* of each function.

Function f	Termination Predicate θ_f	Function f	Term. Pred. θ_f
minus(x, y)	$x \geq y$	dual_log2(x)	$x = 2^n$
half1(x)	even(x)	list_minus(l, y)	$\bigwedge_i l_i \geq y$
half2(x)	even(x) $\wedge x \neq 0$	last(l)	$l \neq$ empty
times(x, y)	true	but_last(l)	$l \neq$ empty
exp(x, y)	true	reverse(l)	true
quotient1(x, y)	$y \neq 0$	list_min(l)	$l \neq$ empty
mod(x, y)	$y \neq 0$	last_x(l, x)	length(l) $\geq x$
quotient2(x, y)	$y \mid x$	index(x, l)	$x = 0 \vee$ member(x, l)
gcd(x, y)	$x = 0 \wedge y = 0 \vee x \neq 0 \wedge y \neq 0$	delete(x, l)	$x = 0 \vee$ member(x, l)
lcm(x, y)	$x \neq 0 \wedge y \neq 0$	sum_lists(l, k)	length(l) = length(k)
log1(x, y)	$x = 1 \vee x \neq 0 \wedge y \neq 0 \wedge y \neq 1$	nat_to_bin(x, y)	$y = 2^n$
log2(x, y)	$x = 1 \vee x = y^n \wedge x \neq 0 \wedge y \neq 1$	bin_vec(x)	$x \neq 0$
dual_log1(x)	$x \neq 0$		

Table 1. Termination predicates synthesized by our method.

Our method proved successful on numerous examples (see Table 1 for some examples to illustrate its power). For each function f in this table the corresponding termination predicate θ_f could be synthesized automatically. Moreover, for all these examples the synthesized termination predicate is not only sufficient for termination, but it even describes the *exact* domain of the functions.

These examples demonstrate that the procedure of Theorem 3 is able to synthesize sophisticated termination predicate algorithms (e.g. for a quotient algorithm it synthesizes the termination predicate "divides", for a logarithm algorithm it synthesizes a termination predicate which checks if one number is a power of another number, for an algorithm which deletes an element from a list a termination predicate for list membership is synthesized etc.). By subsequent application of our simplification procedure one usually obtains very simple formulations of the synthesized termination predicate algorithms.

Up to now, the termination behaviour of the algorithms in Table 1 could not be analyzed with any other automatic method. Those functions in the table which have the termination predicate true are total, but their algorithms call other non-terminating algorithms. Therefore the existing methods for absolute termination proofs failed in proving their totality. See [BG96] for a detailed description of our experiments.

The presented procedure for the generation of termination predicates works for any given measure function $|.|$. Therefore the procedure can also be combined with methods for the *automated* generation of suitable measure functions (e.g. the one we presented in [Gie95a, Gie95c]). For example, by using the measures suggested by this method, for all[5] 82 algorithms from the database of [BM79] our procedure synthesizes termination predicates which always return true (i.e. in this way (absolute) termination of all these algorithms is proved automatically).

Furthermore, with our approach it is also possible to perform termination analysis for *imperative programs*: When translating an imperative program into a functional one, usually each *while*-loop is transformed into a partial function,

[5] As mentioned in [Wal94b] one algorithm (greatest.factor) must be slightly modified.

cf. [Hen80]. Now the termination predicates for these partial "loop functions" can be used to prove termination of the whole imperative program.

Acknowledgements. We would like to thank Christoph Walther and the referees for helpful comments.

References

[BG96] J. Brauburger & J. Giesl. Termination Analysis for Partial Functions. Technical Report IBN 96/33, TH Darmstadt, 1996. Available from http://kirmes.inferenzsysteme.informatik.th-darmstadt.de/~report/ibn-96-33.ps.gz.

[Bi+86] S. Biundo, B. Hummel, D. Hutter & C. Walther. The Karlsruhe Induction Theorem Proving System. *Pr. 8th CADE, LNCS 230*, Oxford, England, 1986.

[BM79] R. S. Boyer & J S. Moore. *A Computational Logic.* Academic Press, 1979.

[BM88] R. S. Boyer & J S. Moore. The Addition of Bounded Quantification and Partial Functions to A Computational Logic and Its Theorem Prover. *Journal of Automated Reasoning*, 4:117-172, 1988.

[Bu+90] A. Bundy, F. van Harmelen, C. Horn & A. Smaill. The OYSTER-CLAM System. In *Proc. 10th CADE, LNAI 449*, Kaiserslautern, Germany, 1990.

[Der87] N. Dershowitz. Termination of Rewriting. *Journal of Symbolic Computation*, 3(1, 2):69-115, 1987.

[Gie95a] J. Giesl. Generating Polynomial Orderings for Termination Proofs. *Pr. 6th Int. Conf. Rewr. Tech. & App., LNCS 914*, Kaiserslautern, Germany, 1995.

[Gie95b] J. Giesl. Automated Termination Proofs with Measure Functions. In *Proc. 19th Annual German Conf. on AI, LNAI 981*, Bielefeld, Germany, 1995.

[Gie95c] J. Giesl. Termination Analysis for Functional Programs using Term Orderings. *Pr. 2nd Int. Stat. Analysis Symp., LNCS 983*, Glasgow, Scotland, 1995.

[Gie96] J. Giesl. Termination of Nested and Mutually Recursive Algorithms. *Journal of Automated Reasoning*, 1996. To appear.

[Hen80] P. Henderson. *Functional Programming.* Prentice-Hall, London, 1980.

[Hol91] C. K. Holst. Finiteness Analysis. In *Proc. 5th ACM Conf. Functional Prog. Languages & Comp. Architecture*, LNCS 523, Cambridge, MA, USA, 1991.

[Man74] Z. Manna. *Mathematical Theory of Computation.* McGraw-Hill, 1974.

[NN95] F. Nielson & H. R. Nielson. Termination Analysis based on Operational Semantics. Technical Report, Aarhus University, Denmark, 1995.

[Plü90] L. Plümer. *Termination Proofs for Logic Programs. LNAI 446*, Springer-Verlag, 1990.

[SD94] D. De Schreye & S. Decorte. Termination of Logic Programs: The Never-Ending Story. *Journal of Logic Programming* 19,20:199-260, 1994.

[Ste95] J. Steinbach. Simplification Orderings: History of Results. *Fundamenta Informaticae* 24:47-87, 1995.

[UV88] J. D. Ullman & A. van Gelder. Efficient Tests for Top-Down Termination of Logical Rules. *Journal of the ACM*, 35(2):345-373, 1988.

[Wal88] C. Walther. Argument-Bounded Algorithms as a Basis for Automated Termination Proofs. In *Proc. 9th CADE, LNCS 310*, Argonne, IL, 1988.

[Wal94a] C. Walther. Mathematical Induction. In D. M. Gabbay, C. J. Hogger, and J. A. Robinson (eds.), *Handbook of Logic in Artificial Intelligence and Logic Programming*, vol. 2, Oxford University Press, 1994.

[Wal94b] C. Walther. On Proving the Termination of Algorithms by Machine. *Artificial Intelligence*, 71(1):101-157, 1994.

A Freeness and Sharing Analysis of Logic Programs Based on a Pre-interpretation

Maurice Bruynooghe[1], Bart Demoen[1], Dmitri Boulanger[2], Marc Denecker[1] and Anne Mulkers[1]

[1] K.U.Leuven, Department of Computer Science, Celestijnenlaan 200A, 3001 Heverlee, Belgium
email: {maurice,bimbart,marcd,anne}@cs.kuleuven.ac.be***
[2] CNUCE Istituto del CNR, via S.Maria,36, 56126, Pisa, Italy
email: dima@orione.cnuce.cnr.it†

Abstract. Recently, a technique was presented for using pre-interpretations for abstract interpretation of the correct answer set $\mathcal{C}_P$ of a logic program P. So far it was an open problem whether pre-interpretations could also be used for deriving non-downward closed properties of the computed answer set $\mathcal{O}_P$ such as definite freeness. This paper shows that it is possible to do so.

1 Introduction

Cousot and Cousot [13, 14] have developed a widely applicable framework for abstract interpretation and obtained the following basic result: if an abstract operator $\mu^{\mathcal{A}}$ over an abstract domain $Dom^{\mathcal{A}}$ of data descriptions γ-approximates a corresponding concrete operator $\mu^{\mathcal{C}}$ over a concrete domain $Dom^{\mathcal{C}}$ of data elements, and both operators are monotonic functions, then the fixpoints of both operators are such that $lfp(\mu^{\mathcal{A}})$ γ-approximates $lfp(\mu^{\mathcal{C}})$.

For logic programs, the concrete operator $\mu^{\mathcal{C}}$ can be a bottom-up semantic function or a top-down one. In both cases, the execution essentially consists of sequences of unifications and projections. The latter ensure that the involved substitutions have finite domains. The construction of the abstract operator $\mu^{\mathcal{A}}$ involves replacing unification and projection by corresponding abstract operations. These abstract operations then can be plugged into the bottom-up or top-down frameworks which compute the fixpoint of the abstract operator $\mu^{\mathcal{A}}$.

A pre-interpretation J of a language is a model semantics concept [20], which can be extended to map a tuple of terms $\bar{t}$ to $J(\bar{t})$, a set of tuples of domain elements, a so called *domain relation*. The domain relation $J(\bar{t})$ encodes properties

*** Research supported by the Flemish section of "National Fund for Scientific Research", GOA "Non-standard applications of abstract interpretation", project IT/IF/04, project ISC-IL-90-PARFORCE, HCM project CHRX-CT94-0624, INTAS project 93-1702.

† Research supported by the ERCIM Grant No.95-01. A part of this work has been done at the GMD FIRST, Berlin.

of the tuple. In particular, the pre-interpretation used in this paper expresses freeness, groundness and sharing properties.

Following work of Giacobazzi et al [17] on a generalised algebraic semantics for constraint logic programs, [2, 1] introduced pre-interpretations based abstractions of constraint computations and used them to approximate the *s*-semantics of logic programs. However, a safe abstraction of non-downward closed properties of computed answers was only ensured when execution of the program did not require the so called "peel"-rule of the Martelli-Montanari unification algorithm [21] and the papers did not offer algorithms for checking the latter. The ideas led Gallagher et al. [16] to use pre-interpretation based models for the derivation of a wide range of *declarative* properties (for declarative properties, the above safety problem disappears). Their experiments showed that this is an approach with great practical value. Also the compiled approach of [8] can be understood as computing a model of the program under some pre-interpretation.

We return to the problem of pre-interpretations based analysis for non-downward closed properties of computed answers. Our abstract domain is the powerset of the original one. The paper explains how familiar properties can be extracted from elements in this abstract domain and develops a 3 element pre-interpretation (*gif*). It gives an algorithm for abstracting unification and extends the notion of "peel-free" unification. It compares the domain with the well-known *Share+Free* domain [18, 23] and reports on a first implementation. Our analysis not only allows to derive definite freeness and possible sharing but also to derive definite sharing. The latter information is useful for the AND-parallelisation of logic programs. It allows to reduce independence conditions to false and to identify parts of the program which are inherently sequential [7].

Our analysis is not obtained just by the systematic lifting to the powerset of the original domain as studied e.g. in [15]. That approach cannot lead to the derivation of non-downward closed properties.

Section 2 recalls some preliminaries and explains the use of tuples. Section 3 recalls what a pre-interpretation is and introduces domain relations. Section 4 introduces the *gif* abstract domain and section 5 explains how to extract properties from an element in this abstract domain. The abstract operations are introduced in section 6. Section 7 makes a comparison with the *Share+Free* domain and reports on an implementation.

2 Preliminaries

Terms in a language are syntactic objects built from a finite set of functors and a enumerable set of variables. With o denoting an object, $\bar{o}$ denotes a tuple of objects. $Var(o)$ denotes the set of variables in a syntactic object o. Variables are denoted by capital letters $X, Y, \ldots$. Abusing notation, we use $\overline{X}$ not only to denote a tuple of variables, but in some contexts also to denote the corresponding set of variables. $\bar{o}_1.\bar{o}_2$ denotes the tuple which is the concatenation of the tuples $\bar{o}_1$ and $\bar{o}_2$. A tuple constructed from $\bar{o}_1$ and $\bar{o}_2$ but with elimination of duplicates is denoted $\bar{o}_1 \cup \bar{o}_2$. A substitution is a function mapping a syntactic object to a syntactic object by simultaneously replacing a finite set of variables by terms. They are denoted by $\sigma, \theta, \ldots$. We write $t\theta$ for the application of a substitution to a term. $Dom(\theta)$ denotes the domain of the substitution θ, i.e. the variables which are replaced by terms. An equation system E is a finite set of equations between terms. Abusing notation, we write $\{\overline{s} = \overline{t}\}$ for the equation system $\{s_1 = t_1, \ldots, s_n = t_n\}$. In the well-known ***solved form*** as computed by the Martelli-Montanari unification algorithm [21], left-hand sides are distinct variables which do not occur in the right-hand sides. We make also use of a ***pre-solved*** form which is a system of equations which is in solved form after removal of all equations of the form $X = X$. We fix a partial function $mgu(E)$ mapping an equation system E to a most general unifier. With θ a substitution, $eqn(\theta)$ denotes the equations system $\{X = X\theta \mid X \in Dom(\theta)\}$.

As stated in the introduction, an analysis is constructed by replacing primitive operations over concrete data in an appropriate concrete semantics by abstract operations over data descriptions. For logic programs, the relevant data in the concrete operational semantics are usually considered to be (accumulated) substitutions. In our setting, it is more convenient to consider pairs $\overline{X}, \overline{t}$ where $\overline{X}$ is a so called ***reference domain***, a set of so called ***reference variables*** and $\overline{t}$ is a tuple of terms such that $\overline{X} = \overline{t}$ is in pre-solved form. For example, where usually the computed answer is defined as $\sigma \uparrow \overline{X}$, the restriction of the accumulated substitution σ to the variables $\overline{X}$ of the query, we say $\overline{X}$ is the reference domain and $\overline{X}\sigma$ is the computed answer. There is an obvious one to one correspondence between pairs $\overline{X}, \overline{t}$ such that $\overline{X} = \overline{t}$ is in pre-solved form and idempotent substitutions σ with $Dom(\sigma) \subseteq \overline{X}$: the tuple corresponding to σ is $\overline{X}\sigma$ and the substitution corresponding to $\overline{t}$ is $mgu(\{\overline{X} = \overline{t}\}) = \{X/\overline{t}_X \mid \overline{t}_X \neq X\}$. Variable names inside tuples are irrelevant to the extent that the tuple remains in pre-solved form wrt. the reference domain. This corresponds to the irrelevance of variable names of the clause variants used in SLD-derivations, to the extent that they do not conflict with variable names already in use.

3 Pre-interpretations

Following [20], a pre-interpretation J for a language $\mathcal{L}$ is characterised by a domain D_J and, for each n-ary functor f/n of the language, a function f_J mapping elements of D_J^n to D_J. A variable assignment V associates an element of D_J with each variable in $\mathcal{L}$. Let $V(o)$ denote the syntactic object obtained by replacing the variables of o by the domain elements specified by V. We can define a function $\tilde{J}$ which maps a term without variables but with domain elements of D_J to a domain element: $\tilde{J}(f(t_1, \ldots, t_n)) = f_J(\tilde{J}(t_1), \ldots, \tilde{J}(t_n))$ for $f/n \in \mathcal{L}$ and $\tilde{J}(d) = d$ for $d \in D_J$.

Using this mapping, we can extend J into a mapping from a tuple of non-ground terms to a ***domain relation***, called the ***pre-interpretation*** of the tuple: $J(\langle t_1, \ldots, t_n \rangle) = \{\langle \tilde{J}(V(t_1)), \ldots, \tilde{J}(V(t_n)) \rangle \mid V \text{ is a variable assignment}\}$. Notice that tuples which are renamings of each other have the same pre-interpretation. Another consequence of this definition is the following trivial proposition:

Proposition 1. *$\bar{t}_1 \leq \bar{t}_2$ implies $J(\bar{t}_1) \subseteq J(\bar{t}_2)$.*

The pre-interpretation on which the freeness and sharing analysis in this paper is based is the *gif* pre-interpretation J^{gif}. It is based on a three element domain $D = \{g, i, f\}$. The pre-interpretation of a functor f/n is defined as: if $\forall j : 1 \leq j \leq n : d_j = g$ then $f_{J^{gif}}(d_1, \ldots, d_n) = g$ else i. It gives distinct domain relations for free variables, ground terms and partially instantiated terms. The domain element f is not in the range of the pre-interpretation of any functor, it is called a *non-term element* [2, 1].

Example 1. $J^{gif}(\langle X \rangle) = \{\langle f \rangle, \langle i \rangle, \langle g \rangle\}$.
$J^{gif}(\langle X, X \rangle) = \{\langle f, f \rangle, \langle i, i \rangle, \langle g, g \rangle\}$.
$J^{gif}(\langle X, Y \rangle) = \{\langle f, f \rangle, \langle f, i \rangle, \langle f, g \rangle, \langle i, f \rangle, \langle i, i \rangle, \langle i, g \rangle, \langle g, f \rangle, \langle g, i \rangle, \langle g, g \rangle\}$.
$J^{gif}(\langle f(Y), f(Z) \rangle) = J^{gif}(\langle f(X,Y), f(X,Z) \rangle) = \{\langle i, i \rangle, \langle i, g \rangle, \langle g, i \rangle, \langle g, g \rangle\}$.
$J^{gif}(\langle f(X), f(X) \rangle) = \{\langle i, i \rangle, \langle g, g \rangle\}$.

4 Abstract Domain based on a pre-interpretation J

Besides the notation $\bar{t}$ for a n-tuple of terms, we need several others. We use $\overline{T}$ for a set of n-tuples of terms and $\overline{\mathcal{T}}$ for the set of *all* n-tuples. Finally, $\mathcal{P}(\overline{\mathcal{T}})$ is the powerset of all n-tuples. For domain tuples, we need even more. We use $\bar{d}$ for a n-tuple of domain elements from some domain D, and DR for a set of domain tuples (a Domain Relation), which is a subset of D^n, the set of all domain tuples. Finally, we use SDR for a Set of Domain Relations, $\mathcal{SDR}$ for the set of *all* domain relations and $\mathcal{P}(\mathcal{SDR})$ for the powerset of SDR.

The reference domain $\overline{X}$ associated with a tuple of terms $\bar{t}$ or domain elements $\bar{d}$ can be considered as attributes. To select the tuple consisting of components from a subset $\overline{Y}$ of the attributes, we use the notations $\bar{t}_{\overline{Y}}$ and $\bar{d}_{\overline{Y}}$ (and $\bar{t}_Y$ if a single attribute is selected).

The establishment of an abstract domain and a Galois connection between a concrete and abstract domain is a first step towards a program analysis. We extend the pre-interpretation as introduced in section 3 into an abstraction function from a set of tuples into a set of domain relations and obtain a Galois connection.

Proposition 2. *Let $\alpha : \mathcal{P}(\overline{\mathcal{T}}) \to \mathcal{P}(\mathcal{SDR})$ be defined as $\alpha(\overline{T}) = \{J(\bar{t}) \mid \bar{t} \in \overline{T}\}$. Let $\gamma : \mathcal{P}(\mathcal{SDR}) \to \mathcal{P}(\overline{\mathcal{T}})$ be defined as $\gamma(SDR) = \{\bar{t} \mid J(\bar{t}) \in SDR\}$. Then the quadruple $((\mathcal{P}(\overline{\mathcal{T}}), \subseteq), \alpha, (\mathcal{P}(\mathcal{SDR}), \subseteq), \gamma)$ is a Galois connection.*

Notice that this is not a Galois insertion; $\mathcal{P}(\mathcal{SDR})$ has spurious elements, due to the existence of non empty domain relations which cannot be the pre-interpretation of any tuple, e.g $\{\langle f \rangle, \langle g \rangle\}$.

Pre-interpretation based analyses or more precisely, model based analyses so far [16, 3] use the standard notion of a model to approximate the set of correct answers of a program. A model only provides approximations describing downward closed sets of tuples. Therefore, only downward closed properties can be derived.

5 Decoding an element of the abstract domain

Given a tuple of terms $\bar{t}$ with reference domain $\overline{X}$, we can formulate predicates and one function (sharegroups) expressing mostly familiar [5] properties of a tuple of terms[5]: $free(X,\bar{t})$ iff $\bar{t}_X$ is a variable; $ground(X,\bar{t})$ iff $\bar{t}_X$ is ground; $instantiated(X,\bar{t})$ iff $\bar{t}_X$ is instantiated but not ground; $sharegroup(\overline{Y},\bar{t})$ iff $\exists U$ s.t. $\overline{Y} = \{Y \in \overline{X} \mid U \in Var(\bar{t}_Y)\}$; $sharegroups(\bar{t}) = \{\overline{Y} \mid sharegroup(\overline{Y},\bar{t})\}$; $indep(\overline{Y},\overline{Z},\bar{t})$ iff $Var(\bar{t}_{\overline{Y}}) \cap Var(\bar{t}_{\overline{Z}}) = \emptyset$. They can be lifted to sets expressing either a $\mathcal{D}$efinite property or a $\mathcal{P}$ossible property. For example: $\mathcal{D}sharegroup(\overline{Y},\overline{T})$ iff $\forall\bar{t} \in \overline{T} : sharegroup(\overline{Y},\bar{t})$; $\mathcal{P}sharegroup(\overline{Y},\overline{T})$ iff $\exists\bar{t} \in \overline{T} : sharegroup(\overline{Y},\bar{t})$. They can be further extended towards domain relations. For example: $\mathcal{P}sharegroups(DR) = \mathcal{P}sharegroups(\overline{T})$ where $\overline{T} = \{\bar{t} \mid DR = J(\bar{t})\}$. We need constructive definitions for the properties of interest. Straightforward ones are[6]:

Proposition 3. *Let DR be a domain relation in J^{gif}, and X a reference variable in reference domain $\overline{X}$.*
$\mathcal{D}free(X,DR)$ iff $\mathcal{P}free(X,DR)$ iff $\exists\bar{d} \in DR : \bar{d}_X = f$.
$\mathcal{D}ground(X,DR)$ iff $\mathcal{P}ground(X,DR)$ iff $\forall\bar{d} \in DR : \bar{d}_X = g$.
$\mathcal{D}instantiated(X,DR)$ iff $\neg\mathcal{D}free(X,DR)$ and $\neg\mathcal{D}ground(X,DR)$.

How to compute $\mathcal{D}sharegroups(DR)$ and $\mathcal{P}sharegroups(DR)$ is less obvious. We define $\mathcal{P}os(\overline{Y},\overline{X}) = \bar{d}$ *where* $\bar{d}_{\overline{Y}} = \bar{i}$ *and* $\bar{d}_{\overline{X}\setminus\overline{Y}} = \bar{g}$ and look at an example.

Example 2. For a reference domain $\langle X,Y,Z\rangle$, consider the domain relation $DR = \{\langle g,g,g\rangle, \langle i,g,g\rangle, \langle i,i,g\rangle, \langle g,g,i\rangle, \langle i,g,i\rangle, \langle i,i,i\rangle\}$. Typical tuples are $\bar{t}_1 = \langle f(U,V), f(V), f(W)\rangle$ and $\bar{t}_2 = \langle f(U,V,S,T), f(V,S), f(W,S,T)\rangle$. The two tuples have sharegroups $\{X\}, \{X,Y\}, \{Z\}$, but $\bar{t}_2$ has additional sharegroups $\{X,Y,Z\}$ and $\{X,Z\}$. Careful investigation shows that all tuples described by DR share this characteristic, i.e. $\mathcal{D}sharegroups(DR) = \{\{X\},\{X,Y\},\{Z\}\}$ and $\mathcal{P}sharegroups(DR) = \mathcal{D}sharegroups(DR) \cup \{\{X,Z\},\{X,Y,Z\}\}$. The application of $\mathcal{P}os$ on the sharegroups yields elements of DR e.g. $\mathcal{P}os(\langle X,Y\rangle, \langle X,Y,Z\rangle) = \langle i,i,g\rangle \in DR$. Also, non-definite possible sharegroups (e.g. $\{X,Y,Z\}$) can be obtained as the union of strictly smaller sharegroups, while definite sharegroups cannot.

For the definition below, we use the order $g < i < f$. We call an element $\bar{d} \in DR$ primitive iff $\bar{d}$ is not the arguments-wise maximum of a subset $S \subseteq DR$ which does not contain $\bar{d}$. Formally, with $\overline{X}$ the reference domain of DR:
$Primitive(\overline{Y},DR)$ iff $\mathcal{P}os(\overline{Y},\overline{X}) \in DR$ and
$\forall S : S \subseteq (DR \setminus \{\mathcal{P}os(\overline{Y},\overline{X})\})$ implies $\mathcal{P}os(\overline{Y},\overline{X}) \neq max(S)$
where $max(\{\bar{d},\bar{d}',\bar{d}'',\ldots\})_Y = max(\{\bar{d}_Y,\bar{d}'_Y,\bar{d}''_Y,\ldots\})$.
The proposition below states that for J^{gif} the primitive sharegroups are the definite sharegroups. Candidate possible sharegroups are the sharegroups

[5] A more complete set is in the full version of the paper [6].

[6] Notice that J^{gif} provides a strong encoding of freeness, groundness and instantiatedness.

$\overline{Y}$ such that $\mathcal{P}os(\overline{Y},\overline{X}) \in DR$. However, in case freeness occurs, some of these candidates can be rejected, as shown in the following example.

Example 3. For a reference domain $\langle X, Y\rangle$, consider the domain relation $DR = \{\langle g,g\rangle, \langle i,g\rangle, \langle f,g\rangle, \langle g,i\rangle, \langle i,i\rangle, \langle f,i\rangle\}$. $\mathcal{D}sharegroups(DR) = \{\{X\},\{Y\}\}$. Moreover, for any $\bar{t}$ such that $J(\bar{t}) = DR$, $\bar{t}_X$ is free and does not occur in $\bar{t}_Y$, otherwise $\langle f,g\rangle$ would not be an element of DR. Hence, there cannot be sharing between X and Y. So here is a case in which $\mathcal{P}sharegroups(DR) = \mathcal{D}sharegroups(DR)$.

Proposition 4. *Let DR be a domain relation in J^{gif} with reference domain $\overline{X}$. Let $\overline{Y} \subseteq \overline{X}$ such that $\mathcal{P}os(\overline{Y},\overline{X}) \in DR$, then:*
$\overline{Y} \in \mathcal{D}sharegroups(DR)$ iff $Primitive(\overline{Y}, DR)$.
$\overline{Y} \in \mathcal{P}sharegroups(DR)$ iff $(\exists Y \in \overline{Y} : \mathcal{D}free(Y, DR)) \rightarrow Primitive(\overline{Y}, DR)$.

Independence can be extracted through its relationship with sharegroups: *$indep(\overline{X}_1, \overline{X}_2, \bar{t})$ iff $\forall \overline{Y} \in sharegroups(\overline{X}, \bar{t}) : \overline{Y} \cap \overline{X}_1 = \emptyset$ or $\overline{Y} \cap \overline{X}_2 = \emptyset$:*

Proposition 5. *$\mathcal{D}indep(\overline{X}_1, \overline{X}_2, DR)$ iff $\forall \overline{Y} \in \mathcal{P}sharegroups(DR) : \overline{Y} \cap \overline{X}_1 = \emptyset$ or $\overline{Y} \cap \overline{X}_2 = \emptyset$. $\mathcal{P}indep(\overline{X}_1, \overline{X}_2, DR)$ iff $\forall \overline{Y} \in \mathcal{D}sharegroups(DR) : \overline{Y} \cap \overline{X}_1 = \emptyset$ or $\overline{Y} \cap \overline{X}_2 = \emptyset$.*

Finally, to decode an element of the abstract domain, we extend these predicates for a set of domain relations. The extension is straightforward. $\mathcal{D}$efinite properties hold if they hold for each domain relation, $\mathcal{P}$ossible properties hold if they hold for at least one domain relation. Further on, sets of domain relations which are the powerset of a single one, will be of special importance. Their concretisation gives a set of downward closed tuples of terms. For our analysis to be practical, we should have a more effective way of computing their properties of interest. One can prove:
$\mathcal{D}free(X, SDR)$ *iff* $\forall DR \in SDR : \mathcal{D}free(X, DR)$.
$\mathcal{P}sharegroup(\overline{Y}, SDR)$ *iff* $\exists DR \in SDR : \mathcal{P}sharegroup(\overline{Y}, DR)$.
$\mathcal{D}free(X, \mathcal{P}(DR)) = false$.
$\mathcal{D}ground(X, \mathcal{P}(DR)) = \mathcal{D}ground(X, DR)$.
$\overline{Y} \in \mathcal{P}sharegroups(\mathcal{P}(DR))$ *iff* $\forall X \in \overline{Y} : \neg\mathcal{D}ground(X, DR)$.
$\mathcal{D}indep(\overline{X}_1, \overline{X}_2, \mathcal{P}(DR))$ *iff* $\forall X \in \overline{X}_1 : \mathcal{D}ground(X, DR)$
or $\forall X \in \overline{X}_2 : \mathcal{D}ground(X, DR)$.

6 Abstract Operations

Two key operations are unification and conjunction. In our setting, unification is a partial function, defined for $\overline{X} = \bar{t}$ a pre-solved form and $\bar{t}$ and E *standardised apart*[7]: $unif(\overline{X}, \bar{t}, E) = (\overline{X} \cup Var(E))\sigma$ where $\sigma = mgu(\{\overline{X} = \bar{t}\} \cup E)$. Conjunction is also a partial function, defined for $\overline{X}_1 = \bar{t}_1$ and $\overline{X}_2 = \bar{t}_2$ pre-solved

[7] Apart from variables in $\overline{X}$, $\bar{t}$ and E do not share variables.

forms and $\bar{t}_1$ and $\bar{t}_2$ *standardised apart*[8]: $conj(\overline{X}_1, \bar{t}_1, \overline{X}_2, \bar{t}_2) = (\overline{X}_1 \cup \overline{X}_2)\sigma$ where $\sigma = mgu(\overline{X}_1 = \bar{t}_1 \cup \overline{X}_2 = \bar{t}_2)$.

Because conjunction can be defined in terms of relational operators, we define abstract unification in terms of abstract conjunction[9] :
$Abstr\_unif(\overline{X}, SDR, E) = Abstr\_conj(\overline{X}, SDR, Var(E), \alpha(\{Var(E)mgu(E)\}))$

Proposition 6. *If* $Abstr\_conj(\overline{X}_1, SDR_1, \overline{X}_2, SDR_2)$ *γ- approximates* $conj(\overline{X}_1, \bar{t}_1, \overline{X}_2, \bar{t}_2)$ *for* $\bar{t}_1 \in \gamma(SDR_1)$ *and* $\bar{t}_2 \in \gamma(SDR_2)$ *then* $Abstr\_unif(\overline{X}, SDR, E)$ *γ-approximates* $unif(\overline{X}, \bar{t}, E)$ *for* $\bar{t} \in \gamma(SDR)$.

The abstract elements are sets of domain relations. Therefore we define *Abstr_conj* in terms of an operator on pairs of domain relations (the relational conjunction operator *Aconj*): $Abstr\_conj(\overline{X}_1, SDR_1, \overline{X}_2, SDR_2) = \bigcup\{Aconj(\overline{X}_1, DR_1, \overline{X}_2, DR_2) \mid DR_1 \in SDR_1, DR_2 \in SDR_2\}$.

Proposition 7. *If* $Aconj(\overline{X}_1, DR_1, \overline{X}_2, DR_2)$ *γ-approximates* $conj(\overline{X}_1, \bar{t}_1, \overline{X}_2, \bar{t}_2)$ *for* $\bar{t}_1 \in \gamma(\{DR_1\})$ *and for* $\bar{t}_2 \in \gamma(\{DR_2\})$ *then* $Abstr\_conj(\overline{X}_1, SDR_1, \overline{X}_2, SDR_2)$ *γ-approximates* $conj(\overline{X}_1, \bar{t}_1, \overline{X}_2, \bar{t}_2)$ *for* $\bar{t}_1 \in \gamma(SDR_1)$ *and for* $\bar{t}_2 \in \gamma(SDR_2)$.

How can *Aconj* be implemented? Let $\overline{X}_1 = \overline{X}.\overline{Y}$, $\overline{X}_2 = \overline{X}.\overline{Z}$ with $\overline{Y} \cap \overline{Z} = \emptyset$. For tuples $\bar{t}_1, \bar{t}_2$ standardised apart, let $\sigma = mgu(\overline{X}_1 = \bar{t}_1 \cup \overline{X}_2 = \bar{t}_2) = mgu(\overline{X} = \bar{t}_{1\overline{X}} \cup \overline{X} = \bar{t}_{2\overline{X}} \cup \overline{Y} = \bar{t}_{1\overline{Y}} \cup \overline{Z} = \bar{t}_{2\overline{Z}})$. $(\overline{X}.\overline{Y})\sigma$ is an instance of $\bar{t}_1$; so, according to Proposition 1, $J((\overline{X}.\overline{Y})\sigma) \subseteq J(\bar{t}_1) = DR_1$. Note that $J((\overline{X}.\overline{Y})\sigma)$ is the projection of $J((\overline{X}.\overline{Y}.\overline{Z})\sigma)$ on $\overline{X}.\overline{Y}$. Similar, the projection of $J((\overline{X}.\overline{Y}.\overline{Z})\sigma)$ on $\overline{X}.\overline{Z}$ is $J((\overline{X}.\overline{Z})\sigma)$ which is a subset of DR_2. But this means that $J((\overline{X}.\overline{Y}.\overline{Z})\sigma) \subseteq DR_1 \bowtie DR_2$, where $\bowtie$ is the *equijoin* [26] of the two domain relations. So, we can define a first relation conjunction operator: $Aconj_1(\overline{X}_1, DR_1, \overline{X}_2, DR_2) = \mathcal{P}(DR_1 \bowtie DR_2)$[10].

Proposition 8. $Aconj_1(\overline{X}_1, DR_1, \overline{X}_2, DR_2)$ *γ-approximates* $conj(\overline{X}_1, \bar{t}_1, \overline{X}_2, \bar{t}_2)$ *for all* $\bar{t}_1 \in \gamma(\{DR_1\})$ *and* $\bar{t}_2 \in \gamma(\{DR_2\})$.

The definition of $Aconj_1$ is independent of a particular pre-interpretation, alas it produces abstractions describing downward closed sets. We introduce two refinements, specific for the *gif* pre-interpretation.

A first improvement is based on a condition under which $J((\overline{X}.\overline{Y}.\overline{Z})\sigma) = DR_1 \bowtie DR_2$. Let $\bar{t}_1$ and $\bar{t}_2$ be standardised apart and let $\sigma = mgu(\overline{X}_1 = \bar{t}_1 \cup \overline{X}_2 = \bar{t}_2)$. It is straightforward that $DR_1 = J(\bar{t}_1) = \{V(\overline{X}_1) | J, V \models \overline{X}_1 = \bar{t}_1\}$. Analogously, $DR_2 = J(\bar{t}_2) = \{V(\overline{X}_2) | J, V \models \overline{X}_2 = \bar{t}_2\}$. It follows then that $DR_1 \bowtie DR_2 = \{V(\overline{X}.\overline{Y}.\overline{Z}) | J, V \models \overline{X}_1 = \bar{t}_1 \wedge \overline{X}_2 = \bar{t}_2\}$.

The Martelli-Montanari unification algorithm produces a sequence of equation systems $E_0 = (\overline{X}_1 = \bar{t}_1 \cup \overline{X}_2 = \bar{t}_2), E_1, .., E_n = eqn(\sigma)$. Now assume that

---

[8] Apart from variables in $\overline{X}_1 \cap \overline{X}_2$, $\bar{t}_1$ and $\bar{t}_2$ do not share variables.

[9] $unif(\overline{X}, \bar{t}, E) = conj(\overline{X}, \bar{t}, Var(E), Var(E)mgu(E))$.

[10] To see the need for the $\mathcal{P}$-operator, consider $\overline{X}_1 = \overline{X}_2 = X$, $DR_1 = DR_2 = \{\langle i \rangle, \langle g \rangle\}$ and $\bar{t}_1 = f(a, U)$, $\bar{t}_2 = f(V, b)$.

for all $1 \leq j < n$, it holds that $J \models \forall(E_j \Leftrightarrow E_{j+1})$, where $\Leftrightarrow$ expresses logical equivalence i.e. that each rewrite step preserves the set of value assignments which are solutions. This implies that $DR_1 \bowtie DR_2 = \{V(\overline{X}_1 \cup \overline{X}_2) | J, V \models \forall(eqn(\sigma))\} = J((\overline{X}_1 \cup \overline{X}_2)\sigma)$.

So, the question now is which rewrite rules are equivalence preserving in J? With respect to any finite J, the only (non-failing) rewrite rule which is not equivalence preserving is the peel-rule: the equivalence $\forall(f(\overline{X}) = f(\overline{Y}) \Leftrightarrow \overline{X} = \overline{Y})$ is not satisfied. This explains why e.g. $\{V(\langle X \rangle) | J^{gif}, V \models X = f(a, U) \wedge X = f(W, b)\} = \{\langle i \rangle, \langle g \rangle\} \neq \{V(\langle X \rangle) | J^{gif}, V \models X = f(a, b) \wedge W = a \wedge U = b\} = \{\langle g \rangle\}$. However, even for the peel-rule, an infinite set of instances are satisfied in J^{gif}: one easily verifies that for any ground atom $\overline{t}$, $J^{gif} \models \forall(f(\overline{X}) = f(\overline{t}) \Leftrightarrow \overline{X} = \overline{t})$. We have the following proposition:

Proposition 9 ng-peel-free rewrite step. *If E is reduced to E' by a remove step (removal of an equation $X = X$), a switch step (replacing an equation $X = t$ by $t = X$), a substitute step (with $X = t$ an equation, X is substituted by t in the other equations) or a peel step (replacement of an equation $f(t_1, \ldots, t_n) = f(s_1, \ldots, s_n)$ by $t_1 = s_1, \ldots, t_n = s_n$) with at least one of the peeled terms a ground term then: $J^{gif} \models \forall(E \Leftrightarrow E')$.*

In [6], we describe and prove a condition in terms of the domain relations which guarantees the existence of a ng-peel-free rewriting to solved form. It allows to define: $Aconj_2(\overline{X}_1, DR_1, \overline{X}_2, DR_2) =$ if the conjunction is ng-peel-free then $\{DR_1 \bowtie DR_2\}$ else $Aconj_1(\overline{X}_1, DR_1, \overline{X}_2, DR_2)$.

Proposition 10. *$Aconj_2(\overline{X}_1, DR_1, \overline{X}_2, DR_2)$ γ-approximates $conj(\overline{X}_1, \overline{t}_1, \overline{X}_2, \overline{t}_2)$ for all $\overline{t}_1 \in \gamma(\{DR_1\})$ and $\overline{t}_2 \in \gamma(\{DR_2\})$.*

To implement an analysis, one needs $Aconj_2(\overline{X}_1, DR_1, Var(E), \alpha(\{Var(E)mgu(E)\}))$. It can be realised as follows:

```
E = mgu(E);
while ∃e ∈ E s.t. the conjunction of DR1 and α({Var(e)mgu(e)}) is ng-peel-free
do remove e from E;
    X1 = X1 ∪ Var(e);
    DR1 = DR1 ⋈ α({Var(e)mgu(e)});
od;
if E = ∅ then {DR1}
        else Aconj1(X1, DR1, Var(E), α({Var(E)mgu(E)})).
```

The conjunction of $\alpha(\{Var(e)mgu(e)\})$ and DR is ng-peel-free if at least one side of e is a free variable or a ground term under DR.

When the rewriting is not ng-peel-free, all freeness is lost, also of variables which are known to be independent of those in the intersection of the two reference domains. Exploiting independence can prevent this[11]. The idea is to split $\overline{X}_1$

[11] It also improves the precision of the possible sharing which can be extracted from domain relations (e.g. the fourth example in Example 1).

in two independent sub-domains $\overline{X}_{11}, \overline{X}_{12}$ such that $\mathcal{D}indep(\overline{X}_{11}, \overline{X}_{12}, DR_1)$, i.e. terms assigned to variables in the two sub-domains do not share variables. As a consequence, DR_1 can be written as a product $DR_{11} \times DR_{12}$. In addition, we require that $\overline{X}_1 \cap \overline{X}_2 \subseteq \overline{X}_{11}$. Similarly, we split $\overline{X}_2$ in $\overline{X}_{21}.\overline{X}_{22}$ and DR_2 in $DR_{21} \times DR_{22}$ such that $\overline{X}_1 \cap \overline{X}_2 \subseteq \overline{X}_{21}$. Let $\bar{t}_1 = \bar{t}_{11}.\bar{t}_{12}$ and $\bar{t}_2 = \bar{t}_{21}.\bar{t}_{22}$ be standardised apart. One can state:
$mgu(\overline{X}_{11} = \bar{t}_{11} \cup \overline{X}_{12} = \bar{t}_{12} \cup \overline{X}_{21} = \bar{t}_{21} \cup \overline{X}_{22} = \bar{t}_{22}) = mgu(\overline{X}_{11} = \bar{t}_{11} \cup \overline{X}_{21} = \bar{t}_{21}) \bigcup \{\overline{X}_{12}/\bar{t}_{12}, \overline{X}_{22}/\bar{t}_{22}\}$.
We have that $J((\overline{X}_{11}.\overline{X}_{21})\sigma) \in \mathcal{P}(DR_{11} \bowtie DR_{12})$ where $\sigma = mgu(\overline{X}_{11} = \bar{t}_{11} \cup \overline{X}_{21} = \bar{t}_{21})$, $J(\bar{t}_{12}) = DR_{12}$, and $J(\bar{t}_{22}) = DR_{22}$.

So, we define another operator $Aconj_3$: determine maximal sub-domains $\overline{X}_{12}, \overline{X}_{22}$ such that $\overline{X}_1 = \overline{X}_{11}.\overline{X}_{12}$, $\overline{X}_2 = \overline{X}_{21}.\overline{X}_{22}$, $\overline{X}_1 \cap \overline{X}_2 \subseteq \overline{X}_{11} \cap \overline{X}_{21}$ and $\mathcal{D}indep(\overline{X}_{11}, \overline{X}_{12}, DR_1)$ and $\mathcal{D}indep(\overline{X}_{21}, \overline{X}_{22}, DR_2)$; then define:
$Aconj_3(\overline{X}_1, DR_1, \overline{X}_2, DR_2) = \mathcal{P}(DR_{1\overline{X}_{11}} \bowtie DR_{2\overline{X}_{21}}) \times DR_{1\overline{X}_{12}} \times DR_{2\overline{X}_{22}}$.
$Aconj_3$ preserves definite freeness of variables in $\overline{X}_{12}$ and in $\overline{X}_{22}$[12]. The following proposition holds:

Proposition 11. *$Aconj_3(\overline{X}_1, DR_1, \overline{X}_2, DR_2)$ γ-approximates $conj(\overline{X}_1, \bar{t}_1, \overline{X}_2, \bar{t}_2)$ for all $\bar{t}_1 \in \gamma(\{DR_1\})$ and $\bar{t}_2 \in \gamma(\{DR_2\})$.*

To combine both improvements, $Aconj_3$ replaces $Aconj_1$ in the definition of $Aconj_2$.

7 Evaluation of the *gif* domain

A logic program analysis using sets of possible sharegroups (the *Share* domain) has been introduced in [18]. In [23] it has been extended with a component expressing definite freeness (the *Share+Free* domain) and has further been refined with a linearity component [4, 22] (the *Share+Free+Linear* domain). All these domains express definite groundness and possible sharegroups, the latter two also definite freeness. As explained in Section 5, definite freeness and possible sharegroups can also be extracted from abstractions in our domain. We present a preliminary investigation about precision and performance of the *gif* domain.

7.1 Definite groundness

With respect to definite groundness, the *gif* domain is as precise as the analysis based on the $\{g, i\}$-pre-interpretation[13], which is known to be equivalent with the Prop-domain which is in turn more precise than *Share* [12]. So, wrt. definite

[12] A domain relation can express independence between a free variable and other variables. The result of $Aconj_3$ is a product of three independent relations. Keeping the result as this product can maintain more independence than what is expressed by the domain relation which is the result of evaluating the product.

[13] Functors are interpreted in *gi* as in *gif*, the only difference is the absence of the non-term element f.

groundness, our analysis is more precise than *Share*. A formal comparison with *Share+Free* and *Share+Free+Linear* is not available[14]. As the precision of Prop is based on the very precise covering information, it is unlikely that there are cases where *Share+Free+Linear* can obtain better groundness information than Prop and the *gif* domain[15]. So, while in theory *gif* is more precise, in practice, we expect that both domains derive the same groundness.

7.2 Definite Freeness

Let us consider a situation with abstract state a_{in}, and an equation E over the reference domain of the form $X = t[Y_1, \ldots, Y_n]$ with $Y_1, \ldots, Y_n$ variables in the term t. Abstract unification derives a new abstract state a_{out}. We analyse cases where freeness, present in a_{in}, is preserved in a_{out}:

- the equation is $X = Y$, X and Y are free in a_{in}. *Share+Free* preserves all freeness. In the *gif* domain, the equation is abstracted as $\{\langle f, f\rangle, \langle i, i\rangle, \langle g, g\rangle\}$, the subsequent conjunction is ng-peel-free and the equijoin preserves all freeness in a_{in}.
- The equation is $X = t[Y_1, \ldots, Y_n]$, X is free in a_{in}. *Share+Free* preserves all freeness of variables Z independent of X[16]. In the *gif* domain, the conjunction is again ng-peel-free (X is free in a_{in}). Also here, the equijoin preserves freeness of all variables which are independent of X (free variables are either equal to, or independent of X, this is expressed in a_{in}).
- The equation is of the form $X = t[Y_1, \ldots, Y_n]$, neither X nor $t[Y_1, \ldots, Y_n]$ is a free variable in a_{in}. *Share+Free* preserves freeness of variables which are independent of $X, Y_1, \ldots, Y_n$. The independence optimisation $Aconj_3$ in the *gif* domain also preserves freeness of those variables.

This suggests that both domains have the same precision wrt. definite freeness. So far, we have been unable to construct an example where *Share+Free* derives more freeness.

7.3 Possible Sharegroups

Here the comparison is not that simple. The interesting case is where the equation is of the form $X = t[Y_1, \ldots, Y_n]$ where both sides are neither free nor ground in a_{in}. In this case, *Share* (and *Share+Free*) performs a kind of closure under union of all sharegroups containing one of $X, Y_1, \ldots, Y_n$. By taking the $\mathcal{P}(DR_1 \bowtie DR_2)$, where DR_1 is the part of a_{in} dependent on the variables

[14] We are not aware of examples of pure programs where more precise groundness is obtained than with *Share*.

[15] A typical example where *Share*, *Share+Free* and *Share+Free+Linear* are less precise than Prop [12] is: $p(U, U, V)$. $p(U, V, U)$. $q(U, V, W)$:- $p(U, V, W)$, $U = a$, $V = W$. However such cases rarely occur in real programs.

[16] Typically, also the Y_i are independent from X.

$X, Y_1, \ldots, Y_n$ and DR_1 of the equation, the *gif* domain performs a somewhat similar closure operation on sharegroups.

Concerning the relative precision of the three share domains, *Share+Free* takes the "closure" in less cases than *Share*, which gives rise to more precise possible sharing. *Share+Free+Linear* avoids the "closure" in even more cases, though benchmarks show that this not so often further enhances precision[17].

As said above, the *gif* domain sometimes gives better groundness. Because of the better groundness, the same example mentioned above gives also a better possible sharing than in *Share+Free+Linear*. However, also in other cases, the sharing can be better. Consider the similar example $p(U, U, V)$. $p(U, V, U)$. $q(U, V, W)$:- $p(U, V, W)$, $V = W$. In the *gif* domain, we obtain $\{U, V, W\}$ as single sharegroup for $q(U, V, W)$. In *Share+Free+Linear*, one derives $\{U, V, W\}$ and $\{V, W\}$.

On the other hand, as Example 1 showed, the *gif* domain is weak at capturing independence between instantiated terms. This can cause a loss of precision. Consider: $q(X, Y, Z)$:- $X = f(A)$, $Y = f(A, B)$, $Z = f(B)$. *Share* yields sharegroups $\{X, Y\}$ and $\{Y, Z\}$. The *gif* domain also derives $\{X, Y, Z\}$ although all steps are ng-peel-free.

7.4 Implementation

A first implementation has been realised by adapting the bottom-up Prop analyser described in [8]. The prototype implements $AConj_2$ and uses $AConj_1$ when the ng-peel-free condition is violated. The ng-peel-free check extracts all required information (e.g. which are the free and ground variables) from the domain relations according to Proposition 3 each time this information is needed. Profiling has shown that the ng-peel-free check is the most expensive part in our implementation. So, the implementation would certainly benefit from: (1) storing this information together with each domain relation and reusing it instead of recomputing it; (2) labeling at pre-compile time an equation as ng-peel-free when one side of the equation is a ground term or the first occurrence of a variable; (3) reduce the set of reference variables after the last occurrence of a variable which does not occur in the head. The powerset of a domain relation is never computed but a global flag is set, indicating that the result for all domain relations, computed from this point on, needs to be downward closed. This flag could be refined to indicate on a domain relation basis which domain relation denotes its downward closure; such a refinement might increase the precision. To assess performance and precision, we have used the *gif* domain in the bottom-up analyser to abstract computed answers of the predicates in a standard set of benchmarks. The same analysis has been done in the *Share+Free* domain, using the appropriate setting of the abstract equation systems described in [22] and the top-down analysis framework AMAI described in [19]. To do this goal-independent analysis efficiently with a top-down framework, the transformation

[17] They are the same benchmarks for which the combination of set sharing and pair sharing [24] (which enhances set sharing with the linearity of pair sharing) shows an improved precision [11].

described in [10] is applied: without this transformation, the comparison would disadvantage AMAI.

The results are summarised in Table 1.

program	Time		Sh/	#pr	mx	# diff pr			flg	#fr arg		#gr	#	# sh gr	
	gif	S+F	gif		ar	Dg	Df	Ps	st	gif	S+F	arg	arg	gif	S+F
append	0.03	0.17	5.7	1	3	0	0	0	0	1	1	0	3	2	2
boyer	2.43	9.45	3.9	34	5	0	0	6	8	10	10	14	88	111	104
deriv	1.99	4.42	2.2	18	4	0	0	4	5	5	5	8	47	46	38
grammar	0.06	0.56	9.3	6	3	0	0	0	1	4	4	4	17	9	9
peep	11.6	17.1	1.5	23	6	0	1	5	8	15	16	13	75	154	84
qsort	0.24	0.73	3.0	4	4	0	0	0	0	1	1	5	11	4	4
reverse	0.05	0.24	4.8	2	3	0	0	0	1	1	1	0	5	3	3
serialize	0.76	1.19	1.6	7	4	0	0	2	4	0	0	3	17	17	12
Total	17.16	33.86	2.0	95		0	1	17	27	37	38	47	263	346	256

Table 1.

Table 1 contains the name of the benchmark program, the time (in seconds) it takes to analyse the benchmark program in the *gif* domain and in the *Share+Free* domain[18], the speedup of *gif* over *Share+Free*, the number of predicates in each benchmark, the maximal arity of predicates in each benchmark, the number of predicates in each benchmark for which *Share+Free* has more precision than *gif* for groundness, freeness and sharing (*Share+Free* has never less precision in the benchmarks), the number of predicates for which the flag indicates that only downward closed properties are derived, the number of arguments for which freeness was derived, the number of arguments for which groundness was derived (only one number, as it is the same for *gif* and *Share+Free*), the total number of argument positions, i.e. the sum of the arities of all predicates, and the number of sharing groups that were derived.

Both the bottom-up and the top-down analyser are based on precompiling a source program into another form (for the bottom-up analyser to an abstracted Prolog program, for the top-down analyser to intermediate code for an abstract interpretation machine). The time for this precompilation is not included in the timings of table 1: it is similar for both systems and small compared to the analysis time. The timing for *gif* does include a postprocessing step, which given the domain relations of the predicates, computes the groundness, freeness and sharing as described in section 5: this takes about 10% of the total time for the larger benchmarks. The times are averages over 10 runs on a Sparc 20 with ProLog_by_BIM 4.0.12 .

[18] A goal independent analysis.

Discussion. The implementation uses a ground representation of the domain relations. This results in large domain relations for predicates with a large arity and shows up in the table as a relative slow-down for benchmarks with such predicates. We expect that a non-ground representation of the domain relations (as in [9] or [25]) would reduce the influence of large arities and on the whole benefit the implementation. However, with a rudimentary implementation of the *gif* domain, we arrive at a speed-up of 2 on average over AMAI.

The precision of *gif* in deriving groundness is exactly as for Share+Free, as expected, since situations where *gif* is more precise happen not to occur in the benchmarks. For freeness, *gif* loses the freeness of one argument (in benchmark peep). Careful analysis of why this was so, reduced it to the following example in which the freeness of A is lost: $t(A, Z, B) :- q(B), Z = f(A, B)$. Assume q returns the powerset of $\{\langle i\rangle, \langle g\rangle\}$. The use of independence as described in Proposition 11, cannot recover the freeness of A. However, doing separately the analysis for each domain relation in the powerset of $\{\langle i\rangle, \langle g\rangle\}$ recovers the freeness of A. These observations confirm the hypothesis that the our approach can potentially derive the same freeness as *Share+Free*.

On the other hand, the derived information on possible sharing is substantially weaker with *gif*. The source of the imprecision can be illustrated with the following example: $p(X, Y) :- X = f(U), Y = f(V)$. The tuple $\langle f(U), f(V)\rangle$ is the computed answer, the abstraction cannot distinguish this from $\langle f(U, Z), f(V, Z)\rangle$ and our current analysis derives that also $\{X, Y\}$ is a sharing group. Exploiting independence, we would derive that the result is the product of two independent domain relations $\{\langle i\rangle, \langle g\rangle\}$ and would only derive the sharegroups $\{X\}$ and $\{Y\}$, as in *Share+Free*.

We have also made an experimental implementation of $Aconj_3$ as described in Section 6 using the independence of subsets of reference variables. We cannot yet fully report on the results of this implementation, but the following observations were made: the representations of individual domain relations is smaller but more domain relations per predicate are derived; the precision concerning freeness is the same but that concerning the possible share groups is greatly improved (no loss of precision in examples such as in the previous paragraph); the efficiency is much worse, among others, because more domain relations are derived: we currently do not know how to control this explosion.

Conclusion and future work. Our implementation of the gif-domain by means of $Aconj_2$ shows that pre-interpretations are a practical means for deriving non-trivial information about logic programs without losing too much precision. More precision can be obtained by using the concept of independence, as in $Aconj_3$. A first attempt to implement $Aconj_3$ reduced the number of possible sharegroups drastically but resulted in a prohibitive slow-down of the analysis. We currently explore how to reduce this slow-down. $Aconj_3$ is based on the idea to use the concept of independence to reduce the subset of reference variables for which the domain relation has to be be downward closed. This notion is not as powerful as one would like: the example where freeness is lost shows that not the notion of independence, but rather the notion of "being affected by a unification" is needed. It follows that another interesting line of research consists in exploring alternatives to *Aconj*$_3$ which would improve precision and hopefully have less impact on efficiency. One possibility is to have a flag for each reference variable.

Another line of future work consists of exploring pre-interpretations that are capable of describing other interesting properties, like for example linearity, and still result in computationally well behaving analysis.

Acknowledgments. We are grateful to G. Janssens for the help with the benchmarks in the *Share+Free* domain and to the referees for many useful comments.

References

1. D. Boulanger and M. Bruynooghe. A systematic construction of abstract domains. In B. Le Charlier, ed., *Proceedings of the first International Static Analysis Symposium, SAS'94*, pp. 61–77. LNCS 864, Springer-Verlag, Sept. 1994.
2. D. Boulanger, M. Bruynooghe, and M. Denecker. Abstracting S-semantics using a model-theoretic approach. In M. Hermenegildo and J. Penjam, ed., *Proceedings of the Sixth International Symposium on Programming Language Implementation and Logic Programming, PLILP'94*, pp. 432–446. LNCS 844, Springer-Verlag, Sept. 1994.
3. D. Boulanger. Complete Analysis for Definite Logic Programs. Proc. 11th Workshop Logische Programmierung, Technische Universität Wien, GMD-Studien Nr.270, September, 1995, 101–110.
4. M. Bruynooghe and M. Codish. Freeness, sharing, linearity and correctness – all at once. In P. Cousot, M. Falaschi, G. Filé, and A. Rauzy, ed., *Proceedings of the Third International Workshop on Static Analysis*, LNCS 724, pp. 153–164, Padova, Italy, Sept. 1993. Springer-Verlag.
5. M. Bruynooghe, M. Codish and A. Mulkers. Abstracting Unification: A key step in the design of logic program analyses. In *Computer Science Today, Recent Trends and Developments*, Jan van Leeuwen ed. LNCS Vol 1000, pp. 406–425, 1995. Springer-Verlag.
6. M. Bruynooghe, B. Demoen, D. Boulanger, M. Denecker and A. Mulkers. A Freeness and Sharing Analysis of Logic Programs Based on a Pre-interpretation. Report CW 233, Dept. Computer Science, KULEUVEN, May 1996.
7. F. Bueno, M. García de la Banda and M. Hermenegildo. Effectiveness of Global Analysis in Strict Independence-Based Automatic Program Parallelization. In *International Logic Programming Symposium*, pp320–336, 1994, MIT Press.
8. M. Codish and B. Demoen. Analysing logic programs using "prop"-ositional logic programs and a magic wand. *The Journal of Logic Programming*, 25(2):249–274, Dec. 1995. A preliminary version appeared in proc. ILPS'93.
9. M. Codish and B. Demoen. Deriving polymorphic type dependencies for logic programs using multiple incarnations of Prop. In B. Le Charlier, ed., *Proceedings of the first International Static Analysis Symposium, SAS'94*, pp. 281–296. LNCS 864, Springer-Verlag, Sept. 1994.
10. M. Codish, M. García de la Banda, M. Bruynooghe, and M. Hermenegildo. Goal dependent vs. goal independent analysis of logic programs. In *Proceedings of the International Conference on Logic Programming and Automated Reasoning, LPAR'94*, LNAI 822, pp. 305–319. Springer-Verlag, 1994.

11. M. Codish, A. Mulkers, M. Bruynooghe, M. García de la Banda and M. Hermenegildo. Improving Abstract Interpretation by Combining Domains. ACM Trans. Prog.Lang. Syst. 17(1):28-44, 1995.
12. A. Cortesi, G. Filé and W. Winsborough. Optimal groundness analysis using propositional formulas. *The Journal of Logic Programming*, 27(2):103–179, May 1996. A preliminary version appeared in ICALP92.
13. P. Cousot and R. Cousot. Abstract interpretation: A unified lattice model for static analysis of programs by construction or approximation of fixpoints. In *Proceedings of the Fourth ACM Symposium on Principles of Programming Languages*, pp. 238–252, Los Angeles, 1977.
14. P. Cousot and R. Cousot. Abstract interpretation and application to logic programs. *The Journal of Logic Programming*, 13(2 and 3):103–179, 1992.
15. G. Filé and F. Ranzato. Improving abstract interpretations by systematic lifting to the powerset. In M. Bruynooghe, ed., *Proceedings of the 1994 International Logic Programming Symposium*, pp. 655–669, MIT Press.
16. J. Gallagher, D. Boulanger, and H. Saglam. Practical model-based static analysis for definite logic programs. In J. Lloyd ed., *Proceedings of the 1995 International Symposium on Logic Programming*, pp. 351–365, 1995, MIT Press.
17. R. Giacobazzi, S.K.Debray, and G. Levi. Generalized semantics and abstract interpretation for constraint logic programs. *The Journal Logic Programming*, 25(3):191–247, Dec.1995. A preliminary version appeared in Proc. FGCS92.
18. D. Jacobs and A. Langen. Static analysis of logic programs for independent AND-parallelism. *The Journal of Logic Programming*, 13(2 & 3):291–314, 1992.
19. G. Janssens, M. Bruynooghe, V. Dumortier. A blueprint for an abstract machine for abstract interpretation of (constraint) logic programs. In J. Lloyd ed., *Proceedings of the 1995 International Symposium on Logic Programming*, pp. 336–350, 1995, MIT Press.
20. J. W. Lloyd. *Foundations of Logic Programming.* Springer Series : Symbolic Computation - Artificial Intelligence. Springer-Verlag, second, extended edition, 1987.
21. A. Martelli and U. Montanari. An efficient unification algorithm. *ACM Transactions on Programming Languages and Systems*, 4(2):258–282, Apr. 1982.
22. A. Mulkers, W. Simoens, G. Janssens, and M. Bruynooghe. On the practicality of abstract equation systems. In L. Sterling, editor, *Proceedings of the International Conference on Logic Programming*, pp. 781–795, Kanagawa, Japan, 1995. MIT Press.
23. K. Muthukumar and M. Hermenegildo. Combined determination of sharing and freeness of program variables through abstract interpretation. In K. Furukawa, editor, *Proceedings of the Eighth International Conference on Logic Programming*, pp. 49–63, Paris, France, 1991. MIT Press.
24. H. Søndergaard. An application of abstract interpretation of logic programs: Occur check reduction. In B. Robinet and R. Wilhelm, eds., *ESOP'86 Proceedings European Symposium on Programming*, Lecture Notes in Computer Science 213, pp. 327–338. Springer-Verlag, N.Y., 1986.
25. S. Sudarshan and R. Ramakrishnan. Optimizations of bottom-up evaluation with non-ground terms. In D. Miller, ed. *Proceedings of the 1993 International Symposium on Logic Programming*, pp. 557–574, 1993, MIT Press.
26. J. D. Ullman. *Principles of Database Systems.* Computer Science Press, 1982.

Refinement Types for Program Analysis

Mario Coppo, Ferruccio Damiani and Paola Giannini

Università di Torino, Dipartimento di Informatica, Corso Svizzera 185
10149 Torino (Italy)

Abstract. In this paper we introduce a system for the detection and elimination of dead code in typed functional programs. The main application of this method is the optimization of programs extracted from proofs in logical frameworks but it could be used as well in the elimination of dead code determined by program specialization. Our algorithm is based on a type inference system suitable for reasoning about dead code information. This system relays on *refinement* types which allow to exploit the type structure of the language for the investigation of program properties. The detection of dead code is obtained via type inference, which can be performed in an efficient and complete way, by reducing it to the solution of a system of inequalities between type variables. A key feature of our method is that program analysis can be performed in a strictly incremental way. Even though the language considered in the paper is a simply typed λ-calculus we can generalize our approach to polymorphic languages like ML. Although focused on dead code elimination our type inference method can also be applied to the investigation of other program properties like binding time and strictness. Some hints on these applications are given.

Introduction

Types have been recognized as useful in programming languages because they provide a semantical (non context free) analysis of programs. Such analysis is usually incorporated in the compiling process, and is used on one side to check the consistency of programs and on the other to improve the efficiency of the code produced.

In addition to preventing run-time errors, type systems can be useful for characterizing run-time properties of programs. For instance intersection types, see [4] (and also [1]), in their full generality, provide a characterization of strong normalization. As a consequence of this their type checking is undecidable, and therefore cannot be used in the compiling process of functional languages.

Type systems tailored to specific analysis, such as strictness, totality, binding time analysis etc. have been introduced, see [17, 12, 5, 13, 18]. In this perspective types represent program properties and their inference systems are systems for reasoning formally about them. In this paper we keep a clear distinction between the type structure of the language (types in the usual sense) and the *refinement* types which represent, inside the type structure of the language, particular properties. This distinction is very useful in the design of inference algorithms.

A similar view is taken in [8], in which the authors attempt to unify the analysis, identifying a basic type structure that can be extended to incorporate the various analyses.

The attraction of the type based approach is the possibility of designing efficient algorithms to do the analysis, as compared to the classical approach of semantical analysis using abstract interpretation which is quite inefficient for higher order functions. Type based analyzers are based on an implicit representation of types, either via type inequalities, see [11], or via lazy (implicit) types, see [8]. In our approach we pursue the first approach, reducing the inference problem to the solution of a system of inequalities between atomic types. An interesting feature of our method is that it is naturally compositional.

Type analysis is also used in the area of program extraction from formal proof. The programs extracted from proofs are usually very inefficient, as they contain parts that are useless for the computation of the final result; they therefore require some sort of simplification. One of the more effective simplification techniques is "pruning", and has been developed by Berardi, see [2]. In this technique useless terms are discovered by analyzing the type of terms. Such terms are called "dead code". The method was improved in [3] with the use of type inclusion. With type inclusion an application is well typed if the argument has a type included in the input type of the corresponding function. There are some basic problems with the method of [3]. The optimization algorithm is rather difficult to understand and this makes its proof of correctness even more difficult to follow. The method presented in this paper seems much more self-evident. Moreover in Berardi's algorithm it is assumed that the input term is typed, and the input type information is used for the analysis. So there does not seem to be a clear way to generalize the analysis to untyped terms (or better to do type inference and "pruning" at the same time). In [16] another formalism to represent information about dead code, based on the idea of marking terms and types, is presented. However no marking algorithm is given. This approach seems related to ours.

In our paper we present an inference system for detecting "dead code", and an algorithm that simplifies λ-terms based on the system of [3]. Although our system is tailored for dead code analysis we will show in the last section of the paper how its basic ideas can be applied to the design of inference algorithms for the investigation of other kinds of program properties.

The inference system for dead code relies mostly on Berardi's ideas. The language we consider is a typed (à la Church) λ-calculus with constants for natural numbers, pairs and recursor. The types are then built from the type of natural numbers, nat, using arrow and cartesian product. Starting from a typed term we infer properties of the term. We call such properties refinement types. For the dead code analysis we need two refinements for the basic type nat. The first, δ corresponds to the idea that the value may be used, and so it could only be replaced with a term with the same behaviour (β-equal). The second, ω, corresponds to the fact that the value is not used, and so it does not matter what the term is (it could be any constant of the same type). We consider an order relation $\sqsubseteq$ on refinement types whose interpretation is that a type is more informative than another, in particular $\delta \sqsubseteq \omega$. These properties are propagated to higher types, for instance if a function of type nat $\rightarrow$ nat has the refinement types $\delta \rightarrow \omega$ or $\omega \rightarrow \omega$ then the whole term will not be used (and also any free assumption on which it depends). When we apply a function to an argument we require that the argument have a refinement type that allows its use in every occurrence of the parameter. So it must be more specific, $\sqsubseteq$, than the refinement type of the formal parameter. The soundness of this system and of the optimizing transformation that it induces is proved via a partial equivalence relation semantics of the refinement types, showing that the optimized programs are observationally equivalent to the original ones.

Let us first consider a simple example. Let $M = (\lambda x^{\mathrm{nat}}.\bar{3})P$ where $\bar{3}$ is the numeral 3 and P is a term of type nat. Since x is never used in the body of the lambda we can assign the refined type $\omega \rightarrow$ nat to $\lambda x.\bar{3}$ so we discover that P is not used in the computation of M and could be replaced by any constant of the right type. The information about dead code can be propagated. Consider having a λ-calculus with pairs $\langle\ ,\ \rangle$ and projections π_1 and π_2. Let M be the term $(\lambda x.\pi_1\langle P, Q\rangle)N$ for some term P, Q, and N. Since the projection π_1 returns the first component of the pair the term Q is dead code. Moreover, assume that P does not contain any occurrence of x, in this case also N is not relevant to the computation of the final result. So M in a call by name language behaves like the term P, which is of course simpler.

The main difference between our approach and that of [2] and [3] is in the algorithm that finds the optimized version of a given term. The algorithm presented in these papers is a kind of "data flow" algorithm that analyzes a term by implicitly building a directed graph which represents the input-output relation between the subterms of a given term. In our approach instead we assign to each term a system of inequalities between refinement type variables which can be seen as representing the whole flow of input-output information of the term. This system has always a maximal solution corresponding to the most informative typing of the term. Detecting the best optimization of a term corresponds to looking for a solution that maximizes the number of ω's with the restriction that the whole term must be useful (cannot be refined to ω). Such a solution can be found in a time proportional to the number of atomic type occurrences in the complete typing of a term. The proof of correctness and completeness of the algorithm is rather easy. An important feature of our algorithm is that it is naturally compositional while that of [2] and [3] is not.

Our analysis is for a strongly normalizing language, so we did not consider termination issues. To apply the method to languages including a fixed point operator we need a richer model including some sort of termination order on the terms.

It would be easy to extend the algorithm to deal with Curry-style polymorphism, see [9]. So for instance one could think of doing both type and refinement type inference at the same time. From the algorithmic point of view this extension is quite easy. In this framework it is, however, more difficult to understand the system from a semantical point of view. We can also deal with Milner-style polymorphism, see [15]. That is the presence of the "let $x = N$ in M" construct. Here x in M can be assigned different types, all instances of the same type scheme. In this case we have to handle the refinements of the different types of N in M. The optimizations possible for N would be such that they eliminate code that is useless according to all the different refinements of N.

The underlying type system is not part of the analysis. So the technique could be applied to more informative type systems such as the decidable restrictions of intersection types, like the rank 2 restriction (see [14]) or the simple types of [6] and [7]. Of course having already, at the level of the type system, more information the same refinement type system would be more informative. We think that, maintaining the orthogonality of the two issues: typing and refining the type, we can get the best out of each one of them.

The technique presented can be extended to deal with other properties useful in program optimization, such as binding time analysis and strictness analysis.

The first section introduces the language we are dealing with and the refinement type assignment system along with its semantics. In the second section we introduce a code optimization based on refinement type information, in particular we show that a term and its optimized version are equivalent. In the third section we introduce an algorithm for refinement types inference. The algorithm is articulated in two phases. First given a term we define a set of inequalities whose solutions induce all the derivations of refinement types for the term. Then we give an algorithm that finds the maximum solution of a system of inequalities. In the last section we outline how the technique of refinement types can be used to study binding time and strictness analysis.

1 A Type Assignment for Proving Properties

The aim of this section is to introduce a typed functional language (basically a typed λ-calculus with cartesian product and arithmetic constants) and a type assignment system for deriving flow properties of typed terms. The set of types is defined assuming as unique basic type nat, the set of natural numbers.

Definition 1 Types. The language of *types* ($\mathcal{T}$) is defined by the following grammar: $R ::= \text{nat} \mid R \to R \mid R \times R$.

Types are ranged over by R, S, ... Typed terms are defined from a set of typed *term constants*

$$\begin{aligned}\mathcal{K}_\Lambda = \{\, & 0^{\text{nat}}, \text{succ}^{\text{nat}\to\text{nat}}, \text{rec}^{\text{nat}\to R\to(\text{nat}\to R\to R)\to R}, \text{it}^{\text{nat}\to R\to(R\to R)\to R}, \\ & \text{case}^{\text{nat}\to R\to(\text{nat}\to R)\to R}, \text{if}^{\text{nat}\to R\to R\to R} \qquad \mid R \in \mathcal{T}\} ,\end{aligned}$$

(ranged over by C^S), and a set $\mathcal{V}_\Lambda$ of typed *term variables* (ranged over by $x^R, y^S, \ldots$). The choice of the constants has been done in view of an application to the optimization of terms extracted from proofs. We write $\Gamma \vdash_{\mathcal{T}} M^R$ to mean that M is a typed term of type R whose free variables are among the variables in the context Γ. We use this notation since it allows to attach a type to all subterms of M. Note the difference with the more usual notation $M : R$ in which this is not possible. The set of well typed (well decorated) terms is defined by the rules of the following definition.

Definition 2 Typed terms. A typing statement is an expression $\Gamma \vdash_{\mathcal{T}} M^R$ where Γ is a *context*, i.e., a set of variables x^R containing all the free variables of M. The rules for term formation are the following:

$$(\text{Var})\ \Gamma/x \cup \{x^R\} \vdash_{\mathcal{T}} x^R \qquad\qquad (\text{Con})\ \Gamma \vdash_{\mathcal{T}} C^R$$

$$(\to \text{I})\ \frac{\Gamma/x \cup \{x^R\} \vdash_{\mathcal{T}} M^S}{\Gamma/x \vdash_{\mathcal{T}} (\lambda x^R.M^S)^{R\to S}} \qquad\qquad (\to \text{E})\ \frac{\Gamma \vdash_{\mathcal{T}} M^{R\to S} \quad \Gamma \vdash_{\mathcal{T}} N^R}{\Gamma \vdash_{\mathcal{T}} (M^{R\to S} N^R)^S}$$

$$(\times \text{I})\ \frac{\Gamma \vdash_{\mathcal{T}} M_1{}^{R_1} \quad \Gamma \vdash_{\mathcal{T}} M_2{}^{R_2}}{\Gamma \vdash_{\mathcal{T}} \langle M_1{}^{R_1}, M_2{}^{R_2}\rangle^{R_1\times R_2}} \qquad\qquad (\times \text{E}_l)\ \frac{\Gamma \vdash_{\mathcal{T}} M^{R_1\times R_2}}{\Gamma \vdash_{\mathcal{T}} (\pi_l M^{R_1\times R_2})^{R_l}}\ l \in \{1,2\}\ .$$

Note that with this notation we explicitly mention in M the types assigned to all its subterms. In the following we often omit to write types which are understood.

As usual a substitution is a finite function mapping term variables in terms, denoted $[x_1 := N_1, \ldots, x_n := N_n]$, which respect the types, i.e., each $x_i^{R_i}$ is substituted with a term $N_i^{R_i}$ of the same type.

Let $\Lambda_{\mathcal{T}}$ be the set of all typed terms which are defined according to the previous rules, i.e., $\Lambda_{\mathcal{T}} = \{M^R \mid \Gamma \vdash_{\mathcal{T}} M^R \text{ for some basis } \Gamma\}$. We provide $\Lambda_{\mathcal{T}}$ with a standard operational semantics defined by a notion of reduction. Let $\to_\beta$ denote the usual β reduction relation and $\to_\pi$ denote the following reduction relation for pairs: $\pi_l\langle M_1, M_2\rangle \to_\pi M_l$, for $l \in \{1,2\}$.
The reduction $\to_C$ determined by the constants is defined by the clauses:

$$\begin{array}{ll} \text{rec}\,0\,M\,F \to_C M & \text{it}\,0\,M\,F \to_C M \\ \text{rec}\,(\text{succ}\,n)\,M\,F \to_C F\,n\,(\text{rec}\,n\,M\,F) & \text{it}\,(\text{succ}\,n)\,M\,F \to_C F\,(\text{it}\,n\,M\,F) \\ & \\ \text{case}\,0\,M\,F \to_C M & \text{if}\,0\,M\,N \to_C M \\ \text{case}\,(\text{succ}\,n)\,M\,F \to_C F\,n & \text{if}\,(\text{succ}\,n)\,M\,N \to_C N\ . \end{array}$$

Let $\to_r$ denote the union of $\to_\beta$, $\to_\pi$ and $\to_C$, let $\to_r^*$ denote its reflexive and transitive closure, and let $=_r$ be the equivalence relation induced by $\to_r^*$. Note that every term in $\Lambda_{\mathcal{T}}$ is strongly normalizable.

The *closed term model* $\mathcal{M}$ of $\Lambda_{\mathcal{T}}$ is defined by interpreting each type R as the set of the equivalence classes of the relation $=_r$ on the closed terms of type R. Let $\mathbf{I}(R)$ denote the interpretation of type R in this model, and let $[M]$ denote the equivalence class of term M. An *environment* is a mapping $e : \mathcal{V}_\Lambda \to \bigcup_{R\in\mathcal{T}} \mathbf{I}(R)$ which respects types, i.e., such that, for each x^R, $e(x^R) \in \mathbf{I}(R)$. The interpretation of a term M in an environment e is defined in a standard way by: $[\![M]\!]_e = [M[x_1 := N_1, \ldots, x_n := N_n]]$, where $\{x_1, \ldots, x_n\} = \text{FV}(M)$ and $[N_l] = e(x_l)$ $(1 \leq l \leq n)$.

We want to be able to represent more information about terms of a given type. If we consider the basic type nat, for instance, we want to represent the notion of terms of type nat whose evaluation will possibly be useful to get the final result of a computation from that of terms (of the same type) whose evaluation will certainly be useless to that aim. For instance take the term of type nat: $M = (\lambda x^{\text{nat}}.Q^{\text{nat}})P^{\text{nat}}$, where x does not occur in Q. The evaluation of P will be useless to the evaluation of M. To this aim we define two *refinement* types of nat: δ and ω, which represent, respectively, the notion of values which are (possibly) necessary or (certainly) useless for the determination of the final value of a computation, i.e., we identify δ with *(possibly) live* and ω with *dead.* So we will assign, for instance, type δ to Q and type ω to P.

Refinement types are defined from $\{\delta, \omega\}$ following the type construction rules. So, for instance, $\omega \to \delta$ is a refinement type of nat $\to$ nat (we denote this with $\omega \to \delta :: \text{nat} \to \text{nat}$) which informally represent the set of all functions f which yield a useful output whenever applied to an argument which is not useful for the termination of this output, like $\lambda x.Q$ above. This means that $\omega \to \delta$ characterizes all constant function of type nat $\to$ nat. In general we write $\rho :: R$ to mean that ρ refines type R.

Definition 3 Refinement types. The language $\mathcal{R}$ of *refinement types* (*r-types* for short) and the *refinement relation* :: are defined by the following rules:

$$(\text{nat})\ \frac{\varphi \in \{\delta, \omega\}}{\varphi :: \text{nat}} \qquad (\to)\ \frac{\rho :: R \quad \sigma :: S}{\rho \to \sigma :: R \to S} \qquad (\times)\ \frac{\rho :: R \quad \sigma :: S}{\rho \times \sigma :: R \times S}\ .$$

It it easy to see that each refinement type ρ refines a unique type R, denoted by $\mathbf{T}(\rho)$, i.e., we have $\rho :: \mathbf{T}(\rho)$. Moreover, if R is a type and $\varphi \in \{\delta, \omega\}$, let $\mathbf{R}_\varphi(R)$ denote the refinement type obtained from R by replacing each occurrence of the basic type nat by φ. We have obviously $\mathbf{R}_\varphi(R) :: R$.

ω-refinement types (*ω-r-types* for short) formalize the notion of not being relevant to the computation at higher types.

Definition 4 ω-r-types. The set $\mathcal{O}$ of ω-r-types is inductively defined by: $\omega \in \mathcal{O}$ and if $\rho, \sigma \in \mathcal{O}$ and $\tau \in \mathcal{R}$ then $\tau \to \sigma \in \mathcal{O}$ and $\rho \times \sigma \in \mathcal{O}$.

We now introduce a notion of inclusion between r-types, denoted $\sqsubseteq$, that means to be less informative.

Definition 5 Inclusion relation. The *inclusion relation* $\sqsubseteq$ between refinement types is defined by the following rules:

$$(\delta)\ \delta \sqsubseteq \delta \qquad\qquad (\omega)\ \frac{\sigma \in \mathcal{O} \quad \mathbf{T}(\rho) = \mathbf{T}(\sigma)}{\rho \sqsubseteq \sigma}$$

$$(\to)\ \frac{\rho_1 \sqsubseteq \rho_2 \quad \sigma_1 \sqsubseteq \sigma_2}{\rho_2 \to \sigma_1 \sqsubseteq \rho_1 \to \sigma_2} \qquad\qquad (\times)\ \frac{\rho_1 \sqsubseteq \rho_2 \quad \sigma_1 \sqsubseteq \sigma_2}{\rho_1 \times \sigma_1 \sqsubseteq \rho_2 \times \sigma_2}\ .$$

Note that all ω-r-types which refines the same type are considered equivalent with respect to the $\sqsubseteq$ relation. Moreover we have immediately that for all $\rho_1, \rho_2 \in \mathcal{R}$, $\rho_1 \sqsubseteq \rho_2$ implies $\mathbf{T}(\rho_1) = \mathbf{T}(\rho_2)$.

Refinement types are assigned to typed λ-terms by a set of type inference rules similar to these of the ML type inference system.

If x^R is a term variable of type R an assumption for x^R is an expression of the form $x^R : \rho$, or $x : \rho$ for short, where $\rho :: R$. A basis is a set Σ of assumptions, and we write $\Sigma :: \Gamma$ to mean that Σ contains an assumption $x^R : \rho$ only if x^R

is a variable in Γ. We will prove judgements of the form $\Sigma \vdash_{\mathcal{R}} M^{\rho}$ where M is a typed term in a context Γ, i.e., such that $\Gamma \vdash_{\mathcal{T}} M^{R}$, $\Sigma :: \Gamma$ and $\rho :: R$. Note that we omit to denote explicitly the types of terms. Note also that we do not follow the more usual notation $\Sigma \vdash_{\mathcal{R}} M : \rho$ since we are interested in keeping track of the r-types assigned to the subterms of M in a derivation.

The type assignment rules are similar to the rules for term formation with the only exception that we take into account the inclusion relation. Notice that the types of all the constants C can be described by $T_C[R]$, where $T_C[\,]$ is a type context (with some, possibly none, holes) and R is a type. For instance $T_0[\,] = \text{nat}$ and $T_{\text{if}}[\,] = \text{nat} \to [\,] \to [\,] \to [\,]$. With $\tau_C[\,]$ we denote the r-type context obtained from $T_C[\,]$ by replacing nat with δ. For instance $\tau_0[\,] = \delta$ and $\tau_{\text{if}}[\,] = \delta \to [\,] \to [\,] \to [\,]$. Let $\rho :: R$, then $\tau_C[\rho] :: T_C[R]$ is the r-type obtained from $T_C[R]$ by replacing nat with δ and R with ρ.

Definition 6 Refinement type assignment system. The rules for refined type assignment are the following:

$$(\text{Var})\ \frac{\rho_1 \sqsubseteq \rho_2}{\Sigma/x \cup \{x : \rho_1\} \vdash_{\mathcal{R}} x^{\rho_2}} \qquad (\text{Con})\ \frac{\rho :: R \quad \tau_C[\rho] \sqsubseteq \sigma}{\Sigma \vdash_{\mathcal{R}} C^{\sigma}}$$

$$(\to \text{I})\ \frac{\Sigma/x \cup \{x : \rho\} \vdash_{\mathcal{R}} M^{\sigma}}{\Sigma/x \vdash_{\mathcal{R}} (\lambda x^{\rho}.M^{\sigma})^{\rho \to \sigma}} \qquad (\to \text{E})\ \frac{\Sigma \vdash_{\mathcal{R}} M^{\rho_1 \to \sigma} \quad \Sigma \vdash_{\mathcal{R}} N^{\rho_2} \quad \rho_1 \to \sigma \sqsubseteq \rho_2 \to \sigma}{\Sigma \vdash_{\mathcal{R}} (M^{\rho_1 \to \sigma} N^{\rho_2})^{\sigma}}$$

$$(\times \text{I})\ \frac{\Sigma \vdash_{\mathcal{R}} M_1{}^{\rho_1} \quad \Sigma \vdash_{\mathcal{R}} M_2{}^{\rho_2}}{\Sigma \vdash_{\mathcal{R}} \langle M_1{}^{\rho_1}, M_2{}^{\rho_2} \rangle^{\rho_1 \times \rho_2}} \qquad (\times \text{E}_l)\ \frac{\Sigma \vdash_{\mathcal{R}} M^{\rho_1 \times \rho_2}}{\Sigma \vdash_{\mathcal{R}} (\pi_l M^{\rho_1 \times \rho_2})^{\rho_l}}\ l \in \{1,2\}\ .$$

If $\Sigma \vdash_{\mathcal{R}} M^{\rho}$ then M^{ρ} has written in it the r-types assigned to its subterms. We say that M^{ρ} is an *annotated* term. It is worth mentioning that, in the rule $(\to \text{E})$, the condition $\rho_1 \to \sigma \sqsubseteq \rho_2 \to \sigma$ is used instead of $\rho_2 \sqsubseteq \rho_1$. This is because if $\rho_1 \to \sigma$ is an ω-r-type M can take any argument. Note that, being $\vdash_{\mathcal{R}}$ an inference system, the same terms can have different annotations.

Notice that the previous system is equivalent to the one obtained by removing the use of inclusion in rules (Var), (Con), $(\to \text{E})$ and by adding an explicit inclusion rule. We chose the presentation of Definition 6 to get a syntax directed system which is more suitable to the definition of the type inference algorithm.

The functions $\mathbf{T}$ and $\mathbf{R}$ defined above can naturally be extended to annotated terms. $\mathbf{T}(M^{\rho})$ in particular is simply the term M in which all r-type annotations have been erased. Is is immediate to see that: $\Sigma \vdash_{\mathcal{R}} M^{\rho}$ implies $\mathbf{T}(\Sigma) \vdash_{\mathcal{T}} \mathbf{T}(M^{\rho})$, and $\Gamma \vdash_{\mathcal{T}} M^{R}$ implies, for $\varphi \in \{\delta, \omega\}$, $\mathbf{R}_{\varphi}(\Gamma) \vdash_{\mathcal{R}} \mathbf{R}_{\varphi}(M^{R})$. This last deduction being obtained without the use of the $\sqsubseteq$ relation.

We now introduce a notion of semantics for our type assignment system. We interpret each basic refinement type δ or ω as a partial equivalence relation (p.e.r. for short) over the interpretation of type nat, i.e., the set of equivalence classes of closed terms of type nat with respect to $=_r$. Let $\times$ denote the cartesian product of sets and $[M]$ denote the equivalence class of M in $=_r$.

Definition 7. 1. The interpretation $[\![\rho]\!]$ of an r-type is defined by:

$$[\![\delta]\!] = \{\langle [n],[n]\rangle \mid [n] \in \mathbf{I}(\mathrm{nat})\} \quad [\![\omega]\!] = \mathbf{I}(nat) \times \mathbf{I}(nat) \quad [\![\rho \times \sigma]\!] = [\![\rho]\!] \times [\![\sigma]\!]$$
$$[\![\rho \to \sigma]\!] = \{\langle [M],[N]\rangle \mid \forall \langle [P],[Q]\rangle \in [\![\rho]\!].\langle [MP],[NQ]\rangle \in [\![\sigma]\!]\} \ .$$

2. By $\sim_\rho$ we denote the equivalence relation $[\![\rho]\!]$ on $\mathbf{I}(\mathbf{T}(\rho))$. Two environments e_1, e_2 are Σ-related if and only if, for all $x^\sigma \in \Sigma$, $e_1(x) \sim_\sigma e_2(x)$.
3. Let $\Sigma \vdash_{\mathcal{R}} M^\rho$ and $\Sigma \vdash_{\mathcal{R}} N^\rho$. We write $M \sim_\rho^\Sigma N$ to mean that for all e_1, e_2, if e_1 and e_2 are Σ-related, then $[\![M]\!]_{e_1} \sim_\rho [\![N]\!]_{e_2}$.

The $\sqsubseteq$ relation between refinement types corresponds to inclusion of p.e.r. . In fact: $\rho \sqsubseteq \sigma$ if and only if $[\![\rho]\!] \subseteq [\![\sigma]\!]$. Moreover, if $\rho :: R$ is an ω-r-type, then $[\![\rho]\!] = \mathbf{I}(R) \times \mathbf{I}(R)$, i.e., $[\![\rho]\!]$ is the p.e.r. which relates all pairs of elements of $\mathbf{I}(R)$.

We state now the main theorem for p.e.r. interpretation, which is standard (in various forms) in the literature. The proof of the following theorem is by induction of terms.

Theorem 8. *Let $\Sigma \vdash_{\mathcal{R}} M^\rho$. Then $M \sim_\rho^\Sigma M$.*

Let us now identify a subset of r-typings that assures a correct use of the optimization mapping introduced in the next section.

Definition 9 Faithful refinement. $\Sigma \vdash_{\mathcal{R}} M^\rho$ is a *faithful* refinement typing statement if $\rho = \mathbf{R}_\delta(\mathbf{T}(\rho))$, and for all $x : \sigma \in \Sigma$, if $\sigma \notin \mathcal{O}$ then $\sigma = \mathbf{R}_\delta(\mathbf{T}(\sigma))$.

Let $(\mathcal{C}[\ ]_\Gamma^R)^S$ denote a typed context of type S with a hole of type R in it which (possibly) binds variables in Γ. If $\Gamma \vdash_{\mathcal{T}} M^R$ and $\Gamma \vdash_{\mathcal{T}} N^R$ we say that M and N are *observationally equivalent* ($M =_{\mathrm{obs}} N$) if for all closed contexts $(\mathcal{C}[\ ]_\Gamma^R)^{nat}$ we have $\mathcal{C}[M] =_r \mathcal{C}[N]$.

2 Dead Code Elimination

In this section we introduce an optimization mapping $\mathbf{W}$ that, given an annotated term M^ρ, defines an optimized version of it. Define $\mathbf{W}(M^\rho)$ to be the term obtained by replacing all maximal subterms of M which are assigned an ω-r-type $\sigma :: R$ by Ω^σ, and define $\mathbf{W}(\Sigma) = \{x : \rho \mid x : \rho \in \Sigma \text{ and } \rho \notin \mathcal{O}\}$, where Σ is a r-type assignment basis. We have immediately that if $\Sigma \vdash_{\mathcal{R}} M^\rho$ then $\mathbf{W}(\Sigma) \vdash_{\mathcal{R}} \mathbf{W}(M^\rho)$ and $\mathbf{W}(\Sigma) \subseteq \Sigma$.

Example 1. Let $\Gamma \vdash_{\mathcal{T}} M^R$ where $\Gamma = \{x^{\mathrm{nat}}\}$, $R = (\mathrm{nat} \to \mathrm{nat}) \to \mathrm{nat}$ and $M^R = \lambda f^{\mathrm{nat}\to\mathrm{nat}}.f((\lambda z^{\mathrm{nat}}.3)(f\,x))$.
It is easy to check that $\Sigma \vdash_{\mathcal{R}} M'^\rho$, where $\Sigma = \{x : \omega\}$, $\rho = (\delta \to \delta) \to \delta$ and $M'^\rho = (\lambda f^{\delta\to\delta}.(f^{\delta\to\delta}((\lambda z^\omega.3^\delta)^{\omega\to\delta}(f^{\omega\to\omega}x^\omega)^\omega)^\delta)^\delta)^\rho$, is a faithful r-typing.
Applying the $\mathbf{W}$ optimization mapping we get $\mathbf{W}(\Sigma) \vdash_{\mathcal{R}} \mathbf{W}(M'^\rho)$, where $\mathbf{W}(\Sigma) = \{\}$ and $\mathbf{W}(M'^\rho) = (\lambda f^{\delta\to\delta}.(f^{\delta\to\delta}((\lambda z^\omega.3^\delta)^{\omega\to\delta}\Omega^\omega)^\delta)^\delta)^\rho$, and, erasing the r-type annotations, $\mathbf{T}(\mathbf{W}(\Sigma)) \vdash_{\mathcal{T}} \mathbf{T}(\mathbf{W}(M'^\rho))$, where $\mathbf{T}(\mathbf{W}(\Sigma)) = \{\}$ and $\mathbf{T}(\mathbf{W}(M'^\rho)) = \lambda f^{\mathrm{nat}\to\mathrm{nat}}.f((\lambda z^{nat}.3)\Omega^{\mathrm{nat}})$. □

The following result follows easily from the r-type semantics.

Theorem 10. *If* $\Sigma \vdash_{\mathcal{R}} M^{\rho}$ *then* $\mathbf{T}(M^{\rho}) \sim_{\rho}^{\Sigma} \mathbf{T}(\mathbf{W}(M^{\rho}))$.

This means that if $\Sigma \vdash_{\mathcal{R}} M^{\rho}$ then M and its optimized version are equivalent in ρ. The function $\mathbf{T}$ has been inserted just to point out that the r-type information has a purely static nature and is not relevant in the formation rules and in the operational semantics of terms.

This result is especially interesting when the typing of M is faithful since, using the above theorem, we can prove that that if $\Sigma \vdash_{\mathcal{R}} M^{\rho}$ is a faithful typing statement then $\mathbf{T}(M^{\rho})$ and $\mathbf{T}(\mathbf{W}(M^{\rho}))$ are observationally equivalent.

Theorem 11. *Let* $\Sigma \vdash_{\mathcal{R}} M^{\rho}$ *be a faithful typing. Then* $\mathbf{T}(M^{\rho}) =_{\mathsf{obs}} \mathbf{T}(\mathbf{W}(M^{\rho}))$.

Remark. A strong optimization function $\mathbf{S}$ could be inductively defined on terms in such a way that, if $\Sigma \vdash_{\mathcal{R}} M'^{\rho}$ is the faithful r-typing of Example 1, then $\mathbf{T}(\mathbf{S}(\Sigma)) = \{\}$ and $\mathbf{T}(\mathbf{S}(M'^{\rho})) = \lambda f^{\mathsf{nat}\to\mathsf{nat}}.f\,3$.
The mapping $\mathbf{S}$ could be defined following [2]. The optimizations performed by $\mathbf{S}$ can be much stronger than those performed by $\mathbf{W}$. In certain cases $\mathbf{S}$ can also replace the constants of the language transforming, for instance, a recursor $\mathsf{rec}^{\delta\to\rho\to(\omega\to\rho\to\rho)\to\rho}$ in an iterator $\mathsf{it}^{\delta\to\rho\to(\rho\to\rho)\to\rho}$. A deeper analysis of the r-type structure of the term can allow to detect where this stronger optimization can be done. We do not go into those details since this kind of analysis simply uses the r-type structure determined by our algorithm. □

3 An Algorithm for Refinement Types Inference

In this section we deal with the problem of defining an algorithm for program optimization based on the system defined in the previous section. To this aim the main problem is to use the inference rules to detect the maximal subterms to which ω-r-types can be assigned. The application of the optimization function $\mathbf{W}$ is then trivial. The algorithm, given a typing of a term, returns a decoration of the term with refinement patterns and a set of inequalities between refinement variables. The output of the algorithm characterizes all the possible r-typings of the term.

We start by defining the notions of r-type pattern and r-type scheme.

Definition 12 Refinement type schemes.
1. Let $\mathcal{U}$ be the set of *atomic variables*, ranged by α, β, γ, ...
   The language $\mathcal{P}$ of *refinement type patterns* (*r-patterns* for short) is defined from the rules of Definition 3 by replacing rule (nat) by the following rule:
   $$(\mathcal{U})\ \frac{\alpha \in \mathcal{U}}{\alpha :: \mathsf{nat}}\ ,$$
   r-patterns are ranged over by θ, η,...
2. A *constraint* is a formula of one of the following shapes:

- $\zeta_1 \sqsubseteq \zeta_2$, where $\zeta_1, \zeta_2 \in \{\delta\} \cup \mathcal{U}$
- $\mathcal{G} \Rightarrow \mathcal{E}$, where $\mathcal{G}$ is a finite not empty subset of $\{\delta\} \cup \mathcal{U}$ and $\mathcal{E}$ is a finite set of constraints.

3. A *refinement type scheme* is a pair $\langle \theta, \mathcal{E} \rangle$ where θ is a r-pattern and $\mathcal{E}$ is a finite set of constraints.

R-types and r-typings can be obtained from patterns by instantiation. A constraint is simply an inequality (between atomic variables or the constant δ) or a guarded set of constraints. For instance the set of constraints

$$\{\ \alpha_3 \sqsubseteq \alpha_1,\ \{\alpha_1, \alpha_2\} \Rightarrow \{\alpha_3 \sqsubseteq \alpha_4, \alpha_5 \sqsubseteq \delta\}\ \}$$

can be read as "$\alpha_3 \sqsubseteq \alpha_1$ and if $\alpha_1 = \delta$ or $\alpha_2 = \delta$, then $\alpha_3 \sqsubseteq \alpha_4$ and $\alpha_5 \sqsubseteq \delta$". To give a meaning to constraints we have to say which are the solutions of a set of constraints.

Definition 13 Renaming and instantiations. 1. A *renaming* is a one–to–one mapping $r : \mathcal{U} \rightarrow \mathcal{U}$.

2. An *instantiation* is a mapping $i : \mathcal{U} \rightarrow \{\delta, \omega\}$.

Both renaming and instantiation can be extended to constants by defining $i(\varphi) = \varphi$ and $r(\varphi) = \varphi$, for $\varphi \in \{\delta, \omega\}$.

Definition 14. Let $\langle \theta, \mathcal{E} \rangle$ be a scheme. An instantiation i satisfies $\mathcal{E}$ if

- $\zeta_1 \sqsubseteq \zeta_2 \in \mathcal{E}$ implies $i(\zeta_1) \sqsubseteq i(\zeta_2)$, and
- $\mathcal{G} \Rightarrow \mathcal{E}' \in \mathcal{E}$ implies that, if $\delta \in i(\mathcal{G})$, then i satisfies $\mathcal{E}'$.

The set of all the instantiations that satisfy $\mathcal{E}$ is denoted by $\mathrm{SAT}(\mathcal{E})$. A scheme $\langle \theta, \mathcal{E} \rangle$ represents all the refinement types $i(\theta)$, for any $i \in \mathrm{SAT}(\mathcal{E})$.

Definition 15. Let i_1, i_2 be instantiations. $i_1 \sqsubseteq i_2$ means that, for all $\alpha \in \mathcal{U}$, $i_1(\alpha) \sqsubseteq i_2(\alpha)$.

Fact 16. *Let $\mathcal{E}$ be a finite set of constraints. The set* $\mathrm{SAT}(\mathcal{E})$ *is not empty and has a maximum element.*

Example 2. Consider the sets of constraints:

$$\begin{array}{ll}
\mathcal{E} = \{\ \{\alpha_3'\} \Rightarrow \{\alpha_3 \sqsubseteq \alpha_3', \alpha_2' \sqsubseteq \alpha_2\}, & \\
\qquad \{\alpha_3''\} \Rightarrow \{\alpha_3 \sqsubseteq \alpha_3'', \alpha_2'' \sqsubseteq \alpha_2\}, & \mathcal{E}_1 = \{\ \{\alpha_1\} \Rightarrow \{\alpha_1 \sqsubseteq \delta\}, \\
\qquad \alpha_1 \sqsubseteq \alpha_1', & \qquad \alpha_2 \sqsubseteq \delta, \\
\qquad \{\alpha_3''\} \Rightarrow \{\alpha_1' \sqsubseteq \alpha_2''\}, & \qquad \alpha_3 \sqsubseteq \delta, \\
\qquad \{\alpha_5\} \Rightarrow \{\alpha_3'' \sqsubseteq \alpha_4\}, & \qquad \alpha_3' \sqsubseteq \delta \qquad \} . \\
\qquad \{\alpha_3'\} \Rightarrow \{\alpha_5 \sqsubseteq \alpha_2'\} \qquad \}, &
\end{array}$$

To find the maximum element i_0 of $\mathrm{SAT}(\mathcal{E} \cup \mathcal{E}_1)$ observe that from the last three constraints of $\mathcal{E}_1$ we get $i_0(\alpha_2) = i_0(\alpha_3) = i_0(\alpha_3') = \delta$. Then from the first constraint of $\mathcal{E}$ we get $i_0(\alpha_2') = \delta$, and finally from the last constraint of $\mathcal{E}$ we have $i_0(\alpha_5) = \delta$. Let $\mathcal{I} = \{\alpha_2, \alpha_2', \alpha_3, \alpha_3', \alpha_5\}$, then i_0 defined by: $i_0(\alpha) = \delta$ if $\alpha \in \mathcal{I}$ and $i_0(\alpha) = \omega$ otherwise, is the maximum instantiation in $\mathrm{SAT}(\mathcal{E} \cup \mathcal{E}_1)$. □

R-type inference of a term is reduced to the solution of a finite set of constraints. A maximal instantiation then corresponds to the typing that shows the maximal amount of dead code. The algorithm for finding the maximal instantiation i that satisfies a finite set of constraints $\mathcal{E}$ is presented in natural semantics style using judgements $\mathcal{E} \leadsto \mathcal{I}$ where $\mathcal{I}$ is the set of atomic variables that *represents* i, i.e., such that $\alpha \in \mathcal{I}$ if and only if $i(\alpha) = \delta$. The idea is simply that of recognizing, following the inequalities, all the variables that are forced to represent δ. All other atomic variables are then replaced by ω in the maximal solution.

Definition 17 "Natural semantics" rules for constraints solution.

(AX) $\dfrac{}{\mathcal{E} \leadsto \emptyset}$ if no other rule can be applied

(ATOM) $\dfrac{\mathcal{E}[\delta/\alpha] \leadsto \mathcal{I}}{\mathcal{E} \cup \{\alpha \sqsubseteq \delta\} \leadsto \mathcal{I} \cup \{\alpha\}}$ (GUARD) $\dfrac{\mathcal{E} \cup \mathcal{E}'' \leadsto \mathcal{I} \quad \delta \in \mathcal{G}}{\mathcal{E} \cup \{\mathcal{G} \Rightarrow \mathcal{E}''\} \leadsto \mathcal{I}}$

It is easy to see that, given a finite set of constraints $\mathcal{E}$, we can find $\mathcal{I}$ such that $\mathcal{E} \leadsto \mathcal{I}$ in a time linear in the number of constraints which occur in $\mathcal{E}$.

Proposition 18. *Let $\mathcal{E}$ be a finite set of constraints. Then $\mathcal{E} \leadsto \mathcal{I}$ if and only if $\mathcal{I}$ represents the maximum of* $\mathrm{SAT}(\mathcal{E})$.

We can now proceed to define the refinement type inference algorithm. This algorithm is presented in the natural semantics style using judgements $\langle \Gamma, M^R \rangle \Longrightarrow \langle \Theta, M'^{\theta}, \mathcal{E} \rangle$ where $\Gamma \vdash_{\mathcal{T}} M^R$, Θ is a basis that associates to each term variable in Γ a pattern, and M'^{θ} is a term annotated with patterns. The natural semantics rules follow the inference rules of Definition 6 in a natural way. We will prove that $\langle \theta, \mathcal{E} \rangle$ is a scheme that represents exactly the refined types assignable to M^R. More precisely, for any Σ and M''^{ρ} such that $\mathbf{T}(\Sigma) = \Gamma$ and $\mathbf{T}(M''^{\rho}) = M^R$, we have that $\Sigma \vdash_{\mathcal{R}} M''^{\rho}$ if and only if $\Sigma = i(\Theta)$ and $M''^{\rho} = i(M'^{\theta})$, for some i that satisfies $\mathcal{E}$.

To define the algorithm we need some preliminary notations. Let R be a type. By fresh(R) we denote a pattern of the same shape of R such that to each occurrence of any atom in R is associated a fresh atomic variable. For example: fresh(nat $\rightarrow$ nat) $= \alpha \rightarrow \beta$. For a basis Γ, fresh$(\Gamma) = \{x : \mathrm{fresh}(R) \mid x^R \in \Gamma\}$. The function vars maps an r-pattern α to its finite set of atomic variables.
The function tail, that maps r-patterns and r-types (not containing ω) to finite subsets of $\{\delta\} \cup \mathcal{U}$, is inductively defined by: $\mathrm{tail}(\zeta) = \{\zeta\}$ (for $\zeta \in \{\delta\} \cup \mathcal{U}$), $\mathrm{tail}(\theta \times \eta) = \mathrm{tail}(\theta) \cup \mathrm{tail}(\eta)$, and $\mathrm{tail}(\theta \rightarrow \eta) = \mathrm{tail}(\eta)$.
Let θ', θ'' be r-patterns or r-types (not containing ω) of the same shape, $\mathrm{flat}(\theta' \sqsubseteq \theta'')$ denotes the set of constraints inductively defined by

$$\begin{aligned}
&\mathrm{flat}(\zeta_1 \sqsubseteq \zeta_2) = \{\zeta_1 \sqsubseteq \zeta_2\}, \ \textit{if}\ \zeta_1, \zeta_2 \in \{\delta\} \cup \mathcal{U}\\
&\mathrm{flat}(\theta_1 \times \eta_1 \sqsubseteq \theta_2 \times \eta_2) = \mathrm{flat}(\theta_1 \sqsubseteq \theta_2) \cup \mathrm{flat}(\eta_1 \sqsubseteq \eta_2)\\
&\mathrm{flat}(\theta'_1 \rightarrow \cdots \rightarrow \theta'_n \rightarrow \eta' \sqsubseteq \theta''_1 \rightarrow \cdots \rightarrow \theta''_n \rightarrow \eta'') =\\
&\ \{\mathrm{tail}(\eta'') \Rightarrow (\mathrm{flat}(\eta' \sqsubseteq \eta'') \cup \textstyle\bigcup_{1 \le l \le n} \mathrm{flat}(\theta''_l \sqsubseteq \theta'_l))\},\\
&\ \textit{where } \eta', \eta'' \textit{ are not arrow r-patterns or arrow r-types.}
\end{aligned}$$

For all instances i, $i(\theta) \sqsubseteq i(\eta)$ if and only if $i \in \mathrm{SAT}(\mathrm{flat}(\theta \sqsubseteq \eta))$.

Definition 19 "Natural semantics" rules for refinement typings inference.

$$(\text{VAR})\ \frac{\Theta = \text{fresh}(\Gamma) \quad \theta_1 = \text{fresh}(R) \quad \theta_2 = \text{fresh}(R)}{\langle \Gamma/x \cup \{x^R\}, x^R\rangle \Longrightarrow \langle \Theta/x \cup \{x:\theta_1\}, x^{\theta_2}, \text{flat}(\theta_1 \sqsubseteq \theta_2)\rangle}$$

$$(\text{CON})\ \frac{\Theta = \text{fresh}(\Gamma) \quad \eta = \text{fresh}(T_C[R]) \quad \theta = \text{fresh}(R)}{\langle \Gamma, C^{T_C[R]}\rangle \Longrightarrow \langle \Theta, C^{\eta}, \mathcal{E}\rangle}$$
where $\mathcal{E} = \text{flat}(\tau_C[\theta] \sqsubseteq \eta)$

$$(\text{ABS})\ \frac{\langle \Gamma/x \cup \{x^R\}, M^S\rangle \Longrightarrow \langle \Theta/x \cup \{x:\theta\}, M'^{\eta}, \mathcal{E}\rangle}{\langle \Gamma/x, (\lambda x^R.M^S)^{R\to S}\rangle \Longrightarrow \langle \Theta/x, (\lambda x^{\theta}.M'^{\eta})^{\theta\to\eta}, \mathcal{E}\rangle}$$

$$(\text{APP})\ \frac{\begin{array}{c}\langle \Gamma, M^{R\to S}\rangle \Longrightarrow \langle \Theta_1, M'^{\theta_1\to\eta}, \mathcal{E}_1\rangle \quad \langle \Gamma, N^R\rangle \Longrightarrow \langle \Theta_2, N'^{\theta_2}, \mathcal{E}_2\rangle \\ \Theta_1 = \{x : r(\theta) \mid x:\theta \in \Theta_2\}\end{array}}{\langle \Gamma, (M^{R\to S} N^R)^S\rangle \Longrightarrow \langle \Theta_1, (M'^{\theta_1\to\eta} N'^{\theta_2})^{\eta}, \mathcal{E}\rangle}$$
where $\mathcal{E} = \mathcal{E}_1 \cup r(\mathcal{E}_2) \cup \{\text{tail}(\eta) \Rightarrow \text{flat}(\theta_2 \sqsubseteq \theta_1)\}$
and r *is a renaming of the atomic variables in* Θ_2

$$(\text{PAIR})\ \frac{\begin{array}{c}\langle \Gamma, M_1{}^{R_1}\rangle \Longrightarrow \langle \Theta_1, M_1'{}^{\theta_1}, \mathcal{E}_1\rangle \quad \langle \Gamma, M_2{}^{R_2}\rangle \Longrightarrow \langle \Theta_2, M_2'{}^{\theta_2}, \mathcal{E}_2\rangle \\ \Theta_1 = \{x : r(\theta) \mid x:\theta \in \Theta_2\}\end{array}}{\langle \Gamma, \langle M_1{}^{R_1}, M_2{}^{R_2}\rangle^{R_1\times R_2}\rangle \Longrightarrow \langle \Theta_1, \langle M_1'{}^{\theta_1}, M_2'{}^{\theta_2}\rangle^{\theta_1\times\theta_2}, \mathcal{E}_1 \cup r(\mathcal{E}_2)\rangle}$$
where r *is a renaming of the atomic variables in* Θ_2

$$(\text{PROJ}_l)\ \frac{\langle \Gamma, M^{R_1\times R_2}\rangle \Longrightarrow \langle \Theta, M'^{\theta_1\times\theta_2}, \mathcal{E}\rangle}{\langle \Gamma, (\pi_l M^{R_1\times R_2})^{R_l}\rangle \Longrightarrow \langle \Theta, (\pi_l M'^{\theta_1\times\theta_2})^{\theta_l}, \mathcal{E}\rangle}\ l \in \{1,2\}$$

The rules are in this form to make them as readable as possible. They generate inequalities that could easily be avoided in a real implementation. Correctness and completeness of the inference are expressed by the following theorem.

Theorem 20. $\Gamma \vdash_{\mathcal{T}} M^R$ *and* $\langle \Gamma, M^R\rangle \Longrightarrow \langle \Theta, M'^{\theta}, \mathcal{E}\rangle$ *imply*

1. *for all instantiations* i*, if* i *satisfies* $\mathcal{E}$*, then* $i(\Theta) \vdash_{\mathcal{R}} i(M'^{\theta})$
2. *for all refinement type assignment statements* $\Sigma \vdash_{\mathcal{R}} M''^{\rho}$ *such that* $\mathbf{T}(\Sigma) = \Gamma$ *and* $\mathbf{T}(M''^{\rho}) = M^R$ *there exists* $i \in \text{SAT}(\mathcal{E})$ *such that* $i(\Theta) = \Sigma$ *and* $i(M'^{\theta}) = M''^{\rho}$.

We are interested in faithful refinements, so we want to restrict the set of solutions of the constraints generated by the algorithm to those that correspond to faithful refinements. This can be done as shown by the following corollary.

Corollary 21. *Let* $\Gamma \vdash_{\mathcal{T}} M^R$ *and* $\langle \Gamma, M^R\rangle \Longrightarrow \langle \Theta, M'^{\theta}, \mathcal{E}\rangle$*. Then* $i(\Theta) \vdash_{\mathcal{R}} i(M'^{\theta})$ *is a faithful refinement type assignment if and only if the instantiations* i *satisfies the set of constraints* $\mathcal{E} \cup \text{faithful}(\Theta, \theta)$*, where*
$\text{faithful}(\Theta,\theta) = \bigcup_{x:\eta\in\Theta}\{\text{tail}(\eta) \Rightarrow \{\gamma \sqsubseteq \delta \mid \gamma \in \text{vars}(\eta)\}\} \ \cup\ \{\alpha \sqsubseteq \delta \mid \alpha \in \text{vars}(\theta)\}$.

The constraint $\text{tail}(\eta) \Rightarrow \{\gamma \sqsubseteq \delta \mid \gamma \in \text{vars}(\eta)\}$ means that either η is an ω-r-type or it contains only δ's.

Let $\Gamma \vdash_{\mathcal{T}} M^R$ and $\langle \Gamma, M^R \rangle \Longrightarrow \langle \Theta, {M'}^{\theta}, \mathcal{E} \rangle$. If i_0 is the maximum element of $\mathrm{SAT}(\mathcal{E} \cup \mathrm{faithful}(\Theta, \theta))$ then, by the results of Sect. 1, $\mathbf{T}(\mathbf{W}(i_0({M'}^{\theta})))$ is the best simplification (in our sense) of M^R with the same operational meaning w.r.t. $=_{\mathrm{obs}}$.

Example 3. Let $\Gamma \vdash_{\mathcal{T}} M^R$ be the typing of Example 1. Then $\langle \Gamma, M^R \rangle \Longrightarrow \langle \Theta, {M'}^{\theta}, \mathcal{E} \rangle$ where $\Theta = \{x : \alpha_1\}$, $\theta = (\alpha_2 \to \alpha_3) \to \alpha_3'$,
${M'}^{\theta} = (\lambda f^{\alpha_2 \to \alpha_3}.(f^{\alpha_2' \to \alpha_3'}((\lambda z^{\alpha_4}.3^{\alpha_5})^{\alpha_4 \to \alpha_5}(f^{\alpha_2'' \to \alpha_3''} x^{\alpha_1'})^{\alpha_3''})^{\alpha_5})^{\alpha_3'})^{\theta}$, and

$$\begin{aligned}\mathcal{E} = {} & \mathrm{flat}(\alpha_2 \to \alpha_3 \sqsubseteq \alpha_2' \to \alpha_3') \cup \mathrm{flat}(\alpha_2 \to \alpha_3 \sqsubseteq \alpha_2'' \to \alpha_3'') \cup \\ & \{\alpha_1 \sqsubseteq \alpha_1', \{\alpha_3''\} \Rightarrow \{\alpha_1' \sqsubseteq \alpha_2''\}, \{\alpha_5\} \Rightarrow \{\alpha_3'' \sqsubseteq \alpha_4\}, \{\alpha_3'\} \Rightarrow \{\alpha_5 \sqsubseteq \alpha_2'\}\}\end{aligned}$$

is the first set of constraints introduced in Example 2.

The set $\mathrm{faithful}(\Theta, \theta)$ is the set $\mathcal{E}_1$ in Example 2, so $\mathcal{E} \cup \mathrm{faithful}(\Theta, \theta) \leadsto \mathcal{I}$, where $\mathcal{I}$ is $\{\alpha_2, \alpha_2', \alpha_3, \alpha_3', \alpha_5\}$.

Let i_0 be defined by: $i_0(\alpha) = \delta$ if $\alpha \in \mathcal{I}$ and $i_0(\alpha) = \omega$ otherwise.
We have that $i_0(\Theta) \vdash_{\mathcal{R}} i_0({M'}^{\theta})$, where $i_0(\Theta) = \{x : \omega\}$, $i_0(\theta) = (\delta \to \delta) \to \delta$ and $i_0({M'}^{\theta}) = (\lambda f^{\delta \to \delta}.(f^{\delta \to \delta}((\lambda z^{\omega}.3^{\delta})^{\omega \to \delta}(f^{\omega \to \omega} x^{\omega})^{\omega})^{\delta})^{\delta})^{i(\theta)}$, is the faithful r-typing used in Example 1. □

When using the inference method to analyze a term M we will indeed produce as output a set of constraints that characterizes all possible r-typings of M. The subterms of M which are assigned ω-r-types in a faithful typing are indeed certainly useless in any use of M, and can then be simplified. Moreover the constraints associated to them are irrelevant to further analysis of M and can then be eliminated by the set of constraints for M. More precisely, if $\Gamma \vdash_{\mathcal{T}} M^R$, $\langle \Gamma, M^R \rangle \Longrightarrow \langle \Theta, {M'}^{\theta}, \mathcal{E} \rangle$ and i_0 is the maximum element of $\mathrm{SAT}(\mathcal{E} \cup \mathrm{faithful}(\Theta, \theta))$ then, the set of constraints $\mathcal{E}$ can be replaced by any set of constraints $\mathcal{E}'$ such that

$$\{i \mid i \in \mathrm{SAT}(\mathcal{E}') \text{ and } i_0 \sqsubseteq i\} = \{i \mid i \in \mathrm{SAT}(\mathcal{E}) \text{ and } i_0 \sqsubseteq i\} \ . \tag{1}$$

Example 4. Let $\mathcal{E}$ and i_0 be the set of constraints and the instantiation of Example 3. Consider the following subset $\mathcal{E}'$ of $\mathcal{E}$:

$$\mathcal{E}' = \{\{\alpha_3'\} \Rightarrow \{\alpha_3 \sqsubseteq \alpha_3', \alpha_2' \sqsubseteq \alpha_2\}, \{\alpha_3'\} \Rightarrow \{\alpha_5 \sqsubseteq \alpha_2'\}\} \ .$$

It is easy to see that any instantiation i' that maps to ω more atomic variables than i_0, i.e., such that $i_0 \sqsubseteq i'$, satisfies all the constraints in $\mathcal{E}$ that are not in $\mathcal{E}'$. So, since only the instantiations $i' \in \mathrm{SAT}(\mathcal{E})$ such that $i_0 \sqsubseteq i'$ are relevant to further analysis, we can replace $\mathcal{E}$ by the simplified set of constraint $\mathcal{E}'$ without loss of information. □

The following algorithm, given a finite set of constraints $\mathcal{E}$ and an instantiation $i_0 \in \mathrm{SAT}(\mathcal{E})$, returns a simplified set of constraints $\mathcal{E}'$ such that (1) holds, and so can be used to eliminate from $\mathcal{E}$ all the constraints which are not relevant for further analysis.
The algorithm is presented in natural semantics style using judgements $\mathcal{E}, \mathcal{I} \gg \mathcal{E}'$, where $\mathcal{I}$ represents i_0.

Definition 22 "Natural semantics" rules for simplification of constraints.

$$\text{(AX)}\ \frac{}{\mathcal{E},\mathcal{I} \gg \mathcal{E}} \text{ if no other rule can be applied}$$

$$\text{(ATOM}_1\text{)}\ \frac{\mathcal{E},\mathcal{I} \gg \mathcal{E}'}{\mathcal{E} \cup \{\delta \sqsubseteq \zeta\},\mathcal{I} \gg \mathcal{E}'} \qquad \text{(ATOM}_2\text{)}\ \frac{\mathcal{E},\mathcal{I} \gg \mathcal{E}' \quad \zeta_2 \notin \mathcal{I} \cup \{\delta\}}{\mathcal{E} \cup \{\zeta_1 \sqsubseteq \zeta_2\},\mathcal{I} \gg \mathcal{E}'}$$

$$\text{(GUARD}_1\text{)}\ \frac{\mathcal{E},\mathcal{I} \gg \mathcal{E}' \quad \mathcal{G} \cap (\mathcal{I} \cup \{\delta\}) = \emptyset}{\mathcal{E} \cup \{\mathcal{G} \Rightarrow \mathcal{E}_0\},\mathcal{I} \gg \mathcal{E}'} \qquad \text{(GUARD}_2\text{)}\ \frac{\mathcal{E},\mathcal{I} \gg \mathcal{E}' \quad \mathcal{E}_0,\mathcal{I} \gg \emptyset}{\mathcal{E} \cup \{\mathcal{G} \Rightarrow \mathcal{E}_0\},\mathcal{I} \gg \mathcal{E}'}$$

$$\text{(GUARD}_3\text{)}\ \frac{\mathcal{E},\mathcal{I} \gg \mathcal{E}' \quad \mathcal{E}_0,\mathcal{I} \gg \mathcal{E}_0' \quad \mathcal{G} \cap (\mathcal{I} \cup \{\delta\}) \neq \emptyset \quad \mathcal{E}_0' \neq \emptyset}{\mathcal{E} \cup \{\mathcal{G} \Rightarrow \mathcal{E}_0\},\mathcal{I} \gg \mathcal{E}' \cup \{\mathcal{G} \Rightarrow \mathcal{E}_0'\}}$$

Proposition 23. *Let $\mathcal{E}$ be a finite set of constraints and let $\mathcal{I}$ represent $i_0 \in$ SAT($\mathcal{E}$). Then $\mathcal{E},\mathcal{I} \gg \mathcal{E}'$ implies that (1) holds.*

Example 5. Consider the output of the refinement type inference algorithm in Example 3, i.e., the triple $\langle \Theta, M'^{\theta}, \mathcal{E} \rangle$. The dead code showed by the maximum faithful typing can be immediately removed and, since $\mathcal{E},\mathcal{I} \gg \mathcal{E}'$, the set of constraints can be simplified as shown in Example 4. The triple $\langle \emptyset, M''^{\theta}, \mathcal{E}' \rangle$, where $M''^{\theta} = (\lambda f^{\alpha_2 \to \alpha_3}.(f^{\alpha_2' \to \alpha_3'}((\lambda z^{\alpha_4}.3^{\alpha_5})\Omega^{\alpha_3''})^{\alpha_5})^{\alpha_3'})^{\theta}$, and $\mathcal{E}' = \{\{\alpha_3'\} \Rightarrow \{\alpha_3 \sqsubseteq \alpha_3', \alpha_2' \sqsubseteq \alpha_2\}, \{\alpha_3'\} \Rightarrow \{\alpha_5 \sqsubseteq \alpha_2'\}\}$, is indeed all we need in the analysis of programs that use M. □

We have now all the components for the definition of an efficient incremental analysis of a term M^R with free variables in Γ. Let $\langle \Gamma, M^R \rangle \Longrightarrow \langle \Theta, M'^{\theta}, \mathcal{E} \rangle$ and $\mathcal{E} \cup \text{faithful}(\Theta, \theta) \rightsquigarrow \mathcal{I}$. We can define an optimization mapping $\mathbf{W}'$ such that $\mathbf{W}'(\langle \Theta, M'^{\theta}, \mathcal{E} \rangle, \mathcal{I}) = \langle \Theta', M''^{\theta}, \mathcal{E}' \rangle$, where $\Theta' = \{x : \theta \mid x : \theta \in \Sigma \text{ and } \text{tail}(\theta) \cap \mathcal{I} \neq \emptyset\}$, M''^{θ} is obtained from M'^{θ} by replacing the maximal subterms annotated by a pattern η such that $\text{tail}(\eta) \cap \mathcal{I} = \emptyset$ by Ω^{η}, and $\mathcal{E},\mathcal{I} \gg \mathcal{E}'$. The triple $\langle \Theta', M''^{\theta}, \mathcal{E}' \rangle$ is all we need to perform further analysis of a program containing M. For instance M could be applied to a term or could be itself the argument of function. In such contexts further optimizations of M could be possible. The optimizations performed by $\mathbf{W}'$ are those which are possible in any context.

4 Binding Time and Strictness Analysis

The interpretation of δ and ω can be understood in a different way, as suggested in [10]. The r-type, δ (interpreted as the diagonal relation on $\mathbf{I}$(nat)), characterizes values which are "known" and have a precise identity while ω characterizes values which are completely unknown (they can be any value in $\mathbf{I}$(nat)). These properties are naturally propagated to higher types, for instance if a term of type nat $\to$ nat has the refinement types $\delta \to \omega$ or $\omega \to \omega$ then it is totally unknown, since it can be equated to anything, whereas the refinement $\delta \to \delta$ or $\omega \to \delta$ are given to terms that identify uniquely a function. In $\delta \to \delta$ two functions are equated only if they are extensionally equivalent. In the case of $\omega \to \delta$ we also know more, that is, the function is a constant function, since it identifies uniquely a value from an unknown input. Of course there are refinements that are not in either one of these classes, e.g., $(\omega \rightarrow \delta) \rightarrow \omega \rightarrow \delta$ that identifies all the functions that return a constant function when applied to a constant function. In general ω-r-types correspond to the concept of being totally unknown, indeed all of them represent the relations that identify all the elements of a given type.

With the previous interpretation detecting dead code in a term M can be seen as assuming that M identifies uniquely a value and trying to assign the maximum number of ω's to its subterms (of course keeping the refinement consistent). A subterm with ω-r-type then can be totally unknown, and so it is useless to the evaluation of the final result.

This interpretation led us to explore the use of the system for binding time analysis. For the binding time analysis the question is: given a description of the parameters of a function that will be known we must determine which parts of the program are dependent solely on the known parts. Known parameters correspond to terms identifying a unique value, and unknown parameters correspond naturally to terms having ω-r-types. The first are called static and the second dynamic in the binding time literature. For this analysis we look for a refinement of the term that respect the static and dynamic information of the parameters and that maximizes the number of δ in the term. A subterm of type δ is a subterm whose value does not depend on the values of the variables with dynamic type. So it is a natural candidate for evaluation when all static values are known. Our analysis gives that same results as [10] and [8].

Our framework can be also applied to strictness analysis. If we replace the rule (Zero) of Definition 6 by the rule "(Zero$'$) $\Sigma \vdash_{\mathcal{R}} 0^{\omega}$ " we get a system that can be used to study strictness properties for the λ-calculus with unary and constant operators. The refinement δ now means to be the undefined value of natural numbers and the refinement ω means to be any value. For a refinement of a functional type, say nat $\rightarrow$ nat $\rightarrow$ nat, to specify that a function is strict in the first argument, means that $\delta \rightarrow \omega \rightarrow \delta$ is a refinement of the function. This is because if the first argument of the function is undefined and, regardless of the value of the second, the result is undefined that means that the first argument must be evaluated somewhere in the body of the function. In this context the equivalence of ω-r-types says that non-informative types are all equivalent. Of course strictness analysis makes sense in a language including a fixed point operator. It is not difficult to add to our language a typed fixed point constant, with a suitable refinement rule.

The difference between strictness analysis and dead code (or binding time) analysis arises with the use of constants such as $\text{if}^{\text{nat}\rightarrow R\rightarrow R\rightarrow R}$ which strictness behaviour cannot be described, as for dead code or binding time, by all the refinements σ such that $\delta \rightarrow \rho \rightarrow \rho \rightarrow \rho \sqsubseteq \sigma$ for any $\rho :: R$.
For strictness analysis, "if" has all the refinements σ such that either $\omega \rightarrow \rho \rightarrow \rho \rightarrow \rho \sqsubseteq \sigma$ or $\delta \rightarrow \rho_1 \rightarrow \rho_2 \rightarrow \rho_3 \sqsubseteq \sigma$. (The second case corresponding to a certainly undefined value of the test.) This adds a sort of and/or structure to the system of inequalities. A version of the system tailored to strictness analysis is in preparation.

References

1. H. P. Barendregt, M. Coppo, and M. Dezani-Ciancaglini. A filter lambda model and the completeness of type assignment. *Journal of Symbolic Logic*, 48:931–940, 1983.
2. S. Berardi. Pruning Simply Typed Lambda Terms. *Journal of Symbolic Computation*, to appear.
3. S. Berardi and L. Boerio. Using Subtyping in Program Optimization. In *Typed Lambda Calculus and Applications*, 1995.
4. M. Coppo and M. Dezani-Ciancaglini. An extension of basic functional theory for lambda-calculus. *Notre Dame Journal of Formal Logic*, 21(4):685–693, 1980.
5. M. Coppo and A. Ferrari. Type inference, abstract interpretation and strictness analysis. In M. Dezani-Ciancaglini et al., editors, *A collection of contributions in honour of Corrado Böhm*, pages 113–145. Elsevier, 1993.
6. M. Coppo and P. Giannini. Pricipal Types and Unification for Simple Intersection Types Systems. *Information and Computation*, 122(1):70–96, 1995.
7. F. Damiani and P. Giannini. A Decidable Intersection Type System based on Relevance. In *Theoretical Aspects of Computer Software*, LNCS 789. Springer, 1994.
8. C. Hankin and D. Le Metayer. A Type-Based Framework for Program Analysis. In *Static Analisys*, LNCS 864, pages 380–394. Springer, 1994.
9. R. Hindley. The principal types schemes for an object in combinatory logic. *Transactions of American Mathematical Society*, 146:29–60, 1969.
10. L.S. Hunt and D. Sands. Binding Time Analysis: A New PERspective. In *Proceedings of the ACM Symposium on Partial Evaluation and Semantics-based Program Manipulation*, 1991.
11. P. O'Keefe J. Palsberg. A Type System Equivalent to Flow Analysis. In *Principles of Programming Languages*, 1995.
12. T. P. Jensen. Strictness Analysis in Logical Form. In J. Hughes, editor, *Proceedings of the 5th ACM Conference on Functional Programming Languages and Computer Architecture*, pages 98–105, 1991.
13. H. R. Nielson K. L. Solberg and F. Nielson. Strictness and Totality Analysis. In *Static Analisys*, LNCS 864, pages 408–422. Springer, 1994.
14. D. Leivant. Polymorphic Type Inference. In *Principles of Programming Languages*. ACM, 1983.
15. R. Milner. A Theory of Type Polymorphism in Programming. *Journal of Computer and System Science*, 17:348–375, 1978.
16. F. Prost. Marking techniques for extraction. Technical report, Ecole Normale Supérieure de Lyon, Lyon, December 1995.
17. T.M.Kuo and P.Mishra. Strictness analysis: a new perspective based on type inference. In *Functional Programming Languages and Computer Architecture*. ACM, 1989.
18. D. A. Wright. A New Technique for Strictness Analysis. In *Proceedings of TAPSOFT'91*, LNCS 494, pages 260–272. Springer, 1991.

A Comparison of Three Occur-Check Analysers

Lobel Crnogorac[1], Andrew D. Kelly[2] and Harald Søndergaard[1]

[1] Dept. of Computer Science, University of Melbourne, Parkville Vic. 3052, Australia
[2] Dept. of Computer Science, Monash University, Clayton Vic. 3168, Australia

Abstract. A well known problem with many Prolog interpreters and compilers is the lack of occur-check in the implementation of the unification algorithm. This means that such systems are unsound with respect to first-order predicate logic. Static analysis offers an appealing approach to the problem of occur-check reduction, that is, the safe omission of occur-checks in unification. We compare, for the first time, three static methods that have been suggested for occur-check reduction, two based on assigning "modes" to programs and one which uses abstract interpretation. In each case, the analysis or some essential part of it had not been implemented so far. Of the mode-based methods, one is due to Chadha and Plaisted and the other is due to Apt and Pellegrini. The method using abstract interpretation is based on earlier work by Plaisted, Søndergaard and others who have developed groundness and sharing analyses for logic programs. The conclusion is that a truly global analysis based on abstract interpretation leads to markedly higher precision and hence fewer occur-checks at run-time. Given the potential run-time speedups, a precise analysis would be well worth the extra time.

1 Introduction

Unification is the central operation in the execution of logic programs. For reasons of efficiency, it is common for Prolog systems to omit the so-called occur-check when performing unification, with the result that soundness can no longer be guaranteed. For example, consider the statement $\exists z : p(z,z)$. This statement is not a logical consequence of the statement $\forall x \exists y : p(x,y)$ (for example, read $p(x,y)$ as $y = x+1$ in the domain of natural numbers). However, with the Prolog program

```
q :- p(Z,Z).
p(X,Y) :- Y=s(X).
```

the query ?-q will succeed if occur-checks are not performed. So Prolog without the occur-check is an unsound theorem prover for first-order predicate logic.

In practice such an occur-check problem is rare. It does occur in practical programs though, in particular in connection with meta-programming or with the use of so-called difference-lists. But even then, it is mitigated by the fact that, when it appears, it often manifests itself as a termination problem. For most implementations this would happen, for example, with the query ?-p(Z,Z) and the above program.

Nevertheless, it *is* a problem that unsound deduction may take place without the slightest warning or indication to a user. Marriott and Søndergaard [15] make two observations that emphasise the problem. First, "unification without occur-check" is an ill-defined notion, and Prolog systems do not react to occur-check problems in a uniform way. Second, even for *pure* Prolog, the most basic program transformations are invalid in the absence of occur-checks. For example, to see that unfolding is invalid, consider the program

```
q(X,Y,U,V) :- X=Y, X=a, U=f(X), V=f(Y).
```

Unfolding of the last two equations yields the program

```
q(X,Y,f(X),f(Y)) :- X=Y, X=a.
```

With the query `?-q(X,Y,X,Y)`, the first program finitely fails, but the second program does not terminate.

We are interested in tests which, if successful, ensure that execution of a given program (possibly for a given query or query pattern) never invokes the occur-check in unification. To restrict the cost of such tests to preprocessing or compile time, we consider here only static methods (for a dynamic method, see Beer [4]). Work on static analysis for occur-check elimination started with Plaisted's [19] suggestion for a family of increasingly precise analyses. The idea was to propagate information about how variables would be used at runtime, in particular *groundness*, *sharing* and *non-linearity* information. Plaisted's method assumed a standard computation rule. It was complex and seemed prohibitively difficult to implement. The problem was somewhat helped by Søndergaard's [20] observation that a slight variant of one of Plaisted's methods could be recast as abstract interpretation. Nevertheless, this line of research did not lead to an implementation until now, in spite of the availability of powerful technology in the form of generic abstract interpreters, and groundness and sharing analysers.

Instead, simpler methods have been proposed. Based on work by Deransart and Małuszyński [10], Deransart, Ferrand and Téguia [9] have suggested a test which is strong enough to guarantee absence of occur-check problems for any computation rule (in fact for any resolution strategy), and work in this direction was continued by Dumant [11]. This line is referred to as the NSTO approach (Not Subject To Occur-check).

Chadha and Plaisted [5] have suggested two methods based on assigning mode assignments to all predicates in the program, and Apt and Pellegrini [1, 2] have independently worked along the same line. The mode-based methods are simple and elegant, and since they assume a standard computation rule, they can be expected to achieve a considerably higher precision than the NSTO approach, when they are valid, that is, when the computation rule indeed is the standard left-to-right rule. For this reason we have not implemented the NSTO approach.

The contributions offered in this paper are:

- We have implemented Chadha and Plaisted's "second method" [5]. Chadha and Plaisted did not implement this method but argued that it would be more precise than their (implemented) "first method". (We have implemented both methods and verified this experimentally.)

- We have implemented two of the three methods suggested by Apt and Pellegrini, namely one based on "well-modings" and one also taking "strictness" into account [2]. We have not implemented Apt and Pellegini's method based on "nicely-moded" programs, as it is equivalent to the first method of Chadha and Plaisted. Apt and Pellegrini made the simplifying assumption that programs would already be "moded" when presented for analysis, so that analysis would simply consist of checking certain conditions such as the "well-modedness" of a program. This makes a comparison with other, fully automatic, methods hard. We have therefore implemented an algorithm that generates optimal well-modings.
- We have implemented a method using abstract interpretation, following the Plaisted-Søndergaard approach. It uses a more sophisticated groundness analysis than was proposed by Søndergaard [20].
- We compare the three approaches with respect to precision and efficiency. We have tested them on a standard set of benchmark programs. Apt and Pellegrini's approach had only been tested on small programs so far.

Note that we make a distinction between an "approach" and the "methods" deriving from the approach. For example, Chadha and Plaisted's two "methods" are variations of their "approach". All methods have been implemented in C++ on identical platforms, using comparable tools, techniques, and test environments. For example, the same parser has formed the front-end of all.

Section 2 sketches the approach of Chadha and Plaisted [5] and that of Apt and Pellegrini [2]. Section 3 sketches the abstract interpretation approach which is derived from two basic dataflow analyses for groundness and sharing (with linearity). We discuss some issues that bear on the precision of sharing analysis and thus are of wider interest. In Section 4 we compare the three approaches and show how they perform on standard benchmark programs. Section 5 concludes and discusses future work. We assume that the reader has a basic knowledge of abstract interpretation [7, 17] and the theory of unification. Apt and Pellegrini [2] give a nice introduction to unification and the occur-check.

2 The Mode-Based Approaches

We first describe the two methods of the Chadha-Plaisted approach [5] as well as the Apt-Pellegrini approach [1, 2]. The idea of the mode-based approaches is to verify syntactic conditions that must hold for a program to be definitely free from occur-check problems.

Definition 1. A term or literal is *linear* if it has no repeated variables. A collection of terms or literals is *collinear* if they have, amongst them, no repeated variables. ■

Example 1. The term p(X,Y,Z) is linear. The terms p(X,X), p(X,f(X)) and p(f(X),g(U,X)) are all non-linear. The set {p(X,Y), r(f(Z))} is collinear. The set {p(X), q(X,Y)} is not. ■

Theorem 2. *[5] Suppose we unify terms s and t, where s is linear, and s and t have no variables in common. Then unification without occur-check is equivalent to unification with occur-check.* ■

The basis of the mode-based approaches is the observation (from Theorem 2) that if all heads of clauses in a program are linear then the program is free from occur-check problems. Naturally, most real programs do not satisfy this condition, as typically at least one clause of a predicate has a non-linear head. Theorem 2 is therefore not very useful by itself.

Mode-based analysis is performed on a clause-by-clause basis. Every argument position of a predicate is assigned a "mode". Each clause is checked for conformance to a syntactic condition which is a function of the "moding" given to the predicates in that clause. Only the positions with a particular mode need to be collinear in the head of the clause. We do not need to check other positions. If the syntactic condition is found to hold, then the occur-check can be omitted. Otherwise, the clause must be modified so that all unifications with the head of such a clause use the full unification algorithm. We assume the standard SLD resolution strategy. No assumptions are made about the specific unification algorithm used, except that it is correct.

Note that both Chadha-Plaisted and Apt-Pellegrini use the terms "input" and "output" as names for "modes", but with rather different semantics. To resolve this we use names *in*, *out*, and *dk* ("don't know") in the following.

2.1 Chadha and Plaisted's "First Method" — CP1

In this method we analyse the program and label each argument position of each predicate by either *out* or *dk* in accordance with Definition 3.

Definition 3. [5] The k'th argument position of a predicate p is an *out* position if, in each clause 'L:-L_1,...,L_n.' when the predicate of L_i is p then for all variables v in the k'th argument of L_i:

(1) v is not in L_j, for all $j < i$, nor does it appear in other arguments of L_i.
(2) If v appears in L then it only appears in *out* positions of L.

An argument position that is not an *out* position is called a *dk* (don't know) position. An *optimal* moding of a predicate is one which is valid and has the least number of *dk* positions. Similar restrictions apply in the query '?-L_1,...,L_n.' except that there is no L, so (2) does not apply. ■

Thus there are two modes, *out* and *dk*. Note that to be in an *out* position, a variable v is allowed to appear only once in L_i, hence the *out* positions of p in L_i must be collinear. Also, variables in *out* positions of L_i can be in *dk* positions of L_j for $i < j$. Finally, *out* positions of clause heads need not be collinear, and there are no restrictions on *out* positions of facts.

Theorem 4. *[5] Suppose in a Prolog program, the head of a clause C has all dk positions collinear. Then for each call to C, unification without occur-check is equivalent to unification with occur-check.* ■

Theorem 4 relaxes the restrictions of Theorem 2. Instead of checking all argument positions of all clause heads for collinearity we only have to check the *dk* positions. Clause heads that do not have positions marked *dk* can be ignored.

To understand how Theorem 4 guarantees absence of occur-check problems consider Theorem 2 again. Any unification between a call and a head of its resolving clause will satisfy the second part of the condition (that is, no variables in common). Hence, if at least one of the terms is linear then we can guarantee the absence of occur-checks. We know that *out* positions of a body atom are collinear. However, we need a stronger result, namely that this is an invariant for all left-to-right SLD derivations. But this follows from the definition of *out* modes. Hence, we can allow *out* positions to be non-linear in a clause head since we know that during execution, all calls to that clause will be collinear in the *out* positions (and *out* and *dk* positions do not share). No such guarantee exists for the *dk* positions, so we still need to make sure that heads of clauses are collinear in *dk* positions.

The following example illustrates these concepts and shows the outcome of the algorithm that generates the optimal moding [5].

Example 2. [19] Consider the query '`?-q(X,Y).`' with the program

```
q(X,Y) :- ancestor(X,Y), ancestor(Y,X).
ancestor(father(X),X).
ancestor(mother(X),X).
ancestor(X,X).
```

The analysis infers these combinations: `ancestor(`*dk*`,`*dk*`)` and `q(`*out*`,`*out*`)`. Note that `q(`*out*`,`*dk*`)`, `q(`*dk*`,`*out*`)` and `q(`*dk*`,`*dk*`)` are also valid combinations, but the *optimal* combination is selected. This way there is more chance of the combination's *dk* positions being collinear. The first position of `ancestor` is found to be a *dk* position, because in the first clause's second call to `ancestor`, the variable `Y` already appears in the preceding call. The second position of `ancestor` is deemed a *dk* position for the same reason. The analysis discovers that the last three clauses have heads that are not collinear in their *dk* positions. For example, `father(X)` and `X` share a common variable `X`, and both are deemed *dk* positions. The analysis concludes that to guarantee soundness, any unifications involving these three clauses will require an occur-check. ■

The following example is a variant of a program from Chadha and Plaisted [5]:

Example 3. Consider the query '`?-app(Y,Y,[a,a]), app(X,Y,Y).`' and the program

```
app([],Y,Y).
app([U|X],Y,[U|Z]) :- app(X,Y,Z).
```

All argument positions of app must be marked *dk*. In the first call, Y occurs twice, so the first two argument positions are *dk*, and in the second call, a previously used variable (Y again) occurs in the last two positions. This means that occur-checks are required. ∎

The implementation of the algorithm described above is divided into two passes. The first pass assigns optimal *out*/*dk* combinations to all predicates. This pass involves a fixpoint computation. The second pass just checks for collinearity of *dk* positions in all the heads of clauses in the given program. The complexity of the first pass is quadratic while the second pass is linear.

2.2 Chadha and Plaisted's "Second Method" — CP2

A problem with the analysis in Example 3 is that it maintains only one moding per predicate. This means that if a head of a clause is not linear in its *dk* positions then all unifications with that head must use the occur-check. In many cases this is excessive since there may only be a couple of problematic calls to that clause, while most other calls to the same clause never need an occur-check.

More precise information can be achieved if we aim at producing a *set* of modings corresponding to the different calls that may be made. Each call to a predicate has its own moding. In Example 3, the two app atoms in the query give rise to two calling patterns: (dk, dk, out) and (out, dk, dk). A calling pattern can in turn give rise to new calling patterns, because of recursive calls:

```
app([U|X],Y,[U|Z]) :- app(X,Y,Z).
```

Without knowing whether the call app(X,Y,Z) resulted from the first or second call to app, the analysis needs to take both possibilities into account. The results of the two possibilities form the set of possible modings for the third call to app. In this case no new calling patterns are created, and the final result is $\{(dk, dk, out), (out, dk, dk)\}$. In general, finding the set of calling patterns is a fixpoint computation, and Chadha and Plaisted [5] give the details of an algorithm. Notice how the result (dk, dk, dk) from the first method is the best possible "merging" of the two calling patterns of the second method.

The *set* of possible calling patterns is a definite improvement in the example, because it is now clear that an occur-check will never be needed when the last clause for app is called. For both calling patterns (dk, dk, out) and (out, dk, dk), those terms of app([U|X],Y,[U|Z]) which are in *dk* positions, are collinear.

The price for the higher precision is a higher time complexity. The method becomes exponential because the number of possible calling patterns may grow exponentially with the number of argument positions. However, practical programs rarely give rise to an excessive number of calling patterns, as witnessed by the quite reasonable analysis times reported in Section 4.

2.3 Apt and Pellegrini's Approach — AP

Apt and Pellegrini independently discovered three methods for occur-check analysis [1, 2]. They defined the concepts of well-moded, strictly-moded and nicely-moded programs. As they point out, their concept of nicely-moded programs is equivalent to Chadha and Plaisted's first method, and so we disregard it here. The other two methods use modes *in* and *dk* as follows:

Definition 5. [1] Consider a clause '`L:-L`$_1$`,...,L`$_n$`.`' The k'th argument position of a predicate `p` is an *in* position if, whenever the predicate of $\texttt{L}_i$ is `p` then for all variables v in the k'th argument of $\texttt{L}_i$:

(1) v appears in a *dk* position of $\texttt{L}_j$, for some $j < i$, or
(2) v appears in an *in* position of `L`.

Also, every variable in a *dk* position of `L`,

(3) appears in an *in* position of `L`, or
(4) appears in a *dk* position of some body atom. ■

A query has to satisfy only condition (1), so query G is well-moded if the first occurrence (from the left) of each variable in G is in a *dk* position. Note that changing the query may change the set of valid modings. For instance, the program in Example 3 is well-moded with the query `?-app([1],[2],X)` and moding `app(`*in*`,`*dk*`,`*dk*`)`, but there is no possible moding for the query `?-app(X,X,Y)`. Facts have to satisfy only condition (3). Hence, a fact is well-moded if every variable in a *dk* position occurs in an *in* position of the fact.

Theorem 6. *[1] Let P and G be well-moded. If the head of every clause in P is collinear in its dk positions then $P \cup \{G\}$ is occur-check free.* ■

To understand Theorem 6 observe that during SLD-resolution, all derived goal atoms are ground in their *in* positions. Every unification between a call and a clause is therefore automatically collinear in the *in* positions of the call, hence satisfying the condition of Theorem 2. Consequently, *in* positions do not need to be collinear in the heads of clauses, while *dk* positions do. The fact that all derived goals are ground in their *in* positions follows from Definition 5. A single-atom query has to be ground in its *in* positions. Otherwise, a variable in an *in* position would contradict conditions (1) and (2). Hence *in* positions start off being ground. Moreover, during unification of a query and a clause head, the *in* positions of the query will ground the *in* positions of the head of the clause, and they, in turn, will ground *in* positions of all body atoms that satisfy condition (2). Finally, resolution of a query containing some *dk* positions ultimately results in all the variables in *dk* positions becoming ground, because of condition (3). Hence the *in* positions satisfying condition (1) will also be ground.

An important difference between Definitions 3 and 5 is the worst-case behaviour of the approaches. For example, in Chadha and Plaisted's approach a program can always be moded completely *dk* in the worst case, as no restrictions are imposed on *dk* positions. Furthermore, a moding remains valid if some (or all) *out* positions are changed into *dk* positions. Apt and Pellegrini's well-modedness property does not exhibit such monotonic behaviour. There are programs that cannot be well-moded at all. We cannot simply mode a program completely *dk* because Definition 5 imposes restrictions on *dk* positions (conditions (3) and (4)). For example, the program

```
p(X,Y):- q(X).
q(a).
```

is not well-moded with the query `?-p(X,Y)` (since `Y` does not appear in a *dk* position of the body of the first clause). Chadha and Plaisted's method naturally degrades to Theorem 2 in the worst case, while well-modedness completely breaks down. (This can be alleviated by simply applying Theorem 2 to a program that cannot be well-moded.) If we try the query '`?-q(X),q(Y),p(X,Y).`' the program is well-moded for `p(`*in*`,`*in*`)` and `q(`*dk*`)`, but not for `p(`*in*`,`*dk*`)` and `q(`*dk*`)`. Apt and Pellegrini do not give an algorithm to generate a well-moding for a program, rather they assume that a moding is provided. This makes it hard to compare their approach with other approaches. We have designed and implemented an algorithm to produce a set of well-modings and choose one with the least number of *dk* positions for a given program. The algorithm is not given because of space considerations. The time complexity is quadratic.

Example 4. Consider the program from Example 2. Since the moding of `q` has to be `q(`*dk*`,`*dk*`)`, the moding of `ancestor` has to be `ancestor(`*dk*`,`*dk*`)`. However, this moding contradicts condition (3) of the Definition 5 in all three clauses. The analysis concludes that both calls to `ancestor` may need an occur-check. If we change the query to `?-q(a,Y)` the analysis infers modes `q(`*in*`,`*dk*`)` and `ancestor(`*in*`,`*dk*`)` concluding that there were no possible occur-check problems. Note that in this case the first method of Chadha and Plaisted would report two possible occur-checks while the second method would report one. ■

We have also implemented the "strictly-moded" method described by Apt and Pellegrini [1, 2]. It was implemented on top of the well-modedness analysis in hope of improving that method. However, the additional effort did not make any difference on any of the test programs used.

3 The Abstract Interpretation Approach — AI

The idea behind this approach is to use the *definite independence* between variables to detect possible occur-check problems. Assume that, in the context of some "current substitution" θ, we are faced with the unification `X=f(Y)`. We know that an occur-check could be necessary if `X` and `Y` are not *independent* according to θ, that is, if the set of variables in $X\theta$ and the set of variables in $Y\theta$ are not disjoint. For example, we might earlier have encountered `X=Y`. In other words, an occur-check is called for if `X` and `Y` *may* share.

Moreover, sharing information is not sufficient. We are forced to also consider *linearity*, which incidentally has the useful side-effect of enabling more precise sharing information. Consider the unification `X=f(Y,Y)`. Even if `X` and `Y` do not share, this *could* create an occur-check problem, for example if the current substitution has X bound to f(Z,g(Z)). On the other hand, if X is linear, then no occur-check problem arises.

The abstract domain we use here for sharing is a variant of *Asub* [20], which allows statements about the possible sharing between two variables, as well as about definite linearity. The *Asub* domain is useful for many tasks, not just occur-check reduction. *Asub* incorporates information about definite independence and linearity by keeping track of the complementary cases, possible sharing and non-linearity. Plaisted [19] observed that sharing and non-linearity information are most naturally represented in a uniform way. We use a 2-bag [X,Y] to indicate that X and Y may share and a 2-bag [X,X] to indicate that X may be non-linear. (This is possible because sharing is reflexive, so there is no need to give [X,X] the "sharing" reading that X may be bound to a non-ground term.)

There is one other kind of information that can improve precision significantly. If a variable is bound to a *ground* term then it cannot share with other variables. For this reason, elements of *Asub* are pairs (G, S) where G is a set of variables known to be ground and S is a set of 2-bags of sharing variables as explained above. For example ({X}, {[Y,Y],[Y,Z]}) approximates any substitution that grounds X and binds Z to a linear term (since if Z was possibly bound to a non-linear term, the 2-bag [Z,Z] would be in the set).

Therefore, for detecting occur-checks we utilise three types of program information, *definite independence, definite linearity,* and *definite groundness.* The method we use to obtain this information is based on abstract interpretation. This approach "mimics" the execution of a program by replacing substitutions by "abstract substitutions" that act as approximations (for reasons of finite computability). The desired result of the approach is to produce an "annotated program". This is a representation of the program which has the program points before and after each literal annotated with the abstract substitutions that hold at those points for all run-time derivations from the initial query.

Søndergaard [20] sketched the manipulations (the abstract versions of unification and composition) of abstract substitutions, including the fixpoint computation necessary to reach a stable and correct set of program point annotations. Codish, Dams and Yardeni [6] subsequently provided the details of "abstract unification" and proved its correctness. We have implemented an abstract interpretation based method which is faithful to the basic ideas in those two papers but differs in two important ways:

1. We work with *normalised programs* in which all atoms contain variables only, and heads are linear, which simplifies abstract operations significantly.
2. The groundness information captured by *Asub* is limited to statements of the form "X and Y are ground." Higher precision is possible by keeping track of groundness *dependencies* such as "if X ever becomes ground, so does Y" or even disjunctive information such as "X or Y is ground." We therefore use a more complex domain, *Pos*, for groundness analysis [3, 16]. The abstract domain used is the reduced product [7] of *Pos* and the sharing component of *Asub*.

For proofs of correctness and termination of this approach see [17].

3.1 Independence and Linearity Information with Asub

We use an example to give some intuition about independence and linearity information. Let us simplify the notation for 2-bags: for [X,Y] we simply write XY.

Example 5. Consider the program

$$\texttt{q(U) :-}\ \underset{\langle 1,0\rangle}{\mathbf{true}}\ \texttt{p(X,Y),}\ \underset{\langle 1,1\rangle}{X}\ \texttt{U=f(X,Y),}\ \underset{\langle 1,2\rangle}{X\wedge(U\leftrightarrow Y)}\ \texttt{X=Y.}\ \underset{\langle 1,3\rangle}{U\wedge X\wedge Y}$$
$$\texttt{p(X,Y) :-}\ \underset{\langle 2,0\rangle}{\mathbf{true}}\ \texttt{X=a.}\ \underset{\langle 2,1\rangle}{X}$$
$$\texttt{p(X,Y) :-}\ \underset{\langle 3,0\rangle}{\mathbf{true}}\ \texttt{X=a,}\ \underset{\langle 3,1\rangle}{X}\ \texttt{Y=b.}\ \underset{\langle 3,2\rangle}{X\wedge Y}$$

We have already annotated the clauses with groundness information obtained using the abstract domain *Pos*. For details of how to obtain this information, the reader is referred to Armstrong et al. [3] and the references given there. Suffice it to say that, for example, the groundness information at $\langle 1,2\rangle$, X $\wedge$ (U $\leftrightarrow$ Y), can be read as "X is ground, and if U is ground so is Y, and *vice versa.*"

Assume that nothing is known about how q may be called. That is, we have to assume that U can be non-linear, so at $\langle 1,0\rangle$ we have the information {UU}. The call to p is found not to introduce sharing or non-linearity, so the same approximation holds for $\langle 1,1\rangle$. However, U=f(X,Y) will make U share with both X and Y. Furthermore, as U may be non-linear, X and Y may share (for example, U may be bound to f(V,V)). Finally, U could be bound to f(f(V,V),f(V,V)) which shows that it is also possible for X and Y to become non-linear. Thus the conservative approximation that holds at $\langle 1,2\rangle$ is calculated as {UU,UX,UY,XY,XX,YY}.

At this point the groundness information proves useful. If a variable is known to be ground, then we can delete all bags containing that variable. In the example, X is ground at point $\langle 1,2\rangle$, so the pairs UX, XY and XX can be removed (actually they are never added) from the annotation at $\langle 1,2\rangle$. At $\langle 1,3\rangle$ the groundness information is sufficiently strong to yield the independence approximation $\emptyset$, that is, all variables are independent and definitely linear. ■

While sharing is symmetric, it is not a transitive relation. If the current substitution binds X to f(U,V) then U shares with X and X shares with V, but U and V do not therefore share. A (pair) sharing analysis would not be very precise if it assumed transitivity of the sharing relation.

To see how information about linearity can help sharing analysis, consider a situation where X, U, and V are independent of each other. After the unification X=f(U,V), X clearly shares with U and also with V, but it is tempting to assume that U and V remain independent. That, however, would be wrong: U and V may well share—for example, X could have been bound to f(Y,Y). On the other hand, if X was known to be linear, we could conclude that U and V remain independent.

Groundness analysis using *Pos* can give very powerful groundness information due to the ability to keep track, not only of groundness dependencies, but also of disjunctions such as X $\vee$ Y, which says that either X or Y must be ground. This information can be used to further improve the sharing information, as shown by the following example.

Example 6. Consider a slight modification of Example 5, where a literal has been omitted from the third clause, and the clauses have been annotated with the appropriate groundness information:

$$\texttt{q(U) :-} \underset{\langle 1,0\rangle}{\texttt{true}}\ \texttt{p(X,Y),} \underset{\langle 1,1\rangle}{X \vee Y}\ \texttt{U=f(X,Y),} \underset{\langle 1,2\rangle}{(X \vee Y) \wedge (U \leftrightarrow (X \wedge Y))}\ \texttt{X=Y.} \underset{\langle 1,3\rangle}{U \wedge X \wedge Y}$$

$$\texttt{p(X,Y) :-} \underset{\langle 2,0\rangle}{\texttt{true}}\ \texttt{X=a.} \underset{\langle 2,1\rangle}{X}$$

$$\texttt{p(X,Y) :-} \underset{\langle 3,0\rangle}{\texttt{true}}\ \texttt{Y=b.} \underset{\langle 3,1\rangle}{Y}$$

With the assumptions from before, the approximation is {UU,UX,UY,XY,XX,YY} at point $\langle 1,2\rangle$. No variable is known to be ground, but we do know that *either* X *or* Y is ground, which could allow the deletion of XY. In general, if the groundness annotation is ϕ, a bag XY can be removed if $\phi \models \mathtt{X} \vee \mathtt{Y}$. ■

The example illustrates a number of points pertinent to occur-check reduction. The information at point $\langle 1,1\rangle$ is sufficient to guarantee that the unification U=f(X,Y) can safely be performed without the occur-check. The independence information at $\langle 1,2\rangle$ indicates that both X and Y are not linear, and so X=Y should be unified using occur-checks. However, a more precise, case-based analysis is possible, and it shows that occur-checks are not really needed at all. Namely, either X is ground at $\langle 1,2\rangle$, in which case the independence information reduces to the 2-bag {UU,UY,YY}, or else Y is ground and we get {UU,UX,XX}. In either case X and Y are independent, and at most one of them could be bound to a non-linear term. It follows that X=Y can safely be performed without occur-checks.

3.2 Occur-Check Detection

The global analyser consists of an abstract interpretation engine that provides efficient fixpoint computation, and modules that implement the *Pos* and *Asub* operations. It is generic, and similar to engines such as PLAI [18] and GAIA [14].

The algorithm we use was given by Hermenegildo et al. [12]. It is incremental, which means it can efficiently handle program transformations, including clause specialisation, which promises to be worthwhile for occur-check elimination [8]. The analyser is also used in the optimising compilation of CLP($\mathcal{R}$) programs [13]. It takes a program (or module), initial annotation and query (or export declaration), and returns the resulting annotated program. Analysis finishes when a fixpoint is found, that is, when all annotations are stable. Once the fixpoint is found, we perform a final pass over the program to detect points containing possible occur-check problems. The algorithm is:

> For each literal X=t in each clause body do:
> an occur-check problem exists for this literal if:
> (1) X shares with some variable in t, or
> (2) X is non-linear and some variable in t is non-linear, or
> (3) X is non-linear and two different variables in t share.

where X is a variable and t is a term (possibly a variable). The case of t=X is handled by reversing the arguments of '='. The case $\mathtt{t}_1$=$\mathtt{t}_2$, where $\mathtt{t}_1$ and $\mathtt{t}_2$ are both non-variable terms, does not arise, owing to normalisation. In a normalised program, an occur-check problem can only occur in a call to '='.

The complexity is exponential, but as for CP2, real-world programs are analysed in reasonable time, as shown in the next section.

4 Test Results

The programs used by Apt and Pellegrini [2] to test their methods were all very small. As Apt and Pellegrini did not have an algorithm for generating well-modings of programs, it would have been difficult for them to compare their results with those of Chadha and Plaisted. Apt and Pellegrini assumed that each program had already been given a moding and then proceeded to compare with Chadha and Plaisted's first method on small programs.

We provide the first comparison that quantifies the merits of the three approaches discussed in this paper, based on a common set of benchmarks. These benchmarks are commonly used to test program analyses for logic programs, and they were also used by Chadha and Plaisted [5].

Before we present the results, we briefly discuss some decisions we have had to make, regarding how to measure the accuracy and efficiency of the methods, and how to interpret and compare results in a meaningful way. The major problem has been the fact that the abstract interpretation based technology we use *normalises* a program before applying dataflow analysis. Furthermore, disjunction and if-then-else constructs are eliminated. This simplifies the analysis, and typically the cost in terms of loss of accuracy is very limited.

However, this kind of normalisation leads to considerable loss of accuracy for the mode-based approaches, and so it would not be fair to evaluate those methods on normalised programs. For details about how badly the mode-based approaches handle normalised programs see [8], but as a typical example, the number of occur-check problems reported by CP1 goes from 22 to 262 for `boyer` when the program is normalised. Normalised programs are perfectly valid programs, and normalisation is common in WAM-based compilation and program transformation, so it is a considerable advantage of the AI approach that it handles normalised programs so well. With the mode-based approaches, the disastrous effect is caused by the fact that once '=' is deemed to have an occur-check problem, all calls to '=' will be deemed unsafe and must use the occur-check. This puts in context the observation ([5], page 108) that

> "it is always possible to transform a clause that does not satisfy the collinearity condition ... into one that does, by 'pulling' some of the unifications into the body. ... The way this is handled is to assume that the predicate '='/2 is defined by a single clause `=(X,X).`"

While this is true, the effect on precision will be detrimental. The same is true in the case of AP. A well-moded program may well lose its well-modedness when normalised.

For this reason we do not use normalisation when applying the mode-based methods. For the purpose of comparing the three methods we define

Program	Clauses	Atoms	Oc-size	Query used
asm	287	725	438	`asm(ground,Y)`
boyer	144	257	113	`wff(X), tautology(X)`
browse	40	107	67	`main`
fourqueens	25	65	40	`qu(10)`
func	211	476	265	`func_inf(Prog,Opts,Modes,PredList,FPreds)`
peephole	156	292	136	`peephole_opt(ground,Y)`
preprocess	170	491	321	`preprocess0(ground,Y,Z)`
projgeom	19	46	27	`pdsbm(N)`
read	134	440	306	`read(Answer)`
serialize	12	33	21	`serialize(L,R)`

Table 1. The test suite

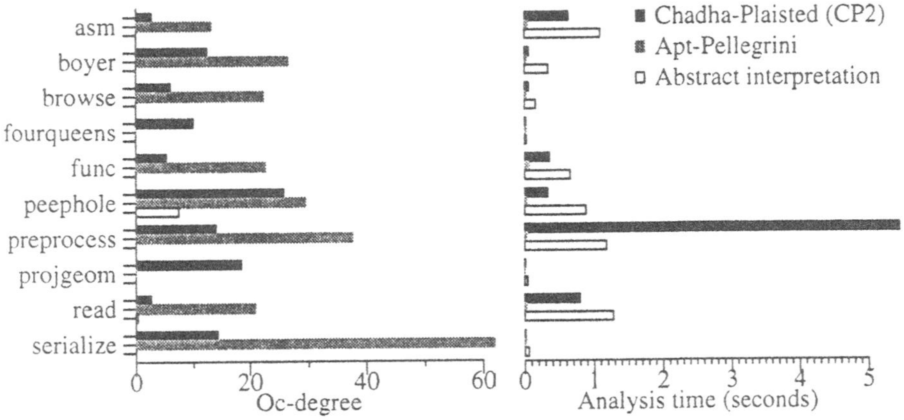

Fig. 1. The three methods compared

- The *oc-size* of a program is the number of literals in clause bodies. Table 1 gives this for all benchmark programs, together with other statistics. It is independent of the method used, since it is measured before normalisation.
- *oc-problems* is the number of calls with occur-check problems reported.

For each method we then consider *oc-degree* = (*oc-problems*/*oc-size*) × 100 as a measure of goodness. The oc-degree should preferably be low. An oc-degree of 0 constitutes proof that a program has no occur-check problems.

The C++ code was compiled with g++ version 2.6.3 with -O3 optimisation and run on a very lightly loaded Sun SPARCstation 5 with 64 Mb physical memory under SunOS 5.4. All times were obtained using a best-of-three approach. Figure 1 shows the results of comparing the approaches. Note that the aim is to minimise both the oc-degree and the analysis time for a program. The left graph shows the relative precision, while the right shows the analysis times.

Abstract interpretation is considerably more precise than the mode-based methods. For all but two programs (`peephole` and `read`), it found that occur-checks could be entirely omitted. AP is highly volatile with respect to precision. When the approach works, it works well, and it is uniformly faster than the other approaches. However, in many cases programs simply are not well-moded, and these cases account for the high oc-degrees often obtained using AP. Concerning CP2, a simple syntax-based metric that correlates with the variation of analysis times appears to be the number of clauses that contain many variables (say, more than 10).

5 Conclusion

We have implemented and compared three approaches for occur-check elimination, and we have given a comparison of three representative methods, based on their behaviour on a standard set of benchmark programs. Two approaches are based on mode assignments, while the third uses abstract interpretation to obtain groundness, sharing and linearity information. For Chadha and Plaisted's approach we have chosen their second method CP2 rather than their first, CP1, since CP2 is considerably more precise, and CP1 is not really competitive on larger programs. Of Apt and Pellegrini's three methods we have chosen the method based on well-modedness. We also implemented the extension to strictly moded programs, but found that this made no difference for the benchmark programs. The method based on nicely moded programs is identical to CP1, and so it has been omitted. More details of the methods we implemented can be found in [8].

Abstract interpretation turns out to be significantly more precise than the mode-based approaches. From the outset it was expected that it would be at least as precise as the other methods, but exactly how it would behave on real-world programs was not clear. However, its use of sophisticated information about *variables*, as opposed to argument positions, appears to be beneficial. For most common program/query combinations, using a realistic, standard set of benchmark programs, it is able to prove that occur-checks can be omitted entirely.

It should be possible to build a version of the Apt-Pellegrini method which considers *sets* of modings similar to Chadha and Plaisted's second method. However, such an improvement is likely to incur the same time cost as we observed for Chadha-Plaisted, while unlikely to match the precision of the abstract interpretation approach. It would be interesting to investigate possible combinations of the methods. More cost-effective hybrid methods could be imagined. The case-based analysis sketched after Example 6 is not currently utilised. Note that the observations we made there apply to sharing analysis rather than to occur-check elimination specifically, so that other applications of sharing analysis, such as parallelisation of logic programs, could also benefit from the resulting precision improvement.

References

1. K. R. Apt and A. Pellegrini. Why the occur-check is not a problem. In M. Bruynooghe and M. Wirsing, editors, *Proc. PLILP '92*, LNCS 631, pages 69–86. Springer-Verlag, 1992.
2. K. R. Apt and A. Pellegrini. On the occur-check-free Prolog programs. *ACM TOPLAS*, 16(3):687–726, 1994.
3. T. Armstrong, K. Marriott, P. Schachte, and H. Søndergaard. Two classes of Boolean functions for dependency analysis. To appear in *Sci. Comp. Prog.*
4. J. Beer. The occur-check problem revisited. *J. Logic Prog.*, 5:243–261, 1988.
5. R. Chadha and D. A. Plaisted. Correctness of unification without occur check in Prolog. *J. Logic Prog.*, 18:99–122, 1994.
6. M. Codish, D. Dams, and E. Yardeni. Derivation and safety of an abstract unification algorithm for groundness and aliasing analysis. In K. Furukawa, editor, *Logic Programming: Proc. Eighth Int. Conf.*, pages 79–93. MIT Press, 1991.
7. P. Cousot and R. Cousot. Abstract interpretation and application to logic programs. *J. Logic Prog.*, 13(2&3):103–179, 1992.
8. L. Crnogorac, A. D. Kelly, and H. Søndergaard. A comparison of three occur-check analyses. Technical Report 96/20, Dept. of Computer Science, The University of Melbourne, 1996.
9. P. Deransart, G. Ferrand, and M. Téguia. NSTO programs (Not Subject To Occur-check). In V. Saraswat and K. Ueda, editors, *Logic Programming: Proc. 1991 Int. Symp.*, pages 533–547. MIT Press, 1991.
10. P. Deransart and J. Małuszyński. Relating logic programs and attribute grammars. *J. Logic Prog.*, 2(2):119–156, 1985.
11. B. Dumant. Checking the soundness of resolution schemes. In K. Apt, editor, *Logic Programming: Proc. Joint Int. Conf. Symp.*, pages 37–51. MIT Press, 1992.
12. M. Hermenegildo, G. Puebla, K. Marriott, and P. Stuckey. Incremental analysis of logic programs. In L. Sterling, editor, *Logic Programming: Proc. Twelfth Int. Conf.*, pages 797–811. MIT Press, 1995.
13. A. D. Kelly, A. Macdonald, K. Marriott, H. Søndergaard, P. Stuckey, and R. Yap. An optimizing compiler for CLP($\mathcal{R}$). In U. Montanari and F. Rossi, editors, *Proc. CP'95*, LNCS 976, pages 222–239. Springer-Verlag, 1995.
14. B. Le Charlier and P. Van Hentenryck. Experimental evaluation of a generic abstract interpretation algorithm for Prolog. *ACM TOPLAS*, 16(1):35–101, 1994.
15. K. Marriott and H. Søndergaard. On Prolog and the occur check problem. *SIGPLAN Notices*, 24(5):76–82, 1989.
16. K. Marriott and H. Søndergaard. Precise and efficient groundness analysis for logic programs. *ACM Letters on Programming Languages and Systems*, 2:181–196, 1993.
17. K. Marriott, H. Søndergaard, and N. Jones. Denotational abstract interpretation of logic programs. *ACM TOPLAS*, 16(3):607–648, 1994.
18. K. Muthukumar and M. Hermenegildo. Compile-time derivation of variable dependency using abstract interpretation. *J. Logic Prog.*, 13(2&3):315–347, 1992.
19. D. A. Plaisted. The occur-check problem in Prolog. *New Generation Computing*, 2(4):309–322, 1984.
20. H. Søndergaard. An application of abstract interpretation of logic programs: Occur check reduction. In B. Robinet and R. Wilhelm, editors, *Proc. European Symposium on Programming*, LNCS 213, pages 327–338. Springer-Verlag, 1986.

Analysis of the Equality Relations for the Program Terms

P.G.Emelianov*

Institute of Informatics Systems
6, avenue Lavrentieva
630090, Novosibirsk, Russia
e-mail: epg@iis.nsk.su

Abstract. In this article an abstract interpretation and formal language based analysis for imperative programs is presented. This analysis makes a lower approximation of the equality relations for the program terms, i.e. for a given program point our analysis produces a set of equalities $t_1 = t_2$ where t_1 and t_2 represent program expressions such that their values are equal for any behavior of the program if this program point is reached. The results of the analysis can be used for debugging, verification, optimization and specialization of programs. An abstract semantics of Pascal–like language is described and some examples of the analysis are given.

1 Introduction

In this section we present our motivation for designing a new semantic analysis and some related works. Modern requirements to the software make the problem of the semantic analysis very important. The results of the analysis can be used on various steps of the elaboration of programs. Unfortunately the most part of the semantic analyses are dealing with no more than one aspect of the program behavior (intervals or congruence relations between integer variables, name aliasing, etc.). Thus they lose the precision since the part of the program behavior is not considered. By practical reasons it is not always possible to use many analyses at the same time (for example, in the case when the analyses are complex or if the different ones require different internal representations). When we apply many passes of different analyses, then the problems of choosing an optimal strategy and passing results arise.

Our analysis is an attempt to take into account various aspects of the program execution in an unified way. All program actions like memory addressing, assignment, branching of control flow, procedure/function call are treated as manipulations with expressions computed in the program. For every program point

* This work performed in part while the author was in Laboratoire d'Informatique de l'École Polytechnique (Palaiseau, France). The work has been partially supported by Russian Committee on Higher Education under grant "Formal methods for program analysis and transformation".

this analysis makes a lower approximation of the set of invariant equations over program memory. The equations are obtained by an interpretation of term equalities representing program expressions and can be used to extract information about program properties. We use formal grammars for an abstract description of term equalities and special computation nets for machine representation of grammars.

Formal grammars and graphs are a popular formalism for representation of semantic properties. We can refer to the following related works (here other references can be found). Special computation nets which are used for grammar representation were first introduced in the Ph.D. thesis of V.Sabelfeld. In this work some acyclic computation nets describing finite sets of term equalities were used for recognizing of the logic–termal equivalence of program schemata [Sa 80]. In [NO 80] term equalities in the form of pairs of labeled graphs (E–graphs) were considered and exploited to the decision procedure for the quantifier–free theory of equality with uninterpreted functional symbols. A semantic analysis for detection of equalities between program variables was described in [AWZ 88]. This analysis makes a list of sets of variables it has discovered to be equal by using of the Hopcroft's partitioning algorithm for finite–state automata. A type inference of Prolog–programs is analyzed in [BJ 92, CCH 95] where sets of substitutions are represented by type graphs which can be seen as a representation of tree automata. Formal grammars are widely used for an analysis of recursive data structures of functional languages (see, for example, [Jo 87]). Formal languages were applied to coding of memory access paths in [Deu 92, Deu 94] and values of program variables in [Hei 92]. Correlation between different approaches and further generalizations are discussed in [CC 95].

2 Analysis of the equality relations

Abstract interpretation [CC 77, CC 79, CC 92a] is a formal method for static and automatic discovering of run–time properties of programs and now we formulate our analysis in the terms of abstract interpretation.

Let $\mathcal{CV}$ be a set of 0–ary symbols (representing variables, constants, names of record fields and indefiniteness) and let $\mathcal{FP}$ be a set of n–ary (functional) symbols (representing primitive operations of programming languages such as arithmetic and logic operations, casting of scalar types, element of array, field of record; usually they are unary or binary). Let $\mathcal{TRS}$ be a set of regular tree terms over $\mathcal{CV}$ and $\mathcal{FP}$, also called program terms. These terms represent expressions which are computed during execution of a program. We note that the memory addressing (as in [Deu 92, Deu 94]) is represented on a high level of abstraction by coding of the memory access paths. Let $\mathcal{EQS}$ be a set of all equalities of the terms from $\mathcal{TRS}$, i.e. $\mathcal{EQS} = \{t_1 = t_2 \mid t_1, t_2 \in \mathcal{TRS}\}$. A set $S \in \wp(\mathcal{EQS})$ is called a computation state and is interpreted in the following way: for each equality $t_i = t_j$ belonging to S the expressions represented by t_i and t_j were computed on an execution trace and their values are equal.

We take the set $\wp(\wp(\mathcal{EQS})) = \wp^2(\mathcal{EQS})$ as the set of the program states.

The initial state for every program point, exclusive of the entry point, is $\emptyset$. It is interpreted as "this point has not been reached yet". The initial state for the entry program point is $\wp(\mathcal{EQS})$. A concrete semantic domain is $\langle \wp^2(\mathcal{EQS}); \sqsubseteq, \emptyset, \sqcup \rangle$ where $\sqsubseteq$ and $\sqcup$ have the usual set-theoretical meaning. An abstract semantic domain is $\langle \wp(\mathcal{EQS}); \sqsupseteq', \mathcal{EQS}, \sqcap' \rangle$ where $\sqsupseteq'$, $\sqcap'$ have the usual set-theoretical meaning. In our case $\langle \wp(\mathcal{EQS}); \sqsupseteq', \mathcal{EQS}, \sqcap' \rangle$ is a meet-semilattice because we do not consider a join-operation for described below model of semantic domain.

The correspondence between the lattice of concrete semantic properties $\langle \wp^2(\mathcal{EQS}); \sqsubseteq, \emptyset, \sqcup \rangle$ and the semilattice of abstract semantic properties $\langle \wp(\mathcal{EQS}); \sqsupseteq', \mathcal{EQS}, \sqcap' \rangle$ is formalized by the pair of monotonic functions $\langle \alpha, \gamma \rangle \in (\wp^2(\mathcal{EQS}) \to \wp(\mathcal{EQS})) \times (\wp(\mathcal{EQS}) \to \wp^2(\mathcal{EQS}))$ satisfying the following condition:

$$\forall x \in \wp^2(\mathcal{EQS}), \tilde{x} \in \wp(\mathcal{EQS}) \;:\; \alpha(x) \sqsupseteq' \tilde{x} \;\Leftrightarrow\; x \sqsubseteq \gamma(\tilde{x}).$$

Let $\pi \in \wp^2(\mathcal{EQS})$ be a concrete property. The abstraction function α is defined by

$$\alpha(\pi) \;=\; \begin{cases} \mathcal{EQS}, & \text{if } \pi = \emptyset, \\ \bigcap_{S \in \pi} S & \text{otherwise} \end{cases}$$

and $\alpha(\pi)$ is the most precise approximation of $\pi \in \wp^2(\mathcal{EQS})$ in $\wp(\mathcal{EQS})$. Let $\tilde{\pi} \in \mathcal{EQS}$ be an abstract property. The concretization function γ is defined by

$$\gamma(\tilde{\pi}) = \{\, \pi \mid \alpha(\pi) \sqsupseteq' \tilde{\pi} \,\},$$

and $\gamma(\tilde{\pi})$ is the most imprecise element of $\wp^2(\mathcal{EQS})$ which can be soundly approximated by $\tilde{\pi} \in \wp(\mathcal{EQS})$.

For the formal description of the analyzed semantic properties we use well-known notions from the formal languages theory [AU 72]. Let us consider a context-free grammar $\mathbf{G} = (\mathcal{N}, \mathcal{T}, \mathcal{P}, S)$ where $\mathcal{N}$ is a finite set of nonterminals denoted by capital letters, $S \in \mathcal{N}$ is the initial symbol of the grammar $\mathbf{G}$, $T = \mathcal{CV} \cup \mathcal{FP} \cup \{\, (,\ ),\ =,\ \mathbf{,} \,\}$ is a finite set of terminal symbols, and $\mathcal{P}$ is a finite set of grammar rules of the following form:

$$\begin{aligned} S &\to A_1 = A_1 | \ldots | A_p = A_p \\ A_1 &\to a | \ldots | h(A_k) | \ldots | f(A_i, A_j) | \ldots \\ &\ldots\ldots \\ A_p &\to \ldots \end{aligned}$$

If the grammar contains a rule $A \to f(\ldots, B, \ldots)$, then the nonterminal B is called an argument of the functional symbol f. The size of the grammar $|\mathbf{G}|$ is defined to be the number of grammar rules.

If $A \overset{+}{\underset{G}{\Rightarrow}} t_1$ and $A \overset{+}{\underset{G}{\Rightarrow}} t_2$, i.e. $t_1 = t_2 \in L(\mathbf{G})$, we say that the nonterminal A and the language $L(\mathbf{G})$ know the terms t_1, t_2. In that way, a state of computation is represented by language $L(\mathbf{G})$ generated by some grammar $\mathbf{G}$ of the described form.

We can suppose that the set of rules $\mathcal{P}$ does not contain rules having identical right parts. It is convenient also to consider the grammars which do not contain

Equality relations	Grammar representation	Machine representation
$a = h(b)$	$S \to A_1 = A_1 \vert A_2 = A_2 \vert A_3 = A_3$	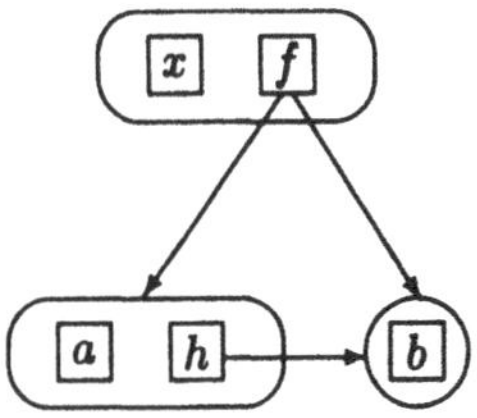
$x = f(a, b)$	$A_1 \to x \vert f(A_2, A_3)$	
$x = f(h(b), b)$	$A_2 \to a \vert h(A_3)$	
$f(a, b) = f(h(b), b)$	$A_3 \to b$	

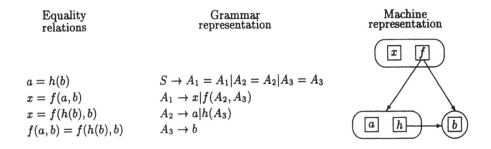

Fig. 1. Semantic properties (only non-trivial equalities are presented).

useless and redundant nonterminals and rules. Such grammars can arise as a result of application of operations on the grammars. We can remove nonterminals and rules (operation of reduction) if they are useless or redundant. To perform this we can use the algorithm from [AU 72].

For the representation of grammars we will use special computation nets. Here nonterminals are represented by ovals containing 0–ary and functional symbols from right parts of rules. Arcs from functional symbols to ovals represent argument dependencies ordered from left to right (see Fig.1).

We use the set–theoretical inclusion of the languages as the order relation $\sqsupseteq'$ of the semantic semilattice. We use the set–theoretical intersection of the languages as the operation of intersection $\sqcap'$ of the semantic semilattice. The intersection of context–free languages is an undecidable problem in the general case. But in our case, for the languages of term equalities, an algorithm exists.

Algorithm. Intersection of the languages of term equalities.
Input: grammars $\mathbf{G_1} = (\mathcal{N}_1, \mathcal{T}, \mathcal{P}_1, S_1)$ and $\mathbf{G_2} = (\mathcal{N}_2, \mathcal{T}, \mathcal{P}_2, S_2)$.
Output: grammar $\mathbf{G} = (\mathcal{N}, \mathcal{T}, \mathcal{P}, S)$ such that $L(\mathbf{G}) = L(\mathbf{G_1}) \cap L(\mathbf{G_2})$.
Description:

1. Let $\mathcal{N} = \{\langle N_1, N_2\rangle | N_1 \in \mathcal{N}_1 \;\&\; N_2 \in \mathcal{N}_2\} = \mathcal{N}_1 \times \mathcal{N}_2$.
2. The set of rules $\mathcal{P}$ is defined as follows:
   - The rule $\langle N_1, N_2\rangle \to t$ is introduced if and only if $t \in \mathcal{CV} \;\&\; N_1 \to t \in \mathcal{P}_1 \;\&\; N_2 \to t \in \mathcal{P}_2$.
   - The rule $\langle N_1, N_2\rangle \to t(\langle N_1^1, N_2^1\rangle, \ldots, \langle N_1^k, N_2^k\rangle)$ is introduced if and only if $t \in \mathcal{FP} \;\&\; N_1 \to t(N_1^1, \ldots, N_1^k) \in \mathcal{P}_1 \;\&\; N_2 \to t(N_2^1, \ldots, N_2^k) \in \mathcal{P}_2$.
3. Add rules $S \to \langle N_1, N_2\rangle = \langle N_1, N_2\rangle$ for the initial nonterminal S of $\mathbf{G}$ and for all $N_1 \in \mathcal{N}_1 \setminus \{S_1\}, N_2 \in \mathcal{N}_2 \setminus \{S_2\}$.
4. Apply the operation of reduction.

During the intersection we can detect the equality of intersected languages. Again, nonterminals which are not arguments and know only one term t can

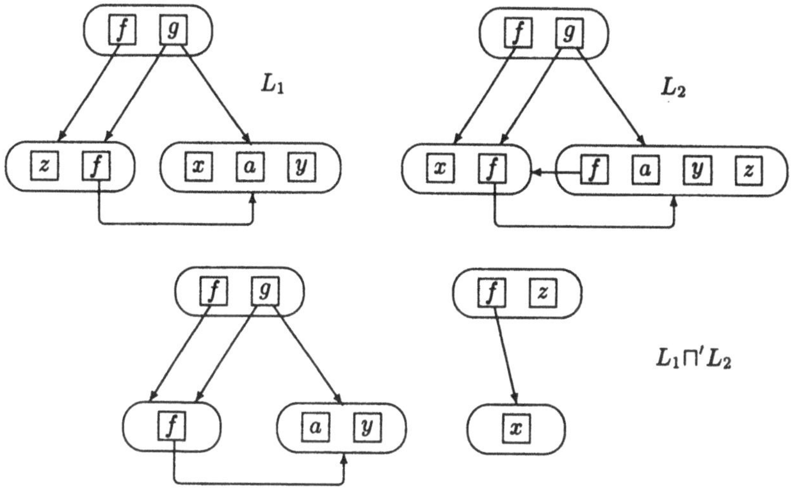

Fig. 2. Intersection of computation states.

be removed because they generate only trivial equalities $t = t$. In what follows we use this correct lower approximation of the intersection of languages of term equalities.

The described algorithm of intersection is very "naïve" and impractical. To improve it we have to choose a more efficient strategy for generating functional symbols. For this end we first do a topological sorting of the functional symbols appearing in the right parts of rules; intersect the 0–ary symbol sets; and then generate the next functional symbol in the conformity with its topological order if and only if all the arguments of this symbol already exist in the new grammar. For practical cases this intersection can be done in an almost–linear average time with respect to the size of grammar and a linear space. It demands the quadratic time in the worst case that is in contrast to [Hei 92] where usage of intersection of languages makes the complexity of analysis to be exponential.

We choose the empty language as infimum $\perp'$ (there are no computed expressions) of the semilattice of abstract semantic properties. The supremum $\top'$ (an inaccessible computation state) is the language generated by the following grammar:

$$\begin{array}{l} S \rightarrow A = A \\ A \rightarrow \underbrace{a| \ldots}_{\textit{all 0-ary symbols}} \mid \underbrace{h(A)| \ldots}_{\textit{all 1-ary symbols}} \mid \underbrace{f(A,A)| \ldots}_{\textit{etc.}} \end{array}$$

It is easy to see that the infimum $\perp'$ and the supremum $\top'$ of the semilattice have the following properties:

$$\forall\, L \in \wp(\mathcal{EQS}) \;\; L \sqcap \perp' = \perp' \;\; \text{and} \;\; L \sqcap \top' = L.$$

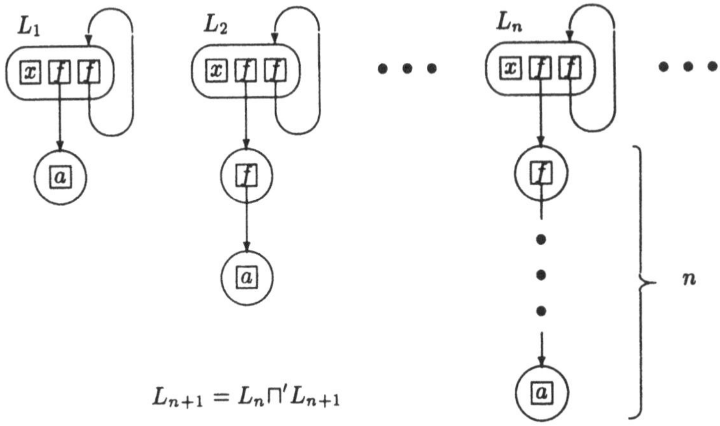

Fig. 3. Infinite chain.

3 Widening operator

Unfortunately this semilattice does not satisfy the ascendant chain condition [CC 79, CC 92a, CC 92b]; this is illustrated by the example in Fig.3. To guarantee the convergence of the abstract interpretation we propose an approach which is dual to the usual widening operator:

- $\forall x, y \in \wp(\mathcal{EQS}) \;\Rightarrow\; x \sqsupseteq' x\tilde{\nabla}y \;\;\&\;\; y \sqsupseteq' x\tilde{\nabla}y$,
- for all increasing chains $x_0 \sqsupseteq' x_1 \sqsupseteq' \ldots$, the increasing chains defined by $y_0 = x_0, \ldots, y_{i+1} = y_i \tilde{\nabla} x_{i+1}, \ldots$ are not strictly increasing.

The upward iteration sequence with widening is convergent and its limit is a sound approximation of the least fixpoint. In our case, if in the course of the abstract interpretation the grammar size becomes greater than some parameter, then it should be destructed the "harmful" cycles so that the new language is finite. The subsemilattice of the finite languages of the semilattice $\langle \wp(\mathcal{EQS}); \sqsupseteq', \mathcal{EQS}, \sqcap' \rangle$ satisfies the ascendant chain condition. To this end we can, for example, remove some functional symbols. In order that the accuracy of analysis would be well it is essential to remove such symbols that the generated language remains so much informative as possible.

Unfortunately this problem is more difficult than the "minimum-feedback-arc-set" (**MFAS**) problem if we consider the computation nets as directed graphs. **MFAS** is a smallest set of arcs (possibly empty) whose removal makes a graph acyclic[2]. In the general case this problem is $\mathcal{NP}$–hard [GJ 79], but there are approximate algorithms which solve this problem in a polynomial or even linear (for example, [ELS 93]) time with respect to the number of graph arcs.

[2] The same purpose can be achieved by consideration of feedback vertices. But it is the author's opinion that there are some reasons for the "feedback arcs" choice.

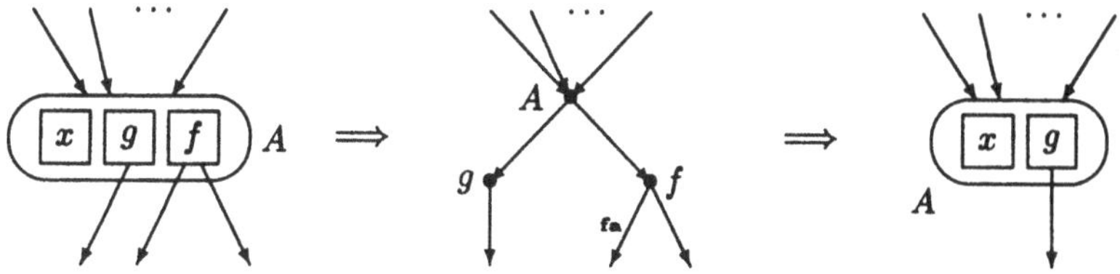

Fig. 4. MFAS–transformation. The **fa** is a feedback arc.

The widening operator for the analysis of equality relations can be defined in the following way. A transformation of grammar graph consisting of detecting **MFAS** and removing those vertices which are adjacent to feedback arcs and represent terminals is said to be the **MFAS**–transformation (an example is shown in Fig.4). Let $L\backslash_{\text{MFAS}}$ be a language which is obtained from L once **MFAS**–transformation is applied to the grammar generated L. We define

$$L(\mathbf{G}_1)\tilde{\nabla}L(\mathbf{G}_2) = \begin{cases} L(\mathbf{G}_1)\backslash_{\text{MFAS}} \sqcap' L(\mathbf{G}_2) & \text{if } |\mathbf{G}_2| > |\mathbf{G}_1| > d, \\ L(\mathbf{G}_1) \sqcap' L(\mathbf{G}_2)\backslash_{\text{MFAS}} & \text{if } |\mathbf{G}_1| > |\mathbf{G}_2| > d, \\ L(\mathbf{G}_1) \sqcap' L(\mathbf{G}_2) & \text{otherwise,} \end{cases}$$

where d is an user defined parameter which depends, for example, on the number of program variables.

Now we choose widening points [Bou 93] in the following simple way. The widening points coincide with heads of cycles and procedure bodies for well structured programs. It should be noted that in our experiences we have not encountered situations as in Fig.3 and their rise seems hardly probable[3].

We apply the recursive strategy of the chaotic iteration. It recursively stabilizes the subcomponent of every component every time the component is stabilized [Bou 93]. A coarse upper bound of time for our algorithm is $O(n^2G^2_{max})$ where n is the size of program and G_{max} is the maximum of sizes of grammars appearing in the course of the analysis. But practical experiences show that the stabilization for heads of cycle bodies come after two iteration steps and the time complexity of analysis does not exceed $O(nG_{max})$.

4 Semantic transformations

Here we describe the abstract semantics of a Pascal–like language. A computation state $L[\![X]\!]$ denotes a result of interpretation of the construction **X** starting in the computation state L. The state L is called an environment for **X**. We assign to each program point a computation state which is called the entry state. All program points, exclusive of the entry point, have $\top'$ as the initial entry state (it means that these points have not been reached yet). Whenever the construction **X** having entry state L' is reached and L is the environment, then a new entry state for **X** becomes $L' \sqcap' L$. The abstract interpretation lasts until the

[3] We failed to construct a program giving such infinite chains.

stabilization: all the entry states are stationary. A notation $L[X][Y]$ means left associativity $(L[X])[Y]$.

There are three basic semantic transformations describing manipulations with the program expressions. All constructions of analyzed programs are expressed by these transformations.

- *Term evaluation.*
  First we define the abstract semantics for the evaluation of a term t in a computation state L. The result is a new state $L' = L[t]$ knowing the term t. Below we give an explicit description how the new state L' is constructed.
  1. If $t = t$ belong to L, then $L' = L$.
  2. Otherwise, if $t \in \mathcal{CV}$, then add the new rules $S \to A = A$ and $A \to t$ to the grammar $\mathbf{G}$, where A is a nonterminal which has not hitherto appeared in $\mathbf{G}$.
  3. Otherwise, if $t = f(t_1, \ldots, t_n)$ where $f \in \mathcal{FP}$ is a functional n-ary symbol and the subterms $t_1, \ldots, t_n$ were calculated (i.e. there exist derivations $A_1 \overset{+}{\underset{G}{\Rightarrow}} t_1, \ldots, A_n \overset{+}{\underset{G}{\Rightarrow}} t_n$), then add the new rules $S \to A = A$ and $A \to f(A_1, \ldots, A_n)$ to the grammar $\mathbf{G}$, where A is a nonterminal which still has not hitherto appeared in $\mathbf{G}$.

  To improve an accuracy of analysis we can take into account the commutativity, associativity, distributivity and other semantic properties of primitive operations.
- *Modification of an access term.*
  The set of the program terms called access terms is formed by the following terms: $x \in \mathcal{CV}$ (representing a variable **x**), $elem(a, i)$ (representing an array element **a**[**i**]), and $field(r, f)$ (representing a record field **r.f**). If in the course of the abstract interpretation a value of an access term t changes (for example, as a result of assignment statement), one should take into account that the current computation state L can contain other access terms which can address the same memory as the term t. It determines the semantics of the access term modification $L[\downarrow t]$. This operation consists of determining and removing a subset of rules $\mathcal{IMP}(t)$ which are used in derivations of these terms. One possible way is described here.
  The notation $A \sim B$ denotes that the nonterminals A and B know some terms which "may be equal" (we have no exact information). The negation of this condition $A \not\sim B$ is true when the nonterminal A knows a term t_1 and B knows a term t_2 such that the values of t_1 and t_2 are not equal. If the nonterminals A and B know terms which represent different record fields, then $A \not\sim B$. The most simple condition guaranteeing the inequality of the values of the terms t_1 and t_2 which represent scalar expressions is $t_2 = c_1$ & $t_1 = c_2$ where $c_1, c_2 \in \mathcal{CV}$ are different constants. It can be used for determining $\mathcal{IMP}(t)$ for the elements of array. Obviously, that many other conditions are admissible.
  Let var be a leftmost 0–ary symbol of the term t and the rule $V \to var$ belongs to the set of the grammar rules. The set $\mathcal{IMP}(t)$ can be obtained by the following procedure:

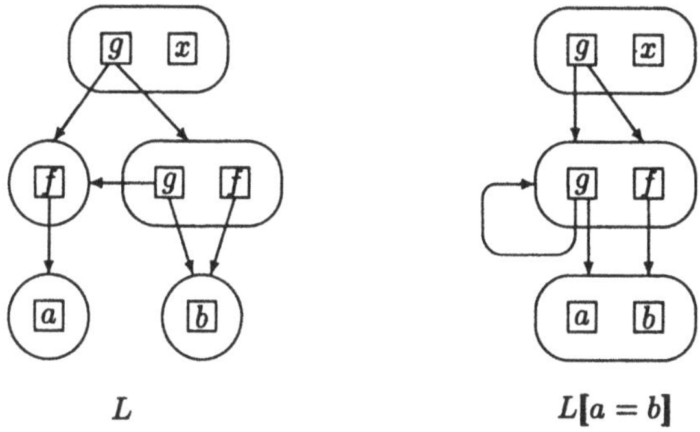

Fig. 5. Unification of values.

1. Introduce a rule $V' \to var'$ into the grammar where V' is a new nonterminal and var' is a new terminal.
2. Let $f(var, x)$ be a subterm of the term t where $f \in \{elem, field\} \subseteq \mathcal{FP}$ and $A \overset{+}{\underset{G}{\Rightarrow}} x$. Introduce a rule $N \to f(V', B)$ for each rule $N \to f(V, B)$ and if $A \sim B$, then add this new rule into the set $\mathcal{IMP}(t)$. Put $\pi = f(var, x)$.
3. Let $f(\pi, x)$ be a subterm of term t where $f \in \{elem, field\}$, $A \overset{+}{\underset{G}{\Rightarrow}} \pi$ and $B \overset{+}{\underset{G}{\Rightarrow}} x$. Introduce a copy of a rule $N \to f(A, C)$ for each rule $N \to f(A, C)$. If $B \sim C$, then $\mathcal{IMP}(t) = \mathcal{IMP}(t) \cup \{N \to f(A, C)\}$ else $\mathcal{IMP}(t) = \mathcal{IMP}(t) \setminus \{r | \text{rule } r \text{ is used in derivations from } A\}$. Put $\pi = f(\pi, x)$. Repeat the step 3 until the stabilization.
4. $\mathcal{IMP}(t) = \mathcal{IMP}(t) \cup \{V \to var\}$.

After determining of $\mathcal{IMP}(t)$ it should be eliminated all the rules from this set; replace var' by var; and apply the operation of reduction.

- *Unification of values.*

This transformation corresponds to the semantic unification of values of expressions during the program execution (for example, in an assignment or for a conditional branching of control flow). The unification gives a possibility to exclude some unexecutable traces and thereby the quality of analysis is increased.

Let terms t_1 and t_2 were calculated in the state L, i.e. $\exists A_1, A_2$ such as $A_1 \overset{+}{\underset{G}{\Rightarrow}} t_1$ and $A_2 \overset{+}{\underset{G}{\Rightarrow}} t_2$ (otherwise, we calculate necessary terms). A new state $L[\![t_1 = t_2]\!]$ where the values of the terms t_1 and t_2 are equal, is obtained beginning at L by the following procedure. In all rules of $\mathcal{P}$, the nonterminal A_2 is replaced by A_1. If thereafter the rules having identical right parts exist, i.e. $\exists\, B_1 \to w$ and $B_2 \to w$, then we replace all occurrences of B_2 by B_1 and continue this procedure to the stabilization. If thereafter some nonterminal knows terms representing different constants (also, there are other suitable conditions), then $L[\![t_1 = t_2]\!] = \top'$. Otherwise, to obtain the result of unification it should be applied the operation of reduction.

In what follows we describe semantic transformations corresponding to the program statements.

- *Program.*
  PROGRAM ;
  VAR x : T ; (∗ variables ∗)
  BEGIN
  S (∗ statements ∗)
  END.

$$\perp'[\![PROGRAM]\!] = \perp'[\![VAR\ \ x : T]\!][\![S]\!][\![HALT]\!]$$

- *Variable declaration.*

$$L[\![VAR\ \ x : T]\!] = L[\![x = \omega]\!]$$

  where ω represents the indefinite value.
- *Assignment statement.*

$$L[\![var := exp]\!] = L[\![exp]\!][\![tmp = exp]\!][\![\downarrow var]\!][\![var = tmp]\!][\![\downarrow tmp]\!]$$

  where *tmp* is a temporary variable.
- *Empty statement.*

$$L[\![\ ]\!] = L$$

- *Sequence of statements.*

$$L[\![S_1; S_2]\!] = L[\![S_1]\!][\![S_2]\!]$$

- *Read statement.*

$$L[\![READ(x)]\!] = L[\![x]\!][\![\downarrow x]\!]$$

- *Write statement.*

$$L[\![WRITE(x)]\!] = L[\![x]\!]$$

- *Conditional statement.*

  IF p THEN $\mathbf{S_t}$ ELSE $\mathbf{S_f}$ END.

$$L[\![IF]\!] = L[\![p]\!][\![p = TRUE]\!][\![S_t]\!] \sqcap L[\![p]\!][\![p = FALSE]\!][\![S_f]\!]\ ,$$

  where *TRUE* and *FALSE* represent the corresponding boolean constants. The results can be improved by an extended consideration of the condition **p**. For example, if **p** = **NOT q**, then

$$L[\![IF]\!] = L[\![p]\!][\![q = FALSE]\!][\![S_t]\!] \sqcap L[\![p]\!][\![q = TRUE]\!][\![S_f]\!],$$

  and if **p** = $\mathbf{q_1}$ **AND** $\mathbf{q_2}$, then

$$L[\![IF]\!] = L[\![p]\!][\![q_1 = TRUE]\!][\![q_2 = TRUE]\!][\![S_t]\!] \sqcap L[\![p]\!][\![p = FALSE]\!][\![S_f]\!],$$

  and so on. It is some variant of conjunctive completion for the semantic properties which was considered in [CC 79, CC 92a]. This completion can lead to a combinatorial explosion, and therefore we have to make a judicious cost/accuracy compromise.

– *Case statement.*

CASE **expr** **OF**

| $\mathbf{c}_{11},\ldots,\mathbf{c}_{1n_1}$: $\mathbf{S}_1$

....

| $\ldots,\mathbf{c}_{ij},\ldots$: $\mathbf{S}_i$

....

| $\mathbf{c}_{m1},\ldots,\mathbf{c}_{mn_m}$: $\mathbf{S}_m$

ELSE

S

END

$$L[CASE] = (\sqcap_{i=1}^{m}\sqcap_{j=1}^{n_i} L_{ij})\sqcap L[expr][S] ,$$

where the states L_{ij} have the following definitions:

$$L_{ij} = \begin{cases} L[expr][expr = c_{ij}][S_i] & \text{if } c_{ij} \text{ is a constant,} \\ L[expr][TRUE = (a \leq expr)][TRUE = (expr \leq b)][S_i] \\ \text{if } c_{ij} \text{ is a constant interval } [a..b] . \end{cases}$$

To improve the precise of the analysis we can make a partitioning of the constant intervals into separate constants and take into account during interpretation of **S** that $\forall i, j : expr \neq c_{ij}$, but it may be quite expensive (see remark for the conditional statement).

– *Cycle statement.*

Cycles of all types (pre–, post–, without–condition and with a parameter) are transformed into cycles of the following form:

CYCLE

S (* **body of cycle** *)

END

where **S** is a composed statement that possibly contains occurrences of exit-of-cycle statements $\mathbf{EXIT}_k$. Let us consider a sequence:

$$L_0 = L,\;\; L_n = L_{n-1}[S] \;\text{ for }\; n > 0 .$$

We define

$$L[CYCLE] = \sqcap_k E_k ,$$

where E_k is a stationary entry state for $\mathbf{EXIT_k}$ and for the sequence $\{L_n\}_{n\geq 0}$ the assertion $\exists N : \forall n > N \Rightarrow L_n = L_N$ is true.

– *Call of a procedure.*

Let a procedure **P** has the following definition:

PROC P(x : T$_1$**; VAR y : T**$_2$ **) ;**

VAR z : T ;

BEGIN

S (* body of procedure *)

END P ;

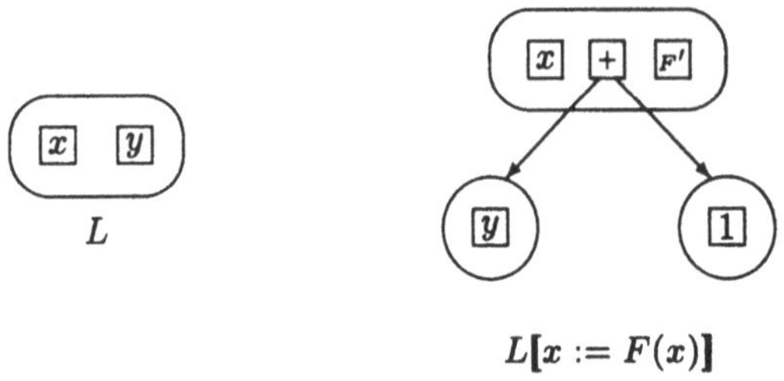

Fig. 6. Function call for $F(a) = a + 1$.

where **S** is a compose statement containing return-statements. We define the result of interpretation of the call statement **P(a,b)** with an environment L as

$$L[\![P(a,b)]\!] = \begin{cases} (\sqcap_k R_k)[b = y][\downarrow z][\downarrow y][\downarrow x] & \text{if } \mathbf{b} \text{ is a scalar variable} \\ (\sqcap_k R_k)[\downarrow z][\downarrow y][\downarrow x] & \text{otherwise,} \end{cases}$$

where R_k is a stationary entry state for return the statement $\mathbf{RETURN}_k$ obtained by the interpretation of the body **S** of **P** with an environment $L[x := a][y := b][z = \omega][\downarrow b]$.

- *Call of a side-effect-free function.*
  The abstract semantics of a function call is similar to the semantics of a procedure call, but there are some details. Namely, if some function $F(...)$ is used for the evaluation of the term t, then a new global variable F' is introduced and all return statements in F are transformed in the following way:

  $$\textbf{RETURN expr} \quad \Longrightarrow \quad \begin{array}{l}\textbf{F}'\textbf{:=expr;} \\ \textbf{RETURN ;}\end{array}$$

  The result $L[\![F(...)]\!]$ of a function call is defined as for a procedure call, but in the term t which is being evaluated, this function call is represented by F'.
- *Halt, exit and return statements.*

  $$L[\![HALT]\!] = L[\![EXIT]\!] = L[\![RETURN]\!] = \top'$$

5 Examples and conclusion

Let us mention briefly the properties which can be discovered by our algorithm of analysis. We can use the given information for a debugging, verification, specialization and optimization of programs:

1. invariants;
2. variable has indefinite value at a program point;

3. infinite cycles and recursion;
4. unused definitions;
5. inaccessible point of program;
6. interval for values of expression;
7. division by zero;
8. redundancy of assignment statement;
9. correlation between parameters of procedures and functions;
10. interprocedural constant propagation;
11. more general: for an expression there exists another expression which always has the same value and is calculated more efficiently (with respect to the given criterion time/space);

Obviously, this list is not complete and there are many other properties which can be extracted from the sets of equalities. For example, closer examination of equations of the form $x = f(x)$ is also interesting: if x is an arithmetic variable and the symbol f is the unary minus, then $x = 0$; if x is a boolean variable and the symbol f is the negation, then this program point is inaccessible. Furthermore, we can consider these sets of equalities as systems of equations (and unequalities) of a general form $\mathbf{F}(\mathbf{v}) = \mathbf{0}$ where $\mathbf{v}$ is a vector of program variables. The theorem prover techniques from [NO 80] can be used for automatic detection of nonsyntactical equalities. The author supposes that the analyzer is well suited for the global specialization of programs. Below a simple example of program analysis is presented:

```
REPEAT
  READ(x,y) ;
  z := y ;
  WHILE  x<=0  DO
    READ(x) ;
    y := x+1 ;
    IF  x=0  THEN
      z := y ;          (* x=0 & y=z=1 *)
    ELSE
      z := x+1 ;        (* y=z & x<>0 *)
      x := y ;          (* x=y=z *)
    END
  END ;
  (* x>0 & y=z *)
UNTIL  y=(z+x) ;        (* always false condition *)
(* infinite cycle, inaccessible program point *)
```

This analysis was implemented for the Modula–programs [ES 94]. The analyzer has three work modes. In the batch mode, the results of the analysis are given in the form of answers to the user's requests inserted into the program text. In the automatic mode, the discovering of all properties does not require the user's participation and they are presented in the listing form; but this output can be very lengthy and unreadable. In the interactive mode, the user formulates requests and receives answers directly.

One way of improving the quality of the analysis is more precise detection of the set $\mathcal{IMP}$ for the elements of arrays. For example, we can use the idea from [Mas 93]. Also, it should be noted that the presented analysis has a syntactical character: the most part of functional symbols are not interpreted. The use of semantics of primitive operations gives a possibility of the analysis improvement. For example, the semantic interpretation of functional symbols can be applied to the constant computations in the states. It corresponds to the constant closure (likewise is the conjunctive completion) of the equality relations.

Analysis of equality relations and Alpern–Wegman–Zadeck's analysis [AWZ 88] are closely related. The AWZ–algorithm can detect some properties which can not be detected by our algorithm. But the identity of values of variables is rare in occurrence. Usually variables are connected by non-trivial equalities $x = y+z+1$ or unequalities $x \geq y+1$ which can be discovered via the analysis of equality relations. In addition, our analysis uses a more general and precise strategy to exploit information about the control flow of programs and provides many possibilities for the conjunctive completion of semantic properties.

Acknowledgments

I would like to thank Mikhail Bulyonkov, Patrick Cousot, Radhia Cousot, Elena Emelianova, Tomas Jensen, Viktor Sabelfeld and Stanislav Tzolovsky for support of my work, useful discussions and comments of this article.

References

[AU 72] A.Aho, J.Ullman. The theory of parsing, translation and compilation. Vol.1 — Prentice-Hall Inc., Englewood Cliffs, NJ, 1972.

[AWZ 88] B.Alpern, M.N.Wegman, F.K.Zadeck. Detecting equality of variables in programs. — Proc. of the 15th *Annual ACM Symposium Principles of Programming Languages*, San Diego, USA, 1988. CA. ACM Press, New York, USA, pages 1–11, 1988.

[Bou 93] F.Bourdoncle. Efficient chaotic iteration strategies with widenings. — Proc. of the *International Conference Formal Methods in Programming and Their Applications*, Novosibirsk, Russia, 1993. LNCS 735, Springer–Verlag, Berlin, Germany, pages 129–141, 1993.

[BJ 92] M.Bruynooghe, G.Janssens. On abstracting the procedural behaviour of logic program. — Proc. of the *First and Second Russian Conferences on Logic Programming*, Irkutsk (1990) and St.Petersburg (1991), Russia. LNAI 592, Springer–Verlag, Berlin, Germany, pages 240–262, 1992.

[CCH 95] A.Cortesi,B.Le Charlier,P.Van Hentenryck. Type analysis of Prolog using type graphs. — *Journal of Logic Programming*, 16(2), pages 179–209, 1995.

[CC 77] P.Cousot, R.Cousot. Abstract interpretation: a unified lattice model for static analysis of programs by construction of approximation of fixpoints. — Proc. of the 4th *Annual ACM Symposium Principles of Programming*

Languages, Los-Angeles, USA, 1977. CA. ACM Press, New York, USA, pages 238–252, 1977.

[CC 79] Cousot P., Cousot R. Systematic design of program analysis frameworks. — Rec. of the 6th *ACM Symposium on Principles of Programming Languages*, San Antonio, USA, 1979. TX. ACM Press, New York, USA, pages 269–282, 1979.

[CC 92a] P.Cousot, R.Cousot. Abstract interpretation frameworks. — *Journal of Logic and Computation*, 2(4), pages 511–547, 1992.

[CC 92b] P.Cousot, R.Cousot. Comparing the Galois connection and widening/narrowing approaches to abstract interpretation, invited paper. — Proc. of the 5th *International Symposium Programming Language Implementation and Logic Programming*, Leuven, Belgium, 1992. LNCS 631, Springer–Verlag, Berlin, Germany, pages 269–295, 1992.

[CC 95] P.Cousot, R.Cousot. Formal languages, grammar and set–constraint–based program analysis by abstract interpretation. — Rec. of the *Functional Programming Languages and Computer Architecture* SIGPLAN–SIGARCH–WG 2.8, La Jolla, USA, 1995. CA. ACM Press, New York, USA, pages 170–181, 1995.

[Deu 92] A.Deutsch. A storeless model of aliasing and its abstraction using finite representation of right–regular equivalence relations. — Proc. of the *IEEE International Conference on Compiler Languages*, pages 2–13, 1992.

[Deu 94] A.Deutsch. Interprocedural may–alias analysis for pointers: beyond k-limiting. — Proc. of the *ACM SIGPLAN'94 Conference on Program Language Design and Implementation*, SIGPLAN Notices, 29(6), pages 230–241, 1994.

[ELS 93] P.Eades, X.Lin, W.F.Smyth. A fast and effective heuristic for the feedback arc set problem. — *Information Processing Letters*, 47(6), pages 319–323, 1993.

[ES 94] P.Emelianov, V.Sabelfeld. Analyzer of semantic properties of Modula-programs. — *Software intellectualization and quality*, Novosibirsk, Russia, pages 13–21, 1994, in russian.

[GJ 79] M.R.Garey, D.S.Johnson. Computers and intractability. A guide to the theory of $\mathcal{NP}$–completeness. — W.H.Freeman and company, New York, USA, 1979.

[Jo 87] N.D.Jones. Flow analysis of lazy higher–order functional programs. — In *Abstract Interpretation of Declarative Languages*, (Eds.: S.Abramsky and C.Hankin), Ellis Horwood, Chichester, UK, pages 103–122, 1987.

[Hei 92] N.Heintze. Set based program analysis. — *Ph.D. Thesis*, School of Computer Sciences, Carnegie Mellon University, Pittsburg, USA, 1992.

[Mas 93] F.Masdupuy. Semantic analysis of interval congruences. — Proc. of the *International Conference Formal Methods in Programming and Their Applications*, Novosibirsk, Russia, 1993. LNCS 735, Springer–Verlag, Berlin, Germany, pages 142–155, 1993.

[NO 80] G.Nelson, D.C.Oppen. Fast decision procedures based on congruence closure. — *Journal of the ACM*, 27(2), pages 356–364, 1980.

[Sa 80] V.Sabelfeld. The logic–termal equivalence is polynomial–time decidable. — *Information Processing Letters*, 10(2), pages 102–112, 1980.

An Even Faster Solver for General Systems of Equations

Christian Fecht

Universität des Saarlandes
Postfach 151150
D-66041 Saarbrücken
Tel.: +49–681–302–5573
fecht@cs.uni-sb.de

Helmut Seidl

Fachbereich IV – Informatik
Universität Trier
D-54286 Trier
Tel.: +49–651–201–2835
seidl@psi.uni-trier.de

Abstract. We present a new algorithm which computes a partial approximate solution for a system of equations. It is *local* in that it considers as few variables as necessary in order to compute the values of those variables we are interested in, it is *generic* in that it makes no assumptions on the application domain, and it is *general* in that the algorithm does not depend on any specific properties of right-hand sides of equations. For instance, monotonicity is not required. However, in case the right-hand sides satisfy some weak monotonicity property, our algorithm returns the (uniquely defined) least solution.
The algorithm meets the best known theoretical worstcase complexity of similar algorithms. For the application of analyzing logic languages, it also gives the best practical results on most of our real world benchmark programs.

1 Introduction

In numerous application areas the information one is interested in can be specified most conveniently by systems of *equations* $x = f_x, x \in V$, where V is a (usually finite) set of unknowns. Important examples include the description of first and follow sets for grammars in the area of parser generation [18], control flow resp. data flow information for imperative programs [13, 10, 15], abstract interpretation [6] of functional and logic languages, and system verification [8, 4].

Given system S of equations, the main goal in all applications consists in efficiently computing a *solution* over some complete lattice D, i.e., an assignment of the variables of S to values in D in such a way that the left-hand side and the right-hand side of each equation evaluate to the same value. If the right-hand sides denote *monotonic* functions, system S is guaranteed to have a *least* solution which usually is also the best information to be obtained. Surprisingly enough, monotonicity of right-hand sides can not always be assured. Well–known and important program analyses introduce *non–monotonic* right-hand sides. In a non-monotonic setting, system S need not have any solution at all. The best we can hope for in this general case is an *approximate solution*, i.e., a variable assignment where the values of left-hand sides either equal the corresponding right-hand sides or exceed them. A *solver* is an algorithm which, given system S of equations, tries to compute a non-trivial approximate solution. If system S is monotonic, the solver should return the least solution, i.e., should have *maximal precision*.

Unfortunately, most solvers presented so far have been developed and presented in an application dependent way, often using different notation. Therefore, it is hard to capture the essentials of the solver algorithms and the key ideas underlying different optimization strategies. Since it is difficult to compare these algorithms, the same algorithmic ideas and optimizations have been reinvented by different people for different applications. Also, specialized algorithms do not allow for reusable implementations. On the contrary, introducing both efficient and application independent solvers offers a lot of promising possibilities. The algorithmic ideas can be pointed out more clearly and are not superseded by application specific aspects. Correctness for the solver can therefore be proven more easily. Once proven correct, a general purpose algorithm can be instantiated to different application domains. Thus, for the overall correctness of the application it simply remains to check whether or not system S correctly models the problem to be analyzed. Reasoning about the approximation process itself can be totally abandoned.

Recently, two efficient application independent solvers have attracted attention, namely *topdown solver* **TD** of Le Charlier and Van Hentenryck [2] and an enhanced version **W** of Kildall's worklist algorithm [13, 12, 17]. The first one has been successfully used to implement analyzers for logic languages [3] and behaves extremely well in this application area – although a better worstcase complexity can be proven for the second one.

In this paper we present a new application independent solver **WRT** which has the same worstcase complexity as **W** but whose instantiation as an analyzer of logic programs additionally outperforms topdown solver **TD** on almost all our benchmark programs. Similar to the known solvers **W** and **TD**, our new solver **WRT** is both *local* and guided by *dynamic* dependencies between variables. The reason is that often in practice the set of all variables is very large where at the same time the subset of variables whose value one is interested in is rather small. In model checking, for instance, one only wants to determine whether or not the initial system state satisfies a given property. A *local* solver, therefore, tries to compute the values only of as few variables as necessary in order to compute the values of the interesting variables. For a local solver, precomputation of all variable dependencies as in the original global version of **W** [13] is no longer feasible. It may even happen that variable dependencies change unpredictably during execution of the algorithm. Therefore, dependencies between variables have to be determined and changed *dynamically* during the execution process.

The overall structure of our paper is as follows. In the first three sections we introduce basic concepts for our exposition. Especially, we introduce the notion of *weak monotonicity* which is more liberal than ordinary monotonicity but still ensures both existence of a least solution together with maximal precision of our algorithms. The following three sections succinctly present solvers **W**, **TD** and

WRT. We use here an ML–style language as algorithmic paradigm. We included descriptions of **W** and **TD** to demonstrate that not only new algorithm **WRT** but also the existing ones benefit from this kind of approach. Section 8 presents our test application, namely abstract interpretation of logic programs, and points out how, based on this technology, efficient Prolog analyzers can be generated. Finally, Section 9 summarizes results from our practical experiments. Especially, it compares all three solvers and concludes.

2 Systems of Equations

Assume $\mathcal{D}$ is a complete lattice. Operationally, $\mathcal{D}$ is given as an abstract datatype consisting of a set of values D together with a designated least element $\bot$, an equality predicate "$=$", and a binary least upper bound operation "$\sqcup$". Note that $\mathcal{D}$ possibly supports other kinds of (monotonic) operations which may be used by right-hand sides of equations. These, however, are not used by our generic solvers. Especially, they do not depend on any implementation of the partial ordering relation "$\sqsubseteq$" on D as opposed to those in [17, 12, 2].

A *system of equations* S is given as a pair $(V, \mathcal{F})$ where V denotes a set of variables and $\mathcal{F}$ denotes (a representation of) the right-hand sides f_x for every $x \in V$. Right hand sides f_x are meant to be (not necessarily monotonic) mappings of variable assignments in $V \to D$ to values in D. In case when set V is "small", $\mathcal{F}$ simply may consist in a collection of corresponding function definitions. In the interesting case however where set V is big, the f_x are only *implicitly* given through some total function F of type $F : V \to ((V \to D) \to D)$. The right-hand side f_x for $x \in V$ then is obtained by $f_x = F\ x$.

In the sequel, we do not distinguish between the algorithm realizing a function f in $(V \to D) \to D$ and the function itself. The only assumption we make is that the only way the algorithm realizing f has access to variable assignment σ provided as its parameter is to call σ on variables $x \in V$.

Similar to Le Charlier and Van Hentenryck in [2], we present our solvers in a very general setting. Nevertheless, we insist on the following three further assumptions:

1. set V of variables is always finite;
2. complete lattice D has finite height h, i.e., every strictly increasing sequence contains at most $h+1$ elements;
3. evaluation of right-hand sides is always terminating.

All three assumptions are satisfied in many applications. In [2], however, it is pointed out how such assumptions still can be relaxed (at least to some extent). It is for clarity of presentation, that we refrain from doing so as well.

3 Approximate Solutions

A variable assignment $\sigma : V \to D$ is called

- *solution* for S if $\sigma\, x = f_x\, \sigma$ for all $x \in V$.
- *approximate solution* for S if $\sigma\, x \sqsupseteq f_x\, \sigma$ for all $x \in V$.

Note that by definition, every solution is also an approximate solution, and that every system S has at least one approximate solution, namely the trivial one mapping every variable to $\top$, the top element of D. In general, we are interested in computing a "good" approximate solution, i.e., one which is as small as possible or, at least, non–trivial.

For function $G : (V \to D) \to V \to D$ define the n–th iterate of G by $G^0 \bot = \bot$ (where $\bot$ denotes the minimal variable assignment mapping every x onto $\bot$), and for $n > 0$, $G^n \bot = G(G^{n-1} \bot)$. With system S we associate function $G_S : (V \to D) \to V \to D$ defined by $G_S\, \sigma\, x = f_x\, \sigma$. In general, sequence $G_S^n \bot, n \geq 0$, may not even be ascending. If we are lucky, all right-hand sides f_x are monotonic. Then G_S is monotonic as well, and therefore has a least fixpoint which is also the least (approximate) solution of S. Often, however, we are less lucky and right-hand sides f_x are not monotonic in general. As a consequence, function G_S is also not monotonic.

Example: Consider complete lattice $D = \{0 \sqsubset 1 \sqsubset 2\}$ and system S with variables $V = \{\langle d \rangle \mid d \in D\}$ and right-hand sides $f_{\langle d \rangle}\, \sigma = \sigma\, \langle \sigma\, \langle d \rangle \rangle$. Right-hand sides of this kind are common when analyzing programs with procedures or functions. Variables $\langle d \rangle$ and their values in the solution of the system represent the input-output behavior of a given procedure p. Thus, nesting of procedure calls introduces "indirect addressing" of variables. Now consider variable assignments σ_1, σ_2 where

$$\begin{array}{lll} \sigma_1\, 0 = 1 & \sigma_1\, 1 = 1 & \sigma_1\, 2 = 0 \\ \sigma_2\, 0 = 1 & \sigma_2\, 1 = 2 & \sigma_2\, 2 = 0 \end{array}$$

Clearly, $\sigma_1 \sqsubseteq \sigma_2$. However, $G_S\, \sigma_1\, \langle 1 \rangle = 1$, but $G_S\, \sigma_2\, \langle 1 \rangle = 0$. Hence, G_S is not monotonic. □

Even if function G_S of system S is not monotonic in general, there might be some partial ordering "$\leq$" on V, such that G_S is monotonic at least on monotonic variable assignments. As usual, variable assignment $\sigma : V \to D$ is called monotonic iff $x \leq x'$ implies $\sigma\, x \sqsubseteq \sigma\, x'$. G_S (and equally well S) is called *weakly monotonic* with respect to variable ordering "$\leq$" iff G_S has the following properties:

- If $x \leq y$ then for all monotonic σ, $f_x\, \sigma \sqsubseteq f_y\, \sigma$;
- If $\sigma_1 \sqsubseteq \sigma_2$ and at least one of the variable assignments σ_i is monotonic then for every $x \in V$, $f_x\, \sigma_1 \sqsubseteq f_x\, \sigma_2$.

Observe that monotonicity is a special case of weak monotonicity where the variable ordering is equality. System S of the example above is weakly monotonic w.r.t. variable ordering "$\leq$" given by $\langle d_1 \rangle \leq \langle d_2 \rangle$ iff $d_1 \sqsubseteq d_2$. Also, both the systems of equations investigated by Jørgensen in his paper on fixpoints in finite function spaces [12] and those systems derived in Section 8 from a generic abstract interpretation framework for logic programs are weakly monotonic. In the latter case, the variables of the equation system are of the form (p, β) where p is a predicate symbol and β an abstract substitution. Similar to the small example above, the ordering is given by $(p_1, \beta_1) \leq (p_2, \beta_2)$ iff $p_1 = p_2$ and $\beta_1 \sqsubseteq \beta_2$. We have:

Fact 1 If G_S is weakly monotonic then the following holds:

1. Sequence $G_S^n\bot, n \geq 0$, is ascending;
2. S has a least approximate solution μ which is also a solution of S and monotonic. μ is given by $\mu = G_S^n\bot$ for some $n \leq h \cdot \#V$. □

Furthermore, it will turn out that weak monotonicity is sufficient for our solvers not only to compute approximate solutions but precisely the minimal solutions according to Fact 1.

4 Partial Variable Assignments

Assume we are given a system of equations $S = (V, \mathcal{F})$ where the set V of variables is tremendously large. One way to deal with large sets of variables is *functional partitioning* as described in [1]. If, however, we are only interested in the values for a rather small subset X of variables, we could try to compute the values of an approximate solution only for variables from X and all those variables y that "influence" values for variables in X. In the following we are going to make this idea precise.

Consider some function $f : (V \to D) \to D$. Evaluation of f on its argument σ does not necessarily consult *all* values $\sigma\ x, x \in V$. Therefore, evaluation of f may also be defined for some *partial* variable assignment $\sigma : V \rightsquigarrow D$. Now assume evaluation of f on σ succeeds. Then we can define set $dep(f, \sigma)$ as the set of all variables y such that the evaluation of f on input σ accesses value $\sigma\ y$.[1]

As a consequence we have, $f\ \sigma = f\ \sigma'$ also for every variable assignment $\sigma' : V \rightsquigarrow D$ as long as $dep(f, \sigma) \subseteq dom(\sigma')$ and σ' agrees with σ on $dep(f, \sigma)$.

Given a partial variable assignment $\sigma : V \rightsquigarrow D$, we put up a *dependence graph* $G(\sigma)$ (relative to σ). The node set of $G(\sigma)$ is given by V itself whereas the set of edges consists of all pairs (y, x) such that $f_x\ \sigma$ is defined and $y \in dep(f_x, \sigma)$. Then variable y is said to *influence* variable x relative to σ iff there is a path in $G(\sigma)$ from y to x. Let furthermore $X \subseteq V$ denote the set of variables which we are interested in. Then we call (partial) variable assignment σ *X–stable* iff for every $y \in V$ influencing some $x \in X$ relative to σ, $f_y\ \sigma$ is defined with $\sigma\ y \sqsupseteq f_y\ \sigma$.

Using this terminology, our goal can be precisely stated as follows:
Given: system S and set X of interesting variables,
Compute: a partial assignment σ with the following properties:

1. σ is X–stable;

[1] In fact, it is this definition which does not really refer to f considered as a function but to f considered as an algorithm. Therefore, it is not really a formal one. To make it precise it would be necessary to formally introduce the programming language to express f and its operational semantics – which we happily refrained to do.

2. If S is weakly monotonic w.r.t. some variable ordering and μ is its least (approximate) solution, then $\sigma\, y = \mu\, y$ for all y influencing some variable in X (relative to σ).

In other words, our algorithm when given S and X should not only return an X–stable partial variable assignment but also should behave "well" in a "well-behaving" context. An algorithm with these properties is called *solver*.

In order to formally compare different solvers with respect to their worstcase complexities we additionally make the following assumptions:

1. We only count the number of evaluations of right-hand sides f_x.
2. The sizes of all sets $dep(f, \sigma)$ are bounded by some constant.

In our applications we found the second one to be a reasonable abstraction. The first assumption, on the contrary, means that we ignore organizational overhead like computing the transitive closure of a certain relation in **TD** or maintaining a priority queue in **WRT**. This is at least justified when (as in our example application) the overall running time is drastically dominated by the calculations in lattice D.

5 The Worklist Solver W

The first and simplest algorithm we consider is solver **W** (Fig. 1). Variants of it were proposed by Jørgensen for the demand driven evaluation of systems of (possibly recursive) first order function definitions in [12] and by Vergauwen, Wauman and Lewi in [17] in a monotonic setting. **W** extends the usual worklist algorithm for systems with statically known variable dependencies, e.g., the one of Kildall [13] and his followers, to the case where system S is dynamically constructed and dependencies between variables may vary.

The algorithm proceeds as follows. The set of variables yet to be evaluated is kept in data structure W, called *worklist*. It is initialized with the set X of variables in which we are interested. For every variable x considered so far, we (globally) maintain the current value $\sigma\, x$ together with a set $infl(x)$ of certain variables y such that the evaluation of f_y (on σ) may access value $\sigma\, x$ or more formally, x may be contained in $dep(f_y, \sigma)$.

As long as W is nonempty, the algorithm iteratively extracts some variable x from W and evaluates right-hand side f_x of x on the current partial variable assignment σ. If the least upper bound of the old value $\sigma\, x$ and $f_x\, \sigma$ is different from the old value (and hence larger!), the value of σ for x is updated. Since the value for x has changed, the values of σ for all $y \in infl(x)$, may no longer be valid; therefore, they are added to W. Afterwards, $infl(x)$ is reset to $\emptyset$.

However, right-hand side f_x is not evaluated on σ directly. There are two reasons for this. First, σ may not be defined for all variables y the algorithm for f may access; second, we have to determine all y such that $f_x\, \sigma$ depends on $\sigma\, y$. Therefore, f_x is applied to auxiliary function $\lambda y.eval(x, y)$. When applied to variables x and y, *eval* first checks whether σ is indeed defined for y. If this

```
fun eval(x : V, y : V) : D
begin
  if y ∉ dom(σ) then σ(y) := ⊥; infl(y) := ∅; W := W ∪ {y} fi;
  infl(y) := infl(y) ∪ {x};
  return σ(y)
end;

begin
  σ := ∅; infl := ∅; W := ∅;
  forall x ∈ X do σ(x) := ⊥; infl(x) := ∅; W := W ∪ {x} od;
  while W ≠ ∅ do
    choose an x ∈ W; W := W − {x};
    let new = σ(x) ⊔ f_x (λy. eval(x, y) ) in
        if σ(x) ≠ new then σ(x) := new; W := W ∪ infl(x); infl(x) := ∅ fi
    end
  od;
  return σ
end
```

Fig. 1. Algorithm **W**.

is not the case, y is added to the domain of σ and $\sigma\ y$ is set to some safe initial value (e.g., $\bot$). Also, variable $\mathit{infl}(y)$ is created and initialized with $\emptyset$. Finally, since y has not yet been considered its future evaluation is initiated by adding y to W. In any case (i.e., whether $y \in dom(\sigma)$ or not), x is added to $\mathit{infl}(y)$, and the value of σ for y (which is now always defined) is returned.

Remarks: We use accumulating updates of entries $\sigma\ x$ in order to handle non–monotonic systems as well. The elegant use of function *eval* is made possible by our ML–style algorithmic paradigm: on the one hand we rely on partial applications and on the other hand on side effects. In contrast to Vergauwen, Wauman and Lewi's formulation, our version also works in a non–monotonic setting. In contrast to Jørgensen's algorithm we need not make any assumptions on the nature of right-hand sides. Also, we need not ensure monotonicity of σ which in practice turns out to be rather costly. Last but not least, in our version sets $\mathit{infl}(x)$ are emptied after use (which is also the case in Verhauwen, Wauman and Lewi's variant, but not in Jørgensen's).

Generalizing the proof of [12], we find:

Theorem 1. *1.* **W** *terminates after at most $O(h \cdot N)$ steps where $N \leq \#V$ is the number of considered variables.*
2. Algorithm **W** *is a solver.* □

6 The Topdown Solver TD

Algorithm **TD** (cf. Fig. 2) originally was proposed by Le Charlier and Van Hentenryck [2] and applied by them to the analysis of logic programs [3].

According to its name, solver **TD** proceeds in a topdown fashion. The basic idea is as follows: If variable y is accessed during the evaluation of a right-hand side, the value of y is not just returned as in algorithm **W**. Instead, **TD** first tries to compute the best possible approximation for y. In order to realize this idea, the algorithm must take precaution that no new iteration is started for variable y provided

1. one iteration process for y has already be initiated; or
2. iteration for y will not result in a new value for y, i.e. y is stable with respect to the current state.

Therefore, **TD** maintains (additionally to σ and *infl*) two extra sets, namely *Called* and *Stable*. A variable y is in *Called* iff a computation for y has been started but not yet terminated. $y \in$ *Stable* means the iteration for y has been completed and since then value $\sigma\ y'$ has not changed for any variable y' possibly influencing y.

Execution of **TD** starts by iteratively calling procedure *solve* for all x whose values we are interested in. In contrast to algorithm **W**, procedure *solve* when applied to variable x, does not evaluate the right-hand side f_x just once but iteratively continues to reevaluate f_x until $x \in$ *Stable*. In detail, procedure *solve* first checks whether its argument x is in *Called* or in *Stable*. In this case, *solve* immediately returns. Otherwise, it proceeds as follows. If x has not been considered so far, x is added to $dom(\sigma)$, $\sigma\ x$ is initialized with $\bot$; also variable *infl*(x) is created and initialized with $\emptyset$. Then x is added to set *Called*. It follows an accumulating iteration on x. Finally, x is removed again from *Called*.

The accumulating iteration on x first adds x to set *Stable* (which is kind of an optimistic decision which in the sequel may need revision). Now, right-hand side f_x is evaluated and the least upper bound of the result with the old value of σ for x is computed. If this value *new* is different from the old value $\sigma\ x$ (and hence strictly larger), then the value of σ for x is updated and all values of σ for variables (possibly) affected by this update *destabilized*. This is repeated until x remains stable, i.e., x has not been removed from *Stable* during the last iteration.

For destabilization, the set *infl*$^+(x)$ of (possibly) affected variables is computed by taking the transitive closure of set *infl*(x), i.e., the smallest set I containing *infl*(x) and for every $y \in I$ also *infl*(y). Now destabilization means that all variables in *infl*$^+(x)$ are removed from *Stable*. Finally, procedure *destabilize* resets set *infl*(x) to $\emptyset$.

It remains to explain that (similar as in **W**) procedure *solve* does not directly evaluate right-hand side f_x on σ but on auxiliary function $\lambda y.eval(x, y)$. Function *eval* when applied to parameters x and y first calls *solve*(y). Then it adds x to set *infl*(y) and, finally, returns $\sigma\ y$.

Remarks: Our presentation of **TD** is closely related to that of Le Charlier and Van Hentenryck in [2]. We only removed all monotonicity constraints (which to maintain can be costly in practice). Also – at least to our taste – our treatment of variable dependencies is much more elegant.

Similar to [2] we find:

```
proc solve(x : V)
begin
  if not(x ∈ Stable or x ∈ Called)
  then
    if x ∉ dom(σ) then σ(x) := ⊥; infl(x) := ∅ fi;
    Called := Called ∪ {x};
    repeat
      Stable := Stable ∪ {x};
      let new = σ(x) ⊔ f_x (λy. eval(x, y)) in
        if σ(x) ≠ new then σ(x) := new; destabilize(x) fi
      end
    until x ∈ Stable;
    Called := Called − {x}
  fi
end;

fun eval(x : V, y : V) : D
begin
  solve(y); infl(y) := infl(y) ∪ {x}; return σ(y)
end

proc destabilize(x : V)
begin
  foreach y ∈ infl⁺(x) do
    Stable := Stable − {y};   infl(y) := ∅
  od;
  infl(x) := ∅
end;

begin
  σ := ∅; Stable := ∅; Called := ∅; infl := ∅;
  foreach x ∈ X do solve(x) od;
  return σ
end
```

Fig. 2. Algorithm **TD**

Theorem 2. *1.* **TD** *terminates after at most* $O(h \cdot N^2)$ *steps where* $N \leq \#V$ *is the number of considered variables.*
2. Algorithm **TD** *is a solver.* □

7 The Time Stamps Solver WRT

It turns out that – despite its theoretically worse worstcase complexity – solver **TD** performs extremely well (see, e.g., our numbers in Section 9). Theoretically, it can be proven to be "optimal" for the case of acyclic variable dependencies – which is not the case, e.g., for solver **W**. In our example application, deficiencies occur only for large and medium sized input programs to be analyzed like *aqua-c*, *chat-parser* or *readq* of our benchmark suite. We conclude that **TD** does not adequately treat larger strong components in the dependence graph.

Opposed to that, solver **W** – despite its theoretically better worstcase complexity – gives worse practical results. One source of inefficiency clearly is its insufficient treatment of variables y newly encountered during evaluation of some right-hand side f_x. Evaluation of f_x simply proceeds while assuming $\bot$ as value for $\sigma\, y$. Computing a better value for $\sigma\, y$ is postponed. It follows that the (possibly) new value for x is most likely to be recomputed later on. Therefore, **W** cannot be proven optimal even for systems of equations with *acyclic* static variable dependencies.

It is for this reason that we propose two improvements to solver **W**. First, we add recursion (the "**R**") in order to compute a better initial value for $\sigma\, y$ than $\bot$ in case y is newly encountered. This modification already guarantees optimality for the case of acyclic static variable dependencies. It does not, however, guarantee that (still in case of static variable dependencies) iteration is performed in one strong component after the other. The best idea therefore might be to add something like an algorithm detecting strong components "on the fly". Since dependencies vary over time in that dependencies both can be added and removed, such an approach seems not very practical. The second best idea is to use *time stamps* (the "**T**").

The resulting algorithm is presented in Fig. 3. Additionally to the data structures of solver **W**, we maintain for every $x \in dom(\sigma)$ its time stamp $time(x)$ which is a positive integer. It records the last time $solve(x)$ has been called. Accordingly, worklist W now is organized as a (max) priority queue where the priority of an element is given by its time stamp. Moreover, we need a stack *Stack* for the time stamps of variables in the recursion stack.

Solver **WRT** works as follows. Initially, variables $x \in X$ are put into worklist W. While doing so, each such variable is equipped with a new time stamp. Then the main loop consists in extracting the variable with maximal time stamp from W and applying procedure *solve* to it until W is empty.

Procedure *solve* when applied to variable x first checks whether $x \in dom(\sigma)$. If not, x is removed from W (if it has been there) and added to the domain of σ, and $\sigma\, x$ and $infl(x)$ are initialized with $\bot$ and $\emptyset$, respectively. In any case, x now receives the next time stamp; this value is pushed onto *Stack*. Similar to **W**, the least upper bound is computed of the old value of σ for x and f_x evaluated on σ. If this new value is different from the old one, σ is updated, the variable set $infl(x)$ is included into W and afterwards reset to $\emptyset$. Then the top element is popped from *Stack*.

The modification now is that procedure *solve* need not return immediately. Instead if *Stack* is nonempty, we compare the current top of *Stack* t and the time stamps of the elements in W and apply *solve* to all those variables y in W whose times are less than t.

It remains to explain that, as with solvers **W** or **TD**, evaluation of right hand side f_x in *solve* is not performed directly on the current value of σ but on auxiliary function $\lambda y.eval(x, y)$. Function *eval* is the same as function *eval* of algorithm **TD**, i.e., when applied to variables x and y where y is not yet contained

```
proc solve(x : V)
begin
  if x ∉ dom(σ) then W := W − {x}; σ(x) := ⊥; infl(x) := ∅ fi;
  time(x) := nextTime();
  push(Stack, time(x));
  let new = σ(x) ⊔ f_x (λy.eval(x, y)) in
    if new ≠ σ(x)
    then σ(x) := new; W := W ∪ infl(x); infl(x) := ∅ fi
  end;
  pop(Stack);
  if not(isEmpty(Stack))
  then while W ≠ ∅ and top(Stack) < time(max(W))
         do let y = max(W) in
              W := W − {y}; solve(y)
            end
         od;
  fi
end;

fun eval(x : V, y : V) : D
begin
  if y ∉ dom(σ) then solve(y) fi;
  infl(y) := infl(y) ∪ {x};
  return σ(y)
end;

begin
  σ := ∅; time := ∅; Stack := empty; infl := ∅; W := X;
  foreach x ∈ X do time(x) := nextTime() od;
  while W ≠ ∅ do
      let x = max(W) in
        W := W − {x}; solve(x)
      end
  od;
  return σ
end
```

Fig. 3. Algorithm **WRT** with time stamps

in $dom(\sigma)$, function *eval* not only initializes both values $\sigma\, y$ and $infl(y)$, but additionally calls $solve(y)$ before returning current value $\sigma\, y$.

Remarks: Solver **WRT** has no equivalent either in Le Charlier and Van Hentenryck's paper [2], Jørgensen's work [12] or Vergauwen, Wauman and Lewi's overview [17]. It can be seen as an effort to combine the nice features of both solver **W** and solver **TD**. From **TD** it inherits the recursive descent on variables not yet considered whereas from **W** it receives the more flexible treatment of strongly connected components in the (dynamically changing) dependence graph. A simpler algorithm **W-DFS** can be obtained from **WRT** if each variable obtains a new time stamp only once, namely when it is added to $dom(\sigma)$. Algorithm **W-DFS** can be seen as the dynamic version of *priority-queue iteration* in [11]. Two variables are arranged by **W-DFS** according to the *first* dependency between them that was established by the algorithm. This is a reasonable choice in case of *static* variable dependencies. However, in the dynamic case dependencies may arbitrarily change during the fixpoint iteration, meaning that any worklist algorithm with fixed variable priorities may show poor performance.

Theorem 3. *1.* **WRT** *terminates after at most $O(h \cdot N)$ steps where $N \leq \#V$ is the number of considered variables.*
2. Algorithm **WRT** *is a solver.*

8 Generic Abstract Interpretation of Logic Programs

As an example application for our implementations of solvers **W**, **TD**, **WRT** and **W-DFS** the first author integrated the four solvers into a tool (GENA) [9] for generating Prolog analyzers from specifications. The generated analyzers are based on the principle of abstract interpretation [7, 14, 3]. More specifically, the analyzers are based on the generic abstract interpretation framework for logic programs of Le Charlier and Van Hentenryck [3]. This framework assumes logic programs to be *normalized.* The set of *normalized goals* is inductively defined by the following rules:

$$
\begin{array}{lll}
G ::= & \mathbf{true} & \\
& \mid X_i = t & X_i \notin vars(t) \\
& \mid p(X_{i_1}, \ldots, X_{i_n}) & i_1, \ldots, i_n \text{ are distinct indices} \\
& \mid G_1, G_2 &
\end{array}
$$

where $X_1, X_2, \ldots$ are *program variables*, t ranges over terms built up from program variables by formal applications of function symbols, and p denotes predicate symbols (of arities n). A *normalized program* is a set of *normalized clauses* $p(X_1, \ldots, X_n) \leftarrow G$. If a clause contains m variables, these variables are necessarily $X_1, \ldots, X_m$.

The abstract semantics is parametrized on an *abstract domain*. The abstract domain provides a finite complete lattice $(Asub, \sqcup, \bot)$ of abstract substitutions and functions for abstract unification (*aunify*), procedure entry ($restrG$, $extC$), and procedure exit ($restrC$, $extG$). The abstract semantics of P with respect to a given abstract domain $\mathcal{A}$ is a function $[P]_{\mathcal{A}} : Pred \times Asub \rightarrow Asub$. It assigns an abstract success substitution to every abstract call. The abstract semantics $[P]_{\mathcal{A}}$ is defined denotationally by means of functions $solveP$, $solveC$, and $solveG$ which define the meaning of predicates, clauses, and goals, respectively.

$$solveP :: (Pred \times Asub \rightarrow Asub) \rightarrow (Pred \times Asub \rightarrow Asub)$$
$$solveP\ \sigma\ (p, \beta) = \bigsqcup\{solveC\ \sigma\ (c, \beta) \mid c \in Prog \text{ and head predicate of } c \text{ is } p\}$$

$$solveC :: (Pred \times Asub \to Asub) \to (Clause \times Asub \to Asub)$$
$$solveC\ \sigma\ (p(X_1, \ldots, X_n)\ \leftarrow\ G,\ \beta_{in}) = restrC(\beta_{exit}, n)$$
$$\text{where } \beta_{exit} = solveG\ \sigma\ (G, \beta_{entry})$$
$$\beta_{entry} = extC(\beta_{in}, p(X_1, \ldots, X_n)\ \leftarrow\ G)$$

$$solveG :: (Pred \times Asub \to Asub) \to (Goal \times Asub \to Asub)$$
$$solveG\ \sigma\ (\mathbf{true}, \beta) = \beta$$
$$solveG\ \sigma\ (X_i = t, \beta) = aunify(\beta, X_i, t)$$
$$solveG\ \sigma\ (p(\bar{X}), \beta) = extG(\beta, \bar{X}, \sigma\ (p, restrG(\beta, \bar{X})))$$
$$solveG\ \sigma\ ((G_1, G_2), \beta) = solveG\ \sigma\ (G_2, solveG\ \sigma\ (G_1, \beta))$$

The abstract semantics $[\![P]\!]_{\mathcal{A}}$ is defined as the least fixpoint of function *solveP*. Existence of the least fixpoint follows from the facts that *Asub* is a finite complete lattice and that all abstract operations are monotonic.

In goal-dependent analyses of logic programs, we are only interested in that part of $[\![P]\!]_{\mathcal{A}}$ that is needed in order to evaluate $[\![P]\!]_{\mathcal{A}}(p, \beta)$ for a given initial abstract call (p, β). Given this part of the abstract semantics, one can compute, for instance, call modes for those predicates in P which are valid with respect to all concrete calls described by the initial abstract call. Therefore, we rephrase $[\![P]\!]_{\mathcal{A}}$ as a system of equations:

$$V = Pred \times Asub \qquad D = Asub \qquad f_x\ \sigma = solveP\ \sigma\ x$$

Since the abstract semantics assigns an abstract substitution to every abstract call (p, β), the variables of the system of equations are exactly the abstract calls $Pred \times Asub$. The lattice of values of the system is the lattice of abstract substitutions. The right-hand side function associated with variable (p, β) is simply $\lambda\sigma.\ solveP\ \sigma\ (p, \beta)$. Unfortunately, this system of equations is not monotonic. This is a consequence of the fact that semantic function *solveG* is not monotonic in general. However, we can consider ordering "$\leq$" on the set of variables from Section 3 defined by $(p_1, \beta_1) \leq (p_2, \beta_2)$ iff $p_1 = p_2$ and $\beta_1 \sqsubseteq \beta_2$. It turns out that for every program the corresponding system of equations is weakly monotonic - at least if the abstract operations *aunify, restrG, extG, restrC* and *extC* are monotonic.

The core of the implementation of analyzer generator GENA is module **ASem** which implements the above system of equations. The implementation of **ASem** was easily obtained by rewriting the above denotational semantics as SML code. **ASem** is parametrized on abstract domains and on general equation solvers. As general equation solvers, we considered solvers **W**, **TD**, **WRT** and **W-DFS**. In case of solver **W**, the worklist is implemented as a stack. In order to get complete program analyzers, the first author also implemented various abstract domains. For lack of space, we confined ourselves in this paper to report only on our numbers found for **Pos**[2] [5, 16]. **Pos** is a conceptually simple and elegant abstract domain to compute *groundness* information for Prolog programs

[2] Similar results have been obtained also with other abstract domains, e.g., for sharing analysis.

program	time				#rhs			
	W	TD	WRT	W-DFS	W	TD	WRT	W-DFS
action	16.25	3.23	3.25	3.30	390	198	198	198
aqua-c	147.40	57.40	51.26	53.56	11135	3797	3529	3517
ann	0.44	0.23	0.22	0.23	237	110	107	107
b2	1.29	0.72	0.70	0.68	1000	437	418	418
chat	21.96	12.11	10.23	10.45	2946	1625	1276	1281
chat-parser	4.86	3.10	2.08	1.85	1149	751	501	500
flatten	0.27	0.10	0.10	0.11	207	69	67	67
nand	0.58	0.39	0.35	0.36	148	67	67	67
peep	0.23	0.11	0.11	0.12	67	42	42	41
press	0.66	0.39	0.34	0.36	461	245	245	245
read	0.51	0.26	0.29	0.25	171	88	92	89
readq	0.91	0.55	0.51	0.51	408	239	201	195
scc	0.10	0.09	0.08	0.08	61	36	35	35
sdda	0.21	0.14	0.14	0.14	164	82	82	82

Table 1. Experimental evaluation of **W**, **TD**, **WRT** and **W-DFS**

where abstract substitutions are represented by Boolean functions. Recall that logical variable X is ground with respect to substitution ϑ if $X\vartheta$ does not contain any variable. By plugging implementations of **W**, **TD**, **WRT** and **W-DFS** into **ASem** + **Pos** we obtained four analyzers for Prolog.

9 Comparison and Conclusion

The generated analyzers were tested on large real-world programs. The program *aqua-c* (16.000 lines of code), for example, is the source code of Peter Van Roy's Aquarius Prolog compiler. Programs *read* and *readq* are Prolog readers. *b2* is a large mathematical program and *chat* (5.000 lines of code) is Warren's chat-80 system. The analyzers were run on a Sun 20 with 64MB main memory with SML-NJ-109. Table 1 shows the results of our experiments. Column *time* gives the total running times of the analyzers (in seconds) including system and garbage collection times. Column *rhs* shows how often right-hand sides of the equation system have been evaluated during the solution process.

As a first result, it should be noted that our versions of all four solvers do reasonably well on all given benchmarks. Thus, the *absolute* numbers indicate that analysis engines generated by GENA are efficient enough to be included into production quality compilers. Secondly, we find that the maximal advantage one solver gains over the other on our benchmark programs is approximately a factor of 5 (which indeed is still moderate). Not surprisingly, worklist solver **W** turns out to be the least efficient. Top-down solver **TD** is amazingly fast even despite its bad (theoretical) worst-case complexity. On programs *aqua-c*, *chat* or *chat-parser*, **TD** is outperformed by our new solvers **WRT** and **W-DFS**. The gain in efficiency here ranges between 6% and 30%. There is just one program, namely *read*, where **TD** needs less evaluations of right-hand sides than **WRT**. On all other programs **WRT** evaluates equally many right-hand sides or less. On *chat* and *chat-parser*, the savings are more than 20%. The runtimes of the two solvers **WRT** and **W-DFS** turn out to be very similar. Note, however, that **W-DFS** – despite (or because of) its static treatment of variable dependencies – is sometimes a tick faster. In fact, the dynamic treatment of variable priorities of solver **WRT** pays off in reducing the number of evaluations of right-hand sides only for program *chat.* Nevertheless we suggest to use solver **WRT** instead of **W-DFS** since it seems to be more robust against non-well-behaving inputs.

To summarize, we found new application independent local solvers for general systems of equations. Both in theory and practice, these algorithms favorably compete with existing algorithms of the same kind, namely worklist solver **W** and topdown solver **TD**. Secondly, we showed that based on such general algorithms, very efficient program analyzers can be generated. Further directions of research must include evaluation of such kind of solvers also in other areas of application. Also, we would like to investigate methods of constructing solutions with are not based on (more or less cleverly guided) iteration.

Acknowledgements. We are indepted for valuable discussions on fixpoint iteration strategies to Andreas Neumann and the German Scholar Olympic Team for Computer Science.

References

1. F. Bourdoncle. *Abstract Interpretation by Dynamic Partitioning.* Journal of Functional Programming, **2**(4), 1992.
2. B. Le Charlier and P. Van Hentenryck. *A Universal Top-Down Fixpoint Algorithm.* Technical report 92–22, Institute of Computer Science, University of Namur, Belgium, 1992.
3. B. Le Charlier and P. Van Hentenryck. Experimental evaluation of a generic abstract interpretation algorithm for Prolog. *TOPLAS*, 16(1):35–101, 1994.
4. R. Cleaveland and B. Steffen. A Linear-Time Model Checking Algorithm for the Alternation-Free Modal Mu-Calculus. In *CAV'91.* Springer, LNCS 575, 1991.
5. A. Cortesi, G. Filé, and W. Winsborough. Prop revisited: Propositional formulas as abstract domain for groundness analysis. In *LICS'91*, 322–327, Amsterdam, The Netherlands, 1991.
6. P. Cousot and R. Cousot. Abstract Interpretation: A Unified Lattice Model for Static Analysis of Programs by Construction or Approximation of Fixpoints. In *POPL'77*, 238-252, 1977.
7. P. Cousot and R. Cousot. Abstract Interpretation and Application to Logic Programs. *Journal of Logic Programming*, 13(2):103–179, 1992.
8. A. Dicky. An Algebraic and Algorithmic Method of Analysing Transition Systems. *TCS*, 46:285–303, 1986.
9. Christian Fecht. GENA – a Tool for Generating Prolog Analyzers from Specifications. *SAS'95*, 418–419. Springer Verlang, LNCS 983, 1995.
10. M.S. Hecht. *Flow Analysis of Computer Programs.* Amsterdam: Elsevier North-Holland, 1977.
11. S. Horwitz, A. Demers and T. Teitelbaum. An Efficient General Iteration Algorithm for Dataflow Analysis. *Acta Informatica*, **24**, 679–694, 1987.
12. N. Jørgensen. Finding Fixpoints in Finite Function Spaces Using Neededness Analysis and Chaotic Iteration. In *SAS'94*, 329–345. Springer, LNCS 864, 1994.

13. G.A. Kildall. A Unified Approach to Global Program Optimization. In *POPL'73*, 194–206, 1973.
14. K. Marriott, H. Søndergaard, and N.D. Jones. Denotational Abstract Interpretation of Logic Programs. *ACM Transactions of Programming Languages and Systems*, 16(3):607–648, 1994.
15. M. Sharir and A. Pnueli. Two approaches to interprocedural data flow analysis. In S.S. Muchnick and N.D. Jones, editors, *Program Flow Analysis: Theory and Application*, 189–233. Prentice-Hall, 1981.
16. P. Van Hentenryck, A. Cortesi, and B. Le Charlier. Evaluation of the domain Prop. *The Journal of Logic Programming*, 23(3):237–278, 1995.
17. B. Vergauwen, J. Wauman, and J. Lewi. Efficient fixpoint computation. In *SAS'94*, 314-328. Springer, LNCS 864, 1994.
18. R. Wilhelm and D. Maurer. *Compiler Construction*. Addison-Wesley, 1995.

Inferring Program Specifications in Polynomial-Time

Robert Givan

Massachusetts Institute of Technology,
NE43-430, Cambridge, MA 02139, USA
rlg@ai.mit.edu, http://www.ai.mit.edu/people/rlg/rlg.html

Abstract. We consider the problem of automatically inferring properties of programs. Our approach is to explore the application of familiar type inference principles to a "type system" sufficiently expressive that the typing problem is effectively the checking of program specifications. We use familiar syntax-directed type inference rules to give a polynomial-time procedure for inferring type theorems in this rich type system. We discuss examples of simple functional programs and the specification information this procedure automatically infers. The enriched notion of type allows the definition of any recursively enumerable set as a type, and includes argument-dependent output types for functions. The inference procedure is capable for example of automatically inferring that an insertion sort program always returns a sorted permutation of its input.

Keywords: Functional Programming, Type Inference, Verification, Induction

1 Introduction

Many researchers have studied type inference systems for functional programming languages[10, 6, 11, 2]. The typical goal of such research is to allow the programmer to omit type declarations without losing the benefits they provide. The types inferred by such systems are typically similar to the primitive types of a typed programming language with typings for functions added (so that $\alpha \rightarrow \beta$ is a type whenever α and β are). Many such type inference systems can be described by sets of locally-acting syntax-directed type inference rules.

More recently, effective type inference systems have been given for more expressive type systems, e.g., allowing conditional types[1]. The stated motivation for such increased expressiveness is to be able to infer types for more programs to ensure type safety. These systems, like most type inference systems, typically have poor worst-case complexity while retaining practical effectiveness.

We believe that there is a continuum between checking type safety and verifying program correctness. As the language of the types inferred becomes more expressive, the type inferences can more precisely characterize the outputs of the programs being analyzed. Rather than inspire our type system from the types present in programming languages, we suggest we draw inspiration from the types present in programmers' analysis of their own programs. Not only do programmers use a very expressive type language (natural language), but we observe that they are effective at quickly analyzing their own programs to draw expressive typing conclusions. For example, a programmer writing an insertion sort program can typically quickly and easily verify that his program returns a sorted permutation of its input—we view this as the typing conclusion that the output of "sort(l)" has the "types" "a sorted list" and "a permutation of l".

We take this human capability, along with the above-stated trend in type inference systems, as evidence that there must exist fast and effective "type inference" algorithms for very rich type systems. We define in this paper a generalization of the traditional notion of "type" to a much more expressive notion of "specification", or "spec", and then give a type inference style algorithm for inferring specifications for functional program expressions. Our algorithm runs in polynomial-time, and is capable of automatically inferring specifications such as the fact that insertion sort returns a sorted permutation of its input.

Note that the specifications "a permutation of the input" and "a sorted list" differ from types in traditional type systems in at least two ways. The first specification depends on the actual input to the function (not just the input's type). Such types are known as *dependent types*[13, 4], and our system depends critically on including such types in our "specification" language. Second, the set of "sorted lists" is not definable by a simple grammar, and so is not a *regular* type. [14, 12, 3, 15] Our specification language allows any $\mathcal{RE}$ set to be defined as a program specification. Note that this property allows one program, possibly very inefficient but simple to understand, to serve as a correctness specification for another program, more efficient but harder to understand.

We envision an interactive programming system in which programmers write programs that include information about the specifications the programs are intended to meet, using an expressive specification language. As the program is written, the system checks that it is well-typed in the sense that no function is applied to arguments that don't provably meet the declared argument specifications for the function. Ideally, the system would be able to infer specifications for expressions quickly and with human-level competence. Where necessary, the programmer would switch to a theorem proving mode and prove lemmas necessary to aid the verification of the well-typedness.

Note that such a system would not require programmers to prove any more than they desired about the program. By providing more, or less, specification information to the system, the programmer can control where on the continuum from checking run-time type safety to verifying program specifications the programming process falls. By adding more specification information, the programmer can be sure that not only is "plus" receiving only numerical inputs, but that "merge" is in fact passed two sorted lists, for example. By adding even more, it may become verifiable that "mergesort" correctly sorts its input.

Short of achieving human-level specification inference, we believe that the simplicity of the inference rules defining our algorithm makes it possible for a programmer to develop the ability to predict what expressions the system will be able to compute specifications for, and where and how it will need help. This property may make an interactive environment based on this system acceptable to some programmers in spite of below human-level specification inference.

The remainder of this paper is structured as follows: first, we present several examples of simple programs and their automatically computed specifications; second, we present the formal syntax and semantics of our programming and specification languages; third, we present our inference algorithm, and then revisit the examples to demonstrate how it works.

2 Some Examples of Quickly Verifiable Specifications

We begin with an informal discussion of our programming and specification languages, and examples of simple programs and their automatically computed specifications. Later sections will contain a more formal treatment.

2.1 Example Programs

The programming language we will use is a simplified, typed first-order variant of LISP. We call it *first-order* because it does not include first-class functions; rather, user functions are introduced only through definitions (possibly recursive) and used only by being applied to arguments.[1] We call it *typed* because every variable is given at its introduction a user-provided *specification* (sometimes abbreviated *spec*). These specifications function much like types in a simply typed programming language, except that they range over our specification language, which is much more expressive than any familiar type system. Because the specification language is so expressive, we don't expect providing specifications for variables to be a significant burden on programmers, though it will still carry some of the advantages of simply typed languages.

The programming language includes constructor and selector symbols (e.g. `cons`, `car`, `cdr`) and has the intended semantics that each program expression denotes some term in the Herbrand closure of the constructor symbols.[2]

Unlike LISP, our language syntax has a distinguished formula category, with formulas of the form *e*:*s* meaning "*e* meets the spec *s*". We will discuss the computation implied by such formulas later. We now discuss computing specs for three example programs. The user-provided definitions of the specification functions (e.g. `(a-number)`) in these examples are shown and explained below.

Our first example program recursively defines `+` on numbers represented in unary as lists of the symbol `'a`. This program defines `+` to be a function that operates on two arguments. Each of the arguments is declared to meet the spec `(a-number)`. Our system automatically determines that `(+ x y)` is always greater than or equal to `x` and `y` (i.e., meets the specs `(≥ x)` and `(≥ y)`).

Our second example program defines insertion sort on a list of numbers, using functions `insert` and `sort`. Our system automatically finds that `(insert x l)`

[1] We omit first-class functions only for simplicity here. We believe this work extends naturally to higher-order languages.

[2] We require recursive definitions to be syntactically terminating.

returns a sorted permutation of (cons x l), i.e., meets the specs (a-permutation-of (cons x l)) and (a-sorted-list) and that (sort l) always returns a sorted permutation of the list l.[3]

Our third and last example program is a first-order version of LISP's mapcar. Here, we map a fixed function f across a list of numbers. Our system automatically infers the spec (samelength-as l) from reading the definition of map-f.

```
(define (+ (x (a-number))
           (y (a-number)))
  (if x:'nil
      y
      (cons 'a (+ (cdr x) y))))

(define (insert (x (a-number))
                (l (a-sorted-list)))
  (if l:'nil
      (cons x l)
      (if x:(> (car l))
          (cons (car l)
                (insert x (cdr l)))
          (cons x l))))

(define (map-f (l (a-numlist)))
  (if l:'nil
      l
      (cons (f (car l))
            (map-f (cdr l)))))

(define (sort (l (a-numlist)))
  (if l:'nil
      l
      (insert (car l)
              (sort (cdr l)))))
```

Fig. 1. Example program definitions.

2.2 Example Specifications

The specification language is less familiar. This language is essentially our programming language extended by a nondeterministic either combinator.[9, 8] Expressions in the specification language can take on more than one possible value. The set of possible values of a specification expression can be viewed as the type defined by that expression.

The either combinator applied to two expressions yields an expression that can nondeterministically take on any of the values of either of the two arguments. For example, the expression (either 'a 'b) can take on either of two the values 'a or 'b, and is our way of representing the type {'a, 'b}. Note that with recursion, a single nondeterministic expression have an infinity of values.

We add two other new combinators to the language to take the intersection or the set complement of the possible values of their arguments (both and not,

[3] As we will exhibit below, the system has no built-in knowledge of permutations. (a-permutation-of l) is a spec defined by the user for arbitrary list l. Once the user (or a specification library) provides that definition and proves two simple and natural theorems about it, the system can infer that sort has the desired spec.

respectively). Finally, we add a universal spec (a-thing) that nondeterministically returns any value at all, and an empty spec $\perp$ that returns no values.

Note that specs, like programs, can contain variables. Moreover, a specification variable can be bound by a program, in which case it refers to the object that the program variable is eventually instantiated with. This means that specs can represent dependent types, i.e., types that depend on an argument to the function being defined. This added expressiveness is an important element of our system, and the examples described in this section centrally involve dependent types.

Figure 2 exhibits the definitions for all the specification functions used in the examples above. Consider, e.g., the definition shown of the function a-number. Given this definition, (a-number) denotes the set of all flat lists of 'a symbols.

```
;; all lists with samelength as l
(define (samelength-as (l (a-list)))
  (if l:'nil
      l
      (cons (a-thing)
            (samelength-as (cdr l)))))

(define (a-list-member-of (l (a-list)))
  (if l:'nil
      bottom
      (either (car l)
         (a-list-member-of (cdr l)))))

;; sorted lists starting with x
(define (an-slist-from (x (a-number)))
  (either 'nil
     (cons x (an-slist-from (>= x)))))

(define (delete (x (a-thing))
                (l (a-list)))
  (if l:'nil  'nil
      (if x:(car l)
          (cdr l)
          (cons (car l)
                (delete x (cdr l))))))

(define (a-permutation-of (l (a-list)))
  (if l:'nil
      l
      (let ((x (a-list-member-of l)))
        (cons x
              (a-permutation-of (delete x l))))))
```

```
(define (a-number)
  (either 'nil
          (cons 'a (a-number))))

(define (a-list)
  (either 'nil
          (cons (a-thing)
                (a-list))))

;; any list of numbers
(define (a-numlist)
  (either 'nil
          (cons (a-number)
                (a-numlist))))

;; a sorted list of numbers
(define (a-sorted-list)
  (an-slist-from (a-number)))

;; the numbers >= x
(define (>= (x (a-number)))
  (either x
          (cons 'a (>= x))))

;; the numbers > x
(define (> (x (a-number)))
  (both (>= x) (not x)))
```

Fig. 2. Example Specification Definitions

Finally, we say that a program expression e *satisfies* a spec s, written $e{:}s$, if the value denoted by e is one of the possible values taken on by s. Abusing notation, we also say that a spec t *satisfies* another spec s, written $t{:}s$, if every value of t can be taken by s (analogous to the standard notion of *subtype*).

As a simple example, consider the spec expression for "non-zero number", `(cons 'a (a-number))`. Every value of this expression is a value of `(a-number)`, so the expression satisfies the spec `(a-number)`.

In the definition of `insert` above we used the formula `x:(> (car l))` in an `if` test. However, > is a specification function, defined by a nondeterministic program. As in this case, our nondeterministic expressions often have infinitely many values, and so cannot be executed. To use the > function in an `if` test we must require > to have associated with it a means of computing membership in the resulting specification, given particular arguments. This *implementation attachment* can be written in our programming language, and proven to compute the desired result with a theorem prover. These steps are straightforward for >.

We choose to write our `if` tests in this manner because it makes the extraction of relevant type information from the test as straightforward as possible for the inference mechanism. In the next section we will discuss the general restriction we need to place on formulas appearing in programs to ensure that they are computable. The use of attachment can always be avoided with no loss in clarity or program effectiveness, all that is lost is those specification inferences that depend on the type information in the `if` test in question.

3 A Programming Language with Specifications

Program Expressions . The program expressions are a first-order typed LISP with constructor and selector functions, recursive definitions, `let`, and `if`:

$$e ::= x \mid (\texttt{let}\ x{:}e\ e_1) \mid (f\ e_1 \cdots e_n) \mid (\texttt{if}\ e : s^*\ e_1\ e_2)$$

where f can be n-ary constructor, selector or n-ary program function-symbol, and s^* must be *testable* (see below). We often write a quoted symbol as an abbreviation for the application of a 0-ary constructor.[4]

Specification Expressions . Specification expressions are formed from the same grammar extended with `either`, `both`, `not`, $\bot$, and `a-thing`:

$$s ::= x \mid (\texttt{let}\ x{:}s\ s_1) \mid (f\ s_1 \cdots s_n) \mid (\texttt{if}\ s_1{:}s_2\ s_3\ s_4)$$
$$\mid (\texttt{either}\ s_1\ s_2) \mid (\texttt{both}\ s_1\ s_2) \mid (\texttt{not}\ s) \mid \bot \mid (\texttt{a-thing})$$

where f can now be any n-ary constructor or selector, or n-ary program *or specification* function-symbol that is defined or being defined. Note that every program expression is also a specification expression.[5]

[4] A full language would also include boolean operations in the formulas in `if` tests. No extra difficulties are presented by this extension.

[5] We include `both` and `not` for convenience—they can also be taken to abbreviate appropriate expressions using `let` and `if`, recognized by the inference process.

Programs . We consider a sequence of function-symbols definitions to be a program. A function-symbol definition assigns to a new function-symbol either of (`lambda` $x_1 : s_1, \cdots, x_n : s_n\ s$) or (`fix` $f\ x_1 : s_1, \cdots, x_n : s_n\ s$) where the body s must be deterministic (i.e. a program expression) if the symbol being defined is a program function-symbol. The specs s_j *can* reference and depend on the variables $x_1, \ldots, x_{j-1}$. Note that we differentiate between defined program function-symbols and defined specification function-symbols.

We must restrict recursive definitions to ensure that every `fix` expression accepted has a well-defined least fixed point. For this language it suffices to prohibit recursive calls in positions that are not *syntactically monotone*—we exclude recursive calls inside the test of an `if`, inside an odd number of `not` expressions, or inside the type specifications of the parameters of the definition. In addition to this restriction, we require definitions of function symbols to be used in program expressions to be *syntactically terminating*. Checking termination is a deep problem itself[7], but here we simply require that there be some argument to the function whose Herbrand size is reduced in each recursive call.

Semantics . Our semantic domain is the Herbrand closure over the constructor functions, with an error (ϵ) element adjoined. When a function is applied to objects outside its domain (as indicated by the specs on its formal parameters) it returns ϵ. Each program expression denotes either a Herbrand term or the error element. Each specification expression denotes a subset of the domain.

Assigning meanings to the various expressions compositionally is routine; we discuss only the unusual cases in specification meaning. Because a specification denotes a *set* of objects, the meaning of function application may not be obvious: to apply a function f to sets $\alpha_1, \ldots, \alpha_n$, choose objects $x_1, \ldots, x_n$ from the α_i respectively, and compute $f(x_1, \ldots, x_n)$. The function application will denote the set of values that can be obtained in this manner. Viewed as a nondeterministic computation, we first nondeterministically compute arguments for the function, and then apply the function, with many possible results. The `s1:s2` test of an `if` expression is true exactly when `s1` denotes a subset of `s2`'s denotation. `(a-thing)` denotes the set of all domain objects, and $\perp$ denotes the empty set. `Either`, `both`, and `not` are computed with union, intersection, and set complement relative to the domain, respectively. Any time a program expression is used as a specification, it's denotation is the set containing the object it denotes.

Note that in both specifications and program expressions, `fix` and `lambda` expressions have only one meaning (not nondeterministically many): in each case it is a relation over the domain, a functional relation for program expressions.

Implementation Attachments We require the user to attach verified program expressions to any specification function used in a way requiring it to be computed (in this language, in the test of an `if`). We also place sufficient restrictions on the use of specifications in programs to ensure that the programs can be run.

A spec s^* is *testable* if it is either a program expression or the application of a *computable* specification function to program expressions.[6] A specification

[6] The application of a specification function to a non-program expression is not directly computable even if all the functions involved have attachments.

function is computable if it has been given a proven program implementation.

As an example, consider the `if` test `x:(> (car l))` in `insert`. Our language forces us to write this uncomputable test rather than the more familiar `(> x (car l))`. However, to avoid this restriction we can just write the program for the predicate form of > returning `'true` or `'false`, and then use `'true: (> x (car l))`. Doing this will lose the advantages our system gains from extracting type information about the formal parameter x from the `if` test.

To retain these advantages, our user must take the same predicate definition (call it `>-imp`), shown in Fig. 3 and prove the attachment theorems shown. Our system recognizes theorems of this form and will then allow the implemented specification function to appear in program expressions, as in `insert`.

```
(define (>-imp (x (a-number))
               (y (a-number)))
  (if x:'nil
      'false
      (if y:'nil
          'true
          (>-imp (cdr x) (cdr y)))))
```

```
forall y:(a-number) x:(> y)
  (>-imp x y):'true

forall y:(a-number) x:(not (> y))
  (>-imp x y):'false
```

Fig. 3. The implementation of the function > and the associated attachment theorems.

4 Program Analysis: Inferring Specifications

For each new user definition our system extracts type lemmas which are then used in the analysis of future definitions. Our algorithm thus operates in the context of a library of previously derived knowledge. This library is just a set of known universally quantified specification formulas `forall` $x_1{:}s_1 \cdots x_n{:}s_n$. $s{:}t$. We call such formulas *type theorems*. The general problem that the algorithm in this section attacks we call the *specification inference problem*. Given a library $\mathcal{L}$ of type theorems (about already processed definitions) and a new definition assigning some `lambda` or `fix` expression e to some new function symbol g, analyze e to generate new type theorems about g to add to the library $\mathcal{L}$. We present the algorithm and then discuss its application to the examples above.

4.1 An Inference Algorithm

There are three parts to our central analysis algorithm. First, a forward-chaining inference closure intended as a notion of "obvious consequence" ($\vdash_e$); second, a syntax-directed, type-inference inspired inference relation ($\vdash\!\circ_e$) that manages the application of $\vdash_e$; and third, a preprocessing stage which prepares the new definition for analysis by $\vdash\!\circ_e$. Our solution to the specification inference problem is to add to $\mathcal{L}$ those theorems inferred when $\vdash\!\circ_e$ is applied to the definitions generated by preprocessing.

The Forward-Chaining Inference Relation $\vdash_e$ We now define a polynomial-time computable inference relation $\vdash_e$, where e is the `lambda` or `fix` expression being analyzed. Given a premise set Σ of formulas (e.g. $s{:}t$), we say that $\Sigma \vdash_e s{:}t$ for specs s and t whenever $s{:}t$ is in the closure over Σ of the inference rules given below. Note that in addition to reasoning about specification formulas, the inference rules draw (and use) conclusions of the form Dom (s) for specification expression s. These ***domain analysis*** conclusions have no intended semantic meaning and are used by the algorithm to limit the scope of the reasoning to remain within polynomial time. We will prove that there are at most polynomially many conclusions Dom (s) inferred. The intended intuition is that the inference process reasons only about expressions in this polynomial-sized "domain". $\vdash_e$ is defined by the inference rules given in Fig. 4.

Sym
p:q
———
q:p

Trans
r:s
s:t
———
r:t

Not-Sym
Dom (d)
d:(not e)
———
e:(not d)

Either1
r:(either s t)
r:(not s)
———
r:t

Either2
s:r, t:r
Dom (either s t)
———
(either s t):r

Under-Both
Dom (both s t)
r:s, r:t
———
r:(both s t)

Basic-Either
Dom (either s t)
———
s:(either s t)
t:(either s t)

Basic-Both
Dom (both s t)
———
(both s t):s
(both s t):t

Always
Dom (s)
———
s:s, ⊥:s
s:(a-thing)

Selectors1
Dom (cons p q)
———
p:(car (cons p q))
q:(cdr (cons p q))

Selectors2
Dom (r)
r:(cons s t)
———
(car r):s
(cdr r):t

Strictness
Dom (f s1...sn)
si:⊥
———
(f s1...sn):⊥

Monotonicity
s1:t1...sn:tn
d:(f s1 ...sn)
Dom (f t1...tn)
———
d:(f t1 ...tn)

Constructors
Dom (c1 s1...sn)
Dom (c2 t1...tm)
c1 ≠ c2
———
(c1 s1...sn) : (not (c2 t1...tm))

Dom-Always
———
Dom (a-thing)
Dom (⊥), Dom (e)

Dom-Subexp
Dom (r)
s a subexp of r
———
Dom (s)

Univ-Dom
forall $x{:}s$ Φ
———
Dom (s)

Univ-Inst
forall $x{:}s$ Φ
$p{:}s$, *p appears in e*
———
$[p/x]\,\Phi$
Dom ($[p/x]\,\Phi$)

Fig. 4. Basic Inference Rules for $\vdash_e$. p and q must be ***program expressions.*** r, s and t can be any specification expressions. f can be any function symbol, constructor or selector. c is any constructor. The selector rules are shown for cons/car/cdr. In the rule Univ-Inst, the notation $[r/x]\,s$ denotes s with each free occurrence of x replaced by r.

Let Σ be a premise set of type theorems. Let $\mathcal{A}$ be the set of all expressions s such that Dom (s) is inferred by forward-chaining the above rules from Σ. We observe the following two complexity bounds:

1. $\mathcal{A}$ has at most polynomially many members in the size of Σ, and
2. The forward-chaining can be computed in polynomial-time in the size of $\mathcal{A}$.

The first bound follows from the observation (provable by induction on the length of derivation) that every spec in $\mathcal{A}$ is either $\perp$, `(a-thing)`, a subexpression of e, or a subexpression of a universal formula `forall` $x_1 : s_1 \ldots x_n : s_n \;\; \Phi$ in Σ with its variables replaced by subexpressions of e. The last case forces us to limit the quantification depth of formulas in Σ to some constant—then there are only polynomially many instances of universal formulas in Σ on subexpressions of e.[7]

To see the second bound, observe that by induction on the length of derivation every spec in any new conclusion is of the form: `s`, `(not s)`, `(car s)`, or `(cdr s)` for some s in $\mathcal{A}$. There are only polynomially many such conclusions and for any not yet closed premise set we can find a new conclusion in polynomial time.

We wish to point out that, although there are a large number of rules given above, they are clearly not designed for the specific examples we've exhibited. Each rule is a natural and simple local rule capturing a small piece of the meaning of one language construct. The important thing about these rules is that they capture a large polynomial time fragment of the quantifier-free inference problem. For any new language features, we can always capture some polynomial-time portion of the possible new inferences in similar forward-chaining rules. The examples serve to demonstrate the power this kind of simple rule set can wield.

The Syntax-Directed Inference Relation $\vdash\!\circ_e$ We now use the $\vdash_e$ relation just defined to define a stronger $\vdash\!\circ_e$ relation that handles `let`, `if`, `lambda`, and `fix` by adding the sequent inference rules shown below. These rules are roughly analogous to typical type inference rules: they are syntax directed, so that typing of any expression can be done in a linear number of $\vdash_e$ closures. The Analyze-Fix, Analyze-Lambda, and Beta-Abstract-e rules are shown for one-argument expressions, but the analogous rules for arbitrary arity are intended. We use the expression $\mathit{THMS}_{\Sigma,e}(s)$ to abbreviate the set of all specification formulas of the form $s\!:\!t$ provable from Σ using $\vdash\!\circ_e$.

The analyze-if rule does a simple case analysis on the `if` test. Because our $\vdash_e$ inference rules reason only about positive specification formulas, we negate formulas with the meta-function *Neg*, which takes as input a formula `s:t` and returns `s:(not t)` if `s` is a program expression, and `s:(a-thing)` otherwise. Analyze-let is implicitly doing universal generalization when r is not a program expression. Analyze-Nondet-App provides rudimentary reasoning about nondeterministic applications. The Analyze-Lambda, Analyze-Fix, and Beta-Abstract-e rules are needed only at the top level of function symbol definitions.

It remains to specify how induction hypotheses for the rule Analyze-Fix are selected. Space allows only the following concise description: we compute a sequence of hypotheses $\Upsilon_0, \Upsilon_1 \cdots$ where each Υ_i is a set of specifications which is a subset of Υ_{i-1}. This sequence eventually reaches the desired fixed point

[7] For lemmas that were derived by the system, the bound on quantification depth can derive from bounds on the arity of functions and the depth of `Let` nesting within analyzed definitions.

Analyze-If

$$\frac{\begin{array}{l}\Gamma = \Sigma \cup THMS_{\Sigma,e}(r) \cup THMS_{\Sigma,e}(s)\\ \Gamma,\ \mathrm{r{:}s} \vdash\!\!\circ_e \mathrm{u1{:}t}\\ \Gamma,\ Neg(\mathrm{r{:}s}) \vdash\!\!\circ_e \mathrm{u2{:}t}\end{array}}{\Sigma \vdash\!\!\circ_e (\mathrm{if\ r{:}s\ u1\ u2}){:}\mathrm{t}}$$

Analyze-Let

$$\frac{\begin{array}{l}\Gamma = \Sigma \cup THMS_{\Sigma,e}(r)\\ \Gamma,\ \mathrm{x{:}r} \vdash\!\!\circ_e \mathrm{s{:}t}\\ \mathrm{x\ not\ in}\ \Gamma\ \mathrm{or\ t}\end{array}}{\Sigma \vdash\!\!\circ_e (\mathrm{let\ x{:}r}\ s){:}\mathrm{t}}$$

Analyze-Nondet-App

$$\frac{\begin{array}{l}\Sigma \vdash\!\!\circ_e (\mathrm{let\ x1{:}s1\ldots xn{:}sn\ (f\ x1\ldots xn)}){:}t\\ \mathrm{No}\ x_i\ \mathrm{in}\ \Sigma\ \mathrm{or}\ t,\ \mathrm{some}\ s_i\ \mathrm{non\text{-}program}\end{array}}{\Sigma \vdash\!\!\circ_e (\mathrm{f\ s1\ldots sn}){:}t}$$

Beta-Abstract-e

$$\frac{e\ \mathrm{is}\ (\mathrm{lambda}\ x{:}s\ B)}{\Sigma \vdash\!\!\circ_e \mathrm{forall}\ x{:}s\ B{:}(e\ x)}$$

Analyze-Lambda

$$\frac{\begin{array}{l}\Gamma = \Sigma \cup THMS_{\Sigma,e}(r)\\ \Gamma,\ x{:}r \vdash\!\!\circ_e B{:}t\\ x\ \mathrm{and}\ x_1\ \mathrm{not\ in}\ \Gamma,\ x_1\ \mathrm{not\ in}\ B\end{array}}{\Sigma \vdash\!\!\circ_e \begin{array}{l}\mathrm{Forall}\ x_1{:}r\\ \quad((\mathrm{lambda}\ x{:}r\ B)\ x_1){:}[x_1/x]t\end{array}}$$

Analyze-Fix

$$\frac{\begin{array}{l}\Gamma = \Sigma \cup THMS_{\Sigma,e}(r)\\ \Gamma,\ \begin{array}{l}\mathrm{Forall}\ x_1{:}r\\ \quad (f\ x_1){:}[x_1/x]I\end{array},\ x{:}r \vdash\!\!\circ_e B{:}I\\ x\ \mathrm{and}\ x_1\ \mathrm{not\ in}\ \Gamma,\ x_1\ \mathrm{not\ in}\ B\end{array}}{\Sigma \vdash\!\!\circ_e \begin{array}{l}\mathrm{Forall}\ x_1{:}r\\ \quad((\mathrm{fix}\ f\ x{:}r\ B)\ x_1){:}[x_1/x]I\end{array}}$$

Fig. 5. Sequent Rules for $\vdash\!\!\circ_e$. *Neg* is discussed in the text. r, s, t, u, I, and B are any specification expressions.

hypothesis. The sequence is defined as follows:

$$\mathcal{T}(\Upsilon) = \left\{ t \;\middle|\; \mathcal{L} \cup \left\{ \begin{array}{c}\mathtt{Forall}\ x_1{:}s_1\ldots x_n{:}s_n\\ (g\ x_1\ldots x_n) : \mathcal{B}(\Upsilon)\end{array} \right\} \vdash\!\!\circ_e B{:}t \right\}$$

$$\Upsilon_0 = \mathcal{T}(\{\bot\})$$
$$\Upsilon_{i+1} = \mathcal{T}(\Upsilon_i) \cap \Upsilon_i$$

where $\mathcal{B}(\Upsilon)$ is the `both` expression intersecting all the members of Υ

Definition Preprocessing Suppose we are presented with a new definition to analyze, defining the symbol f to be a function with arguments $x_1 \ldots x_n$ of types $s_1 \ldots s_n$ and (possibly recursive) body B. Rather than simply apply the $\vdash\!\!\circ$ relation directly to f, we begin by *factoring* the definition of f into a set of definitions $f_1, \ldots, f_n$ such that f is semantically the same function as one that nondeterministically picks one of the f_i and applies it. Our purposes in factoring are twofold: it enables the easy statement of some useful theorems; and it supports some limited case analysis in reasoning about applications of the function.

We first factor the definition of f into the set of definitions $f, f_1, \ldots, f_k$ where $f_1, \ldots, f_k$ are all definitions that can be produced from f by the rewrite rules in figure 6 but cannot be further rewritten (if two definitions differ only in the ordering of their formal parameters, we include only one of them in the f_i). We note that the size of $f_1, \ldots, f_k$ is linear in the size of f.

Either-Def	Let-Def
`(define (f...) (either B1 B2))`	`(define (f x1:s1...xn:sn) (let x:s B))`
`(define (f...) Bi), i=1 or 2`	`(define (f x1:s1...xn:sn x:s) B)`

If-Def

```
(define (f x1:s1...xn:sn) (if xi:s B1 B2))
y1:t1...yn:tn is a suitable reordering of the xi:si
--------------------------------------------------
(define (f y1:t1...yi:(both s ti) yn:tn) B1)
(define (f y1:t1...yi:(both (not s) ti) yn:tn) B2)
```

Fig. 6. Rewrite Rules for Definition Factoring. In the If-Def rule, a reordering is suitable if it yields an output definition with no free variables.

To try and convey some intuition about the f_i defined by this rewrite process, consider an f_i with arguments $y_1 \ldots y_m$ of types $t_1 \ldots t_m$ and body B_i. The y_j are made up of the (possibly reordered) original formal parameters of f (the x_j) and the `let` variables in scope around B_i in B. The t_j restrict the y_j to exactly those values that those variables can take in B_i during an evaluation of f. Thus, $(f_i\ t_1 \ldots t_m)$ can take on exactly the values that B_i contributes to f. We call this the *output type of* f_i.

Now consider an application of f, $(f s'_1 \cdots s'_n)$. We seek to characterize the contribution of B_i to the values of this application. We will write $t_{x_j,i}$ for the type spec of the variable x_j in the parameter list of f_i. We claim that $[(\texttt{both}\ t_{x_1,i}\ s'_1)/t_{x_1,i}] \cdots [(\texttt{both}\ t_{x_n,i}\ s'_n)/t_{x_n,i}]\,(f_i\ t_1 \ldots t_m)$ is the characterization we seek. We call this expression the *output type of* f_i *when restricted to the* s'_j. The `either` expression unioning the output types of the f_i restricted to the s'_j is equivalent to $(f s'_1 \cdots s'_n)$. We called this union expression the *factored application of* f *to the* s'_j.

Finally, we eliminate f entirely from the bodies of the f_i by replacing each application of f with its factored form, to get new definitions $f'_1, \ldots, f'_k$, and redefine f to be the union (`either`) of the f'_i. We use the $\vdash_{\circ}$ relation from the previous section to analyze the mutually recursive f'_i, and then f, and add the resulting theorems to our library $\mathcal{L}$.

The combination of definition factoring with the $\vdash_{\circ}$-rule Beta-Abstract-*e* yields many useful theorems which we call *factoring theorems*. Several examples of these are shown in Fig. 7. Factoring also enhances the conditional analysis done by the recursive descent algorithm.

4.2 Inferring the Specifications in Our Examples

We now return to our example programs and discuss their analysis

The theorems shown in Fig. 7 are among those generated automatically when reading the specification definitions shown in Sect. 2. These and others like them are used in calculating the specifications cited for the example programs.

```
(1) forall l:(both (a-list) (not 'nil))
      (cons (a-thing) (samelength-as (cdr l))) : (samelength-as l)

(2) forall l:(both (a-list) (not 'nil))
           z:(not (car l))
      (cons (car l) (delete z (cdr l))) : (delete z l)

(3) forall l:(both (a-list) (not 'nil))
           z:(a-list-member-of l)
      (cons z (a-permutation-of (delete z l))) : (a-permutation-of l)

(4) forall l:(both (a-list) (not 'nil)) (cdr l):(delete (car l) l)
(5) forall l:(both (a-list) (not 'nil)) (car l):(a-list-member-of l)
(6) forall x:(a-number) (either x (cons 'a (>= x))) : (>= x)
(7) forall x:(a-number) (> x):(both (>= x) (not x))
(8) (a-numlist):(a-list)
(9) (a-numlist):(either 'nil (cons (a-number) (a-numlist)))
(A) (either 'nil (cons (a-number) (a-list))):(a-numlist)
```

Fig. 7. Some automatically generated theorems used in the examples. All but (8) and (9) are generated by factoring analysis of specification definitions. (8) and (9) are generated by the inferential closure analysis of `a-numlist`.

Each example requires the presence of some additional simple and natural theorems, shown in Fig. 8. We intend either that the user have proven these theorems using a theorem prover or that he is using a specification library containing the definitions and theorems. Each theorem captures a basic property of the definitions, rather than a property targeted to any of our examples.[8] Most of the theorems can be proven automatically by a simple inductive theorem prover.

To conclude our discussion of these examples, we show some of the critical inference steps involved in drawing one of the tougher conclusions. To determine that `(insert x l)` has the specification `(a-permutation-of (cons x l))`, the system must first choose that specification as an inductive hypothesis. This happens because it is a specification of the base case `(cons x l)`, by the theorem that any list is a permutation of itself—and a simple inference chain that demonstrates that `(cons x l):(a-list)`. Once we have `(a-permutation-of (cons x l))` as an inductive hypothesis, the analysis of the recursive case of the `if` body goes as shown in Fig. 9. Similar chains of reasoning are involved in automatically drawing the other specification conclusions cited above.

[8] An exception to this is the second lemma on the right, which mitigates a weakness in our reasoning about nondeterminism. Stronger polynomial-time reasoning about non-determinism is possible and is addressed in the full paper[5].

```
forall l:(a-list)
  l:(samelength-as l)

forall l:(a-list)
  l:(a-permutation-of l)

forall x:(a-number)
       y:(not (> x))
  x:(>= y)

forall n:(a-number)
  (>= (>= n)):(>= n)

forall l:(both (a-sorted-list) (not 'nil))
  l:(an-slist-from (car l))

forall n:(a-number)
       l:(both (an-slist-from (>= n))
               (not 'nil))
  (car l):(>= n)

forall l:(a-list)
  (a-permutation-of (a-permutation-of l)):
  (a-permutation-of l)

forall n:(a-number) (cons 'a (>= n)):(>= (cons 'a n))
```

Fig. 8. The theorems needed from the user or the specification library.

```
(cons x (cdr lst))
   by theorem (4) above is under  (cons x (delete (car lst) lst))
   by selectors rule is under     (cons (car (cons x lst))
                                        (delete (car lst)
                                                (cdr (cons x lst))))
   by theorem (2) is under        (delete (car lst) (cons x lst))  (*)

(cons (car lst) (insert x (cdr lst)))
   by ind hyp is under  (cons (car lst)
                              (a-permutation-of (cons x (cdr lst))))
   by (*) is under      (cons (car lst)
                              (a-permutation-of
                               (delete (car lst) (cons x lst))))
   by theorem (3) is    (a-permutation-of (cons x lst))  as desired.
```

Fig. 9. The main inference chain involved in analyzing `insert`. First, `(cons x (cdr lst))` is analyzed to get the result labelled (*). This result is used to analyze the recursive branch of `insert`. The inductive hypothesis puts `(insert x (cdr lst))` under `(a-permutation-of (cons x (cdr lst)))`. Not every inference rule used is cited.

5 Conclusion

We presented a polynomial-time type inference inspired algorithm for inferring properties, viewed as types, of functional programs. We also gave an expressive language for defining new types to extend the "type system" of the algorithm. Several extensions to this work are addressed in the full version[5].

An important remaining task is developing a better understanding of what properties this algorithm and related algorithms can infer. This algorithm is capable for example of checking the correctness of merge-sort much like it checks insertion sort. In contrast, difficulties arise in a naive attempt to check quick-sort. It remains an open problem to cleanly characterize the set of checkable properties.

There are many natural specification theorems that this algorithm will not infer. Exploration of such examples will suggest many ways of enriching the set of checkable properties while remaining within polynomial time. One of the difficulties in working in an area where completeness is out of reach lies in knowing when you've done enough, or whether there is such a point.

An interesting area for future research is the question of how to identify for the programmer the place where a proof is failing. When a forward-chaining process fails to generate a desired formula, it is not clear where to place the blame. Explaining failure may require backward chaining from the goal.

6 Acknowledgment

I would like to thank David McAllester for his significant role in creating the paradigm for this research.

References

1. A. Aiken and E. Wimmers. Soft typing with conditional types. In *ACM Symposium on Principles of Programming Languges*, pages 163–173, 1994.
2. Alexander Aiken and Edward Wimmers. Type inference with set constraints. Research Report 8956, IBM, 1992.
3. J. A. Brzozowski and E. Leiss. On equations for regular languages, finite automata, and sequential networks. *Theoretical Computer Science*, 10:19–35, 1980.
4. R. L. Constable et. al. *Implementing Mathematics with the Nuprl Development system*. Prentice-Hall, 1986.
5. Robert Givan. *Automatically Inferring Properties of Computer Programs*. PhD thesis, Massachusetts Institute of Technology, 1996. http://www.ai.mit.edu-/people/rlg/papers/thesis.ps.
6. P. Jouvelot and D. Gifford. Algebraic reconstruction of types and effects. In *Proceedings of ACM Conference on Principles of Programming Languages*, 1991.
7. D. McAllester and K. Arkoudas. Walther recursion. Submitted to CADE-13, available at http://www.ai.mit.edu/people/dam/termination.html, 1996.
8. D. McAllester and R. Givan. Taxonomic syntax for first order inference. *JACM*, 40(2):246–283, April 1993. internet file ftp.ai.mit.edu:/pub/users/dam/jacm1.ps.
9. J. McCarthy. A basis for a math. theory of computation. P. Braffort & D. Hirschberg, eds., *Computer Programing & Formal Systems*. North-Holland, 1967.
10. Robin Milner. Type polymorphism in programming. *JCSS*, 17:348–375, 1978.
11. John C. Mitchell. A type inference appproach to reduction properties and semantics of polymorphic expressions. In *Proceedings 1986 ACM Symposium on Lisp and Functional Programming*, pages 308–319, 1986.
12. P. Mishra and U. S. Reddy. Declaration-free type checking. In *Proceedings of the Twelfth Annual ACM Symposium on Principles of Programming Languages*, pages 7–21. ACM, 1985.
13. John C. Reynolds. Towards a theory of type structure. In *Proceedings Colloque sur la Programmation*. Springer-Verlag, 1974.
14. J.W. Thatcher. Tree automata: an informal survey. In A. V. Aho, editor, *Currents in Theory of Computation*, pages 143–172. Prentice-Hall, 1973.
15. W. Thomas. Automata on infinite objects. In *Handbook of Theoretical Computer Science, Volume B, Formal Methods and Semantics*, pp. 133-164. MIT Press, 1990.

Automated Modular Termination Proofs for Real Prolog Programs

Martin Müller
Thomas Glaß
Karl Stroetmann

Siemens AG
ZT SE 1
D–81730 München, Germany

{Martin.Mueller,Thomas.Glass,Karl.Stroetmann}@zfe.siemens.de
phone: +49 89 636 41687
fax: +49 89 636 42284

Abstract. We present a methodology for checking the termination of Prolog programs that can be automated and is scalable. Furthermore, the proposed method can be used to locate errors. It has been successfully implemented as part of a tool that uses static analysis based on formal methods in order to validate Prolog programs. This tool is aimed at supporting the design and maintenance of Prolog programs.

Our approach is based on a natural extension of the notion of *acceptable* programs developed in Apt and Pedreschi [AP90, AP93]. The main idea is to assign a measure of complexity to predicate calls. Then the termination of a program is shown by proving this measure to be decreasing on recursive calls. While this measure is a natural number in [AP90, AP93], we extend this idea by using *tuples* of natural numbers as a measure of complexity. These tuples are compared lexicographicly. The use of this kind of measure enables us to refine the notion of *acceptable* programs to the notion of *loop free* programs. This notion can be used to modularize the termination proof of Prolog programs to a greater extend than previously possible.

Keywords: Prolog, termination, formal methods, static analysis, automated theorem proving

1 Introduction

As software gets more and more complex, the problem of guaranteeing the reliability of a software system is getting increasingly difficult. Formal methods can make a valuable contribution towards solving this problem. However, at least for the time being, a complete specification and verification of most software systems is economically not viable since the process of verification can, in general, not be automated. Nevertheless, recent progress in automated deduction has shown that for declarative programming languages it is possible to verify certain kinds of properties automatically.

Of course, the question whether a program is terminating is, in general, undecidable. However, the paper of Apt and Pedreschi [AP90, AP93] gives a useful characterization of terminating programs: A program is terminating iff there exists a *norm* $|.|$ and an *interpretation* I such that the program is *acceptable* with respect to $|.|$ and I. We refine this notion into the notion of a program being *loop free* with respect to $|.|$ and I. This notion has been inspired by the work of De Schreye, Verschaetse and Bruynooghe [SVB92]. Related work can be found in [MP94]. The property of a program being loop free with respect to a fixed norm $|.|$ and interpretation I becomes decidable if we restrict ourselves to the use of *linear norms*. Moreover, our practical experiences have shown that the notion of *loop freeness* is sufficiently strong to deal with most programs encountered in practice.

On a theoretical level, our work is a refinement of the ideas found in Apt and Pedreschi [AP93] and a variation of the approach suggested in Gröger and Plümer [GP92]. The question of the modularization of termination proofs is the main theme of [AP93]. Unfortunately, this solution is not entirely satisfactory: If two programs P and Q are given such that P *extends* Q, i.e. predicates from Q are used in P but not vice versa, then the termination proof for P can not be given independently from the termination proof for Q. Furthermore, [AP93] does not discuss the question of automating the termination proofs in sufficient detail.

The paper of Gröger and Plümer [GP92] is concerned with the question of automating the termination check. Although the methods presented in [GP92] are successful to prove the termination of programs, they seem to be not as well suited to locate errors leading to non-termination. The reason is that the approach of Gröger and Plümer does not require to specify either *inter-argument relations* or *norm definitions* but rather aims at computing this information automatically. This causes their method to fail for some programs that can be dealt with by our method. Furthermore, it prevents them from locating errors. However, in practice the ability to locate errors is one of the features that distinguishes a useful tool.

We present a method that supports modular termination proofs, is capable of being fully automated and, furthermore, can be used to locate errors in programs. It has been successfully implemented as part of a tool that is aimed at supporting the development and maintenance of software written in Prolog. Methodologically our approach is a natural extension of the notion of *acceptable* programs developed in [AP90, AP93]. The main idea there is to assign a measure of complexity to atomic formulas. The termination of a program is then shown by proving this measure to be decreasing on recursive calls. While this measure is a natural number in [AP90, AP93], we extend this idea by using *tuples* of natural numbers as a measure of complexity. These tuples are then compared lexicographicly. The first component of these tuples is the *level* of a predicate as defined in Clark [Cla78], while the second component is determined by the size of the arguments. The fact that the first component is independent of the arguments but only reflects the recursion structure of the program enables us to come up with a truly modular termination criterion.

The next section introduces some basic notions and notations. Section 3 introduces modes and types which are a prerequisite for our method. In Section 4 we define the central notion of the *norm* of an atomic formula. This norm is the measure of complexity which has been cited above. We refine the notion of Apt and Pedreschi of an *acceptable program* to the notion of a program being *loop free* in Section 5. This notion is the basis for the modular termination criterion given in Theorem 19 of Section 6. The question how this criterion can be automated is then tackled in Section 7, while the last section discusses an implementation of the method introduced in this paper.

2 Some Basic Notions

In the following we use $t, t_1, \ldots$ to denote terms, $p, q, p_1, \ldots$ to denote predicate symbols and $P, Q, R, P_1, \ldots$ to denote atomic formulas. If $P_1, \ldots, P_n, P$ are atomic formulas, then $(P_1, \ldots, P_n)$ is a query and P:- $P_1, \ldots, P_n$ is a clause. We use $\mathcal{Q}, \mathcal{R}, \ldots$ to denote queries and C to denote clauses. Given a fixed Prolog program we write

$$(P_1, \ldots, P_n) \rightarrow^{\mu}_{\text{res}} (Q_1\mu, \ldots, Q_m\mu, P_2\mu, \ldots, P_n\mu)$$

if there is a variant of a clause P:- $Q_1, \ldots, Q_m$ and a most general unifier μ of P and P_1. This is called an LD-resolution step. We write $\mathcal{Q} \rightarrow^{*\mu}_{\text{res}} \mathcal{Q}'$ as an abbreviation for $\mathcal{Q} \rightarrow^{\mu_1}_{\text{res}} \mathcal{Q}_1 \rightarrow^{\mu_2}_{\text{res}} \ldots \rightarrow^{\mu_n}_{\text{res}} \mathcal{Q}'$ and $\mu = \mu_n \circ \ldots \circ \mu_1$. We call μ a *solution* of $\mathcal{Q}$ if $\mathcal{Q} \rightarrow^{*\mu}_{\text{res}} ()$. The *search tree* belonging to a query $\mathcal{Q}$ has $\mathcal{Q}$ as its root node and for every node $\mathcal{Q}'$ appearing in this tree we have that $\mathcal{Q}''$ is a child of $\mathcal{Q}'$ iff $\mathcal{Q}' \rightarrow^{\mu}_{\text{res}} \mathcal{Q}''$. The set of solutions of a given query which is found by a certain search strategy – we think of Prologs 'depth first' search strategy – may be a real subset of the set of all solutions of this query if the search tree is infinite.

We call a query $\mathcal{Q}$ *terminating* w.r.t. a Prolog program **P** if there is no infinite sequence $\mathcal{Q} = \mathcal{Q}_1 \rightarrow^{\mu_1}_{\text{res}} \mathcal{Q}_2 \rightarrow^{\mu_2}_{\text{res}} \mathcal{Q}_3 \rightarrow^{\mu_3}_{\text{res}} \ldots$ In this case the search tree is finite (by Königs Lemma, as a Prolog program has only a finite number of clauses) and all solutions are found by Prologs search strategy.

Referring to a given Prolog program we define the following relations between predicate symbols:

Definition 1. Let p, q be predicate symbols.

1. We define $p \rightarrow_{C,i} q$ if *p calls q in clause C at position i* that is C has the form $p(\ldots)\text{:-}\ q_1(\ldots), \ldots, q_n(\ldots)$ and $q = q_i$. We write $p \rightarrow q$ if $p \rightarrow_{C,i} q$ for some C and i.
2. We define $\sqsupseteq$ to be the reflexive and transitive closure of $\rightarrow$. We say *p depends on q* if $p \sqsupseteq q$.
3. We define p and q to be *mutually recursive* or *in the same recursive clique* and write $p \simeq q$ if $p \sqsupseteq q \wedge q \sqsupseteq p$.
4. We define $p \sqsupset q$ if *p calls q as a subprogram* that is $p \sqsupseteq q \wedge \neg q \sqsupseteq p$.

Observe that $\sqsupseteq$ is a preorder, $\simeq$ is a equivalence relation and $\sqsupset$ is a well-founded order, since there is only a finite number of predicate symbols in a Prolog program.

Definition 2. We assign a natural number to every predicate symbol p by defining $\text{level}(p) := \max\{\text{level}(q) + 1 : p \sqsupset q\}$, $(\max \emptyset = 0)$.

Observe that level is well-defined, as $\sqsupset$ is well-founded. This is in essence the level mapping given in Lloyd [Llo87, p. 83]. We extend these notions to atomic formulas in the obvious way, $\text{level}(p(\ldots)) = \text{level}(p)$, $p(\ldots) \simeq q(\ldots)$ iff $p \simeq q$, etc.

Lemma 3. *1. If $p \sqsupset q$ then level$(p) >$ level(q)*
2. If $p \simeq q$ then level$(p) =$ level(q) ∎

Definition 4. The *call graph of a Prolog program* is the hypergraph which has the predicate symbols as vertices and edges $p \rightarrow_{C,i} q$.

We have $p \simeq q$ iff there is a cycle in the call graph containing both p and q.

We assume the reader to be familiar with:

- *well-orderings*: A linear ordering $>$ is called well-ordering, if there is no infinite sequence $a_1 > a_2 > \ldots$).
- *lexicographic ordering*: if $>_1$ is a well-ordering on a set M_1 and $>_2$ is a well-ordering on a set M_2, then $>_{\text{lex}}$ is a well-ordering on the set $M_1 \times M_2$, where $\langle a, b\rangle >_{\text{lex}} \langle c, d\rangle$ is defined by $a >_1 c$ or $a = c \wedge b >_2 d$.
- *multiset ordering*: If $>$ is a well-ordering on M, then $>_{\text{mul}}$ is a well-ordering on the set of finite multisets of M, where $M >_{\text{mul}} N$, iff N can be obtained from M by iteratively replacing an element by a finite number of smaller elements.
- *ordinal numbers*: A canonical well-ordering; every well-ordering is isomorphic to an initial segment of ordinal numbers.

For ordinal numbers cf. Pohlers [Poh89], for multiset and lexicographic orderings cf. Bachmair [Bac91] or Avenhaus [Ave95].)

3 Typed Prolog

In this section we briefly explain "well-typedness". For that purpose we first explain the notion of types and then define well-typed queries and well-typed programs, respectively.

Definition 5. A type is a set of terms that is closed under substitution, i.e. if τ is a type and $t \in \tau$, then for all substitutions μ we have $t\mu \in \tau$.

Example 1. A recursive definition of the form

```
list := [] + '.'(term, list)
```

denotes that the type `list` consists of the constant `[]` and all terms of the form `'.'(T,L)` where `T` is of type `term`, i.e. `T` is an arbitrary term, and `L` is of type `list`. Obviously `list` and `term` are types, i.e. they are closed under substitution. Similarly, the type `nat` which is defined by

```
nat := 0 + s(nat)
```

denotes the set of terms consisting of the constant `0` and all terms of the form `s(N)` where `N` is of type `nat`.

Next we define *predicate signatures*: we specify the input and the output types of a predicate by a signature. In general we write

$$p(\sigma_1 \rightarrow \tau_1, \ldots, \sigma_n \rightarrow \tau_n) \qquad (1)$$

for the predicate p/n with *input types* $\sigma_1, \ldots, \sigma_n$ and *output types* $\tau_1, \ldots, \tau_n$, respectively. We abbreviate $\sigma \rightarrow \sigma$ by $+\sigma$ and $\texttt{term} \rightarrow \tau$ by $-\tau$.

Example 2. A signature for `append/3` is given by:

```
append(+list,+list,-list)
```

which means that whenever $\texttt{append}(r, s, t)$ is called with r, s of type `list` and returns a solution μ, we have that $r\mu$,$s\mu$ and $t\mu$ are of type `list`. This is formalized as follows (suppressing argument lists):

Definition 6. Let $p_0, \ldots, p_n$ be predicates with signatures $p_i(\sigma_i \rightarrow \tau_i)$ for $i \leq n$ be given. We call the clause $p_0(s_0)$:- $p_1(s_1), \ldots, p_n(s_n)$ *well-typed* iff the following holds for all substitutions μ:

1. For all $i = 1, \ldots, n$ the following holds: If $s_0\mu$ is of type σ_0 and $s_1\mu, \ldots, s_{i-1}\mu$ are of type $\tau_1, \ldots, \tau_{i-1}$, respectively, then $s_i\mu$ is of type σ_i.
2. If $s_0\mu$ is of type σ_0 and $s_1\mu, \ldots, s_n\mu$ are of type $\tau_1, \ldots, \tau_n$, respectively, then $s_0\mu$ is of type τ_0.

A program is called *well-typed* iff all clauses are. For the rest of this paper we will assume that all programs are well-typed.

We call a query $(p_1(s_1), \ldots, p_m(s_m))$ *well-typed* iff for all substitutions μ and all $i = 1, \ldots, m$ such that $s_1\mu, \ldots, s_{i-1}\mu$ are of type $\tau_1, \ldots, \tau_{i-1}$ we have that $s_i\mu$ is of type σ_i.

A literal $p(s_1, \ldots, s_n)$ is called *well-typed* w.r.t. the signature (1) iff $s_1, \ldots, s_n$ are of type $\sigma_1, \ldots, \sigma_n$, respectively.

Example 3. The usual implementation of **append/3** is well-typed:

```
append([], L, L).
append([H|T], L, [H|TL]) :- append(T, L, TL).
```

The literal **append([1],[2],L)** is well-typed, whereas **append([1],2,L)** is not.

The property of a query being well-typed is invariant under resolution and substitution. For a proof compare Lemma 3.8 in [AM94].

4 Norms on Prolog Terms and Atomic Formulas

To prove termination we need a mapping from terms, atomic formulas and queries into a well-founded ordering. We use *norms* to assign natural numbers to terms. This mapping is then extended to atomic formulas.

Definition 7. A *norm* on terms is a mapping $|.|$: ground terms $\rightarrow \mathbb{N}$. A *linear norm* is a norm which can be defined by assigning to every n-ary function symbol f some natural numbers $a_1, \ldots, a_n, a \in \mathbb{N}$ and defining inductively on ground terms

$$|f(t_1, \ldots, t_n)| := a_1\,|t_1| + \ldots + a_n\,|t_n| + a.$$

We call a term t *rigid* (cf. [BCF94]) w.r.t. a norm $|.|$ if $|t_1| = |t_2|$ for all ground instances t_1, t_2 of t. We extend the norm $|.|$ to rigid terms t by defining $|t| = |t'|$ where t' is a ground instance of t. We call a type τ *rigid* w.r.t. a norm $|.|$ if every $t \in \tau$ is rigid w.r.t. $|.|$.

Example 4. A linear norm which assigns to every list its length is given by $|[]| = 0, |[A\,|\,L]| = |L| + 1$. The type **list** (cf. Example 1) is rigid w.r.t. this norm.

Definition 8. A *predicate norm* is a mapping $|.|$: atomic formulas $\rightarrow$ On from atomic formulas to ordinal numbers such that $|P'| \leq |P|$ for every instance P' of P.

In a characterization of terminating programs (i.e. equivalence of termination and acceptability, cf. Apt and Pedreschi [AP90, AP93]) arbitrary predicate norms have to be taken into account. To get manageable norms (i.e. acceptability becomes decidable) we use *linear predicate norms* $|.|$: ground atomic formulas $\rightarrow$

$\mathbb{N}^K$, where $K \in \mathbb{N}$ and $\mathbb{N}^K$ is ordered lexicographically. These norms are defined in the following way using a linear norm on ground terms:

$$|p(t_1, \ldots, t_n)| := \langle \sum_{j=1}^{n} a_{1,j}\, |t_j| + b_1, \ldots, \sum_{j=1}^{n} a_{K,j}\, |t_j| + b_K \rangle \tag{2}$$

where $a_{i,j}, b_i$ are natural numbers depending on p. If $K = 1$ we will omit the brackets and write s instead of $\langle s \rangle$.

The lexicographically ordered set $\mathbb{N}^K$ is isomorphic to the set of ordinal numbers up to ω^K. The isomorphism is $\langle a_K, \ldots, a_1 \rangle = \omega^{K-1} a_K + \ldots + \omega^0 a_1$. We can lift the predicate norm (2) to arbitrary atomic formulas by defining

$$|P| := \sup\{|P'| : \ P' \text{ is a ground instance of } P\ \} \tag{3}$$

Notice that we always have $|P| \leq \omega^K$ and (3) defines a predicate norm in the sense of Definition 8.

Definition 9. We call an atomic formula P *rigid* w.r.t. a predicate norm $|.|$ if $|P| = |P'|$ for every ground instance P' of P. We call a predicate norm *rigid* (w.r.t. a signature) if every well-typed atomic formula P is rigid w.r.t. the predicate norm.

A linear predicate norm defined as in (3) is rigid if for every predicate symbol p with signature $p(\sigma_1 \to \tau_1, \ldots, \sigma_n \to \tau_n)$ and every argument position $j \in \{1, \ldots, n\}$ either τ_j is rigid w.r.t. the term norm or $a_{i,j} = 0$ for all $i \in \{1, \ldots, K\}$.

Example 5. If we have the signature `append( + list, + list, - list )` and the predicate norm definition `|append( L1, L2, L )| = |L1|` where the norm of a list is its length (cf. Examples 2,4), then this predicate norm is rigid.

5 Acceptable Prolog Programs

In this section we extend the concept of *acceptable* Prolog programs from Apt and Pedreschi [AP93] by the use of ordinal numbers. Our predicate norm is a generalization of the level mapping given in [Bez89, Bez93, AP90, AP93]. The use of ordinal numbers will allow us to prove that every *loop free* program (cf. Definition 17) is *acceptable* (c.f. Definition 10). This can not be done using the original definition of acceptability given in [AP90, AP93] where the value of a predicate norm is a natural number. Within this section let **P** be a well-typed Prolog program, I a (not necessarily Herbrand) interpretation of **P** and $|.|$ a rigid predicate norm.

Definition 10 (Apt,Pedreschi). A clause C of **P** is called *acceptable w.r.t.* $|.|$ *and* I if I is a model of C, $|.|$ is rigid, and $|P| > |Q_i|$ for every ground instance P:- $Q_1, \ldots, Q_n$ of C and every i such that $I \models Q_1 \wedge \ldots \wedge Q_{i-1}$.

A program **P** is called *acceptable w.r.t.* $|.|$ *and* I if all its clauses are. **P** is called *acceptable* if it is acceptable w.r.t. some predicate norm and some interpretation of **P**.

Example 6. The sorting algorithm in Figure 1 with signatures and type definitions

```
nat := 0 + s(nat)
nat_list := [] + '.'( nat, nat_list )
sort( + nat_list, -nat_list )
minlist( + nat_list, -nat )
min( + nat, + nat, - nat )
delete( + nat, + nat_list, - nat_list )
le( + nat, + nat )
```

is acceptable with respect to a predicate norm $|.|$ and an interpretation I defined in the following way: $|\mathtt{le}(n,m)| = |n|$, $|a\backslash\texttt{=}b| = 0$, $|\mathtt{delete}(a,l_1,l_2)| = |l_1|$, $|\mathtt{min}(a,b,m)| = |a|+|b|+1$, $|\mathtt{minlist}(l,m)| = |l|+1$, $|\mathtt{sort}(l,s)| = |l|+2$, where the norm on terms is defined by $|\mathtt{0}| = 0$, $|\mathtt{s}(n)| = |n|+1$, $|\mathtt{[]}| = 0$, $|\mathtt{[}a\,|\,l\mathtt{]}| = |a|+|l|+1$. Notice that in this example the norm of a list is not its length, but the sum of its length and the values of its elements.

$$
\begin{aligned}
I = \{&\mathtt{sort}(l,s) : l,s \text{ ground}\} \\
&\cup\{\mathtt{minlist}(l,m) : l,m \text{ ground, } m \text{ is a member of } l\} \\
&\cup\{\mathtt{min}(a,b,a) : a,b \text{ ground}\} \cup \{\mathtt{min}(a,b,b) : a,b \text{ ground}\} \\
&\cup\{\mathtt{delete}(e,l_1,l_2) : \ e,l_1,l_2 \text{ ground, } |l_2| \le |l_1|, \\
&\qquad\qquad |l_2| < |l_1| \text{ or } e \text{ is not a member of } l_1 \ \} \\
&\cup\{\mathtt{le}(a,b) : a,b \text{ are ground}\}
\end{aligned}
$$

Definitions of this kind are needed to establish acceptability in the sense of Apt and Pedreschi [AP90, AP93], however these definitions are a bit overloaded for the purpose of proving termination. Therefore we will introduce the notion of *loop freeness* in the next section. We will exemplarily show that the conditions of Definition 10 are satisfied for the second clause. Obviously I is a model of the second clause, because its head is true in I. Let

$$\mathtt{sort}(l,\ \mathtt{[}m\,|\,s\mathtt{]})\mathtt{:-}\ l\backslash\texttt{=}\mathtt{[]},\mathtt{minlist}(l,m),\mathtt{delete}(m,l,l_2),\mathtt{sort}(l_2,s)$$

be a ground instance of the second clause. Then we trivially have $|l\backslash\texttt{=}\mathtt{[]}| < |\mathtt{sort}(l,\ \mathtt{[}m\,|\,s\mathtt{]})|$, $|\mathtt{minlist}(l,m)| < |\mathtt{sort}(l,\ \mathtt{[}m\,|\,s\mathtt{]})|$ and $|\mathtt{delete}(m,l,l_2)| < |\mathtt{sort}(l,\ \mathtt{[}m\,|\,s\mathtt{]})|$. If $I \models l\backslash\texttt{=}\mathtt{[]} \wedge \mathtt{minlist}(l,m) \wedge \mathtt{delete}(m,l,l_2)$, that is m is a member of l and $|l_2| < |l|$, then $|\mathtt{sort}(l_2,s)| < |\mathtt{sort}(l,\ \mathtt{[}m\,|\,s\mathtt{]})|$.

Example 7. The Ackermann function (cf. Figure 2) is acceptable w.r.t. the trivial interpretation $I = \{\mathtt{ack}(t_1,t_2,t_3)\ :\ t_1,t_2,t_3 \text{ ground}\}$ and the predicate norm $|\mathtt{ack}(n,m,a)| = \langle |n|\,,|m|\rangle$, where the norm on terms is defined by $|\mathtt{0}| = 0$ and $|\mathtt{s}(n)| = |n|+1$. To verify this you only have to observe that $\langle |n|\,, |\mathtt{s(0)}|\rangle < \langle |\mathtt{s}(n)|\,, |\mathtt{0}|\rangle$, $\langle |\mathtt{s}(n)|\,, |m|\rangle < \langle |\mathtt{s}(n)|\,, |\mathtt{s}(m)|\rangle$ and $\langle |n|\,, |a|\rangle < \langle |\mathtt{s}(n)|\,, |\mathtt{s}(m)|\rangle$ for all terms m,n,a.

```
sort( [], [] ).
sort( L, [ Min | S ] ) :-
     L \= [],
     minlist( L, Min ),
     delete( Min, L, L2 ),
     sort( L2, S ).

minlist( [E], E ).
minlist( [ E | L ], Min ) :-
        L \= [],
        minlist( L, M1 ),
        min( E, M1, Min ).

min( A, B, A ) :- le(A, B).
min( A, B, B ) :- A \= B, le( B, A ).

delete( _E , [], [] ).
delete( E, [ E | L ], D ) :- delete( E, L, D ).
delete( E, [ F | L ], [ F | D ] ) :-
        E \= F,
        delete( E, L, D ).

le( 0, _ ).
le( s(X), s(Y) ) :- le( X, Y ).
```

Fig. 1. sorting

```
ack( 0, Y, s(Y) ).
ack( s(X), 0, Z ) :- ack( X, s(0), Z ).
ack( s(X), s(Y), Z ) :- ack( s(X), Y, A ), ack( X, A, Z ).
```

Fig. 2. Ackermann Function

Our aim is to show that LD-resolution terminates for every well-typed query if the Prolog program is acceptable. Modifying the notions from [AP93] we obtain the following definition.

Definition 11. With every query $Q = (P_1, \ldots, P_n)$ we associate n sets of ordinal numbers defined for $i \in \{1, \ldots, n\}$ as follows:

$$|Q|_i^I := \{|P_i'| + 1 : \ (P_1', \ldots, P_n') \text{ is a ground instance of } Q \text{ and } I \models P_1' \wedge \ldots \wedge P_{i-1}'\}$$

We define a multiset $|Q|^I$ of ordinal numbers as follows

$$|Q|^I := \{\sup |Q|^I_1, \ldots, \sup |Q|^I_n\}_{\text{mul}}.$$

Lemma 12. *If Q is a query and Q' is an instance of Q, then we have*

$$|Q|^I \geq_{\text{mul}} |Q'|^I.$$

Proof. For every i we have $|Q'|^I_i \subseteq |Q|^I_i$. ■

Lemma 13. *If P :- $Q_1, \ldots, Q_n$ is an instance of some clause which is acceptable w.r.t. $|.|$ and I, furthermore $\mathcal{R} = R_1, \ldots, R_m$ are atomic formulas such that $(P, \mathcal{R})$ is a well-typed query, then we have*

$$|(P, \mathcal{R})|^I >_{\text{mul}} |(Q_1, \ldots, Q_n, \mathcal{R})|^I.$$

Proof. First we have for every $i \in \{1, \ldots, n\}$

$$\sup |(Q_1, \ldots, Q_n, \mathcal{R})|^I_i < \sup |(P, \mathcal{R})|^I_1. \tag{4}$$

This follows from the following observations:

1. $|(P, \mathcal{R})|^I_1 = \{|P| + 1\} = \{|P'| + 1\}$ for every ground instance P' of P as P is a well-typed literal by Definition 6 and $|.|$ is rigid.
2. $\sup |(P, \mathcal{R})|^I_1 = |P| + 1$ is not a limit ordinal.
3. For every $\alpha \in |(Q_1, \ldots, Q_n, \mathcal{R})|^I_i$ we have $\alpha < |P| + 1$, as we know : $\alpha = |Q'_i| + 1$ for some ground instance $(Q'_1, \ldots, Q'_n)$ of $(Q_1, \ldots, Q_n)$ which satisfies $I \models Q'_1 \wedge \ldots \wedge Q'_{i-1}$ (Definition 11). So for a ground instance P' :- $Q'_1, \ldots, Q'_n$ of the acceptable clause P :- $Q_1, \ldots, Q_n$ we have by Definition 10 $|Q'_i| < |P'|$. We conclude $|Q'_i| + 1 < |P| + 1$ using 1.
4. If $\sup |(Q_1, \ldots, Q_n, \mathcal{R})|^I_i$ is not a limit ordinal, then there is a maximal element $\alpha \in |(Q_1, \ldots, Q_n, \mathcal{R})|^I_i$ and we have $\sup |(Q_1, \ldots, Q_n, \mathcal{R})|^I_i = \alpha < |P| + 1$ using 3.
5. If $\sup |(Q_1, \ldots, Q_n, \mathcal{R})|^I_i$ is a limit ordinal, then $\sup |(Q_1, \ldots, Q_n, \mathcal{R})|^I_i \leq |P| + 1$ holds by 3. and $\sup |(Q_1, \ldots, Q_n, \mathcal{R})|^I_i \neq |P| + 1$ by 2.

From 4. and 5. we conclude (4). Further we have for every $j \in \{1, \ldots, m\}$

$$\sup |(Q_1, \ldots, Q_n, R_1, \ldots, R_m)|^I_{j+n} \leq \sup |(P, R_1, \ldots, R_m)|^I_{j+1} \tag{5}$$

since by Definition 11

$$\begin{aligned}
&|(Q_1, \ldots, Q_n, R_1, \ldots, R_m)|^I_{j+n} \\
&= \{|R'_j| + 1 : (Q'_1, \ldots, Q'_n, R'_1, \ldots, R'_m) \text{ is a ground instance of} \\
&\qquad (Q_1, \ldots, Q_n, \mathcal{R}) \text{ and } I \models Q'_1 \wedge \ldots \wedge Q'_n \wedge R'_1 \wedge \ldots \wedge R'_{j-1}\}
\end{aligned}$$

[as for some P', P' :- $Q'_1, \ldots, Q'_n$ is an instance of P :- $Q_1, \ldots, Q_n$ and I is a model of **P**]

$$\begin{aligned}
&\subseteq \{|R'_j| + 1 : (P', R'_1, \ldots, R'_m) \text{ is a ground instance of} \\
&\qquad (P, R_1, \ldots, R_m) \text{ and } I \models P' \wedge R'_1 \wedge \ldots \wedge R'_{j-1}\} \\
&= |(P, R_1, \ldots, R_m)|^I_{j+1}
\end{aligned}$$

The claim follows by definition of the multiset ordering from (4) and (5). ■

Lemma 14. *Let* **P** *be a well-typed program that is acceptable w.r.t. a predicate norm* $|.|$ *and an interpretation* I. *Let* Q_1 *be a well-typed query and* Q_2 *a LD-resolvent of* Q_1. *Then we have* $|Q_1|^I >_{mul} |Q_2|^I$.

Proof. Let $Q_1 = (P_1, \ldots, P_n)$. There is a variant of a clause P:- $Q_1, \ldots, Q_m$ such that P_1 and P are unifiable with most general unifier μ and we have $Q_2 = (Q_1\mu, \ldots, Q_m\mu, P_2\mu, \ldots, P_n\mu)$. By Lemma 12 we have $|(P_1, \ldots, P_n)|^I \geq_{mul} |(P_1\mu, \ldots, P_n\mu)|^I$ and since an instance of a well-typed query is well-typed we know $|(P_1\mu, \ldots, P_n\mu)|^I >_{mul} |(Q_1\mu, \ldots, Q_m\mu, P_2\mu, \ldots, P_n\mu)|^I$ using Lemma 13. ∎

Because the multiset extension of a well-founded order is well-founded and well-typedness is invariant under resolution we have proven:

Theorem 15. *If* **P** *is an acceptable and well-typed program and* Q *is a well-typed query, then* Q *is terminating with respect to* **P**. ∎

6 A Modular Termination Criterion

In this section we are going to explain our termination criterion and prove its correctness. In contrast to the notion of acceptability, we only want to compare predicate norms of literals which are in the same recursive clique in order to obtain termination. We will show how from a predicate norm satisfying *loop freeness*,which is a much weaker condition than acceptability (Definition 10), a predicate norm can be constructed which establishes acceptability.

We divide the edges in the call graph into three classes:

Definition 16. Let **P** be a Prolog program, $|.|$ be a predicate norm and I a model of **P**.

- $p \rightarrow_{C,i} q$ is a *non-recursive call* if $p \sqsupset q$.
- $p \rightarrow_{C,i} q$ is a *descending recursive call w.r.t.* $|.|$ *and* I if $p \simeq q$ and $|P| \geq |Q_i|$ for every ground instance P:- $Q_1, \ldots, Q_n$ of the clause C such that $I \models Q_1 \wedge \ldots \wedge Q_{i-1}$.
- If $p \simeq q$ and $p \rightarrow_{C,i} q$ is not descending, then we call $p \rightarrow_{C,i} q$ a *recursive call which violates the termination conditions.*

Descending recursive calls are split into two subclasses:

- $p \rightarrow_{C,i} q$ is a *strongly descending recursive call w.r.t.* $|.|$ *and* I if $p \simeq q$ and $|P| > |Q_i|$ for every ground instance P:- $Q_1, \ldots, Q_n$ of the clause C such that $I \models Q_1 \wedge \ldots \wedge Q_{i-1}$.
- $p \rightarrow_{C,i} q$ is a *weakly descending recursive call w.r.t.* $|.|$ *and* I if it is descending but not strongly descending.

Definition 17. A program is called *loop free w.r.t.* $|.|$ *and* I if I is a model of **P**, every edge $p \rightarrow_{C,i} q$ such that $p \simeq q$ is descending w.r.t. $|.|$ and I, and every cycle in the call graph of the program contains at least one strongly descending edge $p \rightarrow_{C,i} q$. It is called *loop free* if it is loop free w.r.t. some predicate norm and some interpretation.

Note that every edge which appears in a cycle of the call graph of a loop free program is descending, as a cycle cannot leave a mutual recursive clique.

The concept of loop freeness has two advantages if it is compared with the concept of acceptability: First modular termination proofs become possible since predicate norms of atomic formulas have to be compared only if their predicate symbols are in the same recursive clique, no artificial offsets are needed in the definition of the predicate norm. Secondly mutual recursion can be handled with simpler norms, as every cycle in the call graph has to contain only one strongly descending edge (compare to the parser in Example 4.5 in De Schreye et al. [SVB92]).

Example 8. We can show the loop freeness of the sorting algorithm given in Figure 1 with less effort than its acceptability (cf. Example 6). Let $|.|$ be a norm on terms which assigns to every list its length (cf. Example 4) and to every natural number its value.

Define $|\mathtt{le}(n,m)| = |n|$, $|a\backslash\texttt{=}b| = 0$, $|\mathtt{delete}(a,l_1,l_2)| = |l_1|$, $|\mathtt{min}(a,b,m)| = 0$, $|\mathtt{minlist}(l,m)| = |l|$, $|\mathtt{sort}(l,s)| = |l|$ and define I as in Example 6. Then this program is loop free w.r.t. the predicate norm $|.|$ and the interpretation I.

This can be shown with less effort than acceptability in Example 6. Let $\mathtt{sort}(l, \texttt{[}m|s\texttt{]})\texttt{:-}\ l\backslash\texttt{=[]}, \mathtt{minlist}(l,m), \mathtt{delete}(m,l,l_2), \mathtt{sort}(l_2,s)$ be a ground instance of the second clause. We only have to observe that $|\mathtt{sort}(l_2,s)| < |\mathtt{sort}(l, \texttt{[}m|s\texttt{]})|$ if $I \models l\backslash\texttt{=[]} \wedge \mathtt{minlist}(l,m) \wedge \mathtt{delete}(m,l,l_2)$.

Definition 18. If **P** is loop free w.r.t. $|.|$ and I, then we assign to every predicate symbol p a natural number layer(p), defined as the longest path in the call graph of **P**, which starts from p and contains only weakly descending edges. In other words

$$\text{layer}(p) = \max\{m : \begin{array}{l}\text{There is a path } p = p_0 \rightarrow_{C_1,i_1} \cdots \rightarrow_{C_m,i_m} p_m \\ \text{such that every } p_{j-1} \rightarrow_{C_j,i_j} p_j \text{ is weakly descending}\}\end{array}$$

The function layer is extended to atomic formulas in the obvious way, that is layer($p(\ldots)$) = layer(p).

Notice that layer is well-defined, since every cycle contains at least one strongly descending edge and the length of cycle free paths is limited by the number of predicate symbols.

Theorem 19. *If a program* **P** *is loop free w.r.t.* $|.|$ *and* I*, then there is a predicate norm* $|.|'$ *such that* **P** *is acceptable w.r.t.* $|.|'$ *and* I.

Proof. Define $|P|' := \langle \text{level}(P), |P|, \text{layer}(P)\rangle$ to be a mapping into $\mathbb{N} \times \alpha \times \mathbb{N}$ ordered lexicographicly, where $\alpha \subset \mathsf{On}$ is a set of ordinal number such that $|P| \in \alpha$ for every atomic formula P. Since $\mathbb{N} \times \alpha \times \mathbb{N}$ is a well-founded linear order it is order isomorphic to some initial segment of the ordinal numbers. Therefore we can identify $|P|'$ with an ordinal number. We claim that **P** is acceptable w.r.t. $|.|'$ and I. By assumption I is a model of P. Let $P\texttt{:-}\ Q_1, \ldots, Q_n$

be a ground instance of a clause C and choose any $i \in \{1, \ldots, n\}$ such that $I \models Q_1 \wedge \ldots \wedge Q_{i-1}$. We have to show $|P|' > |Q_i|'$. We distinguish the following cases:

1. If $P \sqsupset Q_i$, then we have level(P) > level(Q_i) and we are done.
2. If $P \simeq Q_i$ and $P \rightarrow_{C,i} Q_i$ is strongly descending, then we have level(P) = level(Q_i) by Lemma 3 and $|Q_i| < |P|$ by Definition 16.
3. $P \simeq Q_i$ and $P \rightarrow_{C,i} Q_i$ is weakly descending. Therefore we have level(P) = level(Q_i) by Lemma 3, $|P| \geq |Q_i|$ by Definition 16 and layer(P) > layer(Q_i) by Definition 18. ■

As an immediate consequence of Theorems 15 and 19 we obtain the following theorem.

Theorem 20. *If* **P** *is a loop free and well-typed program and* Q *is a well-typed query, then* Q *is terminating with respect to* **P**. ■

7 Linear Inter-Argument Relations

The question whether a given program is loop free w.r.t. a predicate norm $|.|$ and an interpretation I is decidable, if we restrict norms to linear predicate norms and interpretations to interpretations defined by *linear inter-argument relations*. A linear inter-argument relation for an n-ary predicate symbol p is an inequation

$$a_1 |X_1| + \ldots + a_n |X_n| + b \geq 0$$

where a_i, b are integers. Given a set of linear inter-argument relations for every predicate symbol p, an interpretation I can be defined by $I \models p(t_1, \ldots, t_n)$ iff the instance $a_1 |t_1| + \ldots + a_n |t_n| + b \geq 0$ of every every inter-argument relation for p is satisfied. Linear norms can be partially evaluated, that is for every term t and atomic formula P, respectively, we can find integers such that

$$|t\mu| = c_1 |X_1\mu| + \ldots + c_m |X_m\mu| + d$$
$$|P\mu| = \langle \sum c_{1,j} |X_j\mu| + d_1, \ldots, \sum c_{K,j} |X_j\mu| + d_K \rangle$$

where the X_i are the variables occurring in t and P, respectively. Therefore in the case of linear norms and an interpretation I defined by linear inter-argument relations the problem of being loop free w.r.t. I and $|.|$ can be reduced to the question whether a formula in Presburger arithmetic (cf. [End72, Pre29]) is true. In our implementation we used Bledsoe's Sup-Inf-method (cf. [Ble75]) for solving Presburger formulas.

For some examples like the sorting algorithm in Figure 1 (cf. Example 8) we need *conditional linear inter-argument relations*. These take the form

$$a_1 |X_1| + \ldots + a_n |X_n| + b \geq 0 \text{ if } P$$

where a_i, b are integers and P is an atomic formula such that only the variables $X_1, \ldots, X_n$ occur in P. The predicate symbol of P has to be defined explicitly, i.e. it must have a fixed interpretation identical to its interpretation in the least Herbrand model of the program. An interpretation I satisfies a conditional inter-argument relation if $I \models p(t_1, \ldots, t_n)$ implies

$$a_1 |t_1| + \ldots + a_n |t_n| + b \geq 0 \text{ or } \mathcal{H} \models \neg P[X_1 \leftarrow t_1, \ldots, X_n \leftarrow t_n]$$

where $\mathcal{H}$ is the least Herbrand model of the program.

In the case of conditional inter-argument relations we have no decision procedure for loop freeness, but we claim that in most cases loop freeness can be established by an automatic theorem prover from the conditional linear inter-argument relations and explicit definitions of the predicates used in the conditions. The treatment of conditional inter-argument relations was inspired by the work of Walther [Wal90].

8 Implementing Termination Checking

Automated termination checking is implemented within the framework of a general static analysis tool for Prolog programs, cf. Stroetmann, Glaß [SG95] and Stroetmann, Glaß, Müller [SGM96]. Naturally in practice we have to deal with certain problems which have not been described in the theoretical part, e.g. negative literals, predefined predicates, etc. Below we describe briefly some of the details which have to be dealt with to obtain a useful tool for automated termination checking of real Prolog programs.

8.1 Implementing Type Checking

The design of a type language has to respect the following conditions: it should be possible to define types such that a well-typed program (in the sense of Definition 6) is type safe, i.e. there should be no run-time type errors in the sense of [DEDC96]. Further, a type checking algorithm should catch as many programming mistakes as possible, therefore the usual data structures of a Prolog program have to be supported. In contrast to these conditions, nearly no program should have to be rewritten just to make it well-typed.

The language design is inspired by Hill and Topor [HT92], Yardeni, Frühwirth and Shapiro [YFS92] and Bronsard, Lakshmann and Reddy [BLR92]. We start from a finite set of so-called basic types (in the sense of [YFS92, 2.4]) which are necessary to describe the signatures of all ISO-Prolog predicates correctly, cf. [DEDC96], as e.g. the types `atom`, `float`, `int`. Then we define new types out of these by recursive equations (type rules in [HT92, 1.5], type definitions in [YFS92, 2.1]) similar to Example 1.

The main features of the implemented type system are:

- parametric polymorphism, i.e. the use of type parameters
- inclusion polymorphism, i.e. the use of a subtype relation
- support of strong typing, i.e. types are distinguished by names
- support of negation as failure

- restricted support of second-order predicates like `findall/3`, `bagof/3`
- restricted support of database manipulating predicates like `assert/1` and `retract/1`

In fact the main problem of type checking is to combine the first two aspects.

8.2 Automated Termination Checking

This subsection explains how the procedure of termination checking works in practice. We will start with an untyped program, cf. Figure 3, and augment it with information for the analysis tool.

```
minus(X, 0, X).
minus(X, s(Y), Z) :-  minus(X, Y, s(Z)).

lt(0, s(Y)).
lt(s(X), s(Y)) :- lt(X, Y).

le(0, Y).
le(s(X), s(Y)) :- le(X, Y).

mod(X, Y, X):- Y \= 0, lt(X, Y).
mod(X, Y, Z):- Y \= 0, le(Y, X), minus(X, Y, W), mod(W, Y, Z).
```

Fig. 3. modulo

To add type information we define the type `nat` of Example 1 and add signatures for all predicates to the source code. Since the code should run on an arbitrary Prolog system, we start all lines containing analysis information with the pragma `%#`, cf. Figure 4.

```
%# nat := 0 + s(nat).

%# predicate: minus(+nat, +nat, -nat).
%# predicate: lt(+nat, +nat).
%# predicate: le(+nat, +nat).
%# predicate: mod(+nat, +nat, -nat).
```

Fig. 4. adding type information

We continue to explain the steps to augment the program by annotations for proving termination: the norm $|.|$ on the type `nat` given by the equations: $|0| = 0$, $|s(N)| = |N| + 1$ is assumed by our system if there is not explicitly given a different definition of the norm.

Termination of `minus/3`, `lt/2`, `le/2` can be proved by observing that these predicates are defined via simple recursions on the second arguments. This is expressed via linear predicate norms:

```
%# pnorm: |minus(X, Y, Z)| = |Y|.
%# pnorm: |lt(X, Y)|       = |Y|.
%# pnorm: |le(X,Y)|        = |Y|.
```

Proving loop freeness for these predicates automatically does not make use of inter-argument relations, i.e. they are loop free w.r.t. the trivial interpretation

$$I = \{\texttt{minus}(x, y, z) : x, y, z \text{ ground}\} \cup \{\texttt{lt}(x, y) : x, y \text{ ground}\} \cup \\ \{\texttt{le}(x, y) : x, y \text{ ground}\} \cup \{\texttt{mod}(x, y, z) : x, y, z \text{ ground}\}.$$

More involved is proving loop freeness for `mod/3`. The first clause of `mod/3` is obviously loop free since `mod/3` calls `\=` and `lt` as subprograms. The second clause

```
mod(X, Y, Z):- Y \= 0, le(Y, X), minus(X, Y, W), mod(W, Y, Z).
```

contains a recursive call of `mod/3`. We know that $|W|$ is less than $|X|$ in the recursive call. Thus we choose the linear norm for `mod/3` as follows:

```
%# pnorm: |mod(X, Y, Z)| = |X|.
```

But, in fact, the program is not loop free w.r.t. to the trivial interpretation I. Termination for `mod/3` depends on conditional linear inter-argument relations for `minus/3` which are annotated as follows:

```
%# dependency(minus(X, Y, Z)): |Z| =< |X|, |Z| < |X| if  Y \= 0.
```

It can be shown automatically that there is an interpretation I which satisfies this inter-argument relation, such that the program is loop free w.r.t. I and $|.|$.

8.3 Error Detection

One further benefit of the method of adding annotations to program code is that this allows a simple kind of error location. Assume that we have coded `mod/3` by the clauses:

```
mod(X, Y, X):- Y \= 0, lt(X, Y).
mod(X, Y, Z):- le(Y, X), minus(X, Y, W), mod(W, Y, Z).
```

This means that we have forgotten the test `Y \= 0` in the second clause. Trying to prove termination automatically, will end up with the following message (pointing to the recursive call of `mod/3` in the second clause):

```
>>> One of the following conditions has to be valid:
>>> le(Y,X) -> Y \= 0
```

The second clause is loop free if we can find an interpretation which satisfies this implication in addition to the program clauses and conditional inter-argument relations. Obviously this is impossible since every model of the program satisfies `le(0,0)`. Actually the query `mod(s(0),0,Z)` will cause the program to loop.

9 Conclusion: Practical Experiences

We have added annotations for the termination check to all clauses of our tool for static analysis of Prolog programs (22k lines of Prolog code with 14.1% annotations including type and signature definitions and including 3.9% annotations for the termination check, i.e. norm definitions and inter-argument relations).

Run time with IF/Prolog 5.0 on a Sun SPARCclassic with 48 MB main memory for the termination check (without parsing and type checking) is: 6.67 sec. cpu time for an average file containing 1k lines of annotated Prolog code, whereas type checking takes 9.93 sec.

References

[AM94] Krzysztof R. Apt and Elena Marchiori. Reasoning about Prolog programs: From modes through types to assertions. *Formal Aspects of Computing*, 6A:743–764, 1994.

[AP90] Krzysztof R. Apt and Dino Pedreschi. Studies in pure Prolog: Termination. In John W. Lloyd, editor, *Symposium on Computational Logic*, pages 150–176. Springer-Verlag, 1990.

[AP93] Krysztof R. Apt and Dino Pedreschi. Modular termination proofs for logic and pure prolog programs. In G. Levi, editor, *Proceedings of Fourth International School for Computer Science Researchers*. Oxford University Press, 1993.

[Apt92] Krzysztof R. Apt, editor. *Proceedings of the Joint International Conference and Symposium on Logic Programming*, Washington, D. C., USA, November, 9–13 1992. The MIT Press.

[Ave95] Jürgen Avenhaus. *Reduktionssysteme – Rechnen und Schließen in gleichungsdefinierten Strukturen*. Springer-Verlag, 1995.

[Bac91] Leo Bachmair. *Canonical Equational Proofs*. Birkhäuser Boston, Inc., Boston, MA, 1991.

[BCF94] Bossi, Coco, and Fabris. Norms on terms and their use in proving universal termination of a logic program. *Theoretical Computer Science*, 124,2:297–328, 1994.

[Bez89] Marc Bezem. Characterizing termination of logic programs with level mappings. In Ewing L. Lusk and Ross A. Overbeek, editors, *Logic Programming, Proceedings of the North American Conference*, volume 1, pages 69–80, Cleveland, Ohio, USA, October 16–20, 1989. The MIT Press, Cambridge, Massachusetts.

[Bez93] Marc Bezem. Strong termination of logic programs. *Journal of Logic Programming*, 15(1&2):79-98, 1993.

[Ble75] W. W. Bledsoe. A new method for proving Presburger formulas. In *4th International Joint Conference on Artificial Intelligence*, September 1975. Tibilisi, Georgia, U.S.S.R.

[BLR92] François Bronsard, T. K. Lakshman, and Uday S. Reddy. A framework of directionality for proving termination of logic programs. In Apt [Apt92], pages 321–335.

[Cla78] K. L. Clark. Negation as failure. In H. Gallaire and J. Minker, editors, *Logic and Data Bases*, pages 293–322. Plenum Press, New York, 1978.

[DEDC96] P. Deransart, A. A. Ed-Dbali, and L. Cervoni. *Prolog: The Standard*. Springer-Verlag, 1996.

[End72] Herbert B. Enderton. *A Mathematical Introduction to Logic*. Academic Press, 1972.

[GP92] Gerhard Gröger and Lutz Plümer. Handling of mutual recursion in automatic termination proofs for logic programs. In Apt [Apt92], pages 336–350.

[HT92] P. M. Hill and R. W. Topor. A semantics for typed logic programs. In Pfenning [Pfe92], pages 1–62.

[Llo87] J. W. Lloyd. *Foundations of Logic Programming*. Springer–Verlag, Berlin, second edition, 1987.

[MP94] Mascellani and Pedreschi. Proving termination of prolog programs. In M. Alpuente, R. Barbuti, and I. Ramos, editors, *Proceedings of GULP-PRODE'94, Joint conference on declarative programming*, pages 46–61, 1994.

[Pfe92] Frank Pfenning, editor. *Types in Logic Programming*. MIT, Cambridge, Mass./London, 1992.

[Poh89] Wolfram Pohlers. *Proof Theory. An Introduction*. Number 1407 in Lecture Notes in Mathematics. Springer-Verlag, Berlin/Heidelberg/New York, 1989.

[Pre29] M. Presburger. Über die Vollständigkeit eines gewissen Systems der Arithmetik ganzer Zahlen, in welchem die Addition als einzige Operation hervortritt. *Sprawozdanie z I Kongrescu Matematykow Krajow Slowkanskich Warszawa*, pages 92 - 101, 1929.

[SG95] Karl Stroetmann and Thomas Glaß. Augmented PROLOG — An evolutionary approach. In Donald A. Smith, Olivier Ridoux, and Peter Van Roy, editors, Proceedings of the Workshop *Visions for the Future of Logic Programming: Laying the Foundations for a Modern Successor to Prolog*, pages 59–70, 1995. The Proceedings of this workshop are available at: `ftp://ps-ftp.dfki.uni-sb.de/pub/ILPS95-FutureLP/`.

[SGM96] Karl Stroetmann, Thomas Glaß, and Martin Müller. Implementing safety-critical systems in Prolog: Experiences from the R&D at Siemens. In Peter Reintjes, editor, *Practical Applications of Prolog '96*, pages 391–403, 1996.

[SVB92] D. De Schreye, Kristof Verschaetse, and Maurice Bruynooghe. A framework for analysing the termination of definite logic programs with respect to call patterns. In *Proceedings of the International Conference on Fifth Generation Computer Systems*, pages 481–488. ICOT, 1992.

[Wal90] Christoph Walther. *Automatisierung von Terminierungsbeweisen*. Vieweg, Braunschweig, Germany, 1990.

[YFS92] Eyal Yardeni, Thom Frühwirth, and Ehud Shapiro. Polymorphically typed logic programs. In Pfenning [Pfe92], pages 63–90.

Data-Flow-Based Virtual Function Resolution*

Hemant D. Pande[1] and Barbara G. Ryder[2]

[1] TRDDC, 1 Mangaldas Road, Pune, 411050, India
[2] Department of Computer Science, Rutgers University, Hill Center, Busch Campus, Piscataway, NJ 08855 USA

Abstract. Determining the type of an object to which a receiver may point at a virtual call site is crucial for compile time virtual function resolution in C++ programs. We show the close interdependence of *type determination* and *pointer-induced aliasing* in C++ and present the first data-flow-based algorithm to solve these problems simultaneously. Our polynomial-time approximation method incorporates information about program flow. Initial experiences with our prototype implementation have shown our technique to be more effective than others that use only inheritance hierarchy information. We present initial empirical results demonstrating the precision of our approach and state the intrinsic difficulty (i.e., NP-hardness) of the type determination problem for programming languages with general-purpose pointers and dynamic binding.

1 Introduction

Optimizing object-oriented programs requires dealing with dynamic binding and polymorphism, properties which differentiate object-orientation from the imperative programming paradigm. Dynamic binding prevents us from understanding the calling structure of a program by mere observation of the code; in this respect the challenge it presents to compiler writers is much like that of function pointers in C. In C++ general-purpose pointer usage exacerbates the difficulty of dealing with dynamic binding, because discerning object types may involve tracing aliases through pointers. Our analysis technique deals with general-purpose pointers and combines the problems of pointer-induced aliasing and type determination for C++, solving them with a single data-flow-based approximation algorithm.

Contributions Previously, we presented a static type determination algorithm for C++ programs restricted to those using only single level pointers [PR94a]. In this context, type determination can be solved independent of aliasing. However, in the presence of multiple level pointers, these two problems cannot be precisely solved separately, but are interdependent (see Section 3). Ours is the first combined approximation algorithm for these problems. Because the combined problem is provably NP-hard (see Section 2), our polynomial-time algorithm computes an *approximation* of the solution, which has been shown to have acceptable precision in our initial empirical experiments (see Section 4). We also show the gains our analysis realizes over methods based solely on the inheritance hierarchy.

---

* This research was supported, in part, by funds from NSF grants GER90-23628, CCR-92-08632 and Siemens Corporate Research.

Motivating Example Discerning the type of an object to which a receiver may point at a virtual call site not only reveals the possible calling structure of the program, but also can enable many optimizations, even if the type is not uniquely determined. The example in Figure 1 illustrates the significance of virtual function resolution in practical issues of run-time efficiency and benefits to other optimizations. We assume that the boolean conditions in *if* statements are side-effect-free and hence inconsequential to the analysis.

```
class Base {
public:
        virtual void foo ( );
        virtual void bar ( );
        virtual void baz ( );
} *a, *p, *q;

void Base::foo ( ) {
   n0 : a = new Base;}

void Base::bar ( ) {...}

void Base::baz ( ) {...}
```

```
class Derived : public Base {
public:
        void foo ( );
        void bar ( );
} r, *s;

void Derived::foo ( ) {
   n1 : a = new Derived;
   n2 : printf ("hello world\n");}

void Derived::bar ( ) {
   Derived *t;
   n3 : t = s;}
```

```
main ( )  {
    if (-) n4 : p = new Base;
    else   n5 : p = new Derived;
    n6  : s = &r;
    n7 : r.bar ( );
    n8 : q = new Base;
    n9 : q->foo ( );
    n10 : a->bar ( );
    n11 : p->baz ( );}
```

Fig. 1. Example for virtual function resolution

At statement *n8* in Figure 1, the pointer *q* is made to point to an object of class *Base*, and then immediately used at statement *n9* as the receiver for a virtual function invocation. Under these circumstances *Base* :: *foo*() will be invoked on all executions notwithstanding the virtual nature of the invocation. Since the virtuality of *Base* :: *foo*() is not utilized, the invocation can be compiled as a direct function call, thereby reducing the run time overhead of virtual invocation.

Limiting the scope of invocation to *Base* :: *foo*() and eliminating *Derived* :: *foo*() from consideration may benefit other analyses. The assignment at statement *n1* and printing of *hello world* at *n2* will not appear as possible side effects of the invocation at statement $n9$. Significantly, our algorithm will be able to determine that $n10$ is a call of *Base* :: *bar*() and never *Derived* :: *bar*(), because the receiver a may only point to an object of type *Base*. Therefore, call site $n10$ can be considered non-virtual. Given the potential disparity in side effects of different implementations of a virtual function, this ability to perform unique resolution can significantly improve the precision of subsequent analyses. Note that this improvement required the ability to do type determination while accounting for interprocedural flow from *main* to *Base* :: *foo*() and back.

Resolving a virtual function invocation to a unique function call also may create possibilities for inlining, resulting in elimination of function call overhead. Inlining a function call may also provide opportunities for various intraprocedural optimizations which would have been impossible if attempted in the untransformed program.

A transformation from virtual invocation to function call is sometimes possible without unique resolution of the receiver type. For example at statement $n11$, the receiver p may point to an object of class *Base* or *Derived*, because of the assignments at $n4$ and $n5$. Since the receiver type is not unique, a naive approach may result in retaining the invocation as virtual. However, since class *Derived* inherits the function *baz*() from class *Base* without redefining it, $n11$ may still be safely compiled as a function call to *Base* :: *baz*(). In general, even if the receiver at the virtual invocation site does not point to a unique class, but all the receiver types in the inheritance hierarchy utilize the same implementation of a virtual function, the virtual invocation may be compiled as a direct function call. Nevertheless, such hierarchy information would fail to resolve the virtual calls at statements $n9$ and $n10$, as there are multiple implementations of *foo*() and *bar*() in the hierarchy. An approach which takes into account the data flow (as we saw earlier) is necessary to uniquely resolve these virtual calls.

For architectures which use deep pipelining and speculative execution, the issue of accurate control flow prediction assumes significant importance. Using type determination to replace virtual invocations with function calls, when the target function is known at compile time, would yield benefits comparable to those obtained by profile-based prediction for C^{++} [CG94]. A uniquely resolved call site would eliminate pipeline stalls, as the target of the call is unambiguously known. A related empirical study of behavioral differences between C and C^{++} programs reveals that C^{++} functions are usually small (in terms of lines of code) and C^{++} programs contain more calls than C programs [CGZ95]. The higher calling frequency usually degrades analysis performance because of the inherent difficulty of interprocedural analysis contrasted with that of traditional intraprocedural analysis. Therefore, these findings suggest that inlining a uniquely resolved function may be a crucial optimization.

Even when unique resolution is not possible, short-listing the functions may allow the compiler to replace the late binding mechanism of virtual call with appropriate function calls within a decision statement. Branch prediction techniques may then be applied to improve the execution performance of the program. Additionally, short-listing can focus further analyses on selected functions, rather than on the entire pool of functions with the same name, potentially saving analysis time and allowing building of a more precise call graph.

While unique resolution of virtual functions seems to contradict the encouraged usage of polymorphism in object-oriented languages, run-time analyses have shown that polymorphism is used selectively, leaving much room for unique resolution of non-polymorphic calls as well as optimization of polymorphic calls [CG94].

Outline Section 2 presents key concepts used in our analysis and defines the ICFG, our internal graph representation of the C^{++} program. We also state our theoretical complexity theorem and outline its proof. Section 3 introduces our approximation algorithm and compares it to the *conditional analysis* approach we previously used for C programs. Our algorithm is a flow-sensitive propagation of information on paths in the ICFG: Figure 2 of Section 3 gives a high level overview of the algorithm which follows a typical data flow worklist scheme. Section 4 includes our implementation results, starting with a description of our test suite of 19 C^{++} programs. We discuss our experiences with virtual function resolution and compare our approach with simpler approaches (see Figure 6(b)). We conclude with our future research plans. Because of space limitations, we have excluded our related work section and some of our empirical results; they are available in technical report number LCSR-TR-269, at **ftp://www.cs.rutgers.edu/pub/technical-reports**.

2 Problem Definition

Program Representation A *control flow graph* (CFG) for a function consists of nodes which represent single-entry, single-exit regions of executable code, and edges which represent possible execution branches between code regions. We represent a program with an interprocedural control flow graph (ICFG), which intuitively is the union of CFGs for the individual functions comprising the program [LR91, PR94a]. Formally, an ICFG is a triple $(\mathcal{N}, \mathcal{E}, \rho)$ where $\mathcal{N}$ is the set of nodes, $\mathcal{E}$ is the set of edges and ρ is the *entry* node for `main`. $\mathcal{N}$ contains a node for each simple statement in the program, an *entry* and *exit* node for each function, and a *call* and *return* node for each invocation site. An intraprocedural edge into a *call* node represents the execution flow into an invocation site, while an intraprocedural edge out of a *return* node represents control flow from an invocation site once the invoked function has returned.[3] For a non-virtual function call, we represent the control flow into the called function by an interprocedural edge from a *call* node to the corresponding *entry* node. Similarly, we represent the return of control from the called function by an interprocedural edge from the *exit* node to the *return* node. However, virtual function invocation makes it impossible to determine the correspondence between a *call* and *entry* before analysis, since the function invoked depends on the type of the receiver at the call site. Establishing the interprocedural edge(s) from a *call* node representing

[3] We use the terms *call* and *invocation* interchangeably.

a virtual function invocation to appropriate *entry* node(s) and from *exit* node(s) to the corresponding *return* node(s), (i.e., resolving virtual functions), is a major goal of the algorithm presented in this paper.

- An ICFG path is *realizable* if, whenever a called function on that path returns, it returns to the corresponding *return* node of the call site which invoked it [LR91]. Not all ICFG paths are realizable.
- A realizable path is *balanced* if for each intermediate *call* node, the path contains a corresponding *return* node representing the return of control from the called function.[4] Intuitively, the first and the last node on a balanced path belong to the same function. Moreover, they are in the same incarnation of that function since every called function on the path (perhaps recursively) must return control before the path terminates.
- *Objects* correspond to locations that can store information; *object names* provide ways to refer to them. We associate names with static memory locations and dynamic (i.e., heap) locations (created by *new*). For static storage, the name-storage association is created through a variable declaration statement. For each heap location, we create a name new_{pp} where *pp* is the program point representing the creation site for the location. An *object name* is a variable name or a heap location name, and a possibly empty sequence of dereferences.
- An *alias* exists at a program point when two or more object names refer to the same location as a result of program execution to that program point. We represent aliases by unordered pairs of object names (e.g. $<v, *p>$). The order is unimportant since the alias relation is symmetric.
- *Type determination* involves calculating the type of the object pointed to by a pointer at a program point as a result of an execution to that program point. We represent this information by a pair consisting of a pointer and an associated type (e.g. $<p \Rightarrow C>$), called a *pointer-type* pair.
- A realizable path from ρ is called *consistent* if, for every edge $\ll$`call`, `entry`$\gg$ on the path, where `call` represents a virtual call with receiver *rec*, the execution defined by the subpath from ρ to `call` implies a pointer-type pair $<rec \Rightarrow C>$ at `call` such that the virtual function represented by `entry` is invocable from `call`. Non-consistent paths do not correspond to any possible execution sequence.
- The *precise*[5] solution for static type determination and aliasing at a program point is a set of pointer-type and alias pairs, each of which is a result of an execution on some consistent path to that program point.

Theorem 1. *In the presence of pointers and virtual functions in* C^{++}, *precise program-point-specific type determination and aliasing is NP-hard.*

The theorem proof works by reducing the 3-SAT problem to type determination and aliasing [Pan96].

---

[4] We defined the terms *realizable* and *balanced* paths independently [LR91, PR94b], and found later that the ideas already existed in literature, referred to as *valid* and *complete* respectively in [SP81]. [RHS95] also addresses these issues.

[5] Under the standard assumption of static analysis that all intraprocedural paths are executable.

3 Type Determination and Aliasing Algorithm

Aliasing and Type Determination In programs restricted to single level pointers, one pointer cannot be aliased to another, as this requires multiple levels of indirection [LR91]. As a result, when a pointer changes its value (to point to an object of another type), it does not affect the value of any other pointers [PR94a]. In this context, type determination impinges on aliasing since the receiver types decide which virtual function is invoked at a call site, and the invoked function can affect aliasing. Nevertheless, aliasing plays no part in type determination.

Such a separation does not occur when we allow multiple level pointers. As an example, the ICFG node "`m : p = &q;`" creates alias $<*p, q>$. Suppose subsequently on an execution path, "`n : *p = &r;`" creates pointer-type pair $<*p \Rightarrow type(r)>$. In the absence of information that the alias pair $<*p, q>$ holds before node `n`, we would not be able to infer $<q \Rightarrow type(r)>$ at `n` and the type determination would be rendered incorrect and unsafe. Thus, aliasing affects type determination and *vice versa.*

In this section, we formulate the combined problem and state our tractable approximation of it. Then, we describe our algorithm at a high level, aided by examples.

Problem Formulation *Conditional analysis* [LR91] involves analyzing execution flow in a function, assuming that certain information holds at the entry of the function. We use this approach to define the following terms.

- A balanced path to an ICFG node `n` from entry node `e` of the function containing node `n` is called *conditionally consistent* with respect to an assumption set S of alias and pointer-type pairs, if for every edge $\ll$`call`, `entry`$\gg$ on the path, where `call` represents a virtual call with receiver *rec*, the following is true:

  Given that all the alias and pointer-type pairs in S hold at `e`, the execution defined by the subpath from `e` to `call` implies a pointer-type pair $<rec \Rightarrow C>$ at `call` such that the virtual function represented by `entry` is invocable from `call`.

  We denote such a path by $\mathcal{P}_{n,S}$.
- We define the *conditional type determination problem* as deciding for an ICFG node `n`, a pointer-type pair PT, and a set of alias and pointer-type pairs S, whether:

  there exists a conditionally consistent path with respect to S to node `n` on which PT holds, **and** there exists a consistent path from ρ, the entry node of `main` in the ICFG, to the entry node of the function containing `n` on which every pair in S holds.
- Similarly, we define the *conditional aliasing problem* as deciding for an ICFG node `n`, an alias AP, and a set of alias and pointer-type pairs S, whether:

  there exists a conditionally consistent path with respect to S to node `n` on which AP holds, **and** there exists a consistent path from ρ to the entry node of the function containing `n` on which every pair in S holds.

Approximation Formulation Since the above formulation is computationally intractable, we approximate the joint solution of these two related problems by considering an approximate assumption set S' to contain at most *one* alias or pointer-type from S, chosen arbitrarily.[6] We use the pair in S' (i) to approximate a conditionally consistent path to n, and (ii) as the only necessary assumption for conditional analysis. This approximation leads to a safe overestimate of consistent paths and conditional analysis solution [Pan96].

A major difficulty in interprocedural data flow analysis is ensuring that the propagation of information only occurs on realizable paths in the program representation. The reaching alias pair used by the Landi-Ryder pointer aliasing algorithm [LR92] acts as an approximation of the call stack at the call site; that is, when data flow information is gathered within a called procedure, the corresponding reaching alias determines to which possible call sites this information will be propagated by choosing those sites with "matching" reaching aliases. Our algorithm similarly uses the assumptions in our predicates (i.e., S') to approximate possible consistent paths in the ICFG.[7] Thus, our algorithm is *context sensitive* (although approximate), thereby analyzing called functions within different calling contexts. It is *flow sensitive* because it propagates data flow information across calls to called procedures and then along paths within those procedures and back again to the calling procedure.

We define two predicates, *points-to-type*[8] and *may-hold*, with the following interpretations.

points-to-type (n, $AAPT$, $<p \Rightarrow C>$) if there exists a consistent path from ρ to the *entry* node of the procedure containing node n, on which an alias or pointer-type pair $AAPT$ (if any)[9] holds **and** there exists a conditionally consistent path $\mathcal{P}_{n,\{AAPT\}}$ to n on which $<p \Rightarrow C>$ holds. In Figure 1, we will have a *true* valued *points-to-type* ($n3$, $<s \Rightarrow Derived>$, $<t \Rightarrow Derived>$), as $<s \Rightarrow Derived>$ holds on the path $\rho{\cdot}n4{\cdot}n6{\cdot}n7{\cdot}entry_{Derived::bar}$ **and** $<t \Rightarrow Derived>$ holds on the path $entry_{Derived::bar} \cdot n3$ assuming $<s \Rightarrow Derived>$ holds at $entry_{Derived::bar}$. Similarly, *may-hold* (n, $AAPT$, $<a, b>$) if there exists a consistent path from ρ to the *entry* node of the procedure containing node n, on which $AAPT$ (if any) holds **and** there exists a conditionally consistent path $\mathcal{P}_{n,\{AAPT\}}$ to n on which $<a, b>$ holds. In Figure 1, we will have a *true*-valued *may-hold* ($n3$, $<*s, r>$, $<*t, r>$), as $<*s, r>$ holds on the path $\rho \cdot n4 \cdot n6 \cdot n7 \cdot entry_{Derived::bar}$ **and** $<*t, r>$ holds on the path $entry_{Derived::bar} \cdot n3$ assuming $<*s, r>$ holds at $entry_{Derived::bar}$. For efficiency, we have designed our approximation algorithm so that only those *may-hold* and *points-to-type* predicates are created which

[6] The choice of one alias or pointer-type was suggested by the use of one alias pair to encapsulate calling context in the Landi-Ryder pointer aliasing algorithm [LR92]. It was shown in [LR91] that a single alias pair precisely represents calling context, if a program is restricted to only a single level of dereferencing.

[7] Our algorithm is *approximate* and *safe* in the sense that it will propagate information on all consistent paths as well as possibly some inconsistent paths.

[8] In our previous papers [PR94a, PR94b], *points-to-type* was called *points-to*.

[9] We will consistently use $AAPT$ to denote a specific "Assumed Alias or Pointer-Type" pair. $AAPT$ may be $\emptyset$.

would return *true* for the conditional aliasing and type determination problems, respectively. Having obtained a solution for these predicates, solving the aliasing and type determination problems is easy. For example, if *points-to-type* (n, $AAPT$, $<p \Rightarrow C>$) is *true*, $<p \Rightarrow C>$ is in the type determination solution at node n.

Algorithm Overview Our combined algorithm for aliasing and type determination is a worklist based, fixed point iteration method which is both *safe* and *approximate*: If there exists an execution path to ICFG node n on which a pointer p points to an object of type C, our algorithm will report *points-to-type* (n, $AAPT$, $<p \Rightarrow C>$) for some entry assumption $AAPT$. Similarly, if there exists an execution path to node n on which $<a, b>$ holds, our algorithm will report *may-hold* (n, $AAPT$, $<a, b>$) for some $AAPT$.

The worst case complexity of our algorithm is polynomial in the number of ICFG nodes. However, we can show that in practice the algorithm runs in time linear with respect to the size of *may-hold* and *points-to-type* solution generated by our method [Pan96].

A high level description of our algorithm appears in Figure 2. The algorithm has three main phases which are discussed using examples in Sections 3.1–3.3. Firstly, the predicates *points-to-type* and *may-hold* and the worklist are *initialized* (see Section 3.1). Secondly, we *introduce* certain *true*-valued predicates at pointer assignments (using **intra-alias-type-introduction**) and at parameter binding sites (using **inter-alias-type-introduction**) (see Section 3.1). These initial predicates are placed on the worklist. Thirdly, the algorithm performs the usual fixed point iteration, until the worklist is empty. That is, a predicate is removed from the worklist and *propagated* through successor nodes using appropriate functions determined by the node type. This propagation of information occurs in the `while` loop of Figure 2. Intraprocedural propagation is explained in Section 3.2; the interprocedural propagation functions (e.g., **alias-type-propagation-from-call**) are explained in Section 3.3. The propagation functions make additional predicates *true* and put them on the worklist. Whenever a predicate becomes *true* for the first time, it is placed on the worklist. We refer to this action as **make-true**. Once marked *true*, a predicate stays *true*. A predicate goes on the worklist at most once, guaranteeing the termination of our algorithm.

The calculation of a fixed point for *points-to-type* and *may-hold* is tantamount to the solution of a standard monotone data flow framework defined on a lattice whose elements are sets of (*assumption, alias/pointer-type*) tuples. For simplicity, we have chosen to provide an intuitive explanation of the monotone transfer functions and solution procedure. A formal treatment, including the underlying program representation, lattice definition and monotone function space appears in [Pan96].

Calculation of Approximate Assumption Sets Before providing algorithm details, we briefly describe some auxiliary functions used to capture type and aliasing effects on entry of an invoked function from the types and aliases present

```
// initialization of information (Section 3.1)
lazily set all possible predicates to false;
set worklist to empty;
// introduction of aliases and pointer-type pairs (Section 3.1)
intra-alias-type-introduction ( ); // (Figure 4)
for each non-virtual call to entry
      inter-alias-type-introduction (call, entry);
// propagation of aliases and pointer-type pairs
while worklist is not empty
      remove (M, AAPT, APT) from worklist
      if M is a call node // (Section 3.3)
          alias-type-propagation-from-call (M, AAPT, APT);
      elseif M is an exit node // (Section 3.3)
          if APT is an alias pair
                alias-implies-alias-from-exit (M, AAPT, APT);
          if APT is a pointer-type pair
                type-implies-type-from-exit (M, AAPT, APT);
      else // intraprocedural propagation (Section 3.2)
          for each N ∈ successor (M)
                if N is a pointer assignment // (Figure 5)
                     if APT is an alias pair
                           alias-implies-alias-thru-assign (N, M, AAPT, APT);
                           alias-implies-type-thru-assign (N, M, AAPT, APT);
                     if APT is a pointer-type pair
                           type-implies-type-thru-assign (N, M, AAPT, APT);
                           type-implies-alias-thru-assign (N, M, AAPT, APT);
                // propagate directly through N
                elseif APT is an alias pair
                     make-true(may-hold (N, AAPT, APT))
                else
                     make-true(points-to-type (N, AAPT, APT))
```

Fig. 2. A High level description of the algorithm

at the invocation site. These functions calculate the approximate assumption sets described earlier. The first two functions, **bind0** and **type-bind0**, are used during the introduction phase (Section 3.1) and the rest during interprocedural propagation (Section 3.3). In these descriptions, `call` and `entry` represent ICFG nodes whereas *alias* and *pointer-type* are specific pairs.

bind0(`call`,`entry`) : This function calculates those *aliasing effects* from `call` to `entry` requiring no information from the predecessor(s) of `call`. For example, if $\&a$ is passed as an actual to the formal f, $<*f,a>$ is created at `entry` regardless of any aliases a may have at `call`; so $<*f,a> \in$ **bind0**(`call`,`entry`).

type-bind0(`call`,`entry`) : This function calculates those *type effects* from `call` to `entry` requiring no information from the predecessor(s) of `call`. For example, suppose a is an object of class B and $\&a$ is passed as actual to the formal f; then $<f \Rightarrow B> \in$ **type-bind0**(`call`, `entry`).

```
Class B { public:
  int b1;};

Class C { public:
  int foo (int *foo1, int *foo2);
  int bar (D *bar1; B *bar2);};

Class D { public:
  B *d1; };
```

```
C *s;     D *r;
int *p, *q, i;
main () {
  n1 : p = &i;
  n2 : q = p;
  n3 : s = new C;
  c1 : s->foo (p,q);
  n4 : r = new D;
  n5 : r->d1 = new B;
  c2 : s->bar (r, r->d1);}
```

Fig. 3. Example for binding functions

bind(`call`**,**`entry`**,***alias***)** : This function represents the propagation of *alias* reaching the `call` to the corresponding `entry`. Depending on the actual-formal associations, *alias* may manifest itself at `entry` and/or may give rise to additional alias pairs. In Figure 3, $<*p, *q>$ is created at n2 and reaches $call_{c1}$, resulting in:

$$\mathbf{bind}(call_{c1}, entry_{C::foo}, <*p, *q>) = \\ \{<*foo1, *foo2>, <*foo1, *q>, <*foo2, *p>, <*p, *q>\}$$

alias-bind(`call`**,**`entry`**,***pointer-type***)** : This function calculates the *alias effects* of *pointer-type* present at `call` which fall into the following two categories: aliases between appropriate dereferences of two formals (i.e., the first pair below) and aliases between the dereference of an actual and the corresponding formal (i.e., the last pair). In Figure 3, **alias-bind**($call_{c2}, entry_{C::bar}, <r \rightarrow d1 \Rightarrow B>$) includes:

$$\{<bar1 \rightarrow d1 \rightarrow b1, bar2 \rightarrow b1>, <r \rightarrow d1 \rightarrow b1, bar2 \rightarrow b1>\}$$

type-bind(`call`**,**`entry`**,***pointer-type***)** : This function calculates the *type effects* of *pointer-type* present at `call` on `entry`. Depending on the actual-formal bindings at `call`, *pointer-type* may simply propagate to `entry` and/or may create a pointer-type pair involving the corresponding formal. In Figure 3, **type-bind** ($call_{c2}, entry_{C::bar}, <r \rightarrow d1 \Rightarrow B>$) includes:

$$\{<r \rightarrow d1 \Rightarrow B>, <bar2 \Rightarrow B>\}$$

3.1 Initialization and Introduction Phases

Conceptually, the algorithm starts by initializing all the *points-to-type* and *may-hold* predicates to *false*.[10] We also initialize the worklist to empty. The intraprocedural aspects of the introduction phase are summarized in Figure 4. This introduces pointer-type and alias pairs generated locally at a pointer assignment node.

`for each node n in the ICFG`
    `If n is`
        `n : p = new B;`
            make-true(*points-to-type* (n, $\emptyset$, $\langle p \Rightarrow B \rangle$))
            make-true(*may-hold* (n, $\emptyset$, $\langle p \rightarrow mem_k, new_n.mem_k \rangle$))[†]
        `n : p = &r;`
            make-true(*points-to-type* (n, $\emptyset$, $\langle p \Rightarrow type(r) \rangle$))
            make-true(*may-hold* (n, $\emptyset$, $\langle p \rightarrow mem_k, r.mem_k \rangle$))

[†]We use $\langle p \rightarrow mem_k, new_n.mem_k \rangle$ to denote all aliases involving corresponding members of the class.

Fig. 4. Intraprocedural introduction phase : **intra-alias-type-introduction**

The function **inter-alias-type-introduction**(`call`,`entry`) has the following task: for each AP in **bind0**(`call`,`entry`), **make-true**(*may-hold* (`entry`, *AP*, *AP*)); and for each *PT* in **type-bind0**(`call`,`entry`), **make-true** (*points-to-type* (`entry`, *PT*, *PT*)).

3.2 Intraprocedural Propagation

We present the salient features of intraprocedural propagation in Figure 5, referring to appropriate functions from Figure 2. Accompanying each function we list the predicate(s) being propagated from node `m`, the pointer assignment successor `n` through which they propagate, and finally the resulting predicate. We concentrate on pointer assignment nodes, calculating the semantic effects (i.e., transfer functions) of the code at these nodes on the information reaching from an ICFG predecessor. Propagation is trivial through a node which is not a pointer assignment; such a node can neither create nor destroy aliases or pointer-types.

[10] We perform a lazy initialization of all predicates in constant time [LR92].

alias-implies-alias-thru-assign
may-hold (m, $\emptyset$, $\langle *q, a \rangle$)
`n : p = q;`
may-hold (n, $\emptyset$, $\langle *p, a \rangle$)

alias-implies-type-thru-assign
may-hold (m, $\emptyset$, $\langle *u, p \rangle$)
`n : *u = new B;`
points-to-type (n, $\emptyset$, $\langle p \Rightarrow B \rangle$)

type-implies-type-thru-assign
points-to-type (m, $\emptyset$, $\langle q \Rightarrow B \rangle$)
`n : p = q;`
points-to-type (n, $\emptyset$, $\langle p \Rightarrow B \rangle$)

type-implies-alias-thru-assign
points-to-type (m, $\emptyset$, $\langle q \Rightarrow B \rangle$)
`n : p = q;`
may-hold (n, $\emptyset$, $\langle p \rightarrow mem_k, q \rightarrow mem_k \rangle$)

Fig. 5. Example for intraprocedural propagation

3.3 Interprocedural Propagation

Propagation from `call` *node:* For non-virtual function calls, the corresponding `entry` node is easily determined. However if `call` represents a virtual call site, the *points-to-type* predicates involving the receiver at `call` determine the possible functions invoked. Each class associated with the receiver may correspond to a virtual function. For each `entry` so determined, we propagate information from `call` to `entry`. Having described the parameter binding functions already (see Figure 3), we can describe **alias-type-propagation-from-call** as setting *true* at `entry` those *may-hold* and *points-to-type* predicates corresponding to each element of the appropriate **bind, alias-bind** and **type-bind** sets. For example in Figure 3, $\langle r \rightarrow d1 \rightarrow b1, bar2 \rightarrow b1 \rangle \in$ **alias-bind**($call_{c2}$, $entry_{C::bar}$, $\langle r \rightarrow d1 \Rightarrow B \rangle$) results in **make-true**(*may-hold* ($entry_{C::bar}$, $\langle r \rightarrow d1 \rightarrow b1, bar2 \rightarrow b1 \rangle$, $\langle r \rightarrow d1 \rightarrow b1, bar2 \rightarrow b1 \rangle$)).

Propagation from `exit` *node:* Suppose a pair APT holds at `exit` with assumption $AAPT$ at `entry`. Using the parameter binding functions we determine the `call`(s) responsible for imposing $AAPT$ at `entry`, and propagate APT only to the corresponding `return`(s). This pivotal role played by the binding functions allows us to propagate information along a good approximation of consistent paths.

alias-implies-alias-from-exit(`exit`,$AAPT$,*alias*): (i) If the entry assumption $AAPT$ is $\emptyset$, *alias* may hold at `exit` no matter which `call` invokes the function containing `exit`, as this alias pair is created solely due to the execution of the function. As a result, *may-hold* (`return`, $\emptyset$, *alias*) is made *true* for all `returns` corresponding to virtual or non-virtual `calls` invoking this function.

(ii) If AAPT is non-$\emptyset$, it implies that *alias* holds at `exit` if a `call` imposes $AAPT$ at `entry`. Suppose *may-hold* (`call`, $AAPT'$, AP) imposes $AAPT$ at `entry` through **bind**(`call`,`entry`,AP). Using this association, we **make-true**(*may-hold* (`return`, $AAPT'$, *alias*)). Also, for each *points-to-type* (`call`, $AAPT'$, PT) imposing $AAPT$ at `entry` through either **type-bind**(`call`,`entry`, PT) or **alias-bind**(`call`,`entry`,PT), we **make-true**(*may-hold* (`return`, $AAPT'$, *alias*)).

type-implies-type-from-exit(exit,$AAPT$,*pointer-type*): There are two cases similar to the previous function:

(i) If $AAPT = \emptyset$, **make-true**(*points-to-type* (**return**, $\emptyset$, *pointer-type*)),

(ii) For non-$\emptyset$ $AAPT$, **make-true**(*points-to-type* (**return**, $AAPT'$, *pointer-type*)).

4 Implementation Results

The results presented in this section represent our initial efforts to empirically demonstrate the contributions of the algorithm and assess its precision using a prototype implementation. The prototype is written in C and runs on a Sun SPARC-20 with 64MB main memory. We are using the MasterCraft C^{++} system of Tata Consultancy Services as the front end C^{++} parser for the implementation. Our aliasing and type determination algorithm reuses some code from the Landi-Ryder aliasing algorithm [LR92] with suitable modifications. Our prototype was engineered as a *proof of concept* implementation to test the effectiveness of our approach for virtual function resolution. The front end had many constraints to its functionality, which led to the use of test programs of 1000 lines of code or smaller. However, this is a limitation of the current implementation, not the algorithm. Thus, we are currently re-engineering our prototype for performance, with a new front end. We also expect to use a newer, optimized version of the aliasing algorithm, whose performance has been improved several orders of magnitude in space and time over that in the current prototype. This will allow us to analyze much larger programs (e.g., 10,000 lines of code).

Here, we present empirical results of analyzing 19 C^{++} programs obtained from various (publicly available) sources such as textbooks, demonstration programs accompanying a C^{++} compiler and undergraduate projects. We only analyzed programs using a library if a driver program was included.

Table 1 lists some characteristics of programs we analyzed, such as the lines of code (LOC), number of classes, number of functions, number of virtual functions and number of virtual calls. We also list the number of virtual call sites present in those functions which were found unreachable, number of aliases per ICFG node, number of pointer-types per ICFG node and analysis times. As stated above, our new implementation will improve the unacceptable times shown for *city*, *tree* and *employ*. In the remainder of this section (unless otherwise stated) we normalize the data with respect to virtual call sites in reachable functions. We also will list the programs by number (from Table 1) instead of by name.

Virtual function resolution Based on the distinct classes of objects pointed to by the receiver at a virtual call site, the algorithm determines which virtual functions in the inheritance hierarchy may be invoked from the call site. In Figure 6(a), we classify the reachable virtual call sites in terms of the number of virtual functions found invocable. Our results support the observation by Calder and Grunwald that although object-oriented libraries support polymorphism through virtual functions, the target of most indirect function calls can be

name	LOC	#classes	functions	virtual functions	virtual calls	%unreach virt calls	aliases per node	ptr-types per node	time (min:sec)
1. greed	968	2	47	9	17	35	2	2	0:31
2. garage	143	4	19	3	10	0	304	34	0:56
3. vcircle	142	3	16	4	5	0	0	1	0:01
4. office	213	5	12	4	4	0	49	10	0:04
5. family	109	3	22	3	3	0	4	3	0:02
6. FSM	98	4	15	2	1	0	6	2	0:01
7. deriv2	313	7	34	16	66	45	29	3	1:04
8. shapes	267	4	34	12	22	23	38	5	2:19
9. deriv1	192	7	31	13	28	29	20	4	0:15
10. objects	465	6	59	31	39	85	6	1	0:08
11. simul	339	7	54	12	7	15	3	1	0:03
12. primes	46	4	11	4	3	0	48	7	0:26
13. ocean	444	7	64	10	5	0	81	8	1:58
14. NP	31	2	7	2	6	0	0	9	0:01
15. city	519	11	67	2	1	0	322	12	13:27
16. tree	217	5	26	8	3	33	726	34	11:14
17. employ	894	10	58	25	4	0	213	14	7:42
18. life	178	5	21	8	2	0	49	3	0:26
19. chess	392	10	43	12	1	0	58	16	0:54

Table 1. Some characteristics of C^{++} programs analyzed

accurately predicted [CG94]. While their observation is based on execution profiles of programs, our results eliminate the dependence on profile data by using compile time analysis which accounts for *all* possible executions of the program. On examining the data, we ascertained that the virtual calls with non-unique resolution (i.e., calls with 2 or more possible methods) were indeed polymorphic at run-time, and that the non-uniqueness was never due to approximations in analysis. While such results are not guaranteed by our approach, they are encouraging.

We also wanted to find out if there was any relation between the program characteristics from Table 1 and virtual function resolution results in Figure 6(a). For example, it would have been interesting to find that the resolution results were better for programs with greater number of virtual calls or virtual functions. Figure 6(a) measures the utility of our algorithm solution for virtual function resolution - unique resolution is best and > 3-way resolution is worst. The programs in Table 1 are sorted in decreasing order of solution utility. There are no corresponding trends in the program characteristics such as lines of code (LOC), number of virtual functions or the number of virtual calls. We conjecture that it is not these program characteristics but the programming style and the functionality of the program which influence the degree of polymorphism demonstrated by the virtual calls. However, a bigger data set containing larger programs is needed to draw definite conclusions about the program properties affecting virtual function resolution.

In Figure 6(b), we summarize how we obtained the unique virtual function resolutions in programs 1-13, shown as black bars in Figure 6(a). Looking only at those calls uniquely resolved in these 13 programs, we attribute the resolution of some of them either to the fact that there was only one choice of virtual function possible (discernible by examining the inheritance hierarchy) or to the use of the address of an object as receiver of the virtual call (thereby providing a unique type for the receiver). The percentage of virtual calls resolvable by the former method are shown as black bars; for the latter method the results are shown by diagonal-lined bars. The remainder of the virtual call sites were unresolvable with either of these two methods, but required our flow analysis technique. For these calls, we list the number of possible choices in the hierarchy (i.e., 2, $\geq$2) out of which we were able to select the unique function. Thus, Figure 6(b) shows those uniquely resolvable virtual calls for which our method proved stronger than optimized inheritance-based techniques.

Invocable virtual functions at a call site and call graph construction Even when unique resolution is not possible, limiting the number of virtual functions invoked at a call site can help subsequent analyses, in that the side effects of the non-invocable functions can be safely eliminated in the context of that call. Given the potential disparity in various implementations of a virtual function, this can translate into improved precision and efficiency of analysis. Limiting the number of invocable virtual functions at a virtual call is relevant to tools which use branch prediction. In Figure 6(c), we report the average percentage of virtual functions found invocable out of those in the class hierarchy of the receiver type at a (reachable or unreachable) virtual call site. We create edges from a virtual call site only to the functions found invocable using resolution information, implicitly building a smaller and more precise call graph than the one built without such information. Therefore, the values in Figure 6(c) can also be interpreted as the size of virtual function portion of our call graph *vis à vis* that constructed using a naive approach. Viewing only the relevant aspects of the program (using a call graph browser which utilizes the analysis information) can be used for better program understanding. Eliminating non-invocable functions can also be used to prune the class libraries, since we can replace the implementation of a non-invoked virtual method by its signature, reducing the library source code as well as object code size.

As expected, the average percentage of invocable virtual functions was low (implying that a high percentage was eliminated) for those programs for which:

1. a high percentage of virtual calls were found unreachable (see Table 1), or
2. we obtained good virtual function resolution (see Figure 6(a)), or
3. most of the unique resolution was obtained from two or more candidate functions in the class hierarchy (see Figure 6(b)).

5 Conclusions

We have presented the first polynomial-time combined algorithm to perform program-point-specific, interprocedural type determination and aliasing for C^{++}. We have stated the theoretical difficulty of this problem and demonstrated the

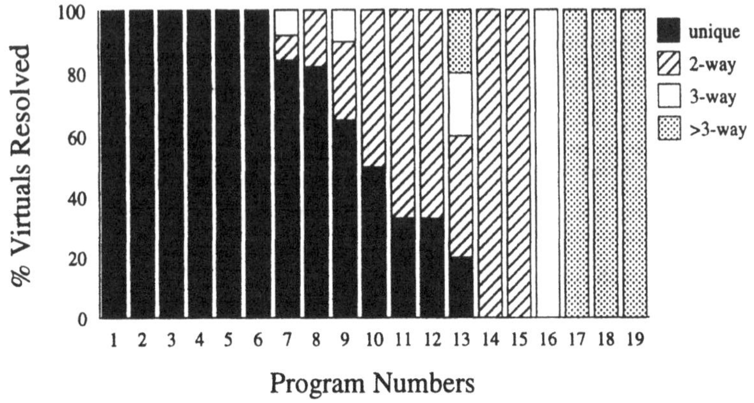

(a) Percentage of virtual calls with 1,2,3,>3 invocable funcs

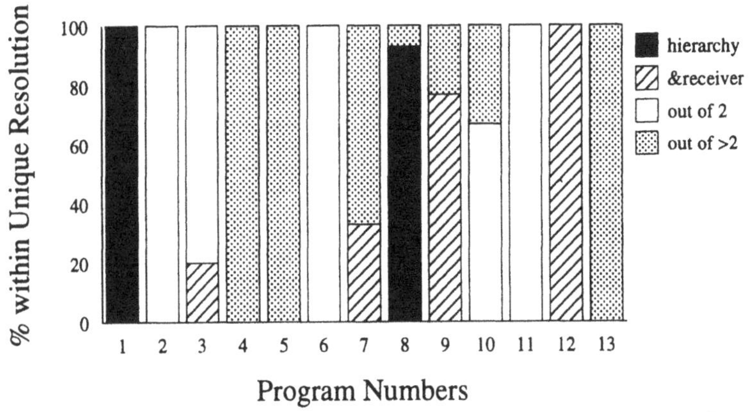

(b) Classification of unique resolution for programs 1-13 from (a)

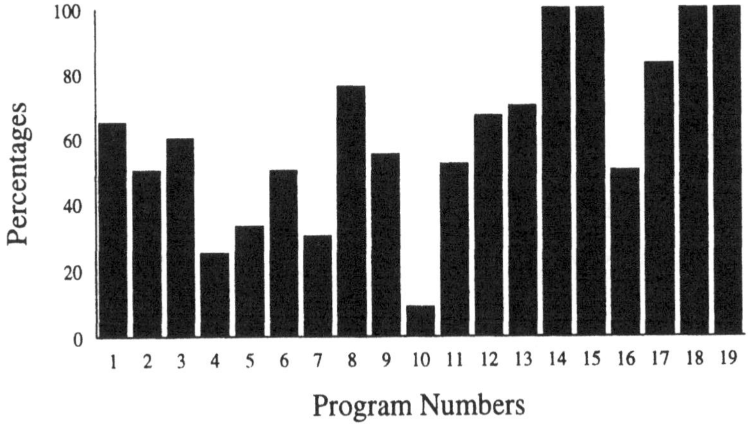

(c) Average percentage of invocable virtual functions out of those in class hierarchy at virtual call

Fig. 6. Empirical Results

utility of its approximate solution in virtual function resolution on a modest dataset using a prototype implementation. Currently, we are redesigning our prototype for performance optimization and to be able to analyze larger C^{++} programs. We also are considering work on useful analyses for other compiler transformations, debugging and testing in a C^{++} programming environment.

References

[CG94] B. Calder and D. Grunwald. Reducing indirect function call overhead in C^{++} programs. In *Conference Record of the Twenty-first Annual ACM Symposium on Principles of Programming Languages*, pages 397–408, January 1994.

[CGZ95] B. Calder, D. Grunwald, and B. Zorn. Quantifying behavioural differences between C and C^{++} programs. *Journal of Programming Languages*, 2:313–351, 1995.

[LR91] W. Landi and B. G. Ryder. Pointer-induced aliasing: A problem classification. In *Conference Record of the Eighteenth Annual ACM Symposium on Principles of Programming Languages*, pages 93–103, January 1991.

[LR92] W. Landi and B. G. Ryder. A safe approximation algorithm for interprocedural pointer aliasing. In *Proceedings of the SIGPLAN '92 Conference on Programming Language Design and Implementation*, pages 235–248, June 1992.

[Pan96] H. Pande. *Compile Time Analysis of C and C^{++} Systems*. PhD thesis, Rutgers University, May 1996.

[PR94a] H. Pande and B. G. Ryder. Static type determination for C^{++}. In *Proceedings of the Sixth USENIX C^{++} Technical Conference*, pages 85–97, April 1994.

[PR94b] H. D. Pande and B. G. Ryder. Static type determination and aliasing for C^{++}. Laboratory for Computer Science Research Technical Report LCSR-TR-236, Rutgers University, December 1994.

[RHS95] T. Reps, S. Horwitz, and M. Sagiv. Precise interprocedural dataflow analysis via graph reachability. In *Conference Record of the Twenty-second Annual ACM Symposium on Principles of Programming Languages*, pages 49–61, January 1995.

[SP81] M. Sharir and A. Pnueli. Two approaches to interprocedural data flow analysis. In S. Muchnick and N. Jones, editors, *Program Flow Analysis: Theory and Applications*, pages 189–234. Prentice Hall, 1981.

Compiling Laziness Using Projections

Ross Paterson

School of Computing, University of North London, Eden Grove, London N7 8DB, UK

Abstract. Projection-based strictness analysis is a powerful technique, able to cope with non-flat domains and latent demand. By analysing the projections as embedding-projection pairs, we develop an algorithm to translate lazy functions into a strict functional language with explicit closures. The translated functions typically operate on simpler types than the originals, in particular types containing fewer liftings, which correspond to the operational notion of closures. Like the analysis on which it is based, our algorithm is restricted to first-order functions.

1 Introduction

A lazy functional language provides great expressive power, but this comes at a cost in both space and time, for delayed computations must be stored as closures on the heap. The management of these closures also adds to execution time, and the frequent context switches frustrate both compile-time optimization and efficient exploitation of hardware.

Strictness analysis [17, 3, 20, 14] aims to ameliorate this situation by identifying strict functions, which can be implemented using call-by-value. The arguments of such functions may be evaluated early and passed unboxed. This has contributed to compiler performance, but the changes to the code generator are seldom formally verified.

There have been some efforts to verify these alterations. Modifications of the CPS translation [2] to use simple strictness information have been described by Danvy and Hatcliffe [6] and by Burn and Le Métayer [4]. Amtoft [1] describes a modification of a type-based strictness analysis to generate code that creates fewer thunks.

Peyton Jones and Launchbury [19, 18] introduce flat domains to their source language, interpreting them operationally as unboxed values. They are thus able to verify unboxing transformations in the source language.

The above systems are based on information about active demand, i.e. statements that a certain amount of a data structure will be required. In the presence of lazy data structures, e.g. streams, one is also interested in latent demand, i.e. statements that though a value may not be required, if it is then so much of it must be evaluated. This sort of strictness information can be obtained by projection-based strictness analysis [20].

This paper extends the projection technique to obtain a new algorithm translating lazy functional programs to more efficient strict forms.

1.1 Projection-based Strictness Analysis

In order to capture strictness over simple domains as well as non-flat domains, Wadler and Hughes [20] introduced projections over extended domains to describe evaluation contexts. An equivalent formulation [15] defines a projection over a type t as a partial function $\alpha : t \circ\!\!\rightarrow t$ satisfying $\alpha \leq id$ and $\alpha \circ \alpha = \alpha$. For example, the projection $\mathsf{Str} : \forall a.\, a_\bot \circ\!\!\rightarrow a_\bot$ is defined only if its argument is not $\bot$. (A type $t_\bot$ consists of the elements of t, which may or may not contain a bottom element, plus a new bottom element.) The projection $\mathsf{Both} : \forall a, b.\, a_\bot \times b_\bot \rightarrow a_\bot \times b_\bot$ is defined only if neither of its arguments are $\bot$.

The analysis of a total function $f : t_\alpha \rightarrow t_\beta$ for a given context projection $\beta : t_\beta \circ\!\!\rightarrow t_\beta$ yields an equation

$$\beta \circ f = \beta \circ f \circ \alpha \tag{1}$$

This equation implies that for an application of f in the context β, the context of the argument of f is given by the projection $\alpha : t_\alpha \circ\!\!\rightarrow t_\alpha$. For example, the iterative factorial function $fact : \mathsf{Num}_\bot \times \mathsf{Num}_\bot \rightarrow \mathsf{Num}_\bot$ (where Num is the set of numbers, without $\bot$) is seen to satisfy

$$\mathsf{Str} \circ fact = \mathsf{Str} \circ fact \circ \mathsf{Both} \tag{2}$$

indicating that it is strict in both arguments. Moreover, such projection equations can also capture latent strictness properties such as *head strictness*, which says that if a list is ever evaluated to weak head normal form, its head will also be evaluated. This analysis has been implemented by Kubiak, Hughes and Launchbury [13]. The present formulation is based on theirs.

1.2 This Paper

The point of departure of this paper is Launchbury's observation [15] that the images of these partial projections correspond to unboxed types. These images may be described using embedding-projection pairs. A partial projection α is factored as $\alpha^{\mathsf{E}} \circ \alpha^{\mathsf{P}}$, for a total function $\alpha^{\mathsf{E}} : t'_\alpha \rightarrow t_\alpha$ and a partial function $\alpha^{\mathsf{P}} : t_\alpha \circ\!\!\rightarrow t'_\alpha$ such that $\alpha^{\mathsf{P}} \circ \alpha^{\mathsf{E}} = id$ and $\alpha^{\mathsf{E}} \circ \alpha^{\mathsf{P}} \leq id$. The type t'_α will be a simpler variant of the type t_α. For example, the projection Str factors as an embedding of a type a in the type $a_\bot$. The latter lifted type might be implemented using closures, the former using unboxed values. Here the embedding component merely boxes the number; the projection component demands the value of a closure, and is therefore partial. Similarly, the projection Both corresponds to an embedding of the type $a \times b$ in the type $a_\bot \times b_\bot$.

Now (2) expands to

$$\mathsf{Str}^{\mathsf{E}} \circ \mathsf{Str}^{\mathsf{P}} \circ fact = \mathsf{Str}^{\mathsf{E}} \circ \mathsf{Str}^{\mathsf{P}} \circ fact \circ \mathsf{Both}^{\mathsf{E}} \circ \mathsf{Both}^{\mathsf{P}}$$

Composing $\mathsf{Str}^{\mathsf{P}}$ on the left to cancel the $\mathsf{Str}^{\mathsf{E}}$'s, this is equivalent to

$$\mathsf{Str}^{\mathsf{P}} \circ fact = \mathsf{Str}^{\mathsf{P}} \circ fact \circ \mathsf{Both}^{\mathsf{E}} \circ \mathsf{Both}^{\mathsf{P}} \tag{3}$$

Now we can fuse the composition $\mathsf{Str}^{\mathsf{P}} \circ \mathit{fact} \circ \mathsf{Both}^{\mathsf{E}}$, yielding a variant fact' : $\mathsf{Num} \times \mathsf{Num} \multimap\!\!\rightarrow \mathsf{Num}$. This function, which operates on unboxed numbers instead of closures, can then be used in place of *fact*. The projection component $\mathsf{Both}^{\mathsf{P}}$ goes on to provide a context for the arguments of *fact*.

General fusion is difficult, so we shall alter projection analysis to generate equations of the form

$$\beta^{\mathsf{P}} \circ f = f_{\beta} \circ \alpha^{\mathsf{P}} \tag{4}$$

for some partial function $f_\beta : t'_\alpha \multimap\!\!\rightarrow t'_\beta$. The rules of our algorithm thus correspond to those of projection-based strictness analysis; the novelty here is the translated version f_β.

The source language of our translation is a small first-order lazy functional language, defined in Sect. 2. The main unusual feature of this language is that lifting is treated as a separate type constructor. This allows us to treat the issues raised by each type constructor separately, and also to deal with unlifted types, which are avoided in most accounts of strictness analysis.

The translation sketched above produces partial functions. The projection components of e-p pairs are also partial functions. To express these, we introduce in Sect. 3 a small first-order strict functional language, with explicit **delay** and *force* constructs, as in Scheme [5].

The usual next step would be to give denotational descriptions of these two languages in a semantic meta-language. However, this meta-language would be essentially equivalent to our source language. Instead, we give an axiomatic description of the lazy language, and define the strict language by a translation to the lazy language. Then the rules of our algorithm expand to formulas over the lazy language.

Since everything is translated back to the lazy language for proof purposes, we could have described our algorithm as a source-to-source transformation on the lazy language. Indeed this was done in an early version of this work, but the transformation rules were far more complex than those presented here. Also, in the strict language closures are exactly the elements of lifted types; in the lazy language the correspondence is not as precise. The strict language is also well suited to the description of sequential computations; failure of any evaluation causes failure of the whole machine. This language may also be used as an interface to existing compilers.

A translation to a strict language driven by strictness analysis is also used by Faxén [9], but there only simple strictness is used. Thunk elimination and unboxing are performed at a later stage using a type-based flow inference [8].

In Sect. 4, we show how the contexts of conventional projection analysis may be factored as embedding-projection pairs. The embedding components, being total functions, are described by the lazy language, while the projection components, being partial, are described in the strict language.

The rules of our translation algorithm are given in Sect. 5, with some examples. Section 6 concludes.

$$
\begin{array}{lll}
\text{Types} & t = \varnothing \mid \mathbb{1} \mid t \times t \mid t + t \mid t_\perp \mid a \mid \mu a.\, t \\
\text{Definitions} & def = f_d \triangleq \lambda x.\, e \\
\text{Expressions} & e = x \mid \perp \mid () \mid (e_1, e_2) \mid f\ e \\
& \quad \mid \textbf{case}\ e\ \textbf{of}\ \mathit{inl}\ x_1 \Rightarrow e_1\ [\!]\ \mathit{inr}\ x_2 \Rightarrow e_2 \\
& \quad \mid \textbf{case}\ e\ \textbf{of}\ \mathit{lift}\ x \Rightarrow e' \\
\text{Functions} & f = f_d \\
& \quad \mid \lambda x.\, e \\
& \quad \mid \mathit{fst} \mid \mathit{snd} \mid \mathit{inl} \mid \mathit{inr} \mid \mathit{lift} \mid \mathit{id} \mid \mathit{empty}
\end{array}
$$

Figure 1. First-order lazy functional language

$$
\begin{array}{l}
\mathit{products} : \mathsf{Num}_\perp \times \mathsf{List\ Num}_\perp \to \mathsf{List\ Num}_\perp \\
\mathit{products}\ (x, ys) \triangleq \textbf{case}\ ys\ \textbf{of}\ \mathit{lift}\ n \Rightarrow \\
\qquad \textbf{case}\ n\ \textbf{of}\ \mathit{inl}\ () \Rightarrow \mathit{lift}\ (\mathit{inl}\ ())\ [\!] \\
\qquad\qquad \mathit{inr}\ (y, ys') \Rightarrow \textbf{let}\ x' \triangleq x * y\ \textbf{in} \\
\qquad\qquad\qquad \mathit{lift}\ (\mathit{inr}\ (x', \mathit{products}\ (x', ys')))
\end{array}
$$

$$
\begin{array}{l}
\mathit{append} : \forall a.\, \mathsf{List}\ a \times \mathsf{List}\ a \to \mathsf{List}\ a \\
\mathit{append}\ (xs, ys) \triangleq \textbf{case}\ xs\ \textbf{of}\ \mathit{lift}\ n \Rightarrow \\
\qquad \textbf{case}\ n\ \textbf{of}\ \mathit{inl}\ () \Rightarrow ys\ [\!] \\
\qquad\qquad \mathit{inr}\ (x, xs') \Rightarrow \mathit{lift}\ (\mathit{inr}\ (x, \mathit{append}\ (xs', ys)))
\end{array}
$$

Figure 2. Example lazy functions

2 A First-order Lazy Language

The source language of our translation algorithm is a simple first-order lazy functional language, whose grammar is given in Fig. 1. This language is the first-order fragment of the language of [16]. The most unusual feature is that not all types have a least element $\perp$. For example, we shall see below that sums are disjoint unions, and we shall later introduce flat types of numbers and so on.

A type is said to be *pointed* if it has a least element $\perp$. The type $\mathbb{1}$ is pointed; $t_1 \times t_2$ is pointed if both t_1 and t_2 are; $t_\perp$ is always pointed; $\mu a.\, t$ is pointed if t is pointed for any a. Note that $t_1 + t_2$ is never pointed; nor is $\varnothing$. The result types of recursive functions, of **case** e **of** *lift* $x \Rightarrow e'$, and of $\perp$ itself, are required be pointed.

Recursive types are considered to be equivalent to their unfoldings. Recursive forms whose initial solution is empty, like $\mu c.\, a \times c$, are forbidden. For example, the list type constructor is defined by

$$\mathsf{List}\ a \triangleq \mu c.\, (\mathbb{1} + a \times c)_\perp$$

Figure 2 contains some example of functions written in this language. (We have used a little syntactic sugar to render the pattern matching more readable.) The function *products* is a typical stream processor, mapping a list of numbers to a list of partial products.

Instead of giving a denotational semantics for the language, we shall give a series of axioms that it satisfies. Firstly, the empty type $\varnothing$ has no elements:

$$\forall\, x : \varnothing.\, \mathsf{false}$$

There is however a function $empty : \forall\, a.\, \varnothing \rightarrow a$.

Next, the unit type $\mathbb{1}$ has a single element $()$:

$$\forall\, x : \mathbb{1}.\, x = ()$$

The product type constructor describes a true product:

$$fst\ (x, y) = x \qquad snd\ (x, y) = y \qquad \forall\, p : a \times b.\, p = (fst\ p, snd\ p)$$

The sum type constructor makes disjoint unions:

$$\begin{array}{l}(\mathbf{case}\ inl\ x\ \mathbf{of}\ inl\ x' \Rightarrow e_1 \ [\!]\ inr\ y' \Rightarrow e_2) = e_1[x' \mapsto x] \\ (\mathbf{case}\ inr\ y\ \mathbf{of}\ inl\ x' \Rightarrow e_1 \ [\!]\ inr\ y' \Rightarrow e_2) = e_2[y' \mapsto y] \\ \forall\, z : a + b.\, (\exists\, x : a.\, z = inl\ x) \vee (\exists\, y : b.\, z = inr\ y)\end{array}$$

Lifted types have constructors $\bot$ and $lift : \forall\, a.\, a \rightarrow a_\bot$:

$$\begin{array}{l}(\mathbf{case}\ \bot\ \mathbf{of}\ lift\ y \Rightarrow e) = \bot \\ (\mathbf{case}\ lift\ x\ \mathbf{of}\ lift\ y \Rightarrow e) = e[y \mapsto x] \\ \forall\, z : a_\bot.\, (z = \bot) \vee (\exists\, x : a.\, z = lift\ x)\end{array}$$

Finally, we assume β- and η-equivalence for functions, and that recursive definitions support unfolding and Scott induction.

Some abbreviations will be convenient. We write $\mathbf{let}\ x \triangleq e\ \mathbf{in}\ e'$ for $(\lambda\, x.\, e')\ e$, and $f \circ g$ for $\lambda\, x.\, f\ (g\ x)$. There are operators on functions corresponding to type constructors:

$$\begin{aligned} f_1 \times f_2 &= \lambda\, z.\, (f_1\ (fst\ z), f_2\ (snd\ z)) \\ f_1 + f_2 &= \lambda\, z.\, \mathbf{case}\ z\ \mathbf{of}\ inl\ x_1 \Rightarrow inl\ (f_1\ x_1)\ [\!]\ inr\ x_2 \Rightarrow inr\ (f_2\ x_2) \\ f_\bot &= \lambda\, z.\, \mathbf{case}\ z\ \mathbf{of}\ lift\ x \Rightarrow lift\ (f\ x)\end{aligned}$$

These operators preserve *id* and composition, i.e. they are functors.

3 A First-order Strict Language

The target language of the strictness translation is a first-order strict functional language, given in Fig. 3. The domain types of this language are identical to those of the lazy language, but there are no pointedness restrictions. Lifted types $t_\bot$

Definitions	$def = p_d \triangleq \lambda\, x.\, v$
Expressions	$v = x \mid \bot \mid () \mid (v_1, v_2) \mid p\ v$
	$\mid$ **case** v **of** $inl\ x_1 \Rightarrow v_1\ []\ inr\ x_2 \Rightarrow v_2$
	$\mid$ **delay** v
Partial functions	$p = p_d$
	$\mid \lambda\, x.\, v$
	$\mid fst \mid snd \mid inl \mid inr \mid id \mid force$

Figure 3. First-order strict functional language

$$[\![p_d \triangleq \lambda\, x.\, v]\!] = p_d \triangleq [\![\lambda\, x.\, v]\!]$$

$$\begin{aligned}
[\![p_d]\!] &= p_d \\
[\![\lambda\, x.\, v]\!] &= \lambda\, x.\, [\![v]\!] \\
[\![fst]\!] &= lift \circ fst \\
[\![snd]\!] &= lift \circ snd \\
[\![inl]\!] &= lift \circ inl \\
[\![inr]\!] &= lift \circ inr \\
[\![force]\!] &= id \\
[\![id]\!] &= lift
\end{aligned}$$

$$\begin{aligned}
[\![x]\!] &= lift\ x \\
[\![\bot]\!] &= \bot \\
[\![()]\!] &= lift\ () \\
[\![(v_1, v_2)]\!] &= \textbf{case}\ [\![v_1]\!]\ \textbf{of}\ lift\ x_1 \Rightarrow \\
&\qquad \textbf{case}\ [\![v_2]\!]\ \textbf{of}\ lift\ x_2 \Rightarrow \\
&\qquad lift\ (x_1, x_2) \\
[\![p\ v]\!] &= \textbf{case}\ [\![v]\!]\ \textbf{of}\ lift\ x \Rightarrow [\![p]\!]\ x \\
[\![\textbf{case}\ v\ \textbf{of}\ inl\ x_1 \Rightarrow v_1\ []\ inr\ x_2 \Rightarrow v_2]\!] & \\
&= \textbf{case}\ [\![v]\!]\ \textbf{of}\ lift\ y \Rightarrow \\
&\qquad \textbf{case}\ y\ \textbf{of}\ inl\ x_1 \Rightarrow [\![v_1]\!]\ [] \\
&\qquad\qquad inr\ x_2 \Rightarrow [\![v_2]\!] \\
[\![\textbf{delay}\ v]\!] &= lift\ ([\![v]\!])
\end{aligned}$$

Figure 4. Semantics of the strict language

have a special role in this language, representing the types of closures. These are built by the **delay** construct, and their values demanded by the function $force : \forall\, a.\, a_\bot \to a$, as in Scheme [5].

The semantics of this language is given in Fig. 4 via a translation into the lazy language, corresponding to the standard denotational semantics of strict languages. Strict computations of type t are modelled by lazy expressions of type $t_\bot$. Thus partial functions, whose types we write as $t \circ\!\!\to t'$, are translated to lazy functions of type $t \to t'_\bot$.

In the strict language we use abbreviations like those for the lazy language. We write **let** $x \triangleq v$ **in** v' for $(\lambda\, x.\, v')\ v$, and $p \circ q$ for $\lambda\, x.\, p\ (q\ x)$. The strict language also has operators (functors) preserving id and composition:

$$\begin{aligned}
p_1 \times p_2 &= \lambda\, z.\, (p_1\ (fst\ z), p_2\ (snd\ z)) \\
p_1 + p_2 &= \lambda\, z.\, \textbf{case}\ z\ \textbf{of}\ inl\ x_1 \Rightarrow inl\ (p_1\ x_1)\ []\ inr\ x_2 \Rightarrow inr\ (p_2\ x_2) \\
p_\bot &= \lambda\, z.\, \textbf{delay}\ (p\ (force\ z))
\end{aligned}$$

$$\begin{array}{rll}
\mathsf{Ide} = \langle id & , id & \rangle : \quad a \trianglelefteq a \\
\mathsf{Abs} = \langle \lambda\,().\,\bot & , \lambda x.\,() & \rangle : \quad \mathbb{1} \trianglelefteq a \\
\mathsf{Fail} = \langle empty & , \lambda x.\,\bot & \rangle : \quad \varnothing \trianglelefteq a \\
\alpha \times \beta = \langle \alpha^{\mathrm{E}} \times \beta^{\mathrm{E}} & , \alpha^{\mathrm{P}} \times \beta^{\mathrm{P}} & \rangle : t'_\alpha \times t'_\beta \trianglelefteq t_\alpha \times t_\beta \\
\alpha + \beta = \langle \alpha^{\mathrm{E}} + \beta^{\mathrm{E}} & , \alpha^{\mathrm{P}} + \beta^{\mathrm{P}} & \rangle : t'_\alpha + t'_\beta \trianglelefteq t_\alpha + t_\beta \\
\alpha_\bot = \langle {\alpha^{\mathrm{E}}}_\bot & , {\alpha^{\mathrm{P}}}_\bot & \rangle : \quad t'_{\alpha\bot} \trianglelefteq t_{\alpha\bot} \\
\alpha_{\oplus} = \langle \mathit{lift} \circ \alpha^{\mathrm{E}} & , \alpha^{\mathrm{P}} \circ \mathit{force} & \rangle : \quad t'_\alpha \trianglelefteq t_{\alpha\bot}
\end{array}$$

Figure 5. Embedding-projection pairs (given $\alpha : t'_\alpha \trianglelefteq t_\alpha$ and $\beta : t'_\beta \trianglelefteq t_\beta$)

4 Embedding-projection Pairs

We need to analyse each projection $\alpha : t \multimap t$ used in strictness analysis [13] as an e-p pair $\langle \alpha^{\mathrm{E}} : t' \to t, \alpha^{\mathrm{P}} : t \multimap t' \rangle$ such that $\alpha = {\alpha^{\mathrm{E}}}_\bot \circ [\![\alpha^{\mathrm{P}}]\!]$. That is, the embedding component is a total function, described in the language of lazy functions, while the projection component is a partial function, described in the language of strict functions. We shall identify α with this pair relating a type t with a reduced representation t'. We write $\alpha : t' \trianglelefteq t$ for this factorization.

The primitive e-p pairs and constructors are listed in Fig. 5.

The trivial e-p pair is the identity Ide, which embeds any type in itself.

The context Abs (absent) is used to indicate that a value is unused, so any value will do, and we may as well implement it using the unit type $\mathbb{1}$ (a form of dead code elimination). Note that $\mathsf{Abs}^{\mathrm{E}}$ is only defined for pointed types, while $\mathsf{Abs}^{\mathrm{P}}$ is defined for all types.

The context Fail is used to indicate that no value is acceptable. Such a value may be represented using the empty type.

We define the composition of e-p pairs $\alpha : t' \trianglelefteq t$ and $\beta : t'' \trianglelefteq t'$ as

$$\alpha \circ \beta = \langle \alpha^{\mathrm{E}} \circ \beta^{\mathrm{E}}, \beta^{\mathrm{P}} \circ \alpha^{\mathrm{P}} \rangle : t'' \trianglelefteq t$$

The above e-p pairs satisfy the following equations:

$$\alpha = \alpha \circ \mathsf{Ide} = \mathsf{Ide} \circ \alpha \tag{5}$$

$$\mathsf{Abs} = \alpha \circ \mathsf{Abs} \qquad \text{if } [\![\alpha^{\mathrm{P}}]\!] \text{ is total} \tag{6}$$

$$\mathsf{Fail} = \alpha \circ \mathsf{Fail} \tag{7}$$

Next are the operators corresponding to the type constructors $\times$, $+$ (unlifted sum) and $\cdot_\bot$. By construction, these operations on e-p pairs preserve Ide and composition.

Liftings are eliminated (performing unboxing) by the variant $\cdot_{\oplus}$ of $\cdot_\bot$. This operator is not functorial; its action on Ide is the strictness projection:

$$\mathsf{Str} = \mathsf{Ide}_{\oplus} = \langle \mathit{lift}, \mathit{force} \rangle$$

The e-p pair corresponding to the projection Both is $\mathsf{Str} \times \mathsf{Str}$.

The interaction of the $\cdot_{\oplus}$ operator with composition is given by the following equations:

$$(\alpha \circ \beta)_{\oplus} = \alpha_{\oplus} \circ \beta \tag{8}$$
$$(\alpha \circ \beta)_{\oplus} = \alpha_{\perp} \circ \beta_{\oplus} \tag{9}$$

For example, the operation on e-p pairs corresponding to List is

$$\mathsf{List}\ \alpha \triangleq (\mathbb{1} + \alpha \times \mathsf{List}\ \alpha)_{\perp}$$

Often we will want to talk about lists in a strict context, so we use the active variant

$$\mathsf{List!}\ \alpha \triangleq (\mathbb{1} + \alpha \times \mathsf{List}\ \alpha)_{\oplus}$$

It would also be possible to eliminate the liftings in the recursive types, giving a context describing tail (or spine) strictness:

$$\mathsf{Tail}\ \alpha \triangleq (\mathbb{1} + \alpha \times \mathsf{Tail}\ \alpha)_{\oplus}$$

However, this kind of unboxing is not always a good idea, as the early evaluation of the whole list may use a great deal of space.

In order to be able to use the fixpoint methods developed for strictness analysis, we need to limit ourselves to a finite set of contexts. In the rest of this paper, we shall use contexts built from Abs, Fail and variables ranging over contexts using $\times$, $+$, $\cdot_{\perp}$ and $\cdot_{\oplus}$. We shall only unfold recursive contexts to one level, as we did with List above. We shall also introduce flat data types, like Num, whose associated contexts are instances of Ide.

4.1 Upper Bounds of Projections

There is a natural ordering on contexts, extending the ordering on simple projections: we write $\eta : \alpha \sqsubseteq \beta$ for $\alpha = \beta \circ \eta$. When we do not need to refer to η, we simply write $\alpha \sqsubseteq \beta$. A smaller e-p pair in this ordering represents less boxing, and is therefore more desirable.

In some of the rules of projection analysis, we require a context β greater than each of a pair of argument contexts α_1 and α_2. The actions on projections are the usual approximate answers [13] built from the primitive contexts and operators of Fig. 5. However, we also require e-p pairs $\eta_i : \alpha_i \sqsubseteq \beta$ to act as witnesses to the orderings, and to mediate between the representations. Since the approximations are defined by syntactic matching of the context terms, the necessary e-p pairs follow from various equations above, as in Fig. 6.

5 Translation from the Lazy Language

The translation of a lazy function f in a context β will be defined by a theorem of the form

$$[\![\beta^{\mathrm{P}}]\!] \circ f = [\![p \circ \alpha^{\mathrm{P}}]\!]$$

$$\begin{aligned}
\mathsf{Ide} &: \alpha \sqsubseteq \alpha \\
\alpha &: \alpha \sqsubseteq \mathsf{Ide} \\
[\![\alpha^{\mathsf{P}}]\!] \text{ is total} \Rightarrow \mathsf{Abs} &: \mathsf{Abs} \sqsubseteq \alpha \\
\mathsf{Fail} &: \mathsf{Fail} \sqsubseteq \alpha \\
\eta_1 : \alpha_1 \sqsubseteq \beta_1 \wedge \eta_2 : \alpha_2 \sqsubseteq \beta_2 \Rightarrow \eta_1 \times \eta_2 &: \alpha_1 \times \alpha_2 \sqsubseteq \beta_1 \times \beta_2 \\
\eta_1 : \alpha_1 \sqsubseteq \beta_1 \wedge \eta_2 : \alpha_2 \sqsubseteq \beta_2 \Rightarrow \eta_1 + \eta_2 &: \alpha_1 + \alpha_2 \sqsubseteq \beta_1 + \beta_2 \\
\eta : \alpha \sqsubseteq \beta \Rightarrow \eta_\perp &: \alpha_\perp \sqsubseteq \beta_\perp \\
\eta : \alpha \sqsubseteq \beta \Rightarrow \eta &: \alpha_\oplus \sqsubseteq \beta_\oplus \\
\eta : \alpha \sqsubseteq \beta \Rightarrow \eta_\oplus &: \alpha_\oplus \sqsubseteq \beta_\perp
\end{aligned}$$

Figure 6. Rules for context orderings

where p is a partial function in the strict language and α is an e-p pair.

The simplest case, corresponding to the transformation discussed by Peyton Jones and Launchbury [19], is where β is Str. This corresponds to the common observation that "an expression is never evaluated unless its value is required in WHNF". Since $[\![\mathsf{Str}^{\mathsf{P}}]\!] = id$, the left side of the above equation reduces to f. In their terminology, the function f is defined as a *wrapper* performing unboxing of the arguments (via the projection α^{P}) for a *worker* function p. For example, we assume that the multiplication function is supplied with a translation

$$[\![\mathsf{Num}_\oplus{}^{\mathsf{P}}]\!] \circ (*) = [\![(*) \circ (\mathsf{Num}_\oplus \times \mathsf{Num}_\oplus)^{\mathsf{P}}]\!]$$

stating that it is strict.

Often the context will be more interesting—in the above example the argument of f will be evaluated in the context α. The environment of the program may also imply a more informative context. For example, in a stream-producing computation the outer context will be both strict and head-strict.

The lazy functions of Fig. 2 interact in interesting ways with latent demand. In different contexts, *products* translates to different partial functions, both defined in Fig. 7:

$$\begin{aligned}
[\![(\mathsf{List!}\ \mathsf{Num}_\perp)^{\mathsf{P}}]\!] \circ \mathit{products} &= [\![\mathit{products}_1 \circ (\mathsf{Num}_\perp \times \mathsf{List!}\ \mathsf{Num}_\perp)^{\mathsf{P}}]\!] \\
[\![(\mathsf{List!}\ \mathsf{Num}_\oplus)^{\mathsf{P}}]\!] \circ \mathit{products} &= [\![\mathit{products}_2 \circ (\mathsf{Num}_\oplus \times \mathsf{List!}\ \mathsf{Num}_\oplus)^{\mathsf{P}}]\!]
\end{aligned}$$

In the first case, *products* is used in a completely lazy context, and the resulting program must build closures for both x' and the tail of the list, just like the original. In a head-strict context, *products* is compiled to a different version that performs the multiplication immediately, but still builds a closure for the tail. Further, $\mathit{products}_2$ expects as arguments an unboxed number and a list of unboxed numbers.

In contrast, a single translation of *append* suffices for all contexts List! α:

$$[\![(\mathsf{List!}\ \alpha)^{\mathsf{P}}]\!] \circ \mathit{append} = [\![\mathit{append}_1 \circ (\mathsf{List!}\ \alpha \times \mathsf{List}\ \alpha)^{\mathsf{P}}]\!]$$

$$\textbf{type } \mathsf{List!}\ a \triangleq \mathbf{1} + a \times \mathsf{List}\ a$$

$$\begin{array}{l}
\mathit{products}_1 : \mathsf{Num}_\perp \times \mathsf{List!}\ \mathsf{Num}_\perp \multimap \mathsf{List!}\ \mathsf{Num}_\perp \\
\mathit{products}_1\ (x, n) \triangleq \textbf{case } n \textbf{ of } \mathit{inl}\ () \Rightarrow \mathit{inl}\ ()\ [] \\
\qquad\qquad\qquad\qquad\qquad\quad \mathit{inr}\ (y, ys) \Rightarrow \textbf{let } x' \triangleq \textbf{delay } (\mathit{force}\ x * \mathit{force}\ y) \textbf{ in} \\
\qquad\qquad\qquad\qquad\qquad\qquad\qquad\qquad \mathit{inr}\ (x', \textbf{delay } (\mathit{products}_1\ (x', \mathit{force}\ ys)))
\end{array}$$

$$\begin{array}{l}
\mathit{products}_2 : \mathsf{Num} \times \mathsf{List!}\ \mathsf{Num} \multimap \mathsf{List!}\ \mathsf{Num} \\
\mathit{products}_2\ (x, n) \triangleq \textbf{case } n \textbf{ of } \mathit{inl}\ () \Rightarrow \mathit{inl}\ ()\ [] \\
\qquad\qquad\qquad\qquad\qquad\quad \mathit{inr}\ (y, ys) \Rightarrow \textbf{let } x' \triangleq x * y \textbf{ in} \\
\qquad\qquad\qquad\qquad\qquad\qquad\qquad\qquad \mathit{inr}\ (x', \textbf{delay } (\mathit{products}_2\ (x', \mathit{force}\ ys)))
\end{array}$$

$$\begin{array}{l}
\mathit{append}_1 : \forall a.\ \mathsf{List!}\ a \times \mathsf{List}\ a \multimap \mathsf{List!}\ a \\
\mathit{append}_1\ (n, ys) \triangleq \textbf{case } n \textbf{ of } \mathit{inl}\ () \Rightarrow \mathit{force}\ ys\ [] \\
\qquad\qquad\qquad\qquad\qquad\quad \mathit{inr}\ (x, xs) \Rightarrow \mathit{inr}\ (x, \textbf{delay } (\mathit{append}_1\ (\mathit{force}\ xs, ys)))
\end{array}$$

Figure 7. Partial functions generated by the translation

Note that append_1 is essentially the same as *append*—the unboxing projections are pushed straight through it onto its arguments.

Similar translations were achieved by the informally verified algorithm of Hall and Wise [10]. They use a single data type, which would be written in the notation of this paper as

$$\mathsf{Structure} \triangleq \mu\, c.\, (\mathsf{Atom} + c \times c)_\perp$$

where Atom is an unpointed set (including *nil* and numbers). Strictness is described by *strictness patterns*, which are equivalent (though with the inverse ordering) to certain contexts over Structure. Their outer strictness pattern corresponds to

$$\mathsf{Printer!} \triangleq (\mathsf{Atom} + \mathsf{Printer!} \times \mathsf{Printer})_\oplus$$

$$\mathsf{Printer} \triangleq (\mathsf{Atom} + \mathsf{Printer!} \times \mathsf{Printer})_\perp$$

They use an infinite domain of contexts, requiring the user to limit the number of versions of a function that may be generated.

5.1 Translation Rules

The rules of the backward analysis correspond to the rules of the conventional analysis [20, 13]; what is new here is the translations.

The translations of the primitive functions are given in Fig. 8. These theorems follow from the axioms of Sect. 2, but the proofs are omitted here. Note that *lift* may also occur in a context of the form $\alpha_\perp$; this case is covered by rule (20), to be discussed later.

$$[\![\alpha^{\mathsf{P}}]\!] \circ fst = [\![fst \circ (\alpha \times \mathsf{Abs})^{\mathsf{P}}]\!] \qquad [\![\alpha_{\oplus}{}^{\mathsf{P}}]\!] \circ lift = [\![id \circ \alpha^{\mathsf{P}}]\!]$$
$$[\![\alpha^{\mathsf{P}}]\!] \circ snd = [\![snd \circ (\mathsf{Abs} \times \alpha)^{\mathsf{P}}]\!] \qquad [\![\alpha^{\mathsf{P}}]\!] \circ id = [\![id \circ \alpha^{\mathsf{P}}]\!]$$
$$[\![(\alpha+\beta)^{\mathsf{P}}]\!] \circ inl = [\![inl \circ \alpha^{\mathsf{P}}]\!] \qquad [\![\alpha^{\mathsf{P}}]\!] \circ empty = [\![id \circ \mathsf{Fail}^{\mathsf{P}}]\!]$$
$$[\![(\alpha+\beta)^{\mathsf{P}}]\!] \circ inr = [\![inr \circ \beta^{\mathsf{P}}]\!]$$

Figure 8. Translations of pre-defined functions

The translation of an expression e in a context β is described by a theorem of the form

$$[\![\beta^{\mathsf{P}}]\!]\ e = [\![v \lhd \rho^{\mathsf{P}}]\!]$$

for some translated expression v and environment ρ. The $\lhd$ operator, applied to an environment π mapping variables $x : t$ to call-by-value functions $\pi_x : t' \circ\!\!\rightarrow t$, is the following abbreviation:

$$v \lhd \pi = \textbf{let } x_1 \triangleq \pi_{x_1}\ x_1 \textbf{ in } \ldots \textbf{ let } x_n \triangleq \pi_{x_n}\ x_n \textbf{ in } v$$

We write $\overline{\alpha}$ for the context environment mapping each variable to the context α.

Figure 9 contains inference rules for every combination of context and expression permitted by the type constraints of our language. The soundness of these follows from the axioms of Sect. 2, but the rules may also be read as a directed logic program.

The first two rules should be given precedence over the others, as they may produce superior results. First, a context of Abs indicates that any value will do, so we use the unit type instead. A context of Fail indicates that no value will do, so the empty type is a suitable representation.

The environment of variable values may be viewed as a product, and variables as projections. Hence their translation (12) is similar to *fst* and *snd* in Fig. 8.

If $\perp$ occurs in a strict context, no value for the free variables will do.

To compile a pair, we must combine the demands of the two components. On each variable, we will have a pair of e-p pairs $\alpha : t_\alpha \trianglelefteq t$ and $\beta : t_\beta \trianglelefteq t$. We require an e-p pair $\gamma : t_\gamma \trianglelefteq t$ and call-by-value functions $\theta^{\mathsf{L}} : t_\gamma \circ\!\!\rightarrow t_\alpha$ and $\theta^{\mathsf{R}} : t_\gamma \circ\!\!\rightarrow t_\beta$ such that

$$(\alpha^{\mathsf{P}}\ x, \beta^{\mathsf{P}}\ x) = \textbf{let } x' \triangleq \gamma^{\mathsf{P}}\ x \textbf{ in } (\theta^{\mathsf{L}}\ x', \theta^{\mathsf{R}}\ x')$$

When this equation holds, we write $\langle \gamma, \theta^{\mathsf{L}}, \theta^{\mathsf{R}} \rangle \in \alpha \,\&\, \beta$. As with the upper bound calculations, we can use the approximations for γ supplied by conventional projection analysis, but we also need the θ's. In Fig. 10, we go through all the rules for & [13] and calculate the θ's. Note the fall-back rule; the other rules give better answers where they apply, but this covers cases like $\alpha_\perp \,\&\, \beta_\perp$. Recursive types can be handled in the same way as for ordinary projections [13].

Applications of primitive or user-defined functions are translated using (16). Applications of λ-expressions, i.e. **let** definitions, are translated using (17). The latter uses & because a **let** definition makes non-linear use of its environment, like the pairing construct.

$$[\mathsf{Abs}^{\mathsf{P}}]\ e = [\![() \lhd \overline{\mathsf{Abs}}^{\mathsf{P}}]\!] \tag{10}$$

$$[\mathsf{Fail}^{\mathsf{P}}]\ e = [\![\bot \lhd \overline{\mathsf{Fail}}^{\mathsf{P}}]\!] \tag{11}$$

$$[\beta^{\mathsf{P}}]\ x = [\![x \lhd (\overline{\mathsf{Abs}}[x \mapsto \beta])^{\mathsf{P}}]\!] \tag{12}$$

$$[\beta^{\mathsf{P}}]\ \bot = [\![\bot \lhd \overline{\mathsf{Fail}}^{\mathsf{P}}]\!] \qquad [\beta^{\mathsf{P}}]\ \text{strict} \tag{13}$$

$$[\beta^{\mathsf{P}}]\ () = [\![() \lhd \overline{\mathsf{Abs}}^{\mathsf{P}}]\!] \tag{14}$$

$$\frac{[\beta_i{}^{\mathsf{P}}]\ e_i = [v_i \lhd \rho_i{}^{\mathsf{P}}] \qquad \langle \rho, \theta^{\mathsf{L}}, \theta^{\mathsf{R}} \rangle \in \rho_1 \,\&\, \rho_2}{[\beta_1 \times \beta_2{}^{\mathsf{P}}]\ (e_1, e_2) = [(v_1 \lhd \theta^{\mathsf{L}}, v_2 \lhd \theta^{\mathsf{R}}) \lhd \rho^{\mathsf{P}}]} \tag{15}$$

$$\frac{[\beta^{\mathsf{P}}] \circ f = [p \circ \alpha^{\mathsf{P}}] \qquad [\alpha^{\mathsf{P}}]\ e = [v \lhd \rho^{\mathsf{P}}]}{[\beta^{\mathsf{P}}]\ (f\ e) = [(p\ v) \lhd \rho^{\mathsf{P}}]} \tag{16}$$

$$\frac{[\beta^{\mathsf{P}}]\ e_2 = [v_2 \lhd \rho_2{}^{\mathsf{P}}] \qquad [\rho_{2_x}{}^{\mathsf{P}}]\ e_1 = [v_1 \lhd \rho_1{}^{\mathsf{P}}] \qquad \langle \rho, \theta^{\mathsf{L}}, \theta^{\mathsf{R}} \rangle \in \rho_1 \,\&(\rho_2 \backslash x)}{[\beta^{\mathsf{P}}]\ \left(\mathbf{let}\ x \triangleq e_1\ \mathbf{in}\ e_2\right) = [\![\left(\mathbf{let}\ x \triangleq v_1 \lhd \theta^{\mathsf{L}}\ \mathbf{in}\ v_2 \lhd \theta^{\mathsf{R}}\right) \lhd \rho^{\mathsf{P}}]\!]} \tag{17}$$

$$\frac{[\beta^{\mathsf{P}}]\ e_i = [v_i \lhd \rho_i{}^{\mathsf{P}}] \qquad \alpha_i = \rho_{i_{y_i}} \qquad \eta_i : \rho_i \backslash y_i \sqsubseteq \rho}{[\beta^{\mathsf{P}}] \begin{pmatrix} \mathbf{case}\ x\ \mathbf{of} \\ \mathit{inl}\ y_1 \Rightarrow e_1\ [] \\ \mathit{inr}\ y_2 \Rightarrow e_2 \end{pmatrix} = [\![\begin{pmatrix} \mathbf{case}\ x\ \mathbf{of} \\ \mathit{inl}\ y_1 \Rightarrow v_1 \lhd \eta_1{}^{\mathsf{P}}\ [] \\ \mathit{inr}\ y_2 \Rightarrow v_2 \lhd \eta_2{}^{\mathsf{P}} \end{pmatrix} \lhd (\rho[x \mapsto \alpha_1 + \alpha_2])^{\mathsf{P}}]\!]} \tag{18}$$

x not free in e_1, e_2

$$\frac{[\beta^{\mathsf{P}}]\ e = [v \lhd \rho^{\mathsf{P}}] \qquad \alpha = \rho_y}{[\beta^{\mathsf{P}}]\ \left(\mathbf{case}\ x\ \mathbf{of}\ \mathit{lift}\ y \Rightarrow e\right) = [\![v \lhd ((\rho \backslash y)[x \mapsto \alpha_{\oplus}])^{\mathsf{P}}]\!]} \qquad \begin{matrix} [\beta^{\mathsf{P}}]\ \text{strict} \\ x \text{ not free in } e \end{matrix} \tag{19}$$

$$\frac{[\beta_{\oplus}{}^{\mathsf{P}}]\ e = [v \lhd \rho^{\mathsf{P}}] \qquad \eta : \rho \sqsubseteq \rho' \qquad \overline{\mathsf{Abs}} \sqsubseteq \rho'}{[\beta_{\bot}{}^{\mathsf{P}}]\ e = [\![\mathbf{delay}\ (v \lhd \eta^{\mathsf{P}}) \lhd \rho'^{\mathsf{P}}]\!]} \tag{20}$$

Figure 9. Translation rules for expressions

$$\langle \alpha, id, id \rangle \in \alpha \,\&\, \alpha \qquad \langle \alpha, id, \lambda x.\, () \rangle \in \alpha \,\&\, \mathsf{Abs} \qquad \langle \mathsf{Fail}, \lambda x.\, \bot, \lambda x.\, \bot \rangle \in \alpha \,\&\, \mathsf{Fail}$$

$$\frac{\langle \gamma_1, \theta_1^{\mathsf{L}}, \theta_1^{\mathsf{R}} \rangle \in \alpha_1 \,\&\, \beta_1 \qquad \langle \gamma_2, \theta_2^{\mathsf{L}}, \theta_2^{\mathsf{R}} \rangle \in \alpha_2 \,\&\, \beta_2}{\langle \gamma_1 \times \gamma_2, \theta_1^{\mathsf{L}} \times \theta_2^{\mathsf{L}}, \theta_1^{\mathsf{R}} \times \theta_2^{\mathsf{R}} \rangle \in (\alpha_1 \times \alpha_2) \,\&(\beta_1 \times \beta_2)}$$

$$\frac{\langle \gamma_1, \theta_1^{\mathsf{L}}, \theta_1^{\mathsf{R}} \rangle \in \alpha_1 \,\&\, \beta_1 \qquad \langle \gamma_2, \theta_2^{\mathsf{L}}, \theta_2^{\mathsf{R}} \rangle \in \alpha_2 \,\&\, \beta_2}{\langle \gamma_1 + \gamma_2, \theta_1^{\mathsf{L}} + \theta_2^{\mathsf{L}}, \theta_1^{\mathsf{R}} + \theta_2^{\mathsf{R}} \rangle \in (\alpha_1 + \alpha_2) \,\&(\beta_1 + \beta_2)}$$

$$\frac{\langle \gamma, \theta^{\mathsf{L}}, \theta^{\mathsf{R}} \rangle \in \alpha \,\&\, \beta}{\langle \gamma_{\oplus}, \theta^{\mathsf{L}}, \theta^{\mathsf{R}} \rangle \in \alpha_{\oplus} \,\&\, \beta_{\oplus}} \qquad \frac{\alpha \sqsubseteq \gamma \qquad \eta : \beta \sqsubseteq \gamma \qquad \langle \delta, \theta^{\mathsf{L}}, \theta^{\mathsf{R}} \rangle \in \alpha \,\&\, \gamma}{\langle \delta_{\oplus}, \theta^{\mathsf{L}}, (\lambda z.\, \mathbf{delay}\ (\eta^{\mathsf{P}}\ z)) \circ \theta^{\mathsf{R}} \rangle \in \alpha_{\oplus} \,\&\, \beta_{\bot}}$$

$$\frac{\eta_1 : \alpha \sqsubseteq \gamma \qquad \eta_2 : \beta \sqsubseteq \gamma}{\langle \gamma, \eta_1{}^{\mathsf{P}}, \eta_2{}^{\mathsf{P}} \rangle \in \alpha \,\&\, \beta} \qquad \text{(used if no other rule applies)}$$

Figure 10. Rules for the & operation

Equations (18) and (19) cover only restricted forms, where the expression being analysed is a variable that does not occur free in the body of the **case**. In this way we avoid aliasing, giving simpler rules. However, no generality is lost, as any **case** expression may be re-written in this form using a **let**.

5.2 Active and Latent Contexts

Equations (13) and (19) have an extra side condition: the function $[\![\beta^{\mathsf{P}}]\!]$ must be strict, corresponding to a context in which the value is demanded.

A similar restriction arises in the translation of recursive functions. A function $f \triangleq \lambda x.e$ will be translated to a different partial function p for each context β. Since our contexts correspond to those of ordinary projection analysis [20, 13], we can use standard fixed point methods to compute the input context α for the required contexts β, and then read off the associated translation p for a particular β. Now the equations $[\![\beta^{\mathsf{P}}]\!] \circ f = [\![p \circ \alpha^{\mathsf{P}}]\!]$ are inductive, so they will hold for the fixed point functions if $[\![\beta^{\mathsf{P}}]\!]$ is strict.

For example, $\gamma_{\oplus}$ has a strict projection component, while $\gamma_{\perp}$ does not. Recall that the translation of *lift* in Fig. 8 also requires the strict form.

Wadler and Hughes [20] made all contexts strict by introducing a *guard rule*. We shall only do this where required by the above rules. They may be extended to contexts of the form $\beta_{\perp}$ using (20). That is, create a boxed closure, whose code evaluates v in an active context.

In most accounts of strictness analysis, all values are assumed to be of lifted type, so (20) covers all cases. In our lazy language, we require of the result type of the evaluation only that it be pointed. Hence it cannot be a sum, but it may be a product of pointed types. Now the context $\gamma \times \delta$ has a strict projection component if either of γ or δ have. Otherwise, in a context $\gamma \times \delta$ we can rewrite an evaluation using the equation

$$\begin{aligned}\textbf{case } x \textbf{ of } \mathit{lift}\ y \Rightarrow e = \textbf{let } z \triangleq (&\textbf{case } x \textbf{ of } \mathit{lift}\ y \Rightarrow \mathit{lift}\ e) \textbf{ in} \\ (&\textbf{case } z \textbf{ of } \mathit{lift}\ p \Rightarrow \mathit{fst}\ p, \\ &\textbf{case } z \textbf{ of } \mathit{lift}\ p \Rightarrow \mathit{snd}\ p)\end{aligned} \tag{21}$$

In the expression on the right-hand side, the first **case** is of lifted type, and thus will have a tractable context. The other two **case** have contexts γ and δ, which we treat inductively. The generated code for such fully latent pairs will not be efficient, but the programmer has left us little choice.

A similar device may be applied to recursively defined functions.

5.3 Polymorphism

Since our language allows expressions of pointed types in these positions, the other possibility is that the result type of an evaluation or recursive function is a type variable, constrained to pointed types. Such a case must be treated by instantiation of the type variable, creating a context more specific than the type of the expression.

Instantiation is also required in the calculation of certain upper bounds of contexts. This is because Fig. 6 gives no general rule for an upper bound of α and Abs.

However, if we constrain the language so that the types of these expressions must be products of lifted types, then our translation procedure will be polymorphic. Even this restriction is less stringent than the situation in languages like Haskell [11], where all expressions are of lifted type.

6 Conclusion

We have developed an algorithm to compile lazy functions to call-by-value forms. By basing the algorithm on projection-based strictness analysis, we were able to make use of latent demand information in the translation. Moreover, the rules of our algorithm are formulas over a simple functional language, and are hence easily verified.

The key step was factoring of the projections as embedding-projection pairs. In the present paper, we used only the projection components in a backwards analysis to expose strictness and perform unboxing. It is also possible (indeed simpler) to define a forwards analysis using the embeddings, delaying creation of closures, possibly permanently. It is also possible that other analyses using projections may benefit from factorization.

The principal shortcoming of our algorithm is inherited from the analysis on which it is based: it is limited to first-order functions. This is an obvious area for future work, perhaps using one of the higher-order extensions of projection analysis [7, 12].

Acknowledgements

John Launchbury suggested that an explicit treatment of lifting might enable the exploitation of projection-based strictness analysis. John Hughes, David Sands and anonymous referees gave suggestions for the presentation of this work. Nurith Goldblatt found some technical errors.

References

1. Torben Amtoft. Minimal thunkification. In Patrick Cousot et al., editors, *Static Analysis: 3rd International Workshop, WSA '93, Padova, Italy*, volume 724 of *Lecture Notes in Computer Science*, pages 218–229. Springer, 1993.
2. Andrew A. Appel. *Compiling with Continuations*. Cambridge University Press, 1992.
3. Geoffrey L. Burn, Chris Hankin, and Samson Abramsky. Strictness analysis of higher order functions. *Science of Computer Programming*, 7:249–278, 1986.
4. Geoffrey L. Burn and Daniel Le Métayer. Proving the correctness of compiler optimisations based on a global program analysis. In *Fifth International Symposium on Programming Language Implementation and Logic Programming*, volume 714 of

Lecture Notes in Computer Science, pages 346–364, Tallinn, Estonia, August 1993. Springer.

5. W. Clinger and J. Rees. Revised[4] report on the algorithmic language Scheme. *ACM Lisp Pointers*, IV, July–September 1991.
6. Olivier Danvy and John Hatcliff. CPS-transformation after strictness analysis. *ACM Letters on Programming Languages and Systems*, 1(3):195–212, 1992.
7. Kei Davis and Philip Wadler. Strictness analysis in 4D. In *1990 Glasgow Workshop on Functional Programming*, Workshops in Computing, pages 23–43. Springer, 1991.
8. Karl-Filip Faxén. Optimizing lazy functional programs using flow inference. In *Static Analysis, Second International Symposium*, volume 983 of *Lecture Notes in Computer Science*, pages 136–153. Springer, 1995.
9. Karl-Filip Faxén. Flow inference, code generation and garbage collection for lazy functional languages. Licentiate thesis, Kungl Tekniska Högskolan, January 1996.
10. Cordelia V. Hall and David S. Wise. Compiling strictness into streams. In *14th ACM Symposium on Principles of Programming Languages*, pages 132–143, Munich, January 1987.
11. Paul Hudak, Simon Peyton Jones, Philip Wadler, et al. Report on the programming language Haskell, a non-strict purely functional language (Version 1.2). *SIGPLAN Notices*, 27(5), March 1992.
12. Sebastian Hunt. *Abstract Interpretation of Functional Languages: From Theory to Practice.* PhD thesis, Imperial College of Science, Technology and Medicine, 1991.
13. Ryszard Kubiak, John Hughes, and John Launchbury. Implementing projection-based strictness analysis. In *1991 Glasgow Workshop on Functional Programming*, Workshops in Computing, pages 207–224. Springer, 1992.
14. T-M. Kuo and P. Mishra. Strictness analysis: A new perspective based on type inference. In *FPCA '89, London, England*, pages 260–272. ACM Press, September 1989.
15. John Launchbury and Gebreselassie Baraki. Representing demand by partial projections. *Journal of Functional Programming*, 6(4), 1996.
16. John Launchbury and Ross Paterson. Parametricity and unboxing with unpointed types. In *European Symposium on Programming*, volume 1058 of *Lecture Notes in Computer Science*, pages 204–218, Linköping, Sweden, April 1996.
17. Alan Mycroft. The theory and practice of transforming call-by-need into call-by-value. In B. Robinet, editor, *International Symposium on Programming*, volume 83 of *Lecture Notes in Computer Science*. Springer, 1980.
18. Simon L. Peyton Jones. Implementing lazy functional languages on stock hardware: the spineless tagless G-machine. *Journal of Functional Programming*, 2(2):127–202, July 1992.
19. Simon L. Peyton Jones and John Launchbury. Unboxed values as first class citizens in a non-strict functional language. In *Conference on Functional Programming Languages and Computer Architecture*, pages 636–666, Cambridge, MA, 1991.
20. Philip Wadler and John Hughes. Projections for strictness analysis. In *Conference on Functional Programming Languages and Computer Architecture*, volume 274 of *Lecture Notes in Computer Science*, Portland, OR, 1987.

Optimized Algorithms for Incremental Analysis of Logic Programs

Germán Puebla and *Manuel Hermenegildo*

{german,herme}@fi.upm.es
Department of Artificial Intelligence
Technical University of Madrid (UPM)

Abstract. Global analysis of logic programs can be performed effectively by the use of one of several existing efficient algorithms. However, the traditional global analysis scheme in which all the program code is known in advance and no previous analysis information is available is unsatisfactory in many situations. Incremental analysis of logic programs has been shown to be feasible and much more efficient in certain contexts than traditional (non-incremental) global analysis. However, incremental analysis poses additional requirements on the fixpoint algorithm used. In this work we identify these requirements, present an important class of strategies meeting the requirements, present sufficient a priori conditions for such strategies, and propose, implement, and evaluate experimentally a novel algorithm for incremental analysis based on these ideas. The experimental results show that the proposed algorithm performs very efficiently in the incremental case while being comparable to (and, in some cases, considerably better than) other state-of-the-art analysis algorithms even for the non-incremental case. We argue that our discussions, results, and experiments also shed light on some of the many tradeoffs involved in the design of algorithms for logic program analysis.

1 Introduction

Global program analysis is becoming a practical tool in logic program compilation and used to perform provably correct program optimizations [HWD92, RD92, MH92, SCWY91, BGH94, Bru91, Deb92]. Several generic analysis engines such as, for example, PLAI [MH92, MH90] and GAIA [CH94] facilitate construction of top-down analyzers. Different description domains and related functions render different analyzers which provide different types of information and degrees of accuracy. The core of such a generic engine is a specialized algorithm for efficient fixpoint computation, a subject that has received considerable attention [CC77, MH90, MH92, LDMH93, VWL94, Jor94].

Incremental analysis of logic programs has been shown to be feasible and much more efficient in certain contexts than traditional (non-incremental) global analysis [HMPS95, KB95]. In particular, [HMPS95] discussed the different types of changes that had to be dealt with in an incremental setting, provided overall solutions for dealing with such changes (in terms of which parts of the analysis graph need to be updated and recomputed), and proposed a basic set of solutions that showed the feasibility of the approach. It was also observed that incremental analysis poses additional requirements on the fixpoint algorithm used since some assumptions on the program that traditional algorithms make are no longer valid. The purpose of this work is to directly address this issue by identifying more concretely such requirements and to improve the performance of the fixpoint algorithm while meeting the requirements. We also aim to define, implement, and evaluate experimentally a novel algorithm for incremental analysis and compare it to some previously proposed algorithms for incremental as well as non-incremental analysis.

To the best of our knowledge, this is the first work dealing with the design and experimentation of fixpoint algorithms specially tailored for incremental analysis of logic programs. Additionally, our results imply performance improvements even in a non-incremental setting. Thus, we believe our discussions, results, and experiments may also clarify some of the many tradeoffs involved in the design of algorithms for logic program analysis in general.

2 Incremental Analysis Requirements

The aim of the kind of (goal oriented) program analysis performed by the analysis engines mentioned in the previous section is, for a particular description domain, to take a program and a set of initial *calling patterns* (descriptions of the possible calling modes into the program) and to annotate the program with information about the current environment at each program point whenever that point is reached when executing calls described by the calling patterns. The program points considered are entry to the rule, the point between each two literals, and return from the call. In essence, the analyzer must produce a program analysis graph. For example, for a standard operational semantics based on AND-OR trees, the analysis graph can be viewed as a finite representation (through a "widening") of the set of AND-OR trees explored by the concrete execution [Bru91]. For a given program and calling pattern there may be many different analysis graphs. However, for a given set of initial calling patterns, a program, and abstract operations on the descriptions, there is a unique *least analysis graph* which provides the most precise information possible. This analysis graph corresponds to the least fixpoint of the abstract semantic equations.

The aim of *incremental* global analysis is, given a program, its least analysis graph, and a series of changes to the program, to obtain the new least analysis graph as efficiently as possible. A simple but inefficient way of computing the new least analysis graph is just to discard the previous analysis graph and start analysis from scratch on the new program. However, much of the information in the previous analysis graph may still be valid, and incremental analysis should be able to reuse such information, instead of recomputing it from scratch.

Unfortunately, traditional fixpoint algorithms for abstract interpretation of logic programs cannot be used directly (at least in general) in the context of incremental analysis for reasons of accuracy, efficiency, and even correctness. This is because such algorithms assume that once a local fixpoint has been reached for a calling pattern, i.e., an *answer pattern* for this calling pattern has been computed, this information will not change and can be used safely thereafter. This assumption is no longer valid in the incremental case, since an answer pattern may become inaccurate if some clauses are eliminated from the program (*incremental deletion*) or even incorrect if more clauses are added to the program (*incremental addition*). When performing *arbitrary change* on the program (i.e., when both additions and deletions are performed), the old answer pattern can be incorrect, inaccurate, or both.

We now discuss two requirements that incremental analysis poses on the fixpoint algorithm.

Detailed Dependency Information: Most practical fixpoint algorithms try to make iterations as local as possible by using some kind of dependency information. Thanks to this information it is possible to revisit only a reduced set of nodes of the graph when an answer pattern changes during analysis. Additionally, dependency information can also be used to detect earlier that a fixpoint has been reached. The more accurate such dependency information is, the more localized (and, thus, less costly) the fixpoint iterations can be.

In the context of incremental analysis, in addition to localizing the fixpoint and detecting termination earlier, dependencies are useful for a third reason: they help locate the parts of the analysis graph that may be affected by program changes and which thus need to be recomputed as required by such changes. Obviously, if more detailed dependency information is kept track of, a smaller part of the analysis graph will have to be recomputed after modifying the program.

Propagation of Incrementally Updated Answer Patterns: Incremental deletion, local change, and arbitrary change ([HMPS95]) do not pose extra requirements on the analysis algorithm, provided that detailed dependency information is available, since such changes only require the analysis algorithms to deal with new calling patterns. However, in incremental addition, i.e., new clauses are added to a program already analyzed, the new clauses may also generate unexpected changes to previously computed answer patterns, i.e., they may update any answer pattern in the analysis graph. Once a global fixpoint has been reached, there is usually no way to propagate this updated information to the places in the analysis graph that may be affected using traditional analysis algorithms. If an algorithm is to deal efficiently with incremental addition it needs to be able to deal incrementally with the update of any answer pattern.

3 A Generic Analysis Algorithm

We now present a generic analysis algorithm taken from [HMPS95], that we will use as the basis for describing the optimized analysis algorithms proposed in the paper. We will refer to this algorithm simply as "the generic algorithm."

We first introduce some notation. CP, possibly subscripted, stands for a calling pattern (in the abstract domain). AP, possibly subscripted, stands for an answer pattern (in the abstract domain). Each literal in the program is subscripted with an identifier or pair of identifiers. $A : CP$ stands for an atom (unsubscripted) together with a calling pattern. Rules are assumed to be normalized and each rule for a predicate p has identical sets of variables $p(x_{p_1}, \ldots x_{p_n})$ in the head atom. Call this the *base form* of p. Rules in the program are written with a unique subscript attached to the head atom (the rule number), and dual subscript (rule number, body position) attached to each body atom (and constraint redundantly) e.g. $H_k \leftarrow B_{k,1}, \ldots, B_{k,n_k}$ where $B_{k,i}$ is a subscripted atom or constraint. The rule may also be referred to as rule k, the subscript of the head atom. E.g., the append program is written:

$$\texttt{app(X,Y,Z)}_1 \texttt{ :- } \texttt{X=[]}_{1,1}\texttt{, } \texttt{Y=Z}_{1,2}\texttt{.}$$
$$\texttt{app(X,Y,Z)}_2 \texttt{ :- } \texttt{X=[U|V]}_{2,1}\texttt{, } \texttt{Z=[U|W]}_{2,2}\texttt{, } \texttt{app(V,Y,W)}_{2,3}\texttt{.}$$

```
analyze(S)
   foreach A : CP ∈ S
      add_event(newcall(A : CP))
   main_loop()

main_loop()
   while E := next_event()
      if (E == newcall(A : CP))
         new_calling_pattern(A : CP)
      elseif (E == updated(A : CP))
         add_dependent_rules(A : CP)
      elseif (E == arc(R))
         process_arc(R)
   endwhile
   remove_useless_calls(S)

new_calling_pattern(A : CP)
   foreach rule A_k ← B_{k,1}, ..., B_{k,n_k}
      CP_1 := Aproject(CP, B_{k,1})
      add_event(arc(
         A_k : CP ⇒ [CP] B_{k,1} : CP_1))
   AP := initial_guess(A : CP)
   if (AP <> ⊥)
      add_event(updated(A : CP))
   add A : CP ↦ AP to answer_table

add_dependent_rules(A : CP)
   foreach arc of the form
         H_k : CP_0 ⇒ [CP_1] B_{k,i} : CP_2
         in dependency_arc_table
      where there exists renaming σ
         s.t. A : CP = (B_{k,i} : CP_2)σ
      add_event(arc(
         H_k : CP_0 ⇒ [CP_1] B_{k,i} : CP_2))

process_arc(H_k : CP_0 ⇒ [CP_1] B_{k,i} : CP_2)
   if (B_{k,i} is not a constraint)
      add H_k : CP_0 ⇒ [CP_1] B_{k,i} : CP_2
      to dependency_arc_table
   AP_0 := get_answer(B_{k,i} : CP_2)
   CP_3 := Acombine(CP_1, AP_0)
   if (CP_3 <> ⊥ and i <> n_k)
      CP_4 := Aproject(CP_3, B_{k,i+1})
      add_event( arc(
         H_k : CP_0 ⇒ [CP_3] B_{k,i+1} : CP_4))
   elseif (CP_3 <> ⊥ and i == n_k)
      AP_1 := Aproject(CP_3, H_k)
      insert_answer_info(H : CP_0 ↦ AP_1)

get_answer(L : CP)
   if (L is a constraint)
      return Aadd(L, CP)
   else  return lookup_answer(L, CP)

lookup_answer(A : CP)
   if (there exists a renaming σ s.t.
      σ(A : CP) ↦ AP in answer_table)
      return σ^{-1}(AP)
   else
      add_event(newcall(σ(A : CP)))
      where σ is a renaming s.t.
      σ(A) is in base form
      return ⊥

insert_answer_info(H : CP ↦ AP)
   AP_0 := lookup_answer(H : CP)
   AP_1 := Alub(AP, AP_0)
   if (AP_0 <> AP_1)
      add (H : CP ↦ AP_1) to answer_table
      add_event(updated(H : CP))
```

Fig. 1. Generic fixpoint algorithm

The program analysis graph is defined in terms of an initial set of calling patterns, a program, and four abstract operations on the description domain:

- *Aproject*(CP, L) which performs the abstract restriction of a calling pattern CP to the variables in the literal L;
- *Aadd*(C, CP) which performs the abstract operation of conjoining the actual constraint C with the description CP;
- *Acombine*(CP_1, CP_2) which performs the abstract conjunction of two descriptions;
- *Alub*(CP_1, CP_2) which performs the abstract disjunction of two descriptions.

The analysis graph has two sorts of nodes: those belonging to rules (also called "AND-nodes") and those belonging to atoms (also called "OR-nodes"). Atoms in the rule body have arcs to OR-nodes with the corresponding calling pattern.

If such a node is already in the tree it becomes a recursive call. The graph is implicitly represented in the algorithm by means of two data structures, the *answer table* and the *dependency arc table*. The answer table contains entries of the form $A : CP \mapsto AP$. A is always a base form. This represents a node in the analysis graph of the form $\langle A : CP \mapsto AP \rangle$. It is interpreted as the answer pattern for calls of the form CP to A is AP. A dependency arc is of the form $H_k : CP_0 \Rightarrow [CP_1]\ B_{k,i} : CP_2$. This is interpreted as follows: if the rule with H_k as head is called with calling pattern CP_0 then this causes literal $B_{k,i}$ to be called with calling pattern CP_2. The remaining part CP_1 is the program annotation just before $B_{k,i}$ is reached and contains information about all variables in rule k. CP_1 is not really necessary, but is included for efficiency. Dependency arcs represent the arcs in the program analysis graph from atoms in a rule body to an atom node.

Intuitively, the analysis algorithm is just a graph traversal algorithm which places entries in the answer table and dependency arc table as new nodes and arcs in the program analysis graph are encountered. To capture the different graph traversal strategies used in different fixpoint algorithms, a priority queue is used. Thus, the third, and final structure is a *prioritized event queue*. Events are of three forms. The first, *updated*$(A : CP)$, indicates that the answer pattern to atom A with calling pattern CP has been changed. The second, *arc*(R), indicates that the rule referred to in R needs to be (re)computed from the position indicated. The third, *newcall*$(A : CP)$, indicates that a new call has been encountered. The priority mechanism for the queue is left as a parameter of the algorithm.

Figure 1 shows the generic analysis algorithm. Apart from the parametric domain dependent functions, the algorithm has several other undefined functions. The functions add_event and next_event respectively add an event to the priority queue and return (and delete) the event of highest priority. When an event being added to the priority queue is already in the priority queue, a single event with the maximum of the priorities is kept in the queue. When an arc $H_k : CP \Rightarrow [CP'']B_{k,i} : CP'$ is added to the dependency arc table, it overwrites any other arcs of the form $H_k : CP \Rightarrow [\_]B_{k,i} : \_$ in the table and in the priority queue. The function initial_guess returns an initial guess for the answer to a new calling pattern. The default value is $\bot$ but if the calling pattern is more general than an already computed call then its current value may be returned. The procedure remove_useless_calls traverses the dependency graph given by the dependency arcs from the initial calls S and marks those entries in the dependency arc and answer table which are reachable. The remainder are removed.

In [HMPS95] the following results are presented:

Theorem 1. *For a program P and calling patterns S, the generic analysis algorithm returns an answer table and dependency arc table which represents the least program analysis graph of P and S.*

The corollary of this is that the priority strategy does not affect the correctness of the analysis.

Corollary 2. *The result of the generic analysis algorithm does not depend on the strategy used to prioritize events.*

4 Optimizing the Generic Algorithm

The algorithm presented in Section 3 is parametric with respect to the event handling strategy in the priority queue, in order to capture the behavior of several possible algorithms. Correctness of the analysis does not depend on the order in which events are processed. However, efficiency does.

The cost of analysis can be split into two components. The cost of computing the arc events, which for a given program P and a queuing strategy q will be denoted $\mathcal{C}_a(P,q)$, and the cost associated with dealing with the event queue which will be denoted $\mathcal{C}_q(P,q)$. There is clearly a trade-off between $\mathcal{C}_a(P,q)$ and $\mathcal{C}_q(P,q)$ in that a more sophisticated event handling strategy may result in a lower number of arcs traversed but at a higher event handling cost. We now discuss some possible optimizations to the generic fixpoint algorithm.

4.1 General Simplifications

Dealing Only with Arc Events in the Priority Queue: The original fixpoint algorithm in Section 3 has to deal with three different kinds of events, namely *updated*, *arc* and *newcall*. This can make the priority mechanism for the queue rather complicated. Looking at the actions performed for each one of these events and the optimizations presented below, it can be seen that the effect of both updated and newcall can be reduced to that of the arc events. Additionally, newcall performs an initial guess of the answer pattern. However, we will always use $\bot$ as the trivial initial guess for newcall events. Therefore, the event queue only needs to deal with arc events. Whenever the generic analysis algorithm would add to the queue an updated or newcall event, the optimized algorithm will directly add to the queue the required arc events.

In what follows, the current event queue will be denoted as Q and will be a set of triples $\langle arc, q(arc), type\rangle$, where *type* can be either newcall or updated and indicates whether such arc was introduced due to a newcall or an updated answer pattern, and q will be a function called ***queuing strategy*** that will assign a priority (a natural number) to each arc event. $\top(Q)$ is a function that returns (and deletes) from a non-empty queue Q an element with highest priority. A ***strongly connected component*** (SCC) in a directed graph is a set of nodes S such that $\forall n_1, n_2 \in S$ there is a path from n_1 to n_2.

Only One Priority per Rule and Calling Pattern: The generic algorithm makes an intensive use of the event queue. Without loss of generality, we will assign priorities to arcs at a somewhat coarser level. Instead of assigning a (possibly) different priority to each arc event, we will always assign the same priority to all the arcs for the same rule and calling pattern.

Never Switching from an Arc to Another with the Same Priority: Once computation for an arc has finished (no other arc with a higher priority can be in the queue), the generic algorithm would add the rest of the arc (if any) to the queue and retrieve one of the arcs with highest priority. Instead, as there cannot be any other arc with higher priority, it is always safe to continue with the arc just added to the queue. Rather than adding the rest of the arc and retrieving it immediately, it is more efficient to process it directly. This optimization allows using the queue only once for each rule and calling pattern.

Indexing the Dependency Arc Table: Whenever a pattern is updated, all the arcs that used the old (incorrect) pattern must be found in order to generate arc events for them. This is done in procedure `add_dependent_rules` by checking all the entries in the dependency arc table against the pattern that has been updated. This process has linear complexity in the size of the analysis graph. The proposed optimization implies keeping a table that for each calling pattern contains the set of arcs that have used this information. In such a way, the set of arcs that depend on a given calling pattern can be found in constant time.

4.2 Restricting the Set of Queueing Strategies

Definition 3 Dynamic Call Graph. The *dynamic call graph* of a program P, denoted as $D(P)$ is the graph obtained from the answer table and the dependency arc table generated for P by the generic analysis algorithm as follows: for each entry $A : CP \mapsto AP_0$ in the answer table create the node $A : CP$ and for each entry $H : CP_0 \Rightarrow [CP_1]\ B_{k,i} : CP_2$ in the dependency arc table create a arc from node $H : CP_0$ to node $B : CP_B$, where $B : CP_B$ is the unique calling pattern for which there exists a renaming σ s.t. $B : CP_B = (B_{k,i} : CP_2)\sigma$.

Definition 4 Reduced Call Graph. The *reduced call graph* of a program P, represented as $D_R(P)$ is the directed acyclic graph obtained by replacing each SCC in $D(P)$ by a single node in $D_R(P)$ labeled with the set of nodes in the SCC, and eliminating all arcs which are internal to the SCC.

Definition 5 SCC-preserving. A queuing strategy q is *SCC-preserving* if $\forall$ program P $\forall\langle A_1, q(A_1), type1\rangle, \langle A_2, q(A_2), type2\rangle \in Q$, where $A_1 = arc(H_k : CP_0 \Rightarrow [CP_1]\ B_{k,i} : CP_2)$ and $A_2 = arc(H_{k'} : CP_{0'} \Rightarrow [CP_{1'}]\ B_{k',i'} : CP_2')$: if there is a path in $D_R(P)$ from $H_k : CP_0$ to $H_{k'} : CP_{0'}$ then $q(A_1) < q(A_2)$.

Theorem 6. *For any program P and any queuing strategy q there is a queuing strategy q' which is SCC-preserving and $C_a(P, q') \leq C_a(P, q)$*

This theorem implies that if $C_q(P, q')$ is low enough, the set of queuing strategies considered can be restricted to those which are SCC-preserving. Definition 5 (SCC-preserving) is not operational because $D_R(P)$ cannot be computed until analysis has finished. It is thus an "a posteriori" condition. Next we give sufficient "a priori" conditions that ensure that a queuing strategy is SCC-preserving.

Definition 7 Newcall Selecting. Let $Q \neq \emptyset$ be a queue with $\langle A, q(A), type\rangle = \top(Q)$ where $A = arc(H_k : CP_0 \Rightarrow [CP_1]\ B_{k,i} : CP_2)$. Let $A_1, \ldots, A_n$ be the set of arc events which the event $newcall(B_{k,i} : CP_2)$ will insert in the queue. A queuing strategy q is *newcall selecting* iff $\forall\langle A', q(A'), type'\rangle \in Q\ \forall i = 1\ldots, n$: $q(A_i) > q(A')$.

The intuition behind a newcall selecting strategy is that analysis processes calling patterns in a depth-first fashion. Note also that if no recursive predicate appears in the program, the least fixpoint would be obtained in one iteration. If the queuing strategy is not newcall selecting, several iterations may be needed even for non-recursive programs.

Definition 8 Update Selecting. Let $Q \neq \emptyset$ be a queue with $\langle A, q(A), type \rangle = \top(Q)$. Suppose that after processing the last literal in A, an *updated*$(H : CP)$ event is generated. Let $A_1, \ldots, A_n$ be the set of arc events which the event *updated*$(H : CP)$ will insert in the queue and let $\langle A_k, q(A_k), newcall \rangle \in Q$ be such that $\forall \langle A', q(A'), newcall \rangle \in Q : q(A_k) \geq q(A')$. A queuing strategy q is *update selecting* iff $\forall \langle A', q(A'), type' \rangle \in Q\ \forall i = 1 \ldots, n : (q(A_k) \geq q(A')) \rightarrow (q(A_i) > q(A'))$.

I.e., the arc events generated by an updated event must have higher priority than any existing arc in the queue except for the arcs of updated type that were introduced after the last newcall.

When update selecting strategies are used together with delayed dependencies introduced below, the analysis algorithm iterates whenever an answer pattern may not be final rather than using this possibly incorrect information in parts of the analysis graph outside the SCC the answer pattern belongs to.

Delaying Entries in the Dependency Arc Table: This modification to the generic algorithm consists in executing "$AP_0 :=$ get_answer$(B_{k,i} : CP_2)$" before the conditional "**if** ($B_{k,i}$ is not a constraint) add (...) to dependency_arc_table" in the procedure process_arc in the generic algorithm. The aim is not no introduce any dependency until an answer pattern is actually used.

Notice than in this case we are not restricting the set of considered queuing strategies but rather we are modifying the generic algorithm itself.

Theorem 9 Delaying Dependencies. *If the queuing strategy is newcall and update selecting then the algorithm obtained from the generic one by delaying dependencies produces the same analysis results as the generic algorithm.*

Theorem 10. *If dependencies are delayed and the queuing strategy is newcall and update selecting then all the arc events generated by an updated$(A : CP)$ event belong to the same SCC as $A : CP$.*

Suppose that when processing the event *arc*$(H_k : CP_0 \Rightarrow [CP_1]\ B_{k,i} : CP_2)$, the answer pattern for $B_{k,i} : CP_2$ is updated m times. In the worst case, the continuation of *arc*$(H_k : CP_0 \Rightarrow [CP_1]\ B_{k,i} : CP_2)$ would be computed m times. Additionally, this computation may generate an *updated*$(H_k : CP_0)$ event which may in turn generate update events for any calling pattern in the analysis graph. This theorem ensures that unless $B_{k,i} : CP_2$ and $H_k : CP_0$ are in the same SCC, the continuation of the arc will only be computed once due to updated values of $B_{k,i} : CP_2$, independently of the number of times the answer pattern for $B_{k,i} : CP_2$ is updated and the number of iterations needed to compute it.

Theorem 11 SCC-preserving. *If dependencies are delayed then if a queuing strategy q is newcall selecting and update selecting then q is SCC-preserving.*

This is a sufficient "a priori" condition to obtain SCC-preserving strategies.

4.3 Parametric Strategies

Ordering Arcs from Newcall Events – the Newcall Strategy: Although SCC-preserving strategies are efficient in general, for any given program P different SCC-preserving strategies may have different values for $C_a(P, q)$ and $C_q(P, q)$. There are still several degrees of freedom associated with the event handling

```
analyze(S)
  foreach A : CP ∈ S
    new_calling_pattern(A : CP)

process_update(Updates)
  if Updates = A1 :: As
    UAs := process_arc(A1)
    NAs :=
    global_updating_strategy(As, UAs)
    process_update(NAs)

insert_answer_info(H : CP ↦ AP)
  AP0 := lookup_answer(H : CP)
  AP1 := Alub(AP, AP0)
  A := {}
  if (AP0 <> AP1)
    add (H : CP ↦ AP1) to answer_table
    foreach arc of the form
      Hk : CP0 ⇒ [CP1] Bk,i : CP2
      in dependency_arc_table
      where there exists renaming σ
      s.t. H : CP = (Bk,i : CP2)σ
      A := A ⋃
        {Hk : CP0 ⇒ [CP1] Bk,i : CP2}
  return:=local_updating_strategy(A)

lookup_answer(A : CP)
  if (there exists a renaming σ s.t.
    σ(A : CP) ↦ AP in answer_table)
    return σ^-1(AP)
  else
    return σ^-1(
      new_calling_pattern(σ(A : CP)))
    where σ is a renaming s.t.
    σ(A) is in base form
```

```
new_calling_pattern(A : CP)
  add A : CP ↦ ⊥ to answer_table
  A0 := {}
  foreach rule Ak ← Bk,1, ..., Bk,nk
    CP1 := Aproject(CP, Bk,1)
    A0 := A0 ⋃
    {Ak : CP ⇒ [CP] Bk,1 : CP1}
  Arcs := newcall_strategy(A0)
  process_newcall(Arcs)
  Let σ be a renaming s.t.
    σ(A : CP) ↦ AP in answer_table
    return σ^-1(AP)

process_newcall(NewCalls)
  if NewCalls = A1 :: As
    UArcs := process_arc(A1)
    process_update(UArcs)
    process_newcall(As)

process_arc(Hk : CP0 ⇒ [CP1] Bk,i : CP2)
  if (Bk,i is not a constraint)
    AP0 := lookup_answer(Bk,i : CP2)
    add Hk : CP0 ⇒ [CP1] Bk,i : CP2
    to dependency_arc_table
  else
    AP0 := Aadd(Bk,i, CP2)
  CP3 := Acombine(CP1, AP0)
  if (CP3 <> ⊥ and i <> nk)
    CP4 := Aproject(CP3, Bk,i+1)
    U := process_arc(
      Hk : CP0 ⇒ [CP3] Bk,i+1 : CP4)
  elseif (CP3 <> ⊥)
    AP1 := Aproject(CP3, Hk)
    U := insert_answer_info(
        H : CP0 ↦ AP1)
  return U
```

Fig. 2. Optimized SCC-preserving analysis algorithm

strategy. The first one, which we will call the *newcall strategy* refers to the priorities among the different arcs generated by a single newcall (there will be one arc event per clause defining the called predicate). We know that all of them should have a higher priority than the existing arcs, but nothing has been said up to now about their relative priorities.

Ordering Arcs from Updated Events – the Updating Strategy: The newcall selecting condition is in a sense stronger than the updating strategy condition. The newcall selecting condition requires the new arcs to be assigned priorities which are higher than any other existing one. Therefore, there is even more freedom to assign priorities to arcs generated by updated events. The approach taken will be to split the updating strategy into two components. One is the relative order of the arc events introduced by a single updated event (*local updating strategy*). The other one is the order of these new arc events with respect to the already existing updated type arc events in the queue that were

```
incremental_addition(R)
  A_0 = {}
  foreach rule A_k <- B_{k,1}, ..., B_{k,n_k} ∈ R
    foreach entry A : CP ↦ AP
      in the answer_table
      CP_1 := Aproject(CP, B_{k,1})
      A_0 = A_0 ∪
        {A_k : CP ⇒ [CP] B_{k,1} : CP_1}
  A := inc_updating_strategy(A_0)
  process_inc_update(A)

process_inc_update(Updates)
  if Updates = A_1 :: As
    U := process_arc(A_1)
    NAs :=
      inc_updating_strategy(As, U)
    process_inc_update(NAs)
```

Fig. 3. Incremental Addition Algorithm

introduced in the queue later than any newcall type arc event (*global updating strategy*).

5 An Optimized Analysis Algorithm

Figure 2 presents an optimized analysis algorithm in which dependencies are delayed. It also ensures that the newcall selecting and updating selecting conditions will hold, thus always providing SCC-preserving strategies (Theorem 11). It is parametric with respect to the newcall strategy and local and global updating strategies introduced above. Different choices of these strategies will provide different SCC-preserving instances of the algorithm with possibly different efficiency.

The two different types of arc events are treated separately by procedures `process_newcall` and `process_update`. Also, rather than having an external data structure for the queue, we will use explicit parameters to store the arc events that have to be processed. The run-time stack of procedure and function calls will isolate and store the arcs. Assuming the the pseudo-code used to describe the algorithm is sequential, the newcall selecting condition is satisfied because if no entry is stored for a calling pattern in the answer table, the procedure `look_up_answer` will have to wait for `new_calling_pattern` to finish before returning control to the calling `process_arc` procedure. The update selecting condition is also satisfied because in the procedure `process_newcall`, `process_update` is called after processing each arc and before executing the recursive call to `process_newcall` for the remaining arcs from the same newcall.

5.1 Augmenting the Algorithm for Incremental Addition

In order to cope with incremental addition, i.e., a set of rules R is added to a program, analysis should process each rule in R with all the existing calling patterns in the answer table for the predicate the rule belongs to. This is done by procedure `incremental_addition` in Figure 3. Note that a specialized version of procedure `process_update` which is called `process_inc_update` is used to start incremental analysis of the new arcs. However, in this case delaying dependencies is not possible because before incrementally analyzing the new clauses, a fixpoint will have been reached and all dependencies will have been introduced. Therefore, for any node $A : CP$ which existed in the analysis graph before incremental analysis started the arc events generated by an event *updated*$(A : CP)$ will not necessarily belong to the same SCC as $A : CP$ and analysis may no longer be SCC-preserving. Thus, it makes sense to use a more involved updating strategy for this case than for the non-incremental one in order to avoid unneeded recomputations. This strategy will be called the *inc_updating_strategy*. Incremental addition will be SCC-preserving or not depending on this strategy. However, for any new calling pattern in the analysis graph it is possible to delay dependencies and thus the algorithm in Figure 2 will be SCC-preserving for them. Thus, for such calling patterns it is profitable to use `process_update` whenever possible rather than `process_inc_update`. This is automatically achieved as the call to `process_arc` in procedure `process_inc_update` will always call `process_update` for any new calling pattern.

6 Experimental Results

A series of experiments has been performed for both the incremental and non-incremental case. The fixpoint algorithms we experiment with have been implemented as extensions to the PLAI generic abstract interpretation system. We argue that this makes comparisons between the new fixpoint algorithms and that of PLAI meaningful, since on the one hand PLAI is an efficient, highly optimized, state-of-the-art analysis system, and on the other hand the algorithms have been implemented using the same technology, with many data structures in common. They also share the domain dependent functions, which is *sharing+freeness* [MH91] in all the experiments.

Three analysis algorithms, as well as PLAI.[1] have been considered. **DD** is the algorithm for incremental analysis used in [HMPS95] (**Incr** or **I** in the experimental results). Both **DI** and **DI**$_S$ are instances of the algorithm presented in Figure 2, with the extensions for incremental addition presented in Figure 3. The difference between **DI** and **DI**$_S$ is the newcall strategy used. **DI**$_S$ uses the more elaborated strategy of computing the SCC of the static graph in order to give higher priority to non-recursive clauses. **DI** simply uses the lexical order of clauses to assign them different priorities. Both use the same updating strategy: the local strategy is to process arcs in the order they were introduced in the dependency arc table, and the global strategy is to use a LIFO stack and eliminate subsumed arcs , i.e., other arcs in the queue exist which ensure that their computation is redundant. Due to lack of space, subsumed arcs are not studied here [PH96]. The incremental updating strategy is to use a FIFO queue and eliminate subsumed arcs. **DD** uses *depth-dependent* and both **DI** and **DI**$_S$ *depth-independent* propagations ([PH96]).

6.1 Analysis Times for the Non-Incremental Case

Table 1 shows the analysis times for a series of benchmark programs using the algorithms mentioned above. Times are in milliseconds on a Sparc 10 (SICStus 2.1, fastcode). A relatively wide range of programs has been used as benchmarks. They can be obtained from `http://www.clip.dia.fi.upm.es`. However, the number of clauses is included in the table (column **Cl**) for reference. **DD_SU**, **DI**$_S$**_SU** and **DI_SU** are the speed-ups obtained in analysis time by each fixpoint algorithm with respect to PLAI. As already observed in [HMPS95], the performance of **DD** is almost identical to that of PLAI (it introduces no relevant

[1] The algorithm used for PLAI is the one in the standard distribution which has been augmented to keep track of detailed dependencies that are later used in multiple specialization [PH95]. This introduces a small overhead over the original algorithm.

Bench.	CI	PLAI	DD	DI_S	DI	DD_SU	DI_S_SU	DI_SU
aiakl	12	3526	3532	2563	2483	1.00	1.38	1.42
ann	170	6572	6593	6615	6906	1.00	0.99	0.95
bid	50	783	779	769	789	1.01	1.02	0.99
boyer	133	2352	2346	2339	2475	1.00	1.01	0.95
browse	29	329	339	343	393	0.97	0.96	0.84
deriv	10	420	436	421	406	0.96	1.00	1.03
fib	3	29	36	29	33	0.81	1.00	0.88
grammar	15	132	128	129	119	1.03	1.02	1.11
hanoiapp	4	579	565	619	539	1.02	0.94	1.07
mmatrix	6	309	306	312	326	1.01	0.99	0.95
occur	8	296	299	316	273	0.99	0.94	1.08
peephole	134	5855	5919	4870	5090	0.99	1.20	1.15
progeom	18	199	199	199	219	1.00	1.00	0.91
qplan	148	1513	1499	1422	1383	1.01	1.06	1.09
qsortapp	7	346	332	323	402	1.04	1.07	0.86
query	52	108	116	109	89	0.93	0.99	1.21
rdtok	54	2528	2509	1316	1209	1.01	1.92	2.09
read	88	44362	44259	14123	11765	1.00	3.14	3.77
serialize	12	629	629	663	616	1.00	0.95	1.02
tak	2	98	99	102	103	0.99	0.96	0.95
warplan	101	3439	3352	2789	2803	1.03	1.23	1.23
witt	160	1902	1902	1762	1738	1.00	1.08	1.09
zebra	18	3376	3356	3362	3259	1.01	1.00	1.04
					Overall	(1.00) 1.00	(1.13) 1.75	(1.12) 1.84

Table 1. Analysis Times for the Non-Incremental Case

overhead) but has the advantage of being able to deal with incremental addition. On the other hand, both **DI** and **DI**$_S$ show significant advantage with respect to **DD** (and PLAI). **DI** is the most efficient of the three, but the margin over **DI**$_S$ is small. Two overall speed-ups appear in the table for each algorithm. The one in brackets represents the overall speed-up after eliminating the **read** benchmark, because of the atypical results. The relative advantage of **DI** and **DI**$_S$ is inverted in this case. The peculiarity in **read** stems from the fact that the dynamic call graph has many cycles with lengths that are as high as 13. However, even when taking **read** out **DI** and **DI**$_S$ are both still somewhat better that **DD** and PLAI.

6.2 Analysis Times for the Incremental Case

Among the different types of incremental change identified in [HMPS95] the one which is really relevant for experimentation is incremental addition. The performance of the fixpoint algorithms in the other types of changes will be directly related to the efficiency of the algorithms in the non-incremental case, as no incremental update propagation is needed. Table 2 shows the analysis times for the same benchmarks but adding the clauses one by one. I.e., the analysis was first run for the first clause only. Then the next clause was added and the resulting program (re-)analyzed. This process was repeated until the last clause of the program. The total time involved in this process is given by **DD**, **DI**$_S$, and **DI**. Columns $\mathbf{SU}_{DD}$, $\mathbf{SU}_{DI_S}$, and $\mathbf{SU}_{DI}$ contain the speed-up obtained with respect to analyzing with the same algorithm the program clause by clause but erasing the analysis graph between analyses. Thus, it is a measure of the incrementality of each algorithm. An important speed-up is observed in $\mathbf{SU}_{DD}$

Bench.	DD	DI_S	DI	SU_{DD}	SU_{DI_S}	SU_{DI}	SD_{DD}	SD_{DI_S}	SD_{DI}
aiakl	3860	3527	3237	1.52	1.38	1.29	1.09	1.38	1.30
ann	41680	25686	8120	12.66	22.82	72.83	6.32	3.88	1.18
bid	4220	2240	1433	3.82	6.54	9.80	5.42	2.91	1.82
boyer	20029	9039	3870	13.00	29.21	69.35	8.54	3.86	1.56
browse	1110	652	556	5.61	3.91	4.82	3.27	1.90	1.41
deriv	3083	1570	1126	0.54	1.63	2.07	7.07	3.73	2.77
fib	57	49	49	1.68	1.96	1.84	1.58	1.69	1.48
grammar	510	300	209	2.41	4.17	5.34	3.98	2.33	1.76
hanoiapp	990	779	816	1.37	1.86	1.46	1.75	1.26	1.51
mmatrix	709	360	343	1.37	2.67	3.12	2.32	1.15	1.05
occur	456	396	322	1.32	3.73	3.97	1.53	1.25	1.18
peephole	59899	15333	8533	8.66	28.19	52.05	10.12	3.15	1.68
progeom	389	360	283	2.63	2.87	3.44	1.95	1.81	1.29
qplan	39890	11303	2342	3.69	12.42	56.94	26.61	7.95	1.69
qsortapp	623	506	466	1.81	2.17	2.73	1.88	1.57	1.16
query	2296	919	277	2.23	7.14	20.32	19.79	8.43	3.11
rdtok	24176	3822	2363	1.66	6.96	10.06	9.64	2.90	1.95
read	176779	35760	22160	5.57	8.16	11.28	3.99	2.53	1.88
serialize	1496	1290	973	2.23	2.63	3.25	2.38	1.95	1.58
tak	139	120	113	1.31	1.75	1.77	1.40	1.18	1.10
warplan	41999	9436	5479	2.69	10.71	17.32	12.53	3.38	1.95
witt	19336	18606	2523	3.08	3.37	17.57	10.17	10.56	1.45
zebra	8580	2716	2480	4.87	15.32	16.44	2.56	0.81	0.76
Overall	6.64	2.13	1	6.15	13.74	28.36	5.69	3.18	1.57

Table 2. Incremental Addition Times

(as already noted in [HMPS95]), but the incrementality of $\mathbf{DI}_S$ is twice as high, and that for **DI** in turn twice as high as that of $\mathbf{DI}_S$.

The last three columns in the table contain the slow-downs for clause by clause incremental analysis with respect to the time taken by the same algorithm when analyzing the file all at once. If we use the **DD** algorithm in an incremental way, the overhead resulting from analyzing clause by clause is greatly reduced with respect to the non-incremental case. However, the time required if we use **DI** incrementally is only about 3/2 of the time required to analyze the program all at once. There is even one case (the `zebra` benchmark) in which using the **DI** algorithm clause by clause is somewhat faster than analyzing the program all at once. However, we believe this is related to working set size and cache memory effects, as the number of arc events processed in both cases (presented in Table 3) is almost the same. In the **Overall** row we give the average analysis times for each algorithm, taking as unit the time for analysis clause by clause using the **DI** algorithm. At least for the benchmark programs **DI** is more than twice as fast as $\mathbf{DI}_S$ and more than 6 times faster than **DD** ([HMPS95]).

6.3 Measuring $C_a(P, q)$: Number of Arc Events

Table 3 shows the number of arc events needed to analyze each benchmark program in both the non-incremental and incremental case using the **DI** algorithm. This is equivalent to counting the number of times the function `process_arc` in the algorithm in Figure 2 is called (including any recursive calls) from (**N**) `process_newcall`, (**U**) `process_update`, and (**UI**) `process_inc_update`. **T** is the total number of arc events processed. $_I$ is used for the incremental case. The last row in the table shows the number of arc events of each type needed to

Bench.	N	U	T	U/T	N_I	U_I	UI_I	T_I	UI_I/T_I
aiakl	50	19	69	0.28	52	8	76	136	0.56
ann	570	179	749	0.24	496	203	101	800	0.13
bid	191	14	205	0.07	144	10	165	319	0.52
boyer	248	70	318	0.22	82	34	330	446	0.74
browse	41	19	60	0.32	21	3	78	102	0.76
deriv	24	1	25	0.04	0	0	52	52	1.00
fib	14	3	17	0.18	6	3	8	17	0.47
grammar	24	0	24	0	2	0	28	30	0.93
hanoiapp	21	15	36	0.42	18	11	26	55	0.47
mmatrix	10	9	19	0.47	2	3	14	19	0.74
occur	15	14	29	0.48	12	12	4	28	0.14
peephole	255	170	425	0.40	180	23	440	643	0.68
progeom	41	9	50	0.18	38	9	3	50	0.06
qplan	384	41	425	0.10	205	31	235	471	0.50
qsortapp	44	15	59	0.25	23	4	41	68	0.60
query	59	0	59	0	0	0	62	62	1.00
rdtok	332	33	365	0.09	145	24	328	497	0.66
read	840	155	995	0.16	720	22	1398	2140	0.65
serialize	43	15	58	0.26	16	1	102	119	0.86
tak	27	5	32	0.16	17	5	10	32	0.31
warplan	330	38	368	0.10	169	13	362	544	0.67
witt	389	39	428	0.09	352	36	44	432	0.10
zebra	51	2	53	0.04	28	2	24	54	0.44
Overall	4003	865	4868	0.18	2728	457	3931	7116	0.45

Table 3. Number of *arc* Events Processed

analyze all the benchmarks. The remaining two columns (**U/T** and $\mathbf{UI}_I/\mathbf{T}_I$) give respectively the ratio of the total arc events that were due to update events in the non-incremental case and those due to the newly introduced clauses in the incremental case. **U/T** gives an idea of how much analysis effort is due to fixpoint computation for recursive calls. These figures show that using a good analysis algorithm, less than 20% of the effort is due to iterations. $\mathbf{UI}_I/\mathbf{T}_I$ gives the ratio of the computation performed by `process_inc_update` (which may use a more complex updating strategy). The ratio between the total number of arcs computed in the incremental and non-incremental case explains the slow-down associated to the analysis clause by clause. It is $7116 \div 4868 = 1.46$ in number of arc events processed and 1.57 in analysis times for the **DI** algorithm. The table also seems to imply that, for the strategies used, counting arc events is a good (and architecture independent) indicator of analysis time.

7 Acknowledgments

This work has benefited greatly from discussions with K. Marriott and P. Stuckey.

References

[BGH94] F. Bueno, M. García de la Banda, and M. Hermenegildo. Effectiveness of Global Analysis in Strict Independence-Based Automatic Program Parallelization. In *International Symposium on Logic Programming*, pages 320–336. MIT Press, November 1994.

[Bru91] M. Bruynooghe. A Practical Framework for the Abstract Interpretation of Logic Programs. *Journal of Logic Programming*, 10:91–124, 1991.

[CC77] P. Cousot and R. Cousot. Abstract Interpretation: a Unified Lattice Model for Static Analysis of Programs by Construction or Approximation of Fixpoints. In *Fourth ACM Symposium on Principles of Programming Languages*, pages 238–252, 1977.

[CH94] B. Le Charlier and P. Van Hentenryck. Experimental Evaluation of a Generic Abstract Interpretation Algorithm for Prolog. *ACM Transactions on Programming Languages and Systems*, 16(1):35–101, 1994.

[Deb92] S. Debray, editor. *Journal of Logic Programming, Special Issue: Abstract Interpretation*, volume 13(1–2). North-Holland, July 1992.

[HMPS95] M. Hermenegildo, K. Marriott, G. Puebla, and P. Stuckey. Incremental Analysis of Logic Programs. In *International Conference on Logic Programming*. MIT Press, June 1995.

[HWD92] M. Hermenegildo, R. Warren, and S. Debray. Global Flow Analysis as a Practical Compilation Tool. *Journal of Logic Programming*, 13(4):349–367, August 1992.

[Jor94] N. Jorgensen. Finding Fixpoints in Finite Function Spaces Using Neededness Analysis and Chaotic Iteration. In *International Static Analysis Symposium*. Springer-Verlag, 1994.

[KB95] A. Krall and T. Berger. Incremental global compilation of prolog with the vienna abstract machine. In *International Conference on Logic Programming*. MIT Press, June 1995.

[LDMH93] B. Le Charlier, O. Degimbe, L. Michel, and P. Van Henteryck. Optimization Techniques for General Purpose Fixpoint Algorithms: Practical Efficiency for the Abstract Interpretation of Prolog. In *International Workshop on Static Analysis*. Springer-Verlag, 1993.

[MH90] K. Muthukumar and M. Hermenegildo. Deriving A Fixpoint Computation Algorithm for Top-down Abstract Interpretation of Logic Programs. Technical Report ACT-DC-153-90, Microelectronics and Computer Technology Corporation (MCC), Austin, TX 78759, April 1990.

[MH91] K. Muthukumar and M. Hermenegildo, Combined Determination of Sharing and Freeness of Program Variables Through Abstract Interpretation. In *International Conference on Logic Programming*, MIT Press, June 1991.

[MH92] K. Muthukumar and M. Hermenegildo. Compile-time Derivation of Variable Dependency Using Abstract Interpretation. *Journal of Logic Programming*, 13(2 and 3):315–347, July 1992.

[PH95] G. Puebla and M. Hermenegildo. Implementation of Multiple Specialization in Logic Programs. In *Proc. ACM SIGPLAN Symposium on Partial Evaluation and Semantics Based Program Manipulation*. ACM, June 1995.

[PH96] G. Puebla and M. Hermenegildo. Optimized Algorithms for Incremental Analysis of Logic Programs. Technical Report CLIP3/96.0, Facultad de Informática, UPM, 1996.

[RD92] P. Van Roy and A.M. Despain. High-Performace Logic Programming with the Aquarius Prolog Compiler. *IEEE Computer Magazine*, pages 54–68, January 1992.

[SCWY91] V. Santos-Costa, D.H.D. Warren, and R. Yang. The Andorra-I Preprocessor: Supporting Full Prolog on the Basic Andorra Model. In *1991 International Conference on Logic Programming*. MIT Press, June 1991.

[VWL94] B. Vergauwen, J. Wauman, and J. Levi. Efficient Fixpoint Computation. In *International Static Analysis Symposium*. Springer-Verlag, 1994.

Tractable Constraints in Finite Semilattices

Jakob Rehof and Torben Æ. Mogensen

DIKU, Department of Computer Science,
Universitetsparken 1, DK-2100 Copenhagen Ø, Denmark.
Electronic mail: {rehof, torbenm}@diku.dk
Fax: +45 35 32 14 01

Abstract. We introduce the notion of *definite* inequality constraints involving monotone functions in a finite meet-semilattice, generalizing the logical notion of Horn-clauses, and we give a linear time algorithm for deciding satisfiability. We characterize the expressiveness of the framework of definite constraints and show that the algorithm uniformly solves exactly the set of all meet-closed relational constraint problems, running with small linear time constant factors for any fixed problem. We give an alternative technique which reduces inequalities to satisfiability of Horn-clauses (HORNSAT) and study its efficiency. Finally, we show that the algorithm is complete for a maximal class of tractable constraints, by proving that *any* strict extension will lead to **NP**-hard problems in any meet-semilattice.

Keywords: Finite semilattices, constraint satisfiability, program analysis, tractability, algorithms.

1 Introduction

Many program analysis problems can be solved by generating a set of constraints over some domain and then solving these. Examples include the binding time analyses described in [11], [2] and [3], the usage count analysis in [17] and the region-size analysis described in [1]. See also Section 6 below.

In this paper we show how to solve certain classes of constraints over finite domains efficiently, and characterize classes that are not tractable. The solution methods can be used as a tool for analysis designers, and the characterization can help the designer recognize when an analysis may have bad worst-case behaviour.

Due to space limitations, details of proofs are left out. Full details can be found in [19].

2 Monotone function problems

Let P be a poset and F a finite set of monotone functions $f : P^{a_f} \to P$ with $a_f \geq 1$ the *arity* of f. We call the pair $\Phi = (P, F)$ a *monotone function problem* (MFP for short.) Given $\Phi = (P, F)$ we let T_Φ denote the set of *Φ-terms*, ranged over by τ, σ and given by $\tau ::= \alpha \mid c \mid f(\tau_1, \ldots, \tau_{a_f})$, where c ranges over constants in P, and α, β, γ range over a denumerably infinite set $\mathcal{V}$ of variables and f is a function symbol corresponding to $f \in F$. Constants and variables are collectively referred to as *atoms*, and we let A range over atoms. We assume a fixed enumeration of $\mathcal{V}$, $\mathcal{V} = v_1, v_2, \ldots, v_n, \ldots$ For each number $m > 0$ we let $\mathcal{V}_m$ denote the sequence of the m first variables in the enumeration of $\mathcal{V}$. Let $\rho \in S^m$ for some set S. We write $[\rho]_i$ for the i'th coordinate of ρ, $i \in \{1, \ldots, m\}$. Any $\rho \in S^m$ is implicitly considered a mapping $\rho : \mathcal{V}_m \to S$ by defining $\rho(v_i)$ to be $[\rho]_i$, for $i \in \{1, \ldots, m\}$. For $\rho \in S^m, 1 \leq k \leq m$ we let $\rho \downarrow k = ([\rho]_1, \ldots, [\rho]_k) \in S^k$.

A *constraint set* C over Φ is a finite set of formal inequalities of the form $\tau \leq \tau'$ with $\tau, \tau' \in T_\Phi$. The set of distinct variables occurring in a term τ is denoted $Var(\tau)$, and if C is a constraint set, then $Var(C)$ denotes the set of distinct variables occurring in C. In this paper, *we always assume that* $Var(C) = \mathcal{V}_m$ *for some* m. If $\rho \in P^m$, τ a (P, F)-term with $Var(\tau) \subseteq \mathcal{V}_m$, then $[\![\tau]\!]\rho$ is given by $[\![\alpha]\!]\rho = \rho(\alpha)$, $[\![c]\!]\rho = c$, $[\![f(\tau_1, \ldots, \tau_k)]\!]\rho = f([\![\tau_1]\!]\rho, \ldots, [\![\tau_k]\!]\rho)$. The function $[\![\tau]\!]$ is monotone for every (P, F)-term τ.

If C is a constraint set over (P, F), $Var(C) \subseteq \mathcal{V}_m$, $\rho \in P^m$, we say that ρ is a *valuation of* C *in* P; we say that ρ *satisfies* C, written $P, \rho \models C$, iff $[\![\tau]\!]\rho \leq [\![\tau']\!]\rho$ holds in P for every $\tau \leq \tau'$ in C. We say that C is *satisfiable* if and only if there exists a valuation ρ of C in P such that $P, \rho \models C$. The set of *solutions* to C, denoted $Sol(C)$, is the set $\{\rho \in P^m \mid P, \rho \models C, Var(C) = \mathcal{V}_m\}$.

If $\Phi = (P, F)$ is an MFP, then we define the decision problem Φ-SAT to be the following: *Given a constraint set* C *over* Φ, *determine whether* C *is satisfiable.* We measure the size of a term by $|\tau|$, the number of occurrences of symbols (constants, variables and function symbols) in τ; the size of a constraint set C, $|C|$, is the number of occurrences of symbols in C. We assume that $f \in F$ are given by a_f-dimensional *operation matrixes* M_f with $M_f[x_1, \ldots, x_{a_f}] = f(x_1, \ldots, x_{a_f})$. Under this representation, evaluating a function f at given arguments $x_1, \ldots, x_{a_f}$ is a constant time operation, and hence evaluating an arbitrary functional term τ is $\mathcal{O}(|\tau|)$. If P is a lattice, the component P is assumed to be given as the set of elements of P together with an additional operation matrix, $M_\sqcup$, defining the least upper bound of L, i.e., $M_\sqcup[x, y] = x \sqcup y$. From this we can recover the order relation of P, using that $x \leq y$ iff $x \sqcup y = y$. This representation will be referred to as the *matrix representation*. As we shall see, this is also an appropriate representation when P is a semilattice, since this case will be reduced to the case where P is a lattice.

There are many problems Φ for which Φ-SAT is **NP**-hard (every problem Φ-SAT is obviously in **NP**, since we can guess and verify a solution non-deterministically in polynomial time.) For instance, for any non-trivial finite lattice L, the problem $\Phi = (L, \{\sqcap, \sqcup\})$ is **NP**-complete, by reduction from CNF-SAT (propositional satisfiability, [9]), since $(P_1 \wedge \ldots \wedge P_k) \Rightarrow (Q_1 \vee \ldots \vee Q_m)$ is logically satisfiable if and only if $(P_1 \sqcap \ldots \sqcap P_k) \leq (Q_1 \sqcup \ldots \sqcup Q_m)$ is satisfiable in a two-point chain. Also, the structure of the poset P is important for complexity, see [18]. Hence we need to impose restrictions on problems to make them tractable. In the following development we shall generally assume that P is a meet-semilattice. Note, though, that the whole development transfers to join-semilattices by lattice-theoretic dualization.

3 Definite problems

Let $\Phi = (P, F)$ be an MFP. A constraint set C over Φ in which every inequality is of the form $\tau \leq A$, with an atom on the right hand side, is called *definite*. A definite set $C = \{\tau_i \leq A_i\}_{i \in I}$ can be written $C = C_{var} \cup C_{cnst}$ where $C_{var} = \{\tau_j \leq \beta_j\}_{j \in J}$ are the *variable expressions* in C, having a variable (β_j) on the right hand side of $\leq$, and $C_{cnst} = \{\tau_k \leq c_k\}_{k \in K}$ are the *constant expressions* in C, having a constant (c_k) on the right hand side. Note that satisfiability of *definite* inequalities over $\Phi = (\mathbf{2}, \{\sqcap\})$, with $\mathbf{2}$ the two-point boolean lattice, is exactly the HORNSAT problem (satisfiability of propositional Horn clauses [10], [7]) since Horn clauses have the form $P_1 \wedge \ldots \wedge P_n \Rightarrow Q$.

A term τ will be called *simple* if τ is a constant, a variable or has the form $\tau = f(A_1, \ldots, A_m)$ *i.e.*, there are no nested function applications; a constraint set C is called simple if all terms in it are simple. The L-normalization $\rightarrow_L$ transforms a definite set into a simple and definite set: let C be definite, $C = C' \cup \{f(\ldots g(\tau) \ldots) \leq A\}$ with $Var(C) = \mathcal{V}_m$ and τ a tuple of terms, and define $\rightarrow_L$ by

$$C \rightarrow_L C' \cup \{f(\ldots v_{m+1} \ldots) \leq A, g(\tau) \leq v_{m+1}\}$$

Lemma 1. *The reduction $\rightarrow_L$ is strongly normalizing, and if C^* is a normal form of a definite set C, then C^* is definite with $|C^*| \leq 3|C|$.*

Monotonicity guarantees that an L-normalized set is equivalent to the original set:

Lemma 2. *If $C \rightarrow_L C'$ then $Sol(C) = \{\rho' \downarrow m \mid \rho' \in Sol(C')\}$ where $Var(C) = \mathcal{V}_m$.*

Figure 1 of Appendix A gives an algorithm, called D, for solving definite constraints over an MFP $\Phi = (L, F)$ with L a finite lattice [1] Algorithm D exploits L-normalization to achieve linear time worst case complexity. Later, we shall change D slightly into an algorithm $D^{\top}$ which works for meet-semilattices. Correctness of algorithm D follows from the properties: (1) after every update of the current valuation ρ at β, $\rho(\beta)$ increases strictly in the order of L, so in particular, termination follows, since L has finite height; (2) the iteration step finds the least solution μ to the set of *variable expressions* in C, so if any solution to C exists, then μ must also satisfy the *constant expressions*, by monotonicity of all functions $[\![\tau]\!]$.

[1] Algorithm D is similar to the technique of Kildall [16] for fast fixed point computation in data-flow frameworks and also to the linear time algorithm of Dowling and Gallier [7] for solving the HORNSAT-problem. In fact, the iteration step is easily seen to be equivalent to a search for the least fixed point of a monotone operator F on a lattice, since the least fixed point of F is identical to the least post-fixed point of F. We already observed (beginning of Section 3) that definite inequalities strictly subsume Horn clauses. See Section 4.1 and Section 4.2 for more on the connection to Horn clauses.

Theorem 3. *(Correctness) If C has a solution over Φ, then it has a minimal solution, and algorithm D outputs ρ the minimal solution of C, and if C has no solution, then the algorithm fails.*

Linear time complexity for algorithm D can be shown by amortizing the number of times the test of the conditional in the **for**-loop, $L, \rho \not\models \sigma \leq \gamma$, can be executed *in total* on input C, in the worst case. We can assume (Lemma 1) that C is in L-normal form modulo an expansion by a factor 3. Let $h(L)$ denote the height of a finite lattice L, *i.e.*, the maximal length of a chain in L, then we have

Theorem 4. *(Complexity) For fixed MFP Φ algorithm D runs in time $\mathcal{O}(|C|)$ and performs at most $3h(L) \cdot |C|$ basic computations on input C.*

Algorithm D operates uniformly in Φ, so it can be considered a decision procedure for the *uniform* problem: *Given Φ and constraint set C over Φ, is C satisfiable?*. In this case, taking $h(L) = |L|$ in the worst case, $|L|^{a_{max}}$ the size of the function matrixes with a_{max} the maximal arity of functions in Φ, we have input size $N = |L| + |L|^{a_{max}} + |C|$. With log-cost for a matrix look-up we get a maximum cost of $\mathcal{O}(a_{max} \cdot \log|L|)$ for a basic computation, resulting in $\mathcal{O}(a_{max} \cdot \log|L| \cdot |L| \cdot N)$ worst case behaviour for the uniform problem.

Algorithm D generalizes to the cases where the poset is a finite meet-semi-lattice, as follows. Let $P^{\top}$ denote the lattice obtained from P by adding a top element $\top$, taking $c \leq \top$ for all $c \in P$. We change algorithm D by adding the test **if** $\exists\alpha.\, \rho(\alpha) = \top$ **then** FAIL at the beginning of the output step. We extend the functions in Φ such that $f(x_1, \ldots, x_{a_f}) = \top$ if any $x_i = \top$. This modification of algorithm D will be referred to as algorithm $D^{\top}$. Algorithm $D^{\top}$ is obviously sound, by soundness of algorithm D, and it is a complete decision procedure for semi-lattices, since if P has no top element and the least solution to the variable expressions in C maps a variable to the top element of $P^{\top}$, then clearly C can have no solutions in P.

4 Relational problems

Inequality constraints are a special case of the much more general framework of relational constraints. A *relational constraint problem* is a pair $\Gamma = (P, \mathcal{S})$ with P a finite poset and $\mathcal{S}$ a finite set of finite relations $R \subseteq P^{a_R}$, with $1 \leq a_R$ (the arity of R.) Any $R \subseteq P^k$ is called a *relation over* P. A *relational constraint set* C over Γ is a finite set of *Γ-terms* of the form $R(A_1, \ldots, A_{a_R})$ where A ranges over variables in $\mathcal{V}$ and constants drawn from P. The size of a constraint term $t = R(A_1, \ldots, A_{a_R})$ is $|t| = a_R$; the size $|C|$ of a constraint set is the sum of the sizes of all terms in C. We say that a constraint set C is *satisfiable* if there exists a valuation ρ of C in P such that $([\![A_1]\!]\rho, \ldots, [\![A_{a_R}]\!]\rho) \in R$ for every term $R(A_1, \ldots, A_{a_R})$ in C. If $Var(C) = \mathcal{V}_m$, then $Sol(C)$ is the set of valuations $\rho \in P^m$ satisfying C. We define the decision problem Γ-SAT to be: *Given a constraint set C over Γ, is C satisfiable?* If $x \in P^m$ and $1 \leq i \leq m$ then $[x]_i$

denotes the i'th coordinate of x. We use the vector notation $\mathbf{x} = (x_1, \ldots, x_m)$, and if $R \subseteq P^m$ we write $R(\mathbf{x})$ as an abbreviation for $R(x_1, \ldots, x_m)$ also when this expression is considered a term.

4.1 Representability

We are interested in the following question: How many relational constraint problems can be (efficiently) solved using algorithm D? This translates to the question: How many problems can be transformed into definite inequality problems and what is the cost of the transformation?

A relation $R \subseteq P^m$ is called *representable* with respect to a constraint problem $\Gamma = (P, \mathcal{S})$ if $R = Sol(C)$ for some constraint set C over Γ. We say that a problem Γ is a *problem with inequality* if the order relation $\leq$ on P is representable with respect to Γ. We say that a problem Γ *has minimal solutions* if $Sol(C)$ has a minimal element with respect to $\leq$ for any constraint set C over Γ with $Sol(C) \neq \emptyset$. If $\Gamma = (P, \mathcal{S})$ with P a meet-semilattice and it holds for all $R \in \mathcal{S}$ that $x, y \in R$ implies $x \sqcap y \in R$, then Γ is said to be a *meet-closed problem*. A relational problem $\Gamma = (P, \mathcal{S})$ is *representable in definite form* if P is a meet-semilattice and there exists an MFP Φ such that for all constraint sets C over Γ there exists a definite set C' over Φ with $Sol(C) = Sol(C')$.

Suppose that $R \subseteq P^m$ is a meet-closed relation, P a meet-semilattice. Then define the *partial* function $H_R : P^m \to P^m$ by $H_R(\mathbf{x}) = \bigwedge \uparrow_R (\mathbf{x})$ where $\uparrow_R (\mathbf{x}) = \{\mathbf{y} \in P^m \mid \mathbf{y} \geq \mathbf{x}, R(\mathbf{y})\}$ and with H_R *undefined* if $\uparrow_R (x) = \emptyset$. Then H_R is monotone when defined, *i.e.*, $\forall \mathbf{x}\mathbf{y} \in dom(H_R).\ \mathbf{x} \leq \mathbf{y} \Rightarrow H_R(\mathbf{x}) \leq H_R(\mathbf{y})$, and if $\uparrow_R (\mathbf{x}) \neq \emptyset$, then $\mathbf{x} \in dom(H_R)$. Moreover, for all $\mathbf{x} \in dom(H_R)$ one has $H_R(\mathbf{x}) \geq \mathbf{x}$, since every $\mathbf{y} \in \uparrow_R (\mathbf{x})$ satisfies $\mathbf{y} \geq \mathbf{x}$, and so we have $\bigwedge \uparrow_R (\mathbf{x}) \geq \mathbf{x}$.

Lemma 5. *$\mathbf{x} \in R$ if and only if $\mathbf{x} \in dom(H_R)$ and $H_R(\mathbf{x}) \leq \mathbf{x}$*

Using Lemma 5 we can characterize the class of relational problems which can be solved using algorithm D, *i.e.*, the problems which can be expressed by definite inequalities, as follows

Theorem 6. *(Representability) 1. Let $\Gamma = (P, \mathcal{S})$ with P a meet-semilattice. Then Γ is representable in definite form if and only if Γ is meet-closed. In particular, if Γ is meet-closed, then any constraint set C over Γ can be represented by a definite and simple constraint set C' with $|C'| \leq m(m+2) \cdot |C|$ where m is the maximal arity of a relation in $\mathcal{S}$.*

2. Let $\Gamma_{\leq} = (P, \mathcal{S})$ be a relational constraint problem with inequality, P arbitrary poset. Then the following conditions are equivalent: (i) $\Gamma_{\leq}$ has minimal solutions. (ii) $\Gamma_{\leq}$ is meet-closed and P is a meet-semilattice. (iii) $\Gamma_{\leq}$ is representable in definite form.

Observe that property 1 of Theorem 6 can be seen as a strict generalization of the well-known fact that a set $R \subseteq \mathbf{2}^k$ of boolean vectors is definable by a set of propositional Horn-clauses if and only if R is closed under conjunction [2] Under this view, the notion of *definite* inequalities generalizes the notion of Horn-propositions from the boolean case of $\mathbf{2}$ to an arbitrary meet-semilattice. [3]

We have seen that any meet-closed problem can be represented by definite, functional constraints. Conversely, consider *distributive constraint sets* over an MFP, *i.e.*, constraint sets C where all $\tau \leq \tau' \in C$ have the *right hand side* τ' built from distributive functions only [4] Distributive sets strictly include the definite ones, but every distributive set can be represented by a relational set over a meet-closed problem, since the functions in F can be regarded as relations (graphs), hence (Theorem 6 (1)) algorithm D can solve any Φ-SAT problem restricted to distributive constraint sets. In practice it may be convenient to translate a distributive set directly into a definite one, using the auxiliary functions H_g, defined thus: let $g : P^m \rightarrow P$ with P a meet-semilattice; then $H_g : P \rightarrow P^m$ is the *partial* function given by $H_g(x) = \bigwedge\{y \in P^m \mid x \leq g(y)\}$ with H_g *undefined* if no $y \in P^m$ satisfies $y \leq g(x)$. If P is a lattice, then H_g is a total function, and it is always monotone. We have

Lemma 7. *Let $f : P^n \rightarrow P$, $g : P^m \rightarrow P$ with g distributive. Then $f(x) \leq g(y)$ if and only if $f(x) \in dom(H_g)$ and $H_g(f(x)) \leq y$.*

The transformation $\rightarrow_R$ given by

$$C \cup \{A \leq g(\ldots h(\tau) \ldots)\} \rightarrow_R C \cup \{A \leq g(\ldots v_{m+1} \ldots), v_{m+1} \leq h(\tau)\}$$

is analogous to L-normalization and satisfies properties corresponding to Lemma 1 and Lemma 2. For MFP $\Phi = (L, F)$, L meet-semilattice, let $\Phi' = (L, F')$ with $F' = F \cup \bigcup_{g \in F_d} \{H_g^i \mid i = 1 \ldots a_g\}$ where F_d is the set of distributive functions in F and $H_g^i(x) = [H_g(x)]_i$. Using $\rightarrow_L$ and $\rightarrow_R$ one has by Lemma 7

Proposition 8. *Let $\Phi = (P, F)$ be an MFP, P a meet-semilattice. Then for any distributive constraint set C over Φ there exists a definite and simple constraint set C' over Φ' with $Sol(C) = \{\rho' \downarrow k \mid \rho \in Sol(C')\}$, where $Var(C) = \mathcal{V}_k$, and with $|C'| \leq 3|C| + 2n(m+2)$ where n is the number of inequalities in C and m is the maximal arity of a function in F.*

---

[2] The definability condition for propositional Horn-clauses is a special case of a much more general model theoretic characterization of Horn-definability in first order predicate logic, by which an arbitrary first order sentence ϕ is logically equivalent to a Horn-sentence if and only if ϕ preserves reduced products of models; see [4] or [12] for in-depth treatments of this result. See also [6]

[3] Note that in definite inequalities we are allowed to use any monotone functions, whereas in the special case of Horn-implications we may use only one function, the meet operation. It is easy to see that one cannot, in general, define an arbitrary meet-closed relation using only the meet operation of the semi-lattice, since, for instance, any set C of inequalities in one variable using only the meet function must be *convex* (*i.e.*, $x, y \in Sol(C)$ and $x \leq z \leq y$ imply $z \in Sol(C)$.) So, for instance, taking L to be the three element chain $0 < 1 < \infty$, the subset $\{\infty, 0\}$ is meet-closed but not convex and hence it cannot be defined using just the meet operation.

[4] A function f is distributive if $f(x \sqcap y) = f(x) \sqcap f(y)$.

4.2 Boolean representation

We show how sets of definite inequalities over finite lattices can be translated into propositional formulae, such that there is a direct correspondence between solutions to the propositional system and solutions to the lattice inequalities.

Given a lattice L with $n+1$ elements, we represent each element of L by an element in 2^n. First we number the elements in $L \setminus \{\bot\} = \{l_1, \ldots, l_n\}$. We then represent each element x in L by a vector of boolean values $\phi(x) : L \to 2^n$ where

$$\phi(x) = (b_1, \ldots, b_n), \text{ where } b_i = 1 \text{ iff } l_i \leq x$$

We also define a mapping $\psi : 2^n \to L$:

$$\psi((b_1, \ldots, b_n)) = \bigvee \{l_i \mid b_i = 1\}$$

It is clear that $x = \psi(\phi(x))$ and $v \leq \phi(\psi(v))$. Moreover, both are monotone. Hence, ϕ and ψ form a galois connection between L and 2^n. We will translate definite inequalities over lattice terms into sets of definite inequalities over 2^n. We will assume that we have already transformed the constraints to the form $f(A_1, \ldots, A_{a_f}) \leq A_0$. We translate constraints over the L-variables $v_1, \ldots, v_k$ into sets of constraints over the boolean variables $v_{11}, \ldots, v_{1n}, \ldots, v_{k1}, \ldots, v_{kn}$. We extend ϕ to variables by setting $\phi(v_i) = (v_{i1}, \ldots, v_{in})$ and define $\phi_i(x)$ to be the i'th component of $\phi(x)$.

Even though we don't use an index for $\bot$ in our representation, we will for convenience assign it index 0 and define $\phi_0(x) = 1$ for all $x \in L$. This corresponds to extending the representation vector with an extra bit, which is always 1 (since $\bot$ is $\leq$ all elements in L).

We first generate, for each variable v_i, the set of constraints $v_{ik} \leq v_{ij}$ whenever $l_j \leq l_k$ (we actually need only do so for a set of pairs $l_j \leq l_k$ whose transitive and reflexive closure yields the ordering on L). These constraints will ensure that any solution to the constraint set will be in the image of ϕ. Note that this only works because we are in a lattice, as when we have two solutions to the constraints for a variable, the meet and join of these are also solutions. Even if we use more general Horn-clauses to model the ordering relation, it will be meet-closed, so at best we can extend the construction to meet semi-lattices.

Let the *i'th frontier of f*, $F_i(f)$ be the smallest subset of L^{a_f} such that $\phi_i(f(y_1, \ldots, y_{a_f})) = 1$ iff there exist $(x_1, \ldots, x_{a_f}) \in F_i(f)$, $(x_1, \ldots, x_{a_f}) \leq (y_1, \ldots, y_{a_f})$. This is well-defined, because the set of all $(x_1, \ldots, x_{a_f})$ such that $\phi_i(f(x_1, \ldots, x_{a_f})) = 1$ is one such, and since the intersection of two such sets is also one. While $F_i(f)$ in the worst case may be of size $\mathcal{O}(|L^{a_f}|)$, it is often smaller. If f is distributive, $|F_i(f)| \leq 1$.

For each i between 1 and n and for each $(x_1, \ldots, x_{a_f}) \in F_i(f)$, we generate from the constraint $f(A_1, \ldots, A_{a_f}) \leq A_0$ a new constraint:

$$\phi_{j_1}(A_1) \sqcap \ldots \sqcap \phi_{j_{a_f}}(A_{a_f}) \leq \phi_i(A_0)$$

where j_k is the index of x_k in L.

The translation of $f(A_1, \ldots, A_{a_f}) \leq A_0$ is the set of all these new constraints.

Theorem 9. *The constraint $f(A_1, \ldots, A_{a_f}) \leq A_0$ is satisfiable iff all the constraints in the translation and all the ordering constraints between the components of the variables are. Moreover, any solution to the translation is in the image of ϕ and maps by ψ to a solution of $f(A_1, \ldots, A_{a_f}) \leq A_0$. Since ϕ and ψ are order-preserving, least solutions map to least solutions.*

Complexity. We have translated a set C of constraints over an $n+1$-point lattice L into a set C' of constraints over the boolean 2-point lattice. The size of the translated constraint set can be calculated as follows:

For any variable v_i in C, we introduce n variables $v_{i1}, \ldots, v_{in}$ in C'. For each v_i, C' contains at most n^2 constraints to ensure that any solution to C' will map $v_{i1}, \ldots, v_{in}$ to an image of an element in L.

For any constraint $f(A_1, \ldots, A_{a_f}) \leq A_0$, we introduce a number of constraints, each of size $a_f + 1$. The number of constraints is $\sum i = 1n|F_i(f)| \leq n \times n^{a_f}$. Since the size of the constraint $f(A_1, \ldots, A_{a_f}) \leq A_0$ is $(a_f + 1)$, the size of the translation is less than n^{1+a_f} times the size of the original constraint.

Bringing these together, we get that $|C'| \leq n^{1+a_{max}} \times |C| + n^2 \times |V|$, where a_{max} is the maximal arity of a function symbol in C and $|V|$ is the number of variables in C. For a fixed lattice and set of function symbols, this is a linear expansion. For the uniform problem, the input is given as operation matrices for the function symbols plus the constraints. The size of an operation matrix for a function with arity a is n^a, so the size of the input is greater than $n^{a_{max}} + |C|$. The size of the output is $n^{1+a_{max}} \times |C| + n^2 \times |V|$. The size of the input is hence the sum of two values and the size of the output is (approximately) the product of these. Hence, we get a quadratic worst-case expansion for the uniform problem.

The exponential dependence on the arity of the function symbols may seem bad, but it can be argued (see [19]) that any reasonable translation to boolean constraints will expand non-polynomially in the arity of the function symbols. Comparing with algorithm D (see Theorem 4) we see that D runs in time linearly dependent on a_{max} for the uniform case, hence boolean representation should, in general, only be used in case arities are known to be small.

Satisfiability of translation. Each constraint in the translation is of the form $a_1 \sqcap \ldots \sqcap a_m \leq a_0$, where the a_i are variables or constants ranging over the lattice $\{0, 1\}$. These constraints are isormorphic to Horn-clauses, and can hence be solved in time linear in the size of the constraint set using a HORNSAT-procedure [7].

5 Intractability of extensions

We have seen that algorithm D efficiently decides the *uniform* satisfiability problem (*i.e.*, uniform in both Γ and C), when instances Γ are restricted to be meet-closed. It is relevant to ask whether this can be extended to cover more relations than the meet-closed ones (perhaps by finding an algorithm entirely different from D.) The main purpose of this section is to demonstrate that, unless $\mathbf{P} = \mathbf{NP}$, *no* such extension is possible for any meet-semilattice L. This shows that algorithm D is complete for a maximal tractable class of problems, namely the meet-closed ones. If L is a meet-semilattice, we say that a problem $\Gamma = (L, \mathcal{S})$ is a *maximal* meet-closed problem if Γ is meet-closed and for any $R \subseteq L^k$ which is not meet-closed, the (particular, non-uniform) satisfiability problem $(L, \mathcal{S} \cup \{R\})$-SAT is **NP**-complete. We first show that *any distributive lattice has a maximal meet-closed problem* and deal with the general case afterwards. The proof is by composing Birkhoff's Representation Theorem for finite lattices [5] with Schaefer's Dichotomy Theorem [20] for the complexity of logical satisfiability problems.

For lattice L, let $\mathbf{Idl}(L)$ be the set of *order ideals* of L and $\mathbf{Irr}(L)$ the set of *join-irreducible* elements of L. If L is a finite, *distributive* lattice with $\mathbf{Irr}(L) = c_1, \ldots, c_n$ any fixed enumeration of $\mathbf{Irr}(L)$, then Birkhoff's Representation Theorem entails that, with $\eta : L \rightarrow \mathbf{Idl}(\mathbf{Irr}(L))$ defined by $\eta(x) = \{y \in \mathbf{Irr}(L) \mid y \leq x\}$, the map $\varphi : L \rightarrow \mathbf{2}^n$ becomes an *order-embedding* by setting $[\varphi(x)]_i = 1$, if $c_i \in \eta(x)$, and $[\varphi(x)]_i = 0$, if $c_i \notin \eta(x)$, for $i = 1, \ldots, n$. We refer to φ as the *canonical embedding* of L. For $R \subseteq L^k$ we let [6] $\varphi(R) = \{\langle \varphi(x_1), \ldots, \varphi(x_k) \rangle \mid (x_1, \ldots, x_k) \in R\}$, so $\mathbf{x} \in R \Leftrightarrow \varphi(\mathbf{x}) \in \varphi(R)$. With $\Gamma = (L, \mathcal{S})$, L distributive, define the problem $\varphi(\Gamma) = (\mathbf{2}, \varphi(\mathcal{S}))$ with $\varphi(\mathcal{S}) = \{\varphi(R) \mid R \in \mathcal{S}\}$. We use $\varphi(R)$ to denote the relation symbol corresponding to the relation $\varphi(R)$. If C is a constraint set over $\varphi(\Gamma)$, one has $\varphi(R) \subseteq \mathbf{2}^{kn}$ for all relations $\varphi(R) \in \varphi(\mathcal{S})$, where $n = |\mathbf{Irr}(L)|$ and k is the arity of R.

Now, we are interested in problems Γ such that $\varphi(\Gamma)$-SAT becomes polynomial time reducible to Γ-SAT. The problem here is that such reduction is not possible in general, because the constraint language of $\varphi(\Gamma)$ is more expressive than that of Γ. For instance, a unary relation symbol R may get translated into a symbol $\varphi(R)$ of arity $n = |\mathbf{Irr}(L)|$ with $n > 1$, so we can write (taking $n = 3$) constraints with patterns like $\{\varphi(R)(x, y, z), \varphi(R)(z, y, x)\}$ expressing that there exists $\mathbf{b} \in \mathbf{2}^3$ such that both that it and its reversal is in $\varphi(R)$; in general this cannot be expressed in the constraint language of Γ. However, if Γ has a certain kind of relations, then this becomes possible. Given distributive lattice L with canonical embedding φ and $|\mathbf{Irr}(L)| = n$ we let Π_L denote the set of "projection relations" $\pi_{ij} \subseteq L^2$, $i, j \in \{1, \ldots, n\}$, defined as follows

$$\pi_{ij} = \{(x, y) \in L^2 \mid [\varphi(x)]_i = [\varphi(x)]_j\}$$

[5] See [5]. We recall also that, for lattice L, an *order ideal* in L is a down-closed subset of L; $x \in L$ is *join-irreducible* if $x \neq \bot$ and $x = y \sqcup z$ implies $x = y$ or $x = z$ for all $y, z \in L$; L is *distributive* if $(x \sqcup y) \sqcap z = (x \sqcap z) \sqcup (y \sqcap z)$ for all $x, y, z \in L$; an *order-embedding* of lattices is an injective map preserving meet and join.

[6] We use the notation $\langle \mathbf{y}_1, \ldots, \mathbf{y}_k \rangle$, for $\mathbf{y}_i \in L^n$, to denote the "flattened" kn-vector $\mathbf{z}$ obtained by concatenating the tuples $\mathbf{y}_1, \ldots, \mathbf{y}_k$ into a single tuple, in that order; in detail, $\mathbf{z} = (z_1, \ldots, z_{kn})$ with $z_1 = [\mathbf{y}_1]_1, \ldots, z_n = [\mathbf{y}_1]_n, \ldots, z_{(k-1)n+1} = [\mathbf{y}_k]_1, \ldots, z_{kn} = [\mathbf{y}_k]_n$. For $\mathbf{x} = (x_1, \ldots, x_k) \in L^k$ we write $\varphi(\mathbf{x})$ for $\langle \varphi(x_1), \ldots, \varphi(x_k) \rangle$.

It is easy to check that π_{ij} are all meet-closed relations, since φ is an order-embedding. If L is non-trivial, there must be $a, b \in L$ with $a < b$, so that $\varphi(a) < \varphi(b)$, and hence $[\varphi(a)]_j = 0$ and $[\varphi(b)]_j = 1$ for some j; we can therefore express that $[\varphi(x)]_i = 0$ and $[\varphi(x)]_i = 1$ by $\pi_{ij}(x, a)$ and $\pi_{ij}(x, b)$, respectively. Constraints of the form $\pi_{ij}(x, y)$ will be written as $[\varphi(x)]_i = [\varphi(y)]_j$ or $[\varphi(x)]_i = b$ ($b \in \{0, 1\}$). One does not, of course, need explicit reference to φ in order to define the projection relations, so long as one can talk about the join-irreducible elements in an appropriate way:

Example 1. Let $\Phi = (L, F)$, $\mathbf{Irr}(L) = c_1, \ldots, c_n$ and suppose we have a function $f_{c_i} \in F$ for each $c_i \in \mathbf{Irr}(L)$ where $f_{c_i}(x) = \top$ if $c_i \leq x$ and $f_{c_i}(x) = \bot$ otherwise. Then all f_{c_i} are distributive functions, and since the condition $[\varphi(x)]_i = [\varphi(y)]_j$ is equivalent to the condition $c_i \leq x \Leftrightarrow c_j \leq y$, the first mentioned condition can be expressed by distributive inequalities over Φ, because $c_i \leq x \Rightarrow c_j \leq y$ is equivalent to the distributive constraint $f_{c_i}(x) \leq f_{c_j}(y)$.

If $\Gamma = (L, \mathcal{S})$ and C is a constraint set over $\varphi(\Gamma)$, we describe a translation of C, called $\varphi^{-1}(C)$, to a constraint set over $\Gamma' = (L, \mathcal{S} \cup \Pi_L)$, as follows. Let $t_1, \ldots, t_m$ be an enumeration of the constraint terms in C. Each t_s can be written as a term of the form $t_s = \varphi(R)(\langle \mathbf{A}_1, \ldots, \mathbf{A}_k \rangle)$, where each $\mathbf{A}_i$ is a vector of n atomic terms, $n = |\mathbf{Irr}(L)|$, k the arity of R. We let $t_s \Downarrow (p, i) = [\mathbf{A}_p]_i$ ($1 \leq p \leq k, 1 \leq i \leq n$.) For each term t_s we let $\alpha_1^s, \ldots, \alpha_k^s$ be k unique, fresh variables to be used in the translation of term t_s. The relational term $t_s = \varphi(R)(\langle \mathbf{A}_1, \ldots, \mathbf{A}_k \rangle)$ then gets translated into the constraint set $C_s = C_{s,1} \cup C_{s,2} \cup C_{s,3}$, where

$$
\begin{aligned}
C_{s,1} &= \{R(\alpha_1^s, \ldots, \alpha_k^s)\} \\
C_{s,2} &= \{[\varphi(\alpha_j^s)]_i = b \mid [\mathbf{A}_j]_i = b \text{ with } b \in \{0,1\}\} \\
C_{s,3} &= \left\{[\varphi(\alpha_p^s)]_i = [\varphi(\alpha_q^u)]_j \,\middle|\, t_s \Downarrow (p, i) \text{ is variable } x \wedge \exists t_u \in C.\, t_u \Downarrow (q, j) = x \right\}
\end{aligned}
$$

For $C = t_1, \ldots, t_m$ we define $\varphi^{-1}(C) = \bigcup_{s=1}^{m} C_s$. The constraints in $\varphi^{-1}(C)$ using π_{ij} can simulate all patterns in $\varphi(C)$, so we can show

Lemma 10. *Let $\Gamma = (L, \mathcal{S})$ with L non-trivial distributive lattice, and let C be a constraint set over $\varphi(\Gamma)$. Then C is satisfiable over $\varphi(\Gamma)$ if and only if $\varphi^{-1}(C)$ is satisfiable over $\Gamma' = (L, \mathcal{S} \cup \Pi_L)$.*

Since each set $C_{s,3}$ in $\varphi^{-1}(C)$ contributes at most $|C|^2$ new constraints, because each new constraint is determined by a distinct pair of occurrences of variables in C, it is straight-forward to show

Lemma 11. *For every constraint set C over $\varphi(\Gamma)$ one has $|\varphi^{-1}(C)| \leq |C|^2 \cdot (2|C| + 3)$.*

We now recall the contents of Schaefer's Dichotomy Theorem [20]. It yields the following very powerful classification (see also [14]):

Theorem 12 Schaefer [20]. *Let $\Gamma = (\mathbf{2}, \mathcal{S})$ be any boolean problem. Then the satisfiability problem Γ-SAT is polynomial time decidable, if one of the following four conditions are satisfied: either (1) every relation in $\mathcal{S}$ is closed under*

disjunction, or (2) *every relation in* $\mathcal{S}$ *is closed under conjunction, or* (3) *every relation in* $\mathcal{S}$ *is* bijunctive, i.e., *it satisfies the closure condition* $\forall x, y, z \in \mathbf{2}^k . x, y, z \in R \Rightarrow (x \wedge y) \vee (y \wedge z) \vee (z \wedge x) \in R$, *or* (4) *every relation in* $\mathcal{S}$ *is* affine, i.e., *it satisfies the closure condition* $\forall x, y, z \in \mathbf{2}^k . x, y, z \in R \Rightarrow x \oplus y \oplus z \in R$, *where* $\oplus$ *is the exclusive disjunction.*

Otherwise, if none of the above conditions are satisfied, the problem Γ-SAT *is* **NP**-*complete under log-space reductions.*

If L is a meet-semilattice which is not a lattice, we let $L^{\top}$ denote the extension of L to a lattice under addition of a top element, as earlier. If L is already a lattice, we let $L^{\top} = L$, by definition. We say that L is a *distributive meet-semilattice* if L is a meet-semilattice such that $L^{\top}$ is a distributive lattice. If L is a distributive meet-semilattice we know by previous remarks that $L^{\top}$ has a canonical embedding into $\mathbf{2}^n$, and this map φ will be referred to as the canonical embedding of L also. For any meet-semilattice L we let $M_L = \{(x, y, z) \in L^3 \mid z = x \sqcap y\}$, the meet-relation of L. The following results are proved in detail in [19].

Lemma 13. *Let L be a non-trivial distributive meet-semilattice, and let φ be its canonical embedding. Then the relation $\varphi(M_L)$ satisfies: $\varphi(M_L)$ is closed under conjunction, $\varphi(M_L)$ is not closed under disjunction, $\varphi(M_L)$ is not bijunctive, and $\varphi(M_L)$ is not affine.*

Let L be distributive and $\mathcal{S} = \Pi_L \cup \{M_L\}$; then the problem $\widetilde{\Gamma} = (L, \mathcal{S})$ is meet-closed. We can show that, for *any* relation R over L which is not meet-closed, the problem Γ^+-SAT with $\Gamma^+ = (L, \mathcal{S} \cup \{R\})$ is **NP**-hard, by reduction from $\varphi(\Gamma)$-SAT, which, in turn, can be shown to be **NP**-hard by Lemma 10, Lemma 11, Lemma 13 together with Schaefer's Dichotomy Theorem. We therefore have

Theorem 14. (Intractability of extensions, distributive case) *For any non-trivial, distributive meet-semilattice L the problem $\widetilde{\Gamma} = (L, \Pi_L \cup \{M_L\})$ is maximal meet-closed.*

By Birkhoff's Theorem we know that L embeds into $\mathbf{2}^n$ if *and only* if L is distributive, hence the method used to prove Theorem 14 will not work for arbitrary finite lattices. However, if L is an arbitrary meet-semilattice we have the following weaker result by direct reduction from CNF-SAT:

Theorem 15. (Intractability of extensions, general case) *Let L be any non-trivial meet-semilattice and let $R \subseteq L^k$ be any relation over L which is not meet-closed. Then there exists a meet-closed problem $\Gamma = (L, \mathcal{S})$ such that the problem $\widetilde{\Gamma}$-*SAT *is* **NP**-*complete with $\widetilde{\Gamma} = (L, \mathcal{S} \cup \{R\})$.*

Theorem 15 entails that the uniform satisfiability problem restricted to meet-closed relations becomes **NP**-hard no matter how it is extended, since the theorem says that there will always be a particular (non-uniform) problem over such an extension which is **NP**-hard; here the hard problem depends on the given extension. In contrast, Theorem 14 asserts the existence of a particular (non-uniform) problem which becomes hard no matter how it is extended. The results given here extend, in the case of finite domains, the results of [13], which considers totally ordered domains. See also [15].

6 Applications to program analysis

An application of the constraint solving technology shown in this paper is program analysis by annotated type systems. In these systems, programs are given types annotated with elements from a finite lattice. The type rules impose constraints between the annotations of the types of a term and its sub-terms. A typing of a program will generate a set of constraints, which must then be solved. Often, the constraints will have a form suitable for solution by the methods presented here.

One such example is the usage count analysis from [17] which has annotations in the lattice $\{0, 1, \infty\}$ with $0 \leq 1 \leq \infty$. The constraints use the following binary operators:

$k_1 + k_2$

$k_1 \backslash k_2$	0	1	∞
0	0	1	∞
1	1	∞	∞
∞	∞	∞	∞

$k_1 \cdot k_2$

$k_1 \backslash k_2$	0	1	∞
0	0	0	0
1	0	1	∞
∞	0	∞	∞

$k_1 \rhd k_2$

$k_1 \backslash k_2$	0	1	∞
0	0	0	0
1	0	1	∞
∞	0	1	∞

$+$ and $\cdot$ are addition and multiplication over counts. $k_1 \rhd k_2$ is 0 if $k_1 = 0$, otherwise $k_1 \rhd k_2 = k_2$.

The constraints are of one of the forms $k_1 = k_2$, $1 \leq k$, $k_1 \leq k_2$, $k_1 + k_2 \leq k_3$, $\infty \cdot k_1 \leq k_2$, $k_1 \cdot k_2 \leq k_3$ or $k_1 \rhd k_2 \leq k_3$. Hence (noting that $k_1 = k_2$ is equivalent to $k_1 \leq k_2, k_2 \leq k_1$), they are of the kind that can be solved by the methods shown, either by the direct method or by translation into boolean constraints. The translation uses the mapping shown below for lattice elements.
Hence, we replace each constraint variable k_i by two variables l_i and r_i over the binary domain, with the constraint $l_i \leq r_i$.

The constraints are translated using the translation shown in section 4.2. The table below shows the result after reduction has been made for the constraints that involve constants.

count	translation
0	00
1	01
∞	11

constraint	translation
$k_1 = k_2$	$l_1 = l_2,\ r_1 = r_2$
$1 \leq k$	$r = 1$
$k_1 \leq k_2$	$l_1 \leq l_2,\ r_1 \leq r_2$
$k_1 + k_2 \leq k_3$	$l_1 \leq l_3,\ r_1 \leq r_3,\ l_2 \leq l_3,\ r_2 \leq r_3,\ r_1 \wedge r_2 \leq l_3$
$\infty \cdot k_1 \leq k_2$	$r_1 \leq l_2$
$k_1 \cdot k_2 \leq k_3$	$r_1 \wedge r_2 \leq r_3,\ l_1 \wedge r_2 \leq l_3,\ l_2 \wedge r_1 \leq l_3$
$k_1 \rhd k_2 \leq k_3$	$r_1 \wedge l_2 \leq l_3,\ r_1 \wedge r_2 \leq r_3$

We end this section by giving some further examples of how our results can be used to reason about problems of interest in program analysis.

Example 2. The problem $\Phi = (\mathbf{2}, \{\wedge\})$ is maximal meet-closed. To see this, represent Φ as relational problem $\Gamma = (\mathbf{2}, \{M_2, \leq\})$. It then follows from Theorem 14 that Γ is maximal, because all relations in the set Π_2 can already be defined in terms of M_2, by Horn-definability (cf. comment after Theorem 6) together with the fact that all relations in Π_2 are meet-closed.

Example 3. Let **3** denote the three-point chain $0 < 1 < \infty$. The distributive lattice **3** occurs in many practical contexts, such as, *e.g.*, program analyses involving usage counting [17], [21],[1].

Let *pred* denote the predecessor function on **3**, with $pred(0) = 0, pred(1) = 0, pred(\infty) = 1$. Then *pred* is a distributive function. Consider the problem $\Phi = (\mathbf{3}, \{\sqcap, pred\})$, it is clearly meet-closed (viewed relationally), and, moreover, it is maximal. To see this, first note that the join-irreducible elements are $\{1, \infty\}$. Now define the function f_1 by setting $f_1(x) = 1 \sqcap x$ and define the function f_∞ by setting $f_\infty(x) = pred(x)$. Then $f_1(x) = 1$ if $1 \leq x$ and $f_1(x) = 0$ otherwise; moreover, $f_\infty(x) = 1$ if $\infty \leq x$ and $f_\infty(x) = 0$ otherwise. Recalling Example 1 we see that the functions f_1 and f_∞ are sufficient to represent the projection relations in Π_3, since we can express the condition $c_i \leq x \Rightarrow c_j \leq y$, for $c_i, c_j \in \mathbf{Irr}(\mathbf{3})$, by the distributive constraint $f_{c_i}(x) \leq f_{c_j}(y)$. It then follows from Theorem 14 that Φ is a maximal problem.

Example 4. Consider the *uniform* function problem restricted to *distributive* inequalities. By Theorem 6 this problem contains all meet-closed problems. Therefore, it follows from Theorem 15 that any uniform extension of the problem becomes **NP**-hard. In other words, if monotone function symbols can occur on the left side of inequalities and *any single* non-distributive function symbol can occur arbitrarily on the right side, then the uniform problem is **NP**-hard.

Example 5. In many applications in program analysis the semilattice L will be thought of as a domain of abstract program properties with lower elements representing more information than higher elements [7] If an analysis can be implemented as a constraint problem with minimal solutions it will have the desirable property that it is guaranteed to yield a uniquely determined piece of information which is optimal relative to the abstraction of the analysis. Theorem 6 says that *all and only* inequality constraint problems with this natural property can be represented as definite inequalities and hence can be solved in linear time using algorithm D.

7 Conclusion

We have studied efficient solution methods for the following classes of constraint problems over finite meet-semilattices:

---

[7] Alternatively, elements with more information may sit higher in the semilattice. Our results still apply, since the whole development in this paper can of course be dualized in the lattice-theoretic sense to encompass join-semilattices and join-closed problems over such.

- Definite inequalities involving monotone functions.
- Distributive inequalities.
- Boolean inequalities (Horn clauses).
- Meet-closed relational constraints.

We have shown that these classes are equivalent modulo linear time transformations for any fixed problem, and we have estimated the constant factors involved. For any fixed lattice and any fixed set of function/relation symbols the methods are linear time in the size of the constraint set, but, in the case of boolean representation, the time depends non-linearly on the maximal arity of relation symbols used. Furthermore, we have shown that these classes can be solved uniformly in polynomial time and that they are are maximal in the sense that any extension leads to **NP**-hard uniform problems.

Acknowledgements We wish to thank Fritz Henglein, Neil Jones, Helmuth Seidl, Mads Tofte and our referees for helpful discussions and comments.

A Algorithm D

Algorithm D is shown in Figure 1. We outline the data-structures and operations assumed for a linear time implementation (more details are in [19].) A list *Ilist* of records representing the inequalities in C. Each record also holds a boolean variable, called *inserted*. An array $Clist[\beta]$ indexed by variables in $Var(C)$. Each entry $Clist[\beta]$ holds an array of pointers to inequalities in *Ilist*, one entry for each inequality in C in which β occurs. Thus, to each item $Clist[\beta][k]$ there corresponds a unique occurrence of β in C. Hence, the number of distinct items $Clist[\beta][k]$ is bounded by $|C|$. The structure NS is a doubly linked list of of pointers to inequalities in *Ilist* which are also in C_{var}, and the item in *Ilist* has a back-pointer set to the representing item in NS. There is a pointer to the head element of NS. The idea is that NS holds holds pointers to those inequalities in C_{var} which are *not satisfied* under the current interpretation ρ (see below.) A finite map ρ mapping each distinct variable of C to an element in L. The map ρ holds the current "guess" at a satisfying valuation for C_{var}. The map $\bot_{Var(C)\rightarrow L}$ is the map which sends every variable of C to the bottom element of L. The map ρ is implemented as an array of lattice elements indexed by the variables. We write $\rho(\beta)$ for $\rho[\beta]$. Evaluating $\rho(\beta)$ is a constant time operation, and so is the operation of updating ρ at β.

Operation POP removes the head element of NS and returns it after setting the corresponding *inserted* field to false. INSERT(i) inserts an inequality pointer i at the front of NS, updating the *inserted* field. If the *inserted* field is true, then INSERT does nothing. DROP(i), removes i, a pointer to an element in NS, from NS, using the *inserted* filed in analogy with INSERT. All these operations can be implemented as constant time operations, using the data-structures above. Operation L-NORMALIZE transforms a definite set into an equivalent L-normal set and runs in time $O(|C|)$ (using Lemma 2 and Lemma 1.)

1. *Input*
   A finite set $C = \{\tau_i \leq A_i\}_{i \in I}$ of definite inequalities over $\Phi = (L, F)$, $F = \{f : L^{a_f} \to L\}$ with each f monotone, L finite lattice, $Var(C) = \mathcal{V}_m$ for some m.
2. *Initially*
   $C :=$ L-NORMALIZE(C)
   $\rho := \bot_{\mathcal{V}_m \to L}$
   $C_{var} := \{\tau \leq A \in C \mid A \text{ is a variable}\}$
   Initialize the lists $Clist[\alpha]$, for every distinct variable α in C.
   Initialize $Ilist$ to hold the inequalities in C.
   $NS := \{\tau \leq \beta \in C_{var} \mid L, \rho \not\models \tau \leq \beta\}$
3. *Iteration*

```
while NS ≠ ∅ do
        τ ≤ β := POP(NS);

        ρ(β) := [[τ]]ρ ⊔ ρ(β);

        for σ ≤ γ ∈ Clist[β] do
                if ρ, L ⊭ σ ≤ γ
                then INSERT(σ ≤ γ)
                else DROP(σ ≤ γ)
        end; (* for *)

    end;(* while *)
```

4. *Output*
   If $L, \rho \models \tau \leq c$ for all $\tau \leq c \in C_{cnst}$ **then** output ρ **else** FAIL.

Figure 1: Algorithm D for satisfiability of definite constraints over Φ

In the algorithm we have followed the convention of writing the pattern of an inequality pointed to by an inequality pointer instead of the pointer itself.

References

1. L. Birkedal, M. Tofte, and M. Vejlstrup. From region inference to von Neumann machines via region representation inference. In *Proc. 23rd Annual ACM Symposium on Principles of Programming Languages (POPL)*, pages 171–183. ACM Press, January 1996.
2. L. Birkedal and M. Welinder. Binding-time analysis for Standard ML. *Lisp and Symbolic Computation*, 8(3):191–208, September 1995.
3. A. Bondorf and J. Jørgensen. Efficient analyses for realistic off-line partial evaluation. *Journal of Functional Programming*, 3(3):315–346, July 1993.
4. C.C. Chang and H.J. Keisler. *Model Theory*. Studies in Logic and the Foundation of Mathematics, Vol. 73, 3rd ed., North Holland, 1990.
5. B. A. Davey and H. A. Priestley. *Introduction to Lattices and Order*. Cambridge Mathematical Textbooks, Cambridge University Press, 1990.
6. R. Dechter and J. Pearl. Structure identification in relational data. *Artificial Intelligence*, 58:237–270, 1992.

7. William F. Dowling and Jean H. Gallier. Linear-time algorithms for testing the satisfiability of propositional horn formulae. *Journal of Logic Programming*, 3:267–284, 1984.
8. Dirk Dussart, Fritz Henglein, and Christian Mossin. Polymorphic recursion and subtype qualifications: Polymorphic binding-time analysis in polynomial time. In *Proc. 2nd Int'l Static Analysis Symposium (SAS), Glasgow, Scotland*, Lecture Notes in Computer Science. Springer-Verlag, September 1995.
9. M. Garey and D. Johnson. *Computers and Intractability – A Guide to the Theory of NP-Completeness*. Freeman, 1979.
10. R. Greenlaw, H.J. Hoover, and W. Ruzzo. *Limits to Parallel Computation. P-Completeness Theory*. Oxford University Press, 1995.
11. F. Henglein. Efficient type inference for higher-order binding-time analysis. In J. Hughes, editor, *Functional Programming Languages and Computer Architecture, Cambridge, Massachusetts, August 1991 (Lecture Notes in Computer Science, vol. 523)*, pages 448–472. ACM, Berlin: Springer-Verlag, 1991.
12. W. Hodges. *Model Theory*. Encyclopedia of Mathematics and its Applications, Vol. 42, Cambridge University Press, 1993.
13. P. Jeavons and M. Cooper. Tractable constraints on ordered domains. *Artificial Intelligence*, 79:327–339, 1995.
14. Peter Jeavons and David Cohen. An algebraic characterization of tractable constraints. In *First Annual Conference on Computing and Combinatorics (COCOON)*, pages 633–642. Springer Verlag, LNCS 959, 1995.
15. Peter Jeavons, David Cohen, and Marc Gyssens. A unifying framework for tractable constraints. In *First International Conference on Principles and Practice of Constraint Programming*, pages 276–291. Springer Verlag, LNCS 976, 1995.
16. G. Kildall. A unified approach to global program optimization. *Proc. ACM Symp. on Principles of Programming Languages (POPL)*, 1973.
17. T. Æ. Mogensen. Types for 0, 1 or many uses. Technical report, In preparation, 1996.
18. Vaughan Pratt and Jerzy Tiuryn. Satisfiability of inequalities in a poset. *Studia Logica, Helene Rasiowa memorial issue (to appear)*, 1996.
19. Jakob Rehof and Torben Mogensen. Report on tractable constraints in finite semilattices. Technical report, DIKU, Dept. of Computer Science, University of Copenhagen, Denmark. Available at http://www.diku.dk/research-groups/topps/personal/ rehof/publications.html, 1996.
20. Thomas J. Schaefer. The complexity of satisfiability problems. In *Tenth Annual Symposium on the Theory of Computing (STOC)*, pages 216–226. ACM, 1978.
21. Mads Tofte and Jean-Pierre Talpin. Implementation of the typed call-by-value λ-calculus using a stack of regions. In *Proc. 21st Annual ACM SIGPLAN-SIGACT Symposium on Principles of Programming Languages (POPL), Portland, Oregon*. ACM, ACM Press, January 1994.

Uniformity for the Decidability of Hybrid Automata

Olivier Roux*, Vlad Rusu**

Abstract. We present some new decidability results on the verification of hybrid automata by symbolic analysis (abstract interpretation using polyhedra). The results include defining a class of hybrid automata for which all properties expressed in the real-time temporal logic TCTL are decidable. The obtained class of automata is shown powerful enough to model reactive applications in which every task eventually terminates within uniformly-bounded time. Indeed, the restrictions we use for obtaining decidability have a physical meaning, and they all impose some kind of uniformity to the runs of hybrid automata.

Keywords: decidability, uniformity, hybrid automata, symbolic verification, temporal logic TCTL

1 Introduction

The verification of concurrent programs is often achieved by modeling programs as transition systems, and by model-checking temporal logic formulas for the desired properties. This approach is acceptable for systems whose time durations and delays are not relevant; but it does not work when one wants to take into account temporal durations of progams in a dense time.

Thus, *timed automata* [ACD90] and *hybrid automata* [ACH+95] arose, allowing specification of both continuous evolutions (such as the passing of time) and discrete changes. Timed automata are quite adapted for the verification of real-time logic properties (e.g. TCTL [ACD90, HNSY94]). But such properties are only *semi-decidable* for hybrid automata [ACH+95]; and even in the decidable cases, the verification algorithms are not very efficient.

For these reasons, the verification problem has been attacked from two directions. The first one is to obtain restricted, decidable classes of hybrid automata [KPSY93, PV94, HKPV95, BER94, BES93, HH95, Hen95, RR94, RR95]. The second consists in using abstractions [HPR94] or compositionality and on-the-fly techniques [BGK+96] to accelerate reaching a result.

Our current proposal lies in the first of these two directions, and it aims at obtaining decidability for classes of reactive and hybrid systems that are useful in practice, by imposing restrictions that have a physical meaning.

We obtain results in two steps:

* Institut Universitaire de France and Laboratoire d'Automatique de Nantes

** Laboratoire d'Automatique de Nantes (CNRS, Univ.Nantes, Ecole Centrale de Nantes) 44072 NANTES Cedex 03, France. E-mail: {roux|rusu}@lan.ec-nantes.fr

- first, we prove that the time-bounded fragment of logic TCTL is decidable on *strongly-non-Zeno* hybrid automata (a relevant subclass of hybrid automata);
- second, we investigate an even more restrictive class of hybrid automata (namely the *uniformly-periodic*) for which the whole logic TCTL is decidable.

These results hold because we progressively introduce some structure (we call it *uniformity*) in the systems, that limits unnatural behaviours and provides decidability: the more uniformity, the more decidability.

As an application, we show that reactive programs in which events do not occur too often so that every task eventually terminates within a uniformly-bounded time, can be modeled by *strongly non-Zeno*, *uniformly periodic* hybrid automata. Decidability of bounded-TCTL then allows to verify such properties as *bounded response* (e.g. 'the system responds within 3 time units'); and the decidability of full TCTL makes it possible to check for *safety* as well as performing the so-called *parametric verification*: instead of verifying a time-bounded property with a given bound, rather synthethise the bound from the program's model.

The rest of the paper is organized as follows. In the next section, we recall the fundamentals of hybrid automata. Section 3 deals with the definition and the decidability of bounded-TCTL for strongly-non-Zeno hybrid automata, together with a decidable equivalent criterion for the strongly-non-Zeno condition, followed by a generalization of this class. Similarly, section 4 contains the definition and the decidability of full TCTL for hybrid automata that are both uniformly-periodic and strongly-non-Zeno, together with a sufficient criterion for uniform periodicity, and followed by a generalization. An experiment is reported in section 5, and we conclude in section 6.

2 Hybrid automata

We use hybrid automata [ACH+95] as a model for reactive applications that consist in lengthing *tasks* that can be preempted and/or launched by instantaneous *events*. We limit ourselves to *asynchronous* systems[3] in the sense that tasks are lengthing and that two events cannot occur at the same time instant[4]. As we shall see in the following, the obtained results apply also to the more general class of *hybrid systems*.

Example. Figure 1 is a graphical representation of a hybrid automaton that describes the iteration of two tasks A, B. Task B is executed either after A completes, or following an event x that preempts task A and launches B; when B completes, A will be resumed at preemption point.

The duration of task A (B) is any real in the interval $[7, 8)$, and respectively the interval $[4, 5)$; and there is a minimum delay of 3 time units between two consecutive events x.

[3] in opposition to the *synchronous* approach, [Hal93]

[4] this is the approach taken in ELECTRE language [RCCE92]

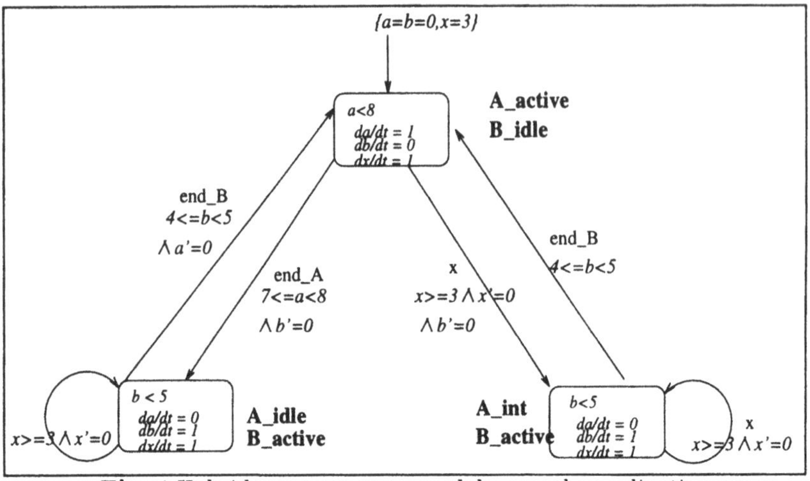

Fig. 1 *Hybrid automaton to model example application*

The states (called *locations*) are labeled with propositions — like **A_active**, **A_int**, **B_idle** — defining at each location which tasks are *active* (executing), *interrupted* (not executing, following some event that has preempted it) or *idle* (neither active nor interrupted). The transitions (called *edges*) are labeled with the possible discrete changes between locations: events or task completions.

There are three *variables* a, b and x, to count the time for tasks A, B and event x. Variables evolve at locations following simple *differential laws* - like $da/dt = 1, db/dt = 0$ at the upmost location, meaning that *task* A *is active (running)* and *task* B *is idle*. The inequalities associated to locations and edges express durations for tasks and events: for instance, when entering the upmost location with variable $a = 0$, we start counting time for task A, and control has to leave the location between 7 and 8 time units after that, by the inequality $7 \leq a < 8$ on the outcoming edge. We now make precise these intuitions.

Syntax of hybrid automata. A hybrid automaton is a sextuple $(X, L, E, \mathcal{I}, \Delta, \mathcal{R})$:

- $X = \{x_1, \ldots x_n\}$ is a finite set of *variables*;
- L is a finite set of *locations*;
- $E \subseteq L \times A \times L$ is a finite set of *edges* (A is an edge-labeling alphabet);
- $\mathcal{I}$ is a function that associates to each location $l \in L$, an *invariant* $\mathcal{I}_l$ which is a system of linear inequalities on variables X;
- Δ is a function that that associates to each location $l \in L$ and each variable $x \in X$, a *differential law* of the form $\frac{dx}{dt} \in [k_{l,x}, K_{l,x}]$ with $k_{l,x}, K_{l,x} \in \mathbb{Q}$;
- $\mathcal{R}$ is a function that maps each edge $e \in E$ to a *relation* $\mathcal{R}_e$, which is a a system of linear inequalities on variables $X \cup X'$ (where $X' = \{x' | x \in X\}$).

Semantics. A *state* (l, v) of a hybrid automaton consists of a location $l \in L$ and a real valuation of the variables $v : X \rightarrow \mathbb{R}$, such that the valuation satisfies the location's invariant: $\mathcal{I}_s(v) = true$ [5].

[5] formally, $\mathcal{I}_s(v)$ denotes the truth value obtained by replacing in the system of linear inequalities $\mathcal{I}_s$, each variable x by its value $v(x)$

A *continuous step* consists in staying at some location l and letting the variables evolve following the corresponding laws (see figure 2(a)) inside the location's invariant. That is, we have a continuous step denoted $(l, v) \xrightarrow{t,f} (l, v')$ if: $t > 0$ and $f = (f_x)_{x \in X}$ is a n-uple of piece-wise continuously differentiable functions, such that: all the derivative values df_x/dt lie in the corresponding interval $[k_{l,x}, K_{l,x}]$; the final values of variables are $v'(x) = v(x) + f_x(t)$; and all the intermediary values of variables satisfy the location's invariant. The real $t > 0$ is the *duration* of the continuous step.

A *discrete step* consists in crossing an edge $(l, a, l') \in E$ such that the values of variables before and after the edge is crossed, satisfy the edge's relation (see figure 2(b)). So we have a discrete step denoted $(l, v) \xrightarrow{e} (l', v')$ if: the edge's relation $\mathcal{R}_e(v, v') = true$ [6]. The duration of a discrete step is 0.

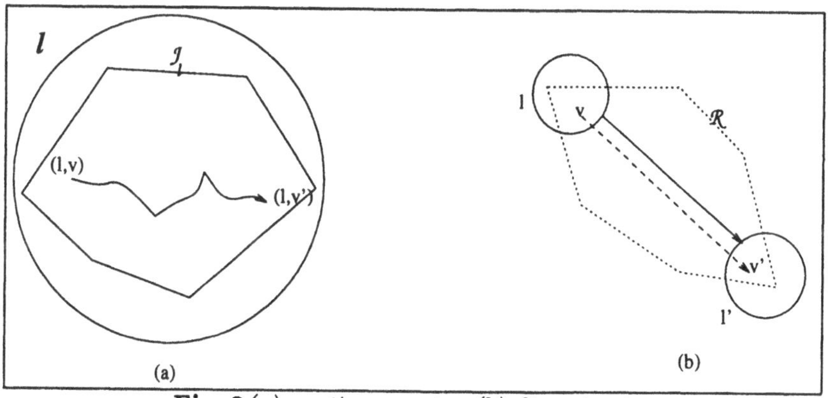

Fig. 2(*a) continuous step (b) discrete step*

A *run* $\rho = (l_0, v_0) \rightarrow (l_1, v_1) \rightarrow \ldots \rightarrow (l_i, v_i) \rightarrow (l_{i+1}, v_{i+1}) \ldots$ is a finite or infinite sequence of steps, such that: all continuous steps have strictly positive durations (by definition); the first step is continuous; and there is at least one continuous step between any two consecutive discrete steps. These restrictions are not usually considered in the literature, but they are imposed by our *asynchronous* context and they will later prove to be useful.

The *duration* of a run is the sum of the durations of all its component steps. A run is *divergent* if its duration is infinite.

2.1 Symbolic analysis

The verification problem for hybrid automata consists in answering questions of the form:

(α) 'starting from an initial set of states, is it possible (or inevitable) to reach some final set of states, in time bounded by constant c (or unbounded time)'

[6] formally, $\mathcal{R}_e(v, v')$ denotes the truth value obtained by replacing in the system of linear inequalities $\mathcal{R}_e$, each variable x by its value $v(x)$ and each variable x' by its value $v'(x')$

It turns out that most practically interesting properties that arise in the analysis of reactive and hybrid systems are of the previous form. But it is obvious that this kind of property cannot be verified directly, since the state space of hybrid automata is continuously infinite. To deal with this, the so-called *symbolic analysis* or symbolic model-checking technique [HNSY94] proposes to represent infinite sets of states by so-called *symbolic states* and infinite sets of runs by *symbolic runs.* A symbolic state is defined by a location and a domain of values for variables indentifiable with a polyhedron in $\mathbb{R}^n$ (such as the pairs (l_1, φ_1), (l_2, φ_2) and (l_3, φ_3) in figure 3); and a symbolic run is a sequence of symbolic states:

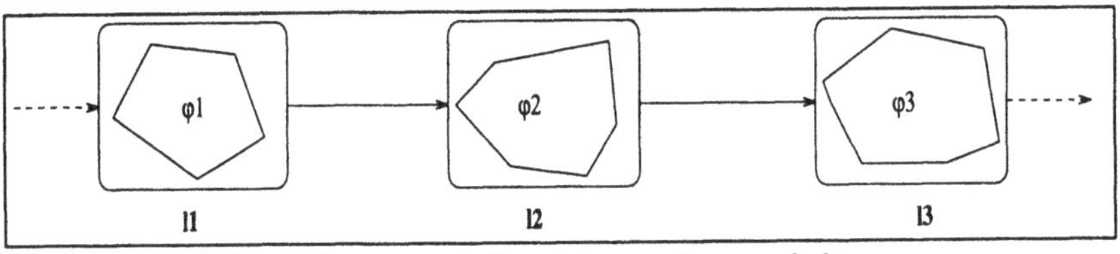

Fig. 3 *Three symbolic states and a symbolic run*

A symbolic run simulates all the runs starting from an initial set of states, that cross a given sequence of edges[7]. It has been shown that symbolic runs can be computed algorithmically by iterating so-called *continous successors* and *discrete successors* of symbolic states [ACH+95]. Computing the continuous and discrete successors comes to performing geometrical operations on n-dimensional polyhedra [HPR94].

So, in order to answer questions of the form (α) above, one should basically compute all the symbolic runs that start from the initial set of states, and see whether the final set of states is reached, by one or by all the symbolic runs. This is the so-called *symbolic forward analysis* algorithm of [ACH+95]. But another serious problem arises: this algorithm is not guaranteed to terminate ever; indeed, properties of the form (α) are only *semi-decidable* on general hybrid automata, and undecidability is shown to affect even quite simple automata [KPSY93, HKPV95]. This is no surprise, because hybrid automata, seen as machines, are extremely powerful (when compared to Turing or to n-counter machines).

However, some partial decidability results exist [KPSY93, PV94, HKPV95, BER94, BES93, HH95, Hen95]. All consist in restricting (drastically) the classes of hybrid automata and/or properties to be verified.

In the following, we systematically pursue such decidability results. The restrictions we impose have an intuitive, physical sense, and they still allow to verify quite large and natural classes of applications. All restrictions have in common some kind of 'uniformity' that is imposed to the continuously infinite sets of runs of hybrid automata, thus reducing their battling undecidability.

---

[7] in this sense, symbolic states and runs perform an *abstract interpretation* of hybrid automata

3 Strongly-Non-Zeno hybrid automata and time-bounded properties

Hybrid automata are subject to the so-called *Zeno paradoxes* that occur at the border of continuous and discrete phenomena. We point out two such paradoxes, and then show they are connected with the undecidability problems.

An infinity of discrete steps in finite time. Consider the automaton in figure 4(a), with one location, one edge and one variable x. Then the edge can be crossed at instants $\frac{1}{2}, \frac{3}{4}, \ldots \frac{2^n-1}{2^n} \ldots$ which makes an infinity of discrete steps in one time unit. We prohibit this kind of pathological behaviour.

Blocking [HNSY94]. Consider the automaton in figure 4(b). When entering location **0** with $x = 1$, there is nothing else to do: the edge cannot be crossed rightaway, since the definition of runs imposes that a non-zero time be spent in location **0**, but this is also impossible - because of incoherence between the location's invariant, differential law, and the edge's relation. The run is blocked. We also prohibit such situations.

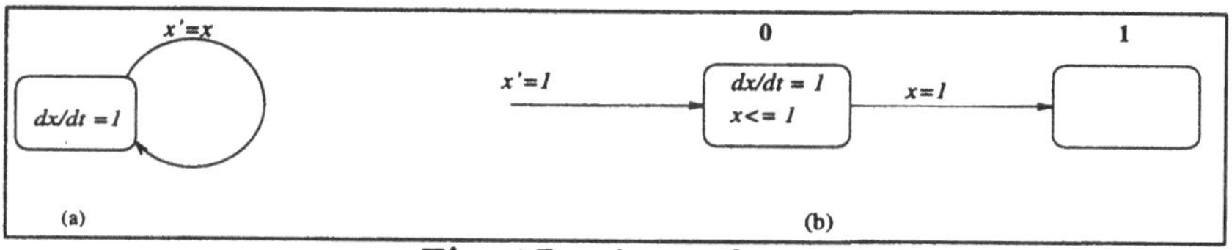

Fig. 4 *Zeno's paradoxes*

Definition: strongly non-Zeno hybrid automata. An *edge-cyclic* run is a run that crosses twice some edge. A *strongly non-Zeno hybrid automaton* respects the following restrictions to avoid Zeno's paradoxes:

- *Uniformly low-bounded:* there exists $\epsilon > 0$ such that all edge-cyclic runs have durations $> \epsilon$;
- *Non-blocking:* all finite runs can be extended to *divergent* runs, by starting with a *continuous* first step.

3.1 Time bounded properties: the logic bounded-TCTL

We present the logic bounded-TCTL, that allows to express *bounded reachability* and *bounded response* properties of hybrid automata. Informally, bounded-TCTL formulas express properties like: starting from an initial set of states ψ, and by remaining in an intermediary set of states ψ_1, it is possible (or inevitable) to reach a final set of states ψ_2, in a time bounded by $c \in \mathbb{Q}$.

Syntax. The bounded-TCTL formulas are $\psi_1 \exists\mathcal{U}_{\prec c}\psi_2$ (called bounded reachability) and $\psi_1 \forall\mathcal{U}_{\prec c}\psi_2$ (called bounded response). The items involved in the formulas are the intermediary and final sets of states ψ_1 and ψ_2, and the *bounded temporal operators* $\exists\mathcal{U}_{\prec c}$ and $\forall\mathcal{U}_{\prec c}$ with $c \in \mathbb{Q}$ and $\prec \in \{<, \leq, =\}$.

Without restricting the generality, we consider that the final set of states is included in the intermediary set : $\psi_2 \subseteq \psi_1$.

Semantics. The meaning of the formulas is:

- *Bounded reachability:* a state (l_0, v_0) satisfies the formula $\psi_1 \exists\mathcal{U}_{\prec c}\psi_2$ if there exists a finite run ρ of duration $d(\rho) \prec c$, originating from (l_0, v_0), such that all its states belong to ψ_1, and its final state belongs to ψ_2;
- *Bounded response:* a state (l_0, v_0) satisfies the formula $\psi_1 \forall\mathcal{U}_{\prec c}\psi_2$ if for any run ρ originating from (l_0, v_0), there exists an initial prefix ρ', of duration $d(\rho') \prec c$, such that all its states belong to ψ_1, and its final state is in ψ_2.

If a state satisfies a formula, we say the formula is *true* at that state. The set of states that satisfy a bounded-TCTL formula ψ is called the *characteristic set* of the formula.

As an example, consider the hybrid automaton in figure 1 and the formula **true**$\forall\mathcal{U}_{\leq 48}$**A_idle**. This formula expresses the fact that task A inevitably terminates within 48 time units. The set of states **true** designs all states of the hybrid automaton, and the set **A_idle** designs all states in the upmost location. The previous formula can be shown to be *false* at all states in location **A_active**.

Symbolic backward analysis. Verifying a bounded-TCTL formula comes to computing its characteristic set. As pointed out in section 2.1, this is impossible to do directly because the state space of a hybrid automaton is a continuously infinite set. However, this problem can be dealt with by *symbolic backward analysis*, which is symmetrical to the symbolic forward analysis presented in section 2.1.

Symbolic backward analysis, when applied to a bounded-TCTL formula, will simulate *backwards* the symbolic runs that arrive in set ψ_2 and that continuously remain is set ψ_1 (we assume that sets ψ_1, ψ_2 are *linear*, so they can be represented by *symbolic states*, cf. section 2.1). By iterating this computation and gathering all the encountered states, one would get all states satisfying the formula. However, an infinity of iterations might be necessary to obtain all these states. It is the same problem (undecidability) pointed out in section 2.1.

3.2 Decidability of bounded-TCTL on strongly non-Zeno hybrid automata

Bounded reachability is decidable. The idea is that, when performing backward analysis for a formula $\psi_1 \exists\mathcal{U}_{\prec c}\psi_2$, the uniformly low-bounded durations of edge-cyclic runs (section 3) make time to 'decrease' uniformly from c to 0, by at least the amount ϵ on each cycle (ϵ is the uniform lower bound for edge-cyclic runs). So, the time bound c is exhausted within a finite number of steps in the symbolic backward analysis, and we obtain all the states that satisfy the formula.

Bounded response is decidable. We now show that bounded response can be translated into bounded reachability. The idea is the following: consider a simple bounded response formula like **true**$\forall\mathcal{U}_{\leq c}\psi$. Roughly, its meaning is that each run eventually encounters a state in set ψ within c time units. This comes to saying: it is impossible to remain in set $\neg\psi$ (the complement of ψ) for c time units. So an equivalent formula could be $\neg(\neg\psi\exists\mathcal{U}_{=c}\neg\psi)$.

This is true, in fact, but the full argument is a little more complicated, and it is essentially based on the *non-blocking* quality of strongly non-Zeno hybrid automata (section 3) and on the particular definition that we have given of runs (section 2: continuous steps have strictly positive durations, and any run starts with a continuous step).

For suppose we drop the non-blocking requirement. Then consider the hybrid automaton in figure 4(b), which we have seen precisely to be blocking. The state $(\mathbf{0}, x = 0)$ satisfies formula $\mathbf{true}\forall\mathcal{U}_{\leq 1}\mathbf{location1}$ since on each *divergent* run, it is possible to find a finite initial prefix of duration ≤ 1 that arrives in location $\mathbf{1}$ — note that divergent (i.e. infinite-duration) runs necessarily exit location $\mathbf{0}$. But the same state $(\mathbf{0}, x = 0)$ does not satisfy the supposedly equivalent formula $\neg(\neg\mathbf{location1}\exists\mathcal{U}_{=1}\neg\mathbf{location1})$ — because it is possible to remain in location $\mathbf{0}$ for 1 time unit. So the equivalence does not hold any more when non-blocking is violated.

Furthermore, suppose we admit runs with continuous steps of 0 duration, or runs that start with a discrete step. Using this relaxed definition of runs, the automaton in figure 4(b) becomes non-blocking. By the same argument as above, we show that the equivalence between formulas $\mathbf{true}\forall\mathcal{U}_{\leq 1}\mathbf{location1}$ and $\neg(\neg\mathbf{location1}\exists\mathcal{U}_{=1}\neg\mathbf{location1})$ does not hold.

So the exact definitions are essential. With these definitions, we can prove that in general, bounded response is equivalent to bounded reachability [Rus96]:

$$\psi_1\forall U_{\leq c}\psi_2 \equiv \neg(\neg\psi_2\exists U_{\leq c}\neg\psi_1) \cap \neg(\neg\psi_2\exists U_{=c}\neg\psi_2)$$

This strengthens an existing result about equivalence between bounded response in time $\leq c$ and *unbounded reachability* (in time > c) [HNSY94].

Equivalent conditions for Strongly non-Zeno. The strongly non-Zeno conditions have been shown to guarantee decidability for the time-bounded properties of hybrid automata. It is then interesting to know when a hybrid automaton satisfies these conditions. For instance, the hybrid automaton in figure 1 is strongly non-Zeno: it has *uniform low-bounds for edge-cyclic runs* because for each cycle (in the sense of graphs) there is a stopwatch[8] a that is reset on some edge of the cycle ($a' = 0$) and tested on some edge of cycle by a condition of the form $c \leq a$ with $c \in \mathbb{Q}^+ \setminus \{0\}$; and it is *non-blocking* since all the upper bounds in invariants and edge guards are *strict*. These syntactical restrictions are sufficient to imply strong-non-Zenoness. But we can give *decidable, equivalent* conditions for a hybrid automaton to be strongly non-Zeno.

Checking uniform low-boundedness. For this, we first enrich the automaton with a new variable z, that systematically evolves like global time (continuously by $dz/dt = 1$, discretely by $z' = z$). Then, for each edge of the hybrid automaton perform the following: let l be the origin and l' be the destination of the edge.

[8] variable a is a *stopwatch* if it evolves continuously only by $da/dt \in [0, 1]$ and discretely by $a' = a$ or $a' = 0$

Consider the symbolic state $(l, z = 0 \wedge \mathcal{I}_l)$ — where $\mathcal{I}_l$ is the invariant of l — a polyhedron in $\mathbb{R}^n$, so $z = 0 \wedge \mathcal{I}_l$ makes a polyhedron in $\mathbb{R}^{n+1}$. We compute each symbolic run (see section 2.1) that originates from symbolic state $(l, z = 0 \wedge \mathcal{I}_l)$ until *the chosen edge from l to l' is crossed once more*, and no other edge is crossed twice. This happens on each symbolic run after a finite number of steps.

When this is done, we look at the polyhedra in the last symbolic states. If all these polyhedra have z-components greater than some $\epsilon > 0$, then all edge-cyclic runs that repeat twice our chosen edge (and no other), have uniformly low-bounded durations (by ϵ). Otherwise uniform low-boundedness is violated.

Checking non-blocking. If the previous test has answered *true*, then we proceed with checking the non-blocking condition. We use the following result [HNSY94]: a hybrid automaton is non-blocking iff all its states satisfy the (bounded reachability) formula $\mathbf{true}\exists\mathcal{U}_{=1}\mathbf{true}$. This bounded reachability formula is decidable because the hybrid automaton has just been shown to respect uniform low-boundedness (cf. section 3.2: note there that uniform low-boundedness is enough to guarantee decidability of bounded reachability formulas).

The two tests, for low-boundedness and non-blocking, allow to decide the strongly-non-Zeno quality.

Generalization: uniform divergence. Uniform low-boundedness was proved sufficient for the decidability of bounded reachability formulas. We now show that there is a strictly weaker condition, *uniform divergence*, that still guarantees decidability.

Definition: uniformly divergent hybrid automata. A hybrid automaton is *uniformly divergent* if: for each $c > 0$, there exists a $N(c) \in \mathbb{N}$ *depending only on* c, such that any run of the automaton that crosses N edges has duration $d(\rho) > c$.

So what happens when symbolic backward analysis (section 3.2) is performed on a bounded reachability formula $\psi_1\exists\mathcal{U}_{\prec c}\psi_2$: the time-bound c decreases on each backwards simulated symbolic run — since it decreases *uniformly* on each run — until it is exhausted, in exactly $N(c)$ steps. Thus, bounded reachability is decidable, and bounded-TCTL is still decidable on the class of *uniformly divergent, non-blocking* hybrid automata.

Obviously, uniformly low-bounded hybrid automata are uniformly divergent. The converse is not true; consider the following *non-linear* hybrid automaton:

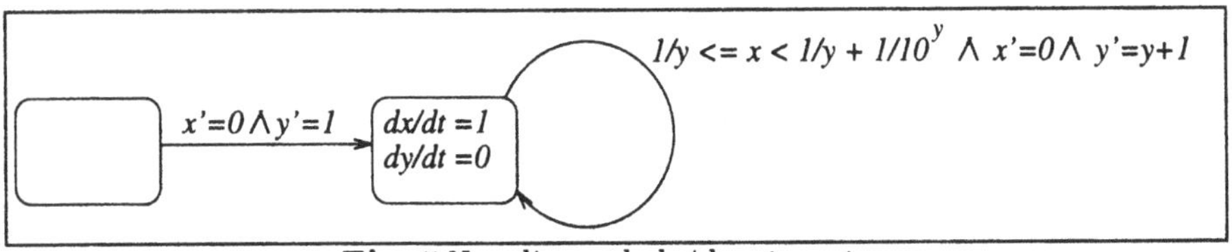

Fig. 5 *Non-linear hybrid automaton*

Variable y takes discrete values: $y = n$ at the n-th crossing of the looping edge. So, the n-th edge-cycle lasts between $\frac{1}{n}$ and $\frac{1}{n} + \frac{1}{10^n}$ time units. Thus, even if individual edge-cycles can be arbitrary brief, the hybrid automaton is uniformly-divergent.

We can also build a *linear* automaton with the same kind of behaviour: just replace the non-linear guard $\frac{1}{y} \leq x < \frac{1}{y} + \frac{1}{10^y}$ in figure 5, by *another hybrid automaton that performs the division of 1 by y with y decimals and affects the result to x*. This can be accomplished by simulating the Euclid algorithm (hybrid automata can perform all the necessary arithmetic operations with the instantaneous, discrete steps); so this 'Euclid hybrid automaton' can generate values between $\frac{1}{y}$ and $\frac{1}{y} + \frac{1}{10^y}$ in arbitrary small time[9], say $\frac{1}{10^y}$.

The linear hybrid automaton obtained by replacing the looping edge by the Euclid hybrid automaton is uniformly divergent, but not uniformly low-bounded.

4 Uniformly-periodic hybrid automata

We now further restrict the hybrid automata in order to obtain decidability for time-unbounded properties. These are also very important: for instance, the basic *safety* is just unbounded reachability of a bad state. For *unbounded response* (e.g. the system will respond eventually), it can be argued that it is not relevant for real-time applications in which precisely the delays are interesting; but we can use unbounded response to *synthethise* such a delay, by model-checking an unbounded response property with a parameter (variable) modelling the delay.

Definition: uniformly periodic hybrid automata. A hybrid automaton is *uniformly periodic* if there exists $T > 0$ and a distinguished state (l, v) (location+ values of all variables) such that any run of the automaton meets state (l, v) every $\leq T$ time units.

So, all the runs of a uniformly periodic hybrid automaton repeat some given state every at most some time T which is *independent of particular runs*.

Unbounded properties: the logic TCTL. To express unbounded properties, the logic bounded-TCTL is extended with the *time-unbounded formulas*. These are, syntactically and semantically, obtained by just dropping the bound c in the corresponding bounded formulas (see section 3.1):

- *Reachability:* a state (l_0, v_0) satisfies the reachability formula $\psi_1 \exists\mathcal{U} \psi_2$ if there exists a finite run originating from (l_0, v_0), such that all its states belong to ψ_1, and its final state belongs to ψ_2;
- *Response:* a state (l_0, v_0) satisfies the formula $\psi_1 \forall\mathcal{U} \psi_2$ if for any run ρ originating from (l_0, v_0), there exists an initial prefix ρ' such that all its states belong to ψ_1, and its final state is in ψ_2.

Other derived properties, for instance *response in at least c time units* denoted $\psi_1 \forall\mathcal{U}_{\geq c} \psi_2$, can be translated into unbounded formulas over modified arguments. For instance, the previous formula can be dealt with by translating it into $\psi_1 \forall\mathcal{U}(\psi_2 \wedge z \geq c)$, where z is a new variable denoting global time.

[9] this shows the extreme computational power of hybrid automata...

Decidability of TCTL on uniformly periodic, strongly non-Zeno hybrid automata. The decidability argument is: since all runs of the (uniformly periodic) hybrid automaton meet some distinguished state every at most T time units, it should be clear that any unbounded property of the automaton is equivalent to a time-bounded property with bound $\leq 2T$; and since time-bounded properties are decidable on the (strongly non-Zeno) hybrid automaton, we have the desired decidability.

Application. Uniformly periodic hybrid automata allow to model systems that are re-initialized to a given state within some time bound. This happens, for instance, in reactive programs (tasks+events) if the tasks are not preempted too often so that they can eventually terminate within *uniformly* bounded time and reset all variables to some fixed value.

Consider for instance the simple reactive program previously modeled in figure 1, which describes the iteration of tasks `A` and `B` disturbed by event `x`. We keep the same durations for tasks `A` (`B`) in interval $[7, 8)$, and respectively $[4, 5)$; but we change the specification for event `x`, imposing that two consecutive events `x` are separated by at least 6 time units. Then, since the maximum duration of task `B` is 5, one less than the minimum interval between the preempting events `x`, task `A` is not systematically preempted and it eventually terminates, in at most 48 time units. When this happens, all variables are set to fixed values (on edge `end_A`):

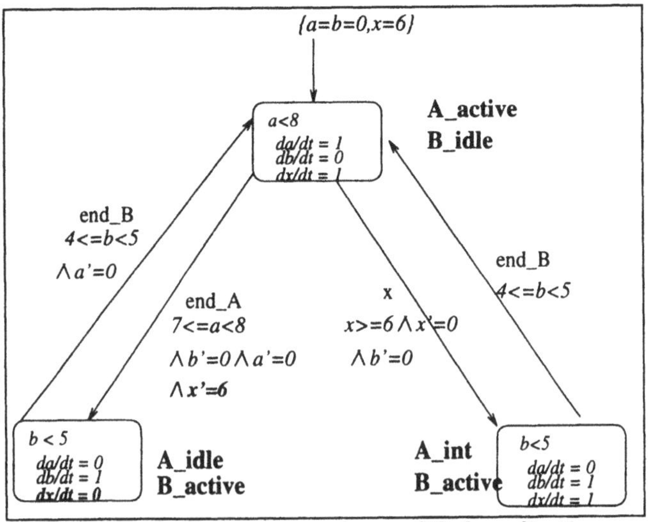

Fig. 6 *Hybrid automaton for modified application*

Note that this resetting slightly changes the timed specification for events `x`: the minimum interval of 6 time units between two consecutive events `x` is *not counted while the concerned task* `A` *is idle*, and the timer `x` is already set to 6 when `A` restarts, so that `x` can occur at once.

We now generalize this idea. Consider a subclass of reactive systems that we shall call *hierarchical*, with the following structure: there is a partial order $\preceq$ on the tasks such that

- tasks which are minimal with regard to $\preceq$ (like **A** in previous example) do not execute in parallel with any others;
- if **B** can be active while **A** is preempted, then necessarily **A** $\preceq$ **B** (this is the case in the previous example)
- there is a minimum interval of time between preemptions such that every task eventually terminates within some uniform time T.

These conditions are met, for instance, in real-time systems with several preemption levels, in which interrupt procedures can be themselves interrupted; but this does not occur too often so that every task manages to terminate. Then it can be argued that such hierarchical systems can be modeled by *strongly non-Zeno, uniformly-periodic* hybrid automata. Indeed, any task eventually terminates within some uniform time T, in particular the ones that are minimal with regard to order $\preceq$. When such a minimal task terminates, all variables can be set to fixed values (task timers to 0 and event timers to their minimal separation value — as x was set to 6 in the previous example) because at that moment, the above conditions guarantee that *there is not other task running or preempted.*

We shall see another example of such hierarchical systems in section 5.

Criterion. We now give a sufficient criterion for a hybrid automaton to be uniformly periodic. The idea is to generalize the automaton of figure 6: we impose that on each cycle of the automaton (in the sense of graphs), there exists a variable a and a location l on the cycle such that:

- the invariant of location l includes an inequality $a < M$ with $M > 0$;
- a has differential law at location l of the form $da/dt = k$ or $da/dt \in [k, K]$ with $k > 0$;
- there is an outcoming edge from l that we call the *resetting edge*, whose relation is of the form $m \leq a < M \wedge \bigwedge_{x \in X} x' = c_x$ where all the $c_x \in \mathbb{Q}$;
- and any edge-cyclic run of the automaton that performs the considered cycle, spends some time $\geq \epsilon$ in location l, for some $\epsilon > 0$.

Then obviously no run can loop on the considered cycle without augmenting the value of a, and so the resetting edge is eventually crossed (in uniformly bounded time): the uniform periodicity is guaranteed.

Note that all the above conditions are checkable: all but the last are syntactical, and the last can be tested by a *forward simulation* of location l's invariant on the cycle (similar to the technique for checking *uniform low-boundedness*, section 3.1).

Generalization: uniform reachability. Uniform periodicity, together with strong non-Zenoness, guarantees the decidability of time-unbounded properties. But uniform periodicity can be relaxed to weaker conditions.

Definition: uniformly reachable hybrid automaton. A hybrid automaton is *uniformly reachable* if: there exists $T > 0$ such that for each pair of states (l_1, v_1) and (l_2, v_2), whenever there is a run from (l_1, v_1) to (l_2, v_2), then there is an initial prefix of the run, of duration $\leq T$, from (l_1, v_1) to (l_2, v_2).

This means that states are not necessarily reachable one from another, but when this is the case, they are reachable in some *uniformly* bounded time. With this definition, it is clear that unbounded properties of hybrid automata reduce to bounded ones, which are decidable under the strongly non-Zeno condition.

A classification of all the obtained decidability results is given in figure 8.

5 Verification example

A real-time application consists of four tasks $\mathtt{A}_{reactive}$, $\mathtt{A}_{back}$, B and C executing on one processor. Task $\mathtt{A}_{reactive}$ lasts between 7 and 8 time units, and it can be preempted by events **x** and **y**; task $\mathtt{A}_{back}$ lasts between 4 and 5 time units, it does not accept events **x**, **y** but it shares the processor with other time-consuming processes outside our application, such that it gets at any moment at least half of processing time.

An event **x** (resp. **y**) launches task B (resp. C) which lasts between 1 and 2 (resp. between 0.5 and 1) time units; these two tasks can run in parallel if their launching events occur one after the other; when they complete, task $\mathtt{A}_{reactive}$ will be resumed at preemption point. Two consecutive events **x** (resp. **y**) are separated by at least 2 (resp. 3) time units, and these intervals are not counted when task $\mathtt{A}_{reactive}$ is idle (at the leftmost location); furthermore, these intervals are reset when $\mathtt{A}_{reactive}$ is launched from its beginning, so that **x** and **y** can occur at any moment after that.

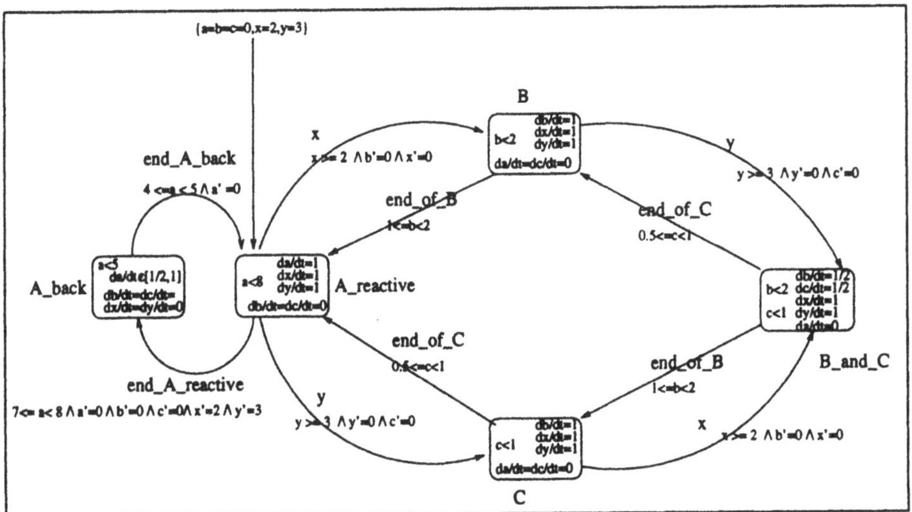

Fig. 7 *Hybrid automaton for example*

This can be modeled by the *strongly non-Zeno* hybrid automaton in figure 7, in which for the sake of simplicity only the active tasks are indicated on locations (like B_and_C at the rightmost location, meaning that B and C are executed in parallel). The differential law $da/dt \in [1/2, 1]$ at location A_{back} is there to model the variable speed of task A_{back} when it shares the processor with other tasks (and gets at least half of processing time), and the laws $db/dt = dc/dt = 1/2$ at location B_and_C mean that the two tasks are scheduled by equal time sharing.

Temporal properties of the example. We verify the following time-bounded properties with our protype verification tool Valet [Rus96] [10] on a Sun Sparc 10:

1. If only events y occur, then task task $A_{reactive}$ inevitably terminates in at most 8 time units:
   true, checked by Valet in 8 steps and 3 seconds of CPU time.
2. If only events x occur, then the task task $A_{reactive}$ inevitably terminates in at most 250 time units:
   false, checked by Valet in 253 steps and 5 minutes of CPU time.

Both are examples of bounded response properties, and they were also chosen to show the behaviour of task $A_{reactive}$ with regards to preemptions. In fact it can be seen on the above figure that in general task $A_{reactive}$ is not guaranteed to terminate ever, because of events x that can occur every 2 time units, launching task B and preempting $A_{reactive}$ too often so that it cannot complete.

Indeed, it would be enough to have a greater interval of time (e.g. 4 time units) between two consecutive events x, in order to obtain the termination of task $A_{reactive}$ in a *uniformly bounded* time. This would make the above automaton *uniformly periodic* and since it was already strongly non-Zeno, all TCTL properties become decidable for this application (in fact, we obtain a so-called hierarchical system, described in section 4).

6 Conclusion

In this paper, we have shown that it is possible to get several decidability results from the structural uniformity of runs in hybrid automata. By imposing increasing uniformity, namely *uniform low-boundedness*, *non-blocking* and *uniform periodicity*, we achieve to prove the decidability of increasingly demanding timed properties expressed in the real-time temporal logic TCTL: first the time-bounded properties, and then the time-unbounded ones. Decidable criteria and generalizations are provided for the most important uniformity conditions.

These classes of automata endowed with uniformity came into sight from experiments of real reactive applications programming. A major result is that general TCTL properties are decidable on a class of hybrid automata powerful

[10] other existing verification tools are Kronos [OSY94], Polka [HPR94], HyTech [HHWT94] and UPPAAL [BGK+96]

enough to model real-time applications in which every task eventually terminates in uniformly bounded time.

The obtained results are gathered in figure 8 (we have emphasized the classes of hybrid automata for which there are also decidable criteria).

	TCTL properties	
	bounded	unbounded
Hybrid Automata (H.A.)	semi-decidable	semi-decidable
Strongly-Non-Zeno H.A.(S-N-Z.H.A.) *uniform low-bound on duration of cycles, non-blocking*	decidable	semi-decidable
Uniformly Divergent H.A. *uniform low-bound on duration of N edges, non-blocking*	decidable	semi-decidable
Uniformly Periodic S-N-Z.H.A. *uniform upper-bound of duration between occurences of periodic state*	decidable	decidable
Uniformly Reachable S-N-Z.H.A. *uniform upper-bound of duration between reachable states*	decidable	decidable

Fig. 8*Summary of main decidability results*

As we have mentionned in the introduction, there are two main directions for improving the verification of reactive and hybrid systems using symbolic model-cheking and hybrid automata. This paper presents some advance in the first direction: restricting hybrid automata in order to obtain decidable subclasses. Now, we are currently starting to work in the second direction: accelerating the verification algorithms. The idea — confirmed until now by experimentation— is that the uniformity we have imposed to hybrid automata, translates into some kind of uniformity in the symbolic states and runs that constitute their abstract interpretation by polyhedra. More precisely, it seems that when a symbolic run completes a cycle, the borders of polyhedra are just *translated* by some fixed amount.

This would mean that any generated symbolic state needs only to visit at most once each location of the hybrid automaton, leading to a substantial improvement of the algorithms implemented in the verification tool Valet.

References

[ACD90] R. Alur, C. Courcoubetis, and D. Dill. Model-checking for real-time systems. In *Proc. IEEE 5th Symp. Logic in Computer Science*, 1990.

[ACH+95] R. Alur, C. Courcoubetis, N. Halbwachs, T. Henzinger, P. Ho, X. Nicollin, A. Olivero, J. Sifakis, and S. Yovine. The algorithmic analysis of hybrid systems. *Theoretical Computer Science B*, 137, January 1995.

[BER94] A. Bouajjani, R. Echahed, and R. Robbana. Verifying invariance properties for timed systems with duration variables. In *Formal Techniques in Real-Time and Fault-Tolerant Systems, LNCS 863*, 1994.

[BES93] A. Bouajjani, R. Echahed, and J. Sifakis. On model checking for real-time properties with durations. In *Proc Symp. on Logic in Computer Science'93, lNCS*, 1993.

[BGK+96] J. Bengtsson, D. Griffioen, K. Kristoferssen, K.Larsen, F.Larsson, P.Petersson, and W.Yi. Verification of an audio protocol with bus collision using UPPAAL. In *Computer-Aided Verification*, 1996.

[Hal93] Nicolas Halbwachs. *Synchronous Programming of Reactive Systems.* Kluwer Academic Publishers, 1993.

[Hen95] T.A. Henzinger. Hybrid automata with finite bisimulations. In *Proc. 22th International Colloquium on Automata, Languages, and Programming, LNCS 944*, 1995.

[HH95] T.A. Henzinger and P.H. Ho. Algorithmic analysis of nonlinear hybrid systems. In *Proc. 7th Conf. Computer-Aided Verification, LNCS 939*, 1995.

[HHWT94] T.A. Henzinger, P.H. Ho, and H. Wong-Toi. A user guide to hytech. In *Proc. 1st. Workshop on Tools and Algorithms for the Analisys of Systems, LNCS*, 1994.

[HKPV95] T.A. Henzinger, P.W. Kopke, A. Puri, and P. Varaiya. What's decidable about hybrid automata. In *STOCS'95, LNCS*, 1995.

[HNSY94] T.A. Henzinger, X. Nicollin, J. Sifakis, and S. Yovine. Symbolic model-checking for real-time systems. *Information and Computation*, (111):193–244, 1994.

[HPR94] N. Halbwachs, Y. E. Proy, and P. Raymond. Verification of linear hybrid systems by means of convex approximations. In *International Symposium on Static Analysis*, 1994.

[KPSY93] Y. Kesten, A. Pnueli, J. Sifakis, and S. Yovine. Integration graphs : a class of decidable hybrid systems. In *Proc. Workshop on Theory of Hybrid Systems, LNCS*, 1993.

[OSY94] A. Olivero, J. Sifakis, and S. Yovine. Using abstractions for the verification of linear hybrid systems. In *Proc. Conference on Computer Aided Verification*, 1994.

[PV94] A. Puri and P. Varaiya. Decidability of hybrid systems with rectangular differential inclusions. In *Proc. Conference on Computer-Aided Verification, LNCS*, 1994.

[RCCE92] O. Roux, D. Creusot, F. Cassez, and J.P. Elloy. Le langage réactif asynchrone ELECTRE. *Technique et Science Informatiques (TSI)*, 11(5):35–66, 1992.

[RR94] O. Roux and V. Rusu. Deciding time-bounded properties for ELECTRE reactive programs with stopwatch automata. In *Proc. Workshop on Hybrid Systems and Autonomous Control (Lecture Notes in Computer Science 999)*, pages 405–416, 1994.

[RR95] O. Roux and V. Rusu. Decidable hybrid automata to model and verify real-time systems. In *Second European Workshop on Real-Time and Hybrid Systems*, 1995.

[Rus96] V. Rusu. *Vérification temporelle de programmes* ELECTRE. PhD thesis, Laboratoire d'Automatique de Nantes, Ecole Centrale de Nantes (FRANCE), 1996.

A Backward Slicing Algorithm for Prolog

Stéphane Schoenig and Mireille Ducassé
IRISA/CNRS IRISA/INSA

Campus Universitaire de Beaulieu F-35042 Rennes Cedex, France

Abstract. Slicing is a program analysis technique originally developed by Weiser for imperative languages. Weiser showed that slicing is a natural tool for debugging, but it has other numerous applications (program integration, program optimization, etc.)
In this article we describe a backward slicing algorithm for Prolog which produces executable slices. The proposed algorithm is applicable at least to pure Prolog extended by some simple built-in predicates that handle the explicit unification =/2 and arithmetic.
To our knowledge, this algorithm is the first one to be proposed for Prolog. Because of the indeterminism and lack of explicit control flow of Prolog, existing algorithms cannot be trivially adapted. The two main contributions of this paper are a general definition of slicing adapted to Prolog and a slicing algorithm that produces executable programs.

1 Introduction

Slicing is a program analysis technique originally developed by Weiser [We84] for imperative languages. It consists of finding all instructions of a program that affect a variable v at a line l. This subset of the original program instructions is called a *slice*. The tuple $\langle v, l \rangle$ is called slicing criterion, and a slice is computed wrt a *slicing criterion*.

Weiser showed that *slicing* is a natural tool for debugging [We82]. Indeed, if the variable v has an incorrect value, the error is very likely to be in the slice. Even if the error is not always in it [Ko93], it always gives interesting information.

Slicing is not restricted to debugging. Horwitz et al. in [HPR88, HR92, HRB90] list other possible applications. For example, slicing can help programmers to understand complex programs, to detect dead code or to find parallelism in programs. Slices can also be used to compute differences between different versions of programs. In the following we will, however, consider slicing mainly in the context of debugging.

An important distinction between slices is pointed out by Hoffner et al. in [HKF95]. Slices can be either *executable programs* or merely a *set of instructions*. It is usually simpler to produce a set of instructions rather than an executable program, but an executable program is more interesting. Indeed, slicing, although helpful, is usually insufficient to locate an error as pointed out by Lyle in [Ly84]. Ducassé in [Du92] has shown that slicing can be combined with various other debugging techniques. If a slice is an executable program, it can be used by a large number of analysis tools, either static or dynamic, hence allowing the debugging process to be more flexible and more accurate.

Slicing can be divided into two categories, *forward slicing* and *backward slicing.* Forward slicing searches for all instructions j of a program P that might have one of its values modified if an instruction i is modified. Backward slicing searches a program P for all instructions j which, if modified, might change the value of a variable at an instruction i. Backward slicing is particularly suited for debugging as it starts from a computed (usually incorrect) value of a variable.

Several slicing algorithms for imperative languages have been developed. After Weiser, who gave the first algorithm [We84, LR87], it is possible to distinguish two main research communities. The first community, interested in the technique of slicing mainly as a basic tool for program transformation, has developed mostly static algorithms. The second community, interested in the problem of debugging, has oriented its researches mainly toward dynamic algorithms. Tip in [Ti95] did a nice survey on existing algorithms of both types.

Logic Programming and Slicing

According to Ducassé and Noyé [DN94], slicing was one of the main debugging techniques missing from logic programming environments. To our knowledge, only two other papers are related to slicing of logic programs. Gyimóthy and Paakki present in [GP95] a very specific algorithm designed to reduce the number of queries for an algorithmic debugging tool à la Shapiro [Sh83]. In particular it does not produce any program. Zhao et al. in [ZCU94] propose an algorithm for concurrent logic programming, but it is not possible to use their algorithm to compute slices as precise as we do (see "Related work" section.)

Designing a slicing algorithm for a logic program is not a simple transposition of existing algorithms designed for imperative languages. From the slicing point of view, mainly two aspects make logic programs very different from imperative programs: indeterminism and lack of explicit control flow. Because of the indeterminism, only considering one result is not sufficient as the computed slice may also produce non-expected results. The lack of explicit control flow makes it more difficult to ensure that the slice produces the trajectory of interest than for imperative programs.

In this article we describe a backward slicing algorithm for Prolog which produces executable slices. The proposed algorithm is applicable to at least pure Prolog extended with some simple built-in predicates that handle the explicit unification =/2 and arithmetic. The analyzed program must succeed for the top level goal of interest.

To our knowledge, this algorithm is the first one to be proposed for Prolog. Furthermore it can abstract away irrelevant *arguments*. This is essential for complex programs with many arguments. As far as we know, only one other algorithm handles abstraction of arguments [HRB90]. That algorithm was designed for imperative languages and does not integrate abstraction of arguments as "naturally" as our does.

The two main contributions of this paper are a general definition of slicing adapted to Prolog and a slicing algorithm that produces executable programs. Furthermore, we define the notion of abstract search tree which should be useful for other debugging techniques.

The section below defines the notion of slicing for Prolog programs and is followed by an example that illustrates the definitions. Then, sec. 4 gives some details about information needed to compute the slice. Our algorithm is then described. Finally, related work is discussed. Due to lack of space, some illustrations and all proofs can be found in an extended version of this paper at `http://www.irisa.fr/lande/schoenig/`.

2 Definitions

Whereas slicing is well defined for imperative languages [Ti95], slices of Prolog programs have neither been formally defined in terms of executable programs, nor defined in terms of their operational semantics.

After some preliminaries, recalling basic notations and definitions, we give our definitions of slicing criterion and slice in the context of Prolog.

2.1 Preliminaries

Throughout the paper we will assume that all clauses of a program P are numbered from c_1 to c_n. Literals of clauses are numbered from left to right, such that the head is numbered 0, the first atom of the body is numbered 1, and so on. Arguments of literals are numbered from left to right starting at 1.

To refer to an argument in a program P, Boye et al. [BPM93] give each argument of P a unique label called *argument position* or simply *position*.

Definition 1 Argument position. If c is a clause, the position of the kth argument of the jth literal is uniquely defined in the program P by the tuple $\langle c, j, p, k\rangle$, where p is the predicate symbol of the jth literal of c.

By convention the fictive position $\langle c, i, p, 0\rangle$ denotes the ith literal of the clause c of which the predicate symbol is p.

$Pos(X)$ is the set of all positions of X, where X can be either an argument, a literal, a clause or a program.

In the definition of positions, the predicate symbol p is redundant, this simplifies some notations further on. Unification of positions is defined as follows:

Definition 2 Unification of positions. Let α and β be the positions of two arguments a and b such that $\alpha = \langle c_1, j, p, k\rangle$ and $\beta = \langle c_2, 0, p, k\rangle$ where $j \neq 0$. $\mathbf{unify}(\alpha, \beta) \Leftrightarrow \exists$ renaming substitution θ such that $a\theta$ has no variable in common with b and $\exists$ substitution σ such that $a\theta\sigma = b\sigma$.

Throughout this paper we will consider that all positions have a mode annotation which is either ***in***, ***out***, ***in/out*** or ***none***. ***in*** is for positions which are either in heads of clauses and ground on invocation (after unification) or in bodies of clauses and ground on success. ***out*** is for positions which are in heads of clauses and ground after the success of the clause or in bodies of clauses and ground on invocation (before unification). ***in/out*** is for positions which are both ***in*** and ***out***. ***none*** is for positions unannotated. The set of input positions of the program P is denoted by $\mathcal{I}(P)$, the set of output positions is denoted by $\mathcal{O}(P)$. More information on annotations can be found in [BPM93].

In order to talk about the operational semantics of Prolog programs, we need the well known notions of SLD-computation and SLD-tree (or *search tree*). We will only recall the definition of search tree. The following definition is taken from [DM93, p. 89] and has been adapted to the computational rule used in Prolog (i.e. top-down and left to right.)

Definition 3 Search tree. The search tree of a Prolog program P and a goal g_0, denoted by $ST_{P \cup g_0}$, is a tree with labeled nodes and edges defined as follows:

- the label of each node is a state of an SLD-computation of P and g_0,
- the label of each edge is a clause of P,
- the root node is labeled by the initial state $\langle g_0, \{\} \rangle$,
- a node n labeled by the state s is connected by an edge labeled c with a node n' labeled s' iff s, c, s' is an SLD-derivation controlled by the selection rule of Prolog.

A state of an SLD-computation is a pair $\langle g_i, \sigma_i \rangle$, where g_i is a goal and σ_i a substitution.

In a search tree, each branch is an SLD-derivation. Finite branches are either *success branches* if they end with the empty goal, or *failure branches* if they end with a non-empty goal. Leaves of success branches are called *success leaves*, leaves of failure branches are called *failure leaves*. Infinite branches are not considered in this paper.

If T is a search tree, we will call $\mathcal{N}(T)$ the set of nodes of T and $\mathcal{E}(T)$ the set of edges of T.

2.2 Slicing Definitions

In our view, to be a slice, a program S must be a "subset" of a program P and must preserve partially the declarative and operational semantics of P:

1. ***Declarative semantics:*** If g_0 is a goal to prove, $S \cup \{g_0\}$ must preserve partially the declarative semantics of $P \cup \{g_0\}$, i.e. if $P \cup \{g_0\} \models A_1, \ldots, A_n$, where A_i are computed answers, then $S \cup \{g_0\} \models$ a subset of $A_1, \ldots, A_n$.
2. ***Operational semantics:*** $S \cup \{g_0\}$ must preserve partially the operational semantics of $P \cup \{g_0\}$, i.e. $ST_{S \cup g_0}$ must be "included" in $ST_{P \cup g_0}$.

In the following, we define formally the meaning of the words "subset" and "included."

Slicing Criterion. To achieve these requirements, the slicing criterion must include (1) a goal, g_0, to be able to talk about semantics and (2) a set of positions, $\mathcal{P}$, the user is interested in preserving the declarative semantics of. Furthermore, as in debugging we are usually interested in an incorrectly computed value, we can focus the analysis on the particular SLD-derivation that produced this value. Hence a slicing criterion for Prolog, as opposed to imperative slicing which does not need to handle indeterminism, has a third component, E, which is the success leaf of the SLD-derivation of interest.

Definition 4 Slicing Criterion. For a program P, a slicing criterion is a triple $\langle g_0, \mathcal{P}, E\rangle$, where g_0 is a goal to prove, $\mathcal{P}$ is a set of positions, subset of $\mathcal{I}(P)$ and E is a success leaf of $ST_{P\cup g_0}$.

Program Abstraction. It was said, the slice should be a *"subset" of an original program*. This notion is formalized in the following in terms of *abstraction*.

Definition 5 Empty term, Empty literal, Empty clause.

- An *empty term*, denoted by $A_\emptyset$ is an *anonymous variable*[1].
- An *empty literal*, denoted by $L_\emptyset$ is the predicate **true**.
- An *empty clause*, denoted by $C_\emptyset$ is a clause that contains no literals.

Definition 6 Abstract argument, literal, clause and program. The binary relation $\succeq$, which can be read as "is an abstraction of", is defined as follows:

- **Arguments**: if a is an argument then (1) $A_\emptyset \succeq a$ and (2) $a \succeq a$.
- **Literals**: if $l = p(a_1, \ldots, a_n)$ is a literal then (1) $L_\emptyset \succeq l$ and (2) $(\forall l_a = p(a_{a_1}, \ldots, a_{a_n})$ where $\forall i = 1, \ldots, n, a_{a_i} \succeq a_i)$, $l_a \succeq l$.
- **Definite clauses**: if $c = l_0 \leftarrow l_1, l_2, \ldots, l_n$ is a definite clause then (1) $C_\emptyset \succeq c$ and (2) $(\forall c_a = l_{a_0} \leftarrow l_{a_1}, l_{a_2}, \ldots, l_{a_n}$ such that (a) there exists a renaming substitution θ and (b) $\forall i = 0, \ldots, n$, $l_{a_i}\theta \succeq l_i$ with $l_{a_0} \neq L_\emptyset)$, $c_a \succeq c$.
- **Definite programs**: if $P = \{c_1, c_2, \ldots, c_n\}$ is a definite program then $(\forall P_a = \{c_{a_1}, c_{a_2}, \ldots, c_{a_n}\}$ where $\forall i = 1, \ldots, n, c_{a_i} \succeq c_i)$, $P_a \succeq P$.

In Def. 6, renaming is only allowed at the level of the clause and not at the level of literals (or arguments). This is to avoid losing aliasing between arguments of the same clause.

Proposition 7. *If P is a definite program then $\forall P_a, P_a \succeq P \Rightarrow P_a$ is a definite program.*

Operational Semantics. Before giving a definition of the slice, we define its intended operational semantics as an abstraction of the operational semantics of the original program, i.e. of its search tree.

Definition 8 Abstract substitution. For a substitution σ, $\sigma_a \succeq \sigma$ iff there exists a renaming substitution θ such that $\sigma_a\theta \subseteq \sigma$.

As the labels of the nodes of a search tree T are states of SLD-computations, therefore the labels of the nodes of an abstract search tree of T are abstract states of some SLD-computations of T.

[1] According to Sterling and Shapiro [SS94, p. 234] an anonymous variable is a variable that appears just once in a clause. Syntactically it is written as an underscore in Prolog.

Definition 9 Abstract SLD-computation state. For a state $\langle g, \sigma \rangle$ of an SLD-computation, $\langle g_a, \sigma_a \rangle \succeq \langle g, \sigma \rangle$ iff $g_a \succeq g$ and $\sigma_a \succeq \sigma$.

In order to define the relation that exists between a search tree and its abstract search trees, we need to have an order relation on the nodes of search trees.

Definition 10 Search tree nodes partial ordering. The binary relation $\leq_T$ over the nodes of a search tree T is defined as follows:

- if s_0 is the root node of T, then for any node $s_i \in T$, $s_0 \leq_T s_i$, and
- $s_i \leq_T s_i$, and
- $s_i \leq_T s_j$ iff the sequence $s_i, c_i, \ldots, c_{j-1}, s_j$ belongs to T.

Proposition 11. *If T is a search tree then $\leq_T$ is a partial order over T.*

Note that $\leq_T$ can only compare nodes of the same SLD-derivation.

The following definition states the requirements for a tree T_a to be an abstract search tree of a search tree T.

Definition 12 Abstract Search Tree. For a search tree T, $T_a \succeq T$ iff:

1. T_a is a search tree,
2. there exists a function f such that:
   (a) $f : \mathcal{N}(T_a) \longmapsto \mathcal{N}(T)$.
   (b) f is injective and total.
   (c) $\forall s_{a_1}, s_{a_2} \in \mathcal{N}(T_a)$ such that there exists an edge $c_a \in \mathcal{E}(T_a)$ from s_{a_1} to s_{a_2}, then $f(s_{a_1}), f(s_{a_2})$ and the edge $c \in \mathcal{E}(T)$ from $f(s_{a_1})$ to $f(s_{a_2})$ are such that $s_{a_1} \succeq f(s_{a_1}), s_{a_2} \succeq f(s_{a_2})$ and $c_a \succeq c$,
   (d) for two states $s_{a_1}, s_{a_2} \in \mathcal{N}(T_a)$, $s_{a_1} \leq_{T_a} s_{a_2} \Rightarrow f(s_{a_1}) \leq_T f(s_{a_2})$.

Intuitively, if T_a is an abstract search tree of T, then there must exist a mapping from T_a to T. This mapping ensures that for each node n_a of T_a there must be a corresponding node n in T such that n_a is an abstract node of n, and for a given node n, there is at most one abstract node. Furthermore because of part 2d of the definition, the relative order of the nodes in T_a and in T is the same.

As was said earlier, the user is interested in partially preserving the declarative semantics of the program, hence intuitively the slice should be an abstract program. Most of the time not all SLD-resolutions need to be taken into account, the derivation which produces the substitutions of interest should be sufficient. However, as we will see later, considering only this SLD-derivation is not enough. Nevertheless, it is easy to show that only the part of the search tree to the "left" of the SLD-derivation of interest is relevant to compute the slice, because the part to the "right" cannot have any effect on the computed answers.

Definition 13 LP-tree. Let T be a tree with labeled edges, $\leq_L$ be a left-most, depth-first total order on $\mathcal{N}(T)$ and E be an element of $\mathcal{N}(T)$. **LP-tree**(T, E) is a tree such that $\forall n \in$ **LP-tree**(T, E), $n \leq_L E$.

Slice. We are now in a position to give a definition of a slice for Prolog.

Definition 14 Slice. A slice S of a definite program P and a slicing criterion $\langle g_0, \mathcal{P}, E\rangle$ is such that:

1. $S \succeq P$,
2. $\mathcal{P} \subseteq Pos(S)$,
3. $\exists E_a \in ST_{S \cup g_0}, E_a \succeq E$,
4. **LP-tree**$(ST_{S \cup g_0}, E_a) \succeq$ **LP-tree**$(ST_{P \cup g_0}, E)$.

The first statement of the definition says that the slice must be an abstract program of the original program. The second ensures that at least the positions of interest are in the slice. The third statement ensures that the slice terminates (if the original program terminates) with an abstraction of the success node of the SLD-derivation of interest. The fourth statement says that the slice computes the same substitutions for the non-abstracted arguments as the original program does and that it does not compute anything else.

Proposition 15. *If S is a slice of a definite program P, then S is a definite program.*

Theorem 16. *Let S be a slice of a program P and a slicing criterion $\langle g_0, \mathcal{P}, E\rangle$. For all positions $s \in Pos(S)$ such that $s \neq A_\emptyset$, for all substitutions computed by $S \cup \{g_0\}$ for s before reaching E_a, there is an identical substitution computed by $P \cup \{g_0\}$ for s.*

The given definition of slice ensures the existence of at least one slice: the program itself. Finding the minimal slice is an undecidable problem [We84].

3 Example

Figure 1 shows two examples of slices of the same program and the same goal but with respect to different arguments. The program simplifies arithmetical expressions. The procedure **simp** decomposes the expression into atomic elements, then recombines them together, and tries to apply one of the simplification rules s. Each time a simplification is made, a message is printed on the screen with **print_reduc** and the number of simplifications is incremented. **simp** has 4 arguments. The first one is the expression to simplify, the second one is the simplified expression, the third one is the number of simplifications already applied to the first argument and the fourth one is the number of simplifications applied to the simplified expression.

An execution of the program with the goal **simp(2 * 3 * x, R, 0, F)** returns `R = 5 * x` and `F = 1`, for the computed solutions. The expected solution was `6 * x` for `R`. A slicing session is then started wrt the goal which produces the erroneous value.

The left column of figure 1 shows the clauses of the original program used to compute the goal **simp(2 * 3 * x, R, 0, F)**. The middle column is a slice for the computed answer `R = 5 * x` and `F = 1` and for the second argument of the head of the first clause **simp**. The right column is a slice for the same computed answers but for the fourth argument of the head of the same clause.

Used clauses (the original program contains 49 clauses)	**Slice (2nd argument)** Criterion: ⟨ g_0 =**simp(2 * 3 * x, R, 0, F)**, $\mathcal{P}$ ={ (1, 1, **simp**, 2) }⟩ E = ⟨ ∅, { `R/5*x, F/1` } ⟩⟩,	**Slice (4th argument)** Criterion: ⟨ g_0 =**simp(2 * 3 * x, R, 0, F)**, $\mathcal{P}$ ={ (1, 1, **simp**, 4) }⟩ E = ⟨ ∅, { `R/5*x, F/1` } ⟩⟩
(c1) simp(E, R, I, F) ← E = X * Y, simp(X, XR, I, IP), simp(Y, YR, IP, FP), s(XR * YR, R, FP, F).	simp(E, R, _, _) ← E = X * Y, simp(X, XR, _, _), simp(Y, YR, _, _), s(XR * YR, R, _, _).	simp(E, _, I, F) ← E = X * Y, simp(X, XR, I, IP), simp(Y, YR, IP, FP), s(XR * YR , _, FP, F).
(c2) simp(E, E, I, I) ← number(E).	simp(E, E, _, _) ← number(E).	simp(E, _, F, F) ← number(E).
(c3) simp(E, E, I, I) ← atom(E).	simp(E, E, _, _) ← $L_\emptyset$.	simp(_, _, I, I) ← $L_\emptyset$.
(c4) s(X * Y, R, I, F) ← number(X), number(Y), +(X, Y, R), /* bug */ +(I, 1, F), print_reduc.	s(X * Y, R, _, _) ← $L_\emptyset$, number(Y), +(X, Y, R), $L_\emptyset$, $L_\emptyset$.	s(X * Y, _, I, F) ← $L_\emptyset$, number(Y), $L_\emptyset$, +(I, 1, F), $L_\emptyset$.
(c5) s(E, E, I, I) ←	s(E, E, _, _) ←	s(_, _, I, I) ←
(c6) print_reduc ← write("Simplification"), nl.	$C_\emptyset$	$C_\emptyset$

Fig. 1. Examples of slices: the left column shows the clauses used to compute the goal `simp(2 * 3 * x, R, 0, F)`, the middle and right columns show 2 slices of the program, respectively for the 2nd and 4th argument of the first clause **simp**.

The slice for the second argument has narrowed the source code to investigate for the bug from the 49 literals of the original program to 12. This makes easier and quicker to find that s (clause 4) adds numbers instead of multiply them.

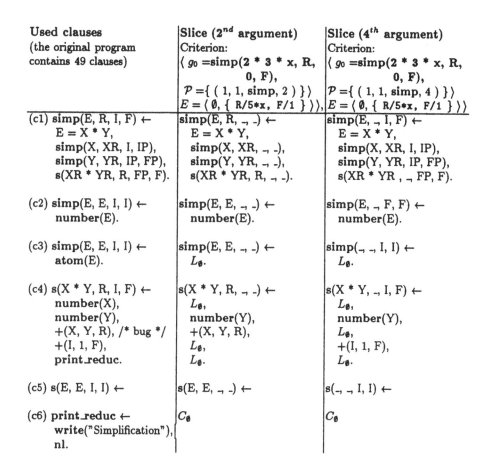

Some observations can be made from this example. The program shown is made of two techniques (for details about techniques, see Vasconcelos in [Va94]). One that simplifies the arithmetical expression and one that counts the number of simplifications. The first two arguments of all clauses are part of the first technique whereas the last two are part of the second. The slice wrt to the second argument eliminates the last technique completely, hence hiding half of the arguments. The slice wrt the fourth argument save the part of the first technique *which is needed to preserve the control flow between clauses.* Indeed if we could remove altogether the first two arguments which are useless for computing the last two arguments as far as data flow is concerned, we would have for the first clause:

```
simp(_, _, I, F) ←
    simp(_, _, I, IP),
    simp(_, _ IP, FP),
    s(_, _, FP, F).
```

which would loop.

Another interesting observation is that only one of the two calls to the built-in **number** in the first clause of **s** is removed. The first one succeeds in the analyzed execution "producing" no value, whereas the second must be kept to ensure that the abstract clause, called with the expression `5 * x`, still fails. Determining which literals must be kept in the slice to preserve the control flow between clauses is one of the main contributions of this paper (see Sec. 4.2).

4 Dependencies

Before actually computing slices, two kinds of analysis must be performed to collect enough information about the program and its execution. The first one is a data dependency analysis and the second one is a control flow analysis.

4.1 Data Dependency

In order to ensure the fourth property of the definition, a slice must compute the same substitutions as the original program does for variables of the non-abstracted arguments. This is partially achieved by a data dependency analysis over the positions of the slicing criterion.

Many works have been carried on data dependency analysis. The purpose of this article is neither to expose in details any analysis nor to compare existing algorithms. We only recall the definitions of Boye et al. [BPM93] concerning *internal* and *external* data dependencies.

Definition 17 Internal Data Dependency. For a clause c, and two positions α and β such that $\alpha \in \mathcal{I}(c)$ and $\beta \in \mathcal{O}(c)$, the internal data dependence relation $\rightarrow_i$ is defined as follows:

- $\alpha \rightarrow_i \beta$ iff α and β have at least one common variable,

Definition 18 External Data Dependency. For two clauses c, d, and two positions $\alpha = (c, j, q, k)$ and $\beta = (d, 0, q, k)$ such that **unify**(α, β) does not fail. The external data dependence relation $\rightarrow_e$ is defined as follows:

- $\alpha \rightarrow_e \beta$ iff $\alpha \in \mathcal{O}(c)$ and $\beta \in \mathcal{I}(c)$, and
- $\beta \rightarrow_e \alpha$ iff $\alpha \in \mathcal{I}(c)$ and $\beta \in \mathcal{O}(c)$.

The data dependency relation $\rightarrow$ is equal to $\rightarrow_i \cup \rightarrow_e$. The transitive closure is denoted by $\rightarrow^*$

4.2 Control Flow

To ensure that the control flow between clauses that arises from the resolution of g_0 is the same in the slice as in the original program, two analyses are needed. The first one, based on the search tree, computes *failure positions*. These positions are used to guarantee that no clauses not executed by the original program are executed in the slice. The other analysis is based on the proof tree and ensures that all the clauses of the slice that should be executed are reachable from the top level goal.

Failure Positions. In order to ensure the fourth property of the definition, a slice must not compute substitutions that were not computed by the original program P. This constraint is achieved by a search for *failure positions* in the search tree $ST_{P \cup g_0}$.

Informally a *failure position* is a position that can be responsible for a failure during the resolution of a goal.

In our subset of Prolog, a failure[2] can have three distinct causes. Firstly, a failure happens when the first literal of the resolvent cannot unify with any clause head because there is no clause with the right predicate symbol and arity in the program. Then, automatically, a failure will also occur in the slice for this literal. Secondly, a failure happens when the first literal of the resolvent cannot unify with any clause head because no substitution can be found for some of the arguments of the two literals. For this case, the first part of the definition of failure positions given below define those arguments in order to be able to preserve them in the slice. Thirdly a failure happens when a built-in predicate fails. If no implementation details are known, all the arguments of the predicate are "responsible" for the failure. The second part of the definition catches these arguments.

Definition 19 Failure Position. Let $ST_{P \cup g_0}$ be the search tree of a program P and a goal g_0. A position $\alpha = \langle c, i, p, k \rangle$ of P is a *failure position* iff:

- $i = 0$ and there exists a position $\beta = \langle D, j, p, k \rangle$ such that:
  1. β is in the first literal of the goal list of a failure leaf of $ST_{P \cup g_0}$, and
  2. $\neg$ **unify**(α, β), or
- $i \neq 0$ and p is the built-in predicate symbol of the first literal of the goal list of a failure leaf of $ST_{P \cup g_0}$.

In the program shown Figure 1 the positions corresponding to the argument Y of **number**(Y) of the first clause **s** is a failure position. Even if it is not needed to compute any substitution, it is needed to preserve the control flow of the original program. It is straightforward to see that if **number**(Y) is removed, goals that should not have been executed will be executed when executing the slice, namely `+(X, Y, R)` for the slice of the middle column and `+(I, 1, F)` for the slice of the right column.

To determine the failure positions of an execution one could use for example Opium [Du92] which provides a *leaf failure analysis*. Discussing analysis algorithms is out of the scope of this paper.

[2] Run-time errors are not considered as failures.

Proof Tree. To satisfy the third and fourth property of the definition, all the clauses of the slice that should be executed must be reachable from the top level goal. This is achieved with an analysis based on the proof tree of the execution.

We use the definition of Deransart and Małuszyński as given in [DM93, p. 27]:

Definition 20 Proof tree. For a program P and a goal g_0, a *proof tree* is a labeled ordered tree T such that:

- The root node is an instance name of g_0.
- Every other node is labeled by an instance name of a clause of P.
- Let n be a node labeled by an instance name $\langle c, \sigma \rangle$, where c is the clause $l_0 \leftarrow l_1, \ldots, l_m$ and $m \geq 0$. Then n has m children and for $i = 1, \ldots, m$, the i-th child of n is labeled $\langle c', \sigma' \rangle$, where c' is a clause with the head l'_0 such that $l_i\sigma = l'_0\sigma'$.

Let T be the proof tree of $P \cup \{g_0\}$ and c be a clause of P such that the slice contains an abstract clause of c. For all such c, the slice must also have abstractions of all calling literals of c which belong to the proof tree. Because of that the abstract clause of c could be reached from the top level goal.

The proof tree can be computed, for example, by using the dynamic tools provided by Opium [Du92].

5 A Slicing Algorithm

In this section, we give a slicing algorithm to compute slices that fulfill definition 14. In the following, the computed slice is called S and is a slice of a program P and a slicing criterion $\mathcal{C} = \langle g_0, \mathcal{P}, E \rangle$. We assume that a set $\mathcal{D}$ of data dependencies, a set $\mathcal{P}_{fail}$ of failure positions and a proof tree **PT** corresponding to the execution that succeeds with E are available.

With our algorithm, a slice is computed in 2 stages:

1. computation of a first set of positions that should belong to the slice,
2. construction of an executable slice from the previously obtained set of positions.

5.1 Stage 1: Computing the set of positions of the slice

The algorithm is shown Fig. 2. It is composed of two loops: one which computes all positions needed to ensure the data flow and another one which computes all positions needed to ensure the control flow.

Data Flow. The data flow is computed by a closure over data dependencies. This closure finds all positions α of the program such that $\alpha \rightarrow^* \beta$ where β is a position of the slicing criterion. Lines 1 to 8 of the algorithm Fig. 2 shows this loop.

```
/* P_prog: the set of all positions of the original program                          */
/* P_criterion: the set of positions of the slicing criterion (subset of P_prog)     */
/* P_fail: a set of failure positions (subset of P_prog)                             */
/* D: a set of data dependencies                                                     */
/* P_slice: the set of positions of the slice                                        */

1    P_slice := ∅

     /* Data flow closure */
2    P_work := P_criterion
3    while P_work ≠ ∅ do
4           select one element p of P_work and remove it
5           if p ∉ P_slice then
6              P_slice := P_slice ∪ closure(p, P_prog, D)
7           fi
8    od

     /* Control flow closure */
9    while ∃p = ⟨d, j, w, k⟩ ∈ P_slice, ∃n_i = ⟨c, σ_n⟩ ∈ PT such that p ∈ Pos(c)
           ∧ ∃n_f = ⟨c_f, σ_f⟩ ∈ PT, c_f ≠ g_0, n_f = father(n_i) in PT,
             n_i is the i^th son of n_f
           ∧ ∄ q ∈ Pos(c_f), q ∈ P_slice do
10               P_slice := P_slice ∪ {⟨c_f, i, w, 0⟩}
11               while ∃r ∈ P_fail, r ∉ P_slice ∃s ∈ P_slice such that
                          r and s belong to the same clause do
12                   P_slice := P_slice ∪ closure(r, P_prog, D)
13               od
14   od
```

Fig. 2. Slicing algorithm: computation of the positions of the slice

Control Flow. To preserve the intended control flow, all the positions computed in $\mathcal{P}_{slice}$ must be in clauses which can be called when executing the top level goal. For example, if a clause is not data dependent of the top level goal but is needed to compute some substitutions, if we only rely on data dependencies to construct the slice, this clause would not be reached when executing the slice.

The purpose of the loop of lines 9 and 10 of Fig. 2 is to ensure that all the clauses that will belong to the slice (i.e. which have at least one position which is in $\mathcal{P}_{slice}$) will also have all their calling literals in the slice. The calling literals are known from the proof tree. If a calling literal l has no argument position in $\mathcal{P}_{slice}$ then the fictive position of l is added to $\mathcal{P}_{slice}$.

The inner loop, lines 11 and 12, adds to $\mathcal{P}_{slice}$ all failure positions that are in clauses that will be in the slice. Each time a failure position is added, all arguments which have a transitive data dependency with it are also added. Of course, if the closure leads to add positions to $\mathcal{P}_{slice}$ such that these positions belong to clauses which did not have any position in $\mathcal{P}_{slice}$ yet, the algorithm must ensure that these clauses are also reachable from the top level goal, hence the inner loop.

This stage returns the set of positions $\mathcal{P}_{slice}$.

5.2 Stage 2: Computing the slice

In order to obtain a program, the elements of $\mathcal{P}_{slice}$ are mapped to the original program. The algorithm applies the following rules:

- $\forall$ clause $c \in P$, **if** $\exists p \in \mathcal{P}_{slice}, p \in Pos(c)$ **then** $\exists!\ c_a \in S, c_a \succeq c \wedge c_a \neq C_\emptyset$.[3]
- $\forall$ clause $c \in P$, **if** $\nexists p \in \mathcal{P}_{slice}, p \in Pos(c)$ **then** $\exists!\ c_a \in S$ such that $c_a \succeq c$ and $c_a = C_\emptyset$
- The abstract clauses c_a in S are in the same relative order as the clauses c in P.

In the next rules, **head**(l, c) holds iff the literal l is the head of c. An abstract clause c_a ($c_a \neq C_\emptyset$) is computed from a clause c by applying the following rules:

- $\forall$ literal $l \in c$, **if** $\exists p \in \mathcal{P}_{slice}, p \in Pos(l)$ **then** $\exists!\ l_a \in c_a, l_a \succeq l \wedge l_a \neq L_\emptyset$.
- $\forall$ literal $l \in c$, $\neg$**head**(l, c) **if** $\nexists p \in \mathcal{P}_{slice}, p \in Pos(l)$ **then** $\exists!\ l_a \in c_a, l_a \succeq l \wedge l_a = L_\emptyset$.
- $\forall$ literal $l \in c$, **head**(l, c), **if** $\nexists p \in \mathcal{P}_{slice}, p \in Pos(l)$ **then** $\exists!\ l_a \in c_a, l_a \succeq l \wedge l_a \neq L_\emptyset$.
- The abstract literals l_a in c_a are in the same order as the literals l in c.

A difference is made between literals inside bodies of clauses and heads of clauses. This is to ensure that there will be no clauses with heads being $L_\emptyset$. Finally, abstract literals l_a ($l_a \neq L_\emptyset$) are computed as follows:

- $\forall$ argument $a \in l$ **if** $\exists p \in \mathcal{P}_{slice}, p = Pos(a)$ **then** $\exists!\ a_a \in l_a, a_a \succeq a$ and $a_a =_s a$[4]
- $\forall$ argument $a \in l$ **if** $\nexists p \in \mathcal{P}_{slice}, p = Pos(a)$ **then** $\exists!\ a_a \in l_a, a_a \succeq a \wedge a_a = A_\emptyset$.
- The abstract arguments a_a in l_a are in the same order as the arguments a in l.

6 Related Work

To our knowledge, this is the second time a slicing algorithm treats abstraction of arguments. The other algorithm was proposed by Horwitz et al. and is designed for imperative languages [HRB90]. In such languages, abstraction of arguments is not "natural": reducing the number of arguments of functions leads to syntactically incorrect programs [HRB90]. In Prolog, the notion of anonymous variables and our definition of control flow make abstraction of arguments a natural task.

One of the two other algorithms related to slicing for Prolog is proposed by Gyimóthy et Paakki [GP95]. Their algorithm computes a slice of the *proof tree* in order to reduce the number of questions asked by an algorithmic debugger à la Shapiro [Sh83]. The slice is computed from a static dependency graph containing only oriented data dependencies. Their algorithm does not, and cannot, be used to compute executable programs such as ours does.

[3] $\exists! x$ means "there exists a unique x."

[4] $=_s$ means "syntactically equal".

In [ZCU94], Zhao et al. defined a program representation of concurrent logic programs called *literal dependence net*. Their concerns are similar to ours in the sense that they want to make explicit both control and data flow of logic programs. However, their representation of programs handles dependencies only between literals and not between arguments as ours does. A slicing algorithm based on their representation cannot yield a program with abstracted arguments. Hence the produced slices are in general bigger.

7 Conclusion and future work

In this paper, we described a backward slicing algorithm for Prolog. At present our algorithm is applicable to a subset of Prolog including pure logic plus simple built-in predicates. We plan to extend its domain of validity.

Our slicing algorithm is the first, to our knowledge, to produce slices for Prolog which are executable programs. It is also the first to integrate "naturally" abstraction of arguments. The two main contributions of this paper are a general definition of slicing adapted to Prolog by use of the notion of *abstract search tree*, and an algorithm that compute slices which are executable programs. Furthermore, the definition of abstract search tree should be useful for other debugging techniques.

We have developed a prototype in Eclipse Prolog that uses both static and dynamic information to compute slices as shown in Example 1. It is freely available at `http://www.irisa.fr/lande/schoenig/`

Acknowledgments

The authors would like to thank Marc Lefur, Jacques Noyé and Olivier Ridoux for their fruitful comments on earlier drafts of this article. They also would like to give special thanks to the anonymous referees for the thoroughness of their remarks.

References

[BPM93] J. Boye, J. Paakki, and J. Małuszyński. Synthesis of directionality information for functional logic programs. In *Third International Workshop WSA '93, Proceeding Static Analysis, Padova, Italy*, volume 724 of *LNCS*, pages 165–177. Springer-Verlag, September 1993.

[De89] S. K. Debray. Static inference of modes and data dependencies in logic programs. *ACM Transactions on Programming Languages and Systems*, 11(3):418–450, July 1989.

[DM93] P. Deransart and J. Małuszyński. *A grammatical view of logic programming*. MIT Press, 1993. ISBN 0-262-04140-5.

[DN94] M. Ducassé and J. Noyé. Logic programming environments: Dynamic program analysis and debugging. *The Journal of Logic Programming*, 19/20:351–384, May/July 1994.

[Du92] M. Ducassé. *An extendable trace analyser to support automated debugging*. PhD thesis, University of Rennes I, France, June 1992. European Doctorate.

[Du95] M. Ducassé, editor. *Second international workshop on automated and algorithmic debugging*, http://www.irisa.fr/manifestations/AADEBUG95/, May 1995.

[GP95] T. Gyimóthy and J. Paakki. Static slicing of logic programs. In Ducassé [Du95].

[GS95] R. Gupta and M.-L. Soffa. Hybrid slicing: an approach for refining static slices using dynamic information. In *3rd ACM Symposium on Foundation of Software Engineering*. University of Pittsburgh, ACM, October 10-13 1995.

[HKF95] T. Hoffner, M. Kamkar, and P. Fritzson. Evaluation of program slicing tools. In Ducassé [Du95].

[HPR88] S. Horwitz, J. Prins, and T. Reps. On the adequacy of program dependence graphs for representing programs. In *Conference record of the 15th ACM Symposium on Principles of Programming Languages (POPL'88)*, pages 146–157, San Diego, CA USA, 1988.

[HR92] S. Horwitz and T. Reps. The use of program dependence graphs in software engineering. In *14th International Conference on Software Engineering (Melbourne Australia)*, pages 392–411, may 1992.

[HRB90] S. Horwitz, T. Reps, and D. Binkley. Interprocedural slicing using dependence graphs. *ACM Transactions on Programming Languages and Systems, TOPLAS*, 12(1):26–60, [1] 1990.

[Ko93] B. Korel. Identifying faulty modifications in software maintenance. In P. A. Fritzson, editor, *First International Workshop On Automated Algorithmic Debugging*, volume 749 of *LNCS*, Linkoeping, Sweden, May 1993. Springer-Verlag.

[LR87] H. K. N. Leung and H. K. Reghbati. Comments on program slicing. *IEEE Transaction on Software Engineering*, SE-13(12):1370–1371, December 1987.

[Ly84] J. R. Lyle. *Evaluating Variations on Program Slicing for Debugging*. PhD thesis, University of Maryland, 1984.

[Sh83] E. Y. Shapiro. *Algorithmic Program Debugging*. MIT Press, Cambridge, MA, 1983. ISBN 0-262-19218-7.

[SS94] L. Sterling and E. Shapiro. *The art of Prolog, 2nd edition*. Advanced Programming Techniques. The MIT Press, 1994.

[Ti95] F. Tip. A survey of program slicing techniques. *Journal of Programming Languages*, 3(3):121–189, September 1995.

[Va94] W. W. Vasconcelos. A method for extracting Prolog programming techniques. Technical Report 27, Dept. Artificial Intelligence, University of Edinburgh, 80 South Bridge, Edinburgh EH1 1HN, Scotland, Great Britain, 1994.

[We82] M. Weiser. Programmers use slices when debugging. *Communications of the ACM*, 25(7):446–452, July 1982.

[We84] M. Weiser. Program slicing. *IEEE Transactions on Software Engineering*, SE-10(4):352–357, July 1984.

[ZCU94] J. Zhao, J. Cheng, and K Ushijima. Literal dependence net and its use in concurrent logic programming environment. In *Workshop on Parallel Logic Programming*, pages 127–141, December 1994.

Combining Slicing and Constraint Solving for Validation of Measurement Software

Gregor Snelting

Technische Universität Braunschweig
Abteilung Softwaretechnologie
Bültenweg 88, D-38106 Braunschweig

Abstract. We show how to combine program slicing and constraint solving in order to obtain better slice accuracy. The method is used in a program analysis tool for the validation of computer-controlled measurement systems. It will be used by the Physikalisch-Technische Bundesanstalt for verification of legally required calibration standards. The paper describes how to generate and simplify path conditions based on program slices. An example shows that the technique can indeed increase slice precision and reveal manipulations of the so-called calibration path.
Keywords: Program Slicing, Constraint Solving, Measurement System, Software Validation, Path Condition.

1 Introduction and Background

The Physikalisch-Technische-Bundesanstalt (PTB) is a national institution which – among other tasks – is responsible for the verification of calibration standards. Every measurement system which is used in medical, commercial, and similar transactions (e.g. an electricity meter or a blood alcohol tester) must stick to legally required standards for accuracy of measurement, robustness and other quality factors. Therefore, the prototype of every measurement system must be certified by PTB. Once the prototype has been thoroughly examined and validated, the numerous specimen of a specific measurement system are (less intensively) checked by local authorities.

Today, 95% of all measurement systems checked by PTB are controlled by software. Even the cheese scale has a built-in microprocessor and a digital display. Thus the validation of measurement software is part of the certification process. In particular, it must be checked that measurement values are not – accidentally or intentionally – manipulated or garbled. The most sensitive parts of measurement software are those which handle the incoming raw values and prepare it for display, while other parts like e.g. user interface control are less important. The data flow path from the sensor input port to the display output port is called the *calibration path* and is subject to most painstaking scrutiny.

At the moment measurement software validation at PTB relies on manual code inspections, which is a time-consuming and error-prone method. PTB is thus strongly interested in tool support for software validation. Therefore, PTB in cooperation with the Technical University of Braunschweig launched a project which aims at a tool for analysis and semiautomatic validation of measurement software. The tool must analyse source code and support the PTB engineer by visualizing the obtained information. It must in particular check that there are no unwanted influences on the calibration path. If the calibration path is not safe, the tool must provide a detailed analysis of the conditions which can lead to a garbling of measurement values. Our ultimate goal is to automatically generate statements like the following: "If CTRL-X is pressed on the keyboard, and the left mouse key is pressed as well, then the measurement value is 8.7% too high".

It is the aim of this paper to describe the underlying technology of the new tool. Basically, the tool is based on program slicing, a technique which has recently received much attention as a device for program analysis, understanding, and validation[1]. But slicing can sometimes deliver too imprecise information, in particular if the program contains complex data structures. We will show how slicing can be combined with constraint solving in order to increase precision. In particular, the method allows to extract precise (and understandable) necessary conditions under which a certain dataflow (e.g. from keyboard to calibration path) can happen. Thus the technique not only improves slicing, but also allows for the generation of error messages as sketched above.

2 Program Slicing

Program Slicing was originally introduced by Weiser as a technique to support debugging [16]. Informally, a slice is defined as follows: Given a statement s and a variable v in s, determine all statements which might affect the value of v at s. Today, there is a wealth of algorithms for slicing, as well as numerous applications besides debugging. It is now possible to handle complex languages like full C (perhaps with some restrictions for pointers), and slicing has found successful applications in program understanding and software maintenance. Tip [15] presents an overview of current slicing technology; [9] describes applications in software engineering. We will only present the most basic definitions.

Definition 1. A *control-flow graph* (CFG) contains one node for each statement and control predicate of a program. An edge from node i to node j indicates the possible control flow from the former to the latter. The variables which are referenced at node i are denoted $ref(i)$; the variables which are defined at i (that is, assigned a value), are denoted $def(i)$.

Usually, a CFG does not contain transitive flow dependencies; we always assume that the CFG is transitively irreducible. Furthermore, we assume that there are special START and STOP nodes corresponding to the beginning and ending of the program or procedure.

[1] In fact, Denning proposed as early as 1977 to use data flow analysis for the validation of safety critical software [6]

Definition 2. A statement j is called *data flow dependent* on statement i, if

1. there is a path p from i to j in the CFG;
2. there is a variable v, where $v \in def(i)$ and $v \in ref(j)$;
3. for all statements $k \neq i$ in p, $v \notin def(k)$.

In this definition, complex data structures like arrays and records are treated as single variables, that is, there are data flow dependencies even if different or disjoint subcomponents of the data structure are involved. Pointers are ignored alltogether in this definition (and in this paper), as well as problems of VAR-parameters and aliasing. There are good conservative approximations to data flow dependencies in the presence of aliases which can easily be integrated into the slicing framework [12, 3]. For pointers and complex data structures, several authors proposed the use of abstract memory locations [8, 1]. The analysis of dependencies between arrays and array components has been studied intensively in the framework of program optimization and parallelization. We will not discuss any of these extensions, but only remark that for pointers, arrays, and VAR-parameters the computed slices may be too big[2]. Thus constraint solving promises to be useful for these extensions as well. For arrays, we will see later how constraint solving can improve slice accuracy.

Definition 3. Statement j is called a *postdominator* of statement i, if any path p from i to STOP must go through j. i is called a *predominator* of j if any control flow from START to j must go through i.

In typical programs, statements in loop bodies are predominated by the loop entry point and postdominated by the loop exit point. In fact, the notion of pre- and postdominators can be used to identify loops in arbitrary flow graphs.

Definition 4. Statement j is called *control dependent* on control predicate i, if

1. there is a path p in the CFG from i to j;
2. j is a postdominator for every statement in p except i;
3. j is not a postdominator for i.

Intuitively, j is control dependent on i if j is "governed" by i. For languages with structured control constructs like IF and WHILE, j is control dependent on i, if i is the condition of an IF or WHILE, and j is in the body of this IF resp. WHILE. For languages with arbitrary GOTOs, the computation of control dependencies is much more expensive [4].

Usually, control dependencies are marked with TRUE or FALSE, in order to distinguish between THEN- and ELSE part of an IF statement. For CASE or SWITCH statements, control dependencies are marked with the value of the selection expression which leads to the statements of a certain case. Thus a

[2] For records and variant records, exact data flow dependencies for record components can easily be determined.

```
read(n);
i:=1;
sum:=0;
product:=1;
WHILE true DO
  BEGIN
    IF i>n THEN
      GOTO L;
    sum:=sum+i;
    product:=product*i;
    i:=i+1
  END;
L: write(sum);
write(product);
```

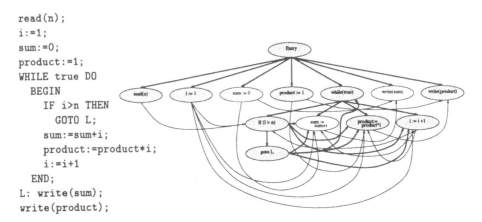

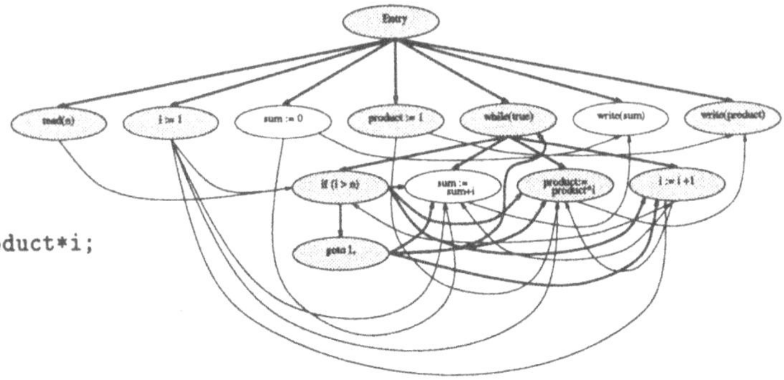

Fig. 1. A program and its PDG

control dependency can actually be followed only if the predicate has the value which is attached to the control dependency edge.

Definition 5. The *program dependency graph* (PDG) consists of all statements and control predicates as nodes, and all data flow and control dependencies as edges. In a PDG, $i \to j$ denotes both a data flow or a control flow edge from i to j. $\to^*$ is the transitive, reflexive closure of $\to$.

There are more elaborated versions of the PDG, but for slicing, this simple definition suffices. Figure 1 shows an example of a program and its PDG.

Definition 6. 1. The *forward slice* of a PDG node i consists of all nodes which depend on i:
$FS(i) = \{j \mid i \to^* j\}$.
2. The *backward slice* of a PDG node i consists of all nodes on which s depends:
$BS(i) = \{j \mid j \to^* i\}$.
3. The *chop* of two nodes i, j consists of all nodes on any path from i to j:
$CH(i, j) = FS(i) \cap BS(j)$.

In case there are procedures, simple PDGs do no longer suffice. First of all, the PDGs of all procedures must be determined. From these PDGs, summary graphs are computed, which contain transitive dependencies between input and output parameters. In the presence of recursion, the computation of summary graphs is nontrivial; an efficient algorithm is described in [13].

Every procedure call in the main PDG is then replaced by the corresponding summary graph (which in turn contains links to the procedure's PDG). The result is called system dependency graph (SDG). From the SDG, slices are computed by a two-step algorithm: first, the top level slice is determined; afterwards slices in called procedures are added as necessary. Due to lack of space, we omit a more detailed description; we just remark that the method described in this paper can easily be extended to system dependency graphs.

3 Path Conditions and Constraint Solving

In this core section, we will explain how slicing can be improved by collecting and solving path conditions. The aim of our technique is twofold:

1. Slices can be made more precise by evaluating additional constraints on PDG edges; it may even happen that PDG edges disappear (which means that data or control flow is in fact impossible).
2. The precise conditions which enable a PDG path or chop to be executed can be determined and – after simplification and pretty-printing – used for diagnostic messages about a program.

As a motivating example, consider the following code piece:

```
(1)   read(i,j);
(2)   a[i+3]:=x;
(3)   IF i>10 THEN
(4)     IF j<20 THEN
(5)       y:=a[2*j-32]
(6)     ELSE
(7)       y:=17;
```

The PDG will contain a dataflow dependency edge (2)→(5). But obviously, a data flow from (2) to (5) is possible only if $i+3 = 2j-32$; this condition is called a *data flow condition*. Furthermore, (5) is executed only if $i > 10 \wedge j < 20$; these conditions are called *control flow conditions*. But the data flow and control flow conditions cannot be satisfied simultaneously, as $i + 3 > 13$ and $2j - 32 < 8$. Thus a dataflow (2)→(5) is impossible! Furthermore, (7) will be executed only if $i > 10 \wedge j \geq 20$, and this control flow condition might be interesting to somebody analysing the program. But note that in general, different occurences of variables must be distinguished, that is, indexed with the PDG node they occur in:

```
(1)  WHILE x<7 DO
(2)    x:=y+z;
(3)    IF x=8 THEN
(4)      p();
     OD;
```

In this example, (4) will only be executed if $x_1 < 7$ and $x_3 = 8$. As we have a dataflow (2)→(3), x_3 is in fact equal to $y_2 + z_2$. Due to this *dependency equation*, the condition governing (4) becomes $x_1 < 7 \wedge y_2 + z_2 = 8$.

We will now precisely describe how path conditions are constructed and solved. The basic idea is to attach an additional constraint to each edge of the PDG. These constraints will be collected appropriately in order to obtain conditions for the execution of single statements or conditions for a data flow along a path in the PDG.

3.1 Dependency Equations

As demonstrated in the above example, all program variables occuring in a flow condition must be labelled with the statement or predicate they occur in. But due to dataflow dependencies, different occurences of the same variable may again be equated. In this section, these equations are formally introduced. The resulting dependency equations are independent of particular slices or execution paths. They are not necessary conditions for certain control or data flow, but are auxiliary conditions, which – as indicated above – can be used to simplify other data or control flow conditions. In contrast to the path conditions defined later, dependency equations always hold during program execution.

Definition 7. Let j be a PDG node, let v be a program variable. The notation v_j denotes the value of v after execution of j. The notation v^j denotes the value of v before execution of j.

Note that j might be executed several times, thus v_j, v^j can change during program execution. If $v \notin def(j)$, $v_j = v^j$.

Definition 8. Let $e_1 = i_1 \to j$, ..., $e_k = i_k \to j$ be dataflow edges to node j, which are due to variable v. The resulting dependency equation is $f(v^j) \equiv v^j = v_{i_1} \vee \ldots \vee v^j = v_{i_k}$. In particular, $k = 1$ leads to $f(v^j) \equiv v_i = v^j$. For a PDG G, the set of all dependency equations is denoted $F(G)$.

We assume $F(G)$ to include all equations $v_j = v^j$, as specified in definition 7. Sometimes it might be worthwile to take an even closer look at variable values, e.g. as resulting from assignments. Therefore, we provide the following definition.

Definition 9. Let i be an assignment `v:=E`, and let $i \to j$ be a dataflow dependency from i to j due to v. Let $\overline{E}$ denote expression E, where all variables $a, b, c, \ldots \in E$ have been replaced by $a_i, b_i, c_i, \ldots$. Then the extended dependency equation is $\overline{f}(v^j) \equiv v^j = v_i \wedge v_i = \overline{E}$. The set of all extended dependency equations is denoted $\overline{F}(G)$.

3.2 Flow Conditions

Control or data flow conditions are attached to certain PDG edges and must be satisfied in order that the edge be included in a slice. They will later be used for the construction of statement or path-governing expressions.

Definition 10. 1. Let $e = i \to^x j$ be a control dependency edge, where i is the predicate and the edge is marked with value x. The corresponding control flow condition is $c(e) \equiv i = x$.[3]

[3] For control dependencies originating from a GOTO statement (see Fig. 1), we define $c(e) = true$.

2. Let $e = i \to j$ be a data dependency edge, where v is the variable carrying the dependency. Let $B(v)$ be any condition on v. The corresponding data flow condition is $d(e) \equiv B(v)$.

   Example: For array references, data flow conditions can explicitely be stated. If v is an array, i is an assignment, $v[E_1]$ is the left hand side of the assignment, and another reference $v[E_2]$ occurs in j, the corresponding data flow condition is $d(i \to j) \equiv B(v) \equiv \overline{E_1} = \overline{E_2}$. [4]
3. The *control dependency graph* (CDG) is the subgraph of the PDG containing only control dependency edges. A missing (control or data) flow condition is considered equivalent to *true*.

Control flow conditions must be true in order that a statement be executed. For example, in

```
(1)  a[u]:=x;
(2)  IF a[v]=y THEN
(3)      p();
```

the control flow condition $a[v] = y$ must be true in order that (3) is executed. On the other hand, data flow conditions are not necessary for the execution of statements, but for a data flow along a certain arc in a PDG. In the example, the dataflow condition for the array references (as given above) is $d((1) \to (2)) \equiv u = v$; it is not necessary for the execution of (2) or (3), but $u = v$ must hold in order that a dataflow from (1) to (2) takes place.

3.3 Execution Conditions

In order to capture the conditions under which a certain statement may be executed, the following definitions are introduced. Obviously, a PDG node i can only be executed if all controlling predicates become successively true during program execution. If there are several paths from START to i, at least one must be executed.

Definition 11. Let i be a PDG node. Let $P = p_1, p_2, \ldots, p_n$ be a path from START to i, where $p_1 =$ START, $p_n = i$, and $p_2, \ldots, p_{n-1}$ are control predicates. The execution condition for P is

$$E(P) = \bigwedge_{\nu=1}^{n-1} c(p_\nu \to p_{\nu+1})$$

Now let $P_1, P_2, \ldots, P_k$ be such paths from from START to i. The execution condition for i is

$$E(i) = \bigvee_{\mu=1}^{k} E(P_\mu)$$

[4] For other language constructs, other data flow conditions may be introduced – the generation of data flow conditions is outside the scope of this paper.

In order that node i is executed, it is necessary to find values for the program variables (indexed with PDG nodes) such that $E(i)$ evaluates to *true*. These values will usually not show up simultanuously during program execution; on the contrary, different instances v_i, v^i, v^j, v_j of variable v will obtain the required values for different program states. But is is a necessary condition that $E(i)$ is solvable, otherwise i cannot be executed. $F(G)$ and $\overline{F}(G)$ must hold as well.

In case there are only structured statements, the control dependencies form a tree, thus for every statement i there is at most one path from START to i, and the computation of $E(i)$ is easy. In general however, the control flow edges form a directed graph which may even contain cycles. In this case, the above formula for $E(i)$ is – albeit correct – not suitable for computation. Even if the control dependency subgraph of the PDG is cycle free, the above expression for $E(i)$ may contain countless copies of the same control predicates.

We therefore develop a simpler formula for $E(i)$. Note that the brute force method of computing a minimal normal form for $E(i)$ can have exponential time complexity – this is the motivation for the following derivations, which utilize the special structure of the $E(i)$.

Definition 12. Let $P_1 = p_1^1 \dots p_{l_1}^1, P_2 = p_1^2 \dots p_{l_2}^2, \dots, P_n = p_1^n \dots p_{l_n}^n$ be the paths from i to j. Then

$$E(i,j) = \bigvee_{\mu=1}^{n} \bigwedge_{\nu=1}^{l_\mu - 1} c(p_\nu^\mu \rightarrow p_{\nu+1}^\mu)$$

The expression $E(i,j)$ generalizes $E(j)$ and collects the control flow conditions between i and j. Obviously, $E(j) = E(\text{START}, j)$. The definition of $E(i,j)$ can easily be generalized for the case that – due to cycles in the PDG – there are infinitely many paths from i to j.

In practice, the paths from i to j will have long common subpaths. This can be used to simplify execution conditions by "factoring out" the subpath. Let $s_1 \dots s_l$ be such a common subpath, where there is no other path from s_1 to s_l. Then by the distributive law,

$$E(i,j) = E(i, s_1) \wedge \bigwedge_{\nu=1}^{l-1} c(s_\nu \rightarrow s_{\nu+1}) \wedge E(s_l, j)$$

as can easily be verified. This formula avoids redundant copies of the $c(e)$ on the common subpaths and can easily be generalized to more than one common subpath. It should be used with common subpaths as long as possible, such that in the remaining $E(x,y)$, the paths between x and y are hopefully disjoint.

Next, we will demonstrate that control dependency cycles can be ignored.

Lemma 13. *Let $P = p_1 p_2 \dots p_{k-1} q \; p_{k+1} \dots p_n$ be the one and only path from i to j (that is, $p_1 = i, p_n = j$), where a cycle $q_0 \dots q_m$ is attached to P (that is, $q_o = q_m = q$). Then the cycle does not contribute to $E(i,j)$ and can safely be ignored.*

Proof. Let μ index over the paths from p_1 to p_n. Then

$$\begin{aligned}
E(p_1,p_n) &= \bigvee_\mu \bigwedge_{\nu=1}^{l_\mu-1} c(p_\nu^\mu \to p_{\nu+1}^\mu) \\
&= \bigwedge_{\nu=1}^{n-1} c(p_\nu \to p_{\nu+1}) \\
&\quad \vee \bigwedge_{\nu=1}^{k-1} c(p_\nu \to p_{\nu+1}) \wedge \bigwedge_{\nu=0}^{m-1} c(q_\nu \to q_{\nu+1}) \wedge \bigwedge_{\nu=k}^{n-1} c(p_\nu \to p_{\nu+1}) \\
&\quad \vee \bigwedge_{\nu=1}^{k-1} c(p_\nu \to p_{\nu+1}) \wedge \bigwedge_{\nu=0}^{m-1} c(q_\nu \to q_{\nu+1}) \wedge \\
&\qquad \bigwedge_{\nu=0}^{m-1} c(q_\nu \to q_{\nu+1}) \wedge \bigwedge_{\nu=k}^{n-1} c(p_\nu \to p_{\nu+1}) \\
&\quad \vee \ldots \\
&= \bigwedge_{\nu=1}^{n-1} c(p_\nu \to p_{\nu+1})
\end{aligned}$$

due to the absorption law ($A \vee A \wedge B = A$). □

The lemma is still true if there are two or more cycles attached to a path. Furthermore, the lemma can be applied to all paths from i to j. Hence we obtain the

Theorem 14. *For the computation of $E(i,j)$, all cycles can be ignored.* [5]

Proof. Let P_μ be the infinitely many paths from i to j. Let $P_1, \ldots, P_n$ be the finitely many "skeleton" paths obtained by removing any cycles attached to a P_ν. Then by the lemma
$E(i,j) = \bigvee_\mu \bigwedge_{p_\nu \to p_{\nu+1} \in P_\mu} c(p_\nu \to p_{\nu+1}) = \bigvee_{i=1}^n \bigwedge_{p_\nu \to p_{\nu+1} \in P_i} c(p_\nu \to p_{\nu+1})$. □

Hence the set of paths from i to j can always be considered finite. A path-finding algorithm can just stop if it encounters the same node for the second time. Intuitively, the reason is that cycles only make execution conditions weaker, and since we are interested in necessary conditions as strong as possible, cycles can be ignored.

Thus we can assume that the set of paths between two nodes is a directed acyclic graph. This can be utilized if all $E(i,p_\nu)$ for successors p_ν of i are needed: all nodes p_ν on paths from i to j can be topologically sorted, and the $E(i,p_\nu)$ are computed in topological order. Trivially, $E(i,i) = \mathit{true}$. Now let j be a PDG node with immediate control predecessors $p_1, p_2, \ldots, p_k$. We assume that $E(i,p_1), E(i,p_2), \ldots, E(i,p_k)$ have already been determined, as the nodes are processed in topological order. Then

$$E(i,j) = \bigvee_{\rho=1}^{k} E(i,p_\rho) \wedge c(p_\rho \to j)$$

Lemma 15. *For any j which is a successor of i, the above formula correctly computes $E(i,j)$.*

[5] This is even true for overlapping cycles, which are ignored here due to space limitations.

Proof. The proof is by induction on the topological order. For $j = i$, the statement is trivial. Otherwise we assume that the $E(i, p_\rho)$ are correct. Then $E(i,j) = \bigvee_{\mu=1}^{n} \bigwedge_{\nu=1}^{l_\mu - 1} c(p_\nu^\mu \to p_{\nu+1}^\mu)$, where $p_1^\mu = i$, $p_{l_\mu}^\mu = j$, and $p_{l_\mu - 1}^\mu = p_\rho$ for a suitable ρ. By grouping the paths which share the last edge $p_\rho \to j$ we obtain $E(i,j) = \bigvee_{\rho=1}^{k} \bigvee_{\mu_\rho=1}^{n_\rho} \bigwedge_{\nu=1}^{l_{\mu_\rho}-1} c(p_\nu^{\mu_\rho} \to p_{\nu+1}^{\mu_\rho}) = \bigvee_{\rho=1}^{k} \bigvee_{\mu_\rho=1}^{n_\rho} \bigwedge_{\nu=1}^{l_{\mu_\rho}-2} c(p_\nu^{\mu_\rho} \to p_{\nu+1}^{\mu_\rho}) \wedge c(i_\rho \to j)$. By induction hypothesis, $\bigvee_{\mu_\rho=1}^{n_\rho} \bigwedge_{\nu=1}^{l_{\mu_\rho}-2} c(p_\nu^{\mu_\rho} \to p_{\nu+1}^{\mu_\rho}) = E(i, p_\rho)$, hence the lemma follows. □

The execution conditions are needed for the computation of path conditions in the PDG. If many such conditions must be determined and solved for the same program, it might be wise to precompute all the needed $E(j) = E(\text{START}, j)$ once and attach them to the PDG nodes j. Computation in topological order will make generation of path conditions much faster.

3.4 Path Conditions

We will now establish necessary conditions which must be fulfilled in order that a data flow between two PDG nodes i and j can take place. Of course, there must be a path from i to j. Furthermore, all nodes on the path must be executable, that is, their execution conditions must be satisfyable. Finally, any data flow conditions on arcs along the path must be fulfilled as well. If there are several paths between i, j, at least one of them must have a satisfyable path condition.

Definition 16. Let $P = p_1, p_2, \dots, p_n$ be any path in the PDG connecting nodes i and j. The path condition for P is

$$PC(P) = \bigwedge_{\nu=1}^{n} E(p_\nu) \wedge \bigwedge_{\nu=1}^{n-1} d(p_\nu \to p_{\nu+1})$$

In case there are several paths $P_1, P_2, \dots, P_k$ from i to j, the path condition is

$$PC(i,j) = \bigvee_{\mu=1}^{k} PC(P_\mu) = \bigvee_{\mu=1}^{k} \bigwedge_{\nu=1}^{n_\mu} E(p_\nu) \wedge \bigwedge_{\nu=1}^{n_\mu - 1} d(p_\nu \to p_{\nu+1})$$

Cycles can safely be ignored, due to the same argument as in the previous section. But again we face the problem that $PC(i,j)$ will contain lots of redundant copies of identical control flow conditions. Again, we try to factor out common subpaths (say, subpath $s_1 \dots s_l$), before more subtle simplification takes place:

$$PC(i,j) = PC(i, s_1) \wedge \bigwedge_{\nu=1}^{l} E(s_\nu) \wedge \bigwedge_{\nu=1}^{l-1} d(s_\nu \to s_{\nu+1}) \wedge PC(s_l, j)$$

Next, we try to simplify $\bigwedge_{\nu=1}^{n} E(p_\nu)$. We first consider the very common situation that the CDG is a tree (or, more precisely, for any $p_\nu \in P$ there is only one PDG path to START). In this case, a redundancy-free formula for $\bigwedge_{\nu=1}^{n} E(p_\nu)$ can easily be obtained. As a first step, "inner" nodes are removed: if $p_\nu \to^* p_\mu$ in the CDG, $E(p_\mu) \Rightarrow E(p_\nu)$, thus by the absorption law, $E(p_\nu)$ does not contribute anything hence P_ν can be ignored. Now let $p_\nu, p_\mu \in P$, and let $a = \text{lca}(p_\nu, p_\mu)$ be their least common anchestor in the CDG. Let $q_1 \ldots q_{\rho_\nu}$ be the path from a to p_ν, and $r_1 \ldots r_{\rho_\mu}$ be the path from a to p_μ. Then by definition of E

$$E(p_\nu) \wedge E(p_\mu) = E(a) \wedge E(q_1 \ldots q_{\rho_\nu}) \wedge E(r_1 \ldots r_{\rho_\mu})$$

The right side does not contain redundant copies of any $c(e)$. Hence by succesively determining least common anchestor and applying the formula, we obtain an expression which contains any $c(e)$ at most once. These observations lead to

Theorem 17. *Let $p_1, p_2, \ldots, p_n$ be CDG nodes (e.g. from a path in the PDG). If the CDG is a tree (or, more precisely, if any p_i has only one CDG path to START), then*

$$\bigwedge_{i=1}^{n} E(p_i) = \bigwedge_{\substack{a \to b \text{ on a path from} \\ \text{START to any } p_i}} c(a \to b)$$

Proof. The proof is by induction on n. For $n = 1$, the statement follows by definition of $E(p_1)$ (note there is only one path from START to p_1). If we add a new node p_{n+1}, let START, $p^1, p^2 \ldots, p^{\mu_{n+1}}, p_{n+1}$ be the unique path from START to p_{n+1}. Then there must exist $p_k \in \{p_1, \ldots, p_n\}$ and a $p^\nu = \text{lca}(p_{n+1}, p_k)$ such that subpath $p^{\nu+1} \ldots p_{n+1}$ is disjoint from all paths from START to any $p_1, \ldots, p_n$, while $START \ldots p^\nu$ occur also in the path from START to p_k. Therefore, for any edge $a \to b$ in path $START \ldots p^\nu$, $c(a \to b)$ already occurs in $\bigwedge_{\substack{a \to b \text{ on a path from} \\ \text{START to any } p_1 \ldots p_n}} c(a \to b)$. Thus

$$\begin{aligned}
\bigwedge_{i=1}^{n+1} E(p_i) &= E(p_{n+1}) \wedge \bigwedge_{i=1}^{n} E(p_i) \\
&= \bigwedge_{i=0}^{\mu_{n+1}-1} c(p^i \to p^{i+1}) \wedge \bigwedge_{\substack{a \to b \text{ on a path from} \\ \text{START to any } p_1 \ldots p_n}} c(a \to b) \\
&= \bigwedge_{i=0}^{\nu-1} c(p^i \to p^{i+1}) \wedge \bigwedge_{i=\nu}^{\mu_{n+1}-1} c(p^i \to p^{i+1}) \\
&\quad \wedge \bigwedge_{\substack{a \to b \text{ on a path from} \\ \text{START to any } p_1 \ldots p_n}} c(a \to b) \\
&= \bigwedge_{i=\nu}^{\mu_{n+1}-1} c(p^i \to p^{i+1}) \wedge \bigwedge_{\substack{a \to b \text{ on a path from} \\ \text{START to any } p_1 \ldots p_n}} c(a \to b) \\
&= \bigwedge_{\substack{a \to b \text{ on a path from} \\ \text{START to any } p_1 \ldots p_{n+1}}} c(a \to b)
\end{aligned}$$

via definition of $E(p_{n+1})$, induction hypothesis and absorption law. □

For programs with non-structured control flow, it might be that $E(p_\nu)$ and $E(p_\mu)$ have common control conditions $c(e)$. By using the distributive law, these can always be factored out, hence $E(p_\nu) \wedge E(p_\mu)$ always has a redundancy-free definition. But these are difficult to obtain in general, and we omit the derivation of the general formula.

3.5 Solving the Path Conditions

We have seen how to construct path conditions which are necessary for a certain dataflow to take place. By construction, the expressions defining the path conditions usually are redundant free, that is, they do not contain multiple copies of the same control flow condition. But this property cannot always be guaranteed – if the CDG is not a tree, and there is more than one path between two PDG nodes, the elimination of multiple control flow conditions during generation of path conditions requires an enourmous effort.

Hence path conditions must be simplified, and even if they are in minimal normal form, they are not necessarily in solved form.

Definition 18. A path condition is in solved form, if all its equations are of the form $v_i = P(\overline{v})$, where $\overline{v}$ is the set of (indexed) program variables, and there are no direct or indirect recursive dependencies between two variables v_i and v_j.

Simplification and subsequent solving can be done in three steps:

1. Simplification based on the following rewrite rules:
$$A \wedge \mathit{true} \to A, \quad A \wedge A \to A, \quad A \vee A \to A,$$
$$A \vee (A \wedge B) \to A, \quad A \wedge B \vee A \wedge C \to A \wedge (B \vee C)$$
A simplifier based on these – and similar – rewrite rules can easily be implemented; it should apply rewrite rules with priority from left to right. Simplification based on rewriting has always polynomial time complexity. Note that factorizing common subpaths as described above can in principle be omitted and replaced by simplification. But it seems simpler to factor out common paths and execution conditions right from the beginning. The example in section 4 will show that simplification alone can produce reasonable understandable path conditions.
2. If the resulting simplified path condition still contains redundant copies of elementary flow conditions, a computation of minimal disjunctive normal form may be appropriate. The standard minimization algorithms (e.g. Quine/McCluskey) all can have exponential time complexity. The Quine-McCluskey algorithm, for example, first determines the set of prime implicands (which is trivial in our application, as there are usually no negated flow conditions); afterwards, a branch-and-bound algorithm computes a minimal cover of prime implicands which already generate the whole path condition.
3. As a last step, one might try to solve the minimized path condition by using a constraint solver or a system for symbolic mathematics. Constraint solving is the basic mechanism in constraint logic programming [11], and CLP(R) was one of the first available systems [10]. Several powerful constraint solvers are available today. The system CLP(BNR) can solve constraints on booleans, integers, and reals; it does not aim at symbolic simplification of constraints, but will try to determine actual intervals for the possible values of variables [5]. Other systems like Mathematica use sophisticated algorithms for symbolic simplification and solution of mathematical problems.

Most constraint solving systems use specialized algorithms for specific problems, e.g. the simplex algorithm for systems of linear inequations. In our case, the generated constraints can contain arbitrary target language expressions (see the example in section 4). Hence it is unlikely that a general-purpose problem solver will produce sophisticated solutions for our application, namely the validation of measurement software. But automatic solving of linear constraints like $(i + 3 = 2 \cdot j - 32) \wedge (i > 10) \wedge (j < 20)$ (see the example at the beginning of the section) is easy for today's systems, and this is at least a starting point. Current research in constraint solving is described in [2].

4 An Example

Figure 2 presents an excerpt of a fictious measurement system program. The example has been modelled after typical programs analysed by PTB. It reads a weight value from hardware port **p_ab** and an article number from port **p_cd**. The article number and the calibrated weight are displayed in an LCD unit. The program contains a calibration path violation: in case the "paper out" signal is active and the keyboard input is "+" or "–", the calibration factor is multiplied by 1.1 and thus 10% too high. It is the aim of this section to demonstrate how slicing discovers the calibration path violation, and how the formulas defined in the previous section yield the precise conditions under which this takes place.

Figure 3 shows the corresponding PDG. Node 1 is the START node (there is no extra START node, as the program contains only one top level statement). The PDG also contains the input and output ports, as well as a port for the initial value of **kal_kg**. Thick edges are control dependency edges. Note that there is no data dependency edge from node (**idx==0**) to (12), as elementary data flow analysis will detect that the loop will be executed at least once.

The backward slice from statement 14 (which is the printout of the weight value) not only contains the calibration statement (statement 3) and the data port for the weight value, but also statements 10 and 11 (modification of the calibration factor) and – via statement 7 – also the keyboard input port. Thus there is a possible influence of the keyboard to the weight value, as $p\_cd \in BS(14)$. This is certainly very suspicious and requires further investigation.

The chop $CH(p\_cd, 14)$ between keyboard and weight value display consists of several paths:

$$(p\_cd) \rightarrow (5) \rightarrow (6) \rightarrow (8) \rightarrow (9) \rightarrow (11) \rightarrow (4) \rightarrow (14)$$
$$(p\_cd) \rightarrow (5) \rightarrow (6) \rightarrow (8) \rightarrow (9) \rightarrow (10) \rightarrow (4) \rightarrow (14)$$
$$(p\_cd) \rightarrow (5) \rightarrow (6) \rightarrow (7) \rightarrow (9) \rightarrow (11) \rightarrow (4) \rightarrow (14)$$
$$(p\_cd) \rightarrow (5) \rightarrow (6) \rightarrow (7) \rightarrow (9) \rightarrow (10) \rightarrow (4) \rightarrow (14)$$
$$(p\_cd) \rightarrow (5) \rightarrow (idx = 0) \rightarrow (6) \rightarrow (8) \rightarrow (9) \rightarrow (11) \rightarrow (4) \rightarrow (14)$$
$$(p\_cd) \rightarrow (5) \rightarrow (idx = 0) \rightarrow (6) \rightarrow (8) \rightarrow (9) \rightarrow (10) \rightarrow (4) \rightarrow (14)$$
$$(p\_cd) \rightarrow (5) \rightarrow (idx = 0) \rightarrow (6) \rightarrow (7) \rightarrow (9) \rightarrow (11) \rightarrow (4) \rightarrow (14)$$
$$(p\_cd) \rightarrow (5) \rightarrow (idx = 0) \rightarrow (6) \rightarrow (7) \rightarrow (9) \rightarrow (10) \rightarrow (4) \rightarrow (14)$$
$$(p\_cd) \rightarrow (5) \rightarrow (idx = 0) \rightarrow (8) \rightarrow (9) \rightarrow (11) \rightarrow (4) \rightarrow (14)$$
$$(p\_cd) \rightarrow (5) \rightarrow (idx = 0) \rightarrow (8) \rightarrow (9) \rightarrow (11) \rightarrow (4) \rightarrow (14)$$

```
(1)  while(TRUE) {
(2)    if ((p_ab[CTRL2] & 0x10)==0) {
(3)      u = ((p_ab[PB] & 0x0f) << 8) + p_ab[PA];
(4)      u_kg = u * kal_kg;
         }
(5)    if ((p_cd[CTRL2] & 0x01) != 0) {
(6)      for (idx=0;idx<7;idx++) {
(7)        e_puf[idx] = p_cd[PA];
(8)        if ((p_cd[CTRL2] & 0x10) != 0) {
(9)          switch(e_puf[idx]) {
(10)            case '+': kal_kg *= 1.1; break;
(11)            case '-': kal_kg *= 0.9; break;
                }
             }
           }
(12)     e_puf[idx] = '\0';
         }
(13)   printf("Artikel: %07.7s\n",e_puf);
(14)   printf("     %6.2f kg     ",u_kg);
       }
```

Fig. 2. Excerpt from measurement software

$$
\begin{aligned}
&(p\_cd) \rightarrow (5) \rightarrow (idx = 0) \rightarrow (7) \rightarrow (9) \rightarrow (11) \rightarrow (4) \rightarrow (14)\\
&(p\_cd) \rightarrow (5) \rightarrow (idx = 0) \rightarrow (7) \rightarrow (9) \rightarrow (10) \rightarrow (4) \rightarrow (14)\\
&(p\_cd) \rightarrow (8) \rightarrow (9) \rightarrow (11) \rightarrow (4) \rightarrow (14)\\
&(p\_cd) \rightarrow (8) \rightarrow (9) \rightarrow (10) \rightarrow (4) \rightarrow (14)\\
&(p\_cd) \rightarrow (7) \rightarrow (9) \rightarrow (11) \rightarrow (4) \rightarrow (14)\\
&(p\_cd) \rightarrow (7) \rightarrow (9) \rightarrow (10) \rightarrow (4) \rightarrow (14)
\end{aligned}
$$

In this list, all cycles involving `idx++` have been ignored, which is allowed according to the previous section.

The path condition is determined according to $PC(p\_cd, 14) = \bigvee_\mu \bigwedge_\nu E(p_\nu)$.[6] There is only one subpath common to all paths, namely $(4) \rightarrow (14)$. We therefore factor out $PC(4, 14) \equiv E(4) \wedge E(14)$. Furthermore, $E(p\_cd) = E(5) = E(14) = true$.[7] Now it turns out that the CDG of the program is a tree. Hence an $E(p_\nu)$ contributes nothing if p_ν is an inner node. This leads to a dramatic reduction of the path condition:

---

[6] There is only one data flow condition: $d((7) \rightarrow (9)) \equiv idx = idx$, which is trivial and hence deleted. Thus the data flow conditions contribute nothing.

[7] The control flow conditions outgoing from (1) are all TRUE and hence deleted.

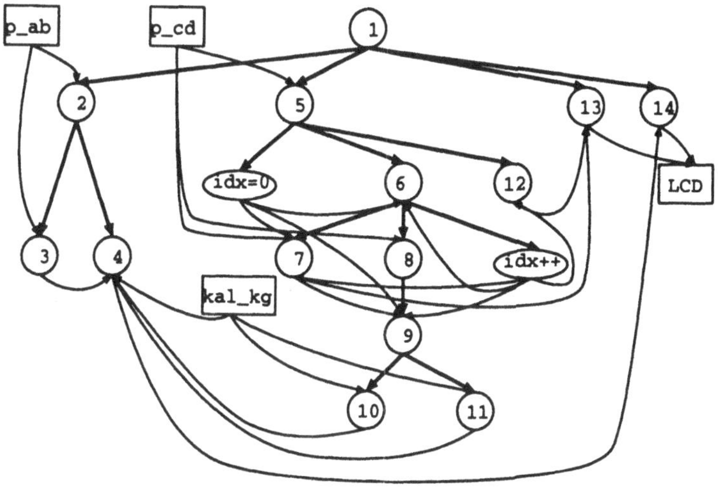

Fig. 3. PDG for Fig. 2

$$
\begin{aligned}
PC(p\_cd, 14) = \Big(&E(11) \vee E(10) \vee (E(7) \wedge E(11)) \vee (E(7) \wedge E(10)) \\
&\vee (E(idx = 0) \wedge E(11)) \vee (E(idx = 0) \wedge E(10)) \\
&\vee (E(idx = 0) \wedge E(7) \wedge E(11)) \vee (E(idx = 0) \wedge E(7) \wedge E(10)) \\
&\vee (E(idx = 0) \wedge E(11)) \vee (E(idx = 0) \wedge E(10)) \\
&\vee (E(idx = 0) \wedge E(7) \wedge E(11)) \vee (E(idx = 0) \wedge E(7) \wedge E(10)) \\
&\vee E(11) \vee E(10) \vee (E(7) \wedge E(11)) \vee (E(7) \wedge E(10))\Big) \\
&\wedge E(4)
\end{aligned}
$$

Simplification via idempotency and absorption laws leads to a collaps of this condition:

$$PC(p\_cd, 14) = \big(E(10) \vee E(11)\big) \wedge E(4)$$

According to the CDG,

$$E(10) \equiv c((5) \to (6)) \wedge c((6) \to (8)) \wedge c((8) \to (9)) \wedge c((9) \to (10))$$

$$E(11) \equiv c((5) \to (6)) \wedge c((6) \to (8)) \wedge c((8) \to (9)) \wedge c((9) \to (11))$$

which leads – after factorization – to the path condition

$$PC(p\_cd, 14) = \big(c((9) \to (10) \vee c((9) \to (11)\big) \wedge c((5) \to (6)) \wedge c((6) \to (8)) \wedge c((8) \to (9)) \wedge c((2) \to (4))$$

The control flow conditions are:

$$
\begin{aligned}
&c((2) \to (3)) \equiv c((2) \to (4)) \equiv p\_ab_2[CTRL2]\&0x10 = 0 \\
&c((5) \to (6)) \equiv c((5) \to (12)) \equiv p\_cd_5[CTRL2]\&0x01 \neq 0 \\
&c((6) \to (7)) \equiv c((6) \to (8)) \equiv idx_6 < 7 \\
&c((8) \to (9)) \equiv p\_cd_8[CTRL2]\&0x10 \neq 0 \\
&c((9) \to (10)) \equiv e\_puf_9[idx_9] = \text{“+”} \\
&c((9) \to (11)) \equiv e\_puf_9[idx_9] = \text{“–”}
\end{aligned}
$$

which leads to the explicit path condition

$$
\begin{aligned}
PC(p\_cd, 14) = \big(&e\_puf_9[idx_9] = \text{``+''} \lor e\_puf_9[idx_9] = \text{``-''}\big) \\
&\land p\_cd_5[CTRL2]\&0x01 \neq 0 \land idx_6 < 7 \\
&\land p\_cd_8[CTRL2]\&0x10 \neq 0 \land p\_ab_2[CTRL2]\&0x10 = 0
\end{aligned}
$$

The dependency equations are $F(G) \equiv u_2 = u_3 \land u\_kg_4 = u\_kg_{14} \land (kal\_kg_4 = kal\_kg_{10} \lor kal\_kg_4 = kal\_kg_{11} \lor kal\_kg_4 = kal\_kg_0) \land e\_puf_7 = e\_puf_9 \land e\_puf_{12} = e\_puf_{13} \land (idx_7 = idx_{idx=0} \lor idx_7 = idx_{idx=0}) \land (idx_9 = idx_{idx=0} \lor idx_9 = idx_{idx++}) \land idx_{12} = idx_{idx++} \land (idx_6 = idx_{idx++} \lor idx_6 = idx_{idx=0})$. Hence $idx_7 = idx_9$, and $\overline{F}(G)$ contains $e\_puf_7[idx_7] = p\_cd_7[PA]$. Applying $\overline{F}(G)$ to the path condition, and removing the conditions which do not invole input ports yields

$$
\begin{aligned}
PC(p\_cd, 14) = \big(&p\_cd_7[PA] = \text{``+''} \lor p\_cd_7[PA] = \text{``-''}\big) \\
&\land p\_cd_5[CTRL2]\&0x01 \neq 0 \land p\_cd_8[CTRL2]\&0x10 \neq 0 \\
&\land p\_ab_2[CTRL2]\&0x10 = 0
\end{aligned}
$$

Further constraint solving does not make sense, thus the last equation is presented to the user. Informally, it reads as follows: "If the keyboard input is + or –, and (not necessarily at the same time) the 'paper out' signal is active, there is data flow from the keyboard to the displayed weight value". A human would have a hard time to extract such statements from large programs!

5 Conclusion

We have shown how to extend program slicing with constraint solving. For any slice or chop, path conditions can be generated, which are necessary conditions for data flow along a slice or chop. We have seen how path conditions are constructed, simplified and perhaps solved by a constraint solver. This leads to more precise information than traditional slicing. The method will be applied in a validation tool for measurement software, where any influences on the calibration path must be detected and analysed.

Although the implementation of the tool has just begun, and although several algorithmic details have been omitted in this paper, an example demonstrated the feasibility of the approach. Our ultimate hope is to analyse real-world programs written in full C, thereby providing semi-automatic software validation. We expect our tool to be useful not just for measurement software, but for other safety-critical software as well.

Acknowledgements. The work described in this paper is funded by the Bundesministerium für Bildung und Forschung, FKZ 01 IS 513 C9. U. Grottker provided the example program. The PDG example in section 2 was originally provided by T. Reps. J. Krinke provided valuable comments on a preliminary version of this paper.

References

1. H. Agrawal, R. DeMillo, E. Spafford: Dynamic slicing in the presence of unconstrained pointers. Proc. 4th Symposium on Testing, Analysis, and Verification. ACM 1991, pp. 60 - 73.
2. F. Benhamou, A. Colmerauer (Ed.): Constraint Logic Programming: Selected Research. MIT Press 1993.
3. J. Choi, M. Burke, P. Carini: Efficient flow-sensitive interprocedural computation of pointer-induced aliases and side effects. Proc. 20th Principles of Programming Languages, ACM 1993, pp. 232 – 245.
4. J. Choi, J. Ferrante: Static slicing in the presence of GOTO statements. ACM TOPLAS 16(1994), pp. 1087 – 1113.
5. F. Benhamou, W. Older: Applying Interval Arithmetic to Real, Integer and Bolean Constraints. To appear in Journal of Logic Programming (1995).
6. D. Denning, P. Denning: Certification of programs for secure information flow. Communications of the ACM 20(7), S. 504 – 513, Juli 1977.
7. J. Field, G. Ramalingam, F. Tip: Parametric program slicing. Proc. 21th Symposium on Principles of Programming Languages, ACM 1995, S. 379 – 392.
8. S. Horwitz, P. Pfeiffer, T. Reps: Dependence analysis for pointer variables. Proc. SIGPLAN Programming Language Design and Implementation, ACM 1989, pp. 28 – 40.
9. S. Horwitz, T. Reps: The use of program dependence graphs in software engineering. Proc. 14th Int. Conference on Software Engineering, IEEE 1992, pp. 392 – 411.
10. J. Jaffar, S. Michaylow, P. Stuckey, R. Yap: The CLP(R) language and system. ACM TOPLAS 14(3), pp. 339 – 395 (Juli 1992).
11. J. Jaffar, M. Maher: Constraint logic programming: a survey. To appear in Journal of Logic Programming (1995).
12. W. Landi, B. Ryder: A safe approximation algorithm for interprocedural pointer aliasing. Proc. SIGPLAN Programming Language Design and Implementation, ACM 1992, pp. 93 – 103.
13. T. Reps, S. Horwitz, M. Sagiv, G. Rosay: Speeding up Slicing. Proc. 2nd SIGSOFT Foundations of Software Engineering, ACM 1994, pp. 11 – 20.
14. G. Smolka, M. Henz, J. Würz: Object-Oriented Concurrent Constraint Programming in Oz. DFKI Research Report 93–16.
15. F. Tip: A survey of program slicing techniques. Journal of Programming Languages 3 (1995), pp. 121 – 189.
16. M. Weiser: Program Slicing. IEEE Transactions on Software Engineering, 10(4), pp. 352 – 357, Juli 1984.

Subtyping Constrained Types

Valery Trifonov* ** and Scott Smith*

Department of Computer Science, Johns Hopkins University
Baltimore, MD 21218, USA
http://www.cs.jhu.edu/hog/

Abstract. A *constrained type* is a type that comes with a set of subtyping constraints on variables occurring in the type. Constrained type inference systems are a natural generalization of Hindley/Milner type inference to languages with subtyping. This paper develops several subtyping relations on polymorphic constrained types of a general form that allows recursive constraints and multiple bounds on type variables. Subtyping constrained types has applications to signature matching and to constrained type simplification.

1 Introduction

A constrained type intuitively is a simple type together with a set of subtyping constraints on its type variables. An example is $t \rightarrow \mathbf{int} \setminus \{t \leq \mathbf{int}\}$, a type of functions whose argument type t is constrained to be a subtype of $\mathbf{int}$. It is possible to perform let-polymorphic type inference for constrained types, producing polymorphic types ("type schemes") of the form $\forall t_1, \ldots, t_n . \tau \setminus C$, which generalize the type schemes produced by the Hindley/Milner unification algorithm; constrained type inference is strictly more general than unification-based type inference. The idea of including subtyping constraints as part of typing judgements was first developed by Mitchell [17, 18]. His constraint sets were restricted to be atomic, allowing coercions between type variables only; numerous other systems with restricted forms of constraint inference have been introduced since, including [16, 12, 14, 4].

A type inference algorithm for polymorphic constrained types of the form studied here was first discovered by Curtis [8], and later independently discovered in somewhat different form, and first proven sound, by Aiken and Wimmers [1]. These constraint systems are less restrictive than the previously cited formulations: they allow recursive constraints such as $t \leq t \rightarrow \mathbf{int}$, and thus subsume recursive types. Additionally, both upper- and lower-bound constraints on variables are legal, and multiple bounds may be placed on a single variable (multiple bounds such as $\{t \leq \tau_1, t \leq \tau_2\}$ are expressed equivalently as $t \leq \tau_1 \cap \tau_2$, where $\cap$ is the type intersection operator of [1]). This extra flexibility allowed in the constraint sets gives a more powerful, but computationally more complex, inference algorithm.

Constrained types are particularly appropriate for object-oriented programming languages [10, 9]: these types incorporate subtyping and recursive dependence, both critical

* Partially supported by NSF grant CCR-9301340
** Partially supported by AFOSR grant F49620-93-1-0169

in an object-oriented setting, and their greater flexibility gives a reasonable solution to the binary methods problem [5].

The objective of this paper is to address the problem of subtyping between polymorphic constrained types:

$$\forall t_1, \ldots, t_n.\tau \backslash C \ \leq^{\forall} \ \forall t_1, \ldots, t_n.\tau' \backslash C'$$

Considering the generality of these types, the relation $\leq^{\forall}$ should be expected to subsume both the "more general than" relation between type schemes in the Hindley/Milner system, and the subtyping relation on recursive types of Amadio/Cardelli [3].

This relation, which has not received the deserved attention in the literature, has at least two important applications. The first is separate compilation via modules and functors, and the subsequent need for signature matching. To a first approximation, in a module system based on Hindley/Milner style of type inference the program specifies a polymorphic type (signature) S for the parameter of a functor F to allow uses of the parameter at different types (which is not possible for parameters of functions); the polymorphic signature S' inferred for the actual argument M is then matched against S at the point of application $F(M)$. In a constrained type setting S and S' are polymorphic constrained types; "matching the signature" thus requires verifying that the $S' \leq^{\forall} S$. Another application is the justification of simplification operations on constrained polymorphic types. In this case a proof is required that the simplified type is equivalent to the original (*i.e.* both a subtype and a supertype).

In this paper we define several variants of $\leq^{\forall}$. The "optimal" form $\leq^{\forall}_{obs}$ may be characterized observationally by analogy with Morris/Plotkin contextual expression equivalence, replacing expression contexts with proof contexts. We then define a semantic form $\leq^{\forall}_{sem}$ based on a regular tree interpretation, and prove it is a good model by showing it is exactly $\leq^{\forall}_{obs}$, a *full type abstraction* property. The ideal model [15] may also be used as a basis of a constrained type ordering $\leq^{\forall}_{ideal}$ [2], but it is not fully abstract. The relation $\leq^{\forall}_{sem}$ is surprisingly complex: we leave open the question whether it is decidable, and develop a powerful decidable approximation $\leq^{\forall}_{dec}$.

In the process of defining these subtyping relations, other results of independent interest are derived. First, an entailment relation $C \ \vdash \ \tau \leq \tau'$ over simple types τ is axiomatized. The set C is a system of arbitrary type constraints, thus generalizing the system of [3] which only allows one upper, non-recursive bound of each variable in C. We define two reduced forms of constraint sets, *constraint maps* (*kernels*) and *canonical* maps, which are also of use as more compact representations of constraint sets in algorithms such as type inference. Next, the subtyping relations on constrained types are defined, and their relationship is established. Finally, soundness of a system of typing rules with constrained types is proved by a simple method of reduction to soundness of a system without constrained types. A principal typing property is established for our type inference algorithm.

In this paper we work over a simple language with only function, top, and bottom types to reduce clutter. However, previous work [10, 9] shows how state, records, variants, classes, and objects all may be incorporated in a constrained type framework, and we explicitly avoid semantic tools (such as the ideal model of types [15]) which lack a strong potential to generalize to such constructs.

2 Simple and Constrained Types

We illustrate our ideas by studying an extension of the call-by-name λ-calculus with constants and let-binding. The abstract syntax of the expressions in the language is

$$e ::= x \mid \lambda x.\, e \mid e\, e' \mid X \mid \mathsf{let}\ X = e\ \mathsf{in}\ e'$$

To simplify the presentation we assume that the λ-bound and let-bound variables are in different syntactic classes, that λ-bound variables are not re-bound, and that constants are a special case of let-variables, bound in the initial environment. We write $\lambda\_.\, e$ for $\lambda x.\, e$ where x is not free in e, and $(e;\ e')$ for $(\lambda\_.\, e')\, e$.

The *simple types* are

$$Typ \ni \tau ::= t \mid \bot \mid \top \mid \tau \to \tau' \mid \ldots$$

where t ranges over the set *TyVar* of type variables, $\bot$ and $\top$ are "minimal" and "maximal" types. In addition to the function types there may be a set of basic types which we leave unspecified. We call $\bot$, $\top$, $\to$, etc. *type constructors*, and all simple types in *Typ* − *TyVar constructed*.

A constrained type κ has the form $\forall \bar{t}.\, A \Rightarrow \tau \setminus C$, where the *context* A is a finite map from variables to simple types, written $\langle \overline{x_i : \tau_i} \rangle$, the *root type* τ is a simple type, and the *constraint set* C is a set of *subtyping constraints* on simple types, each of the form $\tau' \leq \tau''$.[2] We use this new notion for constrained types in order to more appropriately present the binding structure of type variables. The context A represents the assumptions about the types of λ-bound variables free in the term, and C is the set of subtyping constraints (a.k.a. coercions) under which the term is typable; they are both part of the type itself instead of the environment. Thus all constrained types in a type sequent are closed, so we can compare constrained types with different sets of type variables, and avoid giving meaning to constrained types with constrained but free type variables.

Definition 1. A constraint set C is *closed* if it is closed under transitivity (*i.e.* $\{\tau \leq \tau', \tau' \leq \tau''\} \subseteq C$ entails $\tau \leq \tau'' \in C$) and decomposition ($\tau_1 \to \tau_1' \leq \tau_2 \to \tau_2' \in C$ entails $\{\tau_2 \leq \tau_1, \tau_1' \leq \tau_2'\} \subseteq C$).

We denote by $Cl(C)$ the least closed superset of C. Thus, for example, if $C = \{t \to t \leq (\bot \to t) \to \top \to \top\}$, then $Cl(C) = C \cup \{\bot \to t \leq t, t \leq \top \to \top, \bot \to t \leq \top \to \top, \top \leq \bot, t \leq \top, \bot \to t \leq \top\}$.

A constraint set is *consistent* if for each constraint $\tau \leq \tau'$ in it at least one of the following is true: $\tau = \bot$, $\tau' = \top$, both sides have the same outermost type constructor, or one of them is a type variable.

[2] We only consider closed constrained types, for which $\{\bar{t}\} \supseteq FTV(A) \cup FTV(\tau) \cup FTV(C)$, where $FTV(\tau)$ as usual denotes the set of type variables free in τ. Constrained types are considered identical under α-renaming of bound type variables.

3 Primitive Subtyping

In order to define notions of $\leq^{\forall}$, a theory of primitive subtyping under a set of subtyping constraints, $C \models \tau \leq \tau'$, and its decidable axiomatization are developed. Due to space limitations most of the proofs have been elided; currently they can be found on the World Wide Web at URL `http://www.cs.jhu.edu/hog/subcon.ps.gz`.

3.1 Regular Tree Semantics of Constraints

Sequents $C \models \tau \leq \tau'$ may be defined as valid if they hold for all instantiations of type variables in C, τ, and τ'. There are many possibilities for the notion of "instance." The simplest is to allow instances to range over the variable-free types constructed from $\top$, $\perp$, and $\rightarrow$. However, for our purposes this does not give enough points in the space of instances, *e.g.* when typing binary methods [5] we have to work with recursive constraint sets such as $\{t \rightarrow t \leq t,\ t \leq t \rightarrow \top\}$, which have no solutions in this space. This is an example where differences arise when recursive constraint sets are allowed—if recursive constraint sets were not allowed, the simple type basis would have been appropriate. Another candidate is the ideal model [15] used in [2], but conversely it has too many points, allowing polymorphic types such as $\forall t.t \rightarrow t$ to be substituted for type variables; since our system is "shallow" these points are superfluous in our framework. It turns out that the addition of the solutions of recursive type equations to the ground types gives just enough points to define an appropriate semantics. In the next section a theorem will be proven which rigorously demonstrates this fact. We use the convenient notion of regular trees [7, 3] to model solutions of recursive type equations.

We present the semantics of constraint sets in terms of regular trees over a ranked alphabet. Let us review some definitions and results from [7, 3]. Given a ranked alphabet L, a *tree* φ is a partial function from finite sequences of natural numbers $\mathbb{N}^*$ (*paths*) to L such that $Dom(\varphi)$ is prefix-closed and for each $\pi \in \mathbb{N}^*$ we have $\{k \mid \pi k \in Dom(\varphi)\} = \{0, \ldots rank_L(\varphi(\pi)) - 1\}$. The *subtree at* $\pi \in Dom(\varphi)$ is the function $\lambda\pi'.\varphi(\pi\pi')$; $|\pi|$ is the *level* of that subtree. A tree is *regular* if the set of its subtrees is finite.

Define $\mathbb{T}$ as the set of regular trees over the ranked alphabet L_τ of type constructors in our language, the nullary $\perp$ and $\top$ and the binary $\rightarrow$; we reuse the syntax of types as a notation for trees. A *regular system* in this context is a set of equations of the form $\overline{t_i = \tau_i}$ between type variables $t_i \in TyVar$ and simple types τ_i (*i.e.* finite trees over $L_\tau \cup TyVar$ where the type variables are nullary); a regular system is *contractive* if it has no subset of the form $\{t_0 = t_1, \ldots, t_{n-1} = t_n, t_n = t_0\}$. An *assignment* ρ on $V \subset TyVar$ is a total map in $V \rightarrow \mathbb{T}$; it is homomorphically extended on simple types τ with $FTV(\tau) \subseteq V$: $\rho(\perp) = \perp$, $\rho(\top) = \top$, and $\rho(\tau \rightarrow \tau') = \rho(\tau) \rightarrow \rho(\tau')$. An assignment ρ on $\overline{t_i}$ is a *solution* of the regular system $\overline{t_i = \tau_i}$ if $\overline{\rho t_i = \rho\tau_i}$.

Proposition 2. *Each contractive regular system has a unique solution, and each regular tree is the image of some variable in a solution of a contractive regular system.*

A *level-k cut* $\varphi|_k$ of $\varphi \in \mathbb{T}$ for $k \in \mathbb{N}$ is defined as the (finite) tree obtained by replacing all subtrees at level k of φ (if any) by $\top$.

A partial order over L, in which $\bot$ is the minimal element and $\top$ is the maximal, together with variance specifications for the arguments of non-nullary constructors (in this case, contravariance in the domain and covariance in the range of $\rightarrow$) induce a partial order $\leq_{tree}$ over $\mathbb{T}$ as follows: $\bot \leq_{tree} \varphi$ and $\varphi \leq_{tree} \top$ for each finite tree φ, and $\varphi_1 \rightarrow \varphi_1' \leq_{tree} \varphi_2 \rightarrow \varphi_2'$ if $\varphi_2 \leq_{tree} \varphi_1$ and $\varphi_1' \leq_{tree} \varphi_2'$; finally, $\varphi \leq_{tree} \varphi'$ if $\varphi|_k \leq_{tree} \varphi'|_k$ for each $k \in \mathbb{N}$.

Returning to our type system, within a set of constraints we model simple types by regular trees satisfying these constraints:

Definition 3. (i) An assignment ρ *k-satisfies* a constraint $\tau \leq \tau'$, written $\rho \rhd_k \tau \leq \tau'$, if $\rho(\tau)|_k \leq_{tree} \rho(\tau')|_k$.

(ii) ρ *satisfies* $\tau \leq \tau'$ ($\rho \rhd \tau \leq \tau'$, also ρ is a *solution* of $\tau \leq \tau'$) if $\rho \rhd_k \tau \leq \tau'$ for each $k \in \mathbb{N}$.

(iii) The above properties are extended over a set of constraints C if they hold for each constraint in the set.

Regular trees may now be used to define the theory $C \models \tau \leq \tau'$.

Definition 4. (i) $C \models \tau \leq \tau'$ if for every assignment ρ on $FTV(C \cup \{\tau \leq \tau'\})$, if $\rho \rhd C$, then $\rho \rhd \tau \leq \tau'$.

(ii) $C \models C'$ if $FTV(C') \subseteq FTV(C)$ and for each solution ρ of C there is a solution ρ' of C' which agrees with ρ on $FTV(C')$.

(iii) C and C' are *equivalent* if $C \models C'$ and $C' \models C$.

Lemma 5. *C and $Cl(C)$ are equivalent. Thus, if C is satisfiable, then $Cl(C)$ is consistent.*

We leave open the decidability of $C \models \tau \leq \tau'$, and in the sequel we develop decidable approximations to it.

3.2 Constraint Map Representation

We now define *constraint maps* as an equivalent form for representing consistent closed constraint sets. Closed constraint sets may contain significant redundant information. To a constraint set $\{\tau_1 \rightarrow \tau_1' \leq \tau_2 \rightarrow \tau_2'\}$ the closure adds $\{\tau_2 \leq \tau_1, \tau_1' \leq \tau_2'\}$, and the original constraint between functions is completely captured by the additions and can be removed. Constraint maps in fact do not allow constraints between two constructed types, since they can always be expressed by an equivalent family of constraints, provided the constraint set was consistent to begin with. We reuse some of the notation previously defined for constraint sets C on constraint maps K.

Definition 6. A *constraint map* is a finite map $K \in TyVar \rightarrow (2^{Typ})^2$, assigning sets of upper and lower bounds to each type variable in its domain; we use the more intuitive notation $t \leq \tau \in K$ and $t \geq \tau' \in K$ for $\tau \in \pi_1(K(t))$ and $\tau' \in \pi_2(K(t))$, respectively, and $(K, t \leq \tau)$, $(K, t \geq \tau)$ for the maps extending the sets $\pi_1(K(t))$, respectively $\pi_2(K(t))$, to contain τ. We write $t \geq \tau$ instead of $\tau \leq t$ since K is not required to be antisymmetric, *i.e.* $t' \in \pi_1(K(t))$ does not imply $t \in \pi_2(K(t'))$; we use $t = \tau \in K$ for the pair $t \leq \tau \in K, t \geq \tau \in K$.

$(\bot)\ K \vdash \bot \leq \tau$	$(\top)\ K \vdash \tau \leq \top$
$(=)\ K \vdash t \leq t, \quad t \in Dom(K)$	$(\rightarrow)\ \dfrac{K \vdash \tau_1' \leq \tau_1 \quad K \vdash \tau_2 \leq \tau_2'}{K \vdash \tau_1 \rightarrow \tau_2 \leq \tau_1' \rightarrow \tau_2'}$
$(\uparrow)\ \dfrac{(K, t \leq \tau, t \leq \tau') \vdash \tau \leq \tau'}{(K, t \leq \tau) \vdash t \leq \tau'}$ if $(K, t \leq \tau, t \leq \tau')$ is contractive	$(\downarrow)\ \dfrac{(K, t \geq \tau, t \geq \tau') \vdash \tau' \leq \tau}{(K, t \geq \tau) \vdash \tau' \leq t}$ if $(K, t \geq \tau, t \geq \tau')$ is contractive

Fig. 1. Rules for primitive subtyping

Definition 7. The *kernel* $Ker(C)$ of a constraint set C is the constraint map defined by the set of constraints $\{\tau \leq \tau' \in Cl(C) \mid \{\tau, \tau'\} \cap TyVar \neq \emptyset\}$; a constraint of the form $t \leq t'$ sets the appropriate bounds on both variables.

For example, since the closure of the constraint set $C = \{(\top \rightarrow t) \rightarrow t \leq t \rightarrow t \rightarrow \bot\}$ is $Cl(C) = \{(\top \rightarrow t) \rightarrow t \leq t \rightarrow t \rightarrow \bot, t \leq \top \rightarrow t, t \leq t \rightarrow \bot\}$, the kernel of C is $Ker(C) = (t \leq \top \rightarrow t, t \leq t \rightarrow \bot)$.

Proposition 8. *For consistent constraint set* C, $Ker(C)$ *and* C *are equivalent.*

The kernel form of a constraint set has significant advantages from an implementation perspective: a type inference algorithm may maintain constraint sets in their equivalent kernel form, which is considerably more compact than the closure.

3.3 Rules for Primitive Subtyping

We take advantage of the equivalent constraint map representation K of a constraint set C, and with the rules in Fig. 1 define a decidable sound approximation $K \vdash \tau \leq \tau'$ of the theory $C \models \tau \leq \tau'$.

An implicit requirement for $K \vdash \tau \leq \tau'$ is $FTV(\tau) \cup FTV(\tau') \subseteq Dom(K)$. As is usually the case in the presence of recursive types, a notion of contractiveness plays an important role in detecting ill-defined constraint maps.

Definition 9. A constraint map K is *contractive* if $\pi_1 \circ K$ and $\pi_2 \circ K$ as relations on *TyVar* have no cycles, *i.e.* if there do not exist variables $\{t_1, \ldots, t_n\} \subseteq Dom(K)$ such that $t_n = t_1$ and $t_i \leq t_{i+1} \in K$ (respectively $t_i \geq t_{i+1} \in K$) for each $i \in \{1, \ldots, n-1\}$.

For instance, neither $(t \leq t)$ nor $(t \geq t', t' \geq t)$ is contractive, while $(t \geq t', t \leq t')$ is (recall a constraint map is not necessarily symmetric on type variables). However note that contractiveness of constraint maps, as opposed to regular systems, does not entail satisfiability, *e.g.* $(t \leq \bot, t \geq \top)$ is a contractive map with no solutions. Contractiveness is required in order to ensure soundness by disallowing proofs in which *e.g.* a constraint introduced to K by one rule $(\uparrow)$ is used in another $(\uparrow)$ with no intervening uses of $(\rightarrow)$.

Rules $(\bot)$, $(\top)$, $(\rightarrow)$, and $(=)$ for reflexivity of the relation on type variables are standard. The novel rules $(\uparrow)$ and $(\downarrow)$ provide the only access to constraints in K; in fact, were the constraint map in its premise identical to the one in its conclusion, rule $(\uparrow)$ would have been just the standard rule for proving an upper bound on a type variable in a system of rules with eliminated transitivity. With the extra assumption these are induction rules, similar to the (FIX) rule of [11].

Some standard subtyping rules [3] are derivable from those given in Fig. 1 and thus omited, for instance general reflexivity ($K \vdash \tau \leq \tau$ is always provable for $FTV(\tau) \subseteq Dom(K)$, and $(K, t \leq \tau) \vdash t \leq \tau$ is provable by $(\uparrow)$ and general reflexivity. In contrast, transitivity only holds for consistent constraint maps.

Definition 10. A constraint map K is *consistent* if for each t, τ, and τ', if $t \geq \tau \in K$ and $t \leq \tau' \in K$, then $K \vdash \tau \leq \tau'$.

The following lemma shows that a kernel contains all of the information of a consistent set C, and that computing the closure of C is equivalent to the construction of a constraint map K such that $K \vdash C$.

Lemma 11. *If $Cl(C)$ is a consistent constraint set, then $Ker(C)$ is a consistent constraint map, and $Ker(C) \vdash Cl(C)$.*

3.4 Soundness and Decidability of Primitive Subtyping

Next we establish soundness of the proof system $\vdash$ with respect to the relation $\models$; the main idea is to show that all assignments which approximate solutions of a constraint map K also approximate solutions of all subtyping constraints provable from K.

Lemma 12. *If K is contractive, $K \vdash \tau \leq \tau'$ has a proof, and the assignment ρ k-satisfies K, then*

(i) if the proof of $K \vdash \tau \leq \tau'$ has an instance of a rule other than $(\uparrow)$ or $(\downarrow)$ at its root, then $\rho \rhd_{k+1} \tau \leq \tau'$;
(ii) if there is an instance of $(\uparrow)$ or $(\downarrow)$ at the root of the proof of $K \vdash \tau \leq \tau'$, then $\rho \rhd_k \tau \leq \tau'$.

Theorem 13 (Soundness). *If K is contractive and $K \vdash \tau \leq \tau'$, then $K \models \tau \leq \tau'$.*

The system $\vdash$ is incomplete with respect to the relation $\models$; it is not even possible to prove that $(t \leq t \to \bot, t \leq \top \to t) \vdash t \leq \top \to \bot$ since the bound we need is stronger than each of the two given. However $\vdash$ is useful because of the following property.

Lemma 14. *The relation $K \vdash \tau \leq \tau'$ is decidable.*

3.5 Canonical Constraint Maps

We can obtain a stronger proof system if we place the constraints in an equivalent *canonical* form that has pre-computed least upper and greatest lower bounds. In a canonical constraint map each variable has exactly one constructed upper and one constructed lower bound. For instance, a canonical equivalent of $(t \leq t \to \bot, t \leq \top \to t)$ is $K = (t \geq \bot, t \leq \top \to \bot)$. The upper bounds $t \to \bot$ and $\top \to t$ on t have the lub $\top \to \bot$ computed for them. For this set we can indeed prove $K \vdash t \leq \top \to \bot$. The canonicalization process also has potential as an implementation technique.

Definition 15. A constraint map K is *canonical* if

- K assigns exactly one upper and one lower constructed bound (*canonical* bounds) to each type variable in its domain (with no restriction on the number of variable bounds);
- if $t \leq t' \in K$ and $t' \leq t'' \in K$, then $t \leq t'' \in K$, and
- for each $(t \leq t', t \leq \tau, t' \leq \tau') \subseteq K$, where $\{\tau, \tau'\} \cap TyVar = \emptyset$, we have $K \vdash \tau \leq \tau'$, and similarly for the lower bounds.

Clearly if K and K' are equivalent on $FTV(\tau) \cup FTV(\tau')$ then $K \models \tau \leq \tau'$ if and only if $K' \models \tau \leq \tau'$. This allows us to upgrade our system by converting each map K to an equivalent canonical map $Can(K)$ and then proving $Can(K) \vdash \tau \leq \tau'$ instead of the original $K \vdash \tau \leq \tau'$. Here we provide an algorithm for computing an equivalent canonical form $Can(K)$ of a map K.

Algorithm 16 *$Can(K)$ is computed as follows.*

Start with $K' = K$, and for some $t \in FTV(K')$ let V be the least set satisfying $V = \{t\} \cup \{t' \mid \exists t'' \in V. t'' \leq t' \in K'\}$, i.e. *the set of upper bounds on t in the reflexive transitive closure of K' on TyVar; the case of lower bounds is similar. Let $B = \{\tau \in Typ - TyVar \mid \exists t' \in V. t' \leq \tau \in K'\}$, the set of constructed upper bounds on t. We compute the canonical upper bound τ of t as the greatest lower bound of the elements of B, as follows.*

> *If $B \subseteq \{\top\}$, then $\tau = \top$; if $\bot \in B$, then $\tau = \bot$. Otherwise let $\{\overline{\tau_i \rightarrow \tau'_i}\}$ be the set of all function types in B, and let $\tau = t^{\wedge}_{T} \rightarrow t^{\vee}_{T'}$, where $T = \{\overline{\tau_i}\}$, $T' = \{\overline{\tau'_i}\}$, and $t^{\wedge}_{T}$ and $t^{\vee}_{T'}$ are in general auxiliary type variables we associate with the respective sets of type terms; in the cases when T is a singleton set $\{t'\}$ we let $t^{\wedge}_{T} = t^{\vee}_{T} = t'$ to ensure termination. Add the bounds $(t^{\wedge}_{T} \geq \tau_j)$ (and similarly for $t^{\vee}_{T'}$) to K'.*

Replace the constructed upper bounds of t by $(t \leq \tau)$; thus the new bounds on t, namely $(t \leq \tau)$ and $(t \leq t')$ for each $t' \in V$, are in canonical form. Continue until all variables in K' are processed. (Adding also all bounds of the form $(t^{\wedge}_{S} \leq t^{\wedge}_{T})$ and $(t^{\vee}_{T'} \geq t^{\vee}_{T})$ if $T \subset S$, when those auxiliary variables appear in the domain of the map, produces an even stronger, with respect to $\vdash$, yet equivalent form.) The resulting K' is the value of $Can(K)$.

The following lemma proves the correctness of this algorithm.

Lemma 17. *For each constraint map K there exists a canonical equivalent $Can(K)$.*

For example computing the canonical equivalent of $K = (t \leq t \rightarrow \bot, t \leq \top \rightarrow t)$ starts by introducing $t_1 = t^{\vee}_{\{t, \top\}}$ and $t_2 = t^{\wedge}_{\{\bot, t\}}$, and transforming K into $K' = (t \geq \bot, t \leq t_1 \rightarrow t_2, t_1 \geq \top, t_1 \leq \top, t_1 \geq t, t_2 \geq \bot, t_2 \leq \bot, t_2 \leq t)$. This map is already in canonical form, and it is possible to prove $K' \vdash t \leq \top \rightarrow \bot$. However, even when $\vdash$ is used on to canonical equivalents it still does not provide proofs for some valid relations; for instance, $(t \geq \bot, t \leq t \rightarrow \top) \models t \leq (\top \rightarrow \bot) \rightarrow \top$.

In the general case, the algorithm implied by Lemma 14 may attempt comparing τ against each upper bound on t currently in K in the process of searching for a a proof of $K \vdash t \leq \tau$. In this process, it may have to backtrack if it fails to find a proof using a particular bound. However, in the case of canonical maps a more efficient implementation is possible which has time complexity of $O(n^2)$, where n is the size of $K \cup \{\tau \leq \tau'\}$. This algorithm only compares new bounds on a variable against its canonical bounds (which can be shown to suffice) and uses a form of memoisation to detect looping; details are omited for lack of space.

A parallel can be drawn between our system of subtyping rules and the system $\vdash_{AC}$ of Amadio and Cardelli [3], which is based on a relation of equivalence between recursive types, and on the inductive rule

$$(\mu)\ \frac{C, t \leq t' \vdash_{AC} \tau \leq \tau'}{C \vdash_{AC} \mu t.\tau \leq \mu t'.\tau'}$$

Since recursive types can be encoded as type variables with identical upper and lower bounds, the corresponding rule for simple types with constraints is

$$\frac{K, t = \tau, t' = \tau', t \leq t' \vdash \tau \leq \tau'}{K, t = \tau, t' = \tau' \vdash t \leq t'}$$

which is indeed derivable in $\vdash$ in a stronger version by successive applications of $(\uparrow)$ and $(\downarrow)$; furthermore, the steps of the proof of $K, t = \tau, t' = \tau' \vdash t \leq t'$ follow closely the steps of the algorithm for computing $C \vdash_{AC} \mu t.\tau \leq \mu t'.\tau'$ presented in [3], which also effectively constructs the type contexts necessary in order to establish type equivalences. Amadio and Cardelli show that their system is complete with respect to the regular tree model of recursive types under certain conditions on C, τ, and τ'; in particular the constraints in C may not be recursive, and no variable may occur in both τ and τ'. An attempt to directly apply the system to prove sequents violating these conditions shows that it is incomplete in the more general setting considered in this paper, *e.g.* $t \leq \top \rightarrow t \not\vdash_{AC} t \leq \mu t'.\top \rightarrow t'$. Our system, while still incomplete with respect to the model we present, is capable of proving the corresponding forms of all sequents provable in [3], in addition allowing multiple recursive upper and lower bounds on type variables, *e.g.* $t \leq \top \rightarrow t, t' = \top \rightarrow t' \vdash t \leq t'$.

3.6 Satisfiability of Canonical Constraint Maps

A constrained type only has meaning if its constraints describe a non-empty set of instances, and hence the satisfiability of a constraint map is an important property. In this section we provide a connection between consistency and satisfiability of canonical constraint maps. This connection also plays a role in establishing the relationship between various notions of subtyping on constrained types in Sect. 4.

Definition 18. The canonical map K' is a *submap* of a canonical map K if $K' \subseteq K$. Note that constraints on variables in $Dom(K) - Dom(K')$ may involve variables in $Dom(K')$, but $FTV(Codom(K')) \subseteq Dom(K')$.

Lemma 19. *If K' is a submap of K, and K is consistent and canonical, then every solution of K' can be extended to a solution of K. Thus, considering the special case of $K' = \emptyset$, every consistent canonical constraint map K is satisfiable.*

Combining these results with canonicalization and soundness of $\vdash$ with respect to $\models$, we can reason about canonical maps instead of their equivalent constraint sets.

Definition 20. $C \vdash \tau \leq \tau'$ if $\mathit{Can}(\mathit{Ker}(C)) \vdash \tau \leq \tau'$.

4 Subtyping Constrained Types

In this section we define three concrete $\leq^{\forall}$ relations of subtyping on constrained types: $\leq^{\forall}_{obs}$, $\leq^{\forall}_{sem}$, and $\leq^{\forall}_{dec}$, as promised in the introduction.

4.1 Operational Subtyping

For an initial definition of $\leq^{\forall}$ we rely on operational notions as a basis. The basic idea is simple, but we could not find any precedent for it in the literature. Expressions of constrained type $\forall\bar{t}.\, A \Rightarrow \tau \setminus C$ are also of type $\forall\bar{t'}.\, A' \Rightarrow \tau' \setminus C'$ if for all possible uses of expressions of the latter type that are consistent, use of the former type is also consistent. Relation $\leq^{\forall}_{obs}$ is defined by this means. The difficult issue is how a "use" of a type should be defined. Informally, each use is a typing proof context, in analogy with Morris/Plotkin expression contexts. We give a particular version of typing proof context which is one of many reasonable and equivalent notions: a "use" is a set of constraints of the form that could be added by the inference rules. The constraints added by the inference rules may only introduce upper bounds on the root types, and dually only lower bounds on the types in the context. As a consequence one may obtain a valid typing derivation after replacing a subterm by another term whose constrained type yields a consistent system when those bounds are added. This leads us to the following observational definition of a subtyping relation on constrained types. (We let $A \leq A'$ abbreviate the set of constraints $\{A(x) \leq A'(x) \mid x \in \mathit{Dom}(A')\}$, defined only when $\mathit{Dom}(A) \supseteq \mathit{Dom}(A')$.[3])

Definition 21. For closed constrained types, $\forall\bar{t'}.\, A' \Rightarrow \tau' \setminus C' \leq^{\forall}_{obs} \forall\bar{t''}.\, A'' \Rightarrow \tau'' \setminus C''$ if for each $\forall\bar{t}.\, A \Rightarrow \tau \setminus C$ such that $\{\bar{t}\}$ is disjoint from $\{\bar{t'}\}$ and $\{\bar{t''}\}$, if $\mathit{Cl}(C \cup C'' \cup (A \leq A'') \cup \{\tau'' \leq \tau\})$ is consistent, then $\mathit{Cl}(C \cup C' \cup (A \leq A') \cup \{\tau' \leq \tau\})$ is consistent.

[3] This "subtyping rule" for contexts is similar to standard record subtyping [6]; the closure conversion $[\![x]\!] = \lambda E.\, E.x$, $[\![\lambda x.\, e]\!] = \lambda E.\, \lambda x.\, [\![e]\!]\{\, \overline{x_i = E.x_i}|_{x_i \in FV(e) - \{x\}},\ x = x \,\}$, and $[\![e\, e']\!] = \lambda E.\, [\![e]\!]\, E\, ([\![e']\!]\, E)$ makes the environment explicit and maps terms of type $\forall\bar{t}.\, \langle \overline{x_i : \tau_i} \rangle \Rightarrow \tau \setminus C$ to closed terms of type $\forall\bar{t}.\, \langle\rangle \Rightarrow \{\, \overline{x_i : \tau_i}\,\} \rightarrow \tau \setminus C$.

4.2 Semantic Subtyping

Next, a semantic notion $\leq^{\forall}_{sem}$ is defined, via the regular tree model: two polymorphic constrained types are ordered if their sets of regular tree instances are ordered.

The context component A of a constrained type corresponds to a finite map Φ from variables to regular trees; the relation $\leq_{tree}$ can be extended on such maps as follows: $\Phi \leq_{tree} \Phi'$ if $Dom(\Phi) \supseteq Dom(\Phi')$ and $\Phi(x) \leq_{tree} \Phi'(x)$ for each $x \in Dom(\Phi')$. An *instance* of the constrained type $\kappa = \forall \bar{t}. A \Rightarrow \tau \setminus C$ is a pair written $\Phi \Rightarrow \varphi$ where $\Phi = \rho \circ A$ and $\varphi = \rho\tau$ for some assignment ρ on $\{\bar{t}\}$ that satisfies C. The set of instances of κ is $Inst(\kappa)$. As in the definition of $\leq^{\forall}_{obs}$, the natural order on instances is $\Phi \Rightarrow \varphi \leq_{tree} \Phi' \Rightarrow \varphi'$ if $\Phi' \leq_{tree} \Phi$ and $\varphi \leq_{tree} \varphi'$. We can now define a semantical notion of subtyping on constrained types.

Definition 22. $\kappa' \leq^{\forall}_{sem} \kappa''$ if for each instance of κ'' there is a smaller instance of κ'.

We may now prove the equivalence of $\leq^{\forall}_{sem}$ and $\leq^{\forall}_{obs}$, demonstrating the appropriateness of the regular tree interpretation.

Theorem 23 (Full Type Abstraction). *The relations $\leq^{\forall}_{sem}$ and $\leq^{\forall}_{obs}$ agree.*

To contrast $\leq^{\forall}_{sem}$ with the ideal model ordering $\leq^{\forall}_{ideal}$, consider the following example, in which we omit contexts and quantifiers when empty. In the regular tree model the only solution of $C = \{\top \to \bot \leq t, t \leq \top \to \top, t \leq \bot \to \bot\}$ is $\rho = [t \mapsto \top \to \bot]$, which satisfies also $t \leq \top \to \bot$; hence $(\top \to \bot) \to \top \to \bot \setminus \emptyset \leq^{\forall}_{sem} \forall t. t \to t \setminus C$. But this fails for $\leq^{\forall}_{ideal}$ since in the ideal model *e.g.* $[t \mapsto \forall t'. t' \to t']$ is a solution of C which does not satisfy $t \leq \top \to \bot$. As a consequence the ideal model ordering does not offer full type abstraction with respect to the operational subtyping $\leq^{\forall}_{obs}$.

4.3 Decidable Subtyping

The question of decidability of $\leq^{\forall}_{sem}$ is open; we show how it may be approximated by a powerful decidable relation. The material of the previous section is used to define this decidable relation.

The informal idea leading to the decidable relation is simple: observe that adding constraints to a set may only shrink the set of its solutions. For constrained types $\kappa' = \forall \bar{t'}. A' \Rightarrow \tau' \setminus C'$ and $\kappa'' = \forall \bar{t''}. A'' \Rightarrow \tau'' \setminus C''$, Definition 22 states that $\kappa' \leq^{\forall}_{sem} \kappa''$ if a certain relation holds for *each* instance of κ'' (that is, for the unrestricted set of solutions of C'') and *some* corresponding instance of κ' (that is, an element of a possibly restricted subset of solutions of C'). Thus, assumming that $\{\bar{t'}\}$ and $\{\bar{t''}\}$ are disjoint, we would have a proof of $\kappa' \leq \kappa''$ if we could show that the relations $\tau' \leq \tau''$ and $(A'' \leq A')$ hold under C'' and C' together with some set C of constraints which do not "constrain further" the type variables $\bar{t''}$ (but possibly add constraints on $\bar{t'}$).

Applying the machinery developed in Sect. 3, these ideas are formalized in the following definition of a relation approximating $\leq^{\forall}_{sem}$.

Definition 24. $\kappa' \leq^{\forall}_{dec} \kappa''$ if $\kappa' = \forall \bar{t'}. A' \Rightarrow \tau' \setminus C'$ and $\kappa'' = \forall \bar{t''}. A'' \Rightarrow \tau'' \setminus C''$ for some $\{\bar{t'}\} \cap \{\bar{t''}\} = \emptyset$, and there exists a consistent canonical map K such that $K \vdash C' \cup (A'' \leq A') \cup \{\tau' \leq \tau''\}$ and $Can(Ker(C''))$ is a submap of K.

Here the map K represents the union of C'', C', and C of our informal discussion: it has $Can(Ker(C''))$ as a submap (meaning $\{\overline{t'}\}$ are not further constrained), it entails C', and its constraints on $\{\overline{t'}\}$ may be stronger that those in C' in order to ensure that the relations between root types and contexts hold. The following theorem shows that $\leq^{\forall}_{dec}$ is indeed an approximation to $\leq^{\forall}_{sem}$.

Theorem 25. *If* $\kappa' \leq^{\forall}_{dec} \kappa''$, *then* $\kappa' \leq^{\forall}_{sem} \kappa''$.

Although the incompleteness of $\vdash$ with respect to $\models$ implies incompleteness of $\leq^{\forall}_{dec}$ with respect to $\leq^{\forall}_{sem}$, the relation $\leq^{\forall}_{dec}$ is still quite powerful: it subsumes the relation of instantiation between type schemes in the Hindley/Milner system, the subtyping relation between recursive types in the Amadio/Cardelli system, and their union on recursive polymorphic types in shallow (prenex) form. Consider Hindley-Milner subtyping in more detail. The type scheme $\forall\overline{t''}.\,\tau''$ is an instance of $\forall\overline{t'}.\,\tau'$ if $\tau'' = \sigma\tau'$, where σ is a simple type substitution on $\{\overline{t'}\} = FTV(\tau')$, and $\{\overline{t''}\} = FTV(\tau'')$; then we have $\forall\overline{t'}.\,\langle\rangle \Rightarrow \tau' \setminus \emptyset \leq^{\forall}_{dec} \forall\overline{t''}.\,\langle\rangle \Rightarrow \tau'' \setminus \emptyset$ by Definition 24, as evidenced by the canonical constraint map $K = (\overline{t' \leq \sigma(t')}, \overline{t' \geq \sigma(t')})$, which entails $\tau' \leq \sigma(\tau')$ and is obviously consistent. Closed recursive types can also be represented as constrained types, with the constraint set effectively encoding a regular system; when restricted to these types, $\leq^{\forall}_{dec}$ is equivalent to the system of Amadio and Cardelli.

Furthermore, $\leq^{\forall}_{dec}$ is sufficiently strong to allow proving correctness of many useful simplifications of types inferred by the system. For example, $\leq^{\forall}_{dec}$ can be used to show the soundness of the constraint set simplification "garbage collection" of [9], which allows the removal of "unreachable" constraints.

Definition 26. Given a constrained type $\forall\overline{t}.\,A \Rightarrow \tau \setminus K$, where K is a canonical constraint map, a type variable t is *positively reachable* if t occurs positively in τ, or negatively in A, or positively in the canonical lower bound in K of some positively reachable t', or negatively in the constructed upper bound in K of some negatively reachable t''; *negative reachability* is defined symmetrically. (Recall that an occurrence of a variable in a simple type is *positive* (resp. *negative*) if it occurs inside an even (odd) number of type subterms in argument position of $\rightarrow$.)

A constraint $t \leq \tau' \in K$ (resp. $t \geq \tau' \in K$) is *reachable* if t is negatively (positively) reachable; $t \leq t' \in K$ is reachable if t is negatively and t' is positively reachable.

This notion of reachability is motivated by the type rules (Sect. 5, Fig. 2), which only set upper bounds on types of subterms. Thus for instance a type variable t in the type κ of a term e can only obtain new upper bounds (when e is used as a subterm) if t is positively reachable in κ; in this case t's lower bounds may be the source of an inconsistency (via transitivity). Conversely, however, if t is not reachable positively, its lower bounds are not going to cause inconsistency in any use of e—hence they may safely be ignored; for example,

$$\forall t.\,\langle\rangle \Rightarrow t \setminus \{\top \rightarrow t \leq t,\, t \leq t \rightarrow \top\} \;\leq^{\forall}_{dec}\; \forall t.\,\langle\rangle \Rightarrow t \setminus \{\top \rightarrow t \leq t\}.$$

Proposition 27. *If $GC(\kappa)$ is the constrained type obtained by removing the unreachable constraints in κ, then $GC(\kappa) \leq^{\forall}_{dec} \kappa$ and $\kappa \leq^{\forall}_{dec} GC(\kappa)$.*

Pottier [20] offers an alternative definition of reachability which ignores the polarity of the occurences of type variables. Our experience with applications of constrained type systems to object-oriented languages [10, 9] shows that keeping track of polarity makes a significant difference when simplifying types inferred for new objects (which are fixed points of classes). Type variables associated with objects have upper bounds inherited from the class definition (before taking the fixed point); they are often unreachable by our definition but not by Pottier's. Additionally, removing more constraints often enables other simplifications, *e.g.* unifying a type variable with its bound.

We present an outline of an algorithm for computing $\forall\overline{t'}.\, A' \Rightarrow \tau' \setminus C' \leq^{\forall}_{dec} \forall\overline{t''}.\, A'' \Rightarrow \tau'' \setminus C''$. The algorithm either fails, if the subtyping does not hold, or it produces a set of constraints C which only put bounds on the type variables in $\{\overline{t'}\}$; the constraint map K required by Definition 24 can then be obtained by extending *Can*(C'') with *Can*(*Ker*$(C' \cup C)$). The algorithm is very similar to the one for computing closure of a constraint set; in fact it is a generalization of the latter.

Algorithm 28 $\forall\overline{t'}.\, A' \Rightarrow \tau' \setminus C' \leq^{\forall}_{dec} \forall\overline{t''}.\, A'' \Rightarrow \tau'' \setminus C''$ *is computed as follows.*

We start by computing $K'' =$ Can(C'') and with an initially empty set C_0 of new constraints on variables in $\{\overline{t''}\}$ which are "pending proof," and proceed as in computing the closure of $C' \cup \{\tau' \leq \tau''\} \cup (A'' \leq A')$, namely, failing on inconsistent constraints, and reducing consistent ones between constructed types to constraints on variables, of the form $t \leq \tau$ (or $\tau \leq t$). When $t \in \{\overline{t'}\}$, if the constraint is already in $C' \cup C$, the search succeeds; otherwise we add these constraints to C and continue as in the closure computation by searching for a proof of $\tau_L \leq \tau$ (resp. $\tau \leq \tau_U$), where τ_L and τ_U represent the lower and upper bound(s) on t in $C' \cup C$ so far. However, when $t \in \{\overline{t''}\}$, we instead attempt to prove *that this constraint is implied (by the rules for primitive subtyping) by the constraints on t in K''. The proof search goes much as described in Sect. 3.4: if τ is already an upper (lower) bound of t in $K'' \cup C_0$, it succeeds, otherwise the new constraint is added to C_0, and we search for a proof of the constraint $\tau_U \leq \tau$ (resp. $\tau \leq \tau_L$), where τ_U and τ_L are the canonical upper and lower bounds on t in K''.*

Thus, the algorithm treats variables in $\{\overline{t'}\}$ and $\{\overline{t''}\}$ differently, but symmetrically: it compares new upper bounds on a t' with its old lower bounds, but new upper bounds on a t'' with its old (canonical) upper bound. (The reader may have noticed that converting C' to a canonical constraint map is not necessary for this algorithm; however it may improve its performance.)

Theorem 29. *The relation $\leq^{\forall}_{dec}$ is decidable.*

5 Soundness of the Type System and Completeness of Inference

The typing rules shown in Fig. 2 infer sequents of the form $\Gamma \vdash^{\mathsf{T}} e : \kappa$; the type environment Γ only assigns constrained types to let-bound variables, while the types

$$(\text{VAR})\ \Gamma \vdash^{\mathsf{T}} x : \forall \bar{t}.\langle \overline{x_i : \tau_i}, x : \tau \rangle \Rightarrow \tau \setminus C, \quad \{\bar{t}\} \supseteq \textstyle\bigcup_i FTV(\tau_i, \tau, C)$$

$$(\text{ABS})\ \frac{\Gamma \vdash^{\mathsf{T}} e : \forall \bar{t}.\langle \overline{x_i : \tau_i}, x : \tau \rangle \Rightarrow \tau' \setminus C}{\Gamma \vdash^{\mathsf{T}} \lambda x.e : \forall \bar{t}.\langle \overline{x_i : \tau_i} \rangle \Rightarrow \tau \rightarrow \tau' \setminus C}$$

$$(\text{APP})\ \frac{\Gamma \vdash^{\mathsf{T}} e' : \forall \bar{t}.A \Rightarrow \tau'' \rightarrow \tau \setminus C \qquad \Gamma \vdash^{\mathsf{T}} e'' : \forall \bar{t}.A \Rightarrow \tau'' \setminus C}{\Gamma \vdash^{\mathsf{T}} e'e'' : \forall \bar{t}.A \Rightarrow \tau \setminus C}$$

$$(\text{LETVAR})\ \Gamma \vdash^{\mathsf{T}} X : \Gamma(X), \quad X \in Dom(\Gamma)$$

$$(\text{LET})\ \frac{\Gamma \vdash^{\mathsf{T}} e : \kappa \qquad \Gamma, X : \kappa \vdash^{\mathsf{T}} e' : \kappa'}{\Gamma \vdash^{\mathsf{T}} \mathsf{let}\ X = e\ \mathsf{in}\ e' : \kappa'}$$

$$(\text{SUB})\ \frac{\Gamma \vdash^{\mathsf{T}} e : \kappa \qquad \kappa \leq^{\forall} \kappa'}{\Gamma \vdash^{\mathsf{T}} e : \kappa'}$$

Note: the closures of the constraint sets in all conclusions must be consistent.

Fig. 2. Typing rules.

of λ-bound variables are included in the context component of κ. Each rule has the implicit side condition that the closure of the constraint set in the constrained type in its conclusion is consistent. Rule (APP) requires the types of the subterms to share the context A, constraint set C, and set of bound variables $\{\bar{t}\}$. Rule (LET) is sound with respect to the call-by-name semantics;[4] constraints on types of variables free in e need not be reflected in κ' unless X occurs free in e'. Finally the subsumption rule (SUB) replaces the constrained type of a term by a supertype; it is thus the only rule that may allow the constraint set in the type of a term to be taken into account or modified. The rules are parametric in the choice of $\leq^{\forall}$, for which we considered a number of different possibilities; the notation $\vdash^{\mathsf{T}}$ represents the rules with abstract $\leq^{\forall}$, and $\vdash^{\mathsf{T}}_{sem}$ for instance represents $\vdash^{\mathsf{T}}$ with $\leq^{\forall}$ defined as the concrete relation $\leq^{\forall}_{sem}$.

Rules for type inference are presented[5] in Fig. 3; there is no rule for subsumption, and the let-related rules are the same as in $\vdash^{\mathsf{T}}$ and hence omitted.

We may now establish soundness of the typing rules of Fig. 2. In our previous proofs of soundness of constrained typing systems [10], a direct subject reduction argument was used. Recent observations concerning the close relation between constrained type systems and simple type systems [19] allow us to establish soundness based on soundness of a simple type system. We believe this direct approach to type soundness of constrained type systems should be applicable to other constrained type languages.

Amadio and Cardelli [3] present a type system $\vdash^{\mu}$ with recursive types (modeled by regular trees) and a subtyping relation on them equivalent to $\leq_{tree}$. This system can be applied to the let-free fragment of our language to produce sequents of the form $\Phi \vdash^{\mu} e : \varphi$, where Φ is a finite map from variables to regular trees whose role in our type system $\vdash^{\mathsf{T}}$ is played by a context A.

---

[4] A version sound with respect to call-by-value can be obtained by defining $\mathsf{let}_v\ X = e\ \mathsf{in}\ e'$ as $\mathsf{let}\ X = e\ \mathsf{in}\ (X; e')$ for type-checking purposes.

[5] We write the inference rules with a top-down propagation of the contexts; a bottom-up presentation with synthesized context components is also possible.

$$(\textsc{Var}^{\text{I}})\ \Gamma \vdash^{\text{I}} x : \forall \overline{t_i}, t.\langle \overline{x_i : t_i}, x : t\rangle \Rightarrow t \setminus \emptyset$$

$$(\textsc{Abs}^{\text{I}})\ \frac{\Gamma \vdash^{\text{I}} e : \forall \overline{t_i}, t.\langle \overline{x_i : t_i}, x : t\rangle \Rightarrow \tau \setminus C}{\Gamma \vdash^{\text{I}} \lambda x.e : \forall \overline{t_i}, t.\langle \overline{x_i : t_i}\rangle \Rightarrow t \rightarrow \tau \setminus C},\ \{\overline{x_i}\} = FV(\lambda x.e)$$

$$(\textsc{App}^{\text{I}})\ \frac{\Gamma \vdash^{\text{I}} e' : \forall \overline{t'}.A \Rightarrow \tau' \setminus C' \qquad \Gamma \vdash^{\text{I}} e'' : \forall \overline{t''}.A \Rightarrow \tau'' \setminus C''}{\Gamma \vdash^{\text{I}} e'e'' : \forall \overline{t'}, \overline{t''}, t.A \Rightarrow t \setminus C' \cup C'' \cup \{\tau' \leq \tau'' \rightarrow t\}}$$

where $\{\overline{t'}\} - FTV(A)$, $\{\overline{t''}\} - FTV(A)$, $FTV(A)$, and $\{t\}$ are all disjoint

Fig. 3. Typing rules modified for type inference.

We now establish that a typing derivation in $\vdash^{\top}_{sem}$ can be viewed as a family of derivations in $\vdash^{\mu}$.

Definition 30. The let-*expansion* $LE(e)$ of a term e is defined as the homomorphic extension of $LE(\text{let } X = e' \text{ in } e'') = (LE(e'); LE(e'')[LE(e')/X])$, where the postfix $[/]$ denotes capture-free substituton.

Theorem 31. *If* $\emptyset \vdash^{\top}_{sem} e : \kappa$, *then* $\emptyset \vdash^{\mu} LE(e) : \varphi$ *for each* $\varphi \in Inst(\kappa)$. *If* $\emptyset \vdash^{\mu} LE(e) : \varphi$, *then* $\emptyset \vdash^{\top}_{sem} e : \kappa$ *for some* κ *such that* $\varphi \in Inst(\kappa)$.

Corollary 32. *The type system* $\vdash^{\top}_{sem}$ *is sound.*

Proof. Implied by the soundness of $\vdash^{\mu}$ [3]: the typability of a term e under $\vdash^{\top}_{sem}$ implies the typability of $LE(e)$ under $\vdash^{\mu}$, which by soundness of $\vdash^{\mu}$ implies that the evaluation of $LE(e)$ will not cause a run-time error. Since the let-expansion of e is observationally equivalent to e, this implies that the evaluation of e is free of run-time errors.

Corollary 33. *The type system* $\vdash^{\top}_{dec}$ *is sound.*

Theorem 34. *The inference system* $\vdash^{\text{I}}$ *is complete with respect to* $\vdash^{\top}_{sem}$.

6 Related Work

Pottier [20] has independently derived results that are related to some results of this paper. He defines a syntactic and a semantic notions of entailment on constraint sets, shows they are equivalent, and presents a type system with subsumption based on this entailment. He also provides an algorithm for an approximation to the entailment relation, which appears equivalent to $K \vdash \tau \leq \tau'$ for canonical K; finally, the theory is used as a basis for proving the soundness of a number of constrained type simplifications. However the entailment relations do not take into account reachability of type variables, which depends on the polarity of their occurrences and hence on the root type; in particular his syntactic entailment $C' \vdash C''$ requires $C'' \cup C$ to be consistent whenever $C' \cup C$ is, for *any* constraint set C, including sets that put bounds on unreachable type variables, which is not possible during type inference. As a consequence both the relation between constrained types, implied by his subsumption rule, and its decidable approximation are strictly less powerful than ours.

Jim [13] also defines a notion of $\leq^{\forall}$ that relates fewer types than ours but is still powerful enough to prove some principal typing properties for constrained type systems.

Previous researchers [21, 4] have addressed the problem of subtyping constrained types in the context of a system where recursive constraints are not allowed. The choice whether to allow or disallow recursive constraints greatly changes the theory.

7 Conclusions

This paper establishes a foundation for constrained type theory, in particular via a powerful characterization of subtyping on constrained types. We introduce two natural notions of subtyping, observational $\leq^{\forall}_{obs}$ and semantic $\leq^{\forall}_{sem}$, and prove that they are equivalent; we further give a decidable approximation $\leq^{\forall}_{dec}$ to these relations. Both results represent improvements over recent work on subtyping of constrained types with recursive constraints [9, 20, 13]. We also introduce a novel closed form of constraint types with contexts, which eliminates the problems associated with free type variables. Finally, we present a type system with principal constrained types, and establish its soundness via reduction to the system of Amadio and Cardelli.

The most generous relations $\leq^{\forall}_{sem}$ and $\leq^{\forall}_{obs}$ may be undecidable, but we believe that $\leq^{\forall}_{dec}$ is powerful enough to be useful in practice for signature matching and constraint simplification. Our confidence in the system stems from the fact that $\leq^{\forall}_{dec}$ subsumes the Amadio/Cardelli subtyping of recursive types, the type scheme instantiation in the Hindley/Milner system, and the subtyping relation of [20]. Additionally, it turns out that the known simplifications of constraint sets do not test the limits of the system based on $\leq^{\forall}_{dec}$; we have shown in this paper that $\leq^{\forall}_{dec}$ can be used to demonstrate the correctness of simplifications not included in other systems. Similarly, functor signatures may generally be produced by starting with an inferred constrained type and transforming it in regular ways, thus avoiding constrained types which $\leq^{\forall}_{dec}$ does not relate to the inferred type. We have yet to find a realistic subtyping example which is semantically sound but is not derivable using $\leq^{\forall}_{dec}$, but most convincing would be the performance of a system that uses it for signature matching and simplifications in practice on real code; we are in the process of constructing an implementation for this purpose.

Acknowledgements We wish to thank Simon Marlow, François Pottier, Didier Rémy, Philip Wadler, and the anonymous referees for many helpful comments and suggestions.

References

1. A. Aiken and E. L. Wimmers. Type inclusion constraints and type inference. In *Proceedings of the International Conference on Functional Programming Languages and Computer Architecture*, pages 31–41, 1993.
2. A. Aiken, E. L. Wimmers, and T. K. Lakshman. Soft typing with conditional types. In *Conference Record of the Twenty-First Annual ACM Symposium on Principles of Programming Languages*, pages 163–173, 1994.

3. R. Amadio and L. Cardelli. Subtyping recursive types. *ACM Transactions on Programming Languages and Systems*, 15(4):575–631, September 1993. Extended abstract in POPL 1991.
4. François Bourdoncle and Stephan Merz. On the integration of functional programming, class-based object-oriented programming, and multi-methods. Technical Report 26, Centre des Mathématiques Appliquées, Ecole des Mines de Paris, 1996. Available at `http://www.ensmp.fr/~bourdonc/`.
5. Kim Bruce, Luca Cardelli, Giuseppe Castagna, The Hopkins Objects Group, Gary T. Leavens, and Benjamin Pierce. On binary methods. *Theory and Practice of Object Systems*, 1(3):217–238, 1995.
6. L. Cardelli. A semantics of multiple inheritance. In *Semantics of Data Types*, volume 173 of *Lecture notes in Computer Science*, pages 51–67. Springer-Verlag, 1984.
7. B. Courcelle. Fundamental properties of infinite trees. *Theoretical Computer Science*, 25:95–169, 1983.
8. Pavel Curtis. Constrained quantification in polymorphic type analysis. Technical Report CSL-90-1, XEROX Palo Alto Research Center, `CSLPubs.parc@xerox.com`, 1990.
9. J. Eifrig, S. Smith, and V. Trifonov. Sound polymorphic type inference for objects. In *OOPSLA '95*, pages 169–184, 1995.
10. J. Eifrig, S. Smith, and V. Trifonov. Type inference for recursively constrained types and its application to OOP. In *Proceedings of the 1995 Mathematical Foundations of Programming Semantics Conference*, volume 1 of *Electronic Notes in Theoretical Computer Science*. Elsevier, 1995. `http://www.elsevier.nl/locate/entcs/volume1.html`.
11. J. Eifrig, S. Smith, V. Trifonov, and A. Zwarico. An interpretation of typed OOP in a language with state. *Lisp and Symbolic Computation*, 8(4):357–397, 1995.
12. Y.-C. Fuh and P. Mishra. Type inference with subtypes. In *European Symposium on Programming*, 1988.
13. Trevor Jim. *Principal typings and type inference*. PhD thesis, MIT, 1996. (to appear).
14. S. Kaes. Type inference in the presence of overloading, subtyping and recursive types. In *ACM Conference on Lisp and Functional Programming*, pages 193–204, 1992.
15. D. B. MacQueen, G. Plotkin, and R. Sethi. An ideal model for recursive polymorphic types. *Information and Control*, 71:95–130, 1986.
16. P. Mishra and U. Reddy. Declaration-free type checking. In *Conference Record of the Twelfth Annual ACM Symposium on Principles of Programming Languages*, pages 7–21, 1985.
17. John C. Mitchell. Coercion and type inference (summary). In *Conference Record of the Eleventh Annual ACM Symposium on Principles of Programming Languages*, 1984.
18. John C. Mitchell. Type inference with simple subtypes. *Journal of Functional Programming*, 1:245–285, 1991.
19. Jens Palsberg and Scott Smith. Constrained types and their expressiveness. *TOPLAS*, 18(5), September 1996.
20. François Pottier. Simplifying subtyping constraints. In *First International Conference on Functional Programming*, pages 122–133, 1996.
21. Geoffrey S. Smith. Principal type schemes for functional programs with overloading and subtyping. *Science of Computer Programming*, 23, 1994.

Abstract Cofibered Domains: Application to the Alias Analysis of Untyped Programs

Arnaud Venet

LIX, École Polytechnique, 91128 Palaiseau, France.
venet@lix.polytechnique.fr

Abstract. We present a class of domains for Abstract Interpretation, the cofibered domains, that are obtained by "glueing" a category of partially ordered sets together. The internal structure of these domains is well suited to the compositional design of approximations and widening operators, and we give generic methods for performing such constructions. We illustrate the interest of these domains by developing an alias analysis of untyped programs handling structured data. The results obtained with this analysis are comparable in accuracy to those obtained with the most powerful alias analyses existing for typed languages.

1 Introduction

Widening operators have originally been used in Abstract Interpretation [CC77] in order to cope with infinite domains on which abstract iteration sequences were not necessarily computable (e.g. [CC76, CH78]). In fact, the notion of widening is much more powerful since it allows the definition of abstract interpretations with very few hypotheses on their structure by *dynamically* constructing the abstract domain [Cou78, CC92a, Cou96]. In this paper we introduce a new class of such abstract domains: the *cofibered domains*.

A cofibered domain consists of a category of partially ordered sets "glued" together in a sense that we will make clear. Like for other composite domains in Abstract Interpretation (e.g. the reduced product of lattices [CC79]), most constructions over a cofibered domain can be achieved *compositionally* by combining the corresponding constructions over its base components. We illustrate the interest of this approach by constructing an alias analysis for a small untyped language with structured data. This analysis gives results comparable in accuracy to those obtained with Deutsch's framework [Deu92a, Deu92b, Deu94] whose applicability is restricted to languages with explicit datatype declarations.

The paper is organized as follows. In Sect. 2 we recall briefly the context of semantic approximation in which our work takes place. Section 3 is devoted to describing the framework of cofibered domains. We use dynamic partitioning [Bou92] as the running example of our presentation. In Sect. 4 we describe a generic construction of widening operators over cofibered domains. We apply the previous techniques to build an alias analysis for an untyped language in Sect. 5.

2 Abstract Interpretation with Widening

Let P be a program of a language $\mathcal{L}$. We suppose that the semantics $\mathcal{S}_P^\natural$ of P is given by the least fixpoint of a $\sqcup^\natural$-complete endomorphism $F^\natural$ over a complete lattice $(\mathcal{D}^\natural, \sqsubseteq^\natural, \perp^\natural, \sqcup^\natural, \top^\natural, \sqcap^\natural)$, where $\mathcal{D}^\natural$ is the *concrete semantic domain* which expresses program properties or behaviours. This is a quite common situation in practice but it is possible to relax significantly the previous hypotheses [CC92a].

Abstract Interpretation provides general frameworks to reason about semantic approximation [CC92a]. We choose one of these that is quite general and well-suited for our purpose, but all the techniques developed in this paper can be adapted to other frameworks. More precisely, following [CC92a] we assume that an abstract semantic specification of P is given by a preordered set $(\mathcal{D}, \preceq)$, the *abstract semantic domain*, related to $\mathcal{D}^\natural$ by a *concretization function* $\gamma : \mathcal{D} \longrightarrow \mathcal{D}^\natural$, an *abstract basis* $\perp \in \mathcal{D}$, and an *abstract semantic function* $F : \mathcal{D} \longrightarrow \mathcal{D}$ such that:

(i) $\perp^\natural \sqsubseteq^\natural \gamma(\perp)$.
(ii) $\forall x, y \in \mathcal{D} : x \preceq y \Longrightarrow \gamma(x) \sqsubseteq^\natural \gamma(y)$.
(iii) $\forall x \in \mathcal{D} : F^\natural \circ \gamma(x) \sqsubseteq^\natural \gamma \circ F(x)$.

In order to compute an approximation $\mathcal{S}_P$ of the concrete semantics of P in $\mathcal{D}$ we introduce the notion of *widening operator*.

Definition 1 Widening operator [CC77, CC92a]. A *widening* on $\mathcal{D}$ is a binary operator $\nabla : \mathcal{D} \times \mathcal{D} \longrightarrow \mathcal{D}$ which satisfies the following properties:

W1- $\forall x, y \in \mathcal{D} : x \preceq x \nabla y$.
W2- $\forall x, y \in \mathcal{D} : y \preceq x \nabla y$.
W3- For every sequence $(x_n)_{n \geq 0}$ of elements of $\mathcal{D}$, the sequence $(x_n^\nabla)_{n \geq 0}$ inductively defined as follows:

$$\begin{cases} x_0^\nabla &= x_0 \\ x_{n+1}^\nabla &= x_n^\nabla \nabla x_{n+1} \end{cases}$$

is ultimately stationary.

□

Example 1 **Intervals [CC76].** Let $(\mathcal{D}_{\mathrm{I}}, \subseteq)$ be the domain of intervals where $\mathcal{D}_{\mathrm{I}} = \{\emptyset\} \cup \{[a, b] \mid a \in \mathbb{Z} \cup \{-\infty\} \wedge b \in \mathbb{Z} \cup \{+\infty\}\}$ and $\subseteq$ is set inclusion. The widening ∇_{I} is defined as follows:

$$\begin{cases} I \nabla_{\mathrm{I}} \emptyset = I \\ \emptyset \nabla_{\mathrm{I}} I = I \\ [a_1, b_1] \nabla_{\mathrm{I}} [a_2, b_2] = [\text{if } a_2 < a_1 \text{ then } -\infty \text{ else } a_1, \\ \qquad\qquad\qquad \text{if } b_1 < b_2 \text{ then } +\infty \text{ else } b_1] \end{cases}$$

In other words, the upper (resp. lower) limit of an interval is extrapolated to $+\infty$ (resp. $-\infty$) whenever it increases (resp. decreases). □

Proposition 2 Abstract iterates [CC92a, CC92b]. *The abstract iteration sequence* $(F_n^{\nabla})_{n\geq 0}$ *given by:*

$$\begin{cases} F_0^{\nabla} & = \bot \\ F_{n+1}^{\nabla} & = F_n^{\nabla} \qquad\qquad \text{if } F(F_n^{\nabla}) \preceq F_n^{\nabla} \\ & = F_n^{\nabla} \; \nabla \; F(F_n^{\nabla}) \text{ otherwise} \end{cases}$$

is ultimately stationary and its limit $\mathcal{S}_P$ *satisfies* $\mathcal{S}_P^{\natural} \sqsubseteq^{\natural} \gamma(\mathcal{S}_P)$*. Moreover, if* $N \geq 0$ *is such that* $F_N^{\nabla} = F_{N+1}^{\nabla}$*, then* $\forall n \geq N : F_n^{\nabla} = F_N^{\nabla}$*.*

3 Cofibered Domains

The intuitive idea of "glueing" a category of posets is formalized by the *Grothendieck construction.*

Definition 3 Grothendieck construction [BW90]. Let $\mathbb{D}$ be a small category and **Pos** be the category of posets and monotone maps. We associate to any functor $\Delta : \mathbb{D} \longrightarrow$ **Pos** the category $\mathbf{G}\Delta$ defined as follows:

(i) An object of $\mathbf{G}\Delta$ is a pair (D, x) where D is an object of $\mathbb{D}$ and x is an element of the poset ΔD.
(ii) An arrow $(D, x) \xrightarrow{f} (E, y)$ of $\mathbf{G}\Delta$ is a morphism $D \xrightarrow{f} E$ of $\mathbb{D}$ such that $\Delta f(x) \sqsubseteq_E y$, where $\sqsubseteq_E$ denotes the order relation on ΔE.
(iii) The composition of two arrows $(D, x) \xrightarrow{f} (E, y)$ and $(E, y) \xrightarrow{g} (F, z)$ is given by $(D, x) \xrightarrow{g \circ f} (F, z)$. It is explicited in the following diagram:

$$\begin{array}{ccccc} D & \xrightarrow{\quad f \quad} & E & \xrightarrow{\quad g \quad} & F \\ x & \xrightarrow{\quad \Delta f \quad} & \Delta f(x) & \xrightarrow{\quad \Delta g \quad} & \Delta g \circ \Delta f(x) \\ & & \downarrow{\scriptstyle \sqsubseteq_E} & & \downarrow{\scriptstyle \sqsubseteq_F} \\ & & y & \xrightarrow{\quad \Delta g \quad} & \Delta g(y) \\ & & & & \downarrow{\scriptstyle \sqsubseteq_F} \\ & & & & z \end{array}$$

□

Definition 4 Cofibered domain. A *cofibered domain*[1] is a preordered set $(\mathcal{D}, \preceq)$ for which there exists a functor $\Delta : \mathbb{D} \longrightarrow$ **Pos** such that:

(i) $\mathcal{D}$ is the set of objects of $\mathbf{G}\Delta$.
(ii) For all $(D, x), (E, y) \in \mathcal{D}$, $(D, x) \preceq (E, y)$ whenever there exists an arrow $(D, x) \xrightarrow{f} (E, y)$ in $\mathbf{G}\Delta$. □

[1] The term *cofibered domain* comes from the fact that such a domain can be endowed with the structure of a *cofibration* [BW90].

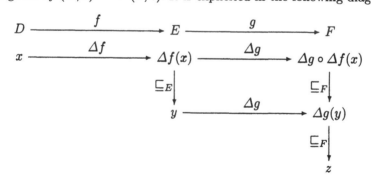

In other words, $(\mathcal{D}, \preceq)$ is the preorder obtained by *flattening* the category $\mathbf{G}\Delta$. We call the functor Δ the *display* associated to the cofibered domain. For each object D in $\mathbb{D}$ we call the poset ΔD the *fiber of Δ over D*.

Example 2 **Dynamic partitioning I.** We illustrate cofibered domains by constructing an approximation of the domain $(\wp(C \longrightarrow L), \subseteq)$, where $C \longrightarrow L$ is the set of functions from a set C into a complete lattice $(L, \sqsubseteq, \bot, \sqcup, \top, \sqcap)$. An interesting instance of this problem arises when C is the set of control points of a program (lexical points, stacks, etc.) and L is the powerset of all memory states. This has been extensively studied in [Bou92] where the powerful abstraction framework of *dynamic partitioning* has been developed. In its simplest form it amounts to abstracting a function $\rho : C \longrightarrow L$ by a partial function μ from $\wp(C)$ into L. The value of ρ at a point x is approximated by the join of the values $\mu(X)$ on the subsets X of C that contain x.

Let $\mathbf{P}(C)$ be the category whose objects are the subsets of $\wp(C)$. An arrow $D \xrightarrow{f} E$ of $\mathbf{P}(C)$ is a function $f : D \longrightarrow E$ such that for any $X \in D$ we have $X \subseteq f(X)$. Composition and identities are the usual ones. One can easily check that this definition is consistent. We define the functor $\Delta_C : \mathbf{P}(C) \longrightarrow \mathbf{Pos}$ as follows:

- For any object D of $\mathbf{P}(C)$, $\Delta_C D$ is the set $D \longrightarrow L$ with the pointwise ordering.
- If $D \xrightarrow{f} E$ is an arrow in $\mathbf{P}(C)$, $\Delta_C f$ maps any $\mu : D \longrightarrow L$ to the function $\lambda X \cdot \sqcup\{\mu(Y) \mid Y \in f^{-1}(X)\}$ of $\Delta_C E$.

We then construct the cofibered domain $(\mathcal{D}_C, \preceq_C)$ associated to the display Δ_C. An element (D, μ) of $\mathcal{D}_C$ represents a partial function from $\wp(C)$ into L, where $D \subseteq \wp(C)$ is the domain of definition of the function. The approximation of the concrete domain is given by the concretization function $\gamma_C : (\mathcal{D}_C, \preceq_C) \longrightarrow (\wp(C \longrightarrow L), \subseteq)$ that maps any (D, μ) in $\mathcal{D}_C$ to the set $\{\rho : C \longrightarrow L \mid \forall x \in C : \rho(x) \sqsubseteq \sqcup\{\mu(X) \mid X \in D \wedge x \in X\}\}$. □

In Sect. 2 we defined the connection between the concrete and abstract semantic domains as a concretization function $\gamma : (\mathcal{D}, \preceq) \longrightarrow (\mathcal{D}^\natural, \sqsubseteq)$. However it is quite rare in practice to directly build the abstract domain $(\mathcal{D}, \preceq)$. In general one proceeds by *stepwise* refinements of the approximation: if $(\mathcal{D}^\sharp, \preceq^\sharp)$ is another preordered set and $\gamma^\sharp : (\mathcal{D}^\sharp, \preceq^\sharp) \longrightarrow (\mathcal{D}, \preceq)$ is a monotone map, then the composite $\gamma \circ \gamma^\sharp : (\mathcal{D}^\sharp, \preceq^\sharp) \longrightarrow (\mathcal{D}^\natural, \sqsubseteq)$ is a further approximation of $(\mathcal{D}^\natural, \sqsubseteq)$. If $(\mathcal{D}, \preceq)$ is cofibered via a display Δ one can obtain an approximation of $(\mathcal{D}, \preceq)$ by means of a *fiberwise approximation* of Δ. In order to describe precisely this idea we need to introduce the notion of lax natural transformation.

Definition 5 Lax natural transformation [Kel74]. A *lax natural transformation* (lax n.t. for short) $\Delta^\sharp \overset{\kappa}{\rightsquigarrow} \Delta$ between two functors $\Delta^\sharp, \Delta : \mathbb{D} \longrightarrow \mathbf{Pos}$ is given by a morphism $\Delta^\sharp D \xrightarrow{\kappa_D} \Delta D$ for each object D in $\mathbb{D}$ and by a collection of commutative diagrams:

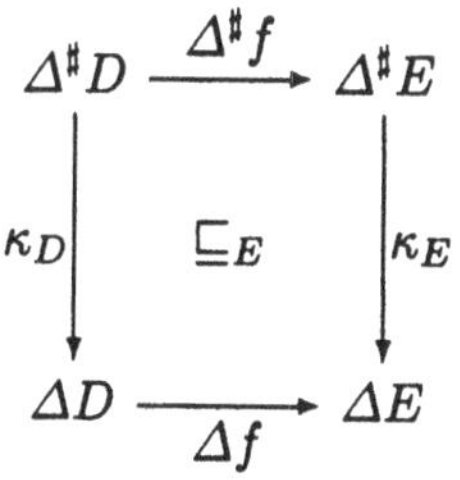

□

The intuition is that a morphism κ_D is a local concretization function that relates the fiber ΔD with its approximation $\Delta^\sharp D$. The commutative diagram above means that $\Delta f \circ \kappa_D \sqsubseteq_E \kappa_E \circ \Delta^\sharp F$, i.e. $\Delta^\sharp f$ is a sound approximation of Δf.

Let $(\mathcal{D}, \preceq)$ and $(\mathcal{D}^\sharp, \preceq^\sharp)$ be two cofibered domains and $\Delta : \mathbb{D} \longrightarrow \mathbf{Pos}$, $\Delta^\sharp : \mathbb{D}^\sharp \longrightarrow \mathbf{Pos}$ be the associated displays. A *fiberwise approximation* of $(\mathcal{D}, \preceq)$ by $(\mathcal{D}^\sharp, \preceq^\sharp)$ is given by a functor $\Gamma : \mathbb{D}^\sharp \longrightarrow \mathbb{D}$ and a lax n.t. $\Delta^\sharp \overset{\kappa}{\rightsquigarrow} \Delta \circ \Gamma$ expressed diagrammatically by:

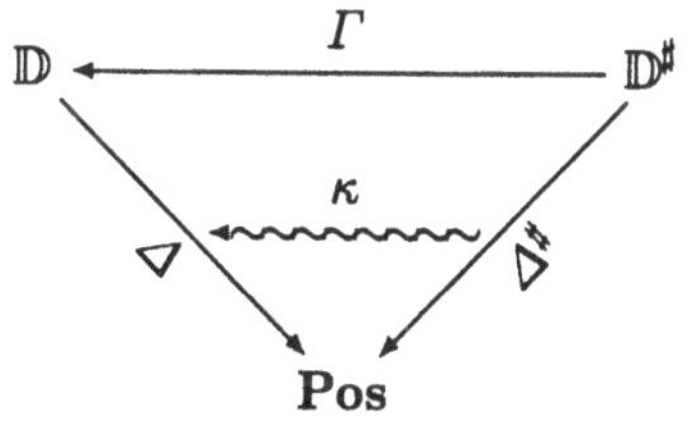

Γ can be seen as a "concretization functor" and $\mathbb{D}^\sharp$ as an abstraction of the shape of the cofibered domain $(\mathcal{D}, \preceq)$. The functor Γ is the *global* part of the approximation and the lax n.t. κ is the *local* part. We can then "glue" these two parts in order to obtain a concretization function $\mathbf{G}(\Gamma, \kappa) : (\mathcal{D}^\sharp, \preceq^\sharp) \longrightarrow (\mathcal{D}, \preceq)$.

Proposition 6. *The function* $\mathbf{G}(\Gamma, \kappa) : \mathcal{D}^\sharp \longrightarrow \mathcal{D}$ *that sends any* $(D^\sharp, x^\sharp)$ *in* $\mathcal{D}^\sharp$ *to* $(\Gamma D^\sharp, \kappa_{D^\sharp}(x^\sharp))$ *is monotone.*

Example 3 **Dynamic partitioning II.** We carry on with Example 2. We suppose that we are provided with two approximations $\gamma_C : (C^\sharp, \subseteq^\sharp) \longrightarrow (\wp(C), \subseteq)$ and $\gamma_L : (L^\sharp, \sqsubseteq^\sharp) \longrightarrow (L, \sqsubseteq)$. We suppose that $L^\sharp$ has the structure of a $\sqcup^\sharp$-semilattice $(L^\sharp, \sqsubseteq^\sharp, \perp^\sharp, \sqcup^\sharp)$ and that γ_C is injective (this is always possible, see [CC79]). Now let $\mathbf{P}_f(C^\sharp)$ be the category whose objects are finite subsets of $C^\sharp$. An arrow $D^\sharp \xrightarrow{f} E^\sharp$ of $\mathbf{P}_f(C^\sharp)$ is a function $f : D^\sharp \longrightarrow E^\sharp$ such that for any $X^\sharp \in D^\sharp$ we have $X^\sharp \subseteq^\sharp f(X^\sharp)$. Let $\Delta^\sharp_C : \mathbf{P}_f(C^\sharp) \longrightarrow \mathbf{Pos}$ be the functor defined as follows:

- For any $D^\sharp$ in $\mathbf{P}_f(C^\sharp)$, $\Delta^\sharp_C D^\sharp$ is the set $D^\sharp \longrightarrow L^\sharp$ with the pointwise ordering.

- If $D^\sharp \xrightarrow{f} E^\sharp$ is an arrow in $\mathbf{P}_f(C^\sharp)$, $\Delta^\sharp_C f$ maps any $\mu^\sharp : D^\sharp \longrightarrow L^\sharp$ to the function $\lambda X^\sharp \cdot \sqcup^\sharp\{\mu^\sharp(Y^\sharp) \mid Y^\sharp \in f^{-1}(X^\sharp)\}$ of $\Delta^\sharp_C E^\sharp$.

Let $\Gamma : \mathbf{P}_f(C^\sharp) \longrightarrow \mathbf{P}(C)$ be the functor that sends any object $D^\sharp$ to $\{\gamma_C(X^\sharp) \mid X^\sharp \in D^\sharp\}$ and any arrow $D^\sharp \xrightarrow{f} E^\sharp$ to the function that maps $\gamma_C(X^\sharp)$ to $\gamma_C(f(X^\sharp))$ for every $X^\sharp \in D^\sharp$. This definition is not ambiguous because γ_C is injective. We now define a lax n.t. $\Delta^\sharp_C \overset{\kappa}{\rightsquigarrow} \Gamma \circ \Delta_C$. Let $D^\sharp$ be in $\mathbf{P}_f(C^\sharp)$, $\kappa_{D^\sharp}$ sends every function $\mu^\sharp$ in $\Delta^\sharp_C(D^\sharp)$ to the function μ that maps $\gamma_C(X^\sharp)$ to $\gamma_L \circ \mu^\sharp(X^\sharp)$, for every $X^\sharp$ in $D^\sharp$. We denote by $(\mathcal{D}^\sharp_C, \preceq^\sharp_C)$ the cofibered domain associated to the display $\Delta^\sharp_C$. By proposition 6 we obtain a fiberwise approximation $\gamma : (\mathcal{D}^\sharp_C, \preceq^\sharp_C) \longrightarrow (\mathcal{D}_C, \preceq_C)$ from (Γ, κ). □

4 Construction of Widenings on Cofibered Domains

Let $(\mathcal{D}, \preceq)$ be a cofibered domain with display $\Delta : \mathbb{D} \longrightarrow \mathbf{Pos}$. We suppose that for every object D in $\mathbb{D}$ the fiber ΔD is provided with a widening operator $\nabla_D : \Delta D \times \Delta D \longrightarrow \Delta D$ satisfying conditions W1, W2 and W3 of Definition 1. Now we need to define a notion of widening on the category $\mathbb{D}$.

Definition 7 ω-chain. An *ω-chain* in $\mathbb{D}$ is a sequence of arrows $(D_n \xrightarrow{f_n} D_{n+1})_{n \geq 0}$. We say that the ω-chain is ***ultimately pseudo-stationary*** if there exists a rank $N \geq 0$ such that for all $n \geq N$, f_n is an isomorphism. □

A *widening operator* ∇ on $\mathbb{D}$ associates to any two objects D, E of $\mathbb{D}$ two arrows:

$$D \xrightarrow{(D \,\nabla\, E)_1} D \nabla E \xleftarrow{(D \,\nabla\, E)_2} E$$

such that for any sequence of objects $(D_n)_{n \geq 0}$, the ω-chain $(D^\nabla_n \xrightarrow{f^\nabla_n} D^\nabla_{n+1})_{n \geq 0}$ defined by:

$$\begin{cases} D^\nabla_0 = D_0 \\ D^\nabla_{n+1} = D^\nabla_n \nabla D_{n+1} \\ f^\nabla_n = (D^\nabla_n \nabla D_{n+1})_1 \end{cases}$$

is ultimately pseudo-stationary. Moreover we require ∇ to be stable under isomorphism, that is, whenever $D \cong D'$ and $E \cong E'$, then $D \nabla E \cong D' \nabla E'$.

Definition 8 Widening on cofibered domains. We assume that $\mathbb{D}$ is provided with a widening operator ∇. If (D, x) and (E, y) are elements of $\mathcal{D}$, we define $(D, x) \overline{\nabla} (E, y)$ as follows:

- $(D, x) \ \overline{\nabla} \ (E, y) \overset{\text{def}}{=} (D, x \nabla_D \Delta((D\nabla E)_1^{-1} \circ (D\nabla E)_2)(y))$ if $(D\nabla E)_1$ is an isomorphism. This is expressed by the following diagram:

$$\begin{array}{ccccc} D & \xleftarrow{\quad (D \,\nabla\, E)_1^{-1} \quad} & D \nabla E & \xleftarrow{(D \,\nabla\, E)_2} & E \\ \Big| & & & & \Big| \\ x \nabla_D \Delta((D\nabla E)_1^{-1} \circ (D\nabla E)_2)(y) & \dashleftarrow & \cdots & \cdots & y \end{array}$$

– $(D,x)\ \overline{\nabla}\ (E,y) \stackrel{\text{def}}{=} (D\nabla E, \Delta(D\nabla E)_1(x)\ \nabla_{D\nabla E}\ \Delta(D\nabla E)_2(y))$ otherwise. That is, graphically:

$$\begin{array}{ccccc} D & \xrightarrow{(D\,\nabla\,E)_1} & D\,\nabla\,E & \xleftarrow{(D\,\nabla\,E)_2} & E \\ \Big| & & \Big| & & \Big| \\ x & \dashrightarrow & \Delta(D\nabla E)_1(x)\ \nabla_{D\nabla E}\ \Delta(D\nabla E)_2(y) & \dashleftarrow & y \end{array}$$

□

Intuitively the first case means that when the fiber is "stable", i.e. $(D\nabla E)_1$ is an isomorphism, we "transfer" the abstract property y into the fiber and we make the widening with x. Otherwise we transfer x and y into the fiber over $D\nabla E$ and we make the widening in this fiber.

Theorem 9. $\overline{\nabla}$ *is a widening operator (i.e. it satisfies conditions W1, W2 and W3 of definition 1).*

Example 4 **Dynamic partitioning III.** We apply this method to the cofibered domain of Example 3. We suppose that the semilattice $(L^\sharp, \sqsubseteq^\sharp, \perp^\sharp, \sqcup^\sharp)$ comes equipped with a widening operator $\nabla_{L^\sharp}$. For each $D^\sharp$ in $\mathbf{P}_f(C^\sharp)$ we define a widening $\nabla_{D^\sharp}$ on the fiber over $D^\sharp$ by pointwise application of $\nabla_{L^\sharp}$. It is not possible to exhibit a widening for $\mathbf{P}_f(C^\sharp)$ in whole generality since it strongly depends on the nature of $C^\sharp$. Therefore we treat a particular instance of C and $C^\sharp$. We suppose that we are analyzing an imperative program P with a set $\mathcal{L}$ which labels the instructions in P. We denote by $\mathcal{C}$ the subset of $\mathcal{L}$ consisting of all labels of procedure calls. We define a control point to be a pair (S,ℓ) where $S \in \mathcal{C}^*$ is a stack of procedure calls and $\ell \in \mathcal{L}$ denotes the current program point. C is the collection of all sets of control points. We do not specify the domain L introduced in Example 2, which is intended to represent sets of memory states.

We define $C^\sharp$ to be the poset $\mathcal{L} \times (\mathcal{C} \longrightarrow \mathcal{D}_{\mathrm{I}})$, where $\mathcal{D}_{\mathrm{I}}$ is the domain of intervals defined in Example 1, the ordering being given componentwise. The injective function γ_C sends a pair (ℓ,ν) to the set $\{(S,\ell) \mid \forall c \in \mathcal{C} : |S|_c \in \nu(c)\}$, where $|S|_c$ denotes the number of occurrences of the label c in S. That is, we abstract a stack by the number of times each procedure call occurs in it. We define a widening operator ∇_C on $C^\sharp$ by componentwise application of ∇_{I}. If $D^\sharp$ is an element of $\mathbf{P}_f(C^\sharp)$ and $\ell \in \mathcal{L}$, we denote by $D^\sharp(\ell)$ the element $\dot{\sqcup}_{\mathrm{I}}\ \{\mu \mid (\ell,\mu) \in D^\sharp\}$ of $C^\sharp$, where $\dot{\sqcup}_{\mathrm{I}}$ is the pointwise extension of the join $\sqcup_{\mathrm{I}}$ on the lattice $\mathcal{D}_{\mathrm{I}}$ of intervals. Now let $D_1^\sharp$ and $D_2^\sharp$ be elements of $\mathbf{P}_f(C^\sharp)$. We define the widening $D_1^\sharp \nabla D_2^\sharp$ as follows:

$$D_1^\sharp \nabla D_2^\sharp \stackrel{\text{def}}{=} \{(\ell, D_1^\sharp(\ell)\ \nabla_{\mathrm{I}}\ D_2^\sharp(\ell)) \mid \ell \in \mathcal{L}\}$$

For $i \in \{1,2\}$, $(D_1^\sharp\ \nabla\ D_2^\sharp)_i$ sends any (ℓ,μ) in $D_i^\sharp$ to $(\ell, D_1^\sharp(\ell)\ \nabla_{\mathrm{I}}\ D_2^\sharp(\ell))$ in $D_1^\sharp \nabla D_2^\sharp$. We readily check that this defines a widening on the category $\mathbf{P}_f(C^\sharp)$. By applying Theorem 9 we obtain a widening $\overline{\nabla}_C$ on the cofibered domain $\mathcal{D}_C^\sharp$.

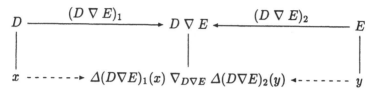

Note that the construction of such a widening (and the proof of its validity) would have been rather intricate without using the cofibered structure of the domain. □

5 Application to the Alias Analysis of Untyped Programs

We apply the previous techniques to sketch the construction of an alias analysis for a small imperative language without datatype declarations. We consider a program P written in this language. Let C be the set of data constructors occurring in P and Σ be the set of associated data selectors. If $f \in C$ has arity n, we denote by $f_1, \dots, f_n$ the corresponding data selectors. We will essentially focus on the two assignment instructions in the language that are involved in the production of aliases: $x := y.w$ and $x := f(x_1, \dots, x_n)$ where $w \in \Sigma^*$, $f \in C$ and x, y are elements of the set V_P of variables occurring in P. The treatment of control structures (conditionals, loops, recursion) is quite standard [CC77, Gra92] and we do not detail it.

Following [Jon81, Deu92b], a semantic configuration is a pair $(L, \equiv)$ where L is a *prefix-closed* subset of $V_P.\Sigma^*$ and $\equiv$ is a *right-regular equivalence relation* over L. Right-regularity means that whenever $v \equiv w$ and $v.a, w.a \in L$, then $v.a \equiv w.a$. L describes the set of access paths in the structures pointed by the variables of the program, and $\equiv$ is the *aliasing* relation on these paths. Right-regularity models equality of pointers in this semantic model.

Example 5. Consider the following program:

```
x := nil; y := nil;
for i:= 0 to N do begin
  h := a;
  x := cons(h, x);
  y := cons(h, y);
end;
```

We suppose that the data selectors associated to **cons** are *hd* and *tl*. Then the semantic configuration at the end of the program is given by $(L, \equiv)$ where L is the set of prefixes of $\{x.tl^n.hd, y.tl^n.hd \mid 0 \leq n \leq N\} \cup \{h\}$ and $\equiv$ is such that $x.tl^n.hd \equiv y.tl^n.hd$ and $h \equiv x.hd \equiv y.hd$. □

We can always assume that none of the variables occurring at the right-hand side of an assignment expression appears at the left-hand side by adding intermediate variables. Let $A \stackrel{\text{def}}{=} V_P \cup \Sigma$. For any prefix-closed subset L of A^* and any binary relation ρ over L, we denote by $[\rho]_L$ the least right-regular equivalence relation over L containing ρ. If $w \in A^*$ and $L \subseteq A^*$, we denote by $w^{-1}L$ the language $\{u \in A^* \mid w.u \in L\}$. The semantics $\{\!|x := y.w|\!\}$ of the instruction $x := y.w$ maps $(L, \equiv)$ to $(L_\bullet, \equiv_\bullet)$ where:

- $L_\bullet \stackrel{\text{def}}{=} (L \backslash x.\Sigma^*) \cup x.((y.w)^{-1}L)$.
- $\equiv_\bullet \stackrel{\text{def}}{=} [(\equiv \cap (L \backslash x.\Sigma^*)^2) \cup \{(x, y.w)\}]_{L_\bullet}$.

The semantics $\{\!|x := f(x_1, \ldots, x_n)|\!\}$ maps $(L, \equiv)$ to $(L_\bullet, \equiv_\bullet)$ where:

- $L_\bullet \stackrel{\text{def}}{=} (L\backslash x.\Sigma^*) \cup \bigcup_{1 \le i \le n} x.f_i.(x_i^{-1}L)$.
- $\equiv_\bullet \stackrel{\text{def}}{=} [(\equiv \cap (L\backslash x.\Sigma^*)^2) \cup \{(x.f_i, x_i) \mid 1 \le i \le n\}]_{L_\bullet}$.

See [Jon81] for more detail on this kind of semantics. The domain $(\mathcal{D}^\natural, \preceq^\natural)$ associated to the collecting semantics of the program is the powerset of all semantic configurations $(L, \equiv)$ ordered by inclusion.

We first approximate $(\mathcal{D}^\natural, \preceq^\natural)$ by a cofibered domain $(\mathcal{D}, \preceq)$. Let $\wp_<(A^*)$ be the set of all prefix-closed languages over A and $\Delta : (\wp_<(A^*), \subseteq) \longrightarrow \mathbf{Pos}$ be the display that sends any $L \in \wp_<(A^*)$ to the powerset of $\{(L', \rho) \mid L' \subseteq L \wedge \rho \in \wp(L' \times L')\}$ ordered by inclusion. The image of an arrow $L_1 \subseteq L_2$ is the natural inclusion map of ΔL_1 into ΔL_2. The concretization function $\mathrm{g} : \mathcal{D} \longrightarrow \mathcal{D}^\natural$ maps any (L, X) to $\{(L', \equiv) \mid L' \subseteq L \wedge (L', \equiv) \in X\}$.

We will make a fiberwise approximation of Δ, but we first need some notations. For any function $f : X \longrightarrow Y$ we denote by $\wp f : (\wp(X), \subseteq) \longrightarrow (\wp(Y), \subseteq)$ its powerset extension. That is, for any $A \in \wp(X)$, $\wp f(A) = \{f(x) \mid x \in A\}$. If $f_1 : X_1 \longrightarrow Y_1$ and $f_2 : X_2 \longrightarrow Y_2$ are two functions, we denote by $f_1 \times f_2 : X_1 \times X_2 \longrightarrow Y_1 \times Y_2$ the function that maps (x_1, x_2) to $(f_1(x_1), f_2(x_2))$.

We choose to abstract the domain L of an alias relation by a regular language. It is represented by an automaton (Q, I, τ) over A which consists of a finite set of states Q, a set of initial states $I \subseteq Q$, and a transition relation $\tau \in \wp(Q \times A \times Q)$. Since L is prefix-closed all states of the automaton are terminal. A morphism $\mathcal{A}_1 \xrightarrow{f} \mathcal{A}_2$ between two automata $\mathcal{A}_1 = (Q_1, I_1, \tau_1)$ and $\mathcal{A}_2 = (Q_2, I_2, \tau_2)$ is given by two functions $f_0 : Q_1 \longrightarrow Q_2$ and $f_1 : \tau_1 \longrightarrow \tau_2$, such that $f_0(I_1) \subseteq I_2$ and for all $(q, a, q') \in \tau_1$, $f_1(q, a, q') = (f_0(q), a, f_0(q'))$. Automata over A with morphisms between them form a category $\mathbb{A}$. In order to keep this category small and representable we suppose that all states come from an infinite and recursively enumerable set $\mathcal{Q}$.

A path π of an automaton $\mathcal{A} = (Q, I, \tau)$ is a sequence of adjacent transitions $(q_0, a_0, q_1)(q_1, a_1, q_2) \ldots (q_n, a_n, q_{n+1})$ such that $q_0 \in I$. Let $\mathrm{Paths}(\mathcal{A})$ be the set of paths of $\mathcal{A}$. We denote by $i(\pi)$ the initial state of π, by $t(\pi)$ its terminal state and by $\ell(\pi)$ the word labelling π. Let $\mathbf{R} : \mathbb{A} \longrightarrow \mathbf{Pos}$ be the functor that sends any automaton $\mathcal{A}$ to the poset $(\wp(\mathrm{Paths}(\mathcal{A}) \times \mathrm{Paths}(\mathcal{A})), \subseteq)$ of binary relations over paths of $\mathcal{A}$. A morphism of automata $\mathcal{A}_1 \xrightarrow{f} \mathcal{A}_2$ induces a function $f^* : \mathrm{Paths}(\mathcal{A}_1) \longrightarrow \mathrm{Paths}(\mathcal{A}_2)$ in the obvious way. We therefore define $\mathbf{R}f$ to be $\wp(f^* \times f^*)$.

Let $\Lambda : \mathbb{A} \longrightarrow (\wp_<(A^*), \subseteq)$ be the functor that sends any automaton to the language that it recognizes and any morphism to the inclusion arrow. For any automaton $\mathcal{A} = (Q, I, \tau)$ in $\mathbb{A}$, let $\kappa^0_{\mathcal{A}} : \mathbf{R}\mathcal{A} \longrightarrow (\Delta \circ \Lambda)\mathcal{A}$ be the morphism in $\mathbf{Pos}$ that sends any relation ρ in $\mathbf{R}\mathcal{A}$ to the set of pairs $(L, \rho_\bullet)$ for which there exists a function $\lambda \in L \longrightarrow \mathrm{Paths}(\mathcal{A})$ such that:

- $\forall w \in L : \ell(\lambda(w)) = w$.
- $\forall w \in L : \forall a \in A : (w.a \in L) \wedge (\lambda(w) = \pi) \Longrightarrow \exists \sigma \in \tau : \lambda(w.a) = \pi\sigma$.
- $\forall u, v \in L : (u, v) \in \rho_\bullet \Longrightarrow (u = v) \vee ((\lambda(u), \lambda(v)) \in \rho)$.

Proposition 10. *κ^0 defines a lax natural transformation* $\mathbf{R} \rightsquigarrow \Delta \circ \Lambda$.

Therefore (Λ, κ^0) induces a fiberwise approximation of $\mathcal{D}$. Following the ideas developed in [Deu92a, Deu92b] we now introduce a numerical abstraction of paths in an automaton. It basically amounts to abstracting a path by the number of times it runs through each arrow of the automaton.

Let $\mathcal{A} = (Q, I, \tau)$ be an automaton of $\mathbb{A}$. We denote by $R(\mathcal{A})$ the set $(I \times Q)^2$. Let $\mathbf{R}^\nu : \mathbb{A} \longrightarrow \mathbf{Pos}$ be the functor that sends an automaton $\mathcal{A} = (Q, I, \tau)$ to the set $R(\mathcal{A}) \longrightarrow \wp((\tau \longrightarrow \mathbb{N})^2)$ ordered by pointwise inclusion. If V and W are two finite sets and $f : V \longrightarrow W$ is a function between them, we define the function $f^\nu : (V \longrightarrow \mathbb{N}) \longrightarrow (W \longrightarrow \mathbb{N})$ as follows:

$$\forall \rho \in (V \longrightarrow \mathbb{N}) : f^\nu(\rho) \stackrel{\text{def}}{=} \lambda y \cdot \sum_{x \in f^{-1}(y)} \rho(x)$$

Let $\mathcal{A}_1 = (Q_1, I_1, \tau_1)$ and $\mathcal{A}_2 = (Q_2, I_2, \tau_2)$ be two automata and $\mathcal{A}_1 \xrightarrow{f} \mathcal{A}_2$ be a morphism between them. We denote by $f_R : R(\mathcal{A}_1) \longrightarrow R(\mathcal{A}_2)$ the function that maps (i, t, i', t') to $(f_0(i), f_0(t), f_0(i'), f_0(t'))$. We define $\mathbf{R}^\nu f$ as follows:

$$\mathbf{R}^\nu f \stackrel{\text{def}}{=} \lambda \rho \cdot \lambda r \cdot \{(f_1^\nu \times f_1^\nu)(\mu) \mid \exists r' \in f_R^{-1}(r) : \mu \in \rho(r')\}$$

For any path π of an automaton (Q, I, τ), we denote by π° its *commutative image*, that is the function $\pi^\circ : \tau \longrightarrow \mathbb{N}$ that associates to each transition $\sigma \in \tau$ the number $|\pi|_\sigma$ of times it occurs in π.

For any $\mathcal{A} = (Q, I, \tau)$ in $\mathbb{A}$, let $\kappa^1_{\mathcal{A}} : \mathbf{R}^\nu \mathcal{A} \longrightarrow \mathbf{R}\mathcal{A}$ be the morphism in $\mathbf{Pos}$ that sends any ρ in $\mathbf{R}^\nu \mathcal{A}$ to the element $\{(\pi_1, \pi_2) \mid (\pi_1^\circ, \pi_2^\circ) \in \rho(i(\pi_1), t(\pi_1), i(\pi_2), t(\pi_2))\}$ of $\mathbf{R}\mathcal{A}$. In other words we approximate a path in an automaton by the pair of its initial and final states together with its commutative image.

Proposition 11. *κ^1 defines a lax natural transformation* $\mathbf{R}^\nu \rightsquigarrow \mathbf{R}$.

If $\mathrm{Id}_{\mathbb{A}}$ is the identity functor on $\mathbb{A}$, $(\mathrm{Id}_{\mathbb{A}}, \kappa^1)$ provides a fiberwise approximation of the cofibered domain given by the display $\mathbf{R} : \mathbb{A} \longrightarrow \mathbf{Pos}$.

Now it remains to give a computable approximation of the poset $(\wp(V \longrightarrow \mathbb{N}), \subseteq)$ for any finite set V, in order to obtain an effective abstract domain. Several abstractions of this kind have been developed like the ***arithmetic intervals*** [CC76], the ***arithmetic congruences*** [Gra89], the ***linear equalities*** [Kar76], the ***linear inequalities*** [CH78] or the ***linear congruence equalities*** [Gra91]. We will not stick to any particular one and leave the choice of the numerical abstraction as a parameter of our domain. We therefore give an abstract description of a numerical domain.

Definition 12 Abstract numerical domain. An *abstract numerical domain* $\mathcal{V}^\sharp$ associates to each finite set V a lattice $(\mathcal{V}^\sharp V, \sqsubseteq_V^\sharp, \bot_V^\sharp, \sqcup_V^\sharp, \top_V^\sharp, \sqcap_V^\sharp)$ together with a concretization $\gamma_V : (\mathcal{V}^\sharp, \sqsubseteq_V^\sharp) \longrightarrow (\wp(V \longrightarrow \mathbb{N}), \subseteq)$. If V and W are finite sets and $f : V \longrightarrow W$ is a function between them, there is a computable function $\mathcal{V}^\sharp f : \mathcal{V}^\sharp V \longrightarrow \mathcal{V}^\sharp W$, such that $\wp f^\nu \circ \gamma_V \subseteq \gamma_W \circ \mathcal{V}^\sharp f$. If $V \overset{f}{\rightarrowtail} W$ is an injection, there are two computable functions $\overrightarrow{f} : \mathcal{V}^\sharp V \longrightarrow \mathcal{V}^\sharp W$ and $\overleftarrow{f} : \mathcal{V}^\sharp W \longrightarrow \mathcal{V}^\sharp V$ such that:

- $\forall \nu^\sharp \in \mathcal{V}^\sharp W : \forall \nu \in \gamma_W(\nu^\sharp) : \nu \circ f \subseteq \gamma_V(\overleftarrow{f}(\nu^\sharp))$.
- $\forall \mu^\sharp \in \mathcal{V}^\sharp V : \forall \mu \in \gamma_V(\mu^\sharp) : \{\nu \in W \longrightarrow \mathbf{N} \mid \nu \circ f = \mu\} \subseteq \gamma_W(\overrightarrow{f}(\mu^\sharp))$.

□

Moreover, if S is a system of linear equations over the set of variables V, there is a computable element $\mathbf{Sol}^\sharp_V(S)$ of $\mathcal{V}^\sharp V$ which upper-approximates the set of solutions of S in $V \longrightarrow \mathbf{N}$. For all previously cited numerical domains, $\mathcal{V}^\sharp$ can be shown to be a functor from the category **Finset** of finite sets and functions to **Pos**. We will omit the subscript V in the previous definitions whenever it will be clear from the context.

Example 6. In Karr's domain [Kar76], an element of $\wp(V \longrightarrow \mathbf{N})$ is upper-approximated by an affine subspace of $\mathbb{Q}^V$, where $\mathbb{Q}$ is the field of rational numbers. An affine subspace of $\mathbb{Q}^V$ can be defined by a system of affine equations over the set of variables V. Any function $f : V \longrightarrow W$ induces a linear map $f_\mathbb{Q} : \mathbb{Q}^V \longrightarrow \mathbb{Q}^W$. Thus $\mathcal{V}^\sharp f$ is the function that sends any affine subspace of $\mathbb{Q}^V$ to its image by $f_\mathbb{Q}$. If f is an injection, $\overleftarrow{f}$ is the orthogonal projection of affine subspaces of $\mathbb{Q}^W$ onto $\mathbb{Q}^V$. If S is a system of equations defining an affine subspace E of $\mathbb{Q}^V$, $\overrightarrow{f}(E)$ is the solution in $\mathbb{Q}^W$ of the system obtained from S by replacing every occurrence of a variable x by $f(x)$. Finally, for any system of affine equations S, $\mathbf{Sol}^\sharp_V(S)$ is computable by standard methods. □

If V and W are finite sets we denote by $V \oplus W$ their disjoint union. We will tacitly use the natural isomorphism $(V \longrightarrow \mathbf{N}) \times (W \longrightarrow \mathbf{N}) \cong (V \oplus W) \longrightarrow \mathbf{N}$ in the sequel. Let $\mathbf{R}^\sharp : \mathbb{A} \longrightarrow \mathbf{Pos}$ be the functor that sends an automaton $\mathcal{A} = (Q, I, \tau)$ to $(\mathcal{V}^\sharp(\tau \oplus \tau), \sqsubseteq^\sharp_{\tau\oplus\tau})$. Let $\mathcal{A}_1 = (Q_1, I_1, \tau_1)$ and $\mathcal{A}_2 = (Q_2, I_2, \tau_2)$ be two automata and $\mathcal{A}_1 \xrightarrow{f} \mathcal{A}_2$ be a morphism between them. We define $\mathbf{R}^\sharp f$ as follows:

$$\mathbf{R}^\sharp f \stackrel{\text{def}}{=} \lambda\rho^\sharp \cdot \lambda r \cdot \sqcup^\sharp_{\tau_2\oplus\tau_2}\{\mathcal{V}^\sharp(f_1^\nu \times f_1^\nu)(\rho^\sharp(r')) \mid r' \in f_R^{-1}(r)\}$$

Now to each automaton $\mathcal{A} = (Q, I, \tau)$ we associate the morphism $\kappa^2_\mathcal{A} : \mathbf{R}^\sharp\mathcal{A} \longrightarrow \mathbf{R}^\nu\mathcal{A}$ in **Pos** defined as follows:

$$\kappa^2_\mathcal{A} \stackrel{\text{def}}{=} \lambda\rho^\sharp \cdot \lambda r \cdot \gamma_{\tau\oplus\tau}(\rho^\sharp(r))$$

Proposition 13. *κ^2 defines a lax natural transformation $\mathbf{R}^\sharp \rightsquigarrow \mathbf{R}^\nu$.*

$(\mathrm{Id}_\mathbf{A}, \kappa^2)$ induces a fiberwise approximation of the cofibered domain associated to $\mathbf{R}^\nu$. If we denote by $\mathcal{D}^\sharp$ the cofibered domain given by the display $\mathbf{R}^\sharp \longrightarrow \mathbf{Pos}$, we obtain a concretization function $\gamma : \mathcal{D}^\sharp \longrightarrow \mathcal{D}$ by composing all previous approximations.

It now remains to define the abstract semantics of the two assignment instructions over $\mathcal{D}^\sharp$. We first need to define the abstract counterpart to the right-regular equivalence closure operator $[-]_L$. Since the closure of a relation by this operator can be seen as a fixpoint computation, we will use the techniques of Sect. 2 to perform an abstract computation locally over a fiber of $\mathcal{D}^\sharp$.

Definition 14. Let $\mathcal{A} = (Q, I, \tau)$ be an automaton. We define the binary relation $\xrightarrow{clo}$ over $\mathbf{R}^\sharp\mathcal{A}$ as follows:

(i) If $\rho^\sharp((q_1, q_2), (q'_1, q'_2)) = \nu^\sharp$, then $\rho^\sharp \xrightarrow{clo} \rho^\sharp_\bullet$ where

$$\rho^\sharp_\bullet(r) = \begin{cases} \nu^\sharp & \text{if } r = ((q'_1, q'_2), (q_1, q_2)) \\ \bot^\sharp & \text{otherwise} \end{cases}$$

(ii) Let $T_1 = T_2 = T_3 = \tau$ and $T = T_1 \oplus T_2 \oplus T_3$. Let $T_1 \oplus T_2 \overset{f_1}{\rightarrowtail} T$, $T_2 \oplus T_3 \overset{f_2}{\rightarrowtail} T$ and $T_1 \oplus T_3 \overset{f}{\rightarrowtail} T$ be the canonical inclusion maps in **Finset**. If $\rho^\sharp((q_1, q_2), (q'_1, q'_2)) = \nu^\sharp_1$ and $\rho^\sharp((q'_1, q'_2), (q''_1, q''_2)) = \nu^\sharp_2$, then $\rho^\sharp \xrightarrow{clo} \rho^\sharp_\bullet$ where

$$\rho^\sharp_\bullet(r) = \begin{cases} \overleftarrow{f}(\overrightarrow{f_1}(\nu^\sharp_1) \sqcap^\sharp \overrightarrow{f_2}(\nu^\sharp_2)) & \text{if } r = ((q_1, q_2), (q''_1, q''_2)) \\ \bot^\sharp & \text{otherwise} \end{cases}$$

(iii) If $\sigma_1 = (q_2, a, q_3)$ and $\sigma_2 = (q'_2, a, q'_3)$ are in τ, then let $T_1 = T_2 = \tau$, $S_1 = \{\sigma_1\}$, $S_2 = \{\sigma_2\}$ and $T = T_1 \oplus T_2 \oplus S_1 \oplus S_2$. Let $T_1 \oplus T_2 \overset{f_1}{\rightarrowtail} T$ be the canonical inclusion map and $T_1 \oplus T_2 \overset{f_2}{\rightarrowtail} T$ be the inclusion map such that $f_2(\sigma_1) \in S_1$ and $f_2(\sigma_2) \in S_2$. Let S be the system of affine equations over T defined as follows:

$$\begin{cases} f_2(\sigma_1) = f_1(\sigma_1) + 1 \\ f_2(\sigma_2) = f_1(\sigma_2) + 1 \end{cases}$$

If $\rho^\sharp((q_1, q_2), (q'_1, q'_2)) = \nu^\sharp$, then $\rho^\sharp \xrightarrow{clo} \rho^\sharp_\bullet$ where

$$\rho^\sharp_\bullet(r) = \begin{cases} \overleftarrow{f_2}(\overrightarrow{f_1}(\nu^\sharp) \sqcap^\sharp \mathbf{Sol}^\sharp(S)) & \text{if } r = ((q_1, q_3), (q'_1, q'_3)) \\ \bot^\sharp & \text{otherwise} \end{cases}$$

Let $\mathrm{F}^\sharp_{clo} \in \mathbf{R}^\sharp\mathcal{A} \longrightarrow \mathbf{R}^\sharp\mathcal{A}$ be the map defined as:

$$\mathrm{F}^\sharp_{clo} = \lambda\rho^\sharp \cdot \bigsqcup^\sharp \{\rho^\sharp_\bullet \mid \rho^\sharp \xrightarrow{clo} \rho^\sharp_\bullet\}$$

Every previously cited numerical domain comes with a widening operator on each lattice $\mathcal{V}^\sharp V$ for any finite set V. Then, for any $\rho^\sharp$ in $\mathbf{R}^\sharp\mathcal{A}$ we define $[\rho^\sharp]^\sharp_{\mathcal{A}}$ to be the limit of the iteration sequence with widening of Proposition 2 applied to $\mathrm{F}^\sharp_{clo}$, using $\rho^\sharp$ as a basis for the iteration and the widening defined locally on the fiber $\mathbf{R}^\sharp\mathcal{A}$. □

We also need the abstract counterpart to the quotient operation $w^{-1}L$ over languages.

Definition 15. Let $(\mathcal{A}, \rho^\sharp)$ be an element of $\mathcal{D}^\sharp$ and $a \in A$. We define $\mathrm{Elim}_a(\mathcal{A}, \rho^\sharp) \stackrel{\mathrm{def}}{=} (\mathcal{A}_\dagger^\sharp, \rho_\dagger^\sharp)$ as follows:

- If $\mathcal{A} = (Q, I, \tau)$, then $\mathcal{A}_\dagger \stackrel{\mathrm{def}}{=} (Q_\dagger, I_\dagger, \tau_\dagger)$, where $Q_\dagger = Q$, $I_\dagger = I$ and $\tau_\dagger = \tau \cap (Q \times (A \setminus \{a\}) \times Q)$.
- If $\tau_\dagger \oplus \tau_\dagger \stackrel{f}{\rightarrowtail} \tau \oplus \tau$ is the natural inclusion map, then $\rho_\dagger^\sharp \stackrel{\mathrm{def}}{=} \overleftarrow{f}(\rho^\sharp)$. □

We can now define the abstract semantics of the assignment instructions. In the following we suppose that we are provided with two distinguished elements Ω and Ω' in $\mathcal{Q}$. Moreover, if $f \in Q \longrightarrow Q'$ is a function between finite subsets of $\mathcal{Q}$, we will denote by $\overline{f}$ the function $f \times \mathrm{Id}_A \times f \in Q \times A \times Q \longrightarrow Q' \times A \times Q'$.

Definition 16 Abstract semantics of $x := y.w$. For any $(\mathcal{A}, \rho^\sharp) \in \mathcal{D}^\sharp$, let $((Q_\bullet, I_\bullet, \tau_\bullet), \rho_\bullet^\sharp) \stackrel{\mathrm{def}}{=} \mathrm{Elim}_x(\mathcal{A}, \rho^\sharp)$ and $P_\bullet \stackrel{\mathrm{def}}{=} \{\pi \in \mathrm{Paths}(\mathcal{A}_\bullet) \mid \ell(\pi) = y.w\}$. We put

$$Q_\dagger \stackrel{\mathrm{def}}{=} Q_\bullet \oplus \bigoplus_{\pi \in P_\bullet} Q_\bullet \oplus \bigoplus_{\pi \in P_\bullet} \{\Omega\}$$

Let $Q_\bullet \stackrel{e}{\rightarrowtail} Q_\dagger$, $Q_\bullet \stackrel{e_\pi}{\rightarrowtail} Q_\dagger$ and $\{\Omega\} \stackrel{o_\pi}{\rightarrowtail} Q_\dagger$, $\pi \in P_\bullet$, be the canonical inclusion maps in **Finset**. We put $I_\dagger \stackrel{\mathrm{def}}{=} e(I_\bullet) \cup \{o_\pi(\Omega) \mid \pi \in P_\bullet\}$ and $\tau_\dagger \stackrel{\mathrm{def}}{=} \overline{e}(\tau_\bullet) \cup \{(o_\pi(\Omega), x, e_\pi(t(\pi))) \mid \pi \in P_\bullet\}$. We then define the automaton $\mathcal{A}_\dagger \stackrel{\mathrm{def}}{=} (Q_\dagger, I_\dagger, \tau_\dagger)$. Let $\mathcal{A}_\dagger \stackrel{\iota^1}{\longrightarrow} \mathcal{A}_\dagger \coprod \mathcal{A}_\dagger \stackrel{\iota^2}{\longleftarrow} \mathcal{A}_\dagger$ be a coproduct diagram in $\mathbb{A}$ and let $\pi \in P_\bullet$. We define the system of affine equations S_π over $\tau_\dagger \oplus \tau_\dagger$ as follows:

$$\begin{cases} \sigma = \begin{cases} 1 & \text{if } \sigma = \iota_1^2(o_\pi(\Omega), x, e_\pi(t(\pi))) \\ |\pi|_{\sigma'} & \text{if } \sigma = \iota_1^1 \circ \overline{e}(\sigma') \\ 0 & \text{otherwise} \end{cases} \\ \sigma \in \tau_\dagger \oplus \tau_\dagger \end{cases}$$

We define the element $\rho_\pi^\sharp$ of $\mathbf{R}^\sharp(\mathcal{A}_\dagger)$ as follows:

$$\rho_\pi^\sharp(r) \stackrel{\mathrm{def}}{=} \begin{cases} \mathbf{Sol}^\sharp(S_\pi) & \text{if } r = ((\iota_0^1 \circ e(i(\pi)), \iota_0^1 \circ e(t(\pi))), (\iota_0^2 \circ o_\pi(\Omega), \iota_0^2 \circ e_\pi(t(\pi)))) \\ \bot^\sharp_{\tau_\dagger \oplus \tau_\dagger} & \text{otherwise} \end{cases}$$

Finally we put

$$\{\!|x := y.w|\!\}^\sharp(\mathcal{A}, \rho^\sharp) \stackrel{\mathrm{def}}{=} (\mathcal{A}_\dagger, [\mathcal{V}^\sharp(\overline{e} \oplus \overline{e})(\rho_\bullet^\sharp) \sqcup^\sharp \bigsqcup_{\pi \in P_\bullet}{}^\sharp \rho_\pi^\sharp]^\sharp_{\mathcal{A}_\dagger})$$

□

Definition 17 Abstract semantics of $x := f(x_1, \ldots, x_n)$. For any $(\mathcal{A}, \rho^\sharp) \in \mathcal{D}^\sharp$, let $((Q_\bullet, I_\bullet, \tau_\bullet), \rho_\bullet^\sharp) \stackrel{\text{def}}{=} \text{Elim}_x(\mathcal{A}, \rho^\sharp)$ and $P_\bullet \stackrel{\text{def}}{=} \{(\pi_1, \ldots, \pi_n) \mid \forall i \in \{1, \ldots, n\} : \pi_i \in \text{Paths}(\mathcal{A}) \wedge \ell(\pi_i) = x_i\}$. We put

$$Q_\dagger \stackrel{\text{def}}{=} Q_\bullet \oplus \bigoplus_{\alpha \in P_\bullet} \left(\bigoplus_{i=1}^{n} Q_\bullet \right) \oplus \bigoplus_{\alpha \in P_\bullet} \{\Omega, \Omega'\}$$

Let $Q_\bullet \stackrel{e}{\rightarrowtail} Q_\dagger$, $Q_\bullet \stackrel{e^i_\alpha}{\rightarrowtail} Q_\dagger$ and $\{\Omega, \Omega'\} \stackrel{o_\alpha}{\rightarrowtail} Q_\dagger$, $\alpha \in P_\bullet$, $1 \leq i \leq n$, be the canonical inclusion maps in **Finset**. We put $I_\dagger \stackrel{\text{def}}{=} e(I_\bullet) \cup \{o_\alpha(\Omega) \mid \alpha \in P_\bullet\}$ and $\tau_\dagger \stackrel{\text{def}}{=} \overline{e}(\tau_\bullet) \cup \{(o_\alpha(\Omega), x, o_\alpha(\Omega')) \mid \alpha \in P_\bullet\} \cup \{(o_\alpha(\Omega'), f_i, e^i_\alpha(t(\pi_i))) \mid \alpha = (\pi_1, \ldots, \pi_n) \in P_\bullet\}$. We then define the automaton $\mathcal{A}_\dagger \stackrel{\text{def}}{=} (Q_\dagger, I_\dagger, \tau_\dagger)$. Let $\mathcal{A}_\dagger \xrightarrow{\iota^1} \mathcal{A}_\dagger \coprod \mathcal{A}_\dagger \xleftarrow{\iota^2} \mathcal{A}_\dagger$ be a coproduct diagram in $\mathbb{A}$. Let $\alpha = (\pi_1, \ldots, \pi_n) \in P_\bullet$ and $i \in \{1, \ldots, n\}$. We define the system of affine equations S^i_α over $\tau_\dagger \oplus \tau_\dagger$ as follows:

$$\begin{cases} \sigma = \begin{cases} 1 \text{ if } \sigma = \iota^2_1(o_\alpha(\Omega), x, o_\alpha(\Omega')) \ \text{ or } \sigma = \iota^2_1(o_\alpha(\Omega'), f_i, e^i_\alpha(t(\pi_i))) \\ 1 \text{ if } \sigma = \iota_1 \circ \overline{e}(\pi_i) \\ 0 \text{ otherwise} \end{cases} \\ \sigma \in \tau_\dagger \oplus \tau_\dagger \end{cases}$$

We define the element $\rho^\sharp_{\alpha,i}$ of $\mathbf{R}^\sharp(\mathcal{A}_\dagger)$ as follows, where we put $I_i \stackrel{\text{def}}{=} i(\pi_i)$ and $T_i \stackrel{\text{def}}{=} t(\pi_i)$:

$$\rho^\sharp_{\alpha,i}(r) \stackrel{\text{def}}{=} \begin{cases} \mathbf{Sol}^\sharp(S^i_\alpha) \text{ if } r = ((\iota^1_0(e(I_i)), \iota^1_0(e(T_i))), (\iota^2_0(o_\alpha(\Omega)), \iota^2_0(e^i_\alpha(T_i)))) \\ \bot^\sharp_{\tau_\dagger \oplus \tau_\dagger} \quad \text{otherwise} \end{cases}$$

Finally we put

$$\{\!\!\{ x := f(x_1, \ldots, x_n) \}\!\!\}^\sharp(\mathcal{A}, \rho^\sharp) \stackrel{\text{def}}{=} (\mathcal{A}_\dagger, [\mathcal{V}^\sharp(\overline{e} \oplus \overline{e})(\rho_\bullet^\sharp) \sqcup^\sharp \bigsqcup_{\alpha \in P_\bullet}{}^{\sharp} \bigsqcup_{1 \leq i \leq n}{}^{\sharp} \rho^\sharp_{\alpha,i}]^\sharp_{\mathcal{A}_\dagger})$$

□

Theorem 18 Soundness of the abstract assignment. *Let α be an assignment instruction. For any $(\mathcal{A}, \rho^\sharp) \in \mathcal{D}^\sharp$ and any $(L, \equiv) \in \mathrm{g} \circ \gamma(\mathcal{A}, \rho^\sharp)$, we have:*

$$\{\!\!\{ \alpha \}\!\!\}(L, \equiv) \in \mathrm{g} \circ \gamma(\{\!\!\{ \alpha \}\!\!\}^\sharp(\mathcal{A}, \rho^\sharp))$$

where g *is the concretization function from $\mathcal{D}$ into $\mathcal{D}^\natural$ defined previously.*

It remains to define a widening on the category $\mathbb{A}$. The idea is to fold states in an automaton that "look similar". This is achieved via the *quotient* of an automaton by an equivalence relation.

Definition 19 Quotient of an automaton. Let $\mathcal{A} = (Q, I, \tau)$ be an automaton of $\mathbb{A}$ and $\sim$ be an equivalence relation on Q. We denote by $\pi_\sim \in Q \longrightarrow Q/_\sim$ the canonical projection onto the quotient set[2]. We define $\mathcal{A}/_\sim \stackrel{\text{def}}{=} (Q/_\sim, \pi_\sim(I), \tau_\sim)$ where $\tau_\sim \stackrel{\text{def}}{=} \{(\pi_\sim(q), a, \pi_\sim(q')) \mid (q, a, q') \in \tau\}$. □

Let $\mathcal{A} = (Q, I, \tau)$ be an automaton and $k \geq 1$ be a fixed integer. For any $q \in Q$ we denote by $\Lambda_q^k(\mathcal{A})$ the set of words $w \in A^*$ of length less than or equal to k such that there exists a path originating from q in the automaton which is labelled by w. We define $\equiv_\nabla^k$ to be the least equivalence relation on Q such that:

- $(i \in I) \wedge (i' \in I) \Longrightarrow (i \equiv_\nabla^k i')$.
- $((q, a, q_1) \in \tau) \wedge ((q, a, q_2) \in \tau) \Longrightarrow (q_1 \equiv_\nabla^k q_2)$.
- $(\Lambda_q^k(\mathcal{A}) = \Lambda_{q'}^k(\mathcal{A})) \wedge (\Lambda_q^k(\mathcal{A}) \cap A^k \neq \emptyset) \Longrightarrow (q \equiv_\nabla^k q')$.

Now let $\mathcal{A}_1 = (Q_1, I_1, \tau_1)$, $\mathcal{A}_2 = (Q_2, I_2, \tau_2)$ be two automata, $\mathcal{A}$ their coproduct and $\mathcal{A}_1 \stackrel{\epsilon_1}{\rightarrowtail} \mathcal{A}$, $\mathcal{A}_2 \stackrel{\epsilon_2}{\rightarrowtail} \mathcal{A}$ the canonical inclusion maps. We define

$$\mathcal{A}_1 \nabla_k \mathcal{A}_2 \stackrel{\text{def}}{=} \mathcal{A}/_{\equiv_\nabla^k}$$

We can extend the projection $\pi_{\equiv_\nabla^k}$ to a morphism of automata $\overline{\pi}_{\equiv_\nabla^k} \in \mathcal{A} \longrightarrow \mathcal{A}_1 \nabla_k \mathcal{A}_2$. For $i \in \{1, 2\}$, we define

$$(\mathcal{A}_1 \nabla_k \mathcal{A}_2)_i \stackrel{\text{def}}{=} \overline{\pi}_{\equiv_\nabla^k} \circ \epsilon_i$$

In other words, we make $\mathcal{A}$ deterministic and we fold two states that cannot be distinguished by only looking at prefixes of length at most k of the paths originating from them. This widening criterion is inspired from the *k-limiting* approximation of [JM81].

Proposition 20. *For any $k \in \mathbb{N}$, ∇_k is a widening operator on $\mathbb{A}$.*

Example 7. Consider the program of Example 5. We use Karr's abstract numerical domain. Since it satisfies the ascending chain condition the widening is given by the join. We use the widening ∇_1 on automata. The analysis computes the element $(\mathcal{A}, \rho^\sharp)$ of $\mathcal{D}^\sharp$. The automaton $\mathcal{A}$ is given by the following diagram[3] where a distinct name in the set $\tau = \{i, j, k, l, m\}$ has been assigned to each transition:

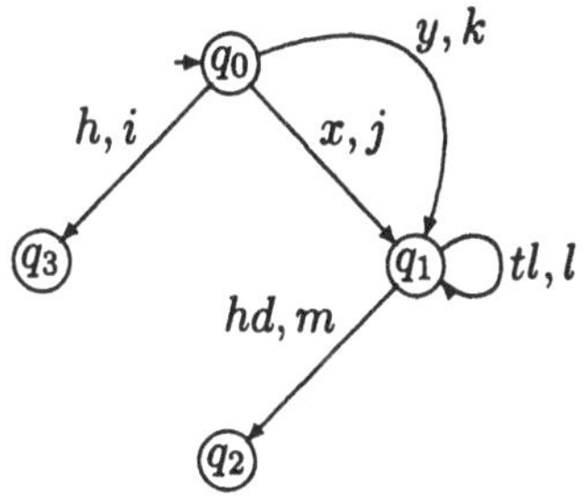

[2] Strictly speaking $Q/_\sim$ is a representative of the quotient set in Q.

[3] The auxiliary variables introduced to guarantee the linearity of assignment instructions have been removed. We have also trimmed the automata produced during the analysis by eliminating all useless transitions.

If we denote by $\tau \xrightarrow{\iota_1} \tau \oplus \tau \xleftarrow{\iota_2} \tau$ a coproduct diagram in **Finset**, $\rho^\sharp((q_0, q_2), (q_0, q_2))$ is given by the following system of affine equations:

$$\begin{cases} \iota_1(j) = \iota_2(k) = 1 \\ \iota_2(j) = \iota_1(k) = 0 \\ \iota_1(l) = \iota_2(l) \\ \iota_1(m) = \iota_2(m) = 1 \\ \iota_1(i) = \iota_2(i) = 0 \end{cases}$$

This means that no spurious alias relation has been inferred. □

6 Conclusion

We have described the core of an alias analysis for untyped programs based upon cofibered domains. Deutsch's framework [Deu92b, Deu94] can be applied to such programs by extracting datatype declarations from the results of a first analysis phase (using for example a grammar-based analysis [CC95]). However the precision of the alias information heavily relies on the approximation of access paths in data structures by a regular automaton. A separate analysis would produce poor results whenever the alias information interfers with the control flow (pointer equality tests, closures). This is especially obvious for mobile processes where the evolution of a program entirely depends on the sharing of communication ports. The techniques described in this paper have been successfully applied to design an analysis of the communications in the π-calculus [Ven96]. Work in progress investigates the application of cofibered domains to analyses based upon the class of context-sensitive tree grammars introduced in [CC95].

Acknowledgements: I am grateful to Radhia Cousot for helpful comments on first versions of this work. All diagrams in this paper have been designed using Paul Taylor's and Paul Gastin's LaTeX packages.

References

[Bou92] F. Bourdoncle. Abstract interpretation by dynamic partitioning. *Journal of Functional Programming*, 2(4), 1992.

[BW90] M. Barr and C. Wells. *Category Theory for Computing Science.* Prentice Hall, 1990.

[CC76] P. Cousot and R. Cousot. Static determination of dynamic properties of programs. In *Proceedings of the* 2nd *International Symposium on Programming,* pages 106–130, Paris, 1976. Dunod.

[CC77] P. Cousot and R. Cousot. Abstract interpretation : a unified lattice model for static analysis of programs by construction or approximation of fixpoints. In *Conference Record of the* 4th *ACM Symposium on Principles of Programming Languages*, pages 238–252, Los Angeles, California, U.S.A., 1977.

[CC79] P. Cousot and R. Cousot. Systematic design of program analysis frameworks. In 6th *POPL*. ACM Press, 1979.

[CC92a] P. Cousot and R. Cousot. Abstract interpretation frameworks. *Journal of logic and computation*, 2(4):511–547, August 1992.

[CC92b] P. Cousot and R. Cousot. Comparing the Galois connection and widening/narrowing approaches to abstract interpretation. In M. Bruynooghe and M. Wirsing, editors, *Programming Language Implementation and Logic Programming, Proceedings of the Fourth International Symposium, PLILP'92*, volume 631 of *Lecture Notes in Computer Science*, pages 269–295, Leuven, Belgium, August 1992. Springer-Verlag, Berlin, Germany, 1992.

[CC95] P. Cousot and R. Cousot. Formal language, grammar and set-constraint-based program analysis by abstract interpretation. In *Conference Record of FPCA'95*. ACM Press, 1995.

[CH78] P. Cousot and N. Halbwachs. Automatic discovery of linear restraints among variables of a program. In 5th *POPL*. ACM Press, 1978.

[Cou78] P. Cousot. *Méthodes itératives de construction et d'approximation de points fixes d'opérateurs monotones sur un treillis, analyse sémantique des programmes.* PhD thesis, Université Scientifique et Médicale de Grenoble, 1978.

[Cou96] P. Cousot. Abstract interpretation in categorical form. To appear, 1996.

[Deu92a] A. Deutsch. *Operational models of programming languages and representations of relations on regular languages with application to the static determination of dynamic aliasing properties of data.* PhD thesis, University Paris VI (France), 1992.

[Deu92b] A. Deutsch. A storeless model of aliasing and its abstraction using finite representations of right-regular equivalence relations. In *Proceedings of the 1992 International Conference on Computer Languages*, pages 2–13. IEEE Computer Society Press, Los Alamitos, California, U.S.A., 1992.

[Deu94] A. Deutsch. Interprocedural may-alias analysis for pointers : beyond k-limiting. In *ACM SIGPLAN'94 Conference on Programming Language Design and Implementation.* ACM Press, 1994.

[Gra89] P. Granger. Static analysis of arithmetical congruences. *International Journal of Computer Mathematics*, 30:165–190, 1989.

[Gra91] P. Granger. Static analysis of linear congruence equalities among variables of a program. In *TAPSOFT'91*, volume 493. Lecture Notes in Computer Science, 1991.

[Gra92] P. Granger. Improving the results of static analyses of programs by local decreasing iterations. In 12th *Foundations of Software Technology and Theoretical Computer Science*, Lecture Notes in Computer Science. Springer Verlag, 1992.

[JM81] N. Jones and S. Muchnick. Flow analysis and optimization of lisp-like structures. In *Program Flow Analysis: Theory and Applications*, pages 102–131. Prentice Hall, 1981.

[Jon81] H.B.M Jonkers. Abstract storage structures. In De Bakker and Van Vliet, editors, *Algorithmic languages*, pages 321–343. IFIP, 1981.

[Kar76] M. Karr. Affine relationships among variables of a program. *Acta Informatica*, pages 133–151, 1976.

[Kel74] G.M. Kelly. On clubs and doctrines. In A. Dold and B. Eckmann, editors, *Category seminar*, volume 420 of *Lecture Notes in Mathematics*, pages 181–256. Springer Verlag, 1974.

[Ven96] A. Venet. Abstract interpretation of the π-calculus. 5th LOMAPS Workshop on Analysis and Verification of High-Level Concurrent Languages, 1996.

STAN: A Static Analyzer for CLP($\mathcal{R}$) Based on Abstract Interpretation

Maria Handjieva

LIX, Ecole Polytechnique
91128 Palaiseau Cedex, France
email: handjiev@lix.polytechnique.fr

Abstract. STAN is an implementation of a static analysis for CLP($\mathcal{R}$) based on abstract interpretation. The semantics of the program is achieved using unfolding operator. The abstract domain is a space of convex polyhedra. Three types of program analysis are implemented - backward, forward and combined.The results of the analysis can be used in program optimization. The implementation is complemented by a graphic user interface.

1 Theoretical basis

The basis of the implementation is drawn from the following principal ideas. The CLP Scheme is a family of rule-based constraint programming languages firstly defined in [7]. The instance of this scheme we are interested in, is the CLP($\mathcal{R}$) language [8]. STAN is a CLP($\mathcal{R}$) static analyzer based on abstract interpretation [2, 3]. The core of the concrete semantics is the unfolding operator [6]. The main advantage of using this operator is the possibility to use the same function for both forward (top/down) and backward (bottom/up) analysis. The constraint space is approximated by convex polyhedra. A specific widening operator for polyhedra [4] is introduced to accelerate the convergence of the iterative fixpoint computation. Polyhedra operation library is based upon Chernikova's algorithm [1] kindly provided by N. Halbwachs. The theoretical basis of this implementation is developed by the author in [5].

2 Overview of the analyzer

The analyzer is written along the lines of a compiler. It comprises of about 3000 lines of C++ split in 15 modules. Only a subset of CLP($\mathcal{R}$) is treated. The uninterpreted functors and non-linear constraints are ignored.

Our experience is that the result can be used as a stronger constraint from which the computation can start. Indeed, if :- $c \diamond B$ is a goal with answer constraint c_a and a is an approximated constraint for c_a (i.e. $c_a \subseteq a$) then the query $c \wedge a \diamond B$, being applied to a stronger constraint, may be executed more efficiently than the original query. The advantage is that the new constraints make information available earlier and can improve the execution of the program. The new constraints are such that the semantics for the CLP program is preserved.

For example, the McCarthy's 91-function (A) is transformed automatically by STAN to the program (B).

$$
\begin{array}{llll}
(A) & mc(N,M) & \text{:-} & N \geq 101, M = N - 10. \\
 & mc(N,M) & \text{:-} & N \leq 100, K = N + 11 \diamond mc(K,L), mc(L,M). \\
(B) & mc(N,M) & \text{:-} & N \geq 101, M = N - 10. \\
 & mc(N,M) & \text{:-} & N \leq 100, M = 91.
\end{array}
$$

A significant speedup is obtained, because the optimized program (B) has no recursion, is deterministic, does not make use of the constraint solver.

To our knowledge, this is the first application of the convex polyhedra to CLP($\mathcal{R}$) analysis. The application of linear inequality analysis to logic programming presented in [3] was implemented for deriving linear size relations in Prolog programs by StJohn [9]. Moreover, a general-purpose Graphic User Interface (GUI) offers a comfortable environment to analyze CLP($\mathcal{R}$) programs. The GUI has been designed to provide a uniform abstract interpretation interface over a wide range of abstract interpreters. It is written using Motif for X Window Systems to allow maximum portability and OSF (Open Software Foundation) compatibility.

References

1. N.V. Chernikova , Algorithm for discovering the set of all the solutions of a linear programming problem. *U.S.S.R. Computation Mathematics and Mathematical Physics*, 8(6):282-293, 1968
2. P. Cousot and R. Cousot, Abstract interpretation: a unified lattice model for static analysis of programs by construction or approximation of fixpoints. In *Proceedings Fourth Annual ACM Symposium on Principles of Programming Languages*, 238-252, Los Angeles, California, 1977
3. P. Cousot and R. Cousot, Abstract Interpretation and Application to Logic Programs. *Journal of Logic Programming, special issue on Abstract Interpretation*, June 1992
4. P. Cousot and N. Halbwachs, Automatic discovery of Linear Restraints among Variables of a Program. *Fifth Annual ACM Symposium on Principles of Programming Languages*, 84-96, 1978
5. M. Handjieva, Abstract Interpretation of Constraint Logic Programs over Numeric Domains, *URL http://lix.polytechnique.fr/~handjiev/HANDJIEVpapers.html*
6. R. Giacobazzi, Semantic aspects of Logic Program Analysis. *Ph.D. Dissertation*, Università di Pisa, March 1993
7. J. Jaffar and J.-L. Lassez, Constraint Logic Programming. In *Fourteenth Annual ACM Symposium on Principles of Programming Languages*, 111-119, San Francisco, California, 1987
8. J. Jaffar, S. Michaylov, P. Stuckey and R. Yap, The CLP($\mathcal{R}$) Language and System. *ACM Transaction on Programming Languages and Systems*, 14(3):339-395, July 1992
9. C. StJohn, Implementation of a static analysis for deriving linear size relations in Prolog programs, *Technical Report, LIX, Ecole Polytechnique, France*, 1993

Two Applications of an Incremental Analysis Engine for (Constraint) Logic Programs

Andrew D. Kelly[1], Kim Marriott[1], Harald Søndergaard[2] and Peter J. Stuckey[2]

[1] Dept. of Computer Science, Monash University, Clayton Vic. 3168, Australia
[2] Dept. of Computer Science, University of Melbourne, Parkville Vic. 3052, Australia

High-level programming languages based on logic programming have developed considerably over recent years. Many real world problems have solutions naturally expressed in logic, and the combination of constraint programming and logic programming has made available new powerful programming languages that allow solutions to be expressed neatly and with minimal effort. An unfortunate but expected initial disadvantage of these new programming languages is their lack of efficiency compared to imperative languages. However, sophisticated optimization techniques based on abstract interpretation are now being included into the next generation of compilers for these languages, often causing dramatic efficiency improvements.

We present a global analyser for (constraint) logic programs. The analyser is

- *Generic*: It is easily instantiated to new analyses, similarly to other analysis engines such as GAIA [4] and PLAI [5], both originally developed for Prolog and recently extended to constraint logic programming.
- *Flexible*: It is easily incorporated into meta-programming tools, and we give two examples below.
- *Incremental*: It allows stepwise program transformation without requiring redundant re-analysis.

The implementation is in C++ and based on the algorithm of Hermenegildo et al. [2]. Central to the object oriented design is an *Annotated Program* class with related iterators. PLAI performs a limited form of incremental analysis for multiple specialisation of rules, but our analyser is, to our knowledge, the first fully incremental analyser for logic programs, efficiently computing the effects of substantial program transformations and analysing hypothetical goals. The analyser is currently used in two applications, a highly optimising compiler for CLP($\mathcal{R}$) and an occur-check eliminator for Prolog.

CLP($\mathcal{R}$) compilation. Global analysis is an essential part of the highly optimizing compiler for CLP($\mathcal{R}$) presented in [3]. CLP($\mathcal{R}$) is an extension of Prolog incorporating arithmetic constraints over the real numbers. The development of the analyser has occurred in parallel with the development of the compiler, and many of the features of the analyser have been specifically designed to fulfil the needs of CLP($\mathcal{R}$) optimization. Optimizing compilation, involves continually modifying the underlying program throughout the compilation process. In particular, compilers need to perform different program transformations such as rule splitting, constraint reordering, and constraint removal [3]. As the underlying program changes, it is essential to reuse the analysis information, as most changes involve only a small region of the program. Incremental analysis allows the analyser to compute only the new analysis information that results from program transformations.

Occur-check elimination. A well known problem of most Prolog interpreters and compilers is the lack of occur-check in the implementation of the unification algorithm. While this greatly improves the efficiency of the implementations, such systems are unsound with respect to first-order predicate logic. We use the analyser to detect cases where occur-checks can be safely omitted [1]. For the large majority of commonly occurring program/query combinations, we can show that occur-checks can be avoided entirely. A Prolog interpreter or compiler using this information can guarantee soundness without losing efficiency.

The analysis engine is not limited to these two applications. The analysis information provided could easily be adapted for the optimizing compilation of other declarative languages, including concurrent constraint logic languages and database languages. Furthermore, the flexibility of the analyser allows many applications within those languages. The analyser performs an ever increasing number of different program analyses. However, these are all based on a common set of basic analyses, deducing properties such as groundness, sharing, freeness, type, liveness, non-linearity for arithmetic variables, and bounds. These basic analyses can be efficiently performed both in combination and in isolation. Experiments on both CLP($\mathcal{R}$) and Prolog benchmarks have shown the analyser to be both practical and efficient [1, 3].

References

1. L. Crnogorac, A. Kelly, and H. Søndergaard. A comparison of three occur-check analysers. In this volume.
2. M. Hermenegildo, K. Marriott, G. Puebla and P. Stuckey. Incremental analysis of logic programs. In L. Sterling, editor, *Proc. Twelfth Int. Conf. Logic Programming*, pages 797–811. MIT Press, 1995.
3. A. Kelly, A. Macdonald, K. Marriott, P. Stuckey, and R. Yap. Effectiveness of optimizing compilation for CLP($\mathcal{R}$). To appear in M. Maher, editor, *Proc. Thirteenth Joint Int. Conf. Symp. Logic Programming.* MIT Press, 1996.
4. B. Le Charlier and P. Van Hentenryck. Experimental evaluation of a generic abstract interpretation algorithm for Prolog. *ACM Transactions on Programming Languages and Systems* **16** (1): 35–101, 1994.
5. K. Muthukumar and M. Hermenegildo. Compile-time derivation of variable dependency using abstract interpretation. *Journal of Logic Programming* **13** (2&3): 315–347, 1992.

PAN – The Prolog Analyzer

Martin Müller, Thomas Glaß, and Karl Stroetmann

Siemens AG, ZT SE 1, D–81730 München, Germany

{Martin.Mueller,Thomas.Glass,Karl.Stroetmann}@zfe.siemens.de

PAN is a tool that performs static analysis of Prolog programs. Its main purpose is to detect errors and inconsistencies during the coding and maintenance phase of software development. To use PAN the programmer has to equip the Prolog program with *signature specifications*. Version 2.0 is able to check the following properties of a Prolog program:

- well-typedness
- completeness
- termination
- unintended backtracking
- adherence to certain coding standards

To check *well-typedness* a type language is needed which is expressive enough for practical purposes. PAN's type system supports parametric polymorphism (e.g. `list(T)` denotes the set of all lists of type `T`, where `T` is a parameter), inclusion polymorphism (e.g. `list(int)` is a subtype of `list(term)`) and base types (e.g. `atom`, `ground`, `int`, `term`, etc.). For every predicate, the user has to specify the type of every argument position. Additionally every argument position has to be classified as either an *input* or an *output* position. This is done by providing a *signature* for every predicate. For example a signature for `reverse`, which takes a list at its first argument position and returns the reversed list at its second argument position, looks like

```
%# predicate: reverse( +list(T), -list(T) ).
```

A program is *well-typed* if input of the specified type leads to output of the specified type and to well-typed subcalls.

An easy but useful check is the detection of unintended backtracking. PAN gives a warning whenever a predicate is backtrackable without being explicitly declared as. In addition the user may want to declare a predicate to be a *function, test* or *generator*. If this is done, the adherence to certain coding standards is checked. For the parts of the program which fit this coding standards, there is a simple declarative semantics [SG96]. Functions and tests have to be free of backtracking, a function returns at most one solution for every input, whereas a test has no output arguments at all. A generator is allowed to return several solutions on backtracking. A call to function, test or generator is not allowed to have any side effects, e.g. it is not permitted to perform i/o-operations. Using this feature the specification of `reverse` might be refined to

```
%# function: reverse( +list(T), -list(T) ).
```

PAN is able to check, if a predicate is *completely defined*, i.e. a well-typed call with uninstantiated output positions of this predicate will only fail by explicitly calling the predicate **fail**. In particular, it may be verified that a well-typed call of a certain predicate will never fail, i.e. if resolution is terminating, then there is always at least one solution. Thus for **reverse** we may specify:

```
%# function: reverse( +list(T), -list(T) ) never_fails.
```

The next feature offered by PAN is to verify the termination of Prolog programs. It turns out that methods for proving termination of algorithms are much better applicable to logic (or functional) languages than to imperative ones. Although the halting problem is not decidable we claim that we have a sufficient criterion which captures the programmer's intuitive ideas about termination. The user has to define *predicate norms* for the predicates involved. After this has been done it is decidable whether a program is *loop free w.r.t. these predicate norms*. Checking whether a program is loop free w.r.t. the specified norms helps the programmer in locating errors which lead to non-termination. The termination check depends on the type check, because we are only interested in proving the universal termination of well-typed queries, i.e. the Prolog resolution procedure terminates in finding all solutions of a well-typed query. As a matter of fact, in many cases resolution does not terminate for queries that are not well-typed, e.g. the query **reverse(Xs,Ys)** with two unbound variables will not terminate. The norm maps well-typed predicate calls into a well-founded ordering such that the norm of every recursive call in the body of a clause is less than the norm of the head of this clause. The definition of the predicate norm of **reverse** would look like

```
%# pnorm : |reverse(Xs,Ys)| = |Xs|.
```

This definition defines the norm of a call **reverse(Xs,Ys)** as the length **|Xs|** of its first argument **Xs**.

Our experience shows that the use of PAN can reduce the costs of program maintenance considerably. This is due to the fact that the type check and the completeness check are able to uncover inconsistencies caused by local modifications of a program.

References

[SG96] Karl Stroetmann and Thomas Glaß. A declarative semantics for the Prolog cut operator. In Roy Dyckhoff, Heinrich Herre, and Peter Schröder-Heister, editors, *Extensions of Logic Programming*, volume 1050 of *Lecture Notes in Computer Science*, pages 255–271. Springer Verlag, 1996.

[SGM96] Karl Stroetmann, Thomas Glaß, and Martin Müller. Implementing safety-critical systems in Prolog: Experiences from the R&D at Siemens. In Peter Reintjes, editor, *Practical Applications of Prolog '96*, pages 391–403, 1996.

Author Index

Aiken, A., 1
Alstrup, S., 42
Alt, M., 52

de Boer, F.S., 83
Borgia, R., 98
Boulanger, D., 128
Brauburger, J., 113
Bruynooghe, M., 128

Coppo, M., 143
Crnogorac, L., 159

Damiani, F., 143
Degano, P., 98
Demoen, B., 128
Denecker, M., 128
Ducassé, M., 317

Emelianov, P.G., 174

Fecht, C., 189
Ferdinand, C., 52

Gabbrielli, M. , 83
Giannini, P., 143
Giesl, J., 113
Givan, R., 205
Glaß, T., 220, 387

Handjieva, M., 383
Hermenegildo, M., 270
Holst Andersen, P., 67

Kehler Holst, C., 67
Kelly, A.D., 159, 385

Lauridsen, P.W., 42
Leth, L., 98

Marriott, K., 385
Martin, F., 52
Mogensen, T.Æ., 285
Mulkers, A., 128
Müller, M., 220, 387

Nielson, F., 2

Palamidessi, C., 83
Pande, H.G., 238
Paterson, R., 255
Priami, C., 98
Puebla, G., 270

Rehof, J., 285
Roux, O., 301
Rusu, V., 301
Ryder, B.G., 238

Schoenig, S., 317
Seidl, H., 189
Smith, S., 349
Snelting, G., 332
Søndergaard, H., 159, 385
Steffen, B., 22
Stroetmann, K., 220, 387
Stuckey, P.J., 385

Thomsen, B., 98
Thorup, M., 42
Trifonov, V., 349

Venet, A., 366

Wilhelm, R., 52

Springer-Verlag and the Environment

We at Springer-Verlag firmly believe that an international science publisher has a special obligation to the environment, and our corporate policies consistently reflect this conviction.

We also expect our business partners – paper mills, printers, packaging manufacturers, etc. – to commit themselves to using environmentally friendly materials and production processes.

The paper in this book is made from low- or no-chlorine pulp and is acid free, in conformance with international standards for paper permanency.

Lecture Notes in Computer Science

For information about Vols. 1–1071

please contact your bookseller or Springer-Verlag

Vol. 1072: R. Kasturi, K. Tombre (Eds.), Graphics Recognition. Proceedings, 1995. X, 308 pages. 1996.

Vol. 1073: J. Cuny, H. Ehrig, G. Engels, G. Rozenberg (Eds.), Graph Grammars and Their Application to Computer Science. Proceedings, 1994. X, 565 pages. 1996.

Vol. 1074: G. Dowek, J. Heering, K. Meinke, B. Möller (Eds.), Higher-Order Algebra, Logic, and Term Rewriting. Proceedings, 1995. VII, 287 pages. 1996.

Vol. 1075: D. Hirschberg, G. Myers (Eds.), Combinatorial Pattern Matching. Proceedings, 1996. VIII, 392 pages. 1996.

Vol. 1076: N. Shadbolt, K. O'Hara, G. Schreiber (Eds.), Advances in Knowledge Acquisition. Proceedings, 1996. XII, 371 pages. 1996. (Subseries LNAI).

Vol. 1077: P. Brusilovsky, P. Kommers, N. Streitz (Eds.), Mulimedia, Hypermedia, and Virtual Reality. Proceedings, 1994. IX, 311 pages. 1996.

Vol. 1078: D.A. Lamb (Ed.), Studies of Software Design. Proceedings, 1993. VI, 188 pages. 1996.

Vol. 1079: Z.W. Raś, M. Michalewicz (Eds.), Foundations of Intelligent Systems. Proceedings, 1996. XI, 664 pages. 1996. (Subseries LNAI).

Vol. 1080: P. Constantopoulos, J. Mylopoulos, Y. Vassiliou (Eds.), Advanced Information Systems Engineering. Proceedings, 1996. XI, 582 pages. 1996.

Vol. 1081: G. McCalla (Ed.), Advances in Artificial Intelligence. Proceedings, 1996. XII, 459 pages. 1996. (Subseries LNAI).

Vol. 1082: N.R. Adam, B.K. Bhargava, M. Halem, Y. Yesha (Eds.), Digital Libraries. Proceedings, 1995. Approx. 310 pages. 1996.

Vol. 1083: K. Sparck Jones, J.R. Galliers, Evaluating Natural Language Processing Systems. XV, 228 pages. 1996. (Subseries LNAI).

Vol. 1084: W.H. Cunningham, S.T. McCormick, M. Queyranne (Eds.), Integer Programming and Combinatorial Optimization. Proceedings, 1996. X, 505 pages. 1996.

Vol. 1085: D.M. Gabbay, H.J. Ohlbach (Eds.), Practical Reasoning. Proceedings, 1996. XV, 721 pages. 1996. (Subseries LNAI).

Vol. 1086: C. Frasson, G. Gauthier, A. Lesgold (Eds.), Intelligent Tutoring Systems. Proceedings, 1996. XVII, 688 pages. 1996.

Vol. 1087: C. Zhang, D. Lukose (Eds.), Distributed Artificial Intelliegence. Proceedings, 1995. VIII, 232 pages. 1996. (Subseries LNAI).

Vol. 1088: A. Strohmeier (Ed.), Reliable Software Technologies – Ada-Europe '96. Proceedings, 1996. XI, 513 pages. 1996.

Vol. 1089: G. Ramalingam, Bounded Incremental Computation. XI, 190 pages. 1996.

Vol. 1090: J.-Y. Cai, C.K. Wong (Eds.), Computing and Combinatorics. Proceedings, 1996. X, 421 pages. 1996.

Vol. 1091: J. Billington, W. Reisig (Eds.), Application and Theory of Petri Nets 1996. Proceedings, 1996. VIII, 549 pages. 1996.

Vol. 1092: H. Kleine Büning (Ed.), Computer Science Logic. Proceedings, 1995. VIII, 487 pages. 1996.

Vol. 1093: L. Dorst, M. van Lambalgen, F. Voorbraak (Eds.), Reasoning with Uncertainty in Robotics. Proceedings, 1995. VIII, 387 pages. 1996. (Subseries LNAI).

Vol. 1094: R. Morrison, J. Kennedy (Eds.), Advances in Databases. Proceedings, 1996. XI, 234 pages. 1996.

Vol. 1095: W. McCune, R. Padmanabhan, Automated Deduction in Equational Logic and Cubic Curves. X, 231 pages. 1996. (Subseries LNAI).

Vol. 1096: T. Schäl, Workflow Management Systems for Process Organisations. XII, 200 pages. 1996.

Vol. 1097: R. Karlsson, A. Lingas (Eds.), Algorithm Theory – SWAT '96. Proceedings, 1996. IX, 453 pages. 1996.

Vol. 1098: P. Cointe (Ed.), ECOOP '96 – Object-Oriented Programming. Proceedings, 1996. XI, 502 pages. 1996.

Vol. 1099: F. Meyer auf der Heide, B. Monien (Eds.), Automata, Languages and Programming. Proceedings, 1996. XII, 681 pages. 1996.

Vol. 1100: B. Pfitzmann, Digital Signature Schemes. XVI, 396 pages. 1996.

Vol. 1101: M. Wirsing, M. Nivat (Eds.), Algebraic Methodology and Software Technology. Proceedings, 1996. XII, 641 pages. 1996.

Vol. 1102: R. Alur, T.A. Henzinger (Eds.), Computer Aided Verification. Proceedings, 1996. XII, 472 pages. 1996.

Vol. 1103: H. Ganzinger (Ed.), Rewriting Techniques and Applications. Proceedings, 1996. XI, 437 pages. 1996.

Vol. 1104: M.A. McRobbie, J.K. Slaney (Eds.), Automated Deduction – CADE-13. Proceedings, 1996. XV, 764 pages. 1996. (Subseries LNAI).

Vol. 1105: T.I. Ören, G.J. Klir (Eds.), Computer Aided Systems Theory – CAST '94. Proceedings, 1994. IX, 439 pages. 1996.

Vol. 1106: M. Jampel, E. Freuder, M. Maher (Eds.), Over-Constrained Systems. X, 309 pages. 1996.

Vol. 1107: J.-P. Briot, J.-M. Geib, A. Yonezawa (Eds.), Object-Based Parallel and Distributed Computation. Proceedings, 1995. X, 349 pages. 1996.

Vol. 1108: A. Díaz de Ilarraza Sánchez, I. Fernández de Castro (Eds.), Computer Aided Learning and Instruction in Science and Engineering. Proceedings, 1996. XIV, 480 pages. 1996.

Vol. 1109: N. Koblitz (Ed.), Advances in Cryptology – Crypto '96. Proceedings, 1996. XII, 417 pages. 1996.

Vol. 1110: O. Danvy, R. Glück, P. Thiemann (Eds.), Partial Evaluation. Proceedings, 1996. XII, 514 pages. 1996.

Vol. 1111: J.J. Alferes, L. Moniz Pereira, Reasoning with Logic Programming. XXI, 326 pages. 1996. (Subseries LNAI).

Vol. 1112: C. von der Malsburg, W. von Seelen, J.C. Vorbrüggen, B. Sendhoff (Eds.), Artificial Neural Networks – ICANN 96. Proceedings, 1996. XXV, 922 pages. 1996.

Vol. 1113: W. Penczek, A. Szałas (Eds.), Mathematical Foundations of Computer Science 1996. Proceedings, 1996. X, 592 pages. 1996.

Vol. 1114: N. Foo, R. Goebel (Eds.), PRICAI'96: Topics in Artificial Intelligence. Proceedings, 1996. XXI, 658 pages. 1996. (Subseries LNAI).

Vol. 1115: P.W. Eklund, G. Ellis, G. Mann (Eds.), Conceptual Structures: Knowledge Representation as Interlingua. Proceedings, 1996. XIII, 321 pages. 1996. (Subseries LNAI).

Vol. 1116: J. Hall (Ed.), Management of Telecommunication Systems and Services. XXI, 229 pages. 1996.

Vol. 1117: A. Ferreira, J. Rolim, Y. Saad, T. Yang (Eds.), Parallel Algorithms for Irregularly Structured Problems. Proceedings, 1996. IX, 358 pages. 1996.

Vol. 1118: E.C. Freuder (Ed.), Principles and Practice of Constraint Programming — CP 96. Proceedings, 1996. XIX, 574 pages. 1996.

Vol. 1119: U. Montanari, V. Sassone (Eds.), CONCUR '96: Concurrency Theory. Proceedings, 1996. XII, 751 pages. 1996.

Vol. 1120: M. Deza. R. Euler, I. Manoussakis (Eds.), Combinatorics and Computer Science. Proceedings, 1995. IX, 415 pages. 1996.

Vol. 1121: P. Perner, P. Wang, A. Rosenfeld (Eds.), Advances in Structural and Syntactical Pattern Recognition. Proceedings, 1996. X, 393 pages. 1996.

Vol. 1122: H. Cohen (Ed.), Algorithmic Number Theory. Proceedings, 1996. IX, 405 pages. 1996.

Vol. 1123: L. Bougé, P. Fraigniaud, A. Mignotte, Y. Robert (Eds.), Euro-Par'96. Parallel Processing. Proceedings, 1996, Vol. I. XXXIII, 842 pages. 1996.

Vol. 1124: L. Bougé, P. Fraigniaud, A. Mignotte, Y. Robert (Eds.), Euro-Par'96. Parallel Processing. Proceedings, 1996, Vol. II. XXXIII, 926 pages. 1996.

Vol. 1125: J. von Wright, J. Grundy, J. Harrison (Eds.), Theorem Proving in Higher Order Logics. Proceedings, 1996. VIII, 447 pages. 1996.

Vol. 1126: J.J. Alferes, L. Moniz Pereira, E. Orlowska (Eds.), Logics in Artificial Intelligence. Proceedings, 1996. IX, 417 pages. 1996. (Subseries LNAI).

Vol. 1127: L. Böszörményi (Ed.), Parallel Computation. Proceedings, 1996. XI, 235 pages. 1996.

Vol. 1128: J. Calmet, C. Limongelli (Eds.), Design and Implementation of Symbolic Computation Systems. Proceedings, 1996. IX, 356 pages. 1996.

Vol. 1129: J. Launchbury, E. Meijer, T. Sheard (Eds.), Advanced Functional Programming. Proceedings, 1996. VII, 238 pages. 1996.

Vol. 1130: M. Haveraaen, O. Owe, O.-J. Dahl (Eds.), Recent Trends in Data Type Specification. Proceedings, 1995. VIII, 551 pages. 1996.

Vol. 1131: K.H. Höhne, R. Kikinis (Eds.), Visualization in Biomedical Computing. Proceedings, 1996. XII, 610 pages. 1996.

Vol. 1132: G.-R. Perrin, A. Darte (Eds.), The Data Parallel Programming Model. XV, 284 pages. 1996.

Vol. 1133: J.-Y. Chouinard, P. Fortier, T.A. Gulliver (Eds.), Information Theory and Applications. Proceedings, 1995. XII, 309 pages. 1996.

Vol. 1134: R. Wagner, H. Thoma (Eds.), Database and Expert Systems Applications. Proceedings, 1996. XV, 921 pages. 1996.

Vol. 1135: B. Jonsson, J. Parrow (Eds.), Formal Techniques in Real-Time and Fault-Tolerant Systems. Proceedings, 1996. X, 479 pages. 1996.

Vol. 1136: J. Diaz, M. Serna (Eds.), Algorithms - ESA '96. Proceedings, 1996. XII, 566 pages. 1996.

Vol. 1137: G. Görz, S. Hölldobler (Eds.), KI-96: Advances in Artificial Intelligence. Proceedings, 1996. XI, 387 pages. 1996. (Subseries LNAI).

Vol. 1138: J. Calmet, J.A. Campbell, J. Pfalzgraf (Eds.), Artificial Intelligence and Symbolic Mathematical Computation. Proceedings, 1996. VIII, 381 pages. 1996.

Vol. 1139: M. Hanus, M. Rogriguez-Artalejo (Eds.), Algebraic and Logic Programming. Proceedings, 1996. VIII, 345 pages. 1996.

Vol. 1140: H. R. Kuchen, S. Doaitse Swierstra (Eds.), Programming Languages: Implementations, Logics, and Programs. Proceedings, 1996. XI, 479 pages. 1996.

Vol. 1141: H.-M. Voigt, W. Ebeling, I. Rechenberg, H.-P. Schwefel (Eds.), Parallel Problem Solving from Nature – PPSN IV. Proceedings, 1996. XVII, 1.050 pages. 1996.

Vol. 1142: R.W. Hartenstein, M. Glesner (Eds.), Field-Programmable Logic. Proceedings, 1996. X, 432 pages. 1996.

Vol. 1143: T.C. Fogarty (Ed.), Evolutionary Computing. Proceedings, 1996. VIII, 305 pages. 1996.

Vol. 1144: J. Ponce, A. Zisserman, M. Hebert (Eds.), Object Representation in Computer Vision. Proceedings, 1996. VIII, 403 pages. 1996.

Vol. 1145: R. Cousot, D.A. Schmidt (Eds.), Static Analysis. Proceedings, 1996. IX, 389 pages. 1996.